THE
MAY FOURTH
MOVEMENT

五四運動史

周策縱自署

THE
MAY FOURTH
MOVEMENT

Intellectual Revolution in Modern China

Chow Tse-tsung

Originally published in
the Harvard East Asian Series

STANFORD UNIVERSITY PRESS
Stanford, California

Stanford University Press
Stanford, California
© Copyright 1960 by the President and Fellows of Harvard College
First published in 1960 by Harvard University Press
Paperback edition first published in 1967 by Stanford University Press
by arrangement with Harvard University Press
Printed in the United States of America
Last figure below indicates year of this printing:
78   77   76   75   74   73   72   71   70

To the Memory of My Beloved Father

CHOW P'ENG-CHU
(1887–1952)

Poet   Scholar   Calligrapher

PREFACE

THERE are few major events in modern Chinese history so controversial, so much discussed, yet so inadequately treated as the May Fourth Movement. For some Chinese it marks a national renaissance or liberation, for others a national catastrophe. Among those who discuss or celebrate it most, views vary greatly. Every May for the last forty years, numerous articles have analyzed and commented on the movement. Several books devoted entirely to the subject and hundreds touching on it have been published in Chinese. The literature on the subject is massive, yet most of it offers more polemic than factual accounts. Most Westerners possess but fragmentary and inaccurate information on the subject. For these reasons, preparation of this volume recounting the events of the movement and examining in detail its currents and effects has seemed to me worthwhile.

More personal motives have also impelled me to undertake this task. I have been interested in the subject since my boyhood in Changsha where I was a student in the same high school from which Mao Tse-tung had graduated fifteen years before. There I was active in the current student movement and became a central figure in the student "storms" and strikes. We of course looked back to the May Fourth Movement with pride and admiration. Significantly, my first poem in the new vernacular, written in this period following over one thousand verses in the classical style which I had composed earlier, was entitled "May Fourth, We Are Not Failing You." It was published in a newspaper edited by Kuo Mo-jo and T'ien Han. Even then I dreamed of some day writing a book on the May Fourth Movement. This intention was strengthened later when I attended a Kuomintang university where student movements were normally prohibited.

The study and presentation of this movement as a many-faceted intellectual and sociopolitical phenomenon has not been an easy task. Aware of the controversial nature of the subject, I have tried to introduce as many factual records as possible. A large number of quotations have been included in the text so that the records and the people concerned might speak for themselves. Translations are my own unless otherwise noted.

Underlying the general theme of the writing is the belief that, while economic conditions and ideological interplay may be major factors in defining an event such as the May Fourth Movement, other elements are also very influential. These include historical background, political setting, social organization and social psychology, personal leadership and participation, as well as some small but probably key incidents. Efforts have been made to analyze some of these factors with respect to the movement.

The book falls into two parts. In the first part, activities and events are described and analyzed in chronological order, with the exception of Chapter VIII which has been inserted somewhat out of sequence to provide background for the following chapter. In the second part of the book, main literary and intellectual currents are separately analyzed and examined in some detail. A full Bibliography, a Glossary of Chinese and Japanese Names and Terms, with characters, and an annotated list of periodicals current during the May Fourth period are published separately.

I am deeply indebted to Professor Robert E. Ward of the University of Michigan. Without his encouragement, guidance, and assistance the study could not have been accomplished. I am most grateful to Professor John K. Fairbank of Harvard University and to Mrs. Wilma Fairbank for their incessant encouragement and help in the writing and publishing of the work. In the preparation of the manuscript for publication, Mrs. Fairbank has not only extended extremely painstaking editorship, but also made a number of critical and helpful remarks which greatly improved the presentation of the subject. Profound gratitude should also be expressed to Professor Benjamin Schwartz of the same university for many inspiring discussions and for his reading of most of the manuscript and making a number of valuable comments and suggestions. I am grateful to Mr. Bertrand Russell for his letter discussing his stay in China during the latter part of the movement. I also thank Dr. Hu Shih and Dr. Carsun Chang for interesting and illuminating discussions of the subject. To my colleague at Harvard University, Professor Lien-sheng Yang, and former colleague, Professor Masataka Banno, I owe great appreciation for saving me from many errors in romanizations in the footnotes. I wish to acknowledge the valuable comments on certain chapters made by Professors James I. Crump, Jr., Russell H. Fifield, John W. Hall, and James H. Meisel of the University of Michigan. Professor Nathaniel Peffer of Columbia University, an eyewitness of the movement in China from 1915 to 1921, has given me firsthand information. I am also much indebted to the following friends for reading parts of the manuscript: Mr. Morton Abramowitz, Mr. William F. Danielson, Dr. Albert Feuerwerker, Professor Wolfgang Franke, Professor Bayard Lyon, Mr. Roderick L. MacFarquhar, and Mr. Mark Mancall. Acknowledgment is also made of the assistance received from Dr. Arthur W. Hummel, Dr. Edward Beal, Jr., Dr. K. T. Wu, and particularly Mr. Liang Hsü, all of the Library of Congress, from Dr. A. K. Ch'iu and other librarians of the Harvard-Yenching Library, from those of the University of Michigan Library and Mr. Kuang-huan Lu of the Columbia University Library. None of those mentioned above, of course, bears responsibility for the views expressed. Finally, I wish to thank Harvard University Press for its great assistance in the publication of this volume.

CHOW TSE-TSUNG

Cambridge, Massachusetts
October 1959

CONTENTS

CONTENTS · xiii

THE
MAY FOURTH
MOVEMENT

CHAPTER I

INTRODUCTION

Definition of the Movement

O<small>N</small> May 4, 1919, students in Peking demonstrated in protest against the Chinese government's humiliating policy toward Japan. There resulted a series of strikes and associated events amounting to a social ferment and an intellectual revolution. This rising tide was soon dubbed by the students the May Fourth Movement (*Wu-ssu yün-tung*), a term which acquired a broader meaning in later years than it had originally.[1]

In the ensuing pages, the term May Fourth Movement will be used in this broader sense. It covers the period roughly from 1917 through 1921 and includes the events summarized briefly as follows. Supported by the rising patriotic and anti-Great-Power sentiments of the public which had been ignited first by the Twenty-one Demands of Japan in 1915 and then by the Shantung resolution of the Versailles Peace Conference in 1919, the students and new intellectual leaders promoted an anti-Japanese campaign and a vast modernization movement to build a new China through intellectual and social reforms. They stressed primarily Western ideas of science and democracy. Traditional Chinese ethics, customs, literature, history, philosophy, religion, and social and political institutions were fiercely attacked. Liberalism, pragmatism, utilitarianism, anarchism, and many varieties of socialism provided the stimuli. The protest of May 4 marked the pivot of these developments. Its aims soon won sympathy from the new merchants, industrialists, and urban workers, and the Peking government was forced to compromise in its foreign and domestic policies. This victory of the new coalition facilitated the expansion of the cultural and intellectual reforms it advocated. Shortly after this, the movement gradually became involved in politics, and the united front of the new intellectuals collapsed. The liberals lost their zeal or turned away from political activity, whereas the left wing of the movement took the expedient political step of allying itself with the Nationalists to overthrow the warlord Peking regime. Western attitudes shifting from sympathy to antagonism towards the movement constituted one major factor in this split. Thereafter socialism and nationalism became ascendant, and a multitude of complicated controversies were precipitated.

The effects of the movement were widespread. It contributed to the rise of the student and labor movements, the reorganization of the Kuomintang, and the birth of the Chinese Communist Party and other political and social groups. Antiwarlordism and anti-imperialism developed. A new vernacular literature was established and popular education was greatly facilitated thereby. The Chinese press and public opinion made great progress. The movement also accelerated the decline of the old family system and the rise of feminism. And above all, the authority of Confucianism and traditional ethics suffered a fundamental and devastating stroke and new Western ideas were exalted.

At first the term "May Fourth Movement" as used by the students and the press did not refer to all of the events mentioned above. It was rather applied only to the student demonstration in Peking on May 4. By analogy the mass arrests that occurred after June 3, 1919, were called the "June Third Movement." In later years, people talking of the May Fourth Movement may not consciously have taken such a narrow view, but they rarely failed to equate the movement with the May Fourth Incident (*Wu-ssu shih-chien*) and its consequences. The term May Fourth Movement was, then, in many cases interchangeable with the term May Fourth Incident.

A second and more serious question of scope has also been raised: should the term May Fourth Movement embrace on the one hand both the social and political activities of the students and intellectuals, and, on the other, the new literature and new thought movements, which started earlier, in 1917, and later came to be called the new culture movement? Some people held that the May Fourth Movement and the new culture movement were different and bore little relation to each other. They thought that the movement was not directly caused by the new culture movement and the leaders of the latter did not in general guide or even support the former. They admitted only that the new culture movement probably somewhat facilitated the May Fourth Movement, while the latter served to intensify and to aid in the expansion of the former.[2]

The advocates of this interpretation overlooked the necessary relation between the students' actions and the development of their thought. They seem to have adopted such a view with the intention of belittling the significance of the new culture movement and of exaggerating the influence of other factors, such as anarchism, upon the students. Their view is not accepted by many who have closely observed and studied the history of the May Fourth Movement.[3]

Still another group, who recognized the close relation between the students' aspects of the May Fourth Movement and the new culture movement, rejected the idea that the term May Fourth Movement should cover the latter. The principal proponents of this opinion were Hu Shih and certain other scholars. Basically, Hu regarded the May Fourth Movement as a patriotic movement of the students and emphasized the significance of its cultural rather than its social and political activities.[4] He accepted Sun Yat-sen's view that the students' activities in the May Fourth Movement had a close relation to the literary and intellectual movements. While Sun rated the new thought movement higher than the others, Hu paid more attention to the new literature movement, and the vernacular problem in particular. Works in English by Hu and others who hold the same view have familiarized many Westerners with the new culture movement under the epithet, "the Chinese Renaissance."

Though the adoption of the vernacular in writing was one of the most prominent achievements of the movement, the literary revolution should be considered merely one aspect of the great general advance which occurred during the period. To this writer the political, social, and ideological events of the time do not seem less significant than the adoption of the vernacular. Moreover, the movement cannot be regarded solely as a student or youth movement. The term "student" (*hsüeh-sheng*) as employed in China denotes only a person studying in a school. This usage, which is followed in this study, differs from the English use of the word, which may also refer to scholars or learners not engaged in active study in an institution.[5] While it is true that students or youths provided the most powerful driving force in the movement, adult intellectuals such as the professors and writers of the new thought group assumed the leadership of the ideological aspects of the movement, and both young and adult intellectuals played a part in its development outside of the schools also. Consequently, though the movement may properly be viewed from the angle of a student or youth movement, it should not be regarded exclusively as such.

The question whether to give primary emphasis to the literary or to the youth and political aspects of the May Fourth Movement has been a subject of political controversy in China. In March 1939, when the Communist-sponsored Youth Association of China (*Chung-kuo ch'ing-nien lien-ho-hui*) was established in Yenan, it suggested that May fourth of each year be proclaimed "Youth Day" (*ch'ing-nien chieh*). Its proposal was accepted by many other organizations throughout the country and by the Chinese government. Later, on April 16, 1944, the Kuomintang government in Chungking, accepting the proposal of the Association of Chinese Literature (*Chung-kuo wen-i-chieh hsieh-hui*) changed this to "Literature Day" (*wen-i chieh*), and substituted March 29 as Youth Day (on that date in 1911, seventy-two young members of the Kuomintang died in an attack on the provincial government at Canton under the Manchu regime). In December 1949, after taking over power on the mainland, the Communist government formally reaffirmed May fourth as Chinese Youth Day. Subsequently, both parties have clung to their different celebrations on May fourth. This does not mean that the Communist Party regards the movement solely as a youth movement or that the Kuomintang views it as an event of merely literary significance. But the episode does shed some light on their different views of the meaning of the movement.

In addition to the above views, the term May Fourth Movement has to many Chinese intellectuals a broader meaning. In popular usage, it often implies both the student and the new culture movements. In this sense it includes all aspects of this period of intellectual ferment before and after 1919. For instance, when Fung Yu-lan talked about the May Fourth Movement, he referred to the currents concerning new thought and Westernization.[6] If an average Chinese student were asked about the movement, one would surely elicit an answer embracing both the social reform activities of the intellectuals and the new literature and thought movements. Discussing the programs of the new intelligentsia in the period, few would fail to refer to science and democracy. In the years after the movement, political leaders of the Kuomintang, Communist, and other parties eventually subscribed to the same view. "The May Fourth Movement," said a writer with hardly any political coloration, "means, of course, not merely the movement which took place on the day of May 4, 1919; it denotes a cultural process resulting from China's contact with Western civilization. The May Fourth Incident was but a signal in this process."[7]

This wider use of the term is eminently justified. First of all, many of those who played leading roles in instigating the demonstrations, strikes, and boycotts were actually the new intellectuals who had been promoting the new literature, new thought, and social reforms. Their opponents, both in action and in thought, were or pretended to be representatives of the Chinese tradition. Secondly, the theoretical basis of the antiwarlord and anti-Great-Powers activities of these intellectual reformers was the idea of democracy, popularized earlier by a group of intellectuals. Considered in this light, the May fourth demonstration was but a logical conclusion of the new thought movement which had begun two or three years earlier. Thirdly, many of the important student leaders concerned in the incident felt from the beginning that the real spirit of their movement was not one of simple patriotism, but was bound up with concepts of the supremacy of public opinion, people's rights, and an intellectual renaissance. Their activities were not confined to antiwarlordism, nor were they only concerned with diplomatic problems. As the incident developed, they paid as much attention to social and intellectual reforms as to patriotic agitation. Subsequently, the most profound and lasting impression of the movement of 1919 and 1920 was that of an intellectual revolution and a social transformation; its keynote was social and intellectual as well as political iconoclasm. In view of these facts, it seems best to accept the broad definition and regard the movement as a vast upheaval affecting many aspects of society.

The May Fourth Movement then may be defined as a complicated phenomenon including the "new thought tide," the literary revolution, the student movement, the merchants' and workers' strikes, and the boycott against Japan, as well as other social and political activities of the new intellectuals, all inspired by the patriotic sentiments after the Twenty-one Demands and the Shantung resolution, and by the spirit of Western learning and the desire to reevaluate tradition in the light of science and democracy in order to build a new China. It was not a uniform or well-organized movement, but rather a coalescence of a number of activities often with divergent ideas, though not without its main currents.[8]

Furthermore, the time span of the movement has also become a confused problem. The term "May Fourth period" (*Wu-ssu shih-tai*) has actually been very loosely used by many Chinese authors. It denotes sometimes the months, sometimes the years, immediately following the incident; it implies, for others, a period extending from 1915 or 1916 to 1923.[a] Some writers extend it to 1925 when the famous "May Thirtieth Incident" began a new phase.[b] Ch'en Tu-hsiu

---

[a] Hu Shih agrees with Chang Hsi-jo that the May Fourth Movement includes the new thought movement developed in 1917 and 1918 and in the few years following the May Fourth Incident. Ho Kan-chih claims that the May Fourth Movement started from the time *New Youth* was established and ended at the time of the conclusion of the polemic on science and metaphysics, that is, Sept. 1915–Dec. 1923.[9]

[b] On May 30, 1925, more than two thousand Chinese students and workers demonstrated in Shanghai protesting the killing of a Chinese worker by guards of a Japanese textile factory on May 15 in that city. At least eleven students and workers in the demonstration were killed and twenty wounded by the British police. A strike of one hundred thousand Chinese workers ensued on June 1. Consequently over twenty foreign warships entered the Whangpoo River and marines of five nationalities landed. At least eight more Chinese were killed and forty-four wounded after May 30. Sympathy strikes and demonstrations in twenty-eight other Chinese cities and in Hong Kong protested the British and Japanese actions. A boycott resulted, lasting for almost sixteen

maintained that the period lasted to "the present," writing in 1938.[11] In this study, since the movement is treated as a phenomenon with many facets, its time span is regarded as variable, not strictly or uniformly fixed. Nevertheless, an examination of the main currents of the movement reveals that most of the important events in it took place during the five years from the beginning of 1917 to the end of 1921. In 1917 the new thought and new literature reforms started to gather momentum due to the rallying of the new intellectual leaders around *New Youth* (*Hsin ch'ing-nien*) magazine and the National University of Peking. After 1921, the movement revealed itself more in direct political action, and for a few years intellectual and social reforms were more or less neglected. Therefore, the May Fourth period may be reasonably defined as 1917–1921 inclusive, which period may be divided into two phases separated by the May Fourth Incident proper. During the first phase, some new intellectuals concentrated on instilling their ideas in the students and youth of China. During the second phase an all-out attack on tradition and conservatism was launched principally by students, and the movement was carried beyond purely intellectual circles.

The period however cannot be strictly limited to these years. Some of the nationalist sentiments and new thoughts started to take hold at least as early as 1915, the year when a feeling of national humiliation was aroused by the Twenty-one Demands, when some students started to consider more seriously than ever before the national problem, and when *New Youth* was established. Nor should the movement be considered as coming to a full stop in 1921. Ideological controversies developed in the period are still a part of the contemporary Chinese scene. The polemics on Eastern versus Western civilizations, and on science and metaphysics, which took place in 1922 and 1923, were direct results of the movement. The latter cannot be fully understood and evaluated, if the polemics of this later period are left out of consideration. At any rate, the movement must be considered as a stage of a whole historical development, in fact one of the most eventful and crucial stages in the long process of China's transformation to adjust herself to the modern world after the Western impact in the last century.

Economic, Social, and Political Background

If this understanding of the movement is acceptable, the question may be raised: why was the process of adjustment accelerated during this period? To

---

months. The incident and its consequences bore some marks of the May Fourth Movement and exerted deep and far-reaching political influence on Chinese society.[10]

answer this, even partially, it is necessary to mention the changes in China's economic, social, and political situation and international influences on China after the beginning of World War I.

China's economy was agricultural and preindustrial in nature before she came into contact with the modern West. In this economy most of the wealth was owned by landlords and merchants. They ordinarily accumulated it through four main channels: by buying more land with their profits from land products, by trade, by moneylending, and by the emoluments, legal and illegal, of bureaucratic position. As the economy continued to be agricultural through the two thousand years before this century, the second and third methods of wealth accumulation usually depended on agricultural production. Consequently traditional Chinese economic thought was dominated by the concept of capital accumulation in the form of land investment, a concept which was well illustrated by the proverbial folksong, "It is as impossible to be rich without possession of land as to kiss through a piece of glass." The abolition of the institution of primogeniture in the third century B.C. prevented the overconcentration of landownership or the large accumulation of wealth.[12] Family and village became basic economic units and were self-sufficient. Handicraft establishments, which were maintained by apprenticeships and served as homes as well as shops, were the only industries. Production and exchange were for the most part fixed by local guilds. All these practices kept the domestic market from expansion and prevented large-scale development of industry.

This self-sufficing agrarian economy began to change after the opening of China by the West during the last century. In 1863 China built her first factory, a state-owned arsenal. Yet in the latter half of the century her industry still had little opportunity to expand, partly because foreign manufactured goods of lower price and better quality were dumped into Chinese markets under the privileges obtained by the Great Powers either by force or by diplomatic means.

The pressure of foreign commercial competition never eased until the outbreak of World War I, when the Western Powers became preoccupied with military production. From that moment Chinese national industry and commerce obtained a breathing space and an opportunity to grow, owing to the lowered excess of imports. Native production by textile and flour mills and other light industries developed markedly from 1914 to 1920. These years of prosperity have often been considered in retrospect the Golden Age of Chinese industrial history, at least by comparison with the previous situation.[13] Because of this expansion and the long-term penetration of the forces of Western capitalism, the collapse of China's traditional self-sufficing agricultural and village economy was quickened. Investment in land showed some slight signs of shifting to that in industrial, commercial, and financial enterprises. New joint-stock corporations to foster industries grew faster than before. Toward the end of the second decade of this century the Chinese national dollar (*yuan*) had largely displaced the Mexican dollar, and thus provided a uniform currency over some areas of the nation and gave impetus to the development of financial activities. More modern-style banks were established in big cities and many old-style money shops were transformed into banks. The years 1912, 1915, 1919, 1920, and 1921 were landmarks in the development of modern Chinese money and credit system. And a tendency toward capital concentration and growth of the urban economy began to manifest itself. Yet this economic transformation was still most rudimentary and spotty. Although the economic character of the big cities became partially that of the twentieth-century West, the vast rural districts of the hinterland retained the character which they had had in antiquity and in the Middle Ages. The agrarian economy was beginning to give way, but it still had not been replaced by a modern economic system. A pattern of socioeconomic change embracing, successively, destruction, clearance of ruins, reconstruction, and reforms was expected in China at the beginning of the twentieth century. But on the contrary, shortly after the end of World War I, the international conditions which had fostered this economic surge in China ceased to exist. With the increase of Japan's influence and the return of other powers to the Chinese market, China's infant industries ran into great difficulties and showed violent ups and downs.[14] Conflict of interests between native and foreign economic forces tended to be acute. This sequence of economic transformation, national prosperity, crisis, and struggle for survival significantly affected contemporary political and cultural activities at each of its stages.

Accompanying these economic changes were important social ones. The traditional equilibrium of social forces in which the old oligarchy maintained its power by way of a united front combining, on the one hand, the imperial house or military groups and, on the other, the landlords, with the gentry as a middle group, was thrown seriously off balance. The civil service examination system had been abolished in 1905 and no new effective recruitment system had been substituted. Able and ambitious young men and women were often unable to enter the government through normal channels. Self-sufficient and cooperative family and village devices which customarily provided remedies for the society in times of stress were unequal to a crisis of this magnitude. New merchants, industrialists, and urban workers arose along with the growth of new cities. The speed of urban growth in the first few decades of this century was remarkable. Peking for example had a population of about 600,000 in 1919 when the May Fourth Incident took place in that city, while four years later, in 1923, it had increased to 1,100,000, almost twice the 1919 figure.[15] Because of civil wars (between 1915 and 1922 there were ten major civil wars which lasted altogether for forty-eight months),[16] calamity, and the collapse of the rural economy the number of landless peasants and unemployed increased. Many of these impoverished people left their villages and became professional soldiers, others became bandits or roamers. This uneasy population nourished warlordism, which reached its most rapid growth in the years just prior to the May Fourth period. At the same time, a factor of fundamental long-range importance began to assert itself in Chinese society. As the power of landlords and the old gentry waned, a new intelligentsia with some degree of modern Western knowledge emerged.[c] In the ten years after 1907, when the new Western-style educational system started functioning on an appreciable scale, there were some 10,000,000 persons who had received or were receiving the new education in one form or another (see Appendix A). Their various contacts with modern Western civilization and increasing alienation from the traditional ideology and ruling class enabled them to lead other restless people in a "save China" crusade. The movement reflects the regrouping of all these social forces.

Meanwhile, the political situation of China after 1915, both internal and external, provided a fertile soil for a revolt. During and right after World War I sentiments of nationalism and democracy prevailed in the world and in Asia in particular. Woodrow Wilson's political idealism, such as his advocacy of the abolition of secret diplomacy, the guaranty of the political independence of small states, and national self-determination, had great appeal to Chinese intellectuals. The hopes of the Chinese were also reinforced by the new tide of political changes in Europe, the increase of new republics, the rise of women's suffrage, the devices of initiative, referendum, and recall, and industrial democracy. But when the Great Powers attempted to re-establish their colonial policies at the Paris Peace Conference, the Chinese fell from a

[c] The term "intelligentsia" (*chih-shih fen-tzu*), used here in a broader sense than in the Western usage, refers to the intellectuals as a fluid group, including the more or less well educated people, teachers, scholars, the students in middle or higher schools, and the gentry, as well as other professionals such as journalists, writers, artists, and lawyers. In later discussion we will use the words "old gentry" to denote the traditionally educated literati who, owning land or not, formed part of the local ruling forces over all the country or remained bureaucratic candidates; and the "new intelligentsia" or "new intellectuals" to denote those with a somewhat new education or Western learning. The use of these terms in China seems to be particularly meaningful because about 80 per cent of the Chinese people were illiterate throughout the period of the May Fourth Movement.

visionary hope to deep despair, and nationalist feeling ran higher than ever before. On the other hand, revolutions breaking out in many countries during this period demonstrated the possibilities of change by popular uprisings. The Russian October Revolution of 1917 and socialist revolts in Finland, Germany, Austria, Hungary, Bavaria, and other countries influenced the political climate of the East. The "Rice Riots" of Japan occurred in August 1918, and Korea experienced her "March First Movement" in 1919. Two months before the May Fourth Incident, the Third Communist International was organized and its First World Congress was held in Moscow.

In contrast to this revolutionary flux abroad, the Chinese lived in a dark domestic political scene. Party politics were tried for the first time in the Republic, under the manipulation of warlords. In 1914 Parliament was dissolved and the constitution was annulled by the warlord president Yüan Shih-k'ai. In 1915 and 1917 two unsuccessful monarchical restoration movements were staged. Yüan's abolition of the Republic lasted eighty-three days and the restoration of the Manchu boy Emperor to the throne by Chang Hsün, the *tuchun* of Anhwei Province, ended in twelve days after Chang's pig-tailed troops in Peking were disbanded. Thereafter, while the whole country was in fact controlled by local competing *tuchuns*, the power of the central government was left in the hands of Tuan Ch'i-jui, the wardlord who was Yüan's long-time subordinate. Tuan was the leader of the Anfu Club, a political group of warlords and bureaucrats with Japanese financial support. To oppose the Peking regime, Sun Yat-sen established the rival Military Government in Canton on September 1, 1917. From this time on, a number of indecisive civil wars between the North and the South stirred the country. Shortly before the May Fourth Incident, a fruitless and wearisome internal peace conference between Peking and Canton began its lengthy deliberations in Shanghai under the encouragement of Woodrow Wilson, an ironical foreshadowing of a similar settlement suggested by the United States after World War II. Psychologically, the ups and downs of the two peace conferences in Shanghai and Paris disturbed Chinese social sentiments to a high degree. It should be remembered that, throughout the years following the 1911 Revolution, Chinese political thinking and behavior had not been very far from tradition. Most of the people were still the victims of oppressive ultraconservative officials and were, as before, obedient to authority, to armed force, and to the traditional ethical and political dogmas. This political chaos and backwardness convinced the new intellectuals that vast and fundamental reforms were necessary to rejuvenate the old nation.

Significance of the Movement in Historical Perspective

In Chinese history, a number of events may be found which bear some similarity to aspects of the May Fourth Movement. Examples of students' taking a lead in criticism of and interference in political affairs are not scarce. The first recorded incident of gatherings in village schools to criticize the government occurred in 542 B.C., nine years after the birth of Confucius. The criticism was tolerated by the current premier of the Cheng State, Tzu Ch'an. His policy of toleration has since been praised by most Chinese historians.[17] In the first century B.C., during the Former Han period, thirty thousand students at the Imperial College, led by a student Wang Hsien, protested against the punishment of an upright censor by the government. This was the first case in Chinese history of direct interference in domestic politics by students. During the second century A.D., in the Later Han period, student Kuo T'ai and others allied with officials and intellectual leaders indulging in criticism of the government and eunuchs, and later several hundred officials and students were imprisoned and executed. It was the first significant factional controversy in China.[18] Student movements became more common than ever before in the Sung dynasty (960–1279). In 1125 students at the Imperial College led by Ch'en Tung (1087–1128) petitioned the Emperor to execute the premier and military leaders, accusing them of mishandling state affairs; but their efforts were in vain. In the following year, Ch'en and several hundred other students led hundreds of thousands of ordinary citizens as well as some soldiers in an appeal to the Emperor to punish the premier and to adopt a strong foreign policy of resistance to the aggression of the northern invaders. There was a violent attack on the Emperor's attendants, several score of whom were killed. As a result, the government executed some citizens held responsible for the violence, but was forced by public opinion to change its foreign and domestic policies. This was the first time that Chinese students in schools had led ordinary citizens to interfere in foreign policy. Ch'en Tung and many other students were later put to death. However, half a dozen similar student movements occurred during the latter part of the Sung dynasty and it is recorded that students took part in strikes. Cases of professors encouraging or supporting student movements against the government are also found in the Sung records.[19] Following such examples, student movements of the Ming dynasty (1368–1643) were continuously involved in the feuds of political factions.[20]

How did this phenomenon of student interference in Chinese political affairs arise? In a monarchy without a genuine legislature or system of popular representation, it was perhaps inevitable that the educated minority should under duress seek to express itself. And, in fact, the government-supported schools, through their faculties and student bodies, did throughout Chinese history occasionally assume in moments of crisis the role of spokesmen for public opinion. This practice has been generally approved by Chinese commentators both in earlier periods and in modern times. In the seventeenth century, for example, the famous scholar and thinker Huang Tsung-hsi (1610–1695) actually advocated a political system in which schools would perform the functions of informed tribunals of public opinion or of a kind of legislature, a system he considered to have originated in the ancient Golden Age.[21]

This traditional concept of the students' political mission was accepted by the students in the May Fourth Movement as their publications repeatedly stated.[22] But there is an important distinction between the twentieth-century student movements and their traditional prototypes. The meaning of "school" and "student" in old China differed from that in general usage at the time of the movement, and, in fact, from that at the turn of the nineteenth century when the school system was reformed to accord more with Western practice. The traditional government schools, which generally commenced at, in modern terms, the middle school stage, were closely linked to the old civil service examination system, and functioned both as reservoirs of civil servants and as institutes for learning. Hence, they were attended by more adult and by fewer juvenile literati than their modern counterparts. These adult literati were more concerned with public affairs than the ordinary younger students who were commonly dispersed throughout the land with their private tutors. That is, the traditional Chinese private tutorial schools (ssu-shu), usually isolated, and organized on a comparatively small scale, were apparently less involved than the government schools in student movements, although a few big private and semipublic schools (shu-yüan) sometimes exerted an influence on public opinion.

Similarly, there were precedents from history for the literary and intellectual changes of the May Fourth period. Literature and thought made great progress in the latter part of the Chou dynasty (1122?–221 B.C.). More elements of the vernacular were then brought into the written language. An important literary reform took place in the T'ang dynasty (618–907). New poetry and new prose achieved much, and Ch'an (Zen) Buddhism was developed. Later, in the Sung period, Neo-Confucianism was established in the teeth of medievalism. Under the Yüan dynasty (1279–1368), a new drama form was evolved, and under the Ming vernacular novels and short stories became popular. Then in the Ch'ing period (1644–1911) classical scholarship rose to oppose the Neo-Confucianist philosophy.

Despite all the precedents, however, the May Fourth Movement was unique both in breadth of activity and in depth of significance.[23] First of all, this was the first time Chinese intellectuals recognized the need for a complete transformation of traditional Chinese civilization. Before China came into contact with the modern West, her civilization had never been seriously challenged *in toto* by any foreign influence except Indian Buddhism, which had touched closely many aspects of Chinese intellectual and social life but had affected the political and economic systems less. Several hundred years of advance in science and other spheres, and many additional factors arising from differences between the societies made the West's impact on China beyond comparison. After the Opium War of 1840–42 had demonstrated the irresistible power of the West, leading Chinese intellectuals began to awaken to the fact that China needed to learn Western scientific technology, though they held that traditional Chinese institutions and traditional thought were superior to their Western equivalents and did not need reform. This first stage of China's response to Western civilization ended after her defeat by Japan in 1894–95. From that time on, young Chinese intellectuals, impressed by the achievements of the Meiji Restoration in Japan, believed that, in addition to learning scientific techniques, China should also model her laws and political institutions after those of the West. They still maintained that Chinese philosophy, ethics, and the fundamental principles of the traditional society, more basic and substantial, in their view, than laws and institutions, should not be changed. This idea was well summarized by Chang Chih-tung in 1898 in the phrase, "Chinese studies as the fundamental structure, Western studies for practical use." [d] The proposed changes in laws and political institutions failed of realization in the Hundred Days' Reform of 1898 and were achieved only in part by the 1911 Revolution. After the establishment of the Republic, the resurgence of warlord rule and the two attempts at monarchical restoration proved that the mere transplantation of laws and political institutions unaccompanied by other changes did not work. Then came the third stage, the era of the May Fourth

---

[d] This formula, *Chung-hsüeh wei t'i, Hsi-hsüeh wei yung*, for a synthesis of Western learning and Chinese studies, and a similar Japanese idea might have influenced each other or developed along parallel lines. For the justification of their Chinese learning, the Japanese had a saying, "Japanese spirit, Chinese skill" (*Wakon, Kansai*), which was attributed to Sugawara Michizane (A.D. 845–903). Later, in the nineteenth century, Sakuma Shōzan (1811–1864), one of the pioneers of Western learning, suggested "Eastern spirit, Western crafts" (*Tōyō seishin, Seiyō gigei*). Even the ardent Westernizer Fukuzawa Yukichi (1834–1901) coined a popular phrase "Japanese spirit, Western skill" (*Wakon, Yōsai*) probably derived from the earlier one.

Movement. The new intellectuals in the movement claimed that not only Western scientific technology, laws, and political institutions ought to be introduced, but also China's philosophy, ethics, natural science, social theories and institutions should be thoroughly re-examined and modeled after those of the West. It was not half-hearted reform or partial renovation which was being advocated, but a vast and fervent attempt to dethrone the very fundamentals of the old stagnant tradition and to replace it with a completely new culture.[24]

The May Fourth Movement also marked an accelerated awakening of the Chinese intelligentsia to the ideas of individual human rights and national independence. It hastened the unification of China in the nation-state pattern by drawing the people together in thought and action. The emancipation of the individual and the promotion of a sense of nationality and social equality among such a great number of people — as Bertrand Russell put it, "a quarter of the human race" [25] — was, of course, far from accomplishment even decades afterward. But the increased consciousness and activity of Chinese intellectuals along these lines at this period must surely be recognized by historians as an event of world-wide significance.

Furthermore, since the movement introduced or coincided with many new factors in the economic, social, political, and intellectual fields, it serves as a most important key to the understanding of modern China during the last forty years. So many furious controversies and struggles in the following decades were initiated by the movement that without a study of it one would miss the origin and nature of the real issues. In fact, the current Chinese political situation may be regarded as, directly or indirectly, a result of the movement. The issue is not dead. It remains to the present and may point to the future. Moreover, most contemporary Chinese leaders, in fields varying from literature and philosophy to economics and politics, were educated and trained during the May Fourth period and started their careers by joining the movement. This experience still influences their thinking and psychology. While some conservatives blame it for all the evils that developed in China later, almost all the younger generation consider that its benefits to them have been "bountiful and undiminished." [26] "At any rate," as one of China's leading journalists declared, "the influence the May Fourth Movement exerted upon my mind will not be effaced as long as I live." [27] Considering all these facts, one may reasonably assert that the temper of modern China cannot be fully understood without knowing the currents of the movement.

Finally, the movement cannot be ignored when reviewing Western relations with China. As is known, the major challenge to Chinese traditional ethics, customs, and institutions in the period was Western thought in the guise of ideas like liberalism, democracy, and science. The wide influence of the West, especially the United States, is not to be denied. Yet, with nationalist sentiments on the rise, fed by the example of Soviet Russia defying the West, socialist ideas became more influential in later years. The shift in emulation from liberalism to socialism may be explained in terms of such factors as China's need to industrialize rapidly, her humiliating defeats, her authoritarian political heritage, and the appeal of socialist idealism to a society based on cooperation rather than individualism, as well as the policies of the Nationalists in and after the movement. On the other hand, inadequacies of the West are exemplified by the hated imperialist methods of their economic interests in China, and by the misguided policies and ineffectuality of the Chinese liberals. In addition to these, an examination of the policies and attitudes of the Western countries toward the movement per se may also shed some light on the reasons for this rise and fall.

The foregoing pages have outlined in brief the scope and significance of the May Fourth Movement and, in particular, the setting in which it arose. The ensuing detailed examination of its events and ideas will, it is hoped, present a full picture of the twentieth-century intellectual revolution which shook China to her roots and which, after forty years, is still reverberating.

PART ONE

DEVELOPMENT OF THE MOVEMENT

CHAPTER II

FORCES THAT PRECIPITATED
THE MOVEMENT, 1915–1918

I N order to understand the sentiments and ideas of the May Fourth Movement, we must trace the Chinese reaction to the Japanese policies toward China and the activities of Chinese students abroad during World War I. With regard to the former, there were essentially two articulate groups which expressed Chinese public opinion and which came to constitute the two major elements of the movement. One group, as a reaction to modern imperialism, gradually developed strong patriotic sentiments in their desire to save China. The other group, influenced by the impact of Western civilization upon China, suggested various reforms for the modernization of the nation. The former, composed of literate as well as illiterate people, supplied the movement with emotional impetus, the latter, mainly young Chinese intellectuals, furnished its ideological content.

These sentiments on the part of the general public and the agitation for reform on the part of the intellectuals indeed had their beginnings during the latter part of the last century. But not until early in World War I did Chinese public feeling of national humiliation start to assume a powerful form as a result of the policies and actions of the Japanese government toward China. At the same time the new intellectuals recognized the necessity to arouse themselves and lead their countrymen to thorough modernization.

Furthermore, the number of Chinese students abroad increased substantially at this time. Their close contact with the West gave them new ideas which later inspired other new intellectuals and helped to activate the May Fourth Movement.

Humiliation of Patriots at Home (Impact of the Twenty-one Demands)

Unlike the Chinese of the late Ch'ing period who, unaware of the ultimate dangers of imperialism, thought that their task was simply to "enrich and strengthen the nation," the Chinese during the May Fourth period realized urgently that China must be rescued from subjugation. Their rallying cry "save the nation" (*chiu kuo*), first used after China's defeat by Japan in 1894, was widely employed at this time. Its popularity reflected the fact that the Chinese people, and the intellectuals in particular, were awakening to the perils to the nation in its struggle for survival in the modern world. This awakening had been greatly accelerated by the humiliation aroused by Japan's Twenty-one Demands and ensuing episodes.

It was on January 18, 1915, a dark and chilly evening, that Hioki Eki, the Japanese minister to China, instead of following normal diplomatic channels, presented in a private interview to the Chinese President Yüan Shih-k'ai a few sheets of paper watermarked with dreadnoughts and machine guns. On these pages were written the notorious Twenty-one Demands. The minister enjoined "absolute secrecy on pain of serious consequences" before handing Yüan the text of the demands, and opened the discussion with an air of great mystery.[1] The use of the unusually watermarked paper was hardly accidental. It hinted at the whole contents and intention of the paper. The demands hurt the pride of the Chinese people more than any real dreadnoughts or machine guns had ever done.

The demands called in effect for Japanese control of Manchuria, Inner Mongolia, Shantung, China's southeast coast, and the Yangtze Valley. The effect of acceptance of these demands would be Japanese colonization of all these areas and economic and administrative control of the whole country. By the fifth group of demands, which was at first concealed from the other powers by the Japanese government, Japan intended to deprive the Chinese government of virtually any effective control over its own domestic affairs. It demanded the employment of influential Japanese advisers in political, financial, and military affairs; the right of ownership of land for the building of Japanese hospitals, churches, and schools; the joint Sino-Japanese organization and administration of the Chinese police forces in important places; the purchase from Japan of 50 per cent or more of the total quantity of her munitions of war or the establishment in China of Sino-Japanese jointly worked arsenals, and other similar control devices.[2]

Negotiations between China and Japan followed and lasted for almost four months. At last, on May 7, 1915, at 3:00 p.m., Japan presented China with an ultimatum, demanding that she "accept without amendment all items, included in groups I, II, III, and IV, together with the item in group V relating to Fukien."[3] The harsher items of group V were omitted. Faced with this threat and in fact with Japanese troops which had been sent to China since the presentation of the demands, Yüan Shih-k'ai's government, without the consent of Parliament, which had been dissolved by Yüan at that time (the constitution required its consent), accepted on May 9 at 1:00 p.m. all the terms set forth in Japan's ultimatum and concluded on May 25 a treaty based upon them.

In the negotiations the Chinese government adopted an unprecedented policy of using the foreign and Chinese press for moral support.[4] Despite Japanese injunctions to secrecy, the nature of the demands was gradually revealed to the press by Chinese officials. When Chinese newspapers unanimously protested the demands, the government relaxed its traditional policy of censorship and suppression. During the next stage of the negotiations the Japanese Foreign Minister Baron Katō Takaaki asked the Chinese government to censor its press.[5] In the third meeting with the newly appointed Chinese Foreign Minister Lu Cheng-hsiang (1871–1949), Hioki complained that the Chinese government, contrary to its traditional practice, did not suppress the press but "utilized" it to help China's advancement in the negotiations. To this complaint, Lu replied, "times have changed from the days of the Manchus, and now there is freedom of the press in China." [6] Lu's argument was of course specious; under Yüan Shih-k'ai's government there was no real freedom of the press. There seems no doubt, however, that in this negotiation with Japan, Yüan's policy was for the moment to secure the support of public opinion. This policy was in fact officially acknowledged at that time.[a] Furthermore, in reply to Japan's demand for the joint ownership of the Han-Yeh-P'ing Iron and Coal Company by Japan and China, Yüan Shih-k'ai made the point that the company was a private enterprise and the Chinese government could not intervene.[9]

Under the conditions of political chaos, backwardness, and warlord rule, Chinese public opinion for the first time in modern Chinese history had an opportunity to express itself. The voice of the new intelligentsia, conveying the public feeling of national humiliation, was widely heard throughout the country. While the negotiations were going on in Peking, excitement prevailed in many parts of China. Almost all Chinese newspapers demonstrated very strong

---

[a] In a letter to Lu Tsung-yü, Chinese Minister in Tokyo, dated March 5, 1915, Ts'ao Ju-lin, Chinese Vice Foreign Minister and actually the responsible negotiator, acknowledged that Wellington V. K. Koo was in charge of using the "policy of publicity." [7] Paul S. Reinsch also has said, "the Chinese relied on public opinion," and he specifically included Yüan himself.[8] It seems clear that Yüan's "policy of publicity" was primarily aimed at stirring up the sympathy of world opinion toward China rather than at the domestic press. But because of his personal ambition he also desired support of his government by Chinese public opinion.

anti-Japanese feelings. Chinese students in America rejoiced that "patriotic feeling and anxiety" were reported to "have found expression in every corner of the country." The governors of nineteen provinces sent requests to the central government not to yield to the demands. It was said that every day the President's palace was "flooded" with letters and telegrams from the people, expressing their indignation.[10]

After Japan's terms were accepted as a result of the ultimatum, Chinese public indignation reached its climax. Signs reading "Don't Forget the National Humiliation" (*Wu-wang kuo-ch'ih*) could be seen all over the country; this slogan was painted on walls, coined into trade marks, and imprinted on stationery.[11] The dates of May 7 and May 9 were immediately named "Commemoration Days of National Humiliation."[12] The history of the humiliation was also written into textbooks.[13]

Chinese officialdom and the public reacted differently to the Twenty-one Demands. As far as the government was concerned, a program of national salvation, proposed by some of the officials right after the conclusion of the Sino-Japanese Treaty [14] and acknowledged by Yüan Shih-k'ai, was forgotten very soon.[15] As for the people, two significant effects of the demands must be noted. In the first place, a new nationalism gradually developed, and many came to understand that it was necessary to resist foreign aggression in order to survive. This feeling was reflected in later years in the cry "Externally, struggle for sovereignty" (*Wai cheng kuo-ch'üan*), which was later often replaced by "Externally, resist the Great Powers" (*Wai k'ang ch'iang-ch'üan*). It became one of the two leading slogans in the May Fourth Incident. This effect of the Twenty-one Demands on the development of nationalism in China had been noted by many Western observers, for example: "The youth of China saw their fatherland engulfed. The Japanese attitude as expressed in the Twenty-one Demands left no shadow of doubt that the one hope for China lay in the adoption, by the Chinese people, of a vigorous, aggressive policy of nationalism."[16]

In the second place, because of the outside pressure of what was taken to be aggression, a spirit of national unity prevailed in China, for the time being at least. Many political factions rallied to support Yüan Shih-k'ai. The strongest opposition party, the Kuomintang, which had been reorganized in 1914 in Tokyo as an underground revolutionary party, declared its support of the Peking government. "Let us," said one of its leaders, "stop all the internal strife and resolve to apply ourselves to face our common foe."[17] At the same time, just as he was reluctant to intervene in the press campaign, as mentioned before, Yüan sought to increase his own popularity by wooing the revolutionary leaders. During the Sino-Japanese negotiations, it was reported that his government had pardoned Sun Yat-sen, Huang Hsing, and many other revolutionary leaders and offered them high official positions if they were willing to return and declare their loyalty to the government.[18] Finally, since every emergency situation furnishes a chance for the rise of ambitious dictators, Yüan was actually encouraged by the spontaneous support of public opinion and of his political opponents to imagine that his dream of being a monarch had the backing of the people.[19] Yüan's attempt to restore the monarchy warned the Chinese, and the new intellectuals in particular, that to save the country the warlords and the traitors had to be eliminated. This feeling grew and formed later the second of the two prevalent slogans in the May Fourth Incident, namely, "Internally, throw out the traitors" (Nei ch'u kuo-tse).

Although both the nationalist and anti-warlord sentiments derived, directly or indirectly, from the Twenty-one Demands, the anti-warlord aspects were not manifested until a few years later. For the time being, nationalist zeal played the major role in the development of a mass movement against Japan. Not long after January 26, 1915, when the first news of the demands was broken to the Chinese, public meetings were held. On February 19 a Citizen's Patriotic Society was formed in Shanghai to oppose the demands. Late in February, Chinese merchants of San Francisco cabled to Canton suggesting a boycott against Japanese goods, but the Cantonese disapproved of the idea on the ground that it might embarrass the government in the negotiations. Yet by that time a National Association of Comrades against Japan (Kuo-min tui Jih t'ung-chih hui) was organized in Shanghai. It held a public meeting in the International Settlement on March 18, 1915, attended by tens of thousands, and resolved to start the boycott. The boycott spread very rapidly to other cities; even the merchants who were specializing in Japanese goods joined it. This immediately alarmed the Japanese government. Under pressure from Japan, Yüan Shih-k'ai on March 25 gave an order to abandon the boycott.[20] However, the feeling of indignation among the Chinese people could not be controlled. The boycott started to spread to the Yangtze ports and some of the northern cities in April. On May 13, a demonstration and boycott by merchants started in Hankow, following a report that the Japanese Concession would be permitted to hold a lantern parade to celebrate victory over China in the negotiations. Shops were closed. Three Japanese shops were looted and two Japanese injured. British and Russian troops, with fixed bayonets, dispersed the gathered Chinese before the arrival of a regiment of Chinese troops, which had been called out. The Japanese garrison was also ordered out but withdrew later.[21]

The boycott soon spread over Southern China. Special organizations for the boycott were established in Peking, Shanghai, Hankow, Changsha, and Canton, as well as among the overseas Chinese in San Francisco.[22] It caused considerable uneasiness in Tokyo and in the middle of June brought an official Japanese protest to China concerning the anti-Japanese movement in the Republic.[23] On June 29 Yüan Shih-k'ai issued another order to all the provincial governments to forbid the boycott.[24] Consequently, the merchants dropped the name boycott but continued to avoid Japanese goods under the slogan "Encourage the use of native goods," and a Society to Exhort the Use of Native Goods (*Ch'üan yung kuo-huo hui*) was established. The boycott lasted from March to the end of the year. Its most effective period probably was the five months from April through August. It was the fifth boycott movement against foreign goods in Chinese history, but the first which revealed the power of this weapon when employed by a considerable number of people. Japan's export trade to China suffered an unprecedented loss during the period of severest boycotting.

The boycott also played a significant part in the advancement of China's native industry which had been encouraged by the dislocations of international trade during World War I. When the Self-conscious Disgrace Society was organized in May in Shanghai, a National Salvation Fund (*Chiu kuo ch'u-chin t'uan*) with the purpose of raising 50,000,000 *yuan* was established in order to develop home industry. It was reported to have been subscribed to by people in all walks of life from the richest to the poorest.[25] After this boycott, increases in production by many native light industries were evident.[26] The effect of the Twenty-one Demands in awakening the Chinese to a sense of national solidarity and of "economic and commercial possibilities" was realized by an American correspondent shortly after China accepted Japan's demands. He believed that the movement to develop home industries, especially in cottons, might be "far reaching" and thus "vitally" affect the staple trade of Japan. "The feeling of national humiliation, the deep resentment, and the bitterness of soul which pervade so many Chinese," he wrote, "render it unnecessary to start a boycott, for the people have made up their minds to refrain from purchasing Japanese goods as far as possible."[27]

This was probably an overoptimistic estimate of the situation. Although it is true that Chinese were beginning to awaken to the need of national salvation, their efforts in economic construction were rudimentary. Moreover, the problem of what steps must be taken to save China was rarely faced by the average intellectual, not to speak of the ordinary citizen, at this time. The traditional apathy of the Chinese people toward political affairs and national problems did not yield so readily to the rising crisis. This fact had been pointed out by a Japanese writer in an article "The Chinese National Character and Social Organization," and was deplored by Chinese writers of the time, such as Ch'en Tu-hsiu.[28]

Nevertheless, a few active Chinese intellectuals, especially the returned students and those still studying abroad, became more aware than ever before of China's basic problems. They started to ponder whether the traditional Chinese civilization should undergo a basic and thorough change.

Reforming Zeal of Students Abroad

The reform movements of modern China were stimulated in different ways by Chinese students returning from various foreign countries as well as by her own traditional theories and historical examples. But, contrary to the later pattern, almost none of the Chinese students who returned from the West in the late Ch'ing period joined the reform movements which were developing in China. Initiative and leadership were usually taken by those who did not understand Western languages. "Because of this limitation," as Liang Ch'i-ch'ao said, "many of the defects of the early reforms — such as the introduction of Western knowledge piecemeal like a peddler's sales and the obscurity, shallowness, and fallacy of its presentation — could not be avoided. Accordingly, they did not lay a solid foundation for the reform movements even after twenty years of effort. Experiencing every up and down, they were finally disregarded by Chinese society."[29] But by the time of the May Fourth Movement new departures both in ideas and activities were often to be linked with the return of students from abroad.

The patterns of reform current in China in the second half of the nineteenth century were, insofar as they were inspired by the West, set, for the most part, by the social and political thought of the predominant foreign power, Great Britain. Almost all of Yen Fu's famous translations were from British sources, and about two thirds of Lin Shu's translations were from English literature. By the turn of the century, however, most Chinese students abroad were studying in Japan, the United States, or on the European continent, especially in France; and these three countries had become the most important centers of foreign influence. Each country imprinted its own cultural patterns and political and social beliefs. When the students returned home, they displayed the cultural discrepancies among the three countries by their advocacy of different and sometimes contradictory solutions to the problems of China. The May Fourth Movement reflected these divergent influences.

Intellectual and literary controversies developed in the United States

The United States was the first country to which modern China sent her students to study. As early as 1872, 30 Chinese boys were sent to the United States to be educated. Until 1909, however, the number of Chinese students in America did not increase greatly. In that year the United States government began to return the Boxer Indemnity funds to China, to be used to send Chinese students to the United States.[30] By 1915, more than 1,200 Chinese students were studying in schools and colleges in the United States.[b]

The news of the Japanese demands on China had aroused great excitement among these Chinese students, which was reflected in their publication, *The Chinese Students' Monthly*, organ of The Chinese Students' Alliance in the United States of America. It devoted almost the whole March 1915 issue to a discussion of the problem. Some of the students declared that China should fight, emulating Belgium instead of Korea. Some advocated that China should not be "Japanned," and some thought that the crisis called for "great sacrifices and sharp departures from settled plans." "We must do," as one of the editorials said, "what is in the best interest of the nation: die, if necessary. . . . China now needs capable men more than anything else. . . . Our duty is, therefore, plain: Go Home!"[32] Some of the Chinese students even wanted to spend their summer vacation in the military camps conducted by the U.S. War Department.[33]

While the general sentiment of indignation among the Chinese students in the United States ran very high, a warning to keep cool came from a few. Hu Shih (romanized Suh Hu),[c] the "Home News" editor of the *Monthly*, wrote

[b] The official report of the U.S. educational statistics estimated 594 Chinese students in American colleges. A more thorough investigation by the Chinese Students' Alliance in the United States gave 800 in colleges and universities, and the total number in all schools as 1,200.[31]

[c] Hu Shih, a most influential liberal scholar in modern China, generally regarded as the first poet to promote vigorously the vernacular literature, was born in Shanghai in 1891. His family home was Chihsi County, Anhwei Province. His father, an outstanding scholar and an official in Manchuria and Formosa, died when Hu was three years old. From three to twelve, Hu was taught by his uncle and cousin all the important classics, and read a number of old novels and stories in the vernacular. During 1904 he attended schools in Shanghai, where he was exposed to Western learning for the first time and was influenced by Yen Fu's translations and Liang Ch'i-ch'ao's writings. While Hu was at the Chinese Public Institute, from 1906 to 1909 he got the idea of using the vernacular for his literary writing. In 1910 he passed a competitive examination and was sent by the

"An Open Letter to All Chinese Students," pleading for "patriotic sanity"; he said:

> It seems to me that the right course for us students to take at this moment and at this distance from China, is this: *Let us be calm. Let us DO OUR DUTY which is TO STUDY. Let us not be carried away by the turmoil of the newspapers from our serious mission. Let us apply ourselves seriously, calmly, undisturbedly and unshakenly to our studies, and PREPARE OURSELVES to uplift our fatherland, if she survives this crisis — as I am sure she will, — or to resurrect her* from the dead, if it needs be! . . .
>
> The final solution of the Far Eastern Question is not to be sought in fighting Japan at present; nor in any external interference by any other Power or Powers; . . . The real and final solution must be sought somewhere else — far, far deeper perhaps than most of us now suspect. I do not know wherein it lies; I only know wherein it does *not* lie. Let us study it out calmly and dispassionately. . . .[35]

The letter stirred up a furious argument. Hu was denounced by his fellow students as a "traitor."[d] Hsu-kun Kwong, the editor-in-chief of the *Monthly*, who was a student in journalism at the time and later became a diplomat, replied with a lengthy article in answer to Hu's doctrine of nonresistance, which the editor described as based on the teachings of Lao-tzu, Jesus, and Buddha:

> In some dark corner of Suh Hu's thought, he seems to agree with us that his interpretation of the doctrine of non-resistance is inadequate and has to be discarded sometimes. In one place in his open letter, he says: "To resurrect her (China) from the dead, if it need be!" How is he going to resurrect China from the dead? By tucking under one arm the Bible and under the other some equally useful book, say Browning, since Suh Hu seems more familiar with it than with any other book? He must admit that force would be necessary to drive out the Japanese, if they once established themselves in China. To resurrect China from the dead is a much more difficult task than to resist Japan before she comes in.[37]

---

government to the United States for study first in agriculture and later in philosophy. He received his B.A. at Cornell in 1915 and his Ph.D. at Columbia in 1917, both in philosophy. From 1917 to 1927 he was professor of philosophy and later chairman of the department of English literature at Peking University. From 1930 to 1937 he was dean of the School of Letters and from 1945 to 1949 Chancellor of the same university. He was ambassador to the United States from 1938 to 1942, during the Sino-Japanese war years. After 1949 he lived in New York City. In 1958 he took the directorship of the Academia Sinica in Taiwan. He holds more than thirty honorary degrees from American and European universities.[34]

[d] Hu Shih in later time recalled the matter in his autobiographic sketch, "My pacifism and internationalism often brought me into serious trouble. . . . When in 1915 Japan presented the famous Twenty-one Demands on China, every Chinese in the United States was for immediate declaration of war with Japan. I wrote an open letter to *The Chinese Students' Monthly*, counseling calmness and cool-thinking, for which I was severely attacked from all sides and often denounced as a traitor."[36]

The article concluded with the assertion that Hu's suggestion was not "patriotic sanity" but "unpatriotic insanity." In a letter to the editor of the *Monthly* another Chinese student declared that, although he recognized that the duty of a student was to study, he did not think anyone had neglected his duty as a student by paying a great deal of attention to the current crisis at home. Only through a serious consideration of their national crisis could they concentrate their energies on their duty, their duty to find an answer to problems that demanded immediate solution.[38]

The debate over this question, i.e., what the Chinese students' attitudes should be in the national crisis, might be regarded as a trifling incident in the long course of history. Yet it actually touched upon the very controversy that would shape most of the activities of the new intellectuals during the May Fourth period, and to a degree Chinese educational, political, and social developments in later years. It is interesting to note that the principles both sides invoked were based on cool thinking and serious consideration and that the rational element prevailed at last. To Hu Shih, the solution of the Chinese problem lay in something deeper than building an army. "It is not a disgrace," as he wrote in his diary on February 21, 1915, "for a nation to lack a navy; or to lack an army! It is only a disgrace for a nation to lack public libraries, museums, and art galleries. Our people must get rid of this kind of disgrace!" [39] In a letter to an American professor he explained his reluctance to support a revolution and his advocacy of education as a foundation on which to build the new China, as he wrote, "from the bottom up." [40] This idea of building a new China through education was later advocated and put into practice during the May Fourth Movement by Hu Shih and many other new intellectual leaders who had been exposed to American influences.

At the same time another movement was taking shape which was to have far-reaching consequences. Since the end of the last century, Chinese men of letters had discussed the idea of a "literary revolution" but no concrete plan had developed. As late as September 17, 1915, Hu Shih wrote about the literary revolution that "the coming of the new tide cannot be stopped," [41] but he still conceived of it as confined to "a revolution of poetry," by which he meant the writing of poems in "prose diction." [42] The broader concept that *pai hua* (the vernacular language) should be used in place of *wen yen* (the literary language) in all Chinese literature was not developed until later, according to Hu, in the dormitories of Cornell University and Columbia University during the summer term of 1916, when he argued this problem with some of his fellow students.[43] The results of the discussion were subsequently described in a series of articles in English by Chao Yüan-jen (Y. R. Chao) and Hu Shih, published in *The Chinese Students' Monthly*.[44] The articles, however, did not provoke any unusual interest among their readers. The idea of literary reform was not enthusiastically discussed until Hu Shih's article in Chinese on the subject was published and supported by Ch'en Tu-hsiu in the *New Youth* monthly in January 1917.

The Chinese literary revolution really began with the poetry revolution, which had been advocated in China for many years. Almost all the political reformers of the Hundred Days' Reform of 1898 were young poets, and some of them were leaders of the revolution.[45] Hu Shih's program in a sense carried this movement to a new stage. As he himself recalled in 1919, his idea of a poetry revolution was primarily based on his own "experimentalism" and "evolutionary idea of literature," drawn from the lessons of Chinese literary history and of the European Renaissance.[46] It should be noted that Hu was probably also influenced by American literary movements of the second decade of this century. From 1912, when Harriet Monroe's *Poetry: A Magazine of Verse* appeared, a new poetry movement had sweeping influence upon American literature. By 1917, the new poetry was considered by some as "America's first national art." [47] In these years the prairie poets, the imagists, the new lyricists, and the experimentalists made their first major appearances.[48] One of the most distinct characteristics of the new American poetry launched at this time was its freedom from the traditionally stilted poetic diction, and its introduction of verse writing in plain speech. The years 1912 to 1918 were spoken of as the years of a "poetic renaissance." [49] Indeed, the second decade of the twentieth century was a new era not only in poetry but in all American literature and thought. "It was," as an American historian says, "an American Renaissance — It would 'make the Italian Renaissance look like a tempest in a teapot,' said Ezra Pound. It was a day when everything was New: the new woman, the new humanism, the new art, the new nationalism, the new freedom — even, with Robinson and Beard, the new history." [50] It was in this creative and inspiring time that Hu Shih and some other Chinese literary and educational leaders of the May Fourth reforms were educated in the United States.[e] A similar spirit was later to infuse the new era of China during the May Fourth Movement.

It is of course difficult to judge how much Hu Shih was influenced by this

---

[e] Hu Shih studied in the United States from Aug. 1910 to June 1917; Chiang Monlin, from Sept. 1908 to June 1917. Chiang's Ph.D. thesis under the guidance of Dewey at Columbia University was finished in 1917, and later published in China as *A Study on Chinese Principles of Education* (Shanghai, 1924).[51]

American movement in his formation of the idea of a new Chinese poetry
and literature. But it seems safe to say that he did notice this literary development during his last three years in the United States, though he paid more
attention to Wordsworth and Browning. One of his arguments with his literary
opponents revolved about the problem whether colloquialism and slang should
be used in poetry and literary writing.[52] After he made his first experimental
composition of a Chinese poem in the new diction on July 22, 1916, an opponent charged that Hu was "plagiarizing" the worthless European and American "New Tide." "The so-called New Tide," as he wrote to Hu, "is the
most ominous thing in the world; what reform does it have!" By New Tide,
the writer of the letter explained he meant Futurism, Imagism, and free verse
in literature, Symbolism, Cubism, and Impressionism in the fine arts, and
Bahaism, Christian Science, Shakerism, Free Thought, Church of Social Revolution, and Billy Sunday in religion.[53] To this charge Hu replied summarily,
"the really most ominous thing in the world is those who regard the New
Tide as the most ominous thing in the world." [54]

There seems to be some truth in the accusation of Hu's adopting the Western New Tide. Even his widely propagandized "eight-don'ts-ism" (*pa-pu
chu-i*) for the new Chinese literature possibly showed certain influences of
Ezra Pound's "A Few Don'ts," which had been published in *Poetry* three
years before.[55] Hu mentioned his knowledge of the Imagist ideas two decades
later when he published his diary, which contains his statement dated at the
end of 1916 that many of the principles of the Imagist poets were similar to
his own ideas on poetry and literature. This is evident in his article "Some
Tentative Suggestions for the Reform of Chinese Literature" (*Wen-hsüeh
kai-liang ch'u-i*).[56] It is also noticeable that Hu's new poetry was based on his
experimentalism, inspired by the tide which was rising in the West at the
time. The title of the volume of his poetry is indeed *A Book of Experiments*
(*Ch'ang-shih chi*) (1920), and the book is the first of its kind in Chinese literary history written in the vernacular.

Similarly, in the fields of philosophy and the philosophy of education, as
well as of scientific method, the new Chinese intellectuals were led principally
by Chinese students returned from the United States. The first volume, and
only one completed, of Hu Shih's *Outline of the History of Chinese Philosophy*
(*Chung-kuo che-hsüeh shih ta-kang*, published in February 1919 in Shanghai
by the Commercial Press), a pioneering work in the re-evaluation of Chinese
philosophy and logic, was based on his doctoral dissertation, "A Study of the
Development of Logical Method in Ancient China," written at Columbia Uni-

versity, under John Dewey's influence, from September 1915 to April 1917, and later published by the Oriental Book Company in Shanghai in 1922 under the new title, *The Development of the Logical Method in Ancient China*. In the new culture movement in China, Dewey's pragmatism and philosophy of education had predominant influence because of the efforts of his students, Hu Shih, T'ao Hsing-chih (or T'ao Heng-chi, T'ao Chih-hsing, W. T. Tao), Chiang Monlin (Chiang Meng-lin), and Cheng Hsiao-ts'ang, and his own travel there. Dewey arrived with his wife in Shanghai on May 1, 1919, three days before the May Fourth Incident, and left China on July 11, 1921. His lectures and articles were widely circulated among China's new intellectuals.[57]

Military, literary, and revolutionary influences of Japan

While the Chinese students in the United States paid more attention to cultural and educational problems, those in Japan tended in other directions and their various activities produced divergent effects in China. The Chinese government for the first time in modern history sent students to Japan in 1896 after the first Sino-Japanese War of 1894–95. The number was very small until after the Boxer Rebellion, but from 1901 to 1906 it grew rapidly. In 1906 there were about 13,000 Chinese students in Japan.[58] In fact, from 1903 on, including the period of the May Fourth Movement, the preponderance of Chinese students abroad were studying in Japan.[f] These students provided much of the leadership of the May Fourth Movement; they furnished, in the main, the militant elements, most of the leading creative writers of the new literature, and many of the revolutionary extremists including nationalists, socialists, and anarchists. They also included many of the military and civil officials who opposed the movement.

From 1904 on, China sent each year to Japan a considerable number of students to study military technique.[60] A Chinese writer remarked in the twenties with some exaggeration that "the students returned from Japan of course should be considered responsible for the prosperity of China's warlordism." [61] In fact some of these returned students, together with warlords and old gentry, formed the hard core of the opposition to the May Fourth Movement. This effect of the Japanese military training is quite natural and comprehensible. Japanese military schools maintained strict discipline and the cadets viewed their superiors with almost superstitious awe. They could not

---

[f] Statistics show that during this period 41.51 per cent of the Chinese students abroad were in Japan, 33.85 per cent in the United States, and 24.64 in European countries, mostly Germany, France, and Great Britain.[59]

criticize the administration of their schools nor intervene in the policies of the government.[62] This system was contrary to what most of the Chinese new intellectuals in the May Fourth Movement believed to be the moral responsibility of students and of youth in general.

At the same time, the creation of the new Chinese literature during the May Fourth period must also be credited principally to students returned from Japan. It is certainly true that to a great degree modern Chinese literature followed the techniques and themes of Russian and other Western literature; but these works were made available to Chinese readers during the period of the May Fourth Movement through retranslations from the Japanese.[63] Japanese influence was also evident in the new literary style. Liang Ch'i-ch'ao's style, for example, which still remained popular among many of the writers in the early period of the May Fourth Movement, bore traces of Japanese influence. Numerous men of letters in China who played leading roles in the construction of the new literature, such as Lu Hsün (pen name of Chou Shu-jen) and his younger brother Chou Tso-jen, had studied in Japan. "Modern Chinese literature," said Kuo Mo-jo, "has for the most part been created by Chinese students returned from Japan." [64] In fact, Japan had experienced her new literature reform, especially new poetry, and new thought tide a few years earlier than China. These must have affected the Chinese reforms.[65]

The third major effect of study in Japan was the introduction of anarchism and socialism, both of which enjoyed a vogue among Chinese youths in 1919.[66] From 1902 to 1911, socialism was propagated to some extent by both the Chinese Pao-huang-tang (Monarchist Constitutional Party) and T'ung-meng-hui (Alliance Society), the latter the predecessor of the Kuomintang. It was discussed in their literary organs, which were published in Chinese in Japan.[67] Liang Ch'i-ch'ao first mentioned Mo-k'e-shih (Marx) in his *New People's Magazine* (*Hsin min t'sung-pao*) in 1902. One of the earliest books on socialism introduced to China was Fukui Junzō's *Modern Socialism* (*Kinsei shakaishugi*) (1899), which was translated from Japanese into Chinese by Chao Pi-chen in 1903, in which year several other books on socialism and anarchism, translated from Japanese, were also published in Shanghai. The ten proposals in the *Communist Manifesto* were first translated into Chinese by a Kuomintang member, Chu Chih-hsin (1884–1920), in 1906, in its organ, the *People Report* (*Min pao*).[68] The Japanese Socialist Party, which was organized in February 1906, exerted a great influence upon the Chinese students in Japan. They often attended public meetings sponsored by the Japanese Socialist Party, and about 1907 established socialist discussion groups among themselves.[69]

It is believed that many Chinese students in Japan at the time kept contact with, and absorbed socialist ideas from, Japanese socialist leaders, such as Abe Isoo, Katayama Sen (Hisomu), Ōsugi Sakae, Kōtoku Denjirō (Shūsui), and Sakai Toshihiko. They converted a teenage Chinese student, Chiang K'ang-hu (Kiang Kang-hu), to socialism when he studied in Japan in 1900 at the age of seventeen. Inspired by the Japanese and Western socialists and the Chinese anarchists in Japan such as Chang Chi, Wu Chih-hui, Li Shih-tseng, and Ch'u Min-i, as well as by ancient Chinese idealists, Chiang established at Shang-hai on September 2, 1911, a Socialist Propaganda Association and published the *Socialist Star* (*She-hui chu-i ming-hsing-pao*). On November 15, 1911, Chiang reorganized the association into the Chinese Socialist Party (*Chung-kuo she-hui-tang*) and held its first national congress in the. same city.[70] This was the first time a socialist party was established in China. From 1899 to 1923 a major force in the Japanese socialist movement, anarchism likewise became popular in China in the early period of the May Fourth Movement.

Because of the above-mentioned influences, the reaction of the Chinese students in Japan to the Twenty-one Demands differed markedly from that of the Chinese in the United States. A group of those young Chinese, which probably numbered four thousand or more, was able upon hearing the news of the demands to express its strong protest by leaving Japan at once and returning to China in a body.[71] Chinese students in Japan were in general more sensitive to Sino-Japanese relations and more emotional in reacting to them because they were both geographically close to their Chinese homeland and at the same time living in Japan where, in the circumstances, personal irritations easily inflamed national resentments. There were several instances of this "returning-in-a-body": [72]

(1) In 1905 students protested against the "Rules Governing Chinese Students in Japan" proclaimed by the Japanese Ministry of Education. A prominent Chinese student, Ch'en T'ien-hua (b. 1875), one of the important party workers of the T'ung-meng-hui, committed suicide on the occasion.

(2) In 1911 they joined the Chinese Revolution.

(3) In 1915 they protested against the Twenty-one Demands.

(4) In 1918 they protested against the Sino-Japanese Military Mutual Assistance Convention.

The 1905 incident had some unforeseen consequences which should be noted, because they exerted indirect influences upon the May Fourth Movement. The students returning at this time numbered about one thousand. In a wave of indignation they established at Shanghai during the next year the famous Chinese Public Institute (*Chung-kuo kung hsüeh*), of which quite a few students (e.g., Hu Shih, Chu Ching-nung, and Jen Hung-chün) later played important roles in the new culture movement.[73] The institute became one of the foremost centers for the new learning at the time.

In addition to this, the returned students from Japan unified all the Chinese students who were studying in Shanghai and organized in 1906 the Alliance of Students in Shanghai from All Provinces (*Ko-sheng liu Hu hsüeh-sheng tsung-hui*). The aim of the alliance was set forth in its draft program: "to unite student groups of all the schools in order to lead to the establishment of a Parliament in the future." [74] The program of the alliance was unprecedentedly ambitious and, in some aspects, fanciful, but deserves examination as a reflection of the national aspirations of patriotic students at the time. It included, among others, the following aims:

1. To publish magazines and newspapers in the vernacular in each province;
2. To train people to speak the national language (*kuo-yü*) in order to eliminate the dialects of the provinces;
3. To investigate social conditions in all the hinterland provinces;
4. To assist and accelerate the establishment of self-government in all the provinces;
5. To study law and political science in order to be available to the provincial legislative gentry for counsel;
6. To carry on translation work to introduce foreign culture to China;
7. To improve industries in the hinterland of China;
8. To encourage Chinese students to study abroad;
9. To organize art clubs to promote the "national quintessence" (*kuo-ts'ui*) [a term which was used later by conservatives in defense of the Chinese tradition];
10. To establish schools for women in order to train teachers for kindergartens;
11. To encourage all the counties and districts to establish more elementary schools;
12. To encourage people to build railroads and open mines in order to save China from being vanquished.[75]

The alliance was not well organized and disappeared before long. Few items of the program were carried out. But this was the first time modern Chinese students made an effort to unite on a nation-wide basis and to pay attention to the social, cultural, and political reform of China.[g] It also might

---

[g] Another group bearing the name of student organization was the World Association of

be regarded as a prelude to the establishment of the various energetic and active student unions in 1919 after the May Fourth Incident. The alliance's advocacy of the vernacular and *kuo-yü* was remarkable at this early date.

In some aspects, the return home movement of the Chinese students in Japan in 1915 was only a repetition of the students' reaction to Japan's policy toward China in 1905 and during other incidents. This time, however, the cause of the movement was more political and diplomatic than had previously been the case. Among the Chinese students in Japan, strong nationalistic and anti-Japanese sentiments were stirred up. Some of them even developed an unreasonable bias and prejudice against Japanese civilization as a whole.[77] As for the return home movement of May 12, 1918, it influenced the Chinese students' demonstration and petition in Peking which took place nine days afterward. It also contributed to the formation of a few political groups or parties in later years.

During the latter period of World War I a nationalist resurgence among the Chinese students and intellectuals in Japan was sparked by the leadership of the Kuomintang. From the fall of 1913 to the fall of 1916 many leaders of the party were in Japan as exiles because of Yüan Shih-k'ai. It was reorganized by Sun Yat-sen in Tokyo in June of 1914 as a revolutionary party, and in the war years campaigned to oppose the Peking warlord government. By the end of the war the party tended to advocate once again a policy of nationalism which had almost been given up since 1912.

On the whole, Chinese intellectuals in Japan received more militarist, socialist, and nationalist influences than did students in any other country.[78]

Revolutionary political ideologies and activities developed in France

France's influence upon China in this period can hardly be exaggerated. From the beginning of the twentieth century, the political thought of the French Revolution had an almost unrivaled vogue among young Chinese revolutionaries and reformers. In the first two decades of this century it influenced a considerable number of Chinese intellectual and political leaders, such as Liang Ch'i-ch'ao, Ch'en Tu-hsiu, and many of the Kuomintang leaders. Ch'en

Chinese Students (*Huan-ch'iu Chung-kuo hsüeh-sheng hui*), which was established in Shanghai in 1905. It had no considerable expansion until 1911. Its program was less ambitious but more practical than the Alliance of Students. But the association was actually led by professional educators rather than by students themselves.[76] During the May Fourth period it had its own day and night schools. As a member of the Student Union of Shanghai and the Student Union of China, it provided its office in the International Settlement in Shanghai for the offices of the latter two until June 9, 1919. Ts'ao Ju-lin was a permanent member of the association but was dismissed from it a week after the May Fourth Incident.

Tu-hsiu studied the French language in his twenties, and became a great admirer and propagandist for French civilization.[79] In the first issue of *New Youth* he wrote an article, "The French and Modern Civilization" (*Fa-lan-hsi-jen yü chin-tai wen-ming*), declaring that the French were the creators of modern Western civilization. Without accurate factual support he maintained that the French "invented" what he held to be the three most significant modern doctrines: the theory of the rights of man, formulated by Lafayette when he wrote *La declaration des droits de l'homme* (Ch'en alleged that Lafayette also drafted the American Declaration of Independence); the theory of evolution, created by Jean Baptist de Monet de Lamarck who published his *Philosophie Zoologique* in 1809, fifty years earlier than Darwin's publication of his theory; and modern socialism, derived from the French writers Babeuf, Saint-Simon, and Fourier, and developed by the Germans, Lassalle and Karl Marx.[80] More noteworthy is the fact that Ch'en's theory of the Chinese literary revolution resulted from his study of the history of French literature. In fact, in later years the May Fourth Movement was sometimes referred to as a Chinese "French Enlightenment."

Chinese intellectuals in the May Fourth Movement were, in many cases, overwhelmingly dominated by the democratic ideas and liberalism of eighteenth- and nineteenth-century France rather than the ideas of other Western countries. The temper of the Chinese intellectuals in the movement often bore traces of French romanticism. Introduced into China were also France's utopian socialism and anarchism, especially in their theoretical aspects. Early in 1907, Chinese students in Paris established the *New Century* (*Hsin shih-chi*) weekly, propagandizing socialism and the theories of Michael Bakunin and Peter Kropotkin.[81] In the following fifteen years a movement for study in France, led by prominent Chinese anarchists, absorbed the attention of many able and ambitious young Chinese students. In 1912, Li Shih-tseng, Wu Chih-hui, Ts'ai Yüan-p'ei (then Minister of Education), all believers in anarchism, and Wang Ching-wei organized in Peking the Society for Frugal Study in France (*Liu-Fa chien-hsüeh hui*) to encourage and help students to go to France. Preparatory schools for this purpose were established in Peking, Shanghai, Tientsin, and Paoting. About one hundred and twenty students went to France in one year (from 1912 to 1913).[82] Shortly after, the society was dissolved under President Yüan Shih-k'ai's pressure.

But in 1914, in view of the fact that some workers were also studying, Li, Ts'ai, Wang, and the other leaders of the society such as Wu Yü-chang expanded their program to a work-and-study scheme. They also organized in

Paris in June 1915 the Society for Frugal Study by Means of Labor (*Ch'in-kung chien-hsüeh hui*). The aim of the society was to encourage and help poor students to study in France by working their way. During the war, the number of students in this category started to increase. To take care of this situation, a Societé Franco-Chinoise d'Education (*Hua-Fa chiao-yü hui*) was organized in France in March 1916 by Ts'ai and his French and Chinese friends. Ts'ai was elected its president. By the end of 1919, 400 students of this type were in France for study. In the next year, 1,200 more were there. Most of these students had received college or middle school education before they left China. Some had been teachers, shop clerks, technicians, or journalists. Actually less than half of the total were enrolled in schools in France; the rest were employed in factories and elsewhere.[83]

Besides this work-and-study program, an unprecedented migration between China and France developed during the war. Early in 1916, because of lack of labor, the governments of France and Great Britain, probably inspired by the use of Chinese labor in Russia, contracted with the Chinese government to recruit Chinese workers for service in France and elsewhere. The five-year contract provided a daily wage for an average worker of five francs (approximately 0.965 *yuan*) for a ten-hour maximum day, with half of this wage deducted for board, lodging, and sickness, leaving a total of 2.50 francs (0.483 *yuan*) per day. The first group of coolies, numbering about 8,000, arrived in France in the winter of 1916.[84] By the end of 1918, 140,000 Chinese workers were recruited, distributed in more than one hundred camps, and in the employ of the French, British, and American governments. The French government employed 40,000, the British 100,000, and the American Expeditionary Force borrowed 10,000 from the French in 1917.[85] According to a report received at the Chinese Legation in Washington in October 1918, the total number of Chinese workers joining the Allies' work in France, Egypt, the French colonies, Mesopotamia, and Palestine amounted to 175,000. The distribution was: with British forces 125,000, with French forces 40,000, with American forces 6,000, and in Mesopotamia and Africa 4,000.[86] By the beginning of 1919, the number was reported to have reached 200,000.[h] This was the first time in Chinese history that such a considerable number of workers had been sent to work in Western countries.

It must be noted that the contracts for the recruitment of Chinese workers were concluded with the help of the Society for Frugal Study in France, and

---

[h] Secretary Lansing is reported to have stated at the Council of Ten that "China had furnished 200,000 men."[87]

that the recruitment was largely done, under government supervision, by Chinese local educational administrators and teachers of elementary schools in many villages and cities in China.[88] At first, all the recruits were illiterate laborers, but as time went on they included many students and teachers.[89] Moreover, 400 students joined as interpreters. Thus in 1918 there were among the Chinese workers in France about 28,000 Chinese literates, who should be considered as belonging to the intellectual group.

These Chinese workers were assigned to work connected with roads, railroads, mines, factories, fields, forests, ordnance and tank workshops, ammunition dumps, forge shops, docks, or construction of barracks. Many of them were engaged in exhuming and reburying the war dead.[90]

It is clear that these Chinese workers differed greatly in character from other overseas Chinese. They included many intellectuals, they were almost all put to hard and heavy war work, they were scheduled to stay abroad only temporarily — as soon as the war was over they were expected to return to China. Moreover, they were well organized. In individual camps the number of Chinese ranged from 25 to 3,000 and the contracts promised them permission to organize trade unions and to enjoy all the liberty guaranteed by French law to its citizens.[91]

This unprecedentedly large number of Chinese workers employed in the West by Western governments had important consequences for the Chinese mass movement in later years. In the first place, it provided a chance for Chinese intellectuals to live together with the workers and to begin to assume leadership. Previously, Chinese students abroad had come mainly from rich families, and few of them had done any hard work. By contrast, these student-workers came from the poor or middle class and for the first time did not follow the student tradition of belonging to a leisure class.[92] With their assistance, a great number of industrial and social organizations were formed among the Chinese workers in France during the war years, such as the Employment Bureau, the Franco-Chinese Trading Company, the Labor Union, the Workers' Society, the Chinese Laborers' Society, in addition to a considerable number of savings clubs, reading clubs, and "self-government clubs." One of the most important organizations was the Chinese Federation, organized for the most part by permanent Chinese residents in France. It was a superorganization of a half-dozen Chinese societies formed in France during the war. Its program included helping Chinese students in France and improving the welfare of Chinese workers there. It maintained the Chung-hua Publishing House, which printed all the Chinese documents for the Chinese delegation at the Paris Peace Conference. It also subsidized a Chinese weekly which was devoted to the interests of the Chinese workers.

The welfare and educational work for Chinese workers and student-workers in France began in the early period of the war. Ts'ai Yüan-p'ei was one of the intellectual leaders in France in charge of editing textbooks for the Chinese Workers' School in France (*Hua-kung hsüeh-hsiao*) about 1916. (It was apparently his experience with this program for educating workers in France which led him later to encourage similar programs among the students at the National University of Peking.) After 1916, the work was done chiefly under the direction of the International Y.M.C.A. with a staff of over 150 Chinese, British, French, American, Danish, and Dutch secretaries, and financed mainly by a fund of 1,416,000 *yuan* raised in China by the United War Work Campaign. Many of the staff, e.g., T. F. Tsiang, were volunteer Chinese students from American universities. Experimental methods of education in the Chinese language were tested. The literacy of the Chinese workers in France consequently rose from 20 per cent to 38 per cent by the end of 1921.[93] James Yen, one of the workers in the Y.M.C.A. in 1918, utilized his experience in the education of Chinese workers in France to develop his idea of a Mass Education Movement, which became popular in China in the latter period of the May Fourth Movement.[94]

At the same time, because of the social circumstances in which they worked, attitudes of racial and class consciousness gradually developed among the Chinese workers and student-workers in France. By the end of the war, nationalism, anarchism, and Marxism had been severally adopted by some of their leaders. Between November 1916 and July 1918, twenty-five strikes took place among the Chinese workers in French factories. (No information is available about the strikes of the Chinese working for the British and American forces. But it was reported that the Chinese workers with the French were more contented than those with the British because French officers were less race-conscious and imposed less strict discipline.) Most of these disturbances were due to the nonfulfillment of provisions of contracts, rough treatment, no pay, rigid military control, dangerous working conditions, severe punishment for small offenses, or language difficulties.[95] When the war ended and France was at once stricken by an economic recession, a great number of these workers and students found themselves unemployed. In 1920, more than 1,700 Chinese students in France were maintained on relief from various sources. This relief work incited political controversy among the students at the time. Political cliques in China were accused of using government relief funds to buy the students' political support.

Most of the workers and many of the students returned to China. Some of the workers came back penniless.[96]

The workers and students who returned from France after World War I brought with them new experiences and new ideas. Many of the workers had learned to read and write, and had been in contact with the European labor movement and the higher European standard of living. Their nationalist sentiments became so strong that some of them even refused to step ashore at Japanese ports on their way back from France during the period of the Shantung dispute. The experiences of these workers helped the organization and activities of labor unions in Shanghai during the May Fourth period. Before the autumn of 1920 the charge was made that "the returned laborer from the scene of recent conflict in Europe may be said to be the stormy petrel of the Chinese labor world." The returned workers were dreaded even then as "potential Bolsheviks." [97] It seems fair to say that many of these returned work-and-study students and workers were instrumental in driving the May Fourth Movement to extremes in both socialism and nationalism early in the twenties. A certain number of the founders and leaders of the Chinese Communist Party had been work-and-study students in France during and after the war.[i]

Thus, while the Sino-Japanese conflict aroused nationalist sentiments among the Chinese at home, the students who had studied abroad provided most of the new ideas absorbed from the West. When these students returned to China, they began to assume the leadership of the vast reforms being undertaken.

[i] To name a few: Chou En-lai, Ts'ai Ho-sen and his wife Hsiang Ching-yü, Wu Yü-chang, Li Li-san, Chang K'un-ti, Lo Hsüeh-tsan, Li Fu-ch'un and his wife Ts'ai Ch'ang, Wang Jo-fei, Hsü T'e-li, Lo Mai (or Lo Man, alias of Li Wei-han), Ch'en I, and Teng Hsiao-p'ing.[98]

CHAPTER III

THE INITIAL PHASE OF THE MOVEMENT:
EARLY LITERARY AND INTELLECTUAL
ACTIVITIES, 1917–1919

THE literary and intellectual ferment of the May Fourth Movement started shortly after the incident of the Twenty-one Demands during a period when the Chinese political situation deepened in gravity. From the winter of 1915 to the summer of 1917, the whole country was disturbed by the two monarchical movements. Reactionary bureaucrats busied themselves with preparations for the enthronement; and the old gentry propagated, not without distortion, the timeworn doctrines of orthodox Confucianism to provide the monarchical movement with its usual theoretical basis. Rumors about the return of a "real dragon emperor" permeated the minds of the illiterate and uneducated masses. Thus while it suffered national humiliation from abroad, the infant republic was endangered by the plots of warlords, old bureaucrats, and gentry at home. In the midst of such chaos, young Chinese intellectuals looked with growing anxiety for some means of saving the nation.

At this point numerous Chinese intellectuals returned from abroad bringing with them new ideas. Ch'en Tu-hsiu's return from Japan in 1915 and his establishment of the *New Youth* magazine that fall marked the start of a basic reform movement. This was reinforced by Ts'ai Yüan-p'ei's return from France in 1916, and by his campaign for reorganization at Peking University in and after 1917. In the summer of that year Hu Shih also returned from the United States, and joined these new intellectual leaders. In their reform effort, they encountered, in the theoretical arguments of the old gentry and literary men, only weak and passive opposition. Nevertheless, because the military and political authorities adhered to the traditional ethics and institutions, the new intellectuals suffered repression by the warlord government.

In the winter of 1916 Japan started its new policy towards China, attempting to buy influence over the Chinese government. Japanese actions well suited the needs of the Peking regime which intended to resort to arms to unify the country under its rule. The anti-Japanese sentiments among the people persisted, and the conflict of economic interest between Japan and the burgeoning Chinese economy deepened with the progress of the World War. In this setting, the close relation between the regimes of Terauchi and Tuan Ch'i-jui, at first financial and later military, quickly aroused suspicions among the Chinese people in general and the intelligentsia in particular. Consequently, when the intellectuals began gradually to use issues of foreign policy as a stick with which to beat the government, the new reform movement was abetted by the mounting anti-Japanese sentiments of the public and became a focus for the energies of young patriots.

Establishment of New Youth Magazine

In the summer of 1915, following the return of Chinese students from Japan after the Twenty-one Demands, Ch'en Tu-hsiu,[a] a veteran revolutionary

[a] Ch'en Tu-hsiu (1879–1942) was born in Huaining County, Anhwei Province, in the same year as Leon Trotsky, with whom Ch'en's name was often coupled in later years. In his home town, Ch'en's family was regarded as rich. His father, who was once an official in Manchuria, died when Ch'en was only a few months old. Between the ages of five and sixteen he received a strict classical education from his grandfather and elder brother. After passing the Manchu dynasty's first civil service examination in 1896 at seventeen and the second in the following year, he entered the renowned Ch'iu shih shu-yüan (Truth-seeking School) in Hangchow, where he studied naval architecture in French. He fled to Nanking after delivering speeches against the Manchu regime and was pursued by the police. Here he met Chang Shih-chao (b. 1881), a prominent political writer and journalist, with whom Ch'en subsequently started his career as editor of magazines. In 1902, at the age of twenty-three, Ch'en went to Japan to study, enrolling at the Higher Normal School in Tokyo. In Japan he organized, together with Feng Tzu-yu and other friends, the Chung-kuo ch'ing-nien hui (Chinese Youth Society). But he returned to Shanghai in the same year and in 1903 established there with Chang Shih-chao, Chang Chi, Su Man-ju, and Ho Mei-shih the revolutionary Kuo-min jih-jih k'an (Citizens' Daily). He returned to his home province and in 1904 established the An-hui su-hua pao (Anhwei Vernacular Magazine). In 1906 he went to Japan again, with the poet Su Man-ju, but returned to China the same year, teaching with Chang Shih-chao and Liu Shih-p'ei (another well-known scholar who, like Chang, also turned conservative and later opposed the new literature and new thought movements) at a high school in Wuhu, Anhwei. At this time Ch'en started another vernacular magazine. Disliking nationalism, Ch'en, during his stay in Japan, had refused to join the revolutionary T'ung-meng-hui (some say that he possibly joined it) led in Japan by Sun Yat-sen. According to some reports, in 1907 Ch'en went to France and was deeply influenced by French political and literary thought and civilization. He returned to China in 1910 to become a teacher in the Army Elementary School at Hangchow and the next year took part in the Revolution. After the Revolution, he was named commissioner of education in the Anhwei provincial government by Po Wen-wei, the Military Governor of that province and a member of the T'ung-meng-hui. Ch'en joined with Po against President Yüan Shih-k'ai in 1913 and fled to Japan shortly after the failure of the revolution in that year. He stayed in Japan until his return to Shanghai in 1915.[1]

then exiled in Japan, went back to Shanghai and founded a magazine, *New Youth*, which was to play an extraordinary part in the May Fourth Movement. Ch'en had taken part in the abortive "second revolution" of 1913 against Yüan Shih-k'ai. Immediately afterwards he had helped Chang Shih-chao to edit the famous periodical, *The Tiger* (*Chia yin tsa-chih*).[b] The periodical was, however, suspended as a result of pressure by Yüan Shih-k'ai in 1915. Yüan had since 1913 continuously throttled any opposition press except when, as during the negotiations of the Twenty-one Demands, it furthered his interests. After the negotiations came to an end, many antimonarchical newspapers were suppressed.

The atmosphere in which Ch'en Tu-hsiu started publication was not favorable. Freedom of the press was restricted by a number of severe laws. Ostensibly the Provisional Constitution of 1912 granted freedom of speech and assembly, freedom to organize, and freedom of the press.[2] But following the example of the Japanese constitution (Art. XXIX), it also provided that the people's rights might be restricted by law in the interest of promoting public welfare, maintaining peace and security, or in an emergency.[3] Since this proviso could be broadly interpreted and laws and ordinances very easily passed at the discretion of the President and his hand-picked Parliament, a series of laws and ordinances were proclaimed in the years 1912 and 1914 to restrict such popular rights. These included the Emergency Law,[4] the Security and Police Regulation,[5] the Regulation Respecting Preparations for an Emergency,[6] the Press Regulation,[7] and the Publication Law.[c] According to these laws and regulations, a state of emergency might be proclaimed by the President or local military commanders, the people's freedom of person, residence, speech, assembly, association, communication, movement, property, and business might be infringed, the police had the power to control all political and social associations and their publications, women were forbidden to join political groups or attend any meeting involving political discussion, incitement of workers to sever a contract, to strike, to demand an increase of wages, or to "harm good customs"

[b] A monthly established by Chang Shih-chao in Tokyo in May 1914 (tiger year). The magazine advocated a liberal constitutional government and opposed the monarchical movement of Yüan Shih-k'ai. Chang, a jurist educated in Japan and Great Britain, was influenced by the political theory of Walter Bagehot and other British thinkers. His political essays were considered the first in China to exhibit to a considerable degree modern logical thinking. Shortly after 1916 he changed his position and began to resist the application of Western institutions in China; he advocated instead the traditional Chinese literature and civilization as opposed to the new literature and new thought movements. After 1949 he supported the Chinese Communist regime.

[c] In 1918 and 1919 many newspapers and student publications were suppressed under this law on the grounds that they published the secret treaties with Japan or criticized the government's policies.[8]

was forbidden, undefined actions such as "corrupting social morality" and "harming local welfare" were branded as crimes, all publications were to be registered with a deposit of money with the police and approved by them before circulation, and heavy penalties were provided for violations of these provisions.

All these laws were in effect during the rule of Yüan Shih-k'ai and throughout nearly the whole period of the May Fourth Movement. Under so repressive a regime the press of China suffered a great decline after 1915. Immediately after the 1911 Revolution, the Chinese press had grown rapidly. Almost five hundred daily newspapers came into existence, Peking having fifty, Shanghai fifteen, and Hankow six; but during Yüan's monarchical movement, the number of newspapers in Peking decreased to about twenty, in Shanghai to five, and in Hankow to two. The total circulation of newspapers of the nation also declined in the two years after 1913 from 42,000,000 to 39,000,000.[9]

This was the setting in which *New Youth* began publication. From the beginning Ch'en Tu-hsiu had been an anti-Yüan zealot. But from his experience in the ill-fated second revolution he had learned that China could rid itself of warlord control only after an awakening of the Chinese people, in particular the youth, and only after a basic change in the old society and civilization. This, he felt, could not be achieved without a new publication. Consequently, he discussed the matter with Wang Meng-tsou (Wang Yüan-fang), the son of a former schoolmate of Ch'en's and manager of the Oriental Book Company (*Ya-tung t'u-shu-kuan*) in Shanghai.[10] With the support of this publisher and others, Ch'en published on September 15, 1915, in the same city the first issue of the *Youth Magazine* (*Ch'ing-nien tsa-chih*), a monthly journal later renamed *New Youth*, or *La Jeunesse* (*Hsin ch'ing-nien*).[d] Ch'en was the

---

[d] The monthly was entitled *Ch'ing-nien tsa-chih* through the first volume which included six issues, the sixth issue appearing on Feb. 15, 1916. Then publication was suspended "due to several factors" (see Vol. II, No. 1, p. 7) for a half year. Subsequently, Vol. II, No. 1 appeared on Sept. 1, 1916, with its title changed to *Hsin ch'ing-nien*. The first two volumes were printed by the Welfare-Seeking Book Co. (*Ch'iu-i shu-she*) and the Oriental Book Co. in Shanghai. It was edited by Ch'en alone until Jan. 1918, when a committee of editors was formed. The committee consisted of six; besides Ch'en, there were Ch'ien Hsüan-t'ung, Hu Shih, Li Ta-chao, Liu Fu, and Shen Yin-mo (Kao I-han, etc., were later added). Beginning with Vol. IV, No. 1 (Jan. 15, 1918), the monthly was edited in turn each month by one of the members of the committee. A discussion meeting was held each month, attended by the six editors and the major contributors such as Lu Hsün, Chou Tso-jen, Shen Chien-shih, and Wang Hsing-kung. From Jan. 1918 on, almost all articles in the magazine were written in the vernacular. From Vol. III, No. 1 to Vol. VII, No. 6, the magazine was printed by the Public Welfare Book Co. (*Ch'ün-i shu-she*) in Shanghai. The French title *La Jeunesse* was attached from the issue of Jan. 15, 1919 (Vol. VI, No. 1). The magazine was suspended in June 1919 because of the May Fourth Incident and did not resume publication until November. (Thus Vol. VI, No. 5 was published in May 1919 but No. 6 on Nov. 1.) In September of that year Ch'en, just out of prison, organized the New Youth

sole editor. Many of its early contributors, such as Li Ta-chao and Kao I-han, had written for the newly suspended magazine, *The Tiger*.

New Youth was established exactly one hundred years after the first appearance of a modern periodical written in Chinese.[e] Because of the difficult political situation, Ch'en avoided direct political commitments. The purpose of the magazine was declared to be reformation of the thought and behavior of youth rather than the launching of political criticism. In a note published in the first issue Ch'en rejected Wang Yung-kung's suggestion that the magazine should sound the alarm against the monarchical movement, although pointed anti-monarchical remarks are to be found here and there, especially in the "Letters to the Editor" and "Records of Current Affairs."

In Ch'en's opinion, as in Hu Shih's, the roots of China's political problems lay much deeper than people generally thought. While Hu Shih concentrated mainly on the academic, educational, and literary fields, Ch'en Tu-hsiu emphasized the necessity for the destruction of stagnant traditions and the ideological awakening of China's youth on whom rested the hope for the building of a new China. The opening article of the first issue, written by Ch'en and entitled "Call to Youth," began:

> The Chinese compliment others by saying, "He acts like an old man although still young." Englishmen and Americans encourage one another by saying, "Keep young while growing old." Such is one respect in which the different ways of thought of the East and West are manifested. Youth is like early spring, like the rising sun, like trees and grass in bud, like a newly sharpened blade. It is the most

---

Society, and a "Manifesto" and "Regulations of the Organization" were published. All of the editors and most of the main contributors joined the society. The magazine was edited in Peking and printed in Shanghai during the period 1917 to winter, 1919, while Ch'en was in Peking. After the summer of 1920 the society split. The committee of editors was abandoned and Ch'en once again took on the sole editorship. The monthly was suspended again after the issue of May 1920 (Vol. VII, No. 6). With the aid of Comintern agent Gregory Voitinsky, who was in China, Ch'en organized the Socialist Youth Corps in Shanghai in Aug. 1920. The magazine resumed publication on Sept. 1 (Vol. VIII, No. 1), printed and managed by the New Youth Society itself, which had been reorganized, and became an organ of the Communists. After this development, Hu Shih, Ch'ien Hsüan-t'ung, Liu Fu, Lu Hsün, Chou Tso-jen, and all of the other liberals left the society. The manuscripts of Vol. VIII, No. 6 (due to be published on Feb. 1, 1921), were seized by secret police in Shanghai. The magazine was moved to Canton where Vol. VIII, No. 6, appeared on April 1, 1921. The society was dissolved in Oct. 1921. The final issue, Vol. IX, No. 6, was dated July 1, 1922. Later a *New Youth* quarterly, edited by Ch'ü Ch'iu-pai, published four issues, June 1923–Dec. 1924, and an irregular *New Youth* published five issues, April 1925–July 1926, both in Canton.[11]

[e] The first nongovernmental periodical in Chinese in the form of a modern magazine is believed to have been the *Ch'a shih-su mei-yüeh t'ung-chi-chuan* ("Chinese Monthly Magazine") established on Aug. 5, 1815, in Malacca by British Protestant missionaries William Milne and Robert Morrison and a Chinese, Liang Ya-fa. The monthly secretly circulated in Canton and among the overseas Chinese in south Asian islands.[12]

valuable period of life. The function of youth in society is the same as that of a fresh and vital cell in a human body. In the processes of metabolism, the old and the rotten are incessantly eliminated to be replaced by the fresh and living. . . . If metabolism functions properly in a human body, the person will be healthy; if the old and rotten cells accumulate and fill the body, the person will die. If metabolism functions properly in a society, it will flourish; if old and rotten elements fill the society, then it will cease to exist.

According to this standard, then, is the society of our nation flourishing, or is it about to perish? I cannot bear to answer. As for those old and rotten elements, I shall leave them to the process of natural selection. I do not wish to waste my fleeting time in arguing with them on this and that and hoping for them to be reborn and thoroughly remodeled. I merely, with tears, place my plea before the fresh and vital youth, in the hope that they will achieve self-awareness, and begin to struggle. What is this self-awareness? It is to be conscious of the value and responsibility of one's young life and vitality, to maintain one's self-respect, which should not be lowered. What is the struggle? It is to exert one's intellect, discard resolutely the old and the rotten, regard them as enemies and as a flood or savage beasts, keep away from their neighborhood and refuse to be contaminated by their poisonous germs. . . .[13]

Ch'en continued that what China needed was for youth to "use to the full the natural intellect of man, and judge and choose among all the thoughts of mankind, distinguishing which are fresh and vital and suitable for the present struggle for survival, and which are old and rotten and unworthy to be retained in the mind." [14] He suggested that this problem should be treated with no compromises and hesitations, as "a sharp knife cuts hemp." He proposed six principles to govern the actions of youth: to be independent instead of servile, progressive instead of conservative, aggressive instead of retiring, cosmopolitan instead of isolationist, utilitarian instead of formalistic, scientific instead of imaginative (pp. 2–7). The basic purpose of the article was to attack conservatism and advocate the destruction of unworthy traditions; Ch'en continued:

Speaking of conservatism, we indeed do not know which of our traditional institutions may be fit for survival in the modern world. I would rather see the ruin of our traditional "national quintessence" than have our race of the present and future extinguished because of its unfitness for survival. Alas, the Babylonians are gone; of what use is their civilization to them now? As a Chinese maxim says, "If the skin does not exist, what can the hair adhere to?" The world continually progresses and will not stop. All those who cannot change themselves and keep pace with it are unfit for survival and will be eliminated by the processes of natural selection. Therefore, what is the good of conservatism? (p. 3)

In his attempt to destroy the traditional idols, Ch'en did not fail to state his reasons. Because the monarchical and other conservative groups had used traditional teachings, Confucianism in particular, to support their beliefs, Ch'en felt that it was more significant to destroy their "foundations" than merely to criticize their political superficialities — that without such destruction, no positive construction would be possible in a China where social and economic stagnation had been the rule for centuries. When Ch'ang Nai-te, a reader of the magazine and later one of the leaders of the Young China Party, asked him why he did not encourage the Chinese to keep their families small as in the West instead of urging the disintegration of the traditional big families, Ch'en replied that, since the system of big families was based on Confucian ethics, the concept of small families could not take root until the Confucian ethical principles were overthrown. These principles maintained that for a son to leave his parents to establish a small family of his own was unfilial and immoral.[15] The family system and the monarchical movement were but two examples of Chinese social institutions and conventions based on those traditional ethics and ideologies which Ch'en proposed to attack.

This ambitious program of criticizing tradition and awakening the youth was carried on by Ch'en and a few contributors to the magazine until 1917. From 1915 to the end of 1916 Ch'en's activities were centered around Shanghai, and relations among the new leading intellectuals both at home and abroad, such as Wu Chih-hui, Hu Shih, Li Ta-chao, Kao I-han, and Liu Fu (Liu Pan-nung), were casual and unorganized. But at the beginning of 1917 the literary revolution began to take shape. And on December 26, 1916, Ts'ai Yüan-p'ei,[f] the moral leader of the new intelligentsia and one of the greatest educators and liberals in modern China, was appointed chancellor of the National University of Peking by President Li Yüan-hung, successor to Yüan

[f] Ts'ai Yüan-p'ei (also named Ho-ch'ing and Chieh-min) (1876–1940) was born in Shanyin County, Chekiang Province. He passed the second civil service examination in 1889 and the third in 1892 which secured for him the highest degree, *han-lin*. In 1894 he was appointed Imperial Editor (*pien-hsiu*), but resigned in 1898 after the failure of the Hundred Days' Reform, and devoted his life to education, propagating revolution and Russian nihilism. Later he joined the T'ung-meng-hui. From 1907 to 1911 he studied at Leipzig University. He returned to China in 1911 and took part in the Revolution. The following year he was appointed Minister of Education in Sun Yat-sen's cabinet. When Yüan Shih-k'ai became President, Ts'ai resigned the post and returned in the summer of 1912 to Germany. There he studied the history of modern civilization. He returned to China in the summer of 1913, but in the fall went to France to study, promoting education and social service for the Chinese workers in that country and the work-study program for Chinese students going there. In the winter of 1916, following the suggestion of some parliamentary members from Chekiang Province, the Peking government offered to appoint Ts'ai governor of that province; he refused the offer by telegram from France. Shortly after this, the government appointed him chancellor of Peking University to succeed Hu Jen-yüan who had resigned the post for a trip to the United States. It was said that the appointment was recommended by T'ang Erh-ho, chancellor of the Medical College of Peking and a friend of Ts'ai's.[16]

Shih-k'ai.[17] Under Ts'ai's stimulus and protection the new intellectual leaders gathered at Peking University and the reform movement was able to make headway.

Reforms at Peking University

The reforms Ts'ai Yüan-p'ei carried out at the National University of Peking from 1917 on were as significant in the May Fourth Movement as Ch'en Tu-hsiu's establishment of *New Youth*. The university had had its origin in the Society for the Strengthening of Learning (*Ch'iang hsüeh hui*) which had been created by K'ang Yu-wei and his disciple Liang Ch'i-ch'ao in 1895. But it was not until May 1898 that the university was actually established under the name *Ching-shih ta hsüeh-t'ang* (Imperial University), with Sun Chia-nai, the Minister of Civil Service, as chancellor, Hsü Ching-ch'eng as dean of the faculty, and a veteran American Baptist missionary, W. A. P. Martin, as dean of the Western faculty. At that time all the students were recruited from high ranking officials or from those who had passed the civil service examinations. In 1900 Hsü Ching-ch'eng, the newly appointed chancellor, was executed because of his opposition to the Boxer Rebellion, and the university was closed for two years. It did not reopen until the end of 1901. In 1912, the name of the university was changed to the National University of Peking (*Kuo-li Pei-ching ta-hsüeh*), and Yen Fu was for seven months chancellor.[18]

By early 1919, the university was one of only three government-established universities and the only one located in the capital and completely financed by the central government. It was considered the leading institution of higher learning in the country. The university had four schools: The School of Letters, consisting of departments of Chinese literature, philosophy, English literature, French literature, and history; the School of Science, consisting of departments of physics, chemistry, mathematics, and geology; the Law School, consisting of departments of political science, economics, law, and commerce; and the Engineering School which had two departments: civil engineering and mining and metallurgy. The annual budget of the university did not exceed one hundred thousand Haikwan Taels before 1911, and was only 430,000 *yuan* in 1916. After Ts'ai Yüan-p'ei took over the chancellorship, the university expanded; its annual budget for 1918 was 676,800 *yuan*, about six times as much as the average annual budget of other government colleges. Its budget for 1919 and 1920 was 792,459 and 957,579 *yuan* respectively.[19] Early in 1919 the university had about fifty administrative members, and a faculty of 202. The professors and teaching fellows were all Chinese with the exception of four Britons, three Americans, three Germans, and one each from Japan, France, and Denmark.

From 1912 to 1918, the university graduated 612 students, of whom 233 were from the School of Letters, 40 from the School of Science, 209 from the Law School, and 120 from the Engineering School. The increase of enrollment in the university in the decade following 1912 and the enrollment for the spring semester of 1919 are shown by the accompanying figures.[20]

Number of Students Enrolled in the National University of Peking 1912–1921, by Years

1912	818	1917	1,695
1913	781	1918	2,001
1914	942	1919	2,228 (2,413) [21]
1915	1,333	1920	2,565
1916	1,503	1921	2,252

Enrollment Spring Semester 1919 [g]

	Undergraduate	Preparatory	Total
School of Letters	341	415	756
School of Science	134	362	496
Law School	532	415	947
Engineering School	60	154	214
Total	1,067	1,346	2,413

When Ts'ai Yüan-p'ei was appointed chancellor at the end of 1916, the university was well known for its conservative tradition. Students regarded it as a steppingstone to promotion in the government instead of as an institution of learning. The professors, most of whom came from officialdom, were judged not by their teaching or learning, but by their official rank. They were called *chung-t'ang* or *ta-jen* (their excellencies), and the students were called *lao-yeh* (esquires). The morals of both professors and students were notoriously low and they often indulged in gambling and consorted with prostitutes. The university was popularly known as "the Brothel Brigade" (*t'an-yen t'uan*), "the

[g] Each school of the university had its *pen k'o* (undergraduate section) and *yü k'o* (preparatory or preundergraduate section). The *pen k'o* was roughly equivalent to an American graduate school. After 1912, a high school graduate could enter the *yü k'o* by passing an entrance examination. He could enter the *pen k'o* after three years' study and graduation from the *yü k'o*; three years were required to graduate from the *pen k'o* and four from the Law School. After 1918 the time requirement for the *yü k'o* was changed to two years and for the *pen k'o*, to four years. A credit system modeled after the American plan was also adopted.

Gambling Den" (*tu k'u*), and "the Fountainhead of Ribaldry and Bawdiness." [22]

From the time Ts'ai Yüan-p'ei took over the chancellorship, the university underwent a great change. Ts'ai pointed out in his inaugural address in January 1917 that the aim of students coming to the university should be the pursuit of learning, not the acquisition of wealth or official promotion.[23] Later he enunciated a three-point policy for administering the university. First, the university was an institution for academic research. Research did not mean merely the introduction of Western civilization, but also the creation of a new civilization; not merely the preservation of the "national quintessence," but study of it by scientific method. Secondly, students should not regard the university as a substitute for the old government examination and recruitment system, nor should they neglect subjects outside their own specialty. Thirdly, the university should preserve academic freedom. Divergent theories, such as idealism and materialism in philosophy, romanticism and realism in literature, the doctrines of state intervention and *laissez faire* in economics, motivational and utilitarian ethical theories, or optimism and pessimism in basic outlook — to the extent that they had serious academic standing — might find free expression in the university.[24]

On the basis of these liberal and progressive principles, Ts'ai Yüan-p'ei carried out many practical reforms in the university. Professors with divergent points of view were brought into the institution. Various study and advisory groups among the faculty were established. The university was in the main governed by professors rather than administrators or officials. Students were permitted to take part in political activities as individuals. In Ts'ai's opinion, the most important duty of a student in school was to study. He held that no relation should exist between political organizations and the school as such. But students of twenty years of age or over who were interested in politics might join any political organization as individuals. The university could advise them, but would not interfere with their free choice. This point of view was contrary to the policy of the Peking government at that time. The government had often forbidden students to join political parties on the ground that the *sole* duty of students was to study.[h] Students' self-government was encouraged by Ts'ai and student societies for study, speech, discussion, publication, recreation, social service, athletics, and other activities, including a

---

[h] On Feb. 6, 1917, the Ministry of Education reinforced this prohibition with an order to all schools. The Manchu government in Nov. 1907 had even forbidden students to have any organizations or make public speeches.[25]

students' bank, a consumer's cooperative organization, and a museum, were established. A work-and-study program similar to that which had been tried in France was also founded at the university. A spirit of equality was introduced into the institution. The previous barriers between students and professors as well as between them and janitors or workers were to a certain extent removed.[i] The moral standards of the students were greatly improved. A Society for the Promotion of Virtue (*Chin-te hui*) was established in 1918 on the pattern of a similar organization founded in Shanghai in 1912 by Wu Chih-hui, Li Shih-tseng, and Wang Ching-wei. All the members of the society were enjoined not to consort with prostitutes, gamble, or have concubines. A second group of members of the society agreed, in addition to observing the above restraints, not to hold government office or become members of Parliament. Penalty regulations were passed and supervisors were elected by the members of the society, who numbered about one thousand.[27] The agreement to refrain from holding office or becoming parliamentary members reflected both the influence of anarchism and nihilism, and the contempt the new intelligentsia felt for the old bureaucrats.[j] In the eyes of the new intellectuals, the old bureaucrats and warlords were the sources of all vice.

The Alliance of the New Intellectuals and the Establishment of New Tide Magazine

Of all Ts'ai's innovations at Peking University, perhaps the most significant was his practice of permitting the coexistence of divergent opinions. In spite of the fact that he himself was one of the earliest members of the T'ung-meng-hui, the predecessor of the Kuomintang, Ts'ai never allowed partisanship or politics to influence his selection of faculty members. In 1912, when he was appointed Minister of Education in Sun Yat-sen's administration, Ts'ai had explained his views on education. His ideal system of education was one "above politics" or "beyond political control." With regard to the aims of edu-

---

[i] For instance, in Jan. 1918 twenty-five students at the university wrote letters to Ts'ai Yüan-p'ei, reporting that a janitor was studying by himself and doing very well; Ts'ai immediately promoted him to clerk and replied that there was no difference in status between the faculty and other workers in the university. This was of course unusual so far as the traditionally conservative social pattern in Chinese schools was concerned. At the same time, an evening school for workers was established at the university.[26]

[j] The Chinese anarchists proclaimed in 1912 a "Twelve Commandments": (1) vegetarianism, (2) teetotalism, (3) abstention from smoking, (4) abstention from hiring servants, (5) abstention from riding sedan chairs and rickshaws, (6) celibacy, (7) renunciation of family names, (8) refusal to hold government office, (9) refusal to become parliamentary members, (10) refusal to join political parties, (11) refusal to enlist in the Army or Navy, (12) atheism.[28]

cation he proposed five principles: universal military education to avoid the militarists' monopoly of military power, utilitarian education to improve the people's livelihood, moral education based on the principle of mutual assistance, "education for a world view" (*shih-chieh-kuan chiao-yü*) to promote a cosmic concept, and finally, "aesthetic education" (*mei-kan chih chiao-yü*) in the Kantian sense, i.e., to lead the people from the phenomenal world to the realization of the world of reality by means of aesthetic appreciation. The ultimate goal of this final principle was to substitute aesthetics for religion. In discussing education for a world view, Ts'ai emphasized that "we must follow the general rule of freedom of thought and freedom of expression, and not allow any one branch of philosophy or any one tenet of religion to confine our minds, but always aim at a lofty universal point of view which is valid without regard to space or time." [29] Later, when he took office at the university, he reiterated his stand on freedom of thought, insisting that all theories which can be maintained on rational grounds should be propagated in complete freedom at the university. Consequently, the faculty came to include persons with many diverse points of view ranging from well-known monarchists, conservatives, and reactionaries, to liberals, radicals, socialists, and anarchists. "And it is but natural," ventured one Chinese writer, "that all the most virile and gifted among the younger members of the Chinese intelligentsia flocked to take a place under his leadership. The result was the creation, within a few years, of an incredibly productive intellectual life, probably unparalleled in the academic history of the world." [30]

This policy of freedom in education made the university a public forum for debates between the old conservative scholars and the new intelligentsia and made possible an alliance of the new intellectuals. At the beginning of 1917 when he assumed the chancellorship, Ts'ai brought Ch'en Tu-hsiu to the university as dean of the School of Letters.[k] Many others with new ideas were

---

[k] Ts'ai had known Ch'en's name since 1906 when Ts'ai had worked on the *Tocsin Daily* (*Ching-chung jih-pao* or *Alarming Bell Daily News*) in Shanghai. Ch'en Tu-hsiu identified himself at the time as Ch'en Chung-fu. Both were doing revolutionary work. Ts'ai was impressed by Ch'en's persistent support of a vernacular magazine created by Ch'en and his friends in Wuhu, Anhwei Province. Shortly afterwards Ch'en went to Japan and Ts'ai to Europe. At the end of 1916 Ch'en left Shanghai for Peking. In Jan. 1917 Ts'ai, newly appointed the chancellor of Peking University, asked T'ang Erh-ho, president of the National Medical College of Peking, to recommend a dean for the School of Letters of the university. T'ang suggested Ch'en and told Ts'ai that Ch'en Tu-hsiu and Ch'en Chung-fu were the same person, and showed Ts'ai some copies of *New Youth*. Ts'ai then went to see Ch'en and secured his agreement to take the post. It is interesting to note that, almost simultaneously with this appointment, in the Jan. 1, 1917, issue of *New Youth*, Ch'en published, without Ts'ai's knowledge, Ts'ai's two speeches attacking the movement to make Confucianism the state religion. In the same issue a reader suggested that Ch'en ask Ts'ai to become a contributor to the magazine.[31]

also invited to join the faculty about this time. Among them were Ch'ien Hsüan-t'ung, etymologist and phonetician,[1] Liu Fu, linguist and poet,[m] and Shen Yin-mo, poet — all of whom were forerunners of the new poetry in the vernacular and of the literary revolution. In the summer Hu Shih, who had just returned from the United States, joined the faculty. He taught courses in the history of Chinese philosophy with views quite far from tradition. Chou Tso-jen, pioneering author in the new essay and short story form, taught at the university after April 1917. The anti-Confucian scholar, Wu Yü, had close contact with Ch'en Tu-hsiu from the end of 1916 and was invited to teach at the university from 1919. Lu Hsün did not join the faculty until 1920, but he had been working in the Ministry of Education after 1912 when it was headed by Ts'ai, and keeping close relations with quite a few of the liberal professors at the university.[n] In February 1918 Li Ta-chao was appointed chief librarian

[1] Ch'ien Hsüan-t'ung (original name Ch'ien Hsia) (1887–1939) was born in Soochow, Kiangsu. His father was Ts'ai Yüan-p'ei's teacher, and his elder brother a diplomat and political reformer in the Ch'ing period. Ch'ien started to learn Chinese phonetics and etymology at the age of seven. Before he was ten, he could recite the basic Confucian classics. At thirteen, under the influence of his playmates, many of whom joined the Boxer Rebellion, he became conservative and studied hard to prepare for the civil service examinations. But later, when he read K'ang Yu-wei and Liang Ch'i-ch'ao, he began to be a reformer and a follower of the modern text school in classic sudies. After 1903 he became an anti-Manchu revolutionary mainly because of the influence of the writings of Chang Ping-lin and Liu Shih-p'ei. With friends in 1904 he established the *Huchow Vernacular Magazine* (*Hu-chou pai-hua pao*). Next year he went to Japan and studied Japanese language and education at Waseda University. He joined the T'ung-meng-hui in 1906. In the following year, Ch'ien, Lu Hsün, Chou Tso-jen, Hsü Shou-ch'ang, K'ang Pao-chung, Chu Hsi-tsu, and others organized in Tokyo a Society for the Promotion of National Learning (*Kuo-hsüeh chen-ch'i she*) and invited Chang Ping-lin (1867–1936), then editor of *People Report*, to be its director and to teach them Chinese linguistics and literature. About the same time, influenced by Liu Shih-p'ei and Chang Chi in Japan and by the *New Century* group in France, Ch'ien started to learn Esperanto and leaned to anarchism. He returned to China in 1910 and taught linguistics at Peking Higher Normal College during the period 1913–15 and at Peking University from 1915 on. He remained somewhat indifferent to the contemporary intellectual and literary problems for a few years until Yüan Shih-k'ai's monarchical adventure. Ch'ien actually joined the faculty of Peking University earlier than Ch'en Tu-hsiu. According to Ch'ien, he and Shen Yen-mo recommended Ch'en to Ts'ai for dean. During and after the May Fourth period Ch'ien published a number of articles on language reform, ancient history, and phonetics.

[m] Liu Fu (*tzu*: Pan-nung) (1891–1934) was born in Kiangyin County, Kiangsu. In 1912 he was a free-lance writer and an editor of the *China's New Daily* (*Chung-hua hsin-pao*) in Shanghai, and from 1913 to 1916 an editor of the Chung-hua Book Co. (*Chung-hua shu-chü*). During this period he wrote popular short stories in the conventional style. In 1916 he went to Peking and the following year taught at the *yu k'o* of Peking University. In the early period of the new literature movement he wrote many popular, light verses and articles to promote the vernacular literature. Later on, he concentrated on the study of phonetics and lexicography. In 1920 he studied linguistics at London University, and in 1925 received his Lit.D. at Paris University and became a member of the Société Linguistique de Paris. Upon his return to China that year he taught at universities in Peking and worked for language reform.

[n] Lu Hsün (1881–1936) was born of a well-to-do family in Shaohsing County, Chekiang, on Sept. 25, 1881. When he was a young boy, his grandfather, an official in the Manchu court,

of the university library and later professor of history, political science, economics, and law.° (In December of the same year, Ch'en Tu-hsiu and Li established in Peking the *Weekly Critic* [*Mei-chou p'ing-lun*].) Other professors were Kao I-han, political scientist, T'ao Li-kung (L. K. Tao, T'ao Meng-ho), social scientist, Ch'en Ta-ch'i, a pioneering psychologist and logician, and Wang Hsing-kung, one of the first scholars in China studying the scientific method. Under the leadership of Ts'ai Yüan-p'ei, these outstanding intellectuals exerted profound influence upon the students at the university.

---

was jailed. The father's financial condition became so bad that the young Chou had often to resort to pawnshops. He attended the Naval School in Nanking at the age of seventeen and about half a year later transferred to the Mining and Railroad School to study mining. After his graduation he was sent in 1902 on a government scholarship to Japan. He began to study medicine at the Medical College of Sendai in Sept. 1903 but abandoned it in 1906 and took up the new literature. He went back to Tokyo and started with his brother Chou Tso-jen in 1907 the abortive magazine *New Life* (*Hsin sheng*). At this time, he learned Japanese and some German, and read widely in eastern and northern European literature. In July 1909 he returned to China, and in the fall became a teacher of chemistry and physiology at the normal school of Hangchow; in Sept. 1910 he began to teach the same subjects at a middle school in his home town. He went to Nanking in Jan. 1912 and became a minor official in the Ministry of Education of the new Republic then under the ministership of Ts'ai Yüan-p'ei. In May, following the move of the government, he went to Peking. He held the position until 1925 when he was dismissed by Chang Shih-chao, then the minister. In the summer of 1917 he was encouraged by Ch'ien Hsüan-t'ung to join the reform movement of *New Youth* magazine. His satiric short essays and short stories were widely read and contributed greatly to the spread of the new literature and new thought movements. After the split of the May Fourth Movement in 1920 he ceased relations with the New Youth group, and it was not until 1930 that he took the leadership of leftist writers.[32] Chou Tso-jen (born 1885) later became, on the other hand, a leading moderate essayist and a great stylist. Married to a Japanese girl, he remained in Peiping after 1937 and became chancellor of the Japanese-sponsored Peking University and concurrently Minister of Education in the puppet government of North China. After V-J Day, in 1946, he was sentenced to ten years of imprisonment by the National government. He is still writing some reminiscences in Communist China.

° Li Ta-chao (*tzu*: Shou-ch'ang) was born in Loting County, Hopei Province, in 1888. He studied political science and economics first at the Peiyang College of Law and Political Science and after the spring of 1914 at Waseda University in Japan. Returning to China about 1916, he became secretary to T'ang Hua-lung, a leader of the Chihputang, and took editorship of the *Ch'en-pao* supplementary. He was appointed in Feb. 1918 chief librarian of the Peking University library and concurrently professor after Sept. 1920. He became a close collaborator of Ch'en Tu-hsiu and helped him to edit *New Youth* and *Weekly Critic*. In Sept. 1921 he resigned the post of librarian, retaining his professorship and being appointed secretary to the chancellor. At the university he taught courses on modern political science, historiography, historical materialism, socialism and social movements, social legislation, etc. He also taught a history of women's suffrage and sociology at the Girls' Higher Normal College of Peking. During the period of the May Fourth Incident students often convened in the neighborhood of his office at the library. In 1920 he collaborated with Ch'en Tu-hsiu in preparing to found the Chinese Communist Party, and after Ch'en went to Canton in 1921 he became the virtual leader of the party in North China. In Jan. 1924 when the Kuomintang-Communist coalition was established, a move which he had fervently promoted, he was elected a member of the Central Executive Committee of the Kuomintang. On April 9, 1927, he was arrested by Chang Tso-lin's troops in the Soviet Embassy at Peking and was hanged in jail on April 28. In 1918 Mao Tse-tung was one of Li's employees at the library and was profoundly influenced by him.[33]

In the winter of 1918 a group of the able students at Peking who had been converted to support of the new thought and literature movements established *New Tide* (*Hsin ch'ao*), a monthly which also bore the English sub-title "Renaissance." The magazine had been proposed originally by a group consisting of Fu Ssu-nien, Ku Chieh-kang, and Hsü Yen-chih; Lo Chia-lun, P'an Chia-hsün, and K'ang Pai-ch'ing joined later. Most of them were students interested in history and literature. With the help of Ch'en Tu-hsiu and Li Ta-chao, they secured financial and material support from the university for the publication of their monthly. Hu Shih became their adviser and, with Ch'en, Li, and Chou Tso-jen, exercised an inspirational influence upon the shaping of the new forum. The students proposed to adopt three guiding principles for their publication — a critical spirit, scientific thinking, and reformed rhetoric — and they eventually supported the reforms advocated by *New Youth* and *Weekly Critic*. The first issue of the magazine appeared on January 1, 1919, and was immediately welcomed by the literary youth of the nation.

The New Tide Society which published the monthly was a very small organization. When first established on November 18, 1918, it had a membership of twenty-one. Up to December 19, 1919, the society still had only thirty-seven members, all of whom were students at Peking University. The recorded membership seems not to have exceeded forty-one. Most of the members were later student leaders in the May Fourth Incident, and thereafter played important roles in the intellectual and social development of modern China.[p] To name a few:

[p] According to Fu Ssu-nien, the establishment of *New Tide* was "purely a result of the awakening" of the members. In the fall of 1917, Fu, Ku Chieh-kang, and Hsü Yen-chih first conceived the idea of establishing a magazine. Hsü discussed the idea with Ch'en Tu-hsiu in the fall of the following year. As Fu recalled, the students were unexpectedly and enthusiastically supported by Ch'en, who replied, "So long as you are determined to establish it and will maintain it, the university may extend you financial support." Accordingly, the students set about to found their organization. They talked with Lo Chia-lun and K'ang Pai-ch'ing, and were joined by more than ten other students. Hu Shih then became their adviser. The first preparatory meeting, at which the three principles were adopted, was held on Oct. 13, 1918. Meanwhile, Hsü suggested the English title "Renaissance," and Lo the Chinese *Hsin ch'ao* (New Tide), a name which had been used earlier by the Japanese. (The Japanese *New Tide* [*Shin-chō*] magazine had been established in 1904 as one of the promoters of naturalism in literature. A series of literary magazines under the title *New Thought Tide* [*Shin-shichō*] were carried on by students at Tokyo Imperial University after 1907. The Chinese students at Peking University must have been influenced by these Japanese counterparts founded in 1914 and 1916 by such active and prominent writers as Kume Masao, Kikuchi Kan, and Akutagawa Ryūnosuke, who had at the time extolled naturalistic and neo-realistic literature in Japan.) The students thought that the English and the Chinese titles had similar meanings. On Nov. 19 a second meeting was held and officials were elected. Li Ta-chao, the chief librarian, assigned a room of the library for the office of the society. An organizational

Fu Ssu-nien: one of the leading historians and popular writers; later director of the Institute of History and Philology, Academia Sinica, and chancellor of the National University of Formosa after World War II.

Lo Chia-lun: historian, educator, and popular writer; later chancellor of Tsing Hua University in Peking, and National Central University in Chungking; high ranking official in the Kuomintang government.

Ku Chieh-kang: prominent historian of Chinese antiquity and folklorist.

K'ang Pai-ch'ing: romantic lyric poet.

Mao Tzu-shui: educator and historian.

Chiang Shao-yüan: educator, historian of religion.

Wang Ching-hsi (Ging-hsi): writer, professor of psychology and physiology.

Wu K'ang: philosopher.

Ho Ssu-yüan: educator and later Governor of Shantung Province and Mayor of Peiping.

Li Hsiao-feng: publisher (a number of important new literary works were published by his firm, Pei-hsin shu-chü).

Yü P'ing-po: famous prose writer, poet, and literary critic.

Kuo Shao-yü: writer, historian of Chinese criticism.

Sun Fu-yüan: well-known editor and writer.

Chang Sung-nien (Chang Shen-fu, Chang Ch'ih): guild socialist; exponent of Bertrand Russell's philosophy, mathematical logic, and, at other times, dialectical materialism.

Yeh Shao-chün (Yeh Sheng-t'ao): famous novelist, poet, and educator.

---

regulation provided that students of the university or outsiders (in the latter case, an introduction by two members of the society was required) who had three or more articles published in the magazine might become members of the society. It had two departments, editorial and managerial. The chief librarian of the university library was named adviser to the management of the magazine. Fu Ssu-nien was elected editor-in-chief, Lo Chia-lun, editor, and Yang Chen-sheng, secretary of the editorial department; Hsü Yen-chih was elected manager, K'ang Pai-ch'ing, assistant manager, and Yü P'ing-po, secretary of the managerial department. On Nov. 19, 1919, Lo was elected to succeed Fu, because the latter was going to study in England. Meng Shou-ch'un succeeded Hsü as manager, and Ku Chieh-kang, Li Hsiao-feng, and three others were selected assistants for the two departments. The same meeting also decided to expand the organization and business of the society. Several books were published. In May of 1920 Chou Tso-jen joined the society, the sole member from the faculty. A resolution of reorganization was formally adopted in a meeting held on Aug. 15. On Oct. 28 Chou was elected editor-in-chief, Mao Tzu-shui, Ku Chieh-kang, Ch'en Ta-ts'ai, and Sun Fu-yüan, assistant editors; Meng retained his post, and six members, including Li Hsiao-feng, Sun Fu-yüan, and Kuo Shao-yü, were selected to help him. At the end of the year the society faded away, partly because most of the important members had gone abroad for study, and partly because some of them were busy founding the Society for Literary Studies (see below, Chap. IX (p. 283)). The last issue of the monthly (Vol. III, No. 2) was published in March 1922.[34]

Yang Chen-sheng: professor of Chinese literature, once chancellor of the National University of Tsingtao.

Liu Ping-lin: economist.

Meng Shou-ch'un: dean of letters, National Chi-nan University, Shanghai.

Fung Yu-lan: prominent philosopher.

Chu Tzu-ch'ing: prominent prose writer and poet.

The views of the new intellectuals enjoyed much prestige and came to wider notice after the *New Youth* group became associated with the university, partly because of the leading academic position of the latter in the nation, and partly because of the growing support from students.

But it must be noted that this coalition of the new intellectuals at Peking University was only temporary. Among its leaders, views and interests were far from identical. This is well exemplified by Ch'en Tu-hsiu and Hu Shih. Ch'en Tu-hsiu's interest centered primarily on political and social affairs, although he then felt that political innovation must be preceded by the destruction of the old orthodox ideologies. Hu Shih and many other professors at the university, however, were more interested in literary and educational reforms. When they united in 1917 to promote the new movement against the old gentry, they had a loose mutual understanding that their reform movement would concentrate on other than political activities. The coalition was in fact based on general and imprecise ideas such as liberalism, humanitarianism, democracy, and science. Later when Ch'en Tu-hsiu found Tuan Ch'i-jui's activities in the government more and more intolerable, he was unable to refrain from criticism of the government, and after 1918 he turned more radical and came to favor a mass movement. The establishment of *Weekly Critic* as a small but sharp political review was actually to serve his political purpose. Other liberals, on the contrary, gradually became more conservative or moderate and reluctant to involve themselves in politics. The coalition did not break up, however, until after the May Fourth Incident. This development was recalled by Hu Shih in 1932 as follows:

> When in 1917 we worked together for *New Youth*, we had a common ideal that we should for twenty years not talk politics. We promised to keep away from politics for twenty years and to be devoted only to educational, intellectual, and cultural activities, to build a political foundation by way of nonpolitical factors. But this promise was not easy to keep, because even though we resolved to refrain from talking politics, the practical political situation compelled us to become involved in it. In 1918 Mr. Ch'en and Mr. Li Ta-chao, interested in political affairs, founded *Weekly Critic*. I did not criticize it. I remember that when they asked me to write something for them I only sent them my translations of two short stories.[35]

Reform Views of the New Intellectuals

In spite of the nature of their alliance, the new intellectuals did essentially concentrate their efforts on intellectual and cultural matters during the period 1917 to 1918. Before taking the position of dean of the School of Letters, Ch'en Tu-hsiu had already developed, with Yi Pai-sha and Wu Yü, an anti-Confucianist approach, and, in collaboration with Hu Shih, the idea of a literary revolution. All these men were contributors to his magazine. Subsequently, upon taking office, he declared:

My opinion on the problems of the Chinese classics and Chinese literature are twofold. On the one hand, all schools of classical thought should be treated fairly and without favor. On the other hand, we should encourage vernacular literature. We swear to carry out these two programs not only in the School of Letters of the university, but throughout the country.[36]

The program placed emphasis on both ethical and literary reforms. To achieve these the new intellectuals tried not only to introduce Western thought and institutions but also to re-evaluate and criticize the Chinese tradition. This approach was neither planned nor directed by any one person. Rather, it represented a common meeting ground for a number of people with divergent ideas.

While a detailed survey of these new ideas will be reserved for later chapters, a summary outline of the major issues discussed in *New Youth* prior to the May Fourth Incident, listed roughly in order of their appearance, will serve to indicate the temper of the intellectuals during the first stage of the May Fourth Movement. The magazine in the main opposed old patterns of thought and customs, and advocated new learning. It opposed monarchy and political privileges for the few, and advocated democracy, liberalism, and individualism, and later considered socialism. The magazine opposed the traditional ethics, such as loyalty to officials, filial duty to parents, and a double standard of chastity for men and women, and favored equality of individuals in society. It opposed the traditional big family (parents and married children living together as a family unit) and advocated the Western small family system, the equality and independence of women, and freedom of choice in love and marriage instead of marriage arranged by parents. In subsequent issues, the magazine advocated the literary revolution and encouraged language reform, discussed problems of romanization and the use of Esperanto, and introduced punctuation. The magazine was against old superstitions and religions, upholding science, technology, and agnosticism. To oppose the unquestioned traditional Confucianism, the monthly proposed to re-evaluate all the classics.

Authors in the magazine demanded that education should encourage individuality rather than assert the traditional authority of educators. Finally, the magazine attempted to promote unified intellectual leadership against warlordism through social, political, and cultural reforms.

The basic principles underlying these tenets of the new intellectual leaders could be reduced to two, nicknamed "Mr. Democracy" (*Te-mo-k'e-la-hsi hsien-sheng*) and "Mr. Science" (*Sai-yin-ssu hsien-sheng*). These principles were well summarized by Ch'en Tu-hsiu in an article published in January 1919 to celebrate the third anniversary of the publication of *New Youth* and to answer opponents' charges against the magazine:

They accused this magazine on the grounds that it intended to destroy Confucianism, the code of rituals, the "national quintessence," chastity of women, traditional ethics (loyalty, filial piety, and chastity), traditional arts (the Chinese opera), traditional religion (ghosts and gods), and ancient literature, as well as old-fashioned politics (privileges and government by men alone).

All of these charges are conceded. But we plead not guilty. We have committed the alleged crimes only because we supported the two gentlemen, Mr. Democracy and Mr. Science. In order to advocate Mr. Democracy, we are obliged to oppose Confucianism, the codes of rituals, chastity of women, traditional ethics, and old-fashioned politics; in order to advocate Mr. Science, we have to oppose traditional arts and traditional religion; and in order to advocate both Mr. Democracy and Mr. Science, we are compelled to oppose the cult of the "national quintessence" and ancient literature. Let us then ponder dispassionately: has this magazine committed any crimes other than advocating Mr. Democracy and Mr. Science? If not, please do not solely reprove this magazine: the only way for you to be heroic and to solve the problem fundamentally is to oppose the two gentlemen, Mr. Democracy and Mr. Science.[37]

Inspired by the professors and *New Youth*, the students at Peking University, and at other colleges as well, acquired a clearer understanding of the new intellectual currents and became more active in the new thought movement. Members of the New Tide Society were in the vanguard. They regarded the movement as an "intellectual revolution" or "social revolution" and urged their readers to introduce and spread in China the "new thought tide" of the world. They pointed out that the spirit of the movement should be the spirit of criticism, in Nietzsche's catchword, a "transvaluation of values." Most significantly, they desired "to cooperate with the students of all middle schools throughout the country to fight for spiritual emancipation," a point emphasized in the opening article of the first issue of the *New Tide* monthly:

Our society is very strange. Western people used to say that China has "masses" but no "society" and that since Chinese "society" is more than two thousand years old, it is a type of society which does not meet modern needs. Facing the matter honestly, this is not untrue. Consider our evil and inferior customs which are dead rules for dead things, cruel and contrary to human nature! There is no path left for human expression. We human beings are like dogs and sheep, not conscious whether we are living or dead. . . .

Real learning gives one individuality and independence. The Renaissance and Reformation in the Western world show how scholars there declared their independence of tradition.

Through this magazine we desire to cooperate with students of all middle schools throughout the country to fight for spiritual emancipation. Our hope is that all students in the country will interest themselves in modern scientific thought; that they will give up a subjective mind and fixed ideas in order to be objective and critical; that they will consider themselves men of the future rather than men of the present; that they will have personality enough to conquer our society rather than to be conquered by it. The spirit of our publication is the spirit of criticism.[38]

The conception of social revolution held by the leaders of the New Tide Society shows the influence of the Russian October Revolution. In the first issue of the magazine, Lo Chia-lun, discussing tides in the contemporary world, wrote that in world history almost every significant period had had its tide which could not be stopped. The Renaissance was the tide after the Dark Ages, and the Reformation was the tide of the sixteenth century in Europe. The main tide of the eighteenth century was the French Revolution which spread democracy to many countries; that of the nineteenth century, the revolutions of 1848, which resulted in the overthrow of despotism in Germany, Austria, and Italy. The new world tide of the twentieth century, according to Lo, would be the Russian October Revolution. "The present revolution is not like the previous ones! The previous revolutions were of the type of the French Revolution; henceforth revolutions will be of the type of the Russian Revolution!" [39] He considered the French Revolution to have been political, but henceforth revolutions would be of the Russian type, social revolutions in which democracy would defeat monarchism, plain people would defeat warlords, and laborers would defeat capitalists.[40] In the same issue, Fu Ssu-nien, who, as did Lo Chia-lun, later became fervently anti-communistic, expressed the same opinion, saying that Russia would "annex" the world, not in territory or sovereignty but in thought.[41] In a later issue a reader suggested that henceforth revolutions would follow the pattern of the American Revolution. But the idea was rebutted by the editors. By and large, these student opinions seem to have been more radical than those of such professors as Ch'en Tu-hsiu, Hu Shih, or even Li Ta-chao.

It would be wrong, however, to assert that the student leaders were Bolsheviks or Marxists. Their ideas were a vague mixture of socialism and democracy. Lo explained in the above-mentioned article that "after the new revolution, democracy and socialism will surely coexist" and draw closer, that socialism and individualism were mutually complementary, not contradictory forces, and that socialism will develop individuality.[42] This, he believed, was the real meaning of the new tide. In discussing these political ideas Lo was considerably influenced by Walter Edward Weyl's book *The New Democracy* (1912), subtitled "An essay on certain political and economic tendencies in the United States," and Stephen Butler Leacock's *Elements of Political Science* (1906). Lo rejected the idea of reform by violence. Emphasizing humanitarianism and the welfare of the common people, he said, "We would rather worship George Washington than Peter the Great, Benjamin Franklin than Bismarck, Karl Marx's economics than Richelieu's public finance, and Thomas Edison's inventions than Alfred Krupp's manufacture."[43] This indeed well exemplifies the students' love of vague generalizations at this time. Yet their eagerness for learning and enthusiasm for spreading their ideas provided a new impetus to the reform movement. It is dangerous, they proclaimed, to stop or sail against the tossing tide; it is safe to sail with it. "Now that the new tide of the world is coming, why do we not spread canvas and ply the oars to become the world's tide-player boys *(lung ch'ao erh)*?"[q]

The Opposition's Argument and the Rejoinder

While the alliance of the new intellectuals was forming, an opposition group came into existence at Peking University. It consisted of certain conservative professors, research workers, and students. At the end of the Ch'ing period, the faculty of the School of Letters at the university had consisted of a number of men of letters belonging to the T'ung-ch'eng school of literature and some to the Wen-hsüan school.[r] (In the School of Law returned students from Japan

[q] According to an ancient custom associated with the famous Hangchow bore, people in groups carrying colorful flags swim and play with the tossing tide at the estuary of the Ch'ien-t'ang River. This is supposed to welcome the soul of Wu Yüan, a patriotic general of the fifth century B.C. whose body was thrown into the river after he was executed by the king of Wu. The swimmers are called *lung ch'ao erh*, a term used in Chinese classical literature.

[r] T'ung-ch'eng is a county of Anhwei Province (the same province Ch'en Tu-hsiu, Hu Shih and Tuan Ch'i-jui came from) where many famous prose writers in the Manchu dynasty were born. These included Fang Pao (1668–1749), Yao Nai (1731–1815), Liu Ta-k'uei (1698–1780), and others. Since these famous T'ung-ch'eng literary men displayed a similar style in their writing and were imitated widely in China, the school bore the name of the county. It was rejuvenated and popularized by Tseng Kuo-fan (1811–1872), and his disciples and friends in the nineteenth

had held most of the teaching posts and generally were more conservative than those returned from France and the United States.) After the 1911 Revolution, scholars from Kiangsu and Chekiang provinces (ergo "the Kiang-Che faction"), most of whom were disciples or friends of Chang Ping-lin (Chang T'ai-yen), rose to power in the School of Letters of the university in succession to the T'ung-ch'eng school, with which Lin Shu was supposed to be associated. The professors of the Kiang-Che group were the major opposition to the new intellectuals.[44]

This group of advocates of the old literature was led by Liu Shih-p'ei and supported by Huang K'an (Huang Chi-kang), Lin Sun, Ku Hung-ming, Ma Hsü-lun, and the older researchers in the Institute of Chinese History (*Kuo-shih kuan*).[s] Their public forum was the magazine *The National Heritage*

---

century. The name of the Wen-hsüan school came from the book *Wen-hsüan* (An Anthology of Literature) which was compiled by Hsiao T'ung (A.D. 501–531) consisting of exemplary Chinese poetry and prose written between 246 B.C. and A.D. 502. The anthology dominated and guided the traditional Chinese literary style for almost a thousand years.

[s] Liu Shih-pe'i (Liu Kuang-han) (1884–1919) was born of a family of scholars of the modern text school in I-cheng County, Kiangsu Province. In 1904, with Chang Ping-lin, Teng Shih, Huang Chieh, Ma Hsü-lun, and other nationalist writers, Liu established the Society for the Preservation of the National Learning (*Kuo-hsüeh pao-ts'un hui*). Next year it published the *Journal of National Quintessence* (*Kuo-ts'ui hsüeh-pao*) in Shanghai. By 1906, he was a colleague of Ch'en Tu-hsiu, teaching in a middle school. In 1906 and 1907, Liu and other Chinese students established the *T'ien-i pao* in Japan, which was one of the first Chinese magazines to advocate socialism. As Chang Ping-lin, Liu was an anti-Manchu revolutionist before the 1911 Revolution. After that he became a conservative literary man, being one of the "six gentlemen" who founded the Society to Plan for Stability (*Ch'ou-an hui*), which sponsored the monarchical movement of Yüan Shih-k'ai in 1915 and 1916. Liu became notorious among the liberals because of his article "On Restoration of the Monarchy" (*Chün-cheng fu-ku lun*). He was an intimate friend of Chang Ping-lin, Yen Fu, and Yang Tu, the latter two also founders of the Society to Plan for Stability. Liu was introduced to Peking University as a professor by Chang Ping-lin. Liu died on Nov. 20, 1919. A scholar in the old classics, history, and literature, Liu was the author of, among others, *Chung-ku wen-hsüeh shih* (History of Chinese Literature in the Middle Antiquity), *Lun wen tsa-chi* (Miscellaneous Sketches on Literature), and *Tso-an wen chi* (Collected Essays of Liu Shih-p'ei).

Huang K'an (1886–1935) was one of Chang Ping-lin's leading disciples. It was Huang who recommended Ch'ien Hsüan-t'ung to Peking University in 1915, though later they were often at odds in classical studies.

Lin Sun was another old learned literary man.

Ku Hung-ming (1857–1928) was born in Penang, Malaya, of Chinese ancestors from Amoy, Fukien and went to China about 1880, after being educated in English and German classical philosophies at the University of Edinburgh and later in an engineering college in Germany. Upon his arrival in China he worked under Chang Chih-tung as his secretary and adviser for twenty years. An "imitation Western man" who could read English, French, German, Italian, Latin, and ancient Greek, he was unable to speak fluent Mandarin though he wore a queue and was dressed in a Chinese long gown. Hating Western colonialism and republican China, he often defended all the traditional Chinese ethics and customs with whimsical remarks. In his opinion, concubinage was justifiable, because it was as natural as a teapot with several teacups making a tea set. One never finds a teacup with several teapots. Though he stubbornly opposed the ideas of progress and reform, Ku preached before 1910 a so-called "Chinese Oxford Movement," a

(*Kuo-ku*), which advocated the traditional literary language and style, Confucianism, and the old ethics. These scholars had a following among the conservative students at the university and the old gentry.[45]

This conservative opposition was, however, very ineffective in its intellectual propaganda. Lacking readability and sometimes logic, their publications had little appeal to the majority of young Chinese. Some of their writings, overloaded with archaic words, were so hard to understand that even a well-trained scholar could not read them. Consequently, their magazine *The National Heritage* was short-lived, lasting only four issues.[46] The publications of the warlords' government, which usually contained merely official releases, were of little help in the debate. This was in great contrast to the writing ability of the new intellectual leaders, most of whom were excellent essayists. Ch'en Tu-hsiu's essays, passionate and powerful, always appealed to the young. Hu Shih's clear and lucid style had no rival at the time. Lu Hsün's satiric short essays and stories were as sharp and deadly as a double-edged blade. Chou Tso-jen always wrote vivid articles, giving the reader a feeling of taking part in a family parley. Other professors and student leaders of the new literature and new thought movements, such as Ch'ien Hsüan-t'ung, Liu Fu, Lo Chia-lun, and Fu Ssu-nien, were for the most part eloquent and forceful writers, not to mention the galaxy of other young essayists, novelists, playwrights, and poets rising from the movements. The new intellectual leaders outstripped the old scholars (with a few exceptions such as Yen Fu and Ku Hung-ming) not only in their knowledge of Western languages and civilization, but also even in the field of Chinese classical studies. Many of the new intellectual leaders could write very well in both the vernacular and the classical language, while the old scholars were either masters only of the latter or too proud to employ the former, which had already become the far more effective medium for writing.

Outside the university there were two renowned literary leaders who supported the opposition, Yen Fu and Lin Shu, both famous translators. Yen by

---

policy of "intellectual open door" and "soul expansion" for China and the world, and cited St. Paul's words, "Prove all things; hold fast to that which is good" — a spirit not necessarily very remote from what was upheld by the new intellectuals in the May Fourth period, although the aim of his movement was, on the contrary, to fight for China's "moral civilization" against the European "materialistic civilization." When democracy showed such an increasing prestige in China during the May Fourth period, Ku called it "Demo crazy." And to ridicule the naturalistic new literature, he called Dostoyevsky "Dosto-whisky."

For Ma Hsü-lun, see below, Chapter V, n. v.

The Institute of Chinese History was one of the branches of the university at the time. Its staff members were all aged historians, such as T'u Ching-shan (T'u Hsiao-shih's father), Chang Hsiang-wen (Chang Wei-hsi), Hsieh Lang-hsien, T'ung I-han, and Hsü I-sun.

this time had become conservative and opposed both the student movement and the new literature and new thought movements, despite the fact that a number of the reforms advanced by the young intellectuals in the May Fourth period had been suggested by himself twenty years before. Contrary to his opinion in the nineties, Yen thought now that only a return to the ancient Chinese ethics and civilization and rejection of Western influence could save China. He also declared that the classical language was more allusive and elegant than the vernacular, and that the new literature movement would, in the struggle for survival, soon perish as a natural result of its irrationality. Therefore he held active opposition to be superfluous and unnecessary.[t] This left Lin Shu as the only influential outspoken supporter of the opposition outside the university.

Lin Shu was the most popular Chinese translator of European and American fiction during the first two decades of this century though he could read only Chinese.[u] With the help of more than sixteen assistants versed in Western

[t] Yen Fu (1854–1921), in his early days, especially during the years 1895 to 1902, had actually been a leading liberal reformer, one of the first to advocate Westernization, the introduction of modern scientific methods and democratic ideas and institutions into China, and the reform of the Chinese language. He was also one of the first to oppose the civil service examination system and the traditional thought control justified by Confucianism. But after 1902 he gradually became conservative, preferred reform by education to revolution and rejected liberalism and nationalism. He believed ancient Chinese thought had some similarities to modern Western thought and should be preserved. His early optimistic view of Western civilization was also shaken by the increasing criticism of capitalist society in the West late in the nineteenth century. After the 1911 Revolution, Yen was appointed chancellor of Peking University by Yüan Shih-k'ai and later became his political and legal adviser. After Yüan's death following the failure of his monarchical movement, which Yen had been more or less forced to support, Yen's disgust with the Republic and all political parties increased. He thought World War I was a sign of the collapse of Western civilization. Consequently he advocated in his last years the restoration of the ancient Chinese civilization and called Ts'ai Yüan-p'ei a "neurotic." But despite this clash of ideas between Yen and the younger generation, the influence of his translations of social Darwinism, utilitarianism, and logic upon the intellectuals of the May Fourth period can hardly be exaggerated (see Chapter XII). Many of the Chinese phrases he coined skillfully in his literary translations, such as the "struggle for existence," and "survival of the fittest by natural selection," had been used in China almost like native maxims since the first decade of the twentieth century, and later, probably beyond his own expectation and approval, were used as battle cries for the new reformers and revolutionaries. To illustrate, the warlord-revolutionary Ch'en Chiung-ming's nickname, Cheng-ts'un (struggle for existence), and Hu Shih's name, Shih (fit), adopted by himself in 1910 according to Hu's autobiography, were all taken from Yen's translations. Many zealots of the save-the-nation movement used these social Darwinian concepts to argue their case. These ideas were used by Ch'en Tu-hsiu in his opening article for *New Youth*, "Call to Youth," to argue against conservatism. Yen's translations, especially that of *Evolution and Ethics*, greatly influenced Mao Tse-tung also in his high school days.[47]

[u] Lin Shu (*tzu*: Ch'in-nan, *hao*: Hui-lu) (1852–1924) was born in Minghou County, Fukien Province, the same country from which Yen Fu came. At nineteen, he contracted a serious lung disease which had plagued the whole family. In his twenties Lin lived a rather wild life and was regarded as a heretic in his native county. He passed the first civil service examination in 1879 and the second in 1882 but failed in the third for seven times between 1883 and 1898. In

languages he translated 180 novels and other works into classical Chinese in about 281 volumes, a total of about twenty million Chinese words. His assistants rendered orally the original texts into vernacular Chinese, which Lin then retranslated into the classical language. As a great admirer of the prose style of the Wen-hsüan school and T'ung-ch'eng school, he had been the principal rival of the conservative group from Kiang-Che at Peking University. The Kiang-Che group, basing their study on etymology, phonetics, and verification, despised the T'ung-ch'eng prose school, which they considered not scholarly but shallow. To Lin Shu the rise of this classical school, which had after 1911 captured the academic position of the T'ung-ch'eng school at the university, was a sign of the deterioration of Chinese literature. With the advent of the new literary revolution, these two schools of old scholars and men of letters, with a few exceptions, forgot their rivalries and rallied together against the mutual threat.

The conservative opposition was, however, passive, and Lin Shu's joining the battle was belated. Early in 1917, Ch'ien Hsüan-t'ung came out in support of Hu Shih's proposal for literary reform and attacked Lin Shu.[49] Lin answered

---

his early thirties he read some forty thousand *chüan* (chapters) of Chinese classical books. In 1900 he went to Peking where he taught in a middle school and later (about 1905) in the Imperial University, the precursor of the National University of Peking. He became dean of its School of Letters in 1909. With the rise of Kiang-Che group, Lin resigned from the university in 1913. Later, during the May Fourth period, he was the dean of Cheng-chih Middle School (*Cheng-chih chung-hsüeh*), which was established by Hsü Shu-cheng, Tuan Ch'i-jui's right-hand man. The school forbade its students to join the student movement. In the late Ch'ing period Lin had advocated social, political, and literary reforms, writing poems in 1898 in somewhat plain language, but, like many others, he could not keep pace with the fast progress of time. Lin's translations were written in fluent and sometimes archaic classical Chinese following the oral translations read to him by his assistants, among them Wang Tzu-jen, Wei I, Wang Ch'ing-t'ung, and Ch'en Chia-lin. Lin could translate at a rate of 6,000 to 8,000 words a day. (He could produce 1,500 to 2,000 characters an hour in translation, but a short article of his own classical writings sometimes took him several months to finish. In comparison, Hu Shih could produce, according to his own testimony, about 900 characters an hour of his own writing and 400 in translation.) Of the 180 books translated by him, 17 were not published. Among those translated works, 105 were by British authors, 33 by French, 20 by American, 7 by Russian, 2 by Swedish, and 7 by unknown authors. There was also one work each by a Belgian, a Spaniard, a Norwegian, a Greek, and a Japanese. Besides these, he also rendered 15 short pieces, and wrote quantities of Chinese prose fiction and poetry. The most popular of his translations in China were *Ch'a-hua-nü i-shih* (Alexandre Dumas, *fils*, *La Dame aux Camelias*) — this was Lin's first translation, done in 1893 — *K'uai-jou yü-sheng shu* (Charles Dickens, *David Copperfield*), *Sa-k'e-hsün chieh hou ying-hsiung liao* (Walter Scott, *Ivanhoe*), *Hei-nu yo-t'ien lu* (Harriet Beecher Stowe, *Uncle Tom's Cabin*), and *Fu chang lu* (Washington Irving, *The Sketch Book*). Some of these early translations were replaced by new translations after the literary revolution. Nevertheless, Lin remained the most productive translator in China, unsurpassed in quantity by anybody, and some of his best translations became classics in their own right, though it is regrettable that, except for forty great or famous novels, many of the original works he translated are inferior because few of Lin's assistants had much literary ability and he had to depend on their selection.[48]

him at that time only indirectly and moderately, stating simply that literature written in the classical language should not be discarded, but should, like Latin in the West, be preserved.[50] Other gentry and scholars who opposed the new ideas in literature and ethics took only a passive part in the debate. Thus when the editors of *New Youth* wanted to arouse interest by controversy, they had to publish a planted letter to the editor written in the old literary style in a disguised hand by one of their own editors, Ch'ien Hsüan-t'ung. The letter, published on March 15, 1918, and signed by one "Wang Ching-hsüan," made a great number of ridiculous and absurd charges against the magazine, and was answered by another member of the magazine's staff, Liu Fu, at length and with great eloquence. Although the letter was planted, it was a fairly faithful imitation both in style and content of most of the views of the older gentry concerning the problems of Confucianism, old-style ethics, and literature.[51] The episode aroused the interest of the readers and the anger of the old scholars.

Gradually Lin Shu intensified his opposition to the new literary movement. In February and March of 1919 he published in *Hsin Shen pao*, a famous newspaper in Shanghai, two short stories, ridiculing the leaders of the new thought and new literature movements. Ts'ai Yüan-p'ei, Ch'en Tu-hsiu, Hu Shih, and Ch'ien Hsüan-t'ung were pictured in the stories under fictitious names, and were described in abusive language. The general theme of the stories was that of giants punishing heretics. One of them, "Ching-sheng the Giant," only slightly abbreviated, reads:

Three young men visit a Buddhist temple in Peking. One of them is T'ien Ch'i-mei [implying Ch'en Tu-hsiu], another Chin Hsin-i [Ch'ien Hsüan-t'ung], and the third, Ti Mo [Hu Shih].[v] Ti is newly returned from America, and well versed in philosophy. T'ien is the most intelligent and often expresses what others dare not say. Chin specializes in Chinese etymology. They are all intimate friends.

When they arrive at the temple, they see one of its rooms is occupied by Ching-sheng the Giant. They despise and ignore him, thinking him merely a military man and unrefined. They have their feast in the next room, eating, drinking, talking, and laughing.

"Alas, China is going to be subdued," sighs T'ien, who is sitting between the other two. "This is all caused by Confucianism. What is ethics for and what *is* ethics anyway? The foreigners often marry their cousins, and their countries are still strong. So long as there is a human race, there are parents. What single benefit do they really give us?"

---

[v] According to ancient Chinese history, the T'ien clan stemmed from the Ch'en clan. And the Chinese characters *hsiu* and *mei* mean the same thing — beauty. The characters *chin* and *ch'ien* both mean money, and *i* is the antonym of *t'ung* which means similarity. The Chinese characters *hu* and *ti* both have the meaning of a barbarian or savage. Ching-sheng implies General Hsü Shu-cheng because Ching and Hsü are the names of two closely related ancient Chinese prefectures.

"Why, all these miseries are brought by the classical language. Thus we sink into such sufferings," Ti Mo says and laughs.

T'ien beats the table with his fist, replying, "How can a dead language produce living literature and scholarship? We have to overthrow Confucius and destroy ethics!"

"I think we must discard the written language first," Ti replies, "and substitute the vernacular, so that people may learn difficult things easily. But, Chin, why do you still cling to your etymology? What is its use?"

"Well, you know my family name, Chin, means money," replies Chin with a smile. "All those who have Chin as their family name love money, and I do too. My teaching of etymology is for this sake and to fool the illiterate. I just want to help you to preach the vulgar language."

Thus the three throw themselves into ecstasy, swearing to be brothers and to beat Confucius Suddenly, a wall of the room falls in, breaking the table and dishes.

The Giant jumps through the broken wall into the room, pointing to the three and shouting, "What are you talking about? Why do you want to destroy the ethics on which China has been built for more than four thousand years? If Confucius had lived today, he would, of course, have emphasized science too. Do you suppose that he would not take a train to see his very sick father, but rather drive a horse-drawn carriage so that he would not see him until he died? Your parents brought you up and provided you an education. How can you forget this and talk like beasts? . . ."

T'ien attempts to defend himself but is struck on the head by the Giant and falls unconscious. The Giant kicks Ti Mo and breaks Chin's nearsighted glasses. They tremble and fall. The Giant shouts, "I'll not stain my hands to kill you beasts. Get out of here!"

The three, pale as paper, crawl in haste out of the temple, hearing the Giant laughing loudly. . . .[52]

In the concluding part of the story, Lin Shu laments, "In this chaotic world, only people like T'ien and Ti may show off, but where can we find a Ching-sheng the Giant?" In another story, "The Nightmare," Lin pictured a similar scene. One of his students dreamed he visited the lower world where he found a "vernacular school" of which Ts'ai Yüan-p'ei was the principal, Ch'en Tu-hsiu the dean, and Hu Shih the assistant dean. Later he saw them all eaten by Rahu-asura, the titanic demon, who according to the Buddhist sutra had once swallowed the sun and moon.[53] The stories were believed to be an appeal to the warlords, especially General Hsü Shu-cheng, one of the ablest leaders of the Anfu Club and a great admirer of Lin, to intervene in the affairs of the university, though Lin, it should be noted, did not completely share the opinions of the warlords on the government's foreign or domestic policies.[54] Later in response to criticism Lin conceded in the same newspaper with regret that the stories were insulting. The concession won Ch'en Tu-hsiu's praise.

On March 18, 1919, Lin wrote a famous letter to Ts'ai Yüan-p'ei, charging the university with "the destruction of Confucianism and the five virtues and five ethical relations" and "the abolition of the classics and adoption of the vernacular as the Chinese written language." The letter was written in the old style. Its content may be summarized as follows:

(1) Toward the end of the Ch'ing dynasty, the reformers said that China would become strong if the old system of civil service examination and the required "eight-legged" essay style were abolished, people's queues cut off, women's feet unbound, the Manchus expelled, despotism put down, and a modern army established. All of these have now been done; has China become strong?

(2) The new reformers in the Republic went further, attempting to overthrow Confucianism and destroy the five virtues and five ethical relations. This is as if a sick child should refuse to see a good doctor to cure itself, but instead should denounce the "latent disease" of its parents and drive them away. Can it recover in this way?

(3) Although foreigners do not know the doctrines of Confucius and Mencius, they still follow the five virtues, i.e., *jen, i, li, chih*, and *hsin* (benevolent love, righteousness, propriety, wisdom, and faithfulness). Besides these they also admire bravery. In the 123 Western works which I have translated in the past nineteen years I find not a single sentence against these five ethical principles. Therefore, where do the new reformers obtain their queer ideas?

(4) The old Chinese books, such as the histories by Ssu-ma Ch'ien and Pan Ku, will under any circumstances not be read by many. Since those books will be eliminated in time, what is the need for a literary revolution?

(5) As for the contention that literary Chinese is a dead language and will thwart the development of living scholarship, it will not hurt science if scientists do not use it. Charles Dickens often denounced Greek and Latin as dead languages, but they are still read. Even as a writer of great fame Dickens could not extinguish the old languages; who of our Chinese contemporaries can surpass Dickens?

(6) It should be kept in mind that principles should not be given up for the sake of temporary convenience, nor should abuse be allowed in order to satisfy transient desire. Confucius was a sage adjustable to any time in which he might have lived. If he had lived today, he would have tried to prevent U-boats and airplanes from being used to kill people. He would always have

fitted himself to the times. How can we attribute the present weakness of China to him?

(7) Furthermore, only real scholarship and real morality can survive and command respect. If all the old classical books were discarded and the vernacular used, all the rickshaw boys and peddlers in Peking and Tientsin could be regarded as professors because their vernacular is more grammatical and correct than the Fukienese and Cantonese dialects.

(8) *Shui-hu* (All Men Are Brothers) and *Hung Lou Meng* (Dream of the Red Chamber) are indeed the best Chinese novels in the vernacular; but the authors of these novels read and imitated a great number of older books. People will not be able to write well either in the literary language or in the vernacular, if they do not read thousands of books. Because the reader will prefer to read the originals of old works to any translations, the old classical language must not be discarded in its entirety.

(9) Of late the new reformers have suggested the so-called new ethics. They denounce filial piety on the ground that children are borne by parents only because of their sexual passion, not as an act of grace on the part of the parents. This absurd statement comes from "the head of a man with the speech of a beast." They also regard lustful women and disloyal ministers in history as good people. Their ideas are actually based on the theories which vicious persons of the past had advocated. There is no use arguing with these reformers.[55]

To these serious charges, Ts'ai Yüan-p'ei answered on March 18 with a long analytical letter, which was to be widely cited and helped to spread the cause of the new thought and new literature movements. In defense of the university, Ts'ai made the following points, here paraphrased:

(A) About the charges of the destruction of Confucianism, and the five virtues and five ethical relations.

(1) Do the professors teach the students at the university to discard the teachings of Confucius and Mencius? They do not. Hu Shih's work, *An Outline of the History of Chinese Philosophy* is a study of Chinese philosophy in a new light without any intention of destroying the teachings of Confucius and Mencius. Other lecturers, such as Ts'ui Huai-ch'eng [Ts'ui Shih, Kang Yu-wei's follower], Liang Sou-ming, and Hu Mo-ch'ing, are all admirers and exponents of Confucianism.

(2) As for the professors' publishing their comments on Confucianism outside the university, it has no connection with the university. These comments are only to be found in *New Youth* magazine. Moreover, they are not

directed against Confucius but only against the Confucian Society (*K'ung-chiao hui*), which uses Confucius' teachings as a pretext or tool for supporting the monarchical movement and for attacking the new thought movement. As you have said, Confucius is a sage adjustable to any time. If anyone distorts his theory in an effort to restore obsolete feudalism in the modern world, is he not an enemy of Confucius and should he not be denounced?

(3) Next, no professors have taught the students at the university to behave contrary to the five virtues and the five ethical relations. The traditional relation between the emperor and his subjects, however, is invalid in a republic. In recent years the students at the university have organized the Society for the Promotion of Virtue, which restrains its members from consorting with prostitutes. This restraint is of course not against the old ethics. The society also restricts its members from taking concubines; even the teachings of Confucius and Mencius are not this strict. In the course on ethics at the university, benevolent love, freedom, order, and honesty are taught, and science certainly will help the development of the students' wisdom.

(4) The professors do not publish any opinions decrying virtue or reasonable ethical relations outside of the university. Nor has any of them regarded lustful women as good. The opinion that "children were borne by parents only because of their sexual passion, not as an act of grace" was actually expressed about seventeen hundred years ago by two prominent and righteous literary men, K'ung Jung and Mi Heng, and opposed by an acknowledgedly vicious person, Lu Ts'ui.[w]

(B) About the charges of the abolition of the classics and the adoption of the vernacular as the Chinese written language:

(1) The university does not completely discard the old literary language in which many textbooks and lectures are still written. Only Hu Shih's *An Outline of the History of Chinese Philosophy* is written in the vernacular, but its citations from the classes are all in the original instead of vernacular translations.

(2) It is possible and indeed necessary to interpret and explain orally the classics in the modern vernacular language for students in classrooms for otherwise they can scarcely understand them.

---

[w] It is interesting to note that K'ung Jung (A.D. 153–208) of the Han dynasty was recorded as Confucius' descendant in the twentieth generation. He was a victim of false charges of Lu Ts'ui, one of Ts'ao Ts'ao's staff, and executed by Ts'ao.[57] K'ung Jung's remark on children had been cited by Wu Yü in his article "On Filial Piety" to support his argument against filial piety.

(3) People who speak the vernacular language cannot necessarily write valuable literary books. This is true not only of rickshaw boys and peddlers, but also of the Manchu nobility and other gentry. The vernacular and literary languages are merely different media for literature. Thomas Huxley's *Evolution and Ethics*, Montesquieu's *The Spirit of the Law*, and Adam Smith's *The Wealth of Nations* were all written in modern plain language, but Yen Fu translated them into archaic Chinese; the novels by Alexandre Dumas, *fils*, Charles Dickens, and Thomas Hardy were all written in the vernacular, but you translated them into literary Chinese; can you say that Yen's and your translations are better than the originals because you have used a literary language? It is true that one has to read thousands of books in order to master either the literary or the vernacular language; but how can you say that professors such as Hu Shih, Ch'ien Hsüan-t'ung, and Chou Ch'i-meng [Chou Tso-jen] do not read thousands of books and are not able to write in good literary language? As a matter of fact, all of these professors had written excellent classical literature before they started the new movement.

(C) Two principles for the administration of the Peking University:

(1) In regard to any and all theories, the university follows the example of the great universities of the world, adopting the principle of freedom of thought. Any theories which are reasonable and merit retention, and have not suffered the fate of being eliminated by natural selection, even though they disagree with each other, should be allowed to develop freely at the university.

(2) In judging professors, the university considers mainly their academic standing. If they are not opposed to the principles mentioned above, they have complete freedom of speech and activity outside of the university. The university will not interfere with their private speech and activity, nor will it be responsible for that speech and activity. For instance, the idea of a restoration of the Manchu emperor is rejected by the Republic, yet on the faculty of this university there is a professor who wears a long queue and maintains the theory of restoration [i.e., Ku Hung-ming]. But, since he teaches English literature which has nothing to do with practical politics, we let him do as he wishes. The founders of the Society to Plan for Stability [sponsor of Yüan Shih-k'ai's monarchical movement] are considered by public opinion criminals. Among the professors of this university is a member of that society [Liu Shih-p'ei]. We keep him because he teaches ancient Chinese literature, which has no relation to politics. Consorting with prostitutes, gambling, and the taking of concubines are forbidden by the Society for the Promotion of Moral-

ity of the university; yet among our faculty members there are those who like to write love poems [in praise of prostitutes, e.g., Ch'en Tu-hsiu, Huang K'an, and later Wu Yü] and who consider the taking of a concubine and consorting with courtesans as romantic actions, and gambling as a pastime. If they do not neglect their school work and do not mislead the students into falling in with them, they also, for the time being, may keep their posts. Generally, it is very difficult to procure men of ability. If we sought perfection and asked for completeness, it would be very difficult to establish a school. Moreover, a distinction should be made between private and public activities. It would be absurd to hold you guilty of teaching prostitution or adultery in the school where you are teaching ancient Chinese literature and ethics, on the ground that you have translated *La Dame aux Camelias* and similar romances.[56]

The exchange of these letters marked a general attack by the conservative forces on the new movement. Ts'ai's answer, firm and solemn though it was, showed traces of evasiveness at certain points. In some respects he denied or minimized what the professors of the new movement had advocated. Indeed under the circumstances, that is the rule of a backward warlord government and this onslaught by the massed conservative forces, the most important purpose of Ts'ai's reply had to be to keep the university free from intervention by the government. He could not afford to go all out for the new ideas. But even with these restrictions, his answer was a good defense of the new movement.

From the beginning the conservative opposition was doomed to fail, because they worked less for public support than they did for intervention by the government. They attempted to persuade the Anfu-controlled Parliament to impeach the Minister of Education and the chancellor of the university, and they asked the Ministry of Education to dismiss such liberal and progressive professors as Ch'en Tu-hsiu, Hu Shih, and Ch'ien Hsüan-t'ung. The resolution to impeach was proposed in Parliament but failed of passage, because the government feared the strong opposition of the students and public opinion. Yet rumors of intervention became so strong in the spring of 1919 that Ch'en Tu-hsiu was forced to resign in March the post of dean of the School of Letters;[58] and it is possible that if the May Fourth Incident had not taken place, the new thought movement at Peking University and other colleges would have been suppressed by the warlord government.[59] The Governor of Kiangsu Province, Ch'i Yao-lin, on the pretext of preserving the "national quintessence" had already ordered all local governments and schools not to buy or read any publications which criticized the old literature and traditional ethics.[60]

Response of the Youth to the New Ferment

Although the situation had become critical, the new movement, unlike the opposition, had aroused the enthusiastic support of the young intellectuals from the time Ch'en Tu-hsiu established *New Youth*. This can be attributed not only to the numerous bold, new ideas promoted in the monthly, but also to its effective literary style and techniques. Moreover, the letters-to-the-editor section in many aspects became, for the first time in a Chinese magazine, a really free public platform where a number of important problems and ideas were seriously discussed and developed. The magazine was indeed a bombshell of thought. "It came to us," as one of the readers recalled, "like a clap of thunder which awakened us in the midst of a restless dream." [61] According to Wang Meng-tsou, one of the publishers of the monthly, about a thousand copies of each issue were printed. After 1917, during the May Fourth period, circulation increased to sixteen thousand — a considerable number given the conditions of publication in China at the time.[62] Many issues were reprinted several times under the pressure of public demand.

The ardent response of Chinese youth to the magazine may be seen in the letters to the editor that were often written by awakening young people, some of whom later became politically or intellectually prominent in modern China. The young readers, frustrated in their striving for social reforms, found the magazine, as one of them expressed it, the "youth's Polestar." As soon as a new issue appeared in bookstores, they anxiously rushed to buy it, and, upon reading it, "could not refrain from rapture" as if they had obtained "the most precious gem." "The fifth issue of the magazine came out today," a young man wrote the editor, "and I bought and read it earnestly. You must know that before this I had asked the bookstore several times, and could not wait any longer. After reading several pages I felt that every sentence in it deeply penetrated my mind. I was so greatly touched and aroused that I longed to introduce the magazine to vast numbers of the public." [63]

Similar letters may be found in the magazine and reflect the fact that, aroused by the new thought tide, the young people felt the need of organized activity. Since they were introduced to so many unformed and mixed new ideas, their reactions to the new tide were diverse. From 1917 on, many young people of moderate or progressive liberal opinions, as well as radicals, formed various organizations. These societies were inspired primarily by *New Youth*. While they were not particularly influential, some of their members later played important roles in China's political developments.

Among such societies was the New People's Study Society (*Hsin-min hsüeh hui*), which was founded by Mao Tse-tung and his friends in Changsha on April 18, 1918. Before the May Fourth Movement, Mao was still a student in the Hunan Province First Normal School (*Hu-nan sheng-li ti-i ssu-fan hsüeh-hsiao*) in that city. This school, headed after 1913 by a graduate from Peking Higher Normal College who was joined by a number of teachers such as Yang Ch'ang-chi (Yang Huai-chung), Hsü T'e-li, and Fang Wei-hsia, with strong liberal leanings, was a Peking University in miniature and its students were often active leaders of student movements of Hunan. Many of them later became prominent figures in social, political, and cultural reform. Mao very soon became an enthusiastic supporter of *New Youth*, and in the spring of 1917 sent it an article under the strange pseudonym "Erh-shih-pa-hua Sheng" (The Man of Twenty-eight Strokes).[x] The article was insignificant, but the event showed his interest in the monthly. Before long, he began to organize the New People's Study Society under the inspiration of the magazine. The society had seventy or eighty members, many of whom later became leaders of the Chinese Communist Party and some of whom were killed in the civil war after 1927. Others joined the Kuomintang and other organizations.[65] In 1918 the society helped to recruit and organize students in Hunan Province to go to France under the work-and-study program. It was to some extent responsible for the development of radical elements among the Chinese worker-students in France.[y] Mao went to Peking with about twenty such work-and-study students in September 1918 after graduating from normal school early in the year. He had a recommendation to Li Ta-chao from Yang Ch'ang-chi, former teacher of ethics, logic, psychology, education, and philosophy at the normal school and later

[x] The article, entitled "T'i-yü chih yen-chiu" ("A Study of Athletics"), appeared in the issue of April 1, 1917 (Vol. III, No. 2), in the old Chinese literary style. The pseudonym was based on the fact that his name, Mao Tse-tung, was constructed of twenty-eight strokes in Chinese writing. Shortly after the publication of this article, Mao, in the summer of 1917, sent letters to many students at the schools in Changsha to invite those interested in the task of saving China who were hardened and determined and ready to make sacrifices for her to become his friends. He also inserted the letter as an advertisement in a Changsha newspaper. The letter was signed with the same pseudonym used in the article published in *New Youth*. To this letter, Mao received, according to his own recollection, "three and one-half replies." The "half" reply came from a youth named Li Li-san, who came to see him and listened to him but went away without committing himself. Their friendship never developed. Li later became for a time the leader of the Chinese Communist Party and was responsible for the "Li-san line." Shortly after publication of the letter, Mao rallied a group of students around him, and the nucleus was formed for the New People's Study Society. Mao's publication of the article in *New Youth* has scarcely been mentioned by himself or his biographers or comrades in later years. At the time of the article, Mao was an ardent and Spartan physical culturist.[64]

[y] According to a report on Chinese students working in France, Hunan Province sent the largest number.[66]

Mao's father-in-law, at the time a professor at Peking University. Mao was appointed by Li Ta-chao as an assistant librarian with a salary of eight *yuan* a month. At this time, Mao was profoundly influenced by the new thought tide going on at the university. In spite of his low position, he joined the Society of Philosophy and the Society for the Study of Journalism in order to be able to audit university classes. He thus made the acquaintance of some ambitious young men who later became leaders of the Kuomintang or Communist Party, and of some literary leaders, such as Ch'en Kung-po, T'an P'ing-shan, Shao P'iao-p'ing, K'ang Pai-ch'ing, and Tuan Hsi-p'eng. He also met Ch'en Tu-hsiu and Hu Shih, but did not win their attention. Under such circumstances, Mao's interest in politics continued to increase and his views became more and more radical. Influenced by Ch'ü Sheng-pai, a student, Mao accepted many of the anarchist ideas at this time. He did not leave Peking for Shanghai and Changsha until early in 1919.

Societies similar to the New People's Study Society were independently founded in many other cities. About these organizations Mao Tse-tung remarked in the summer of 1936:

Most of these societies were organized more or less under the influence of *New Youth* (*Hsin Ch'ing Nien*), the famous magazine of the Literary Renaissance edited by Ch'en Tu-hsiu. I began to read this magazine while I was a student in the normal college and admired the articles of Hu Shih and Ch'en Tu-hsiu very much. They became for a while my models, replacing Liang Ch'i-ch'ao and K'ang Yu-wei, whom I had already discarded.

At this time my mind was a curious mixture of ideas of liberalism, democratic reformism, and Utopian Socialism. I had somewhat vague passions about "nineteenth-century democracy," Utopianism and old-fashioned liberalism, and I was definitely anti-militarist and anti-imperialist.[67]

It should be noted that this "curious mixture of ideas" was not a particular state of mind belonging to a particular young student at the time. It actually represented the main current of thought of the active and restless youth in the middle of the May Fourth Movement.

The new movement not only appealed to the young intellectuals but also secured the sympathy of liberals and radicals in the political parties, even before the May Fourth Incident. Many leaders of the new intellectuals, such as Ts'ai Yüan-p'ei, Wu Chih-hui, Li Shih-tseng, Ch'ien Hsün-t'ung, and Chiang Monlin, were members of the Kuomintang. Though the party did not take any stand concerning the movement in its early stage, some of its members joined it as individuals.[z] Members of Chinese political parties at this time often acted

---

[z] From 1914 to 1919 the Kuomintang was known as the Chung-hua ke-ming tang (Chinese

quite freely. In addition, the new intellectual currents enjoyed strong support from the moderate conservative party called the Yen-chiu hsi (Study Clique), the descendant of the Chinputang (Progressive Party) — both led by the famous journalist and reformer Liang Ch'i-ch'ao.[a']

By the end of World War I the new reformers actually succeeded in winning the sympathy of the major political parties (except the progovernment groups) and many of the new intelligentsia. Peking University and some of the other colleges in the capital became to all intents the headquarters of the movement, while new ideas and a new spirit started to radiate to young intellectuals in other urban schools throughout the country.[b']

Up to this point, the activists of the new reform movement were principally professors and students in Peking. There was no close relation so far between the new intellectuals and the new merchants and industrialists. Also, the oppo-

Revolutionary Party). Its headquarters was in Tokyo until after the death of Yüan Shih-k'ai in 1916 when it was moved to Shanghai. The name of the party was changed to Chung-kuo Kuo-min-tang on Oct. 10, 1919. Early in 1924, after its first congress, the headquarters were moved from Shanghai to Canton. During the May Fourth period the Kuomintang was the only strong party attempting to overthrow the Peking government. Some of its more moderate members stayed in Peking and in the Peking Parliament.[68]

[a'] The Chinputang was the descendant of the Monarchical Constitutional Party, which was founded by the Hundred Day reformers at the end of the Ch'ing period. Shortly after the 1911 Revolution the monarchical constitutionalists organized the Democratic Party. In 1913 under the protection of Yüan Shih-k'ai, Liang Ch'i-ch'ao, the leader of the Democratic Party, combined this party with Yüan Shih-k'ai's Party and the small Unification Party to establish the Chinputang; this formed an opposition to the majority party in Parliament, the Kuomintang. After Yüan's death, the Chinputang was disbanded. Its members and other moderate politicians established in 1916 the Hsien-fa yen-chiu hui (Constitutional Study Society), which was popularly known as Yen-chiu hsi (Study Clique). The clique in most cases supported Tuan Ch'i-jui and held many posts in Tuan's cabinet. But after Tuan stepped down in Nov. 1917, it retained very few seats in the Anfu-controlled Parliament. (It also held some seats in the Canton Parliament.) From 1918 many of its intellectual leaders, such as Liang Ch'i-ch'ao and Chang Tung-sun, intended to give up practical politics and take part in cultural and intellectual reforms. At the end of that year, the Kuo-min kung-pao (Citizens' Gazette), one of the clique's organs in Peking, published a series of articles discussing and supporting some of the new ideas promoted in New Youth. Early in 1919 Hu Shih, Chou Tso-jen, and Ch'en Tu-hsiu exchanged a few long letters in the magazine with Lan Chih-hsien (Lan Kung-wu), editor of the Gazette, discussing problems of chastity, language, attitudes of the reformers, etc. Other organs, such as the Peking Ch'en pao (Morning Post) and the Shih-shih hsin pao (often called "The China Times") in Shanghai, along with the Kuomintang's Min-kuo jih-pao (Republic Daily), also became pioneers of the new culture movement. Li Ta-chao, before being converted to Marxism, belonged to the Study Clique, being one of the four secretaries of T'ang Hua-lung, who was a leader of the clique and President of the House of Representatives of the Peking government. T'ang was later assassinated in California in Sept. 1918.[69]

[b'] Before the May Fourth Incident there had been some cases of students, under the inspiration of New Youth, establishing magazines in schools to propagate the new thought and new literature, but in the face of great pressure from the school authorities. An example was the establishment of the New Voice Society (Hsin-sheng she) and its publication of New Voice by the students at the middle school of the Chung-hua College in Wuchang in the spring of 1919.[70]

sition, based on a coalition of the warlord government and the old gentry, was not yet at odds with the new merchants and industrialists. In fact, from 1915 to 1917 the conflict between the new intellectuals and old forces was mainly a conflict of ideas rather than of actions. This situation, however, began to change after 1917 when relations between the Chinese government, under Tuan Ch'i-jui's premiership, and Terauchi's Japanese government became more intimate. The pro-Japanese character of the Chinese conservative group led those in the new intellectual movement to join hands with the general public, whose patriotism had been stirred by the Twenty-one Demands in 1915 and by subsequent actions of the Japanese militarist government. Such patriotic sentiments gradually set in motion a joint "save China" movement which became more intense in 1918.

The Anti-Japanese Petition of May 1918

To explain the development of close relations between the Chinese intellectuals and the public in the save China movement, it is necessary to note the change in Japan's policy toward China in October 1916, when Terauchi Masatake succeeded Okuma Shigenobu as Premier. Okuma had supported both the Chinese revolutionary party and the Manchu monarchical party with the hope of checking Yüan Shih-k'ai's power. The Twenty-one Demands had climaxed his policy in China.[71] When Terauchi came to power, Shōda Kazue (Katsuda Shukei) was appointed Minister of Finance. At that time Japan's economy was enjoying an unprecedented wartime boom, with surplus capital everywhere available for new enterprises. Thus Shōda launched the so-called "separation-of-the-chrysanthemums'-roots" (*kiku-no-newake*) policy, which worked toward the establishment of economic roots in, and the colonization of China by way of loans and investments.[c'] In addition, Hayashi Gonsuke, the Japanese minister in Peking, suggested a policy of helping Tuan Ch'i-jui and cutting off support of the antigovernmental Kuomintang. This new policy resulted in the huge Nishihara loans to Tuan's government in the period from January 1917 to September 1918.[d']

[c'] The term was an allusion drawn from a line of one of Shōda's poems which served as a caption for a painting of chrysanthemums. Later he wrote an unfinished memoir with this title in defense of the Nishihara loans. The memoir was translated into Chinese by Kung Te-po and titled *Chü-fen-ken*.[72]

[d'] Hayashi suggested the policy of helping Tuan, but opposed the Nishihara loans, which he thought would hurt the interests of the Great Powers in China and stir up their jealousy. He also charged later that the motive and aim of Terauchi's policy of supporting Tuan were not positively helping to unite China but quite the contrary.[73] The loan was named as such because it was negotiated by Nishihara Kamezo. It amounts to about 145,000,000 yen.

Under the influence of these loans, Tuan Ch'i-jui's government leaned more and more upon Japan, and with its financial support Tuan consolidated his forces in Parliament. On March 7, 1918 (possibly initiated in August 1917), Tuan's chief of staff, Hsü Shu-cheng, with the financial backing of the Ministry of Finance then headed by Ts'ao Ju-lin, established the powerful organization known as the Anfu Club (*An-fu chü-lo-pu*), which bought the support of a majority of the parliamentary members. After the autumn of 1918 it monopolized control of the Peking Parliament and held most of the significant posts in the administration. This aroused jealousy on the part of other groups in the government and dissatisfaction among the public.[e']

The situation deteriorated further when secret military conventions were concluded with Japan. In February 1918 the Soviet Union made a truce with the Central Powers and both made public and renounced a series of secret Russo-Japanese agreements which had been concluded in the period 1907 to

---

[e'] Tuan Ch'i-jui was born in Hofei County, Anhwei Province in 1864. He graduated from the Peiyang Military Academy at Tientsin in 1885 and studied artillery science in Germany in 1889. In 1895 he assisted Yüan Shih-k'ai in training modern troops and was instrumental in suppressing the Boxer Rebellion in Shantung in 1900. During the 1911 Revolution, as one of the commanders of the Government Army, he first fought on the side of the Manchu regime, but later took the lead in asking the Emperor to abdicate. After the revolution, he was appointed Minister of War in Yüan's cabinet; acting Prime Minister in May–July 1913; Prime Minister in 1916–17 and concurrently Minister of War in 1917. After the failure of Chang Hsün's monarchical movement, Tuan was reinstated as Premier and Minister of War in 1918. Tuan had previously established the Chung-ho chü-lo-pu (Moderation Club or, the term "Chung-Ho" might mean "Sino-Japanese") on March 25, 1917, which was actually the precursor of the Anfu Club. In the spring of 1918 Hsü Shu-cheng, then second in command of the Fengtien troops, received from the Ministry of Finance the sum of 10,000,000 *yuan* ostensibly for the payment of these troops. But the sum was said to have been spent in manipulating the elections for the new parliament. When the parliament came into being in the autumn, more than 330 of the 430 parliamentary members were under obligation to Hsü. Among such members Wang I-t'ang, Speaker of the House, was the leader, and his residence on Anfu Street (*An-fu hu-t'ung*) became the meeting place for this group of parliamentarians; hence the name Anfu Club. It was reported that the club paid from 300 to 800 *yuan* per month to any member of Parliament who would record his name as a member. Nominally at least, no party lines were drawn in regard to applicants for membership. Tuan was the real leader of the group, but on the surface he had no relation with it. The whole organization was under the immediate control of Hsü Shu-cheng who was a very shrewd and able young general, well known as "Little Hsü." Through Ts'ao Ju-lin and certain of his intimates, the club maintained close relations with the Japanese. China's President Hsü Shih-ch'ang and some of the military men around him came to feel quite uneasy about this powerful organization. (President Hsü was reportedly receiving support from the American and British legations.) Important members of the club included Li Sheng-to, President of the Senate, Kung Hsin-chan, acting Premier, Chu Shen, Minister of Justice, Ts'ao Ju-lin, Minister of Communications, and his Vice Minister Tseng Yü-chün, Lu Tsung-yü, Director of the Currency Reform Bureau, General Wu Ping-hsiang, Chief of the Constabulary, Chang Hu, director of the Salt Gabelle and head of the Bureau of Labor Emigration, T'ien Ying-huang, Vice-Speaker of the House, the chief secretaries of the two Houses, and many military officers. The club was disbanded by the government on Aug. 3, 1920, after Tuan's troops were defeated by the forces of Ts'ao K'un and Chang Tso-lin.[74]

1917 by the Tsarist government. In these agreements Japan and Russia had planned to wrest Manchuria and Mongolia from China, and to prevent China's receiving political aid from any other powers.[75] After this disclosure, Japan secured Tuan Ch'i-jui's consent to negotiate from March to May 1918 the Sino-Japanese Military Mutual Assistance Conventions. By these conventions the Chinese government conceded to Japan the right to station troops in North Manchuria and Outer Mongolia on the pretext of preventing invasion by the Central Powers or the Soviet Union, to use the Chinese military maps, to provide Japanese training officers for the Chinese army and navy, among other rights. The contents of the conventions were kept secret by the two governments until February 1919 when the Peking representatives made sections of them public at the Shanghai Peace Conference on the demand of Southern representatives.[f']

This diplomatic development, however, could not be completely kept from the public before that date. Already in the spring of 1917 the government's pro-Japanese policy had aroused a furious protest by Chinese public opinion. A Chinese-English bilingual newspaper, *The Peking Gazette* (*Ching pao*), edited by Eugene Chen (Ch'en Yu-jen), published on May 18, 1917, an editorial titled "Selling out China," which disclosed certain negotiations between Japan and China that later developed into the military conventions and which publicly denounced Tuan Ch'i-jui's government as traitorous. Ch'en was consequently imprisoned and the paper was suppressed immediately by the government.[77] Then in the summer of 1918 the people demanded the publication of the conventions. Chinese students in Japan and France demonstrated against secret diplomacy. Despite the intervention of the Japanese police, the Chinese students in Japan resolved in a meeting on May 5 that all of them (about three thousand) would return to China in a body before May 20.[g'] They also organized the Corps of Chinese Students in Japan for National Salvation (*Liu-Jih hsüeh-sheng chiu-kuo t'uan*), with all Chinese students in Japan as members and with financial support from Chinese merchants in that country. In a meeting in Tokyo on May 6, forty-six Chinese student representatives were arrested

[f'] The whole contents of the conventions are still unknown. They were declared void by the Peking and Tokyo governments on Jan. 27, 1921. Some of the texts of the military conventions were given to the press by agreement of the governments of both Japan and China on March 14, 1919.[76]

[g'] During these weeks some Chinese students in Japan organized a Society for the Punishment of Traitors (*Chu Han-chien hui*). Chinese suspected as pro-Japanese were warned and threatened. Kuo Mo-jo, who at the time had been married to a Japanese girl for a year and a half, was, as he later recalled, regarded as a "traitor." He had joined the "returning China" movement in 1915; but this time he was passive. He participated in anti-Japanese activities a year later under the influence of the May Fourth Incident.[78]

by Japanese police. This incident further stirred the students' sentiments.[79]

The Chinese students in Japan started to return home on May 12, 1918. On May 22 the Ministry of Education of the Peking government issued an order to force them back to Japan, saying that the conventions could not be made public because of their military character, and that students could save China only by continuing, not abandoning, their studies.[80] In spite of the government's threats, the returned students maintained their corps in Shanghai, and some of them, e.g., Tseng Ch'i, Wang Chao-jung, and Yü I, established the *Save-the-Nation Daily* (*Chiu-kuo jih-pao*) in that city. Tseng Ch'i published in it a series of articles, asking Chinese youth to join in the task of salvation.[h'] The articles were later reprinted in Peking as a pamphlet titled *State Structure and the Youth* (*Kuo-t'i yü ch'ing-nien*).[82]

On June 30, 1918, vigorous intellectuals and Japan-returned students, Wang Kuang-ch'i (1892–1936), Tseng Ch'i, Li Ta-chao, Ch'en yü (Ch'en Yü-sheng), Lei Pao-ching (Lei Mei-sheng), Chang Shang-lin (Chang Meng-chiu), and Chou Wu (Chou T'ai-hsüan), initiated in Peking the Young China Association (*Shao-nien Chung-kuo hsüeh-hui*).[i'] The sponsors of the association in its early stage of formation promoted nationalism and proposed four aims: (1) to animate a spirit of rejuvenation, (2) to study "true theories," (3) to expand social enterprises, and (4) to overturn declining customs. By social enterprises, they meant education for reform and for new learning and industry and commerce.[84] Among the sponsors were enthusiastic nationalists, such as Tseng Ch'i and Wang Kuang-ch'i, and potential leftists, such as Li Ta-chao; some of them, Li and Wang among others, were connected with *New Youth*. Ch'en Tu-hsiu appears also to have had some relation with the association before the May Fourth Incident, but he refrained from joining it.[85]

The initiation of the Young China Association was only one example of the save-the-nation movement which developed under the stimulus of the pro-Japanese policy of the government. The more apparent this policy became, the

[h'] Tseng Ch'i (1884–1951) was born in Lungchang County, Szechwan Province. He joined the T'ung-meng-hui in elementary school, and was a member of the House of Representatives in 1912. Later he became a newspaperman in Chengtu and Chungking. About 1914 he went to Japan and returned to China in 1918. He was in France and Germany from 1919 to 1924, and founded the Young China Party (*Shao-nien Chung-kuo tang*, later named the Chinese Youth Party or *Chung-kuo ch'ing-nien tang*) in Paris on Dec. 2, 1923. In the winter of 1945 he attended the Political Consultative Council as leader of this party, which was a rightist nationalist organization. He came to the United States in Oct. 1948. After a two months' trip to Europe in 1950 he returned to the United States. He died in George Washington University Hospital, Washington, D.C., on May 7, 1951.[81]

[i'] The Young China Association was not formally established and expanded until July 1, 1919. One source says that Li Ta-chao joined it a little later.[83] For an account of the history of the association see below, Chap. IX, n. q.

closer were the contacts between the advocates of the new literature and new thought movements and public anti-Japanese and patriotic groups.

By May 1918 public sentiment in China against the Sino-Japanese Military Mutual Assistance Conventions was running very high. On May 21 more than two thousand students in colleges and other schools in Peking, including the National University of Peking, the National Higher Normal College, the National College of Law and Political Science, and the National Industrial College, held a demonstration to protest the conclusion of the conventions. The students went to the office of the President, Feng Kuo-chang, to ask the contents of the conventions, and to demand their annulment.[j'] The feelings of the students were soothed momentarily by the President's promise that his government had not done and would not do anything against the interests of China.[k']

Similar demonstrations by students followed in many other cities, including Tientsin, Shanghai, and Foochow. They asked that the local governments require the Peking government to annul the secret conventions.[88] Although the student movement was soon calmed down, it did influence a number of merchants who in the days following held many public meetings and sent telegrams to the government, denouncing Tuan Ch'i-jui and asking a truce in the civil war with the South, which Tuan had insisted on carrying on to the end. The significance of the student demonstrations and petitions of May 1918 did not lie in any immediate effect on the government. Of prime importance is the fact that they marked the beginning of the cooperation on a significant scale of the new intellectuals with other forces in the society, and in a sense were rehearsals for the May Fourth Incident.

Efforts towards the unification of the student movement on a nation-wide basis began when the students of Peking during the summer after the demonstration sent representatives to Shanghai who immediately joined with other

---

[j'] *The Eastern Miscellany* reported that there were four schools involved in the event; see Vol. X, No. 6, pp. 44–45. Hua Kang said that more than ten schools joined, that besides the four colleges there were, among others, the Middle School of the National Normal College and Chung-kuo Ta-hsüeh (China University).[83]

[k'] The students gathered at 9:00 a.m. in front of the reception room of the President's office at Hsin-hua-men (New-China Gate), asking to see the President. President Feng sent Wang Chih-hsiang, the Mayor of Peking, Li Chieh-p'ing, commander-in-chief of the infantry, Wu Ching-t'an, police chief, and Ma Chin-men, chief of gendarmerie, to persuade the students to go back to school, but they failed. At last, the President received thirteen student representatives, including: Tuan Hsi-p'eng, Lei Kuo-neng, Hsü Te-heng, Wang Cheng, Yi k'e-ni, and Fang Hao (all from Peking University); Hsiung Meng-fei (Normal College); and Lu Shih-i, Teng Ch'ang-hai, and Hsia Hsiu-feng (all from Industrial College). They were introduced to the President by Commander Li Chieh-p'ing in the Chü-jen T'ang (Benevolence Hall). A number of students in this group later became leaders in the May Fourth Incident and renowned figures in Chinese politics and educational circles.[87]

students to organize the Patriotic Society of Students (*Hsüeh-sheng ai-kuo hui*). The name was later changed to the Students' Society for National Salvation (*Hsüeh-sheng chiu-kuo hui*).[89]

During the same summer, the society, especially students at Peking University, established a magazine called *The Citizens Magazine* (*Kuo-min tsa-chih*), which was supported also by students from other schools in the capital and other cities. A Citizens Magazine Society was founded with a membership of more than two hundred (some report says one hundred and eighty). Each member paid five *yuan* as dues to finance publications. The first issue of the magazine appeared on January 1, 1919, the same date the *New Tide* monthly was established. While *New Tide* was a publication chiefly concerned with fomenting a purely literary and intellectual revolution, *The Citizens* was devoted to rallying the new intellectuals and the public to patriotic action.[90]

An additional indication of these student demonstrations and petitions of May 1918 was the regrouping of social forces along clearer lines. On the surface the movement was simply a patriotic activity expressing the anti-Japanese sentiments of the people and a protest against the foreign policy of the Peking government. Beneath the surface, however, it indicated a conflict between two groups of social forces, the old and the new.

The old forces in this conflict were strengthened at this time by increased foreign assistance. The warlords had secured after 1915 the support of some of the gentry in their monarchical movements. In fact, the driving force of these monarchical movements, despite some foreign influences, had always come mainly from reactionary domestic elements. The monarchists had failed to secure positive support from most of the Great Powers.[l'] However, in the latter years of World War I, when Japan's influence in China grew as a result of Terauchi's policy toward China, the Chinese warlords came to depend increasingly on the financial and military assistance of the Japanese government to maintain their ruling power, as has been pointed out. Thus from 1917 to 1918 Tuan Ch'i-jui enjoyed support from both domestic and foreign sources, support which, however, brought trouble from social and intellectual groups in China.

On the other side of the conflict, new merchants and industrialists began to find common grounds with the new intellectuals for opposing the government's policies. In 1916 and 1917 the two monarchical movements had failed because of the opposition of political and military forces rather than the re-

[l'] Yüan Shih-k'ai won some sympathy for his monarchical movement from President Wilson. Yüan was said to have sent Wellington Koo to the United States to secure support and Yüan did obtain some assistance from that country. Japan was the first to oppose Yüan's movement.[91]

sistance of merchants and students. In the field of foreign policy Yüan Shih-k'ai had secured some public support as a result of his stand in the negotiation of the Twenty-one Demands with Japan. His intention to become emperor had not perturbed the merchant class to any great extent. When Chang Hsün restored the Manchu boy Emperor to the throne, yellow dragon flags were unfurled immediately on the front doors of shops in Peking accompanied by, as Reinsch reported, "joyous excitement" or curiosity.[92] This action may have been taken under police suasion, yet the merchants' reluctance to protest seemed clear. It is, of course, understandable that the new merchants and industrialists of China were less interested in problems of republic or monarchy than those of competition with Japanese goods. During the latter years of World War I, Japan's control of Chinese markets became a vital threat to Chinese industry and commerce. The Peking government's concessions to Japan were not calculated to win the sympathy of these business groups who, with their emerging patriotism, protested against the Sino-Japanese military conventions. Failure to unify the currency system which was still so chaotic in many areas that internal trade was badly hampered, the heavy burden of taxation which was for the most part spent in supporting an indecisive and prolonged civil war, and the obstructions to industrial development created by existing laws all provided further grievances on the part of these new forces against the government. Such feelings were manifested in the demands presented by the Federation of the Commercial Organizations of Shanghai to the Internal Peace Conference in May 1919.[93]

The new intellectuals, as they had cooperated in an effort to undermine the ideological and ethical foundations of conservative forces both inside and outside of the government, were certainly eager to attain an alliance with the new economic forces. Thus the student and merchant petitions of May 1918 served indeed as a test ground of this alliance, which did not fully mature for another year.

CHAPTER IV

THE MAY FOURTH INCIDENT

T HE May Fourth Incident of 1919 was the center of the whirlwind, the vortex of the whole May Fourth Movement. In the events following this incident, the alliance of the intellectuals with the new economic forces on the common ground of patriotism was vigorously expressed. Meanwhile, the new literature and new thought movements obtained great popularity, the save China sentiments gathered, and the whole movement achieved a peak of power and influence until at last the reformers gradually split up into various factions and produced a rearrangement of social forces in the social, political, and cultural developments of later years.

China's Failure at the Versailles Peace Conference

The immediate cause of the May Fourth Incident was the handling of the Shantung question at the Versailles Peace Conference. Sino-Japanese relations had been China's most urgent and troublesome problem since the beginning of World War I. On August 15, 1914, Japan sent an ultimatum to Germany demanding transfer to Japan before September 15 of "the entire leased territory of Kiaochow," which Germany leased from China in 1898 for ninety-nine years after she seized the area by force because two German Jesuits were killed by disbanded Chinese soldiers in Shantung in the previous year, but at the same time promising "the eventual restoration of the same to China." [1] This promise was viewed with skepticism by the Chinese public from the beginning.[2] In the following year Japan occupied Kiaochow and eventually the greater part of Shantung Province — the "Holy Land" of China, where Confucius and Mencius were born, taught, and died — which has an important economic and strategic position. Japan not only showed no intention of carrying out her promise, but instead served on China the drastic Twenty-one Demands and secured the treaty of May 25, 1915. The Chinese consoled themselves with the hope that the Great Powers would redress this wrong in an equitable settlement at the end of the war.[3]

Consequently, when the war ended on November 11, 1918, the Chinese people were jubilant. A three-day holiday was declared by the government, and there were heartfelt celebrations. The grand parade in Peking took place in the T'ai-ho Tien (Great Peace Palace), where eighteen years before an "Allied victory" had also been celebrated — the victory over the Boxers by the troops of eight countries led by Count Waldersee, the German general and senior Allied commander. The situation now seemed reversed, with China as one of the Allies and Germany the defeated. In keeping with this sentiment, shortly after the armistice the Von Ketteler monument in Peking, which the Chinese had long regarded as an affront, was removed.[a] The general feeling of the Chinese was that the national disgrace would disappear forever with the "stony monument!"[5]

The hopes of the new Chinese intellectual leaders went even further. In celebrating the Allies' victory on November 17, large numbers of students and teachers joined the parade of almost sixty thousand in Peking. At the same time, the new intellectual leaders displayed their optimism in speeches on the celebration and in many articles published in magazines and newspapers. They believed that the Allied victory was a real one of democracy over despotism and militarism, and of the workers and plain people over their oppressors.[6] They thought that the war had destroyed the ideas and practices of secret diplomacy, violation of law, military intervention in politics, and dictatorship.[7] They also assumed that the territory and interests seized by Germany in China since 1898 would be restored, and that the Sino-Japanese treaties and agreements concluded under duress during the war would be readjusted at the ensuing peace conference. Most of them somewhat naively believed that Wilson's Fourteen Points and the war aims declared by the governments of the Allies would be carried out in the postwar years.[8]

This illusion, however, could not be long maintained after the opening of the Versailles Peace Conference on January 18, 1919. News from Paris revealed that Japan was going to take over the position of Germany in China, and the situation would probably be worse than before. The Japanese and Chinese governments had shown a friendly feeling toward each other at the prospect

---

[a] The Von Ketteler monument was erected at the central park of Peking to commemorate the German minister Freiherr von Ketteler, who had been slain by Chinese soldiers in the Boxer Rebellion in 1900. It bore the Chinese inscription, "Right Overcometh Might," on the one side, and on the reverse side, the Latin words, "In Memoriam Juris Vindicati." It was first strafed by over-exultant Allied soldiers in the early morning and then removed by the Chinese government.[4]

of the peace conference. But their attitudes changed suddenly as soon as their missions arrived in Paris. The Chinese delegation changed its attitude partly because of suspicion of Japan and partly because of the pressure of Chinese public opinion.[b] The attitudes of the Chinese and their delegation split at the time along the political cleavage of the North and the South. The appointment as chief delegate of Lu (Lou) Cheng-hsiang, who, as Foreign Minister in both 1915 and 1919, had signed in 1915 the Sino-Japanese treaty resulting from the Twenty-one Demands, was opposed from the beginning by the Canton government. Among the delegates, C. T. Wang represented the South, and V. K. Wellington Koo sympathized with the South and was apparently influenced by Americans. The Southerners advocated a firmer policy against Japan and intended to provoke public suspicion of the Peking government in its pro-Japanese attitude. In March and April 1919, both Chinese and foreign newspapers in China reported that influences which would serve only the interests of Japan were at work among the Chinese delegates.[c] Under such circumstances, furious arguments not only between the Japanese and Chinese delegations, but also among the Chinese factions within their delegation erupted from the beginning of the conference.

The first news from Paris to shock the Chinese public was that the Japanese delegate, Baron Makino Nobuaki, had announced at the plenary session of the five Great Powers (the United States, Great Britain, France, Italy, and Japan) on January 27 that Great Britain, France, and Italy had signed secret treaties with Japan in February 1917, giving assurances that after the war they would "support Japan's claims in regard to the disposal of Germany's rights in Shan-

[b] A box of important documents belonging to the Chinese delegation which was en route to Paris was lost or stolen in Tokyo early in Jan. 1919. This and the route of China's delegation from Peking to France via Japan, as well as the two hour conference in Tokyo between Japanese Foreign Minister Uchida Yasuya (Kōsai) (1865–1936) and Chnia's chief delegate "going over the Kiaochow question somewhat," as reported by Reuter's Pacific Service, aroused a deep suspicion of the Chinese government and its delegation among the Chinese public in general and the Southern Chinese in particular.[9]

[c] The Chinese delegation included five plenipotentiaries, Lu, C. T. Wang (Wang Cheng-t'ing), one of the Southern leaders and the Vice-President of the Senate at Canton, V. K. Wellington Koo (Ku Wei-chün), minister to Washington, Sao-ke Alfred Sze (Shih Chao-chi), minister to London, and Wei Sun-tchou (Wei Jen-tsu), minister to Brussels (later replaced by C. C. Wu), representative from the Southern government and son of Wu T'ing-fang). Its members numbered altogether sixty-two. The mission was split on the question of individual rank and representation.[10] Early in April 1919, C. T. Wang wired to the Shanghai press accusing "certain traitors" among Chinese. The telegram caused wide speculation in China. Late in April it was rumored in Shanghai that Wellington Koo was going to be pro-Japanese, because of his alleged engagement to Ts'ao Ju-lin's third daughter. The news was reported by the Reuter's representative in Peking and later said to be based on a telegram sent by two of the delegates in Paris, other than Koo, to the Canton government.[11]

tung." [d] With these secret pledges Japan's hand was strengthened at the conference, and the United States, to which China had looked for support, found herself isolated.

Moreover, the situation had been further complicated when the Chinese warlord government on September 24, 1918, had negotiated a secret loan (it was one of the Nishihara loans) from Japan for the construction of the Tsinan-Shunteh and Kaomi-Hsüchow railroads in Shantung Province, as a result of which the whole property and income of the two railroads was mortgaged for the repayment of the loan.[13] On the same date, Baron Gotō Shimpei, the Japanese Foreign Minister, proposed to China a seven-point arrangement concerning the question of Shantung. According to this, Japanese troops stationed along the Kiaochow-Tsinan Railroad were to be concentrated at Tsingtao, with a detachment at Tsinan; the railroad was to be guarded by a police force with the Japanese as the chief officers and trainers; and when the status of the railroad was established, it should be worked jointly by Japanese and Chinese. To these proposals, Chang Tsung-hsiang, the Chinese Minister to Tokyo, replied in an exchange of notes, "I beg to acquaint you in reply that the Chinese government gladly agree (*hsin-jan t'ung-i*)." [e] All the arrangements were kept secret until the morning of the meeting on January 28 of the Council of Ten at the Versailles Conference. Until this time they were unknown even to some of the Chinese plenipotentiaries.[f]

The loan for the Tsinan-Shunteh and Kaomi-Hsüchow railroads and the exchange of notes concerning the Shantung question provided Japan with her legal basis for her claims in regard to Shantung and the related railroads. On the evening of January 27, 1919, the American delegation learned from Wellington Koo of the loan and agreement between Japan and China. The American delegation immediately explained to the Chinese delegates its difficulty in supporting China because of these arrangements; the Chinese delegates were also

[d] The Chinese and American delegates in Paris were surprised, though a secret understanding of similar nature concluded between Russia and Japan in the period 1907 to 1917 had been made public and renounced previously by the Soviet government of Russia.[12]

[e] In a later memorandum dated March 20, 1919, in the files of the American Commission to Negotiate Peace, Ch'en Lu, the acting Chinese Foreign Minister, made a statement to Paul S. Reinsch that the Shantung agreement of Sept. 24, 1918, was the one agreement that China would not wish to have published, since it admitted the right of Japan to inherit all the special privileges formerly enjoyed by Germany.[14]

[f] "The secret agreement referred to [i.e., the so-called 'gladly agree to' note] was unknown to the Chinese delegates till the moment when it was shown to the conference." [15] Wellington Koo confirmed this later in an interview with Russell H. Fifield on Oct. 30, 1951.[16] But Lu Cheng-hsiang probably had prior knowledge of it, because it was reported that copies of the secret agreement were in the lost box in Tokyo.[17]

embarrassed by the matter. In a confidential telegram to the Chinese Foreign Ministry they made the following peculiar suggestion: [18]

Under the present circumstances we can only suggest, after careful consideration, that it is better for the administration to submit this contract of loan and notes to Parliament, counseling parliamentary members and asking them to refuse to ratify them. In this way, the administration, backed by the public opinion of Parliament, might strengthen our hands for future argument in the Peace Conference; it would make it easier too for a certain country [the United States] to help us. Otherwise, facing the alliance of Japan and Great Britain, and being isolated, the United States would not be able to help China, and the future would be unthinkable. We ask you to report this situation immediately in person to the President in order to decide what action we should take in this matter. In case the above suggestion be accepted by the President, the administration should summon a secret meeting of the two Houses and submit the matter to them. After the Houses fail to ratify the loan agreement, they should inform the administration in the same secret manner, keeping the public from knowledge of it.

The matter apparently was not submitted to Parliament.[g] However, the loan and the agreement could not be kept secret for long since they had to be debated at the Paris Peace Conference. In presenting her case concerning Shantung to the conference, Japan based its legality on the Sino-Japanese Treaty of May 25, 1915, the contract of the Tsinan-Shunteh and Kaomi-Hsüchow railroads, and the exchange of notes respecting adjustment of the Shantung question of September 24, 1918. To these arguments the Chinese delegation replied that China concluded the treaty of May 25, 1915, under duress, and that "China's entry into the war [in 1917] so vitally changed the situation contemplated in the treaty that, on the principle of *rebus sic stantibus*, it ceased to be applicable." [21] The Japanese delegation countered that the contract respecting the railroads and the exchange of notes respecting the Shantung questions of 1918 were made after China entered into the war and was thus not under duress.[22]

Under these unfavorable circumstances, i.e., the prior assurance of Great Britain, France, and Italy that they would support Japan's claims to Shantung interests and the Sino-Japanese arrangement of 1918, China lost her case at the conference. On April 30, 1919, Woodrow Wilson, Lloyd George, and Clemenceau — the "Holy Trinity," as Lansing called them — resolved in secret in the Council of Four (Orlando of Italy was absent) to transfer to Japan all of

<hr />

[g] Reinsch believed, "The Chinese people will insist that agreements cannot be considered valid as to concessions and securities therein included unless they are ratified by the National Parliament." [19] According to Article 35 of the Provisional Constitution of China, "The Provisional President shall have power, with the concurrence of the National Council [Parliament], to declare war and conclude treaties." [20]

Germany's interests in Shantung without any mention of Japan's promise of 1914 about "the eventual restoration of the same to China." The resolution was later embodied in articles 156, 157, and 158 of section VIII of the Versailles Peace Treaty.[23]

In addition to its argument on the Shantung question, China presented to the Peace Conference in April two memoranda. One stated the "claim of China for the abrogation of the treaties and notes concluded with Japan on May 25, 1915," and the other dealt with the readjustment of the following seven questions: (1) renunciation of spheres of influence or interest, (2) withdrawal of foreign troops and police, (3) withdrawal of foreign post offices and agencies for wireless and telegraphic communications, (4) abolition of consular jurisdiction, (5) relinquishment of leased territories, (6) restoration to China of foreign concessions and settlements, and (7) tariff autonomy.[24]

The latter proposal was prepared spontaneously by the Chinese government but the former, the proposal to abrogate the treaty of 1915, was suggested to the Chinese delegation by Chinese students in Europe, who had organized themselves since the beginning of the conference for the purpose of keeping watch on the delegation.[25] Both proposals were rejected by the conference.

Chinese Public Sentiment in Respect to the Peace Treaty

China's case at Paris had not appeared too hopeless until April 22, when Wilson began to show signs of wavering in the Council of Four. The Chinese public retained some optimism even after this. During the Peace Conference the Chinese people, both at home and abroad, had developed great concern regarding Sino-Japanese diplomacy. They organized a large number of groups to support and check on their delegation in Paris and to publicize its actions. Some members of the delegation also tried to keep in close contact with the public. Articles, pamphlets, and news releases were widely distributed. The Chinese carried on this information campaign so strenuously that some foreign observers regarded it as overdone. It had at least the immediate effect of causing the Japanese to feel that they had lost face.[26]

As an examination of the whole situation indicates, this great interest on the part of the Chinese public, especially the new intellectuals and merchants, was not merely a result of agitation by political parties. Rather, it reflected a real demand by those new groups to free themselves from the threat of colonial control. To justify this evaluation of public sentiment prior to the May Fourth Incident, it is necessary to analyze the character and variety of social, political, and cultural groups which raised their voices concerning the controversies at the Versailles Conference.

It is true that the Southern Chinese had made great efforts to propagate animosity against the Japanese and the Peking governments. A few able Chinese connected with the Kuomintang or the Southern government had gone to the United States and France to prepare this program.[h] Such activity was not limited to the revolutionary party. The Progressive Party (Chinputang) — the Study Group — though sometimes a parliamentary ally of the warlords, also came out in opposition to Tuan Ch'i-jui's pro-Japanese policy at this time. The leader of the group, Liang Ch'i-ch'ao, who while traveling in Europe had been appointed by the Peking government as adviser to the Chinese delegation, sent from Paris on April 24 a telegram to the Citizens' Diplomatic Association (*Kuo-min wai-chiao hsieh-hui*) in Peking opposing Chinese agreement to the peace treaty.[27]

But of more fundamental importance than the activities of these political parties was the rallying of the Chinese people at home and abroad in many private groups to discuss the diplomatic problem. These included, in China, the League of Nations Association (*Kuo-chi lien-meng t'ung-chih hui*) organized by Li Sheng-to and Wang I-t'ang on February 11, 1919, and the abovementioned Citizens' Diplomatic Association organized by Lin Ch'ang-min, Chang Chien, Wang Ch'ung-hui, and other Chinputang and Kuomintang leaders on February 16.[28] Another influential group, the Diplomatic Association (*Wai-chiao tiao-ch'a hsieh-hui*), was founded by the Canton leaders. Public interest was aroused partly by the formal presentation of China's case to the Council of Ten by V. K. Wellington Koo and C. T. Wang on the morning of January 28, 1919.[29] Subsequently, from February 7 to April 10, the Chinese delegation in Paris received eighty-six telegrams from various Chinese groups all over the world in support of China's claims and in protest against Japan's case at the conference. The telegrams represented groups which included thirteen Chinese student organizations in Peking, Tientsin, Shanghai, Wu-Han (Wuchang, Hankow, and Hanyang), and Tsinan, as well as in New York, Boston, Los Angeles, Berkeley, Honolulu, London, and — in Shanghai — returned students from Japan.[30]

---

[h] According to Fifield, Eugene Chen and T. C. Quo [Kuo T'ai-ch'i] were active propagandists in Paris. Before going to France they established a China Agency in the United States that was violently anti-Japanese. Both Chen and Quo were for a while representatives of the Canton government in Washington, and Chen later became Foreign Minister in both the Wu-Han government during the Northern Expedition period and the Nanking government after the Mukden Incident of 1931.

In addition, there were protests from thirty-two commercial and industrial organizations, and labor unions, such as the Chamber of Commerce of China in Peking, the Chinese Merchants Association in Honolulu, the Shantung Industrial Association, and the Overseas Chinese Labor Union in Canton, and from more than sixty-seven political and social groups, such as the provincial assemblies, educational associations, and various overseas Chinese organizations in the United States, Philippines, Cuba, Mexico, Java, Malaya, and many other countries.

In these telegrams the senders emphasized their belief that the Peace Conference was pledged to respect people's rights and that the nation would not recognize secret agreements among the Great Powers. The Peking students' telegram read, "11,500 students of institutions of higher learning in Peking pledge themselves support you defending our national rights. Desire you remain firm to end." [31] The telegram from the Shantung Provincial Assembly, Chamber of Commerce and Agriculture, Shantung Educational Association, and Shantung Industrial Association specifically mentioned the fact that secret agreements like the Japanese Shantung agreements were "directly opposed to" President Wilson's Fourteen Points. It concluded by demanding that "China be saved from those perils into which traitors have betrayed her." [32]

Most of these telegrams were sent to Paris by Chinese literati or members of the middle class. While they reflected public feeling, they seemed to be somewhat emotional and unrealistic. On this point, four months later the conservative Ku Hung-ming, who opposed the adoption of the vernacular for literary use, issued the following sarcastic diatribe (in English):

Your [the *Millard's Review's*] correspondent complains that over 90 per cent of the population in China are illiterate because "literary Chinese is hard to learn." It seems to me that instead of complaining, all of us, foreigners, militarists, politicians and especially we returned students, who are now still having such a good time here in China, should give thanks to God every day in our lives for the fact that 90 per cent of the four hundred million people in China are still illiterate. For just fancy what the result would be, if the 90 per cent of the four hundred million people were to become literate. Imagine only what a fine state of things we would have, if here in Peking, the coolies, mafoos, chauffeurs, barbers, shopboys, hawkers, huxters, loafers and vagabonds, *hoc genus omne*, all became literate and wanted to take part in politics as well as the [Peking] University students. It is said that recently five thousand telegrams were sent to the Chinese delegates in Paris on the Shantung question. Now calculate out the number of the telegrams that would have to be sent and the amount of money it would cost to send the telegrams, if the 90 per cent of the four hundred million people in China all became literate, and wanted to be patriotic like us returned students! [33]

Ku did have a point as far as the overemotional response of the Chinese public was concerned. But this emotion was understandable against the background of earlier hopes and optimism for the results of the Peace Conference, the battle which the new intellectuals were fighting against the pro-Japanese government, and the efforts of the new merchants and industrialists to keep their market in China from falling under Japan's control at the end of the war.

Disillusioning News from Paris

When the disheartening news that the Paris Peace Conference would give Japan Germany's place in Shantung reached China in the latter part of April, the Chinese public suddenly fell into a state of dejection and indignation. First of all they wanted to know who was responsible for the disaster at Paris. Wilson was reported to have asked the Chinese delegates in the meeting of the Council of Four on April 22: "In September 1918, when the Allied forces apparently were about to win the war and the armistice was at hand, and Japan was not able to threaten China, why did the Chinese government still make the exchange of notes stating 'gladly agree' to Japan's terms concerning the Shantung question?" [34] This aroused the Chinese public's suspicions that their government willingly sold out the sovereignty of the nation instead of doing it under duress. A few days later, upon receiving Liang Ch'i-ch'ao's telegram of April 24 to the Citizens' Diplomatic Association reporting that the Paris Peace Conference would turn over Tsingtao to Japan, Lin Ch'ang-min commented in newspapers on May 2 that, since the conference had reversed its earlier proposal to submit the Shantung question to the disposal of the five Great Powers (Great Britain, the United States, France, Italy, and Japan) with the requirement of consent from the nations concerned, and now accepted Japan's demand of Shantung, China was going to be subdued.

Meanwhile the Chinese delegates, fearful of being held responsible for the failure, reported back to China that "two factors had caused China to lose her case in the Peace Conference: one was that Japan had already secured secret pledges from Great Britain and France in February and March of 1917 that she would receive the German concessions in Shantung after the war; another was that our government had made the 'gladly agree' exchange of notes with Japan in September 1918 in respect to the Shantung question. These two *faits accomplis* made it impossible for those who wished to help us to do so." [35] The contents of this report were published by the Peking daily, *China Press*, on May 1, and disclosed to the public by other newspapers and foreign teachers in Peking on May 3. In this way the Chinese at home learned on the eve of the May Fourth Incident that the Paris Peace Conference was, far from what they had hoped, controlled by power politics and that their own government had "sold out" the interests of their nation to Japan even before the conference opened. The students formally explained their disappointment at the failure of Wilson's idealism and promises:

> Throughout the world, like the voice of a prophet, has gone the word of Woodrow Wilson strengthening the weak and giving courage to the struggling. And the Chinese have listened and they too have heard. . . . They have been told that in the dispensation which is to be made after the war unmilitaristic nations like China would have an opportunity to develop their culture, their industry, their civilization, unhampered. They have been told that secret covenants and forced agreements would not be recognized. They looked for the dawn of this new era; but no sun rose for China. Even the cradle of the nation was stolen.[36]

The feeling of unrest among the students and their disappointment with the Western countries in the days immediately preceding May 4 was later described by a graduate of Peking University:

> When the news of the Paris Peace Conference finally reached us we were greatly shocked. We at once awoke to the fact that foreign nations were still selfish and militaristic and that they were all great liars. I remember that the night of May 2nd very few of us slept. A group of my friends and I talked almost the whole night. We came to the conclusion that a greater world war would be coming sooner or later, and that this great war would be fought in the East. We had nothing to do with our Government, that we knew very well, and at the same time we could no longer depend upon the principles of any so-called great leader like Woodrow Wilson, for example. Looking at our people and at the pitiful ignorant masses, we couldn't help but feel that we must struggle![37]

This situation began to look ominous to those in the know. "Even before the demonstration of May 4," Chiang Monlin said, "some of the leaders in the new educational movement who had been observing the spirit of unrest among the students predicted that something was going to happen."[38] Paul S. Reinsch, then American Minister to China and a close observer of the movement, described the public feeling of the Chinese, as well as the Americans and British in China before May 4, as follows:

> Probably nowhere else in the world had expectations of America's leadership at Paris been raised so high as in China. The Chinese trusted America, they trusted the frequent declarations of principle uttered by President Wilson, whose words had reached China in its remotest parts. The more intense was their disappointment and disillusionment due to the decisions of the old men that controlled the Paris Con-

ference. It sickened and disheartened me to think how the Chinese people would receive this blow which meant the blasting of their hopes and the destruction of their
confidence in the equity of nations. . . .

The Americans in China, as well as the British and the Chinese, were deeply
dejected during these difficult weeks. From the moment America entered the war
there had been a triumphant confidence that all this sacrifice and suffering would
establish just principles of world action, under which mankind could live more
happily and in greater security. That hope was now all but crushed.[39]

This dejection and indignation among the Chinese students was by the beginning of May turning into a threat of a furious demonstration in protest
against the "traitors in the government" and the resolutions of the Great Powers
at Paris.

The Students: Their Character and Organization

It is important to note the character and temper of the Chinese students in
general and of those in Peking in particular before describing in detail their
reactions to the Versailles crisis. Chinese students, especially since the beginning
of the twentieth century, have had a more active political and social consciousness than those of the Western democracies. They were more inclined to participate in public affairs and to attempt reform in politics. This characteristic
can be explained by a number of factors.[i]

First of all, China's repeated humiliating defeats by foreign countries which
she had previously considered barbarous and inferior, her corrupt and divided
governments, prolonged civil wars, and backward and collapsing economy, certainly alarmed the young intellectuals. Taught customarily by their teachers
that someday they were bound to be the saviors and hope of the nation, the
Chinese students were more sensitive than other groups to any hurt to their
national and cultural pride. At the same time, they were aware of the long
tradition of influential student political movements and of their own privileged
status among the few who possessed the ability to read and write a difficult
language. Thus they took for granted their own exceptionally significant position in public affairs and their mission to save China.

Moreover, the Chinese students were psychologically prepared to take part
in social and political activities. The abolition of the traditional civil service
examination system in 1905 left the youth uncertain regarding their postgraduate
professional prospects of which the major goal had been and still was, conven-

---

[i] See also above, Chap. I, pp. 11–12.

tionally, to enter government as officials. The fact that this personal frustration was offset by the opportunity of being powerful as leaders of mass action tended to make Chinese students, as Bertrand Russell observed, reformers or revolutionaries instead of, as was the case with some highly educated youths of the West, cynics.[j] Living as they did in a nation without a genuine legislature or election system, they saw that gradual improvement was obstructed and public opinion suppressed; this situation enraged them and justified their resort to revolt or protest in unorthodox political action. Since the old order appeared so hopeless, the appeal of novelty and modernism to youth was strengthened.

In this connection, we must note the striking contrast in age and education between the new intellectuals and their opposition. The college student leaders at the time were all in their early twenties and many of their schoolmates and almost all the middle school students were teen-agers. In 1919, active students like Fu Ssu-nien, Tuan Hsi-p'eng, Lo Chia-lun, and Chou En-lai were all twenty-three years old, and Hsü Te-heng, who was considered an older student than average and was sent as one of the few student representatives of Peking to Shanghai and Nanking and subsequently played a significant role in spurring student, merchant, and worker strikes in those cities, was twenty-four. Their professors purveying the new thought were in their twenties or thirties. In contrast, most of the old scholars in the opposition had passed sixty and the warlord leaders were middle age or older.[k] Generally speaking, they and the majority of the governmental officials had received an old-fashioned education under the former imperial regime, which differed greatly from that given to the new intellectuals, a difference far exceeding that between ordinary successive generations.[l] This discrepancy in education and ideology made the views and

[j] "Throughout the East," said Russell, "the university student can hope for more influence upon public opinion than he can have in the modern West, but he has much less opportunity than in the West of securing a substantial income. But, neither powerless nor comfortable, he becomes a reformer or a revolutionary, not a cynic. The happiness of the reformer or revolutionary depends upon the course of public affairs, but probably even while he is being executed he enjoys more real happiness than is possible for the comfortable cynic. I remember a young Chinese visitor to my school who was going home to found a similar school in a reactionary part of China. He expected the result to be that his head would be cut off. Nevertheless he enjoyed a quiet happiness that I could only envy." [40]

[k] In 1917, when Peking University started its reform, Ch'en Tu-hsiu had just reached 38, Hu Shih 26, Ch'ien Hsüan-t'ung 30, Liu Fu 28, Lu Hsün 36, and Li Ta-chao 29. Even Ts'ai Yüan-p'ei was only 41. In the same year Lin Shu became 65, Yen Fu 63, and Ku Hung-ming 60; Tuan Ch'i-jui was 53.

[l] According to a who's who of contemporary officials of China published in 1919, among 4,764 high ranking officials and educational administrators, 1,545 had passed the old civil service examination under the Manchu dynasty, 1,341 had studied abroad after completing some of the old schooling, 909 had graduated from Chinese schools, and 969 came from merchant and other groups. Almost all middle and lower ranking officials had received only the traditional education." [41]

actions of many government and school authorities unbearable to the young students.

Moreover, several factors facilitated the Chinese students' taking part in mass activities. Unlike their counterparts in the West, they customarily lived together in crowded dormitories and were well regimented in study and recreation activities. Collective and cooperative rather than individualistic attitudes prevailed in Chinese life in general and among the more idealistic young intellectuals in particular. Their concentration in urban centers furthermore alienated them in habit and thinking from their parents, a great number of whom were old gentry or landlords living in the country. The techniques of mass action, such as demonstrations, strikes, and boycotts, which were either introduced by returned students from abroad or learned from Chinese history and Western publications, provided suitable means for the expression of grievances or indignation that could find no other vent. The intellectuals' experiences in frugal study by means of labor and in the work-and-study program in Europe during World War I, as described earlier, had of course helped to draw them closer to the experience of the labor movement which was ascending in the West. On the other hand, there had been in China no strong objection in public opinion to student interference in politics.

While the above analysis might be applied to Chinese students in general during the May Fourth period and since, a few points should be borne in mind with regard to the students in Peking prior to the May Fourth Incident. Peking had long been the political and cultural center of traditional China. Most of the active and ambitious intellectuals, except those with merely economic aspirations, had for centuries gathered in this old capital. The intellectuals came mostly from landlord, bureaucrat, or other well-to-do families. Traditionally, a number of them had maintained close relations with the bureaucracy, and quite a number of the students had been prodigals. Their goals of life had always been, for the most part, to enter officialdom and share power with the old bureaucrats. Not many of them had troubled to pay attention to foreign policy, social problems, or the tide of new thoughts.

The temper of the students, however, underwent a considerable change near the end of World War I, especially after the 1917 reforms of Ts'ai Yüan-p'ei. On the eve of the May Fourth Incident college students in Peking might be classified, according to their character, into three categories: the remnant of the prodigals who still lived more or less luxurious and corrupt lives, the diligent students who devoted their attention more to study than to current affairs, and the third group who were most affected by the new ideas. This third group probably constituted only 20 per cent of the student body, but it was the most active.[42] These students followed foreign and domestic affairs closely and were deeply interested in social, cultural, and intellectual problems. Compared with their fellow students, they absorbed more Western thought, and read more Western literature — Ibsen, Tolstoy, Maupassant, Kropotkin, and Shaw. A consciousness of mission and a spirit of skepticism prevailed among them. These were the students who led the later student movement.

Actually, the thoughts and activities of the whole student body in Peking at the time were quite complex. All the ideas which had been championed in the West and the East in past centuries crowded together and conflicted with each other in the minds of the students. They had not, of course, studied these vast ideas very deeply. But their enthusiasm for what they believed was unsurpassed. It was like a man just coming into a lighted room out of one long darkened and finding everything curious.

As has been mentioned, after the petition of May 1918 the students organized many small groups, public or secret, liberal or radical, among which the New Tide Society and the Citizens Magazine Society were the most influential. (Secret organizations had come into vogue at this time among citizens, politicians, merchants, and some military men.) Though most of the student organizations were nonpolitical, there were a number interested in political events. For many active students, anarchism became popular in Peking early in 1919. Indeed, Ts'ai Yüan-p'ei himself had been an enthusiastic nihilist, anarchist, and socialist propagandist in the first decade of this century. This was true of many other intellectual leaders as well. After the 1911 Revolution many of them had retained their anarchist convictions more in the sense of humanitarianism, liberalism, and altruism than of terrorism. Under the rule of the ruthless warlords, radical ideas mushroomed inevitably among the youth. Revolutionary or anarchist publications such as the *Liberal Record* (*Tzu-yu lu*), *Collected Essays on Tiger Taming* (*Fu Hu chi*), *Voice of the People* (*Min-sheng, La Voco De La Popolo*), and *Evolution* (*Chin-hua*) were secretly passed about among the students.[m] Kropotkin and Tolstoy became popular, and

---

[m] The *Voice of the People* was a magazine published by the anarchist Cock-crow Society (*Hui-ming hsüeh-she*) founded in Canton in 1912 by Liu Shih-fu (1884–1915); its French edition bears the Esperanto title. The magazine was suppressed and the society disbanded by the Canton Governor the next year. In July 1914, Liu established in Shanghai the Comrades for Anarchistic Communism Society (*Wu-cheng-fu kung-ch'an-chu-i t'ung-chih-she*), sometimes known as the Chinese Anarchist Party (*Wu-cheng-fu tang*). The *Collected Essays on Tiger Taming* contains Liu's essays edited by T'ieh-hsin after Liu's death. Liu was critical of Sun Yat-sen's doctrine and of Chiang K'ang-hu's Socialist Party. The title "Tiger Taming" alludes to Chiang K'ang-hu's given name, since the Chinese character *hu* means tiger. The *Liberal Record* was published by the Shih she (Society for

K'ang Yu-wei's *One World* (*Ta-t'ung shu*) and T'an Ssu-t'ung's *Philosophy of Benevolence* (*Jen hsüeh*), as well as the old nationalistic *Record of the Ten Days at Yangchow* (*Yang-chou shih-jih chi*) about the massacre by the Manchu troops, were still widely read and admired by the youth. These works by K'ang and T'an bore some marks of anarchism and utopian socialism.[n] Among the student groups under this ideological influence, a very radical one was the Work-and-Study Society (*Kung-hsüeh hui*), established by a group of students and alumni from the Peking Higher Normal College, predecessor of the Peking Normal University, on February 9, 1919. The society promoted a kind of doctrine of work-and-study (*kung-hsüeh chu-i*). It rejected Mencius' idea that "mental laborers are governors and manual laborers the governed," and attempted to unite the functions in one person, that is, to have mental laborers do physical work and manual laborers, study. The major purposes of the society were to realize certain anarchist ideals in China, to serve the interest of the laboring classes, and to build a nation based on work-and-study units. It also accepted John Dewey's idea that education is life and school is society. Although its members were very iconoclastic and rebellious, they still committed themselves to the belief that social reform should be carried out bit by bit. In the student activities we are going to describe in the following sections, this group performed behind-the-scenes and sometimes pivotal functions in turning them to a positive and radical direction.[o] Other organizations such as the Common Voice Society (*T'ung-yen she*) and the Cooperative Study Society (*Kung-hsüeh hui*) were more moderate but also influential in student circles.[45]

Reality), also an organization promoting anarchism. It is believed that the Anarchist Party was the first to organize the Canton barbers and teahouse workers into labor unions. After 1925 it was merged with the Kuomintang.[43]

[n] K'ang Yu-wei's *Ta-t'ung shu* was written in 1884 but never finished. It was published in part in 1913 and 1919, and *in toto* posthumously in 1935 and 1956. The English translation was by Laurance G. Thompson with the title, *Ta T'ung Shu, the One World Philosophy of K'ang Yu-wei* (New York, 1958). The title had been translated literally by the author as *The Book of the Great Concord*. T'an Ssu-t'ung's *Jen hsüeh*, first published in Yokohama in 1898 by Liang Ch'i-ch'ao, is an iconoclastic work, a blend of Neo-Confucian, Buddhist, Christian, anti-Manchu, and Western scientific ideas. According to T'an, *jen* stands for benevolence, universal love, compassion, soul, love-force, or human nature—the manifestation of "ether," which is a material as well as spiritual basic substance of the universe and life.[44]

[o] The Work-and-Study Society should not be confused with the Work-and-Learning Mutual Assistance Corps (*Kung-tu hu-chu t'uan*) established almost a year later. Although student members of both groups took part in manual work, the Work-and-Study Society was more ambitious in attempting to build a society according to its own image, and was more interested in labor problems than the corps. In May 1922, the society published a "Labor Day" issue of its organ, *Work-and-Study* monthly, and proposed to establish a workers' school.

The May Fourth Demonstration

When the news of China's failure in the Paris Conference reached Peking at the end of April 1919, student organizations, including the New Tide Society, the Citizens Magazine Society, the Work-and-Study Society, the Common Voice Society, and the Cooperative Study Society, held a meeting wherein they resolved to hold a mass demonstration on May 7, National Humiliation Day, the fourth anniversary of Japan's ultimatum in the Twenty-one Demands. This resolution was soon approved by the student bodies of all the universities and colleges in Peking, led by Peking University, the Higher Normal College, the Higher Industrial College, and the College of Law and Political Science, together with a plan for participation in the forthcoming demonstration by all the students of those educational institutions. Thus it is clear that the immediate causes of the May Fourth Incident were not only the disaster at Paris but also the continuing indignation aroused by the Twenty-one Demands of 1915.[p] At the same meeting the students also decided to telegraph the following declaration to the press and public organizations throughout the country:

Our demand for the restoration of Tsingtao is going to fail; and May 7 is near at hand. All of our people must awake to this situation. We hope that you will one and all hold protest meetings on that day to oppose unanimously foreign aggression. Only in this way can our nation survive the crises.

[Signed] 25,000 [q] students of the schools of higher learning (*Chuan-men i-shang hsüeh-hsiao*) [47]

After this meeting, on May 1 and May 3, the news from Paris grew alarming. It was reported that China's demand for a just settlement of the Shantung question was about to be rejected by the Peace Conference and that China's case had been handicapped by the "gladly agree" exchange of notes engineered by the Chinese "traitors." Chang Tsung-hsiang, the Chinese Minister to Japan, hastily returned from Tokyo at this time.[r] After his return, he stayed

[p] On this point Paul S. Reinsch remarked, "Primarily the cause of the student violence [of May 4, 1919] lay in the proximity of the fourth anniversary of the Japanese ultimatum of 1915; but they were also anxious and stirred because of the reported action of the old men at Paris." [46]

[q] Whether the number of the college and university students in Peking reached 25,000 at the time might be questioned. This might have included the cadets. Student literature of the time often claimed this number. Some sources imply that students of this kind in Peking at the time numbered 15,000.

[r] According to Ch'en Tu-hsiu, "When Chang left Tokyo, more than three hundred Chinese students in Japan rushed to the railway station to see him off. They shouted 'traitor!' and threw

in Tientsin for several days. Lu Tsung-yü, another outstanding pro-Japanese official in the government, went to Tientsin to talk with him; on April 30 Chang came to Peking without announcing his purpose and lived in Ts'ao Ju-lin's home, though Chang had his own house in the capital. The following day the foreign press reported that Chang would not return to his post. Rumors also circulated that he would succeed Lu Cheng-hsiang as Foreign Minister and chief delegate to the Paris Peace Conference. This news aroused great suspicion on the part of the public, who believed that persons high in the government were plotting against the interests of the country. On May 3, public sentiment in Peking reached fever heat; political and social groups rushed to hold emergency meetings in an effort to save the situation. The Chamber of Commerce of Peking telegraphed to similar organizations in many other cities, asking them to support China's claims in Paris; the Chamber of Commerce of Shanghai resolved to hold a conference on May 6 to discuss methods of handling the matter. The Citizens' Diplomatic Association sent representatives to see the President, Hsü Shih-ch'ang, requesting him to order the Chinese delegation in Paris to refuse to sign the Peace Treaty in the event that the Shantung question was not reasonably solved. It also resolved on May 3 to invite other social and political groups to join a citizens' meeting (*kuo-min ta-hui*) to be held in Peking on May 7.[49] The Corps of Chinese Students in Japan for National Salvation telegraphed the President that "it would be better to face an open rupture than to live in shameful submission."[50]

Under this public pressure, the Peking government took drastic measures to quell the uproar, which made the public still angrier.[51] The students in Peking felt impelled to hold the scheduled mass demonstration earlier than originally planned. The mounting urge for action during the time from May 1 to May 3 was described by one of the students, who took part in the subsequent events, as follows:

Since May 1st we had been thinking and moving around to seek some way to express our discontent at the corruption of our Government and of the militarists, both Chinese and Foreign. . . . Finally, we came to the conclusion that the only immediate thing we could do was to call a great mass parade of the students in Peking.[52]

A group of the most active students, in view of the emergency, posted a notice at Peking University on May 3 at 1:00 p.m., calling for an informal meeting of student representatives from all the universities and colleges of

---

into his train a snowfall of white flags bearing the inscriptions, 'Traitor,' 'You gave away all our mines and railroads to Japan,' and 'Treason!' His wife was frightened and wept."[48]

Peking.[s] The informal meeting took place that evening at 7:00 in the assembly hall of the Law School (or "Third School") of the National University of Peking, was attended by more than one thousand students, and presided over by Yi K'e-ni, a nationalistic student at Peking University from Hunan, who was a leader of the Citizens Magazine Society and took a moderate attitude to the old and new culture problems. Most of the participants were from Peking University. Shao P'iao-p'ing of the Society for the Study of Journalism at that university delivered a speech analyzing the Shantung question; it was followed by a number of agitating speeches by other students. Several resolutions were adopted, of which the most significant was passed at 11:00 p.m. It called for a mass meeting of all the students of the universities and colleges in Peking the next day, May 4, instead of May 7, to protest against the government's foreign policy. This meeting of May 3 was described later by a student of the National University of Peking:

We first discussed the problem of our national crisis and we all agreed that the Shantung problem was caused by corruption and injustice, and that we as students must fight to show the world that "might should never be right!" Four methods of procedure were then discussed. They were as follows: (1) to get the people of the country to fight together; (2) to send telegrams to the Chinese delegates in Paris and ask them not to sign the treaty; (3) to send telegrams to the people of all provinces in the country asking them to parade on May 7th, National Humiliation Day;[t] (4) to meet [with] on May 4 the students of all the schools in Peking at "Tieng-Ang Mien" [T'ien-an-men] and to show our discontent by a great mass parade.

During the meeting, a student of the Law School, Mr. Tshia [Hsieh Shao-min], deliberately cut open his finger and wrote on the wall in blood "Return Our Tsingtao." The students were all quiet.[53]

Obviously the meeting on the evening of May 3 proceeded in a highly emotional atmosphere. This was also recalled by Hsü Te-heng, a student leader who had spoken at the meeting and was one of thirty-two later arrested in the incident, and by Chang Kuo-t'ao, another student at Peking University, who had also spoken at this meeting and later became a communist leader but left the Party in 1938. It was also said that in the meeting a young student of about

[s] Chang Kuo-t'ao claims in his memoirs that the proposal to hold such an informal meeting was made by him in a staff meeting of the Citizens Magazine Society on May 2 at 7 p.m.
[t] The third resolution had actually been adopted and carried out previously, and the first two were very similar to those adopted in the meeting held on the following morning, May 4. Apparently repeated resolutions were adopted at the various meetings either because the students attending the meetings were not necessarily the same, or the later resolutions were intended only to reinforce the previous ones.

sixteen or seventeen years of age shouted in tears that he would commit suicide on the spot if the meeting did not reach a positive resolution for the demonstration.[54]

It must be pointed out, however, that the meeting was carried on in an orderly fashion and that the majority of students and student representatives had no intention that there should be violence in the scheduled demonstration. The meeting was conducted mainly by members of the New Tide Society and the Citizens Magazine Society, most of whom from the beginning disavowed violent action.[u] The demonstration seemed to have been carefully prepared. John Dewey and his wife, who had arrived in China on May 1, 1919, wrote home from Peking on June 20, 1919:

I find, by the way, that I didn't do the students justice when I compared their first demonstration here to a college boys' roughhouse; the whole thing was planned carefully, it seems, and was even pulled off earlier than would otherwise have been the case, because one of the political parties was going to demonstrate soon, and they were afraid their movement (coming at the same time) would make it look as if they were an agency of the political faction, and they wanted to act independently as students. To think of kids in our country from fourteen on, taking the lead in starting a big cleanup reform politics movement and shaming merchants and professional men into joining them. This is sure some country.[56]

Some of the radical groups, nevertheless, had planned to turn the demonstration into more than mere orderly protest. On the evening of May 3, both before and after the informal meeting of student representatives, many small student groups, secret and public, held meetings at their respective schools to discuss methods and procedures for the forthcoming demonstration. It is reported that some groups in their meetings planned to attack three pro-Japanese officials, Ts'ao Ju-lin, Chang Tsung-hsiang, and Lu Tsung-yü.[57] Ts'ao, Minister of Communications and managing director of the Bank of Communications,[v]

[u] Lo Chia-lun, one of the founders and editors of the *New Tide* monthly and a student leader in the new literature and new thought movements "was among those in charge of the meeting." [55]

[v] Ts'ao Ju-lin was born at Shanghai in 1876. He learned French from the age of thirteen. In 1897 he passed a competitive examination and was sent by the Manchu government to Japan to study law at the Imperial University of Tokyo. After returning to China in 1904, Ts'ao passed the examination for returned students and obtained the degree of *chin-shih* in law. He was appointed a section chief in the Ministry of Commerce and lecturer on law at the Imperial University of Peking. Later he became junior secretary of the Board of Foreign Affairs in the Manchu court, and with the help of Yüan Shih-k'ai, Hsü Shih-ch'ang, and others, he was appointed Vice-Minister of Foreign Affairs by the end of the Ch'ing dynasty. After the 1911 Revolution he was dismissed from the post but remained as Yüan's personal adviser. At the same time, Ts'ao practiced law in Peking and occupied a prominent place in that profession. He seemed to have been a skilful publicity hunter. Once when two girls in Shanghai were sentenced to jail on a charge of "raping" a young man and causing his death on the spot, Ts'ao volunteered to come to their rescue and won the girls' freedom, mainly on the argument that physically it is impossible for a girl to rape a man

Chang, minister to Japan since 1916,ʷ and Lu, the director general of the Currency Reform Bureau, chairman of the Bank of Communications, and

and that the law did not specify such a case.⁵⁸ In the first republican Parliament, Ts'ao was elected a senator, representing Mongolia, despite the fact that he had never resided there. In Parliament he ostensibly belonged to the Chinputang. As Yüan's Vice-Minister of Foreign Affairs in 1915, Ts'ao was responsible for the negotiations on the Twenty-one Demands and the subsequent Sino-Japanese treaty. After the collapse of Yüan's monarchical movement, Ts'ao retired for a short time. On July 17, 1917, he was appointed Minister of Communications in Tuan Ch'i-jui's Cabinet, which post he held until June 1919 through many changes of premiers. He was concurrently Acting Minister of Finance from March 1918 to Jan. 1919. In 1918 he took the leadership of the Hsin Chiao-t'ung hsi (New Communication Clique) in Parliament and worked very closely with the Anfu Club. In the same year he participated in the conclusion of the Nishihara loans and actually took part in all loan transactions with Japanese bankers. During the Paris Peace Conference, he reputedly exerted great economic pressure on the Peking government on behalf of the Japanese government. Through his public and private career, Ts'ao made a large fortune. A report of the Sino-American News Agency on May 16, 1919, listed Ts'ao's property as: "Land in Shanghai in seven places, valued at $3,000,000 [yuan]; land near Tachimen [Ta-chih-men] at Hankow, valued at $2,000,000; deposit in the Yokohama Specie Bank in his family tang name of Tsiaokuotangkee [Chiao-kuo-t'ang chi], Y. 2,500,000 [yen]; shares in the Bank of Communications, to the value of $200,000. Land, houses, gold and piecegoods shops, total $1,500,000; shares in the South Manchuria Railway [Railroad] Co., worth Y. 500,000; land, houses, piecegoods shops and restaurants in Peking, total $500,000; a country residence in Japan worth $20,000; invested together with Little Hsü [Shu-cheng], Tuan Ch'i-jui, and Nyi Tsze-chung [Ni Ssu-ch'ung] in the salt-producing fields at Haichow, $100,000; in company with Liang Shih-yi, Little Hsü, and one of Yüan Shih-kai's relatives, gold mining rights in Tibet, Tsao's share is worth $2,000,000; shares in the Lungkow-Yentai Iron Mining Co. and in the Exchange Bank, total $600,000. There are many other shares, quantities of valuable curios, precious stones, pearls, pictures, etc., too numerous to mention as well as deposits in different banks under fictitious names and kept secret even from his own family and best friends. At a very conservative estimate, Ts'ao's private fortune cannot be less than $20,000,000 [yuan]. Counting his salaries and allowances as minister and vice-minister, and adding a liberal rate of interest to his total income, he should, at the most, possess about $500,000 [yuan] at the present moment." ⁵⁹ Ts'ao was awarded the Third Order of Merit in Jan. 1920 despite his dismissal after the May Fourth Incident. In Jan. 1922 he was appointed High Industrial Commissioner. He held the post until June when he was proscribed in connection with alleged embezzlement in making foreign loans while a Cabinet minister. After this he interested himself in mining enterprises. He was reported living in Peking in 1946, though the house burned by the students had been sold to Liu To-ch'ien, the Military Governor of Jehol Province. Ts'ao is now living in Japan.

ʷ Chang Tsung-hsiang was born in Wuhsing County, Chekiang, in 1879. After passing the first civil service examination in 1895 he went to Japan to study law at the Imperial University of Tokyo, one of the earliest Chinese students to study in that country and a close schoolmate of Ts'ao Ju-lin's. Chang received his LL.B. at Meiji University in 1903. Returning to China, he taught at the Imperial University of Peking for a short time, and was bestowed the title chin-shih by the Manchu court. During 1908–1910 he became superintendent of police at Peking (in the office he protected Wang Ching-wei, when the latter was imprisoned there after an unsuccessful assassination of the Manchu authority), and in June 1911 deputy commissioner of the Constitutional Department of the Manchu Cabinet. After Jan. 1912, Chang retired briefly but returned to the government in Yüan Shih-k'ai's regime, and was appointed Chief Justice of the Supreme Court in July 1912. In Jan. 1914 he became Minister of Justice. In April he was ordered to act concurrently as Minister of Agriculture and Commerce. On June 30, 1916, he was appointed Chinese Minister to Japan to succeed Lu Tsung-yü. Chang had been held responsible for a number of Japanese loans, and in Sept. 1918 he signed the exchange of notes stating "gladly agree" to Japan's proposal concerning her position in Shantung. After his dismissal in June 1919 he received in Jan. 1920 the Fourth Order of Merit from the Peking regime.

Chinese director of the Chinese-Japanese Exchange Bank,[x] were regarded as the most pro-Japanese officials in the Peking regime.

Another report has it that some of the students had also planned in advance to burn Ts'ao's house and that secret student societies, mostly anarchist, had intended in the latter part of April to start a demonstration.[60] According to the story, on the eve of May 4 they convened in secret and resolved to punish the three officials severely. At the time an old member of the T'ung-meng-hui gave these students Chang Tsung-hsiang's photograph so that they might identify him. (Photographs of Ts'ao and Lu were often displayed in various studios, so the students could identify them.) They decided to carry small cans of fuel and matches to burn Ts'ao's house, but kept their plans secret from the majority of the students. Because the societies feared that the secret might leak out, they persuaded the students at the informal meeting on May 3 to carry out the demonstration three days earlier than previously scheduled. This account appears to offer a possible explanation of the later violence. But it would be an exaggeration to say that the demonstration itself was directed by those secret societies. It is more likely that they made use of the popular sentiment as an occasion for using violence.[61]

The students' resolution on May 3 to change the date of the demonstration was apparently known to the administrators of the National University of Peking. Before this student meeting Ts'ai Yüan-p'ei had called a faculty meeting to discuss the problem of the student activities. Because of the hostile attitudes of the warlord government toward the university and their own indignation at the government's weak stand on the Sino-Japanese issue, the faculty did not wish to impede the students' activities. On the eve of May 4, Ts'ai

[x] Lu Tsung-yü (born 1875) was a native of Haining County, Chekiang. He studied political science at Waseda University in Japan. On return to China he passed in 1905 the civil service examination for returned students and obtained the degree of *chu-jen*. In August of that year the Ch'ing government sent five high officials (including Hsü Shih-ch'ang) on a mission to observe constitutional conditions of different foreign countries. Lu was with the mission as its second class counselor. Because of his ability in entertaining officials of the hour, Lu received quick promotion and became a favorite subordinate of Hsü Shih-ch'ang, who was then the Grand Chancellor of the Manchu dynasty. Shortly after Hsü was appointed Viceroy of Manchuria in 1907, he appointed Lu Director-General of the Salt Gabelle for Manchuria. In 1913 he was elected senator of the first Parliament in Peking. Under Yüan Shih-k'ai, Lu served as Chinese Minister to Japan from Dec. 1913 through 1915 when the Twenty-one Demands treaty was negotiated. He was regarded as one of the supporters of Yüan's monarchical movement. After Yüan died, Lu retired and returned to China, where he formed the Japanese financed Chinese-Japanese Exchange Bank through which he contracted many loans from Japan for the Peking militarists. He was held partly responsible for the Nishihara loans. Ironically, like Ts'ao and Chang, he also had been a teacher at the Imperial University of Peking (in 1902). He became a senator in the Anfu Parliament after 1917, belonging to the New Communication Clique as Ts'ao Ju-lin's partner.

called in one of the student leaders, Ti Fu-ting and, reportedly, expressed his sympathy with the students.[62]

On the morning of May 4, a Sunday, at ten o'clock, student representatives met at the Peking College of Law and Political Science, as scheduled by the meeting on the previous evening, to prepare the demonstration.[63] Student representatives from thirteen colleges and universities, including the National University of Peking, attended. An Army Cadets Academy (*Lu-chün hsüeh-hsiao*) also sent student representatives as observers. At this meeting which lasted about an hour and a half, five resolutions were adopted: (1) that telegrams be sent to all organizations concerned at home and abroad urging them to protest the Shantung resolution of the Paris Peace Conference; (2) that efforts be made to awaken the masses of the people all over the country; (3) that a mass meeting of the Peking people be arranged; (4) that a permanent and united organization of all Peking students be established to take charge of student activities and of relations with other organizations; and (5) that the route of the demonstration that afternoon was to be from the T'ien-an Gate, through the Legation Quarter (*Tung chiao-min hang*), and thence to the Hatamen (*Ch'ung-wen-men*) Boulevard business area. At this meeting the student representatives displayed considerable efficiency and harmony in making these important decisions.[64]

By 1:30 in the afternoon over three thousand students had gathered at the T'ien-an Gate (Square of Heavenly Peace) to take part in the demonstration (see Appendix B). They represented thirteen colleges and universities in Peking. The first to arrive were from the National Higher Normal College of Peking and from Hui-wen University (established by American missionaries). They were followed by students from the National College of Law and Political Science, National Industrial College, National Agricultural College, National Medical College, Academy of Police Officers, Institute of Railroad Administration, Institute of Tax Administration, China University, University of the Republic, and Ch'ao-yang University. The National University of Peking students arrived last, but played a leading role in the demonstration (see Appendix C).

The Peking government had made efforts to prevent the mass meeting. A representative of the Ministry of Education accompanied by several garrison and police officers was sent to Peking University on May 4 about 11:00 a.m. and in the presence of Ts'ai Yüan-p'ei advised the students not to join in, but, after a long argument with the representative, they refused to follow his advice.

The only effect of this episode was to delay the students of the university for a time.

When the students had gathered in the big square in front of the T'ien-an Gate, standing in order, group after group by school, a student representative of Peking University introduced the representative of the Ministry of Education to the audience and explained the delayed arrival of the university students. The representative from the ministry "advised the students to go back to their respective schools and to send their representatives to call upon the Government or the Allied Ministers to talk over the matter, instead of parading in such numbers." [65] General Li Ch'ang-t'ai, the commander of the infantry, and Wu Ping-hsiang, the chief of the constabulary, also persuaded them to give up the parade. The students did not accept the proffered advice; they fully realized that their aim was not going to be achieved at once either by petitions or by mass demonstrations anyway. Their immediate purpose was to publicly demonstrate indignation against the warlords and against the national humiliation brought about by power politics.

At the mass meeting and the following demonstration, a printed brief "Manifesto of All the Students of Peking" was distributed describing this purpose: [y]

Japan's demand for the possession of Tsingtao and other rights in Shantung is now going to be acceded to in the Paris Peace Conference. Her diplomacy has secured a great victory; and ours has led to a great failure. The loss of Shantung means the destruction of the integrity of China's territory. Once the integrity of her territory is destroyed, China will soon be annihilated. Accordingly, we students today are making a demonstration march to the Allied legations, asking the Allies to support justice. We earnestly hope that all agricultural, industrial, commercial, and other groups of the whole nation will rise and hold citizens' meetings to strive to secure our sovereignty in foreign affairs and to get rid of the traitors at home. This is the last chance for China in her life and death struggle. Today we swear two solemn oaths with all our fellow countrymen: (1) China's territory may be

[y] The manifesto was drafted by Lo Chia-lun. As he recalls: "On May 4, 1919, at 10 a.m., as soon as I returned from the Higher Normal College in the suburb to the New Tide Society of Peking University at Han-hua-yüan, one of my schoolmates, Ti Fu-ting (also named Chün-wu) [a member of the society] pushed the door open and entered. He said that since we needed a manifesto for the demonstration of the day, the students of the eight schools in Peking had delegated the students of Peking University, and the students of the university had, in turn, delegated me to draft one. I composed it immediately at a long desk, realizing that the demonstration was near at hand and I should not refuse to do so. It was handed by Chün-wu to the Lao-pai-hsing yin-shua-so [Plain People's Press], which was owned by Mr. Li Hsin-pai, to be printed. A printing of fifty thousand copies was planned, but they did not finish twenty-thousand copies for distribution until 1:00 p.m. Although it was composed by an individual student, it completely reflected the hope and enthusiasm of the whole body of students. This was the only printed material distributed by the students on May 4." [66]

conquered, but it cannot be given away; (2) the Chinese people may be massacred, but they will not surrender.

Our country is about to be annihilated. Up, brethren!

This manifesto was written in vivid and clean-cut vernacular Chinese, which reflected the effect of the literary revolution, and was considered an excellent expression of the spirit of the young intellectuals. Besides this, a more formal declaration written in the literary language was adopted at the meeting. It advocated "citizens' meetings," "public speeches," and pistols and bombs for the traitors as last expressions of student reaction. The declaration, which seemed to have been drafted by the militant, nationalistic students before the meeting, was not printed and distributed at the meeting and the demonstration, but it circulated throughout the country afterwards. It reads:

Alas, citizens! Our dearest, most respected, and most patriotic brethren! The five Great Powers first promised to seek our consent for the solution they will reach regarding the humiliating secret and dangerous treaties forced upon us by Japan and the long-prayed-for return to us of Tsingtao and other German privileges in Shantung. But now they leave these problems to direct negotiation between China and Japan. This ominous news robs the light from our skies. When the Paris Peace Conference was convened, was it not our hope and happy anticipation that right, humanitarianism, and justice would prevail in the world? To return Tsingtao to us and to abolish the Sino-Japanese secret treaties and military conventions and other unequal treaties are right and just; to surrender right to might, to place our territory at the disposal of the five Great Powers, and to treat us like the defeated Germany and Austria are not right and are unjust. Now right and justice have been further violated; the Great Powers ask China and Japan to negotiate the Shantung question directly. Japan, tiger-like and wolf-like, has been able to wrest privileges from China simply by sending us a sheet of paper, the Twenty-one Demands. Our further negotiation with her will certainly mean the loss of Tsingtao and Shantung. Shantung, strategically controlling Chihli and Shansi to the north and Hupei and Kiangsu to the south, and situated in the middle of the Peking-Hankow and Tientsin-Nanking Railroads, is actually the throat and heart of the South and North. The loss of Shantung means the subjugation of China. How can our brethren, dwelling in this land as owners of these mountains and rivers, while looking on the insult and oppression and the attempt to enslave us, refrain from crying out for last-ditch salvation? The French in their struggle for Alsace-Lorraine cried, "Give us our wish or give us death." The Italians in their struggle for the Adriatic Straits cried, "Give us our wish or give us death." The Koreans in their struggle for independence also cried, "Give us our wish or give us death." We now approach a crisis in which our country is threatened with subjugation and her territory is going to be ceded. If her people still cannot unite in indignation in a twelfth-hour effort to save her, they are indeed the worthless race of the twentieth century. They should not be regarded as human beings. Are there not some of our brethren who cannot bear the torture of being slaves and beasts of burden and steadfastly desire to save their country? Then the urgent things we should do right now are to hold citizens' meetings, to make public speeches, and to send telegrams to the government in support of our stand. As for those who willingly and traitorously sell out our country to the enemy, as a last resort we shall have to rely on pistols and bombs to deal with them. Our country is in imminent peril — its fate hangs on a thread! We appeal to you to join our struggle.[67]

At two o'clock, after the meeting, the students marched from the T'ien-an Gate southward through Chung-hua Gate. At the head of the procession two janitors carried huge five-colored national flags. After them was a pair of funeral scrolls on which were written traditional Chinese mourning phrases (*wan-lien*) doctored with sarcasm:[z]

The names of Ts'ao Ju-lin, Lu Tsung-yü, and Chang Tsung-hsiang will stink a thousand years;
The students of Peking mourn for them with tears.

Besides distributing leaflets to the spectators on the streets, the students carried white flags made of cloth or paper, bearing slogans written in Chinese, English, and French and caricatures expressing the purposes and sentiments of their demonstration. The slogans may be classified into the following categories:[68]

(A) Externally, struggle for sovereignty, or resist the Great Powers.

Examples:

Return our Tsingtao.
We may be beheaded, but Tsingtao must not be lost.
Reclaim Tsingtao unto death.
Abolish the Twenty-one Demands.
China has been sentenced to death [by the Paris Conference].
Refuse to sign the Peace Treaty.
Boycott Japanese goods.
Protect our country's soil.
Protect our sovereignty.
China belongs to the Chinese.
Self-determination.
International Justice.
Oppose power politics.

---

[z] *Wan-lien* are Chinese funeral scrolls usually of white cloth or paper on which parallel sentences are written to compliment the dead. The couplets are a Chinese literary form akin to an elegy. They are customarily written: "The fragrance of the deceased's name will last a thousand years (*liu-fang ch'ien-ku*), and the giver of the scrolls "mourns for him with tears [or humility]." But now the students changed the phrase "liu-fang ch'ien-ku" to "i-ch'ou ch'ien-ku" (their names will stink a thousand years). White was a sign of mourning in traditional China.

(B) Internally, throw out the traitors.

Examples:

Down with the traitors.

Ts'ao Ju-lin is a traitor.

Death punishment for the traitors, Ts'ao, Lu, and Chang.

The people should determine the destiny of the traitors.

Don't just be patriotic for five minutes.

The people of Peking were deeply impressed by the demonstrators. Many spectators were so touched that they wept as they stood silently on the streets and carefully listened to the students shout their slogans. Many Western spectators greeted them with ovations and by taking off or waving their hats.[69] The students paraded along the streets in order. Boy Scouts and students from elementary schools joined in and distributed leaflets. Even the police and secret agents, who were sent by the government to patrol, did not find any signs of intended violence on the part of the students.

From the Legation Quarter to Ts'ao Ju-lin's House

But the temper of the students changed and became less disciplined during the latter part of the demonstration. Passing the Chung-hua Gate, the procession turned to the east and reached the western entrance of the Legation Quarter.[a'] The students were refused entrance to the extraterritorial district by the Legation Quarter police. After several telephone conversations with legation officials, four student representatives, including Lo Chia-lun and possibly Chang Kuo-t'ao, were appointed to enter the American Legation to see the minister. When they found him absent, the students left for the minister a memorandum.[b'] Paul S. Reinsch later recalled:

[a'] The Legation Quarter was established by the treaty of 1901 after the Boxer Rebellion. An area of over one thousand Chinese acres (*mou*) was set up as a special district for the foreign legations. The quarter on its south side bordered upon the city wall and on the other three sides was surrounded with high fortified walls. Outside of the wall grounds were reserved for military training purposes and for the defense of the quarter. Within the district were located the legations with their barracks and the special police forces of the legations. Chinese armed forces and police were forbidden to enter the area and Chinese people were forbidden to reside in it. Bertrand Russell made this remark in 1921 about the Legation Quarter: "To this day, it [the Legation Quarter] is enclosed by a wall, filled with European, American and Japanese troops, and surrounded by a bare space on which the Chinese are not allowed to build. It is administered by the diplomatic body, and the Chinese authorities have no powers over anyone within its gates. When some unusually corrupt and traitorous Government is overthrown, its members take refuge in the Japanese (or other) Legation and so escape the punishment of their crimes, while within the sacred precincts of the Legation Quarter the Americans erect a vast wireless station said to be capable of communicating directly with the United States."[70] The quarter was legally abolished in 1942 when China's "unequal treaties" with foreign powers were annulled.

[b'] This account is based on the memoir written in 1926 by a student of Peking University and

A crowd of students appeared before the legation gate on the 5th [4th] of May clamouring to see me. I was absent, that day, on a trip to the temple above Men T'ou-kou and so missed seeing them. Their demonstration, as it turned out afterward, was the first step in the widespread student movement which was to make history. Their patriotic fervour had, on that morning [afternoon], been brought to the boiling point by the first inkling of the Paris decision on Shantung. . . .

The Chinese people, discouraged in Peking, had centered their hopes on Paris. When hints of a possible acceptance of Japan's demands were received in Peking, the first impulse of the students was to see the American minister, to ask him whether this news was true, and to see what he had to say. I escaped a severe ordeal.[77]

The student representatives also found the British, French, and Italian ministers absent, and left letters at their legations. After a long wait (about two hours) they failed to secure the permission of the Legation Quarter police to pass through the quarter. At the same time, Chinese police and troops, surrounding the entrance of the quarter, violently intervened and tried to force the students back. Under this double disappointment and pressure, the students, now joined by other citizens, became irritated and angry. Suddenly, they cried, "On to the Foreign Ministry!" "On to the house of the traitor!" At this critical moment, Fu Ssu-nien, as the elected "marshal" of the student demonstration, urged his fellow students not to go; but he could not control the situation in the uproar and agitation.[78]

The students then marched northward along Hu-pu Street and Tungch'ang-an Street, to the Tung-tan Arch and Shih-ta-jen Hu-t'ung (side street).

cited by Tsi C. Wang,[71] and on many similar accounts, such as the gendarme officer's report dated May 5, 1919.[72] Chang Kuo-t'ao's presence as a representative on this occasion is mentioned in his own English memoirs but not recorded in early reports. According to Chu Wen-shu's record of 1923 the student procession had reached the American Legation but was turned back later by the legations of Great Britain, France, and Italy and had to send representatives to the three legations.[73] Chu Wen-shu mistakenly took the American barracks, located at the western entrance of the quarter, to be the American Legation chancery. The students' procession received permission from the American military authorities to pass the barracks and chancery. It did pass the former but was prevented by the Legation Quarter police from reaching any of the chanceries.[74] The 1952 version of a Chinese Communist author, however, was that "the students first decided to see the Japanese imperialists. They entered the western entrance of the Legation Quarter, and were first halted by the American imperialists because the American Legation was located at the western entrance. The American imperialists on the surface sympathized with the students but actually prevented them from going to the east side since the Japanese Legation was there."[75] This is questionable since, by all the evidence, and given the practical situation of 1919, it seems unlikely that the Americans would wish to defend Japan's position in China. According to a report dated May 4, 1919, the first secretary of the American Legation, who was taking his turn as chief of the Legation Quarter police, saw no reason why the students should not be permitted to go on, because they were unarmed, orderly, and claimed nothing but the right to present their letters. But the Chinese police officials refused to let the students visit the legations.[76] It seems possible that both the Legation Quarter police and, to a less degree, the Chinese police were responsible for the refusal.

On the road they shouted slogans and called the traitors by name, including Ts'ao Ju-lin, Lu Tsung-yü, Chang Tsung-hsiang, as well as the leader of the warlords, Tuan Ch'i-jui, and his chief of staff, Hsü Shu-cheng. About 4:30 p.m. the procession arrived at Ts'ao's residence which was at 2 Chao-chia-lou Street, close to the office of the Foreign Ministry.

Up to this time, things had not yet really gotten out of control. As a British correspondent reported, the students "arrived at Ts'ao Ju-lin's house in an orderly procession, quite worthy of the students of an enlightened nation. But the wrath of the demonstrators was roused by the repressive measures taken by the Police, whereupon they broke out into acts of unbridled violence." [79]

The students found the doors of the house all firmly closed and the mansion guarded by police and gendarmes.[c'] The crowd demanded that Ts'ao appear in person and explain why he had made the secret agreements with Japan.[83] To this demand the police and gendarmes turned a deaf ear, and tried to force the students back. At this the demonstrators flew into a rage, yelling loudly, "The traitors! The traitors!" Many of them threw stones and white flags into the windows and over the walls and tried to enter but in vain. When they were about to withdraw and go back to their schools, five intransigents among them climbed up the wall, broke open a window, and jumped into the house.[d'] These five students encountered more than a dozen of Ts'ao's armed body-guard, who, startled by the students, without resistance let them open the front door.[86] Thus the mass of students stormed into the house.

The students supposed that the three pro-Japanese officials were holding a secret conference in the house. But they could not find anyone, except Ts'ao's sick father, son, and young concubine. They let them go away with the body-

[c'] Chou Yü-t'ung says, "Chao-chia-lou Street was not wide, only allowing four persons to walk abreast; and there was only one policeman at the front door of Ts'ao's house." [80] But Rodney Gilbert reported from Peking on May 4, 1919, that there were fifty police assembled at the Cabinet Minister's gate.[81] Other sources reported shortly after the incident that Ts'ao's house was surrounded by two hundred policemen.[82] Ts'ao probably had asked the constabulary chief Wu Ping-hsiang to send two hundred men, but Wu did not send so many at first. Wu did not seem very sympathetic with Ts'ao.

[d'] The identity of the five students who jumped through the window has become legendary. The one who first climbed the wall and jumped into the window was said to be Fu Ssu-yen, Fu Ssu-nien's younger brother.[84] But according to Shen Yin-mo, a professor at Peking University and member of the New Youth Society, the first one to break into the house was Ts'ai Chen-ying, a student of the School of Science of the university. K'uang Hu-sheng later claimed that he was one of the five. (He became the principal of the Li Ta School in Shanghai, and author of *Wu-ssu yün-tung chi-shih* [Factual Accounts of the May Fourth Movement].) Yang Hui, a student of the department of philosophy, School of Letters of the university, was also reported to be one of the five. Another is Yi K'e-ni.[85]

guard, but, shouting and hysterical, smashed all the furniture [e'] and set the house on fire. [f']

At this instant (about 5 o'clock) some of the students found Chang Tsung-hsiang in a sitting room with Ting Shih-yüan, director of the Aviation Department, Ministry of the Army, concurrently managing-director of Peking-Suiyuan Railroad and Peking-Hankow Railroad, and a well-known Japanese journalist Nakae Ushikichi. [g'] Chang was immediately beaten to the ground. When Ting rushed out to call the police, they were reluctant to intervene. Chang lay on the ground pretending to be dead. Seeing the fire, the confused students feared they had overreached themselves and many dispersed to return home or to their schools. Nakae and some of the police took this opportunity to help Chang escape to a dark room in a neighboring salted-egg store. There he was found once again by another group of students who dragged him to the door of the store. When he refused to tell who he was, the students beat him into insensibility with banner staffs and pelted him with eggs; later he was taken to the Japanese T'ung Jen Hospital by the police. [h'] Chang's house in Tientsin was reportedly destroyed by students on the same date. [98]

[e'] According to Ts'ao's report, his father was beaten. Sun Fu-yüan recalled: "When the students of Peking were smashing Ts'ao Ju-lin's house, a young man rushed into Ts'ao's bedroom (or Ts'ao's daughter's bedroom), tore up the colorful silk bedcover, shouted, and ran back out of the room to be subsequently arrested by the police. This man was Chiang Shao-yüan." Chiang was later a famous educator and writer. [87]

[f'] While the way the fire was set remains disputable, on the basis of later memoirs there is no doubt that it was set by some of the students. On the day after the incident Ts'ao charged that the students had burned his house down; but the students denied it and declared that Ts'ao's family had burned it in order to kill the students or to destroy the confidential documents concerning his traitorous career. [88] Many news reports at the time of the incident said that the cause of the fire was unknown. [89] Some say that the fire was caused by the accidental breaking of the electric lights. This seems to be the excuse later adopted by the government in order to release the students arrested. [90] Some reports say Ts'ao's servants set the fire to cover up their robbery of his property during the turmoil. [91] Tsi C. Wang cited in 1927 a student's recollection that "the students dispersed because a fire suddenly broke out in the building and the soldiers fired at them." [92] According to K'uang Hu-sheng the fire was set purposely by some of the radical students. [93] Chou Yü-t'ung said that some of the students burned the house with fuel brought with them. Hsü Te-heng recalled in 1950 that the students burned the house by lighting the bed curtains. [94] According to Shen Yin-mo's memoirs in the same year, the people of the neighborhood thought on the day of the incident that the fire was set by the students. Most of the foreign newspapers stated at the time that the students set fire to the house but did not say how. Judging from the majority of the reports, one may conclude that some of the students, disappointed at missing Ts'ao, set the fire by means which are now uncertain.

[g'] Nakae Ushikichi (1889–1942), son of a liberal thinker, Nakae Chōmin, lived in Peking for thirty years and was an influential Japanese scholar deeply versed in Western (especially German) philosophy and Chinese classical learning. Later he became a student of Marxism inter alia, and the teacher of Suzue Gen'ichi and a friend of Ojima Sukema. One of Nakae's major works is Chūgoku kodai seiji shisō (Political Thought of Ancient China) (Tokyo, 1950). [95]

[h'] It was reported that the salted-egg store was owned by Japanese. Some Westerners and Japanese were among the onlookers when Chang was beaten in the store but Nakae alone tried to

Ts'ao himself had actually been at home in conversation with Chang, Ting, and Nakae at the moment the students attacked the house.[i'] He had escaped in disguise with a servant through a window and a narrow alley, and been driven in a motor car to the foreign-owned Wagons Lits Hotel (*Liu-kuo fan-tien*) in the Legation Quarter.[j'] Lu Tsung-yü had not been present.[k'] The following account of the attack on his house was given in Ts'ao Ju-lin's letter of resignation to the President the next day, May 5:

I was asked to attend the banquet in the office of the President on the morning of May 4. I went to my home on Chao-chia-lou Street in the east side of the city at 2:30 p.m., and had a talk with Mr. Chang Tsung-hsiang, the minister to Japan. All of a sudden, we heard wild shouts and noises coming from afar, as furious tides rolled toward the entrance of the lane, with the patroling police passively looking on. About ten or more minutes later we saw over one thousand students — some of them jumping over the wall and breaking the door — storm into my house. They smashed everything they saw and beat everybody they met. My paralyzed father who was cared for in the house was also beaten. Then they set fire to my house. Its eastern wing which served as my bedroom was immediately burnt to the ground. All the other things were also completely destroyed. Mr. Chang was caught by the mob when he hastily escaped to a neighboring house. He was violently thrown to the ground, and beaten into insensibility with sticks and stones. His head bore nine deep wounds and bled incessantly. . . .[104]

During these disorders there were some struggles between the police and the students in the courtyard. The attitude of the police, however, was very moderate under the circumstances. Some of them actually "observed an attitude of 'benevolent neutrality.'" But they were forced to interfere after several urgent orders were received from the higher commanders.[105] Consequently, in the fight some students and police were wounded. A student of the National University of Peking named Kuo Ch'in-kuang died three days later in a French hospital in

help and to defend him. Most of the students who beat him in Ts'ao's house thought he was Ts'ao, and those who hurt him in the store did not identify him either. But they suspected that he was one of the traitors since he refused to tell who he was.[96] Some reports say that one of the students in Ts'ao's sitting room identified Chang.[97]

[i'] Ts'ao, Lu, and Chang had all attended a banquet at the office of the President that noon. Ts'ao was advised not to go home, but he said, "What is there to fear?" He went home with Chang.[99] Another report says that Chang was invited by Tung K'ang to see peony blossoms at Fa-yüan Ssu (Fa-yüan Temple) that morning and after lunch went to Ts'ao's house.[100] That a Japanese had been present in the conversation was reported by a Reuter telegram from Peking on May 4 at 11 p.m.[101] Another report said, "They [the students] saw one of the traitors conversing with a group of Japanese. . . . They went to question him, but they were stopped by the Japanese."[102]

[j'] The same report stated that "the Legation police stopped the car for exceeding the speed limit, disarmed the four guards [Ts'ao's] and arrested the chauffeur."

[k'] According to most reports, Lu was not in the house. But Chiang Monlin says, "Ts'ao and Lu escaped by the back door."[103]

the city. The death was attributed to injury and overstrain in the incident. This became one of the events which heightened indignation among the students in the days that followed.[l']

The fighting lasted until 5:45 p.m., by which time most of the demonstrators had dispersed and only a few dozen remained to see what would happen. Only then did Wu Ping-hsiang and General Li Ch'ang-t'ai arrive accompanied by troops, police, and gendarmes.[m'] The police and troops, who had been moderate before, suddenly changed their attitude, probably because of the presence of their commanders. They fired a few shots into the air. Upon the orders of Wu, who had been sent by Premier Ch'ien Neng-hsün (*tzu*: Kan-ch'en, 1869–1924), they made several arrests near the scene and more along the streets. As a result, thirty-two students, including Yi K'e-ni, Ts'ao Yün, Hsü Te-heng, Chiang Shao-yüan, Li Liang-chi, Yang Chen-sheng, Hsiung T'ien-chih (Peking University), and Hsiang Ta-kuang (the Higher Normal College), were imprisoned at police headquarters.[108] The students arrested were, judging from all the evidence, distributed as follows: twenty from the University of Peking, eight from the Higher Normal College, two from the Higher Industrial College, and one each from China University and Hui-wen University.[n']

The students arrested, although only a few of them were among the leaders or had participated in the violence, went to the police station with a show of heroism.[o'] As a student later recalled:

[l'] Kuo Ch'in-kuang (1896–1919) was born in Kuangtung and attended the *yü k'o* of the School of Letters of the university in the fall of 1917. Many of the reports assert that Kuo died of injuries. According to Chu Wen-shu, Kuo was a very patriotic student who risked his life to beat the traitor in the demonstration. He spat blood in the incident and died three days later upon hearing the news in the hospital that a number of his fellow students had been arrested.[106]

[m'] According to Meng Shih-chieh, the police and guards sent this time by the constabulary numbered over three hundred.[107]

[n'] Besides the above mentioned students who later became famous, the rest of the thirty-two are: Liang Pin-wen, Hu Chen-fei, Liang Ying-wen, Ch'en Shu-sheng, Hao Tsu-ning, Hsiao Chi-shih, Ch'iu Pin, Sun Te-chung, Ho Tso-lin, Lu Ch'i-ch'ang, P'an Shu, Lin Chün-sun, Yi Ching-ch'üan (Peking University); Ch'en Hung-hsün (might be Ch'en Ch'in-min who later became chairman of the mathematics department of Chi-nan University), Hsieh Jung-chou, Chao Yün-kang, Yang Ch'üan-chün, T'ang Kuo-ying, Wang Te-jun, Ch'u Ming-chin (The Higher Normal College); Li Keng-hsin, Tung Shao-shu (The Higher Industrial College); Liu Kuo-kan (China University); and Chang Te (Hui-wen University). Some reports give Li Liang-chi as Li Liang-chün. According to Ts'ai Hsiao-chou and Yang Ching-kung, the distribution of the students arrested was: Peking University 20, Normal College 8, the College of Law and Political Science 2, China University 2.[109] Ch'en Tuan-chih gives a different account: Peking University 19, Normal College 8, Industrial College, Hui-wen University, and the French Institute together 5. Hsü Te-heng recalled that one of the thirty-two arrested was not a student but a citizen.[110]

[o'] After they were sent to the central police station the students were reportedly treated very badly, undergoing torture on the first day. But next day, after a visit by the chief of the constabulary, they were permitted to have walks in the courtyard. On the third day a copy of the

The students (only ten at first) were taken to the police station in pairs. The soldiers pushed them with the ends of their guns or slapped them if they protested. They were at once put into prison; five being paired off with a group of robbers and thieves. They were not allowed to speak. Three hours later more students arrived at the prison. . . . At 7 p.m. the students were carried to the central police station. On the road these student-prisoners met a few Westerners passing them in an automobile. They greeted the student-prisoners by clapping, and the students returned the salutation. After they reached the station they were put together in a room and not allowed to talk.[111]

After the arrests, martial law was at once proclaimed for the area surrounding the Legation Quarter.[112] Firemen rushed to Ts'ao's house. They came with a fine display of banners and much blowing of horns. A half-inch stream was turned on the buildings which were already burning like tinder. They put out the fire at about eight o'clock. The water flooded adjacent streets carrying with it the gossip that the college boys had burnt the traitor's house. The news immediately spread all over the capital.

The event at once made a profound impression on Chinese political and social circles. The subject of most comment was the fact that in the very brief skirmish before Ts'ao's gates there had been no fierce fighting between the police and the students. "It seems very bitter irony to the local Chinese audience," one of the first reports said, "that the man who has found the money and the arms for all the Northern armies, who through his associates could command several hundred thousand men, should be mobbed in his own house and have no one fire a shot or strike a blow for him." [113]

From the foregoing description, it seems clear that, thus far, the demonstration had been purely a public expression of indignation by the students which had resulted in an uncontrolled disturbance unanticipated by the majority of the demonstrators. Their prime motive had been devoted patriotism. The significance of the demonstration would have been limited if there had been no developments following the events of May 4. It might have been counted merely a defiant gesture on the part of the students against the warlords and a protest against the unpopular resolutions on the Shantung question by the Great Powers at Paris. Or it might have been considered merely a riot by a youthful mob, or at least by its radical wing, as it has in fact been interpreted by a few observers who did not understand the history and development of the movement.

But the students in Peking started immediately after the incident to organize

I-shih pao (Social Welfare Daily), an American-owned anti-Japanese newspaper in China, was given to them.

the new intellectuals of the nation in the support of their cause. They also tried to win over the sympathy of the general public by means of publicity, mass meetings, and demonstrations. In this process they began to establish closer contacts with the masses of illiterate people, and to secure strong and effective support from the new merchants, industrialists, and urban workers. Hence the students' new ideas were spread to an unexpected extent throughout the cities of the country, the antiquated civilization began to crack up, and new sociopolitical developments were set afoot. The unique place occupied by the May Fourth Incident in the history of modern China is due to these consequences rather than to the demonstration alone.

CHAPTER V

DEVELOPMENTS FOLLOWING THE INCIDENT: STUDENT DEMONSTRATIONS AND STRIKES

T HE most critical and important period of the May Fourth Movement was the few months immediately following the incident. The students, by their revolutionary acts, began to exert what was to become a far-reaching influence upon the cultural and political aspects of modern Chinese history. To understand this influence we must observe how the students turned to rallying and organizing the new intellectuals and securing a coalition with other social and economic forces by peaceable methods, and how they spread their new ideas among the mass of the people in this time of *Sturm und Drang*.

The developments during these two months, to be described in detail in this chapter and the next, may be divided into two periods:

(A) A period of student demonstrations and strikes. From May 4 to June 4 the movement was furthered principally by students. This period may be subdivided into two stages. The first, from May 4 to May 18, was devoted to organization and demonstrations by the students. The activities of the students during this time were confined mainly to rallying other intellectual, political, and social leaders, organizing themselves, and holding demonstrations, circulating petitions, and making street speeches. Subsequently, from May 19, a student general strike and intensive boycott against Japanese goods became major weapons against the Peking government and Japan.

(B) A period of alliance of the students with merchants, industrialists, and workers. The mass arrests of students by the government on June 2, 3, and 4 prompted merchants' and urban workers' strikes on June 5 in support of the students. The May Fourth Incident achieved triumphant results when, on June 28, China refused to sign the peace treaty with Germany.

Immediate Reaction of the Government

The first reaction of the Peking government to the May Fourth Incident seemed hesitant and perplexed. At the beginning, President Hsü Shih-ch'ang did not insist upon any harsh treatment to the students. On the evening of May 4, Ts'ao Ju-lin called some of his followers to a secret meeting at the Wagons Lits Hotel to discuss how to deal with the students. The result of this meeting was not disclosed.[1] But in a letter to the President, the next day, he asked to resign his position as Minister of Communications, and defended his career in the government.[2] This was followed by Lu Tsung-yü's letter to the President in a similar vein.[3] On the surface, Ts'ao's attitude toward the students seemed moderate. And the Ministry of Education, with Fu Tseng-hsiang, a moderate member of the old gentry, at its head, seemed to wish to compromise and placate the students. A report dated May 4, 10 p.m., is indicative of this:

The students were persuaded to disperse. The Ministry of Education exhorted all school principals to keep their students under strict control, promising to obtain the release of those arrested by attributing the cause of the fire at Ts'ao's house to accidental breakage of the electric lights. Ts'ao himself was understood to have expressed his unwillingness to deal with the rioters harshly, and if that were true the agitation might subside gradually.[4]

However, this attitude was not acceptable to the military and old bureaucratic groups in the government. On the evening of May 4 the administration convened at the house of the Premier, Ch'ien Neng-hsün, to decide a course of action. The Anfu clique, which was in control of the government and backed Ts'ao and the other pro-Japanese officials, at first insisted with some of the other old bureaucrats on taking drastic steps to discipline the students and the schools, and to this end exerted great pressure on the President and the Premier.[5]

The attitude of these conservatives toward the students and the schools was quite understandable. From the spring of 1917 when Ts'ai Yüan-p'ei had taken over the chancellorship of Peking University, the military and various older men in the Peking government had kept a suspicious and hostile eye on the university, because some of the professors and students were continually attacking Confucianism and traditional ethics and customs, and publicly criticizing warlordism and the government's foreign policies. Tuan Ch'i-jui himself viewed the university with distaste because of some pamphlets attacking him during his term as premier.[6] After the student petition of May 21,

1918, the conflict between the warlords and the Peking schools had deepened. As has been mentioned, in March 1919 government pressure on Peking University had caused Ch'en Tu-hsiu's resignation as dean of the School of Letters.[7] Against this background of long-term conflict, the May Fourth demonstration was in effect a public declaration of war on the part of the new intellectuals against the warlord government. The warlords thus considered it a proper opportunity and pretext for disciplining the schools.

Consequently, at the official meeting on the evening of May 4 in the Premier's home, strong demands were made by the conservative groups that the National University of Peking be closed, that the chancellor of the university be dismissed, and the students arrested be dealt with summarily. All these proposals were approved almost unanimously over the futile opposition of Fu Tseng-hsiang.[8]

The administration then ordered the Ministry of Justice to investigate the matter in order to punish those responsible for the incident.[a] On May 5, an order was given by the Ministry of Education to restrict the students' activities. At the same time police and troops were reinforced in Peking to control the activities of the students. The government was prepared to prosecute the arrested students in court.

Some significant blunders were made by the government from the start in handling the situation after the incident. Facing a delicate situation of long standing, it had hastily adopted a policy of drastic reprisals against the students and schools without an accurate calculation of the support which might be given the young scholars by society in general. Although the leaders of the new literature and new thought movements had played very important roles in the demonstration, they were not the only people involved. For example, the anti-Japanese attitude was actively endorsed not only by the new but also by most of the old intellectuals, including many students and teachers who were in favor of the old literature. Even Lin Shu, whose spirited defense of the old literature has been cited above, a few weeks after the incident declared his sympathy with the boycott against Japanese goods.[b] Ignoring these clues, the government treated the leaders and students of the new literature and new thought movements as if they had been the sole leaders of the demonstration. This gave the new culture group an opportunity to secure sympathy and

[a] From May 5 to 7 there were false reports that Chang Tsung-hsiang had died from his wounds.[9]
[b] Lin said in a letter that he sympathized with the boycott, but preferred to carry it out along with building China's national industry, and to leave foreign affairs to the Peking government instead of to the student strike.[10]

support from other students and teachers, even from those who had been reluctant in their advocacy of the reform in literature and thought. Moreover, the government failed to realize that the violence done to Ts'ao and Chang while it had not been planned by the bulk of the demonstrators had come to be considered justifiable by the public and students, after the fact. The government also failed to take into consideration the fact that the students arrested were not necessarily those responsible for the violence. As a result, when the government indiscriminately made its charges against the thirty-two students arrested, the whole body of students and teachers burned with indignation and felt the need for united action against the government.

In its dealings with the students and schools, the government had ignored or muddled all these factors. In short, it had so acted as to put the issue in an anti-Japanese versus pro-Japanese context, thus insuring that an absolute majority of the Chinese people would of course take the former side.

Establishment of the Peking Student Union and Mobilization of the Intellectuals

The students, right after the incident, started to rally vigorously. When the students of Peking University returned to school from the demonstration, they held a roll call about 7:00 p.m. and found some of their schoolmates missing.[11] News very soon spread among them that the missing students had been arrested by the police and troops, would be tried under martial law, and could be executed summarily. They were infuriated and immediately called a meeting of students of the university for that night. Ts'ai Yüan-p'ei attended. The students complained that they had been treated roughly by the police and explained their fear that their schoolmates arrested by the police might be killed. They felt that all of them, and not only the students arrested, were responsible for the incident. Consequently they resolved to go in a body to the police station and offer to be imprisoned. Ts'ai Yüan-p'ei, sympathizing with the students' patriotic motives, declared that he would take responsibility for the release of the student prisoners. He then went alone to the police station.[12] His effort was fruitless, but his stand for the release of the students remained firm. On the same evening similar meetings were held by students in other colleges.[13]

On the following morning (May 5) at nine o'clock student representatives from all the colleges and universities involved met and resolved to send representatives, led by Fang Hao (later to become an educational administrator, not to be confused with the well-known historian with the same name), to appeal to the chancellors of the schools and the Minister of Education, asking them to petition the President of the Republic to release their schoolmates from prison. They also resolved that, until this had been achieved, none of the students in those schools would attend classes.[c] These resolutions were ratified in the afternoon by a general conference which was held at three o'clock at the Law School assembly hall of Peking University, Tuan Hsi-p'eng presiding. It was attended by more than three thousand students from all the schools involved. A parliamentary member of the Peking government, Fu Ting-i, addressed the meeting and supported their cause. Lo Chia-lun made a report on his successful mission to win the support of merchants and the press. The students at this meeting did not confine their attention to the freeing of their schoolmates, but also insisted upon the purposes of their demonstration. Resolutions to this effect passed by the meeting included that: (1) a letter be presented to the President of the Republic asking for the punishment of the traitors and for the restoration of Tsingtao to China; (2) a letter be presented to the Ministry of Education setting forth the students' case with regard to the occurrences of May 4; and (3) telegrams be sent to all interested organizations and societies at home and abroad asking for united actions. A possible boycott against Japanese goods was also discussed. To finance their activities the students voluntarily contributed several thousand *yuan* at the meeting.[15]

It may be pertinent to mention here the financial situation of the student movement at the time. In the first few months after the incident, most of the newly-founded student unions did not provide in their regulations for regular membership dues as became common practice in later years. It was provided merely that necessary funds would be raised from the membership. Voluntary contributions were allowed. During May and June of 1919 pro-

[c] The student strike eventually spread to the majority of the colleges in Peking after the demonstration. In the meeting the representatives of Peking University insisted on the resolution to strike which was opposed by those from the Higher Normal College on grounds that (1) they should follow the sacrificial spirit of the students arrested and go to jail too and that (2) striking would make it hard to get the students together again. This argument was not accepted by the majority.[14] According to Chang Kuo-t'ao's English memoirs, the meeting held in the morning of May 5 was participated in only by students from Peking University, and at the meeting the Student Union of the university was established and Tuan Hsi-p'eng and Fang Hao were elected representatives of the union, Lo Chia-lun, K'ang Pai-ch'ing, Chou Ping-lin, and Ch'en Chien-hsiao elected to take charge of general affairs and secretariat activities, and Chang himself elected chairman of the public speech corps of the union.

Japanese groups and the Japanese press in both China and Japan accused the American Legation in Peking of having financed and instigated the Chinese student anti-Japanese movement. The charge was flatly denied by Reinsch and the Chinese students and denounced as a patent smear.[16] The students in fact refused outside financial assistance. Judging from the two facts, first, that college students could command the necessary resources since at the time most of them came from rich families and, second, that no evidence turned up then or later to substantiate the charge, we may well assume that the students were essentially independent in financial matters throughout the movement.[d]

At the same meeting a further step of far-reaching consequence was taken by the students. They resolved, for the purposes of rescuing their fellow students and promoting the patriotic movement, to set up a permanent organization of all the students in middle (high) schools and higher educational institutions in Peking. The representatives of Peking University and the Higher Normal College were delegated to draft the articles of organization. These articles were submitted to, and accepted by, a conference of student representatives from all the middle and higher schools in Peking next day (May 6), and the Student Union of the Middle Schools and Institutions of Higher Learning in Peking (*Pei-ching chung-teng i-shang hsüeh-hsiao hsüeh-sheng lien-ho-hui*) was established immediately.[17]

The aim of the union, as described in the articles of organization, was "to facilitate the performance of students' duties and to promote the welfare of the nation." The major action programs, among others, were, in foreign affairs, to insist upon the restoration of Shantung and to initiate a boycott against Japanese goods; and in domestic affairs, to have the traitors (Ts'ao, Lu, Chang) punished and to destroy warlordism.[18]

In order to achieve these aims, the union was organized in two councils.[19] The first was a legislative council (*p'ing-i-hui*) consisting of two student legislators elected from each middle and higher school in Peking without regard to the number of students at the school. This council, meeting every Sunday, was responsible for determining all policies and drawing up resolutions for the union. The function of executing the policies and resolutions adopted by the legislative council was temporarily delegated to the student government of the National University of Peking. Later, an executive council (*kan-shih-hui*) was established and its members were elected by the student bodies of the member schools. The union was to be financed by the students themselves

[d] For the financial problems of the student movement see also Chap. VI, n. e.

and it might be disbanded by a four-fifths majority of the legislative council with more than four fifths of the student legislators present.[e]

The establishment of the Student Union of Peking was significant because it was China's first permanent united student organization of all the middle and higher schools on a city-wide basis. It became the model for numerous similar organizations in almost all the important cities in China during the next few years. It also led to the establishment a month later of the Student Union of the Republic of China which became the headquarters for students' activities throughout the nation.

Moreover, it was the first time in Chinese history that boy and girl students convened jointly, actively participated in the same meetings, and were organized into a single group. At the time there was still no coeducation in China; boys and girls were in different schools and had no common activities. Because the Student Union of Peking contained representatives from all the middle schools, colleges, and universities in Peking, representatives from all the middle schools and colleges for girls were included. From this time on, girl students joined the student movement and provided it with vital stimulus. This contributed to the establishment of coeducation in China the following year, and aided the women's suffrage movement later on.[f]

The establishment of the Student Union of Peking was the first successful step toward unifying the students in that city. Their intention to free their fellow students was immediately supported by an absolute majority of other in-

[e] Each school in turn had its own student government which consisted of two similar departments, the legislative and executive, both elected by the students of the school. The legislative and executive representatives to the union were to be elected by the united assembly of the two departments of the student government of each school from among the legislative and executive representatives themselves, or other students of the school.[20]

[f] Ts'ai Yüan-p'ei publicly advocated coeducation in elementary schools for the poor in a speech delivered in the Y.M.C.A. on March 15, 1919. Several students of the New Tide Society also published some articles in a newspaper upholding coeducation. Shortly before the May Fourth Incident took place, a girl student wrote a letter to Ts'ai asking his permission to study at Peking University. By the time the letter reached Peking, Ts'ai had left the capital because of the incident. After the incident many girl students were aroused by the new thought, and several of them petitioned the authorities of the university for admission. Between the beginning of 1920 and February of that year, nine girls were permitted to audit at the university by the acting dean, T'ao Meng-ho, though many others coming later were refused. The practice stirred up much interest among the male students and was widely discussed on the campus. The Ministry of Education immediately sent a letter to the university, warning that admission of girl students to the university should be carefully considered, since government schools should maintain their "high moral standard." The episode caused such alarm that even the President of the Republic warned the university. But the existing laws of China did not prohibit coeducation. Taking advantage of this, Ts'ai, without asking the permission of the government, formally allowed the nine girls to enroll as regular students after the summer of 1920. This was considered the beginning of coeducation in China, though the Canton Christian College, which was owned by American and Chinese Christians, had actually started it in 1918.[21]

tellectual leaders (especially teachers), and by most of the nation's social and political groups.

On May 5, the chancellors of the thirteen universities and colleges involved also met at Peking University.[22] They resolved that they should take the responsibility of securing the release of the student prisoners and that, after this had been done, they should resign their positions.[g] Besides advising the students to keep calm, they sent telegrams to the educational associations of all provinces asking their united action against the warlord government's arrest and punishment of the students.[23] On the same date they went to see the President, Premier, Minister of Education, and the chief of the constabulary, but were refused an interview by all except the last. The chief of the constabulary told them that he had no power to release the student prisoners.[24]

Right after the incident the Peking government had taken some precautionary steps to prevent the spread of the demonstration. News concerning the demonstration was strictly censored. Cable communications between Peking and foreign countries were cut off. Foreign correspondents reported the event mainly by wireless. This meant that information about the incident abroad was brief and fragmentary.[h] Some students outwitted the government, however, by sending a telegram through a foreign agency to one of the foreign concessions in Tientsin. From there it was relayed to Shanghai on May 5 and thence spread to other cities.[25] Telegrams of protest flooded the government. Most of the press, except a few papers owned by the pro-Japanese warlords and by Japanese, frankly stated their sympathy with the students. The newspapers and magazines supporting the students were the most influential ones. In Peking, for instance, they were the *Ch'en pao* (Peking Morning Post) and the *Kuo-min kung-pao* (Citizens' Gazette), both belonging to the Chinputang and with leanings toward the new culture movement, and the *Yi shih pao* (Social Welfare Daily), a Chinese Catholic newspaper founded in 1915 and newly purchased by Americans, among many other newspapers.[26] The Union of Daily

[g] The chancellors of the six colleges under the Ministry of Education at the time of the incident were Ts'ai Yüan-p'ei (Peking University), Ch'en Pao-ch'üan (Normal College), Hung Yung (Industrial College), Chin Pang-cheng (Agricultural College), Wang Chia-chü (College of Law and Political Science), and T'ang Erh-ho (Medical College). Besides Ts'ai, Ch'en Pao-ch'üan and T'ang Erh-ho were well-known sympathizers of the new culture movement, and T'ang had close relations with some high ranking officials in the Peking government.

[h] There seems to have been no thorough coverage of the May Fourth Incident in U.S. and British newspapers right after the event. A brief dispatch from Washington dated May 8 and appearing in the *New York Times* (May 9, 1919), p. 2, says "The State Department received word today that cable communication with Peking, China, had been cut off. A radiogram was received from Minister Reinsch confirming press reports of disturbances in the capital due to indignation over the action in Paris regarding Shantung Province. . . ." No further detailed information is to be found in the newspaper. The London *Times* did not report the incident at all.

Newspapers in Shanghai, which consisted of most of the newspapers in the city, sent a telegram to the President and the Premier, which approved the students' patriotism and asked that the students be freed "at once to relieve the popular tension." [27]

Other important organizations protesting included the Citizens' Diplomatic Association, the Educational Association of Kiangsu Province, the Technical Research Society, the Corps of the Chinese Students in Japan for National Salvation, the Association of European and American Returned Students, and the Lawyers Association of Shanghai. Numerous commercial organizations also extended their support to the students. On May 6, the Chamber of Commerce of Peking met and resolved that none of its members should buy Japanese goods, that all industrial and commercial relations between Japan and China should be cut off, and that the traitors and oppressive officials should be punished. [28] On the same day, the Federation of Commercial Organizations of Shanghai expressed its sympathy with the students in telegrams to the government and to Ts'ai Yüan-p'ei. The next day it sent another telegram to urge the release of the student prisoners, and declared that "the students were actuated by patriotic sentiments, arousing the highest esteem and greatest admiration of this Federation which hereby swears to support them and guarantee their safety and which will not let them suffer the least harm." [29] These telegrams are significant as evidence of the Chinese merchants' active interest in the matter, and particularly of readiness to protest strongly to the government by a class which had been traditionally apathetic to political affairs and mass movements in the long course of Chinese history. On May 6 T'ang Shao-i, the chief representative from the Southern government to the Peace Conference in Shanghai, sent a telegram to President Hsü Shih-ch'ang in support of the Peking students. On the same day Chu Ch'i-ch'ien, the chief representative of the Peking government to the conference, also dispatched a telegram to the Peking government, reporting public sentiment in that city and urging that the student demonstrators and those arrested should be leniently dealt with. In addition to this, he, partly on his own initiative, joined T'ang Shao-i on May 6 in cabling Paris and asking the Chinese delegates to stand firm in their demand for the return of Tsingtao to China.[i]

The obvious sympathy of the public with the students was soon seized upon by political parties as ammunition against the Peking government. Sun Yat-sen, in Shanghai at the time, immediately expressed his support of the students.

---

[i] Chu had at the time no close relation with the Anfu group. He was a follower of President Hsü Shih-ch'ang.[30]

As soon as the news of the incident spread to the South, he led the other six directors of the Canton government in sending a telegraphic protest to the Peking government in favor of the student movement, which read in part: [j]

The youthful students, whose activities may have slightly exceeded the normal limit because of their patriotic sentiments, should be excused. . . . If the authorities of Peking do not seek a basic solution in their policies but instead oppress the people by brutal force, the people will not be afraid of death. A careless start might result in a serious catastrophe. . . . Accordingly, we hope that you will handle the matter reasonably in order to satisfy the public sentiment of the whole country. . . .

Moreover, the Parliament at Canton, after a joint meeting of the two Houses specifically called to discuss the incident, sent a telegram to all the provincial governments and other groups: [k]

The traitors, Ts'ao Ju-lin, Chang Tsung-hsiang, and Lu Tsung-yü, willingly serve as running dogs of a foreign country, and do business secretly with Japan. In the field of foreign relations, they do everything to thwart the demands of representatives at Paris who are working for China to annul the secret Sino-Japanese treaties and to restore Tsingtao to China. In domestic affairs they intend to break up the Shanghai peace negotiations in order to succeed in their traitorous intrigue. Their crimes are so apparent that both heaven and the people feel indignant about them. The students of Peking, fearing their country will be tragically subjugated, and seeing clearly that the Peking government is controlled by traitors, risked their lives to burn Ts'ao's house and beat Chang Tsung-hsiang. There is nothing in history which is more gratifying than this.

However, the Northern regime, ignoring the fact that those traitors ought to be killed by anybody at any opportune moment, arrested the students. It is reported that those students arrested will be cruelly executed, and the colleges and universities involved will be closed. We, the Senators and Representatives of the Parliament in Canton, surprised by the news, called on May 9 a joint meeting of the two Houses, wherein we, in indignation, resolved unanimously to telegraph you to demand jointly that the Northern regime immediately release the imprisoned students, protect all the schools, and apologize to the people of the whole country by severely punishing the traitors, Ts'ao Ju-lin, Chang Tsung-hsiang, and Lu Tsung-yü. Trusting that your patriotism will not be surpassed by that of the

[j] In May 1918, a Directorate of Seven had been set up in the Canton government in place of the generalissimoship, which had been held by Sun since the fall of 1917. After giving up the supreme command under the Southern warlords' pressure, Sun remained nominally one of the directorate but went to Shanghai immediately. He was there studying the problems of economic, psychological, and social reconstruction of China when the May Fourth Incident took place. Consequently, not all of the orders and declarations of the directorate during this period were sanctioned by him. But this telegram, according to Hu Han-min, was initiated by Sun.[81]

[k] Lin Sen, later President of the Nationalist government, led the signatories of the Canton Parliament.[82]

youthful students, we ask you to rush to their rescue with all vigor, and protest in unity against the Northern regime, in order to maintain justice for human dignity and to wipe out treason from the face of the nation. The situation is very urgent — we hope you will act at once.

The Southerners seem to have seen that the May Fourth Incident would strengthen their hands in the Shanghai Peace Conference. On May 13 their chief representative, T'ang Shao-i, presented, without instruction from Canton or knowledge of his colleagues at the conference, a stronger demand to the North, which caused the breaking off of negotiations on May 15.[33]

The dispute, developing so quickly and so unexpectedly, soon became more a struggle between a pro-Japanese faction of warlords, with a few bureaucrats and backward elements on the one side, and the population of the country on the other, than a struggle between the new intellectuals and the conservatives. Once the news of the incident spread to the entire nation, the fact that a majority hated the pro-Japanese Anfu Club became very apparent. Tuan Ch'i-jui's enemies, within and without the government, were shrewd enough to seize the opportunity to undermine his power.

Some warlords and monarchists also voiced their approval of the students. K'ang Yu-wei, the erstwhile reformer but recently one of the planners of the 1917 monarchical restoration movement and no supporter of the new literature and new thought movements, lauded by public declaration in telegram the student movement of May 4 as "a rare and precious event similar to the students' protest against the government in the Sung dynasty," and said, "No real public opinion and real people's rights have been seen in China in the eight years since the establishment of the Republic in 1912; if there are now any, they are due to the students' actions in this incident." [34] Another example of approval is that of Wu P'ei-fu, a warlord who later became one of the most powerful rulers in Northern China. He, like K'ang, expressed his support of the students publicly. Other warlords, such as Chang Ching-yao, Military Governor of Hunan, and Ch'en Kuang-yüan, that of Kiangsi, also demanded the Peking government to dismiss Ts'ao, Chang, and Lu and to insist upon the return of Tsingtao to China.[1]

These early developments reveal the character of the student movement. The movement started by the students under a banner of protest against Japa-

---

[1] Wu was at the time commander of a division in Hengyang, Hunan, the only troops which had won a few battles over the Southerners. He was a follower of Ts'ao K'un. Ts'ao and Wu were at this time reluctant to carry out Tuan's plan of unifying the country by force.[35]

nese aggression and pro-Japanese officials in the government had now developed into a coalition supported by groups with different interests and understandings of the movement. The students and intellectual leaders of the new thought were, of course, the central figures of the movement. They were temporarily joined by the new merchants and supported morally and politically by other social and political groups. In such a complicated grouping, the long range goal of cultural reform could hardly be accepted by all of the participants. But for the time being, they were united on one point at least, that they wanted to fight the pro-Japanese officials in power. This situation had temporarily strengthened the hands of the new intellectuals in their dealings with the government.

After the arrest of the thirty-two students, the Peking government was under great pressure from the public. A great number of telegrams of protest each day flooded the offices in the Peking palace and the Chinese delegation at Paris.[36] From May 5 on, the Minister of Education submitted his resignation to the Premier three times in as many days, and flatly refused to countersign the order closing the schools involved in the incident. The idea was consequently given up.[37] At the same time, the student strike in Peking was going on and considerable excitement prevailed in the city. News from other cities indicated that demonstrations and strikes were widespread. Under this pressure both from outside and inside, the government on the morning of May 7 released the thirty-two students on bail pending further trial in court.[m] It is probable that the government hoped to ease the public tension by selecting this specific date — National Humiliation Day — to release the students, since it knew that a great number of mass meetings and demonstrations would be held against the government on that date.[39] The students had won the first battle with the government.

The day after the release of the student prisoners, the student strike in Peking ended. But the activities of the students both in Peking and other cities did not cease. On the contrary, they steadily spread and increased. Students in Peking under the leadership of the Student Union of Middle Schools and Institutions of Higher Learning in Peking proceeded to prepare the way for a boycott against Japanese goods. Some Japanese goods stored in schools were taken out and publicly burnt at Hsien-nung T'an (the Temple of Agriculture) in Peking.

[m] Three prominent persons, Wang Ta-hsieh (ex-Premier), Wang Ch'ung-hui (later Premier) (1881–1958), and Lin Ch'ang-min (one of the leaders of the Chinputang), volunteered as bailors. At 10:00 a.m. the students sent thirteen automobiles to the prison to welcome the arrested students shouting "Long live the students," and "Long live the Republic of China!" [88]

Student Support from Other Cities

In the first one or two weeks after the May Fourth Incident, student activities spreading over the country were characterized by: (1) establishment of self-governing student organizations in charge of carrying on various programs; (2) organization of demonstrations in protest against the government's foreign policy, the resolution of the Paris Peace Conference in respect to the Shantung question, and the arrest of the students; (3) initiation of a widespread boycott against Japanese goods. These nation-wide activities were exemplified by those going on in the big cities such as Tientsin, Shanghai, Nanking, and Wu-Han, which merit examination.[40]

In Tientsin, the news of the incident reached the students on May 5. They reacted very quickly and held an excited meeting of protest against the government in the evening of May 6. Next day a provisional student union of the city was formed. On May 12, over a thousand students held a public memorial meeting to mourn the death of Kuo Ch'in-kuang, the student martyr who died because of the May Fourth Incident. After the meeting, street speeches were delivered all over the city and suburbs. The Student Union of the Middle Schools and Institutes of Higher Learning in Tientsin was established on May 14 after the model of that in Peking, with students of the Higher Industrial College of Chihli (Hopei), Nankai Middle School (later University), and Peiyang University as leading members. Even students of the Railroad College of Tangshan (*T'ang-shan lu hsiao*) — which belonged to the Ministry of Communications headed by Ts'ao Ju-lin, and had as chancellor Chang Tsung-yüan, Chang Tsung-hsiang's elder brother who had studied in the United States — joined in the student movement against the government. Leading students in the union were Ch'en Chih-tu and Ma Chün, a Moslem and later communist. Antigovernment activities were strengthened by the creation of the Tientsin Association of Women Patriotic Comrades (*T'ien-chin nü-chieh ai-kuo t'ung-chih-hui*) which was founded on May 25 under the leadership of Liu Ch'ing-yang, an alumna of the Hopei Province First Girls' Normal School, and Li I-t'ao, a teacher of the school's elementary school, and with girl students Wang T'ien-lin (then named Wang Jui-sheng) and Kuo Lung-chen (then Kuo Lin-i) as its nucleus, and later on June 18 by the organization of the Tientsin Alliance of All Circles for National Salvation (*T'ien-chin ko-chieh chiu-kuo lien-ho-hui*) which included over 170 educational, economic, social, and religious groups. Chou En-lai, then a student in Japan after his graduation from the Nankai Middle School, returned to Tientsin after the May Fourth Incident and became the editor of the *Journal of the Student Union* (*Hsüeh-sheng lien-ho-hui pao*), a paper published every three days (which later appeared daily) by the Tientsin Student Union, with a circulation of over twenty thousand. Teng Ying-ch'ao (Teng Wen-shu), who later became Chou's wife and a top communist, was then a student at the First Girls' Normal School, a leader of the speech-making corps of the Association of Women Patriotic Comrades and head of the speech department of the Student Union of Tientsin.[41]

In Shanghai, word of the incident reached the students on May 5 through the telegram relayed from Tientsin. The first reaction to the news was recalled as follows by Chiang Monlin, who was in the city at the time:

The whole city was excited by the news. In the afternoon public organizations such as educational associations, chambers of commerce, and provincial and local guilds sent telegrams to the Peking government demanding the dismissal of the three high officials and the release of the students arrested or detained. Through the following day all Shanghai waited anxiously for a reply from the government but there was none. Then the students of the city went on strike, making the same demands as the public organizations, and went forth lecturing on the streets.[42]

A citizens' meeting was held on May 7, at 1:00 p.m., presided over by Huang Yen-p'ei and attended by more than twenty thousand (some say seven thousand) persons, most of whom were students. After the meeting its representatives went to see the Northern and Southern representatives at the Shanghai Peace Conference and the Military Governor of Shanghai, asking for their support of the Peking students. On May 8 student representatives from all major schools resolved to organize a student union of the city. On May 11 the Student Union of the Middle Schools and Institutes of Higher Learning in Shanghai was established by twelve thousand students from sixty-one colleges and schools. Ho Pao-jen, a student of Futan University, was elected its head. A Shanghai Student Volunteer Corps for the Defense of Shantung and street speechmaking groups were also organized.[n]

In Nanking, students from more than two dozen schools, including at least one of the leading institutions, the Higher Normal College of Nanking, and members of many professional educational organizations held a memorial meeting on National Humiliation Day (May 9) with about ten thousand people present. A student union was also organized. Representatives were

---

[n] Ho Pao-jen was the chairman of the legislative department of the union who was most active in the Shanghai student movement. Li Ting-nien was the chief of the administrative department of the union. Another student leader from Futan University was Ch'eng T'ien-fang, who later became Chinese Ambassador to Germany, Minister of Information of the Kuomintang, and Minister of Education in Formosa after the Nationalist government retreated to the island in 1949.[43]

sent by the meeting to petition the office of the military viceroy, the office of the Governor of Kiangsu Province, and the Provincial Council, asking for their good offices to protest against the resolution concerning Tsingtao at Paris, to expand education, and to improve national industry. Street speechmaking groups, a Save China Corps, and a Save China Fund were also established. Following a similar action in Tsinan and Shanghai on May 9, merchants in Nanking started a boycott against Japanese goods on May 11.

Over two thousand student representatives from fifteen colleges and middle schools in Wu-Han met on May 11 at Wen-hua University, an American missionary school. They discussed steps necessary to support the Peking students and resolved to protest against the Peking government's foreign policy. At the meeting, the students contributed more than two thousand *yuan* to finance their own activities. A student union similar to the Peking model was established on May 14, and resolved at the same time to telegraph the Chinese delegates at Paris urging them to refuse to sign the peace treaty; the union decided also to establish publications in the vernacular to encourage the expression of public opinion and to advocate a Chinese market for national products. A colorful student demonstration was held on May 18.

Students in other cities and provinces showed similar reactions and activities. The provinces in which students were most active in this respect were Kiangsu (especially Soochow, Wusih [Wuhsi], Changchow, Chinkiang, Yangchow, and Nantung), Chekiang (especially Hangchow, Chiahsing, and Huchow), Shantung (especially Tsinan), Hunan (especially Changsha), Shansi (especially T'aiyuan), Shensi, Honan, Anhwei, Kiangsi, Fukien, Kwangtung (especially Canton), and Kwangsi.[44]

Moreover, Chinese students abroad in Europe and Japan were also aroused by the news of the incident. An episode took place in Tokyo which had some effect on the development of the May Fourth Movement in the following days. Most of the Chinese students who had returned to China in a body in 1918 had drifted back to Japan later that year. But before May 4, 1919, some of them had initiated another movement to return to China. Upon hearing the news of the May Fourth Incident, the remaining Chinese students in Japan, numbering about four thousand, prepared to hold a national humiliation memorial meeting in Tokyo on May 7. They could not find a place for the meeting because the Japanese police intervened. Finally, they asked permission to use the office of the Chinese Legation. Chuang Ching-k'o, the acting Minister to Japan, found no reason to refuse them. But on the evening of May 6, the office was surrounded by Japanese police and troops. Next morning, since they had been unable to hold the meeting in the Chinese Legation, the students gathered in front of the German Legation and in nearby parks and paraded in separate groups to the legations of Great Britain, the United States, Russia, and France for the purpose of presenting a petition concerning the Shantung question. Their slogans included: "Destroy militarism," "For the preservation of peace," "Return our Tsingtao," and "In memory of National Humiliation Day!" [45] The groups of students were surrounded and harried by more than a thousand Japanese cavalrymen and armed police, as they proceeded along Futagaya-zaka. Street fights developed in which more than one hundred students were wounded, twenty-nine of them severely. Thirty-nine were arrested by the police and jailed in the police station at Kojimachi-ku. They were released on bail next day.[46] Meanwhile, the Japanese police were reported to have declared in effect that it was not their fault that they attacked the students, as they were asked to do so by the Chinese acting Minister in Tokyo and the supervisor of Chinese students in Japan.[47] Later on, a Japanese local court sentenced seven Chinese students to imprisonment against furious protests by the Chinese public.° The sentences seem to have been suspended in an effort to ease the tension of Chinese public feeling.

The Chinese Legation in Tokyo made a report to the Peking government unfavorable to the students involved. The Chinese government also made no effort to protect the students in Japan. This, of course, added fuel to the student movement at home.[49]

Throughout the first two weeks following the May Fourth Incident, the students' activities listed above had been confined mainly to forming organizations and rallying social support by demonstrations and street speeches. Although some permanent programs had been started, it appears that pressure brought by the new intelligentsia and other social and political forces had not been substantial enough to compel the Peking government to make any major concessions so far as changes in its foreign policy or personnel were concerned.

The President's Disciplinary Mandates and Ts'ai Yüan-p'ei's Departure

After the May Fourth Incident the government had in fact taken some steps to prevent or interfere with patriotic activities by the public. On May 6, the

° The sentences imposed upon the students were: Hu Chun, one year of hard labor; Chang Yün-chang and a certain Wang, four months; Tu Chung and two others, each three months; another unknown. In the 1955 reprinted source materials on the incident, the Chinese Communists omitted all the names of those Chinese students arrested and wounded except P'eng P'ai, who was among the wounded in the incident and later became a communist. Most of the arrested (over 30 per cent) and wounded (over 40 per cent) were from Hunan Province.[48]

day before the thirty-two students arrested in the incident were released, President Hsü Shih-ch'ang issued a mandate, in which he held his subordinates responsible for their failure to prevent the incident, and especially blamed the lower ranks of policemen. Moreover, he ordered the chief of the constabulary "to take adequate measures" to check any further public meeting or demonstration, and directed that if the people refused "to submit to strict control," they should be arrested and punished at once. The English version of the mandate reads:

Referring to the case on the 4th instant, in which the students of the Peking University and other schools collected, held meetings, committed arson and wounded persons, an order was issued at the commencement of the trouble to the Peking Constabulary Bureau to distribute its forces and take proper precautionary measures. Yet, due to its failure to take prompt preventive measures such offences as arson and assault were made possible of perpetration. It was only when Wu Ping-hsiang, Chief of the Constabulary, himself proceeded to the scene and directed matters that some students were arrested and the gathering dispersed.

The said Chief of the Constabulary cannot but be accounted to have seriously blundered in the proper handling of the affair. The officers and men of the Constabulary, delegated to perform outside work, have been lacking in methods of prevention and neglectful of their duty. Let the Chief of the Constabulary ascertain their ranks and names and submit them for the consideration of their penalties. As Peking is our capital upon which Chinese and foreigners alike cast their eyes, the preservation of order and peace therein is of paramount importance. It is the duty of the said Chief of the Constabulary to direct his subordinates to take adequate measures of precaution against any breach of public peace, in which matter he should act carefully in conjunction with civil and military officials of the district. Should there be people again collecting together and disturbing order under one pretext or another, who refuse to submit to strict control, let him at once arrest and punish them in accordance with the law; do not show the least neglect or laxity.[50]

Under this strict order, the new intellectuals in Peking waxed more indignant than ever before. Most of the social, educational, and economic groups in the city had planned to hold a citizens' meeting at the central park on National Humiliation Day (May 7) as sponsored by the Citizens' Diplomatic Association but were forbidden to do so by the government. The gates of the park were locked by the police. Some two hundred representatives of these groups met instead at the office of the association and there passed four resolutions protesting the government's foreign policy and its attitudes toward the students.[51]

The President, embarrassed by the fact that the students never ceased their anti-government activities, issued another mandate on May 8. In it he cited the police report concerning the incident and indicated that the thirty-two students, though released for the time being, were going to be prosecuted in court and punished. He also stated that students whose duty was to study were too young "to interfere in politics." The English version of the mandate reads:

In a memorial from Ch'ien Neng-hsün, he submits a report from Wu Ping-hsiang, Chief of the Peking Constabulary, stating that on the 4th instant, over 3,000 students from thirteen schools, including the Peking University, carrying white flags in their hands, successively arrived in front of Tienanmen (Heavenly Peace Gate), where they assembled and resolved to hold a parade through the streets; that when they reached the west entrance to the Legation quarter, they were held up by the Legation Police, whereupon they went to the house of Ts'ao Ju-lin, Minister of Communications, where they threw stones promiscuously, assaulted people with sticks and paid no attention to the remonstrance and opposition by the troops and police; that subsequently, they broke the windows facing the street, and swarmed into the house, demolishing furniture and articles, setting fire to the windows, and beating the guardsmen, several of whom were seriously wounded; that further they collectively beat Chang Tsung-hsiang, Minister to Japan, who was still more grievously wounded, and that a number of the riotous students were then arrested on the spot, preliminarily examined by the Constabulary Bureau and then handed to the Court of Justice for trial and punishment, etc.

Schools were established chiefly for the purpose of training and developing the ability of men with a view to rendering service to the nation at some future date. As the students at schools are yet youthful, and as their nature and character have not yet been fixedly shaped, it is essential for them to devote their whole heart to their studies; it is inconceivable that they should be allowed to interfere in politics and disturb our public peace. Since the rioters arrested at the spot have been handed by the said Bureau to the Court of Justice, let the latter deal with them in accordance with the law. As Peking is the capital of our nation, the habit of the schools must be speedily and energetically reformed. Let the said Ministry (? of Education) ascertain the true circumstances that have led to the disturbance, and submit a report for our decision.ᴾ Let it at all times diligently exercise its supervision over the students and earnestly exhort them, each and all, to endeavour to become men of accomplishments and to refrain from doing anything to disappoint the Government in its desire to cultivate men of a brilliant and promising character.[52]

The President not only ordered that the students be treated severely, as shown by these mandates, but also refused to accept the resignations of Ts'ao Ju-lin and Lu Tsung-yü. In his replies to them, he praised Ts'ao as "selflessly and sincerely loyal to his country" and Lu as "invaluable in public affairs." [53] This was of course intolerable to the new intellectuals and general public of the country. Furthermore, in the last paragraph of the mandate of May 8, the

---

ᴾ The Chinese text does not name the Ministry of Education specifically. From the context, the *Herald's* interpolation appears correct.

President's implication was clear that he put a great deal of responsibility for the incident on the Minister of Education and all school teachers. Actually, the Minister of Education and the chancellors of the colleges had been under fire ever since the incident from the warlords and the old bureaucrats. As has been said before, the Cabinet did consider removing Ts'ai Yüan-p'ei from the chancellorship. There were also wild rumors that Ts'ao Ju-lin and Chang Tsung-hsiang were, with three million *yuan*, buying someone to assassinate Ts'ai, and that the campus of Peking University would be burned and its students massacred.[q]

Ts'ai, learning of the President's mandate of May 8 and receiving on the evening of the same day at eleven o'clock an intimation that he would be dismissed and succeeded by Ma Ch'i-ch'ang, secretly left Peking for Tientsin on the morning of May 9.[r] Two letters of resignation were left, one for the President and the other for the Minister of Education.[56] But most important of all, he also left a brief bulletin which immediately mystified and excited the students and teachers and had an unexpected influence upon the movement. It has since become famous:

I am exhausted! "Those who killed your horse are the children by the road." "The people indeed are heavily burdened, but perhaps a little rest may be got for them." I want a little rest too! I have formally tendered my resignation of the chancellorship of the National University of Peking; all relations which I previously had with other schools and associations will also cease from May 9. The above is a formal notice of that decision. I hope that those who understand me will forgive me.

The two quotations from ancient poems in the notice contained very ambiguous meanings.[s] Free interpretations spread widely at the schools at the time.

---

[q] John Dewey reported in Peking on June 24: "The provinces were rife with rumors of the readiness of the Chinese militarist clique to go to any extreme in the way of slaughter to put down opposition; rife even with rumors of an impending coup d'etat to fix irretrievably the hold upon the government of the militarist and pro-Japanese party. The Chancellor of the University, whom the militarists hated as the intellectual leader of the liberal elements, resigned and disappeared, because, according to report, not only his life but those of hundreds of students were threatened." [54]

[r] Ts'ai first went to Tientsin, then to Shanghai, and later retired temporarily to Hangchow, where he lived in a friend's house on scenic West Lake.[55]

[s] The first quotation is from an ancient poem. It tells a story of a high official who had a handsome horse, but scarcely ever let it appear in public. Once when he rode it along a road, the children were seized with curiosity about it. Encouraged by the applause of the young spectators, the official rode the horse to death. The second quotation was from the Book of Odes (Shih-ching) the context of which was:

> The people indeed are heavily burdened,
> But perhaps a little rest may be got for them.
> Let us cherish this centre of the kingdom,
> And make it a gathering-place for the people. [Continued, p. 136]

The resignation of Ts'ai Yüan-p'ei under government pressure was viewed by the new intellectuals, both students and teachers, as a public assault by the government upon them. For many reasons Ts'ai had long been considered their moral leader. His reputation in educational circles was unrivaled at the time. Almost all the professors and students at the university respected and supported him enthusiastically, because of his liberal, democratic, and straightforward attitude towards themselves and towards even the minor employees of the university. He had, to the new intelligentsia both moderate and revolutionary, become a symbol of their common cause, although it was doubtful whether he saw the movement completely as they did.[58] Following his example, chancellors of other colleges in Peking, including those of the Medical College, the Industrial College, the Normal College, and the College of Law and Political Science, also tendered their resignations.[59]

On the same day of Ts'ai's flight from Peking, the Ministry of Education gave another order to restrict the students' activities, whereas some parliamentary members proposed to impeach Ts'ao Ju-lin. At the same time, the government decided to bring to trial the thirty-two students on bail. On May 10 they were arraigned at the local court. There they categorically denied that they were responsible for the burning of Ts'ao's house and the beating of Chang. Questioned further by the attorney, they also denied flatly that they were manipulated by any political forces. "It was a completely free action based on our consciences," they declared in court. They also refused to fill out pleas of not guilty on the ground that their action was after all not a crime. In a written statement submitted to the court a few days later they said:

> We, the thirty-two students, Hsü Te-heng and others, declare that Ts'ao Ju-lin and Chang Tsung-hsiang who have committed treason should have been punished. They are hated by everybody who has courage. The May Fourth Incident was simply an outbreak of indignation based upon the consciences of the several thousand students and tens of thousands of citizens in Peking. Because it cannot be considered

---

Let us give no indulgence to the wily and obsequious,
In order to make the noisy braggarts careful,
And to repress robbers and oppressors; —
So the people shall not have such sorrow. . . .

(*The Chinese Classics, The Shi King*, translated by James Legge, Part III, Bk. II, Ode IX, stanza 2.)

Shortly after the disclosure of the notice, students tried to find its real meaning. One of them asked a professor of literature at Peking University and obtained on May 10 an illuminating letter in reply.

Some circles at the time interpreted the poem to mean that the high official in it was a metaphor for the Peking government, the horse, Ts'ao and Chang, and the young spectators, the students. This hardly fitted the case, but the interpretation was prevalent anyway. The implication of the second quotation was more clear. But Ts'ai himself explained a year later that there was no other implication but that he felt tired of the situation and needed a rest.[57]

a crime so far as the intention is concerned, why should we be suspected and prosecuted? If we are a law-abiding people, the prosecuting officers should perform their duty without fearing forceful pressure, and go straight to prosecute the traitors like Ts'ao and Chang according to Articles 108 and 109 of the criminal law. Only doing this the court may conciliate popular feeling. . . . Considering that the plea of "not guilty" is a form used by defendants in criminal cases, we students refuse to accept your order to apply it in our case.[60]

It cannot be stated categorically that the government could not have found any reason to argue the case in terms of law in a court. However, the problem was, or at least was considered by most of the Chinese people at the time, to be social, political, and moral rather than legal. From the beginning, the Peking government's conclusion of secret agreements with Japan, making such vital concessions to the latter without consent of Parliament, could not be regarded as legal by most of the people. As a matter of fact, the Southerners had declared the Peking regime to be unconstitutional after the autumn of 1917. The Peking government had eventually been accepted by many of the people including the new intellectuals as a *de facto* rather than a *de jure* government. Consequently, this appeal to law by the unpopular Peking government had little support from the public. Ultimately the government's attempt to prosecute the students in a law court never materialized because of the Peking students' threat that they would go to the court and to prison in a body.

At the same time, the Peking government increased the pressure on the schools. More arrests of students were made. On May 11, two student street-lecturers at Tsing Hua School were arrested by the government.[61] Distressed by the situation and under fire from the warlords, Fu Tseng-hsiang, the Minister of Education, fled on the evening of May 11 to the Western Hills (*Hsishan*), in the vicinity of Peking, and insisted on resigning.[62] On May 15 he was permitted to resign by the Premier, and Yüan Hsi-t'ao, vice-minister, was appointed acting minister.[63] Meanwhile, on May 14, two special mandates had been issued by the government: one ordered the authorities to suppress the activities of students by military force; the other stated that the students had no right to interfere with government policy.[64]

All these events, the issuance of the President's mandates, the resignation of Ts'ai and Fu, the attempt to prosecute the students, and the further arrests, stirred up the feelings of the new intellectuals. The indignation of the youth was so intense that a student at Tsing Hua College died of fatigue after street speeches and an alumnus from the Imperial University of Peking tragically and dramatically committed suicide.[t]

[t] The alumnus drowned himself. A message was found in his pocket expressing his pessimistic

After Ts'ai's departure, all the chancellors of colleges and universities in Peking united in a protest against the government. Nine representatives were sent to see the Premier, demanding that the government make clear its actual attitude toward educational circles, its plans and means for future handling of the situation, and its sincere desire to keep Ts'ai in office. Owing to this and many other protests, the government reluctantly refused Ts'ai's resignation. But Ts'ai, by telegram, insisted on resigning. Even student representatives who were specifically sent to beg him to return could not prevail upon him to change his mind.[u] Meanwhile, news from the government indicated that the pro-warlord Ma Ch'i-ch'ang, who was political counselor to the Peking government and a man of letters advocating the traditional T'ung-ch'eng literary style, would succeed Ts'ai as chancellor of Peking University, and that T'ien Ying-huang would succeed Fu as Minister of Education. Both these men belonged to the Anfu Club. These were the very things the new intellectuals dreaded most to hear.

Aware of the fact that the warlord government was waging an all-out war on them, the new intellectual leaders in Peking quickly organized. The teachers and professors united and set up the Alliance of Teachers' Unions of the Middle Schools and Institutions of Higher Learning in Peking (*Pei-ching chung-teng i-shang hsüeh-hsiao chiao-chih-yüan lien-ho-hui*), on the model of the Student Union. The teachers' alliance, like the Student Union, consisted not only of adherents of the new literature and new thought movements, but also of those who were reluctant to join or actually against the new movements.[v]

view of the Chinese situation: "With such severe internal and external troubles, China may soon be a dead nation. No one can tell how the Shantung question will end or when there will be peace between the North and the South. What a pitiful sight to see the students rise up empty-handed, risking their lives for the national salvation without the least selfishness or conceit and free from any ulterior motives! With the realization that I am witnessing the passing of a nation and the enslavement of her people, I have decided that I would rather be a free ghost than a living slave. My fellow citizens, be brave and struggle for your country! I have finished my life." [65]

[u] The Ministry of Education resolved on three ways to try to bring Ts'ai back: to ask the President of the Republic to refuse to accept his resignation; to send a departmental director to Tientsin to seek to dissuade Ts'ai from leaving; and to send a telegram to Ts'ai asking him to return.[66]

[v] According to Ma Hsü-lun, the establishment of the teachers' alliance was proposed by the Teachers' Union of the National University of Peking, of which K'ang Pao-chung was the chairman and Ma, the secretary. The alliance also elected K'ang its chairman and Ma its secretary. Later on, after K'ang's death, Ma succeeded to his post and Shen Shih-yüan, another professor at Peking University and a brother of Shen Yin-mo, was elected secretary of the organizations. Ma Hsü-lun (b. 1884) was associated with the conservative Monarchist Party before the 1911 Revolution. In the early years of the Republic he was considered a member or a supporter of the Chinputang which cooperated with the Northern warlords. When he taught at Peking University during the time of the May Fourth Incident, he was criticized by *New Tide*. He actually opposed the new literature movement. But he was a classmate and intimate of T'ang Er-ho, who had recommended Ts'ai Yüan-p'ei to the Peking government to be the chancellor of the university and also Ch'en

Most of them supported the student movement against the government's foreign policy and against the official move to unseat Ts'ai and Fu. It is clear that in some respects the teachers and professors were actually following the students' actions instead of vice versa.[w]

The Students' General Strike

At this critical time, when the majority of teachers and students were indignant over the government's attitude toward them, some students still tried to keep calm and cool. On May 13, the day after Minister Fu left his office, students of all the middle schools, colleges, and universities in Peking met to discuss the situation. A resolution to stage a general student strike came up and was supported by the majority. But after calm consideration and discussion, they resolved to continue attending classes on the ground that the strike would hurt their studies and be ineffective if the government ignored it. A second attempt to stage a general strike also failed.

But this calm between tempests could not be maintained very long against increasing government pressure. Upon learning that the pro-warlord politician, T'ien Ying-huang, was going to head the Ministry of Education, and that the government was determined to discipline the educational groups, the students from eighteen colleges and universities in Peking called an emergency meeting of the Student Union on May 18.[69] There it was resolved to stage a general student strike on May 19. The "Manifesto for a General Strike" addressed to the provincial councils, educational, commercial, agricultural, and labor organizations, schools, other professional societies, and the press, by the Student Union of Peking, declared somewhat emotionally and naively:

"Externally preserve our sovereignty and internally eliminate the traitors!" This

---

Tu-hsiu to Ts'ai to be the dean of letters of the university. Ma claimed later in his autobiography that T'ang's idea of recommending Ts'ai originated from his suggestion. Hu Shih told the present author in the fall of 1956 that he once saw T'ang Er-ho's diary in manuscript and found mention of T'ang's relations with Ch'en and Ts'ai in regard to the university. Hu did not believe Ma's claim was true. After the May Fourth Incident, Ma led some teacher strikes against the Peking government. However, he later became Vice-Minister of Education under both the Northern government (once as acting Minister of Education under Tuan Ch'i-jui in 1924–25) and the Nationalist government. During the Sino-Japanese War he stayed in Shanghai. In 1945, after the war, he organized, with Hsü Kuang-p'ing, Lu Hsün's widow, and others, the Chinese Society for the Promotion of Democracy (*Chung-kuo min-chu ts'u-chin hui*). After 1949 he was appointed one of the People's Commissars, Vice-Chairman of the Cultural and Educational Council, and Minister of Education in the Communist government.[67]

[w] Some people had suggested after the May Fourth Incident that the teachers should follow the students' example and organize their own unions.[68]

is the repeated demand we students make of the government and the incessant call to our fellow citizens since the May Fourth Incident (*Wu-ssu yün-tung*). There has been no response, only some added mischief. We have focussed our appeal on the Shantung question. Yet the government at this critical moment fails to take a firm stand against signing the peace treaty which summarily rejects the Chinese request. Instead, it breaks off the internal peace conference in Shanghai, a move that will help the enemy. We are deeply distressed at this situation. Secondly, we are disappointed to observe that the government, ignoring public opinion, refuses the blackmail resignations of Ts'ao Ju-lin, Chang Tsung-hsiang, and Lu Tsung-yü, whose execution has been demanded by the whole nation, and instead publicly praises them while dismissing Minister Fu. It is also predicted that educational circles will undergo thorough and severe discipline. If this is true, what an inconceivable disaster to the nation it will be! Thirdly, we are dumfounded that the government in its two orders of May 14 prohibits by threat of armed force public meetings and student intervention in government policies and suppresses all expression of patriotic conscience, whereas it turns a deaf ear to the news of the arrests of Chinese students by the Japanese police in Tokyo. We students have to have clear minds in order to pursue our studies; now our minds are confused by these grave disappointments. We resolve to start a general strike on May 19 to continue until we are satisfied with the settlement of the above-mentioned matters. During the period of the strike, we shall abide by the resolutions set forth in our telegram of May 14: first, to organize a Peking Student Volunteer Corps for the Defense of Shantung (*Pei-ching hsüeh-sheng hu-Lu i-yung-tui*) to concern itself with the potential national emergency; second, to establish units in schools to spread popular education by public speeches and awaken the people to the importance of nationhood; third, to organize in schools Groups of Ten (*Shih-jen t'uan*) for the maintenance of order to lessen the danger to our country; fourth, to make more extensive study of the economy in order to benefit our country. We students have been educated and self-cultivated for so long that we will advisedly follow our national traits of wisdom, virtue, and courage and will not by exceeding accepted rules of action shame our national history. We shall behave according to our own natural ability and innate knowledge, and do not care whether you understand or censure us at the present but wait for the judgment of posterity.[70]

At the same time, the Student Union submitted to President Hsü Shih-ch'ang six demands. It urged him (1) to refuse to sign the peace treaty at Paris, (2) to punish the traitors, Ts'ao, Chang, and Lu, (3) to reinstate Fu Tseng-hsiang as Minister of Education and Ts'ai Yüan-p'ei as chancellor of Peking University, (4) to remove the drastic repressive measures imposed upon the students by the government, in order to uphold human rights, (5) to protest the Japanese government's attack on and arrest of Chinese students on May 7, and to secure their release and the punishment of the police, and (6) to resume the peace negotiations with the South in Shanghai, which had been suspended on May 15.[71] The students threatened to continue the strike until the demands were accepted by the government.

The Groups of Ten mentioned in the manifesto were also called "Groups of Ten for National Salvation" (*Chiu-kuo shih-jen t'uan*). According to their regulations, any congenial students could form a group to promote the boycott and propagandize. A particular group was responsible to the student union of its own institution; this local union was answerable to a provincial student union, and, later, the provincial union to the Student Union of China, which was established about one month after the start of the general strike.[x] This pattern of organization later spread to many cities and became the nucleus of both the student unions and labor organizations in action.[y]

The students' decision of May 18 marked a further advance in the developments arising out of the May Fourth Incident. Before this, their activities against the government had produced some agitation; the boycott movement was beginning; and student strikes had sprung up here and there. But without a general strike their activities could not be extensive or intensive enough to attract the attention of the illiterate masses. The decision for a general student strike meant all-out defiance of the government's repression. More important still was the students' shift in emphasis from mass meetings of student groups to smaller but more influential street assemblies involving the average people; from colorful demonstrations to a practical boycott against Japanese goods and the promotion of national industries. The latter development, of course, had great appeal to some of the new merchants and industrialists, who were facing a threat of dumping of Japanese products into Chinese markets at the end of World War I. The students' decision to boycott was certainly not an isolated one. The Chamber of Commerce in Peking had, as mentioned above, promoted

[x] The ten men were to elect from their number: (1) one chairman, who was to put his strength where the group most needed it, (2) one inspector, to take an inventory of the Japanese goods in the shops of the district assigned to his group, (3) one editor, to write leaflets, newspaper articles, and other propaganda material, (4) one disciplinarian, to impose and collect fines for infraction of the group's rules, (5) one treasurer, to look after the finances of the group (one of his main duties was to solicit money to carry on the propaganda), (6) five orators, upon whom fell the burden of exhorting the people to promote native industries and to buy Chinese instead of Japanese goods.[72] The plan also provided that every ten groups were jointly to nominate one representative to be called the Representative of Ten, every hundred groups a Representative of One Hundred, and every thousand groups a Representative of One Thousand, which was the maximum; that on the back of the card of every member of a group should be printed the names of the other nine members of the same group; and that every member should do his best to persuade outsiders to join this movement (each making a point to secure at least ten members). It is, of course, a question how far this plan was ever strictly carried out.[73]

[y] Communists consider that the Groups-of-Ten movement helped the political orientation of the Chinese labor movement and the establishment of the Chinese Communist Party.[74] But Chang Kuo-t'ao, an ex-communist leader, said in his English memoirs that this was not true.

this in its resolution of May 6. The students, who probably took this step to woo the new merchants and industrialists, did in fact gain strong reinforcements because of it.

The general strike started on May 19 with all students at the eighteen colleges and universities in Peking refusing to attend classes. Next day, students of all the middle schools in the city joined the strike. Street speech groups were dispatched all over the city braving the intervention of the police. Printed handbills, leaflets, and newspapers in the vernacular language were widely distributed. What the speakers advocated was for the most part restoration of Tsingtao, denunciation of the Sino-Japanese treaties based on the Twenty-one Demands and other secret agreements, boycott of Japanese goods, and purchase of native products. Such intervention by the police as took place at this time was highly ineffective, because many of them were sympathetic with the students' patriotic sentiments.

The Peking general strike soon spread to other cities. After May 19, a few student representatives were secretly sent from Peking to Tientsin, Nanking, Shanghai, and other cities to promote the movement. Strikes swiftly spread to schools in all important cities in the latter part of May. The Student Union of Tientsin started a general strike on May 23.[75] More than ten thousand students in fifteen institutions including Peiyang University, Nankai Middle School, and the British Anglo-Chinese College refused to attend classes. They presented to the Peking government a six-point demand, closely resembling that submitted by the Peking students.

In Shanghai, the student union resolved on May 19 that a telegram should be sent to the Peking government urging the annulment of the order accepting Minister Fu's resignation; that all students of the schools belonging to the union should refuse to attend classes beginning on May 22 and attendance should not be resumed without instruction from the student union; and that student representatives should be sent to other cities to persuade all public and private schools to join the strike. The union, however, promised to postpone the strike for three days upon the mediation of the teachers and of the Association of Education of Kiangsu Province, of which Chiang Monlin was one of the organizers. Learning that the government would not accept the demands of the Peking students, more than twenty thousand students from more than seventy schools, including Futan University and other important colleges and universities, boycotted classes beginning on May 26. Their demonstration of this day attracted about three hundred thousand observers from the general public.[76]

Students in Shanghai seemed more conscious of their relation to merchants and urban workers. Their union decided on May 27 to dispatch liaison groups to merchant societies, urging all the merchants to hang white flags on their front doors on May 31 as evidence of participation in the mourning ceremony for the martyred Kuo Ch'in-kuang; to establish a labor department in the student union to keep contact with labor; to set up an investigation department to survey Japanese goods stored in all the big shops; to establish a daily publication as its organ; to ask every member to contribute every half year fifty cents (Chinese) to the union; and to send representatives to schools of other cities, to the Chinese students returned from abroad, and to diplomatic legations to ask their cooperation and support.[77] The first three resolutions were important steps which advanced the coalition with the merchants and workers in the following days.

From this time on, Shanghai became the most important center of student activities. Many able student leaders from Peking, Tientsin, and Nanking gathered in this, China's biggest city. The memorial meeting on May 31 was attended by about one hundred thousand citizens and students, the latter from eighty-two local middle schools and institutions of higher learning.[78] Hsü Te-heng and Ch'en Pao-o, student representatives of Peking who had left that city in disguise on May 27, made exciting speeches in the meeting. After the meeting, the students paraded to the Chamber of Commerce of Shanghai County (*Shang-hai hsien shang-hui*) urging that it advise the shops to cooperate with the students. The chamber promised to discuss the matter with student representatives on the following day.[79]

Students in some cities encountered strong suppression and had to resort to different types of action. For example, in Wu-Han, after the student demonstration of May 18, Wang Chien-yüan, the warlord governor of Hupei Province, severely suppressed the students' activities. When the 5,969 students of the middle schools and institutions of higher learning in Wu-Han declared a strike on June 1, Wang dispatched troops to stand guard in all those schools, thus keeping the students under strict surveillance. Almost one hundred student street lecturers were wounded and arrested by the police and troops on the same day. Some of them were crippled. A student from the Higher Normal College of Hupei Province was killed by the troops. On June 3 the Governor, who was just celebrating his acceptance of a medal from the Japanese Emperor, ordered all schools to close immediately upon the pretext that the summer vacation would begin early. About the same time, he declared that any students making anti-Japanese public speeches would be killed on the spot.

The activities of the Student Union of Wu-Han were then driven underground. Next day, it secretly resolved that all the students should go home and carry their campaign to the rural districts. Similarly, students in Hangchow were sent home on May 28 and campaigned there.

Major cities hit by the student strike included Peking (May 19), Kiukiang (May 20), Tientsin (May 23), Tsinan (May 23), Tangshan (May 24), Paoting (May 24), Taiyuan (May 26), Shanghai (May 26), Soochow (May 28), Hangchow (May 29), Nanking (May 29), Foochow (May 30), Anking (May 31), Kaifeng (May 31), Ningpo (May 31), Wusih (May 31), Wu-Han (June 1), Nantung (June 3), Changsha (June 3), Changchow (June 5), Chinkiang (June 6), Wuchin (June 6), Hsüchow (June 9), Canton, Amoy, and others.[80] Altogether the movement affected more than two hundred large and small cities in over twenty-two provinces.

The foregoing account indicates that most events in the first month following May 4 were sparked by the students. Students alone played the major role in protest against the government, first with public demonstrations and next with a widespread student general strike. They achieved in this period, moreover, four things which significantly facilitated their further activities. In the first place, with the establishment of the student unions in many schools, cities, and provinces, they became a well-organized body. In the second place, the students secured the support of intellectual leaders such as professors, teachers, writers, and journalists. Moreover, the student movement inspired these leaders to establish organized activities themselves. True, educators had had their own organizations before; but most of these were purely professional in character. The teachers' organizations created during this period were more political in nature. In the following years, educational circles developed into a special force in the struggle against the militarists and bureaucrats. In the third place, the students awakened many political and social leaders to the fact that youth was a force to be reckoned with in any political struggle. At least, they conceded that it was an effective force in fighting against the Anfu Club. Finally and most importantly, the students, inspired by the rising tide of national consciousness, had seized "protest against the pro-Japanese policy" as their battle cry. Their success in securing public sympathy under the banner of patriotism quickly led to the achievement of united support from urban merchants, industrialists, and workers in the latter part of the period.

CHAPTER VI

FURTHER DEVELOPMENTS: SUPPORT FROM MERCHANTS, INDUSTRIALISTS, AND WORKERS

THE situation gradually changed after May as merchants, industrialists, and urban workers aligned themselves with the students. The coalition was provoked by the government's mass arrests of students early in June and started to manifest itself in the strikes of merchants and workers in Shanghai and elsewhere.

The formation of this united front against the government took place under unprecedentedly favorable circumstances as regards both ideology and economic interest. One of the most important factors, as indicated by succeeding events, was a new wave of patriotism and nationalism which seems to have been ignored by the Japanese and Chinese governments. Another factor, especially where the boycotts and the merchants' strike were concerned, was the conflict of interests with Japan on the part of Chinese and Western economic forces developing during the period of World War I.

The Government's Failure to Secure a Compromise from the Students

The Peking government, embarrassed by the student strike, at first showed signs of wishing to compromise with the students on minor issues. But it also desired to refrain from doing anything that would arouse Japan's objection and hurt the pro-Japanese warlords then in power. On May 21 Premier Ch'ien Neng-hsün answered the students' demands in a statement to the representatives of the Teachers' Alliance: (1) The government could not by law punish without sufficient evidence and due trial any official charged with committing treason. (2) The government could not publicly declare that it would refuse to sign the Peace Treaty in the Paris Peace Conference; by doing so, it would harm its diplomatic relations with other nations. But the government would carefully consider the problem. (3) Ts'ai's resignation had been rejected; Fu was determined to resign although the government had tried to retain him. (4) As for the Shanghai peace negotiations, the Northern representatives would not be withdrawn. The door for negotiation was always open.[1]

The students were not satisfied by this answer. It angered them to know that the three pro-Japanese officials, Ts'ao, Lu, and Chang, were to remain in office and the pro-Japanese policy unchanged. And they were exasperated at the government's disregard of their other demands, which were still neither answered nor accomplished.

At this point the Japanese chose to intervene in the situation. On May 18, 20, and 21, Obata Torikichi, the Japanese Minister to China, served three protests upon the Peking government, demanding the suppression of all the students' anti-Japanese activities. This was followed by demonstrations in force staged by the Japanese troops stationed in China. Japanese warships gathered and maneuvered along the harbors of Tientsin, Shanghai, Nanking, Hankow, and other Chinese ports.[2] Under this threat the Peking government started to try to quell the student movement by force. It first tried to remove Wu Ping-hsiang, the chief of the constabulary, but failed because of objections by the Chamber of Commerce of Peking. Later, on May 21, it was able to remove Li Ch'ang-t'ai, the commander of the infantry, who along with the police chief Wu Ping-hsiang was suspected by the conservatives of being sympathetic with the students. Wang Huai-ch'ing was appointed in his place.[3] On May 23 it suppressed the Peking Student Union's newspaper, *May Seventh Daily* (*Wu-ch'i jih-k'an*), which was edited by Ch'en Pao-o (another name Ch'en Chien-hsiao), and thereafter moved to Tientsin to continue for a time, and other of their publications such as *Save the Nation* (*Chiu-kuo*). Secret publications put out by anarchists and socialists, such as the *Evolution, Workers' Companion, Peace,* and *Voice of the People,* were confiscated; and eleven prostudent newspapers such as the *Social Welfare Daily, Peking Morning Post,* and *Peking Gazette* were also suppressed.[4] On May 25 the Ministry of Education ordered all students to return to their classes within three days. Meanwhile, three measures were planned by the government to deal with the students: to intervene with armed force in the administration of the schools; to dissolve the student organizations; and to dispatch policemen to the schools to put pressure upon individual students to sign a promise to attend classes. Those who refused to sign would be dismissed. The students ignored the order to resume classes. And the teachers in Peking protested at once to the government, threatening to resign as a body if the government took such drastic measures.

Faced with such opposition, the government moderated its tactics. It promised to drop the plan of intervention by armed force for the time being, and in turn asked the teachers to persuade the students to return to classes. Officials from the Ministry of Education were also sent to negotiate with the students. Other lenient measures were tried to ameliorate the situation. Acting Minister Yüan proposed to start the summer vacation a month earlier than usual in order to disperse the students. Eventually the Higher Normal College and the College of Law and Political Science did start their vacations early. But in this tense situation the students could hardly be dispersed. Another proposal, suggested by Lü T'iao-yüan, the Governor of Anhwei Province, was that a special civil service examination should be immediately opened to all students. The aim of this proposal was to draw some of the abler and more ambitious students into the government in order to weaken the student movement. The government was apparently impressed by this novel idea and started plans to carry it out. Although it was somewhat naive and did not in fact materialize, the proposed program reflected a social problem which was felt at the time. As has been pointed out in the introduction, since the abolition of the old civil service examinations, no new personnel recruitment system had been substituted. More than a decade passed with the new intellectuals still finding no normal channel through which they might enter government office; yet to enter government office remained the ideal of their lives, as tradition dictated. This was a problem which had existed for a long time, and it would certainly be wrong to imply that the immediate motive of the students' movement was to get themselves into the government. A sound recruitment system might have helped to re-establish a social equilibrium for the young Republic in the long run; but a hasty gesture of this sort could do little to stop a storm which was caused by so many complex factors.

However, the government's efforts to secure a compromise with the students did have some effect. At first, the students in Peking emphasized anti-Japanese speeches in their activities. About three thousand of them worked in the streets every day. Later, in order to avoid provoking diplomatic difficulties with Japan, they gave up the all-out campaign of anti-Japanese speeches by large groups and shifted their activities to speeches by individuals or small clusters of students (mainly organized as the Groups of Ten) and to promoting the purchase of native goods. They acted as volunteer sales agents for Chinese industrialists and for the merchants who sold native goods. They made a thorough survey of marketing and production in the city, listing more than eighty Chinese factories and companies which could manufacture goods to substitute for those usually purchased from the Japanese, such as straw hats, luxuries, and office equipment. They recommended this list to all shops. Their work included studies of markets, prices, and possibilities for many economic reforms. Several million pamphlets and leaflets were printed and distributed. Their activities became concentrated and intensive, but quite orderly and peaceful.[5]

The Peking government, with a pro-Japanese group behind it, determined to suppress forcibly this intolerable campaign now that student passions appeared outwardly to be a little on the ebb. On June 1 President Hsü of the Republic issued two mandates.[6] The first of them praised Ts'ao, Lu, and Chang, saying that the Republic owed a great deal to them. The second accused the students of jeopardizing public order and security and admonished them to return immediately to their books. It also intimated that such organizations as the student unions and the student volunteer corps would be suppressed. Martial law was proclaimed in the capital.[a]

Mass Arrests of June 2, 3, and 4

The resumption of a stern policy was marked, the afternoon of the next day, i.e., June 2, by the arrest of seven students who were selling Chinese goods in the Tung-an Market in Peking.[b] The students were outraged. Their union met that evening and decided to carry on their work on a bigger scale. They decided that the next day they would set out upon their lecturing tours in larger numbers, fifty in each group. They would not mention any boycott

[a] Reinsch thought that the Peking government made a technical mistake in whitewashing Ts'ao and his confederates, and thus arousing the students at a time of relative quiet. According to Tseng Ch'i, late in May, when he went from Shanghai to Peking as a representative of the Corps of Chinese Students in Japan for National Salvation to support the Peking student movement, he found that the situation had become quiet and people like Li Ta-chao, Ch'en Tu-hsiu, and K'ang Pai-ch'ing tended to encourage moderation among the students. Tseng claimed that, against Li's and K'ang's advice, he made several speeches among the students to incite their protest against the government at this critical time. He also said that Yi K'e-ni, a student at Peking University from Hunan Province, was one of the most earnest and positive student leaders in the event.[7] Yi later became Tuan Hsi-p'eng's secretary in the Kuomintang.

[b] A telegram addressed to the whole country by the Student Union of Peking dated June 3 reads: "Although public speeches in groups have been suspended for the sake of avoiding diplomatic complications, our efforts to promote the purchase of native goods and our individual speeches were not interrupted. Yet the government, taking more and more peculiar actions, arrested seven students yesterday. We students feel greatly indignant."[8] The policy of mass arrests was reportedly suggested and insisted on by Tuan Chih-kuei, the Commander-in-Chief of the Armed Forces for the Protection of the Capital.[9] Hsü Shu-cheng, of the Anfu group, seemed to have been reluctant to support any drastic measures in dealing with the students since his return to Peking after the May Fourth Incident. Chang Kuo-t'ao, who was the head of the public speech corps of the Peking Student Union, said later that he was among the seven arrested on June 2.

against Japan but preach patriotism and persuade the citizens to buy native goods. In case any one of the fifty lecturers was arrested, the rest would go to the jail with him in a body.

On the morning of June 3, more than nine hundred (some reports say about two thousand) students carrying white flags started the lecturing tours, numbering from ten to sixty in each group. Police patrols in the city had been multiplied several times. Cavalrymen galloped along the streets. They tried to disperse the students and their audiences. As a result, a great number of students and bystanders were injured either by horses or by being beaten. The student union immediately telegraphed to the Shanghai press, reporting that 178 students were arrested by soldiers and policemen that morning; by afternoon arrests had increased to 400. This overtaxed the facilities of the prisons in the capital. The government had to turn the big buildings of the Law School of Peking University into a temporary student prison, on the front gate of which a sign "The First Student Prison" was posted. In the telegram to the Shanghai press, the Student Union of Peking said:

Today [June 3] there were over 900 students from all schools making street speeches and 178 of them were arrested by the police and troops. The Law School of Peking University has been seized by soldiers and policemen and converted into a temporary prison for those arrested students. Surrounding the school twenty barracks were set up. All communications in the area were severed. Army and police officers insulted the students at will, seizing and destroying the national flags and school banners held by the students. Those students who resisted the seizure and destruction were badly beaten with guns, and subsequently two of them were severely wounded. They were then imprisoned in the headquarters of the infantry commander and flogged. Whether they will be kept alive is not certain. Besides this, numerous students were wounded by the cavalrymen. . . .[10]

On June 4 a report on the Peking situation of June 3 was sent by telegram from Tientsin to Shanghai:

Yesterday [June 3] at 10 a.m. students in Peking made street speeches on a large scale and many of them were arrested by soldiers and policemen. Four hundred students are now imprisoned in the building of the [former] Institute for Translations (I-hsüeh Kuan) of Peking University. The building was surrounded by armed forces and barracks were erected. No food is allowed to be sent in. Two students were arrested by soldiers of the infantry headquarters, then flogged and imprisoned. Those students who have not been arrested are continuing their speech tours, and send telegrams to students of each province and country asking for their immediate support and help.[11]

John Dewey and his wife reported from Peking on June 4:

We saw students making speeches this morning about eleven, when we started to look for houses, and heard later that they had been arrested, that they carried tooth brushes and towels in their pockets. Some stories say that not two hundred, but a thousand have been arrested. There are about ten thousand striking in Peking alone.[12]

In spite of the arrests, the students did not give up. The street lecturers were reinforced again and again. Finally, by the end of June 4, the government had about 1,150 student prisoners on its hands. The buildings of the School of Science of Peking University were turned into a second temporary prison, and those of the School of Letters were also surrounded by troops.[13] To this threat of armed retaliation, the students not only showed no sign of yielding, but intensified still more their lecturing ventures. On the morning of June 5 more than 5,000 of them lectured on the streets. Every street, lane, park, and market place was turned into a public meeting ground. They stood on boxes and talked in tears. The Peking authorities could not make any more arrests, but dispersed the audiences, who were considerably touched by the boys.

During the height of the mass arrests, most of the students in the city displayed their determination and prepared to go to prison. They had bedding strapped to their backs in order to settle in the detention quarters.[c] In many cases the police were softened by the students' patriotism and sympathized with them. When their superiors were not watching, they would ask the boys to move on and lecture at the next corner: "We are with you, sure, but we want no trouble; please go further down."[15]

The student prisoners had a hard time when they were first imprisoned. About seven hundred soldiers guarded them and twenty temporary barracks were set up surrounding the Law School buildings. Traffic around the area was stopped. On the first day no food was admitted to the buildings. The prisoners got bedding at four in the morning of June 4, but no food till after that time. But "those recently arrested had wisely provided themselves with knapsacks stocked with food before taking their lecture trips."[16] The wounded and the sick in the prison were not cared for at all.[d]

This drastic action by the government aroused fury throughout the country.

[c] It was reported that once when some students were arrested and about to go to prison, they stopped on the spot and allowed several foreign spectators to take photographs of them at the spectators' request. The police tried to interfere. "Wait a minute," the boys chided them for their lack of humor. "Can't you see that we've come fully prepared to be imprisoned? But before we go, let us give these kind foreigners some souvenirs."[14]

[d] Tsi C. Wang recorded: "Observation of the Law School prison, made by Dr. Hu Shih, revealed pitiful conditions, sickness, and hunger almost to the point of starvation. He begged the teachers to send them bread." Hu probably somewhat exaggerated the students' miserable condition in the school prison, for a *Ch'en Pao* reporter who visited the students on the afternoon of June 6 found their living conditions better and saw several hundred of them playing football in

Girl students came forth to join the protest. On June 4 more than a hundred of them went out to make street speeches. On the next day, more than a thousand of them from fifteen girls' schools in Peking assembled and marched to the President's palace to protest against treating students as bandits and using school buildings as prisons, to request the release of the young men under arrest, and to demand the freedom of speech — an action without precedent in Chinese history.[18]

The teachers also came to the students' rescue by sending in provisions and blankets. Eight representatives from the Teachers' Alliance of Peking, including an American professor of Hui-wen University, fought their way into the school prison to comfort the student prisoners.[19] The administrators of colleges and universities protested as had the girl students that educational institutions should not be turned into prisons.[20] On June 4, the Christians of Peking resolved to yield their pulpits and convert them into forums for the students.[21]

As soon as the miserable condition of the student prisoners was reported to the public, a storm of indignation was aroused against the government. Hundreds of individuals as well as representatives from various organizations, such as the Citizens' Diplomatic Association, the Girls' Student Union (Nü-hsüeh-sheng lien-ho-hui), the Peace Association (Ho-p'ing lien-ho-hui), and the Red Cross, each day went to the prisons to comfort the student prisoners, offering them food and other assistance. However, all offers of money were refused by the students.[e] The government was at the same time barraged with protests.

The June Fifth Merchants' and Workers' Strikes in Shanghai

The mass arrests caused passionate indignation in all the cities of China. But the greatest excitement was in Shanghai. The merchants, industrialists, and urban workers, stirred by this tumult, began to follow the leadership of

the courtyard.[17] Huang Yu-ch'ang, a professor at the Law School of Peking University, also visited the prison.

[e] Liang Ch'i-ch'ao's brother, Liang Ch'i-hsiung, presented to the imprisoned students one thousand *yuan*, relating that they were donated by a Ho of Canton. A representative of the student union in the building received the money and presented it to the legislative department of the student union. After a discussion, the department resolved to return it to Liang and subsequently published an advertisement in newspapers stating that such contributions would not be accepted. Even Tuan Ch'i-jui and his right hand man, Hsü Shu-cheng, the head of the Anfu Club, had tried to find a way to contribute to the students, saying that they were actually sympathetic with them but they were rejected. The integrity of the students in the incident remained firm; and as a result, they won the greatest respect from Chinese society.[22]

the new intellectuals in united, if limited, action. Moreover, the new intellectuals, involved in what was to prove a short-lived honeymoon with the new social and economic forces, began to realize that their further success depended on a thoroughgoing mass movement aimed at the transformation of the Chinese economy and society. These trends were manifested in the June fifth strikes, which marked the turn of the May Fourth Movement towards this new orientation.

It must be remembered that ever since the student strikes in Shanghai on May 26, students from all the middle schools and institutions of higher learning in the city had been carrying on their boycott campaign without a letup. Numerous impressive and thrilling episodes occurred in schools and in the community.[23] In the meeting with the student representatives on June 1 as arranged previously, the merchant leaders promised to take action in support of the students.

On June 2 when the government's mass arrests started, student representatives visited again the authorities of the Chamber of Commerce of Shanghai County to persuade them to take immediate action to support the student movement. But that day, the fifth of the fifth lunar month, was a holiday, i.e., the day of the Dragon-boat Festival, a day for settling accounts, and the merchants were busy. An emergency meeting of merchant leaders was scheduled for the next day. At the meeting, which was held at the chamber's office in south Shanghai on June 3 at 5:00 p.m., Ho Pao-jen, student leader of Shanghai, Hsü Te-heng, Huang Jih-k'uei, Tuan Hsi-p'eng, and Ch'en Pao-o, student representatives from Peking, made speeches asking the Shanghai merchants to maintain the boycott, to protest against the government's foreign and domestic policies, and, if the government failed to respond favorably, to cease to pay taxes. When the leadership of the chamber tried to postpone discussing the proposals, other merchant representatives enthusiastically supported the proposals. Agitation and disorder prevailed in the debate and in the presence of a number of uninvited merchants and clerks. At eight o'clock, without reaching a decision, the meeting was adjourned by the chairmen of the chamber until next day at 4:00 p.m.

On the afternoon of June 3, when the Chamber of Commerce of Shanghai County was preparing for the next meeting, it received an order from the Chinese police authority of the city, forbidding any further such gathering. Merchant and student representatives, arriving to attend the meeting, saw the order posted on the front door of the office and were met by a number of policemen and governmental officials, who forced them to leave the place. A crowd of several thousand merchants and other citizens waiting to observe the meeting was insulted and dispersed by the police. Feelings of indignation against the police and the government were roused among them. In the evening students made more speeches and passed handbills along the streets accusing the Shanghai local government of unconstitutional encroachment on people's freedom and rights, and inciting the merchants to take action against the government. At the same time, leaders of the Chamber of Commerce of Shanghai County promised to join with the Association of Education of Kiangsu Province in a petition to the Peking regime in favor of the students, in response to a letter from Huang Yen-p'ei, vice-president of the association.[24]

A more vigorous campaign to secure support from commercial and industrial circles was at once started by the Student Union of Shanghai after receiving on the afternoon of June 4 the telegram from Tientsin concerning the mass arrests at Peking. News extras, handbills, and leaflets carrying the information were immediately distributed. After 7:00 p.m., in every street students wearing white cloth caps [f] delivered their exciting speeches. Particularly active in south Shanghai, they visited all shops asking them to sign a promise to start a strike from the next day on. Almost all shops visited did so.[g] They bought and stored food for the coming event. The students were not dispersed by the armed police until midnight. A prediction was made by the Japanese consul general in Shanghai on June 3 and one by the Peking press on the next day that a commercial strike might take place in Shanghai on June 5.[26]

The strike did begin on the morning of June 5. At dawn, students had resumed their lecturing in the streets. In the morning, shops in south Shanghai did not open their doors. The movement swiftly spread to adjacent areas. About 8:00 a.m., shops in the streets bordering the French Concession joined the strike. It spread into the French Concession about an hour later, and to the British and American sections of the International Settlement between 10 and 11 a.m. It continued to extend like wildfire northward and by noon covered the whole city, and later expanded to the suburbs.[27] All sorts of shops were closed, including places of recreation and food stores. Some of the foreign shops were the only exceptions. This meant that within a few hours a city with a population of 1,538,500 was seized by an impromptu and sketchily organized commercial strike in support of the 13,000 striking students.[h]

[f] After the start of the boycott few Chinese wore straw hats, most of which were made in Japan.

[g] There was only one case reported, in Hsiao-tung-men, where a shopowner refused to sign the promise, but yielded after the students knelt to implore him.[25]

[h] In a letter to all foreign consulates in Shanghai dated June 6, the Student Union of Shanghai

The commercial strike gave the city a bleaker appearance than Westerners can readily imagine. Most of the shops in China do not have plate glass windows and doors in the Western style. They are closed by putting up heavy wooden shutters that seem designed to resist a siege. Consequently, when most of Shanghai's shops were closed at the same time, the city appeared to be expecting invasion or revolution. But in fact all this was carried out in orderly fashion after the first few days of the strike, during which over two hundred students were arrested by the police and soldiers while speaking on the streets. The students were released very soon and the situation quieted down.[29] The city was not deserted. On the contrary, streets were crowded with increasing audiences listening to the student street-corner orators. White paper signs were pasted on shop doors and windows all over the city, bearing legends such as "Merchants and students must unite to save China," "Give us self-government and return us the students," "No more business until the traitors are punished," "Stay in the prisons unto death, we will join you." [30] These legends reflected to an extent a rising consciousness of nationalism and desire for self-government among the merchants. They were aware of the need for uniting with the new intelligentsia in resisting aggression and oppression.

On the afternoon of June 5 a meeting of more than two hundred representatives from various social and political groups was held at the invitation of the Student Union of Shanghai. It was attended by such commercial, social, and political leaders as Yü Ho-te, Huang Yen-p'ei, Chiang Monlin, Yeh Ch'u-ts'ang, and Chang Tung-sun and such students as Tuan Hsi-p'eng, Hsü Te-heng, and Chu Ch'eng-hsün. Ho Pao-jen of Futan University presided over it. The representatives resolved unanimously to sustain the strike in support of the students and to form a permanent association of merchant and labor organizations, the press, and the student union, which became known as the Federation of All Organizations of China (*Ch'üan-kuo ko-chieh lien-ho-hui*, or *Kung shang hsüeh pao lien-ho-hui*). *The North-China Herald* reported that, in this meeting, "several speakers emphasized that the strike was not an anti-foreign movement—even the Japanese were to be spared. All present undertook to advise their friends to help to maintain peace and order." [31] In the following days the federation held a number of meetings to sustain the merchants' and workers' strikes and other mass movements. Later, on November 10, a formal

---

stated that 13,000 students in the city were on strike. A student representative, however, declared in a meeting at the Chamber of Commerce next day that the city had more than 20,000 students. From June 5 on, all students, including college, middle school, and elementary school, had actually joined in the strike. The figure of the population of Shanghai was given by the Chinese post office estimate in 1919.[28]

inaugural meeting of the federation was held and attended by over twelve hundred delegates from all provinces, including political leaders such as Huang Ta-wei (representing Sun Yat-sen), Chang Ping-lin, and Huang Yen-p'ei.

The character of this merchant strike is debatable. First of all, what group was the driving force in this strike? Three major groups were involved in it, the shopowners, the clerks, and the students. Were the shopowners or the clerks the decisive force? How important a role had the students played in the decision to strike? Many contradictory reports emerge.

Some said that most of the shopowners did not wish to strike. Right after the strike, Yü Ho-te (Yü Hsia-ch'ing), the president of the Chamber of Commerce of Shanghai (*Shang-hai tsung shang-hui*, an organization larger than that of Shanghai County), reported to Lu Yung-hsiang, the Military Governor of Shanghai (*Sung-hu hu-chün-shih*) that the strike had not been desired by shopowners, but was carried out by the clerks, who were very sympathetic to the students.[32] On the other hand, some reports suggested that many shops were closed spontaneously by the shopowners. It must be understood that one of the purposes of Yü Ho-te's report to the military governor seems to have been to minimize the responsibility of shopowners in the strike, a strike which was considered highly suspicious by the military forces. (The military governor was the actual ruler of the Chinese section of the city and the Chamber of Commerce of Shanghai represented the interests of the shopowners.)

Normally at this time, the clerks, unorganized and isolated from shop to shop, had scarcely any voice in the management of the shops. They were in a much weaker position in dealing with their employers than factory workers dealing with a manufacturer. It seems unlikely that the clerks could have staged a strike against the shopowners' will and interests under normal conditions. But the conditions were not normal, owing to public indignation over the political situation fanned by the vigorous activities of the students. Under the circumstances, the clerks' desire for a strike, which was of course favored by the students, could not be resisted by the shopowners. Any merchant who refused to cooperate in the anti-Japanese movement at the time might be called a traitor and ruined.

The students' influence upon social events and public sentiment through their propaganda campaign was of course tremendous and its importance in the merchant strike is unquestioned. They had won the sympathy of most of the people, including both clerks and merchants. Yü Ho-te's report to the military governor cannot be interpreted as proving that the merchants were not sympathetic with the students, for the reasons given above. Evidence to the contrary is furnished by the several telegrams in favor of the students sent by the various commercial organizations of Shanghai to the Peking government after the May Fourth Incident. John Dewey reported from Peking on June 24: "There was plenty of evidence that the students had practically succeeded in converting the merchants to their side; that they no longer stood alone, but had effected an alliance, offensive and defensive, with the powerful mercantile guilds. There was talk of a strike against paying taxes."[33]

Dewey's report is to be contrasted with the opinion of the authorities in the foreign concessions of Shanghai who reversed their favorable attitude toward the students after the June fifth strike and accused the students of forcing the merchants to close their shops. With few exceptions, no record has been found of complaints raised by the merchants against this alleged compulsion.[34]

It is true that not every Chinese merchant supported the students in all their activities. Chinese merchants in Shanghai had split in their attitudes toward Japan. Although the Chamber of Commerce of Shanghai expressed its sympathy with the young scholars, it had earlier expressed a somewhat pro-Japanese viewpoint. This had drawn furious criticism from the Federation of the Commercial Organizations of Shanghai (*Shang-hai shang-yeh kung-t'uan lien-ho-hui*), and from the press, including Ch'en Tu-hsiu's editorial in the *Weekly Critic.*[i] Chinese merchants who were carrying exclusively Japanese goods suffered heavy financial loss. They constituted, however, only a small minority at the time.

In any case, such financial loss as resulted from the short strike on the part of the merchants — estimated at over twenty million *yuan* for the seven days' commercial strike[36] — may well have been offset by other factors. After the shortlived wartime boom, China faced a market problem. With the gradual disintegration of the village economy, the purchasing power of the vast agrarian population showed a decline. Both the merchants and the native industrialists were faced with this problem. The exclusion of Japanese goods from the market and the exhortation to buy Chinese products in the boycott, whether a basic

[i] The editorial was written on May 18, 1919. It concerned the episode in which the conservative Chamber of Commerce of Shanghai sent on May 9 a telegram to the Peking government advocating direct negotiation with Japan over the Shantung question. This advocacy was welcomed by the Japanese press, but opposed by the powerful Federation of the Commercial Organizations of Shanghai, which represented fifty-six (later sixty-two) commercial guilds and organizations. Japan had before suggested, fearing intervention of other Great Powers, that the Shantung question should not be submitted to the Paris Peace Conference but directly negotiated between Japan and China. On May 13 the chamber retracted its telegram of May 9 to the government, and its president, Chu Pao-san, and vice-president, Shen Yung, resigned on May 14. Though their resignation was rejected by the Peking government, Chu was in fact succeeded by Yü Ho-te later.[35]

solution or not, brought temporary relief. At the end of May, the prices of native goods showed some sign of going up, as a result of the student movement.[j]

Positive support for the students was not limited to the merchants and their clerks. An unprecedented sympathy strike by urban workers in Shanghai took place on the same day. It started among textile workers and printers and spread to metal workers and others.[38] As there was no united and effective labor organization in China at the time, the starting dates of the workers' strike differed in various factories, ranging from June 5 to June 11. No complete statistics are available on the number of workers involved in the strikes. It was estimated by some at 60,000 to 70,000 and at 90,000 or more by others.[k]

According to available information, the strikes took place in at least forty-three factories, companies, and service trades. Among these were seven textile mills, seven metal mills, eight public utility enterprises such as bus lines, telephone and telegraph companies, seven transportation and communication companies such as railroads (Shanghai-Nanking and Shanghai-Hangchow) and steam navigation, and others including printing, paper milling, petroleum and oil marketing, the tobacco trade, and match milling. Other trades involved were restaurant workers, painters, carpenters, masons, drivers, and scavengers. It was estimated that about one hundred companies and factories were affected by the strikes.[40]

The losses to employers and employees as a result of the workers' strike were not reported. A rough estimate gives the total man-days lost in Shanghai as 350,000, and the wage loss as 204,400 *yuan*. This takes the minimum number of workers involved as 50,000 and is based on the officially estimated average daily wage of 0.584 *yuan*.[41] These figures must be viewed with skepticism.

The significance of the strike does not lie in its economic consequences, but in its nature. It was the first political and patriotic strike in Chinese history, one in which the aim of the workers was not to increase their wages or better their treatment. They were making a protest against the Chinese and Japanese governments. During the period of the strikes, there were negotiations between workers and managers to work out procedures for maintaining order or necessary public services. There was no serious conflict between them except at a

[j] After the students' general strike of May 19, students of Peking adopted a plan to penalize those merchants who raised the prices of native goods.[37]

[k] Teng Chung-hsia gives the number of workers involved in the strikes as from 60,000 to 70,000. According to a speech on June 7 by Mu Ou-ch'u, one of the important textile industrialists in Shanghai, the city had a population of 1,000,000 (the Post Office's estimate: 1,538,500) and 12 per cent were factory workers, the majortiy of whom were textile workers.[39]

few of the Japanese-owned factories. Even in the latter cases, the motives of the workers were not challenged by the management. In most cases, the Chinese owners of the factories and companies involved did not raise any substantial objection to the strike. It seems safe to interpret the strike as a manifestation of positive support for the students by the urban workers with the silent agreement of most of the employers. The effectiveness and significance of the workers' strikes in their political and social aspects were reflected by the following events. During the period of the strike, workers held mass demonstrations on June 9, 10, and 11 in Shanghai.[42] Although not all workers in the factories of Shanghai took part in the strikes, the movement aroused much political interest on the part of labor in general. One of the labor organizations in the city even went so far as to suggest in a telegram dated June 6 to Li Shun, the Military Governor (*tuchun*) of Kiangsu Province with an office in Nanking, that he start a rebellion and declare the province independent of the Peking government.[43]

A great number of citizens outside of organized industrial and commercial establishments joined in the strikes. The movement had such a thorough influence at the grass roots of society that even the beggars, thieves, prostitutes, and singsong girls went on strike. Later on, the postal clerks, policemen, and firemen also threatened that they would stop work if the government maintained its attitude toward the students.[44]

Settlement of the May Fourth Incident: Fall of the Cabinet and Refusal to Sign the Peace Treaty

Meanwhile the Peking government was learning a lesson when its mass arrests produced only stronger opposition from the students. The acting Minister of Education, Yüan Hsi-t'ao, faced double pressure both from the military group and from the students and social circles. He found no way out of the dilemma except to offer his resignation. At the same time the Cabinet, encountering such strong protests, once again wavered in its position. On the evening of the day the government had over one thousand student prisoners on its hands, the Cabinet met at the Premier's private home and resolved to accept Yüan's resignation and to appoint another vice-minister, Fu Yo-fen, to succeed him as acting Minister of Education.[1] From this time on, the govern-

---

[1] The Deweys wrote in Peking on Aug. 4: "It seems that the present acting Minister of Education [Fu] was allowed to take office under three conditions — that he should dissolve the University, prevent the Chancellor from returning, and dismiss all the present heads of the higher schools here. He hasn't been able, of course, to accomplish one, and the Anfu Club is correspond-

ment abandoned all hope of solving the student problem by force and began to try persuasion as a tactic without relaxing its determination to adhere to its foreign policy and to retain the three accused officials. Two actions of the government on June 5 exemplified this new tactic. The acting Minister of Education was replaced opening the way for compromise. And Hu Jen-yüan, former dean of the Engineering School of Peking University, was appointed chancellor of the university, but on a temporary basis and without any indication whether or not Ts'ai Yüan-p'ei's resignation had been accepted.[m] These moves were, however, interpreted by the students as showing that the government still intended to discipline the university.

The new acting Minister of Education immediately suggested a two-fold measure to solve the student trouble: (1) request the military and police authorities to withdraw the garrison of police and troops stationed around the school buildings; (2) through the school authorities and the Ministry of Education, ask the students to return to classes, with the understanding that thereafter the military forces and police should not participate in negotiations with the students.[48] Accordingly, on the afternoon of June 5, all troops and police were withdrawn from the school buildings. This sudden retreat on the part of the government was influenced by news from Shanghai that serious strikes were under way. The far-reaching effect of the merchant and worker strikes can not be overemphasized. The tension in Peking after June 5 was obvious to everyone.[49]

But after the withdrawal of the soldiers and police, the students refused to leave the school prisons until certain demands had been met. When the prisons were established they had begun to organize themselves in the buildings and now took further steps to guard themselves.[n] They immediately sent telegrams to all provincial councils, educational associations, chambers of commerce, agricultural societies, labor organizations, schools, and the press of the country accusing the government of "unlawfully ruining education, destroying the

---

ingly sore. He is said to be a slick politician, and when he has been at dinner with our liberal friends, he tells them how even he is calumniated — people say that he is a member of the Anfu Club." [45]

[m] Since Ts'ai's departure, the university had been governed by a committee selected from among the faculty, though Ts'ai had asked Wen Tsung-yü, dean of the Engineering School, to take care of his duty. The faculty refused to accept the new chancellor after his appointment.[46] Hu Jen-yüan was an official of the Yüan Shih-k'ai group and had become a rich rubber merchant in Malaya. He had also been chancellor of the university before Ts'ai took over the office.[47]

[n] The students in the Law School buildings elected 178 guards from among their number. Those in the Science School buildings elected members of the student Volunteer Corps for the Defense of Shantung as their guards. They also elected liaison officers in charge of receiving guests and other matters.[50]

judicial system, and injuring human rights." [51] At the same time, they presented their four demands to the Peking government: (1) that the three traitors should be dismissed; (2) that the students' freedom of speech should be guaranteed; (3) that they should be allowed to parade through the streets of Peking on being released from the prisons; and (4) that the government should publicly apologize to them for the arrests.[52] The second demand was in a sense a matter of principle, because the students of Peking had been lecturing continually in the streets and urging the purchase of only native goods after the mass arrests with no further intervention by the government.°

The government now became as anxious to get rid of the students as it had been to arrest and imprison them. Four officials from the Ministry of Education were sent to the prison on June 7 as an "unofficial delegation" to persuade the students to leave the jail. They failed. Next day, the government sent a two-man "pacification delegation," one member of which was the secretary of the State Council, to explain that the government recognized its mistake and apologized. The police also apologized and sent automobiles to the prison doors. A great number of social organizations sent consoling representatives, numbering several thousands. They mediated between the students and the government.

It was under such circumstances that the self-imprisoned students marched triumphantly out of the school prisons on June 8, amid firecrackers and cheers, to a fervent mass meeting and parade of welcome given by their fellow students and the citizenry. .Thus the mass arrests ended in the manner of an *opera bouffe* and made the government a laughing stock, a development usually fatal in China, as Western observers remarked.[54]

But the matter was not settled, since the government still had not accepted all the students' demands. Acts of protest against the government's pro-Japanese policies on the part of students, merchants, workers, and other social groups were still going on in many cities. The Shanghai strikes were not terminated by the release of the arrested students. On the contrary, the various social forces there merged for unified action in dealing with the government. On June 6, a total of 1,473 representatives of merchants, workers, students, the press, and others held a joint meeting of their Federation of All Organizations

---

° The Deweys reported on June 7: "The whole story of the students is funny and not the least funny part is that last Friday [June 6] the students were speaking and parading with banners and cheers and the police standing near them like guardian angels, no one being arrested or molested. We heard that one student pouring out hot eloquence was respectfully requested to move his audience along a little for the reason that they were so numerous *in statu quo* as to impede traffic, and the policemen would not like to be held responsible for interfering with the traffic." [53]

of China, in the office of the Chamber of Commerce of Shanghai, attended by a number of economic, political, and social leaders. The representatives demanded that the Peking government severely punish the traitors; otherwise, the strikes would continue and the merchants would refuse to pay their taxes as a gesture of protest.[55]

Two declarations were issued by the joint meeting. One was directed to the foreigners in China:

> The real purpose of the strikes now carried out by the citizens of Shanghai is to awaken the Peking government to annul the unjust and improper treaties [concluded with Japan] which injure the sovereignty of China, and to punish the diplomatic and military authorities who are responsible for these treaties. We will not do anything which will hurt in the least the interests of the citizens of friendly countries. The strikes are the most peaceful and righteous manifestation of patriotism by the Chinese people. We hope that all the people of friendly countries understand our difficulties; we hope that they will help uphold justice and give us spiritual support.[56]

This declaration was apparently countering the Japanese government's charge that the anti-Japanese activities constituted an anti-foreign movement.

In the other declaration, the federation of merchants, workers, students, and the press urged the citizens of Shanghai to maintain order, after explaining that the federation's aim was to fight for freedom within the limits of law.[57] In some parts of the city, boy scouts and students came out to help the police to maintain order. A sense of unity prevailed so deeply among all social forces that even the hobos, robbers, and underworld gangs and societies, such as the members of the Ch'ing-hung Pang (Green-red Society), expressed their loyalty to the movement, and helped to maintain peace and order. Consequently, the city, where vice was as widespread as that of Chicago or New York, saw no disturbances during the period of the strike.[58]

The merchants' and workers' strikes spread rapidly to other cities. The merchants of Nanking closed all shops beginning on June 6. More than twenty-four hundred students mobilized to join the campaign, and a fight with the troops and police resulted. Many students were wounded. From June 6 to 9 merchants in the cities along the Yangtze River joined the strike one after another. Transportation along the river was halted. North China was also involved in the movement.[P] Workers of the Tangshan Station on the Peking-

[P] Major cities in these areas involved in commercial strikes were: Sungkiang, Ningpo, Amoy, Nanking (all started on June 6), Chinkiang (started on June 7), Soochow, Changchow, Wusih, Yangchow, Chiukiang, Wuhu, Anking (all started on June 8), Hangchow (started on June 9), Wu-Han, Tsinan, Tientsin (all started on June 10), and Foochow (started on June 14 because of government intervention in the students' boycott movement).[59]

Mukden Railroad and of the Ch'ang-hsin-tien Station on the Peking-Hankow Railroad also struck. The workers in these places held demonstrations. Labor organizations in embryo form were established.[60]

All these strikes exerted great pressure upon the Peking government. But the most serious blow came from Tientsin, which economically dominated the capital. On June 5 and 6 students in Tientsin had held two demonstrations to protest the mass arrests of students in Peking and the suppression of free speech. On June 9 a mass meeting of citizens was sponsored in Tientsin by the student union, attended by more than twenty thousand citizens. The Chamber of Commerce of Tientsin, under the persuasion and coercion of the students and citizens, decided to call forth a merchants' strike from June 10. On the afternoon of June 9 news of the Tientsin decision reached Peking. The psychological reaction in business circles of Peking at once stirred up a monetary panic. Bank notes issued by the Bank of China and the Bank of Communications suddenly became unpopular on the market. Merchants in the capital also intended to suspend business. The government began to realize the seriousness of the situation. On June 9, Kuo Tse-yün, the Secretary General of the State Council brought to the Student Union of Peking University the news that a presidential mandate accepting Ts'ao Ju-lin's resignation was being printed, but that the other two officials would not be dismissed because their dismissal might provoke irritation in Sino-Japanese relations. Shortly after this, the news from Tientsin became worse. Workers were going to strike on June 10, following the merchants' suit; and all city utilities would stop if the situation continued. A group of Chinese bankers also warned the government: "The financial market cannot be maintained tomorrow, if the problem is not solved today."[61] Wild rumors circulated. There was fear that the soldiers could no longer be counted upon. It was even said that a regiment in the nearby Western Hills was going to start for Peking to side with the students.[q] The students of Peking had already resolved to march to the office of the President of the Republic on the morning of June 10 to urge his action on the dismissal of the three officials.

The Cabinet in the face of this crisis convened at midnight of June 9 and decided to accept the resignation of Ts'ao Ju-lin, Chang Tsung-hsiang, and

---

[q] John Dewey reported: "Undoubtedly the spread of the strike to the merchants and the fear of its further extension, were the actuating motives in the inglorious surrender. But the students had managed to get their propaganda into the army. Rumors were afloat that the armies could not be counted upon for further suppressions — especially as pay was far in arrears. After their triumphant march out from their self-made prison, students were heard to lament that the government changed the guards so often they had not been able to convert more than half their jailers."[62]

Lu Tsung-yü. The orders of dismissal[r] were published on the morning and afternoon of June 10.[63] The Shanghai Chamber of Commerce tried twice to terminate the strikes on June 9 and June 11, but the action was delayed because of the uncertainty of the dismissals.[64] The strikes in the city did not stop until the morning of June 12, having lasted a little more than seven days.[65] About a day or two later all the merchants' and workers' strikes elsewhere stopped. The students had won a major battle.

But to wipe out the traitors was only one of the aims of the movement. Other demands, for example to refuse to sign the Peace Treaty at Versailles and to retain Ts'ai Yüan-p'ei as the chancellor of Peking University, were still unmet. Although the strikes were over, the various social groups and students still insisted on their other demands. On the same day that the orders for the dismissal of the three officials were published, President Hsü Shih-ch'ang submitted his own resignation, but this was rejected by Parliament. However, because of the government's failure in the student trouble and in the Shanghai Peace Conference, Premier Ch'ien Neng-hsün was permitted to resign his post on June 13 (he had been both Premier and Minister of the Interior since February 1918; he resigned both posts), and the Minister of Finance, Kung Hsin-chan, was appointed acting Premier.[66] In the following months the President had difficulty in finding anyone to form a new Cabinet because of the formidable situation caused by the May Fourth Incident and other domestic troubles.[s] The remnant Cabinet was still controlled by the Anfu Club.

At the time the three officials were dismissed, the schools were all near summer vacation. Students went home and carried their propaganda to the villages. But a permanent student headquarters was established in Shanghai.

Previously, late in May, the two student unions of Peking and Tientsin invited each student union in Shanghai, Nanking, Taiyuan, Tsinan, Paoting, Hankow, and Hangchow to send two representatives to Shanghai to organize a student union of all China. On June 1 student representatives from Peking, Shanghai, Nanking, Tientsin, and Japan had resolved in an informal meeting in Shanghai that a Student Union of the Republic of China (*Chung-hua-min-kuo hsüeh-sheng lien-ho-hui*) should be established. They set up a tem-

---

[r] The orders were published separately. The one permitting Ts'ao's resignation was released early in the morning. The one regarding Lu was published in the afternoon under the pressure of Shanghai bankers, and the one regarding Chang a few hours later because of further warnings from the same group and Shanghai Chamber of Commerce. On June 10, Tseng Yü-chün, Vice Minister of Communications, was appointed acting Minister, and on June 18, Li Ssu-hao was appointed to succeed Lu Tsung-yü as Director General of the Bureau of Currency Reform.

[s] It was not until Sept. 24 when Chin Yün-p'eng, a warlord connected with Tuan Ch'i-jui, was appointed acting Premier that a new Cabinet was formed.[67]

porary office in the World Association of Chinese Students in Shanghai for the preparatory work of the organization, and asked all the student unions of individual institutions and cities to send representatives to that city two weeks later to arrange matters. The Student Union of the Republic of China was then established on June 16 in Shanghai by more than thirty student representatives from important provinces and cities, with over two hundred prominent guests from other social and economic groups attending the meeting. On June 18 the representatives elected Tuan Hsi-p'eng as chairman and Ho Pao-jen vice-chairman of the union with a tenure of one year.[t] The Student Union of China was well organized and became a political force in later decades, as attested by a leading Chinese political historian:

Starting from this [May Fourth] Movement, student unions were established in every city and every province all over the country, and a Student Union of All China was also founded. I may venture to say that the then long established Kuomintang was probably not as well organized and active as the newly born Student Union of All China. Later on, the Chinese Communist Party and the Kuomintang relied mainly upon the student unions in provinces under the control of warlords as headquarters for propagating their doctrines and securing young members. This shows how significant the so-called "May Fourth Movement" was in Chinese political history.[69]

After June 11, the issue between the students and the government centered

---

[t] The union was established in a meeting at Ta Tung Hotel, attended by 11 student representatives from Peking, 3 from Nanking, 1 from Tientsin, 2 from Hangchow, 2 from Shanghai, 3 from Japan, 2 from Nantung, 2 from Wu-Han, 2 from Chiahsing, 2 from Ningpo, 2 from Chungming, 2 from Sungkiang, 1 from Paoting, 2 from Soochow, 1 from Chiukiang, 1 from Yangchow, 2 from Shantung Province, 1 from Chilin Province, 2 from Anhwei Province, 2 from Honan Province, and 1 from Chekiang Province. Representatives from other provinces and cities were on the way. Among the student representatives attending the meeting, there were quite a few who later became famous in China, such as Tuan Hsi-p'eng, T'ang Ping-yüan, Lu Mei-seng, Hsü Te-heng, Huang Jih-k'uei, Chang Po-ch'ien, Yang Ch'ien (from Peking), Ho Pao-jen (Shanghai), Ts'ui Shu-hsing (Shantung), Liu Chen-hua (Japan), Chang Ch'i-yün (Ningpo), later Secretary General of the Kuomintang Party and Minister of Education in the Nationalist government in Formosa. Ch'en Pao-o of Peking University must have attended the meeting. His name was probably misprinted as Lu Tsung-o in some reports. Ch'en later received his M.A. from London University and became a professor in psychology at Peking University and Wu-Han University. Some report that Wen I-to (the famous poet and later one of the leaders of the Democratic League, who was assassinated in 1946) and Chou Ping-lin (later dean of the Southwestern Associated University [Hsi-nan lien-ho ta-hsüeh] at Kunming) also attended the meeting. This is not shown in the early records. Among the guests were Huang Yen-p'ei, Chiang Monlin, and Li Teng-hui. Tuan Hsi-p'eng (1896–1948) later studied at Columbia, Berlin, and Paris Universities and became one of the important organizers of the Kuomintang. In 1932 he was Vice Minister of Education, and after V-J Day vice chancellor of the Central University of Political Sciences (Kuo-li cheng-chih ta-hsüeh). Hsü Te-heng was later a prominent professor in Peking, one of the influential members in the People's Political Council which operated in the period 1938–1948, and the head of a minority party, the Chiu-san hsüeh-she, in Communist China after 1949.[68]

principally on the problem of whether China should sign the Peace Treaty. Prior to May 13 the government had no fixed policy concerning the problem.[70] After June 4, when the Chinese delegation at Paris asked Peking for instructions in the matter, the government concluded that it would be more beneficial to China to sign it. Former premier Tuan Ch'i-jui, the Anfu Parliament, the President, and Chinese diplomatic circles all concurred.[71] Consequently on June 24 the government confidentially instructed the delegation to sign the Peace Treaty, if their protests finally failed entirely.[u]

The Chinese public learned this news and was shocked. Numerous groups including merchants, industrialists, and workers denounced the government's action. The Student Union of Peking urged the President of China to change his instructions. Several hundred representatives from various groups petitioned him, standing in front of the President's office for two days and two nights weeping and remonstrating without sleep. Citizens in Shanghai and Shantung held mass meetings and threatened that, if the government signed the treaty, they would declare their independence from the Peking regime.[73] Under such threats from the public, President Hsü on June 25 sent a telegram to Paris from Peking reversing his previous decision, but it was not received by the Chinese delegation before the time set for the signature of the treaty.[74] The belatedness of this instruction was later interpreted by the Canton government as a trick to evade responsibility. "The Peking government sent the later telegram with the certainty," declared the Southerners, "that it would be received only after the treaty had been signed so the Peking government could declare that the delegates acted too hastily and contrary to instructions." [75] Whether this is true or not is difficult to judge, but it seems apparent that the Peking government was very reluctant to give this contrary instruction.

The Chinese delegates in Paris were not enthusiastic about signing the Peace Treaty, which failed to settle the Shantung question satisfactorily. But, knowing the Peking government's soft attitude toward Japan, Lu Chenghsiang, the chief Chinese delegate, hesitated to act against the instructions of the Peking regime, despite the pressure of public opinion.[v] On the other hand,

[u] President Hsü Shih-ch'ang advocated signing the peace treaty. In his letter of resignation of June 10, he stated that one of the reasons for submitting his resignation was that he felt it necessary to sign the treaty, whereas public opinion, "ignorant of diplomatic reality," as he said, objected to it.[72]

[v] The Southerners made this charge, saying, "Although Mr. Lu Ts[Ch]eng-hsiang refrained from any declaration, it appears that among the causes of fears entertained by the Chinese Chief Delegate the principal one was fear of the consequences which would probably ensue if he disobeyed secret instructions given him to sign the treaty. Non-compliance with Peking instructions will mean for him the loss of his portfolio of foreign affairs." [76] This is not necessarily true, since all the delegates extended their resignations after refusing to sign. Judging from Lu's communica-

the Chinese delegates in Paris had been under heavy pressure from the Chinese students, workers, and overseas Chinese in France, who demanded that they refuse to sign the treaty in its present form. They told the delegates that if they signed it, they would be treated as the students of Peking had treated Ts'ao Ju-lin. The number of telegrams received by the delegates from the Chinese people and social organizations asking that they refuse to sign amounted to seven thousand.[78] Under these circumstances, C. T. Wang, the Southern delegate, followed by V. K. Wellington Koo, declared that he was determined to refuse to sign, even if the Peking government insisted on it.[w]

On June 28, the date for the signing of the Peace Treaty, Chinese students, workers, and overseas Chinese in Paris surrounded the headquarters of the Chinese delegation at the Lutitia Hotel and the residence of Lu Cheng-hsiang, a French sanatorium at St. Cloud, where he had suddenly moved, according to the Southerners, in order to avoid "pressure from his colleagues who were against this signature." [81] They surrounded the delegates to prevent their going out to sign the treaty. Only when French guns announced to the world that the Versailles Treaty was signed did the Chinese students and workers leave their self-assigned posts. It was under such circumstances that the Chinese delegation, upon learning that their final proposal, that is China's signature of the treaty be conditional on her reserving her right to reconsider the Shantung question in the future, was unacceptable to the conference, at last unanimously decided, without Peking's approval, to refuse to sign the Peace Treaty with Germany. At the same time, the delegation submitted to the President their resignations as a body.[82]

China's refusal on June 28 to sign the Peace Treaty with Germany marked the successful conclusion of the mass protest which had begun with the May

---

tions to the Peking government, one may assert that originally he did not intend to oppose the weak policy of Peking toward the Shantung question. Nevertheless, he was probably very reluctant to sign the treaty under such circumstances. Writing in his memoirs in 1943 when he had become a monk of the Abbey of Saint-André near Bruges in Belgium, and without mentioning the public pressure during the Paris Conference, Lu stated, "For the first time in my career I believed it to be my duty not to obey. Our country owed it to herself to consent no longer to letting herself be played with. I was not willing to sign my name yet again to unjust clauses, and I took it upon myself alone to refuse my signature. In the evening of that same day, very late, when the closing session of the Conference had come to an end several hours before, an entirely unexpected telegram from my Government gave me the counter-order which I had had the boldness to carry out of my own accord." [77]

[w] In an interview with Fifield in Washington, D.C., on Oct. 30, 1951, Koo noted that Lu and Wang had manifested their willingness to sign and "had already sent their seals to be affixed to the treaty." [79] This statement contradicts Lu's report to Peking before the refusal to sign that Wang was the first and most vigorous opponent of signature.[80] Lu's report seems closer to the truth since Wang was a Southern delegate and a forceful personality.

Fourth demonstration. On July 22 the Student Union of China declared an end to all student strikes. In July, Ts'ai Yüan-p'ei promised to return to Peking and resume the chancellorship of Peking University. On July 30, Chancellor Hu Jen-yüan was removed from the post, and Ts'ai returned to Peking on September 12 and resumed the post on September 20.[83] The chancellors of the other colleges and universities in Peking also resumed their posts.

Attempts to Split the Students after the Settlement

None the less, at the close of this period, a few episodes in Peking exemplified the uneasy character of the truce between the government and the students. When the thirty-two students who had been arrested in the May Fourth Incident were released on bail in May, the heads of the schools gave assurances that the students would not engage in further disorder, and it was understood that the released students were nominally subject to legal summons later. Consequently, when the fall semester began, the government demanded that the heads of the schools submit the students for trial in court. The school officials replied that those students had not returned to their respective schools. Public opinion considered the demand of the government "a breach of faith." [84] The government, which did not really wish to provoke more trouble from the students, probably made the demand as a device to save the face of the warlords. After this gesture, the matter was dropped.

However, when Ts'ai Yüan-p'ei promised to return to the Peking University, some militaristic reactionaries in the government tried to discredit the students at the university and make trouble. On the evening of July 16, some members of the Anfu Club gave a banquet at the Cheng-wen-she (Political News Society) to a few students of the university, and some who intended entering. The banquet was also attended by officials of the secretariat of the Anfu-controlled Senate. The officials tried to bribe the students to start a movement against those students and professors who had been connected with the demonstrations. A meeting for this purpose was scheduled for the next day. Resolutions for the meeting were prepared. These stated that a few noisy, self-seeking individuals, anxious for notoriety, had fostered the whole student movement and coerced their weaker followers. The resolutions also declared, in the alleged name of a thousand students, that the majority had objected to the whole agitation and did not want Ts'ai back.[85] But late in the night, two students who had attended the banquet gave the information to their fellows who had been active in the movement. The next day when the plotters met in the School of Law and Political Science, about one hundred student supporters of the movement broke in and took the five bribed students prisoner, gave them a trial, obtained from them a written statement confessing their plot with the reactionary clique, and locked them up in the School of Science as a punishment, whence they were released by the police in the evening. Consequently, on July 18 warrants were sworn out and several leaders of the punitive group were arrested by the police. The government indicted them in the local law court, charging them with conducting an illegal trial.[86]

This aroused great indignation. Liu Ch'ung-yu (*tzu*: Sung-sheng, d. 1941), an eminent lawyer of the time and a member of the Chinputang, offered to defend the students. Though some of them received sentences from the court on August 26, they actually won the support of the public.[87] The bribery by the reactionary politicians became public scandal, and educators indignantly remarked that "officials had no business interfering in a matter that concerned only the students." [88] Some of the students indicted were members of the New Tide Society and other organizations who were later active as leaders in various fields in China.[x]

As indicated, in the closing period of the agitation following the May Fourth Incident, politicians and militarists tried to infiltrate the student body and failed. The majority of Chinese students, though often naive and emotional, refused to be bribed, and remained true to their cause.

Some Questions Regarding the Settlement

These trials provide some hint of the concept of law in China. The May Fourth Incident was considered by most Chinese intellectuals to have placed moral, social, and political issues above the law. To Westerners who are accustomed to the forms of regular legal procedures, the incident and the subsequent mass actions may seem lawless. However, acute Western observers such as John Dewey saw the movement in terms of "the moral sense of the community" instead of "a purely legal treatment." "It is to be doubted," said Dewey in the spring of 1920, "whether China will ever make the complete surrender to legalism and formalism that Western nations have done. This may be one of the contributions of China to the world. There is little taste even among the advanced elements, for example, for a purely indirect and representative system of legislation and determination of policy. Repeatedly in the last few

---

[x] The students indicted include Lu Shih-i, Wang Wen-pin, Meng Shou-ch'un, Yi K'e-ni, Ti Fu-ting, and Liu Jen-ching.

months popular opinion has taken things into its own hands and, by public assemblies and by circular telegrams, forced the policy of the government in diplomatic matters. The personal touch and the immediate influence of popular will are needed." [89] But more accurately, the incident should be understood as a result of an abnormal political situation. The people, and the new intelligentsia in particular, actually lost confidence in the Peking government. The incident probably took place only because, under the circumstances, the people could not change or control the government through legal process.

Considering as a whole the developments following the incident, one can recognize that the new intellectuals had scored a significant victory over warlordism and conservatism. But the victory was quite superficial in certain respects. Although the German Peace Treaty was not signed by China, the Shantung question was left unsolved. The three pro-Japanese officials were dismissed, but their successors all came from the same pro-Japanese Anfu Club. The new Cabinet was also controlled by the same military group. Even though Tuan Ch'i-jui stepped down from the government a year after the May Fourth Incident, succeeding warlords were worse than he. It must be noted that Tuan was, after all, a more restrained warlord than many. It was he who was responsible for overthrowing Chang Hsün's monarchical restoration — no matter what his motive — and for bringing China into World War I on the side of the Allies. Ch'en Tu-hsiu pointed out at the end of 1919 that other warlords and bureaucrats, either in the North or in Canton, were in no way better than Tuan, Ts'ao, Lu, Chang, and the Anfu Club.[90] Indeed, the Peking government's treatment of the intellectuals in 1919 was not more severe than that adopted by warlords in other times.

Conditions at the time of the movement were unusually favorable for its success. Tuan's control over the Peking government was incomplete at the time. His power was checked in a sense by the Chihli group, another warlord faction under the leadership of Feng Kuo-chang and Ts'ao K'un, and by the moderate Study Clique. Furthermore, the President, Premier, and Minister of Education during the period of the incident were all civilians. They stayed in office by keeping a balance of power among the various military and civilian factions. In addition, the country was in effect divided into North and South. The Southern revolutionary government had a rising favorable reputation with the new intellectuals and the public. The new intellectuals' success in the May Fourth Incident had been achievable because, among other factors, there was a balance of power among those political and military groups. Although Tuan suffered a vital blow to his prestige from the incident and was replaced shortly thereafter by other and stronger military leaders, the intellectuals were never again able to find circumstances as favorable.

Despite the fact that the political accomplishments of the intellectuals' activities in these months were limited, they succeeded in other ways. During this time more of the new intellectuals were brought into closer contact with other groups in the society than ever before. The scholars, previously sheltered in ivory towers, had to come out into the market place. Events brought them experience with merchants, clerks, urban workers, and industrialists, as well as professional politicians and political party workers. In these adventures, the new intellectuals were awakened to the need for prolonged and broad programs "to go among the masses of the people, and enlighten and organize them." This led to the expansion of the new culture movement in the period immediately following.

CHAPTER VII

EXPANSION OF THE NEW CULTURE MOVEMENT, 1919–1920

Increasing Unity among the New Intellectuals

After the May Fourth Incident, the boys and girls of high schools and institutions of higher learning stole the show. But it was not simply a student movement; the vigorous doctrines of the new intellectual leaders, namely, the professors, teachers, and writers, lay behind it. Ch'en Tu-hsiu, Hu Shih, Ts'ai Yüan-p'ei, Li Ta-chao, Ch'ien Hsüan-t'ung, Lu Hsün, Chou Tso-jen, Liu Fu, Kao I-han, and other contributors to *New Youth* and *Weekly Critic* as well as some older political leaders of the Chinputang (such as Lin Ch'ang-min and Wang Ta-hsieh, who were considered pro-American) and the Kuomintang (such as Wang Ch'ung-hui) provided the inspiration for the movement by stimulating the students' interest in current Chinese affairs and awakening them to the realities of the modern world. Although they did not directly suggest the demonstration of May 4, the militant members of this group had been preaching that the youth should take responsibility for keeping watch over the government's policies and carrying out social reforms. In this light, the demonstration may be considered a logical result of the teachings of these new intellectual leaders.

From the time of the incident on, the new intellectual leaders were the most enthusiastic supporters of the students. The protests and resignations of Ts'ai Yüan-p'ei and the chancellors of other universities and colleges were the most effective moral support the students could have obtained. Hu Shih and Chiang Monlin were in Shanghai welcoming John Dewey when the incident took place in Peking, and did not learn of it until May 6,[1] but both they and Dewey immediately sympathized with the student movement. Early in June when the movement was at its climax, Ch'en Tu-hsiu, Hu Shih, Kao I-han, and other professors actually joined the students' action against the warlords and enthusiastically distributed handbills in the streets supporting the students and protesting against the warlords. Ch'en Tu-hsiu was arrested on June 11 for his active participation and his alleged relations with Bolshevik publications in Shanghai and imprisoned for eighty-three days. He was arrested when he was distributing the "Peking Citizens' Manifesto" (*Pei-ching shih-min hsüan-yen*), which demanded, among other things, dismissal of Hsü Shu-cheng and other pro-Japanese officials, abolition of the Peking police headquarters, and guaranty of the citizens' absolute freedom of assembly and speech, and proposed that, if the government failed to comply, the citizens should take "direct action to achieve fundamental reforms." [2]

Although in the incident the students' activities overshadowed those of the professors and teachers, during the two ensuing months the movement became a united action by the majority of the new intelligentsia. The Peking government's indiscriminate pressure on educators fused them more firmly than ever before. Those who had previously been lukewarm to the new literature or new thought movements responded with sympathy when the professors and students closest to these movements proved to be very active leaders of the admired May Fourth demonstration and later developments. And of course the support that other social, political, and economic groups gave the student movement also helped to strengthen and unify the new intellectuals.

The coalescence of the new intellectual leaders and their indignation at the warlords after the conclusion of the May Fourth Incident were clearly manifested in their writings celebrating Ch'en Tu-hsiu's release from prison in September 1919. The first issue of *New Youth* after the May Fourth Incident, which did not appear until November, presented poems on this subject in the vernacular by some leading intellectuals.[a] Hu Shih wrote a poem titled "Authority" (*Wei-ch'üan*), which was later reprinted in many middle school textbooks and widely read by young Chinese. In the poem, he described "Authority" sitting on the top of a hill, directing slaves in chains to dig minerals for him, and after the slaves had dug for ten thousand years, the hill was finally undermined and Authority fell in and was killed.[3] Liu Pan-nung's long poem had a similar theme in protest against authority.[4] Li Ta-chao's spirited contribution was addressed directly to Ch'en:

> We are rejoicing
> That you have come out of prison!
> Your words have been heeded
> By a number of decent youths:

[a] *New Tide* was also interrupted from May to Oct. because the editors and contributors were busy with the movement. This may indicate just how involved these new intellectuals were in the incident.

"Out of study, enter prison;
Out of prison, enter study." [b]
After they all go to prison,
The prisons will become studies.
Then even if you spend your life in prison
You will not suffer solitude.[7]

Ch'en Tu-hsiu answered these sentiments with a long poem, explaining his belief in universal love and forgiveness. At this time, Ch'en's writings expressed a mixture of romanticism and humanitarianism rather than Marxism-Leninism. He believed that all men, including authoritarians, economic exploiters, political oppressors, and militarists, are brothers. They should be saved, awakened, and enlightened, rather than hated. His poem affirmed that "those who really comprehend the truth will see all men as poor brethren, not as hateful enemies." "Sympathy" will unite them all. And this belief was his "true God." [8] It reflected the sense of identity of the new intellectual leaders who were psychologically cemented more firmly than ever before by a spirit of protest.

Though united in protest, they encountered greater difficulty in finding an affirmative doctrine acceptable to all of them. One principle had, however, been generally agreed upon as their basis for action after 1917, that is, the creation of a new society and civilization through the re-evaluation of all Chinese traditions and the introduction of Western concepts. Indeed, the period of the May Fourth Movement in China may well be regarded as an era of the "transvaluation" of all values, as was suggested in that period.[9]

The attack on traditionalism and warlordism was analyzed by Ts'ai Yüan-p'ei at the time in an ingenious parable. His article entitled "Floods and Beasts" began by reminding his readers that 2,200 years ago, Mencius likened the causes of turmoil in Chinese history to floods and beasts. Ts'ai applied this metaphor to the May Fourth Movement. The new thought was a flood. However, Ts'ai did not regard the flood as a purely negative force in the traditional manner, for if rivers were dredged and obstructions removed, the full force of the flood could be controlled and might benefit the people in irrigation. If, on the contrary, these harnessing measures were impeded, it might overflow and destroy everything. Ts'ai identified the beasts in the metaphor as the warlords

[b] This saying was quoted here by Li from Ch'en's "The Study and the Prison" (*Yen-chiu-shih yü chien-yü*), published in *Weekly Critic*, No. 25 (June 9, 1919), two days before his arrest. Ch'en's full text reads: "There are two sources of world civilization: one is the study, another is the prison. We the youth must make up our minds to enter the prison once out of the study, and enter the study once out of the prison. Only these provide the most lofty and sublime life. And only those civilizations born in these two places are true civilizations with life and value." [5] This saying of Ch'en's was also quoted by some student leaders as their watchword for their fight for freedom of thought.[6]

who ate the plain people. The contemporary task of China, as Ts'ai saw it, was to clear the flood channels and tame the beasts.[10]

Invigorated Programs of New Youth and New Tide

The new strength and cohesion among the intellectuals brought about the reorganization and expansion of *New Youth* and *New Tide* in the few months after the incident. *New Youth* magazine apparently had not had any formal organization but only a loosely-knit board of editors since the fall of 1917. There was no stated program for the magazine. Each editor or writer spoke for himself and they had widely differing viewpoints. Later on, more organization was introduced when a New Youth Society (*Hsin ch'ing-nien she*) was established. In the winter of 1919 a "Manifesto of *New Youth* Magazine" (*Hsin ch'ing-nien tsa-chih hsüan-yen*) was published which was said to express the "common opinion of the whole body of its members." Members joining the society were to be bound by it. The essentials of the manifesto were:

We believe that warlordism and mammonism in the world have resulted in numerous vices, and now should be given up.

We believe that, in the traditional ideas of politics, ethics, and economics in all countries of the world, there are many illogical and inhuman elements which thwart the progress of society. In order to seek social progress, it is necessary to break up the prejudices that are upheld as "unalterable principles" (*t'ien-ching ti-i*) or as "established from of old" (*tzu-ku ju-ssu*). Consequently, we are determined to get rid of these antiquated ideas, and, by synthesizing conclusions reached by ancient and modern thinkers and ourselves, to create new ideas in politics, ethics, and economics, and to establish the spirit of the new era, in order to adapt ourselves to the special circumstances of the new society.

Our ideal new era and new society are to be honest, progressive, positive, free, equal, creative, beautiful, kind, peaceful, full of universal love and mutual assistance, and pleasant labor; in short, happiness for the whole society. We hope that the hypocritical, the conservative, the negative, the bound, class-divided, conventional, ugly, vicious, warring, restless, idle, pessimistic elements, happiness for the few — all these phenomena will gradually diminish and disappear.

The new youth of our new society certainly will respect labor; he should according to his own ability and interest treat labor as free, pleasant, and beautiful rather than consider such a sacred thing a mere means for maintaining a subsistence.

We believe that the moral progress of mankind should expand to a standard above the life based on animal impulse (i.e., aggressive and possessive); therefore, we should extend a feeling of friendship and mutual assistance to all peoples of the world. But toward aggressive and possessive warlords and plutocrats we have to be hostile.

We advocate mass movement and social reconstruction, absolutely cutting off any relations with past and present political parties.

Although we do not believe in the omnipotence of politics, yet we recognize that politics is an important aspect of public life. And we believe that in a genuine democracy, political rights must be distributed to all the people. Even though there may be limitations, the criteria for the distribution will be whether they work or not, rather than whether they own property or not. This kind of politics is really inevitable in the process of introducing the new era and a useful instrument for the development of the new society. As for political parties, we also recognize them as a necessary device for political practice, but we will never tolerate membership in parties which support the interests of the few or of one class rather than the happiness of the whole society.

We believe that politics, ethics, science, the arts, religion, and education should all meet practical needs in the achievement of progress for present and future social life.

We have to give up the useless and irrelevant elements of the traditional literature and ethics because we want to create those needed for the progress of the new era and new society.

We believe that it is requisite for the progress of our present society to uphold natural science and pragmatic philosophy and to abolish superstition and fantasy.

We believe that to respect women's personality and rights is a practical need for the social progress at present, and we hope that they themselves will be completely aware of their duty to society.

Because we intend to put our principles to the test and strengthen our position, we welcome thoughtful and faithful opposition rather than unintelligent and indecisive agreement. But unless and until we are convinced by our opponents' reasoning, we will of course bravely and determinedly propagate what we believe. Hypocritical, confused, inertia-nourishing, and progress-blocking compromises from no fixed standpoint, as well as nihilistic, vague, unbelieving, unrealistic, and fruitless "absolute skepticism" are rejected.[11]

Several aspects of this manifesto should be noted. In the first place, it represents a mixture of idealistic socialism with liberalism of a strong international flavor. Shortly after World War I intellectual leaders of many countries had similar ideas. In March 1919, a *Déclaration d'indépendance de l'esprit* was published in France and signed by numerous prominent intellectual leaders of many countries, including Romain Rolland, Henri Barbusse, and Georges Duhamel of France, Bertrand Russell and Israel Zangwill of Great Britain, Georg F. Nicolai and Heinrich Mann of Germany, Benedetto Croce of Italy, Stefan Zweig of Austria, Ellen Key and Selma Lagerlöf of Sweden, Jane Addams of America, and many others.[12] In the declaration they denounced the intellectuals of the world for giving up their independence of thought and spirit and surrendering to force and joining the war for political, partisan, national, or class interests. They advocated democracy for all people and brother-hood among the nations. The declaration was translated into Chinese and published in both *New Youth* (the same issue which published the manifesto of the monthly) and *New Tide* in December of the same year.[13] The "Manifesto of *New Youth* Magazine" was more or less inspired and influenced by this declaration.

In the second place, the manifesto reveals the extent to which John Dewey's pragmatism had gained favor among most of these Chinese intellectual leaders. Marxist-Leninist ideas are not to be found obvious in the manifesto, though it was issued by Li Ta-chao, Ch'en Tu-hsiu, and other students and writers who were to be founding fathers of Chinese communism shortly thereafter. Experimentalism, both as a philosophy and as a scientific method, had in this period an upper hand over dialectic materialism. The idea of class struggle was also definitely rejected by Ch'en Tu-hsiu and most other Chinese intellectual leaders at the time.

Thirdly, when the new intellectual leaders had banded together at Peking University and around *New Youth* magazine in 1917, they had agreed not to involve themselves in politics. But in this manifesto they recognized that politics was one of the important aspects of public life, and that political parties were necessary for the application of political ideas to practical life. They were, however, still very reluctant to tie themselves to established political parties.

The strengthening of the unity of the new intellectuals was also exemplified by the reorganization of the *New Tide* group into a society on November 19, 1919, with an expanded program. Besides issuing the monthly, it began to publish a series of books, including translations from Western languages. Financial assistance from some new industrialists enabled it to do this and to send members abroad for study.[14]

Under such circumstances the activities of the new intellectuals increased considerably. Their activities developed mainly along two lines: an increase in the number of "new thought" publications and the concomitant spread of new ideas on the one hand, and the creation of social organizations and social services on the other.

Rapid Increase of New Publications and Revamping of Old

The Chinese press had made some progress in 1917 and 1918, but prior to the May Fourth Incident most publications were still old-fashioned and stereotyped in content. Chinese periodicals just prior to April of 1919, which were with a few exceptions published in the classical language, may be classified into four categories. The most formalized were the manifold official publications of the government in the form of monthly or weekly bulletins, often of a trifling and bureaucratic nature. In the second category were periodicals published by school or university authorities or by students, which mushroomed at the time. The contents were generally classroom assignments or unenlightening old-fashioned articles on well-worn academic subjects, for example, "On Emperor Han Kao-tsu's Bestowing an Honorary Title on Hsiang Po and Executing Ting Ku" (*Han Kao-tsu feng Hsiang Po tsan Ting-kung lun*), ghost stories, and the like. A third category covered magazines for general readers which commonly discussed everything without taking a stand on anything and had little if any literary value. Journals of opinion constituted the fourth category. They often published essays supporting the traditions and advocating the "national quintessence," as represented, for example, in the ancient ethical principle of "three bonds" (*san-kang*), namely, "the prince is the master of his ministers, the father the master of his sons, and the husband the master of his wife." Only a few of the journals of opinion concerned themselves with current social or scientific problems: *Pacific Ocean, New Youth, Weekly Critic*, and *Science* (*K'o-hsüeh*) represent the foremost of such publications edited by people with a modern outlook.[15] Almost all the periodicals in this last sub-category had either been established or drastically reorganized after 1915 and used the vernacular.

The stagnant and backward situation just described was not limited to the field of periodicals. It characterized all Chinese publications of the time. When Hu Shih returned to China from the United States in the summer of 1917, he could not find a single Chinese book on philosophy published within the past seven years. After a day's intensive search in Shanghai he found a book entitled the *History of Chinese Philosophy*. But, according to Hu, the author's contribution was only to the effect that "Confucius accepted the Mandate of Heaven" and "his concept of morality was to seek harmony between Heaven and Earth." Hu concluded from this that: "As a whole, the world of publication in Shanghai — the world of publication in China — has not produced in the last seven years two or three books worth reading! Not only is there no single book with a high standard of scholarship, but also not a single book one could read for pleasure while traveling. I felt like weeping when I discovered this peculiar situation."[16] The introduction of Western works to China was at the time limited almost entirely to those of the seventeenth or eighteenth centuries. Even teachers of English literature did not know the names of

Galsworthy or Bernard Shaw. One college student of political science and law did not know that Japan was an island country and that the Japanese language differed greatly from English.[17] Although this is an extreme example of public ignorance, it is fair to say that before 1917 the introduction of Western knowledge was very limited and that publishing in China was stagnant. This stagnation may be attributed directly to the series of strict press and publication laws inaugurated after 1914, though the interruption of intellectual development by foreign and domestic wars and other deeper causes underlay it. Some improvement was made between 1917 and 1919 but even this was confined for the most part to the new intellectuals in Peking and to a few schools in other cities.

Chinese publishing underwent a remarkable development, however, after the May Fourth Incident. During May and June of 1919 while the students were carrying on their propaganda for the strikes and boycotts, many of their publications were written in the vernacular except for communications sent to the government and most of their solemn declarations. Writings in the spoken language had proved more effective than those in the old literary style. As a consequence, within half a year after the incident, some four hundred new periodicals in the vernacular appeared in China.[c]

The following are some of the important new periodicals which had great influence in China during this period and in later years (for a more complete and annotated list of 604 new periodicals and newspapers of this period see the separately published volume of additional reference matter, *Research Guide to "The May Fourth Movement"*): [19]

New Youth (monthly)	est. Sept. 1915	in Shanghai	Independent
The Pacific Ocean (monthly)	April 1917	Shanghai	Independent

[c] Chiang Monlin wrote at the end of 1919: "Since May about three hundred and fifty weekly bulletins have been published, either by the students or by those who sympathize with the students. These weeklies are usually printed on one sheet of paper, half the size of a daily paper, doubled over, making four pages." John Dewey reported from Peking at the beginning of 1920, "It is stated that whereas two years ago there were but one or two tentative journals in the vulgar tongue, today there are over three hundred. Since last May the students have started score upon score of journals, all in the spoken tongue and all discussing matters in words that can be understood by the common man." The precise number of periodicals created in this period is not known. Tsi C. Wang says, "Within the four years following the beginning of the literary revolution in 1917, three hundred student magazines have been published, of which only one or two are not in the vernacular." But he also acknowledges that "some writer claims it to be more than 400." Hu Shih asserted in 1922 that in the year 1919 at least 400 periodicals were established in the spoken language. Later an author listed 650 periodicals published during 1919–1927, excluding government publications, newspaper supplements, and many of the official publications by school administrations.[18]

Weekly Critic	Dec. 1918	Peking	Independent
New Tide (monthly)	Jan. 1919	Peking	Independent, student
The Citizens (monthly)	Jan. 1919	Peking	Independent, student
New Education (monthly)	Jan. 1919	Shanghai	Independent
Weekly Review	June 1919	Shanghai	Kuomintang organ
Young China (monthly)	July 1919	Shanghai	Journal of the Young China Association
The Construction (monthly)	Aug. 1919	Shanghai	Kuomintang organ
Emancipation and Reconstruction (semimonthly), later (Sept. 15, 1920) changed to *La Rekonstruo* (monthly)	Sept. 1919	Shanghai	Chinputang organ
Young World (monthly)	Jan. 1920	Shanghai	Journal of the Young China Association

These were the more well-known ones. The other hundreds of new periodicals were generally short-lived or less influential. Their names, however, revealed the temper of the time. There was a monthly entitled *The Dawn*; others had such names as *Youth and Society, The New Voice of Society, New Society, New China, The Progress of Youth, The New Life, The New Atmosphere, The People's Tocsin, The New Man, The Warm Tide, The Plain People, The Light, Save the Nation, Freedom, The New Learning, The New Culture, The New Students, Work-and-Study, Upward, Strife, Awakening, The Ethics of the Plain People, Mass Education,* and *Science and Education*. There were also *The New Woman, The Woman's Bell,* and even *The Elementary Student,* this last established by the students themselves. Some periodicals specializing in philosophy, music, painting, literature, or certain of the natural and social sciences were actually pioneers in their fields. The new publications covered nearly all important aspects of modern knowledge and life, many of which had hardly been brought to public notice in China, and certainly not in the same way, before the period of the May Fourth Movement.

On the other hand, the new periodicals were, like American "little magazines," characterized by their ambition and zeal; in some respects they were pretentious. They often announced their platforms and aims in high-sounding terms. *Young China*, for example, declared itself to be dedicated to "social services under the guidance of the scientific spirit, in order to realize our ideal of creating a young China." *Save the Nation* proposed "to promote popular education and to save society." The object of *The New Woman* was "to rouse women as a means of reforming society," while *The Woman's Bell* had as its aim "to educate women and enable them to take part in the progress of society." The mottos of these new periodicals were phrased with monotonous frequency in such terms as "to reform the nation and society, physically and socially," "to study social and economic problems and introduce new ideas," "to introduce new thoughts to the citizen and uplift his personality while promoting home industries," "to rouse the workingman and reform society," "to bring about a development of learning so as to apply the idea of research and criticism to the reform of society," "to study society and introduce Western ideas," "to advocate the new literature in the vernacular and brave criticism," "to publish the people's opinion on foreign policies, and to point out the significance of diplomacy to the nation," and even, as stated in one of the periodicals, "to introduce new thoughts to the world, and to apply an optimistic but critical attitude to the reconstruction of society." After a survey of these publications, John Dewey remarked in the summer of 1921: "Many of these papers were of course as ephemeral as all of them were ambitious. But they illustrate the spirit of the movement as hardly anything else could." [20] For this ephemeral nature, lack of constancy and perseverance on the part of the youth was partly responsible, but in many cases they were suppressed by the warlord governments or handicapped by the chaotic civil wars and social unrest.

These new periodicals are noteworthy for one fact pre-eminently — they introduced to the public, and provided a channel of communication for, young Chinese intellectuals who became prominent social, political, or literary figures in China during the following decades. Actually, the "periodical fever" during the months following the May Fourth Incident was an epoch-making event both in the development of Chinese public opinion and in the shaping of the new Chinese intellectuals.

The movement not only gave rise to new publications but also stimulated reforms of many old magazines and newspapers. Established periodicals such as the *Eastern Miscellany, Chinese Educational Review, Short Story Monthly, Ladies' Journal, Students' Magazine, Chinese Educational Circles,* and many others shifted to the use of the vernacular and started to introduce modern Western ideas and knowledge. To facilitate and hasten these changes, the older editors were in almost every case replaced by aggressive, modern-minded younger men. In June 1919, the fifteen-year-old leading magazine, *The Eastern Miscellany* (established in 1904), announced a radical change in its editorial policy in order to "keep up with the progress of the world." [21] In July, the editor, reversing its former conservative stand, declared that Chinese magazines should closely follow world tendencies, give up "reactionary conservatism" and recognize the contemporary situation, meet the practical needs of life, and prepare for future progress instead of lingering in the memory of the past.[22] In 1920 and 1921 it started to publish articles in the vernacular and Hu Yü-chih was appointed editor in the latter year. The *Short Story Monthly* changed even more radically. In December 1920, Shen Yen-ping (later famous under his pen name Mao Tun) was appointed editor and in January 1921 the eleven-year-old monthly was completely remade. Contemporary Western literature was translated and new Chinese literature was published for the first time. The *Chinese Educational Review,* under the new editorship of Li Shih-ch'en, later a famous philosopher, reacted with even greater alacrity. After January 1920, its editorials and articles began to appear in the vernacular. The *Ladies' Journal* and *Students' Magazine* also changed their editors. All these long-established periodicals were published by the Commercial Press, which was actually controlled at the time by conservative monarchist remnants. Sun Yat-sen cited it at the beginning of 1920 as a reactionary organization which monopolized the field of Chinese publishing.[23]

Newspapers in all the big cities were also influenced by the revolutionary tide after the May Fourth Incident. Many of them added special columns or published supplementary magazines in order to print new literary works and discuss the cultural and student movements. The fate of those which did not thus respond to popular demand is illustrated by the example of a famous Shanghai daily, *Shih pao (Times)*. Before 1919 it was a favorite in Chinese educational circles. But after 1919 when the thought of the young intellectuals took a new turn, the paper still clung to its traditional form and content. As a result its circulation dropped rapidly, and it was soon forced to cease publication. On the other hand, the *Shih-shih hsin-pao (The China Times)* and *Min-kuo jih-pao (Republic Daily)*, because of their sympathy with the new movement, quickly won favor among the intellectuals and the youths.[24]

New books and translations were also published in larger quantities than ever before. In the years immediately following the incident, there were no less than forty-eight publishers who printed Chinese translations of Western works.[25] The Commercial Press, the largest firm of its kind in China, published 407 books in 1912, 552 in 1915, 602 in 1919, but 1,284 in 1920.[26] An index of the rapid expansion of Chinese publication in 1919 and 1920 may be found in the increase of the amount of paper imported into China in these years, since almost all new Chinese publications were then printed on imported paper. From 1918 to 1921 these imports more than doubled.[d] This is additional evidence of the prosperity of Chinese publications during the post-May-Fourth-Incident period.

The Rising Tide of Iconoclasm

Concurrently with this rapid expansion of publishing there was a growing intoxication with new thoughts. In fact, the year following the incident witnessed an era of mingled skepticism, romanticism, liberalism, realism, and anarchism in the thought of the new Chinese intellectuals. Traditional thought and institutions were criticized and attacked from every side; new doctrines, new isms, and new ideas in many branches of modern knowledge were introduced and discussed in a somewhat superficial manner but with vigor and enthusiasm. John Dewey reported the phenomenon from Peking at the beginning of 1920:

A friend who made a careful study of some fifty of the students' papers says that their first trait is the question mark, and the second is the demand for complete freedom of speech in order that answers may be found for the questions.

In a country where belief has been both authoritatively dogmatic and complacent, the rage for questioning is the omen of a new epoch.[28]

Later in the summer of 1921 he further reported from the same city:

After the upheaval of May 4 [1919] the student unions started periodicals all over China. It is significant that at this moment of the height of the revolt against corrupt and traitorous officials and also of the Japanese boycott, these topics were secondary in the students' journals. . . . Their burden was the need of educational

---

[d] The value of paper imported into China in 1912 was 4,303,712 haikwan taels; in 1913 it was 7,169,255; but in 1914, partly because of World War I, it decreased to 6,470,768. From 1915 to 1918, except in 1916, the value of imports for each year remained static. The value in 1918 was 7,243,564 haikwan taels. However, the figure jumped to 10,212,652 in 1919, to 14,159,186 in 1920, and to 15,311,873 in 1921; while it dropped to 13,689,258 in 1922. Most of the paper reported in these statistics was used for newspapers, periodicals, and books; only an insignificant quantity was for bookcover and other uses.[27]

change; attacks upon the family system; discussion of socialism; of democratic ideas; of all kinds of utopias. . . . Naturally there was much effervescence along with the fermentation. Lacking definite background of experience, the students thought all ideas and proposals much alike, provided only they were new and involved getting away from old customs and traditions.[29]

The traditions under attack from these new intellectuals and the reasons for the attacks will be discussed later. It must simply be noted here that the Chinese attitude toward things old and new underwent a tremendous change in this period. Previously, to the great majority of Chinese, antiquity had been the criterion of excellence. Merchandise to be of any worth was advertised as being old-fashioned. Pharmacies, for example, habitually advertised "medicines and prescriptions handed down from the ancestors" (*tsu-ch'uan tan-fang*). Styles of literary writing, painting, calligraphy, and others followed the ancient models. This was also true with respect to ethical principles, philosophy, and political or economic theories. All in all, the new should obey the old. Even most of the reformers and revolutionaries of the late Ch'ing period (late nineteenth and early twentieth centuries) did not defy but utilized this approach. To justify their advocacy of the adoption of Western technology, science, and institutions, they tried to prove that they were upheld in principle by the ancient sages, including Confucius.

But almost from the time of Yen Fu's translation of *Evolution and Ethics*, Liang Ch'i-ch'ao's and some anarchists' polemics at the turn of the last century, and increasing in intensity during the period after the May Fourth Incident, this idea began to change radically. With the young students of the period, admiration for the old gave way to that of the new. This situation gave John Dewey the impression that "there seems to be no country in the world where students are so unanimously and eagerly interested as in China in what is modern and new in thought, especially about social and economic matters, nor where the arguments which can be brought in favor of the established order and the status quo have so little weight — indeed, are so unuttered."[30] A Christian Chinese lecturer who returned to China in April 1921 after nearly a decade in the United States was deeply impressed by this change in Chinese attitude and life which he encountered on his arrival in Shanghai:

Almost at once I found myself overwhelmed by a kind of invisible power and atmosphere. I felt that there was life vibrating — a "new life" which I had not found a few years ago. The people whom I met, conversations I had with them, the attitude[s] they took, the opinion[s] they expressed, the judgments they gave on various questions of the day; the newspapers I read, the tone of public opinion reflected in their lines, the topics discussed, all indicated the presence of this new life. One evening I roamed through the streets and dropped into various bookstores and newspaper stands and gathered together 47 different kinds of magazines, including weeklies, quarterlies, and semi-annuals. I spent an entire night merely glancing over their contents, finding that there were more up-to-date things discussed and a wider range of opinions expressed in those magazines than in any combination of 47 magazines picked up from American newspaper stands. As I have traveled from one place to another since then, speaking to various audiences and teaching in four or five institutions, I have become more and more interested in this "new life" which seems to be developing all the time.[31]

This enthusiasm for new thoughts on the part of the young Chinese soon caused alarm among both older Chinese conservatives and foreign observers, most of whom approached China, as Dewey said, "with an antecedent belief in its essential conservatism, its aversion to change." [32] Some Chinese teachers complained of the "bumptious" insubordination of students and of their instability of mind.[33] In some respects these complaints seem to have been justified. It is easy to imagine that such a vast change in attitude toward life in so short a time and in such an old country as China occasioned some alarming reactions. The following short sketch given by one of the witnesses of the period illustrates the extreme length to which this new attitude was carried by the Chinese youth of this period:

The thoughts of Chinese youth underwent the most drastic change about the time of the May Fourth Movement. At the time, most of them protested in an uproar against the family system, the old religions, the old morality, and the old customs, in an effort to break up all traditional institutions. I was then studying in a summer school in Nanking. I knew a young man who abandoned his own name and substituted the title "He-you-I" (T'a-ni-wo). Later when I went to Peking, I met at the gate of the School of Letters of Peking University a friend of mine accompanied by a young girl with her hair cut short. "May I ask your family name?" I asked her. She stared at me and screamed, "I don't have any family name!" There were also people who wrote letters to their fathers saying, "From a certain date on, I will not recognize you as my father. We are all friends, and equal." T'ieh-min was among those who had denied their fathers; but when his father died in 1921, he wrote a very touching poem to explain his grievous mourning for him.[34]

Does this illustration indicate that Chinese youth, or at least some of them, at the time were mad or unbalanced? The question must be posed against the background of the practical relations between family members in China of the period, especially the paternal ruling over wives and children. Marriage was prearranged and determined by parents without the agreement or knowledge of the partners directly concerned. A one-sided requirement of chastity was imposed on women. The ethical principles of *chieh* and *hsiao* (wifely fidelity and filial piety) were regarded as iron-clad laws of society. Social ethics, in some extreme cases, encouraged teen-age girls, whose fiancés died, to die after them. Sons who disobeyed and refused to marry the girls picked by their parents were considered unfilial and highly immoral, despised by the community and deprived of their rights of inheritance of the family property.[e] In this kind of family system and under the rule of such ethical principles, the revolt of the Chinese young intellectuals in the manner described above is quite understandable. They explain why a writer, Wu Yü, without due credit to some of its advantages, asserted that the Chinese family and clan system was the basis of despotism, and Fu Ssu-nien went so far as to declare that the corrupt Chinese family system was "the source of all evil."[37]

Although the unreasonableness of the conventional ethics was so apparent, the conservative gentry and the warlord government firmly clung to them and refused to change.[38] Many colleges and schools were still administered by people with little modern knowledge, and many teachers of science unversed in it were kept in the schools.[f]

[e] The following instances, all occurring in 1918, can be cited as examples. A woman, whose husband died and who finally succeeded in committing suicide after trying nine different ways of killing herself and suffering for ninety-eight days, was worshipped in a shrine and held up as a moral model for all women. When an engaged girl of nineteen, desiring to follow this pattern, fasted for seven days but did not die, many people regretted that they lost another moral example. It might not have been quite so objectionable had all the betrothed women and widows who refused to remarry or committed suicide done so willingly and spontaneously. But, because the government had proclaimed a "Reward Regulation" for this kind of chastity, cases of families that compelled young women to commit suicide in order to seek moral fame for the family were not lacking.[35] According to the "Reward Regulation," women who did not remarry in the period at least from thirty years of age to fifty, or who committed suicide for their dead husbands or fiancés or in protest against forceful assault, would be rewarded by the government.[36]

[f] For example, in the spring of 1919 a *Mathematics Magazine* (*Shu-li tsa-chih*) published by the Higher Normal College of Wuchang included two fantastic articles by Yao Ming-hui, chairman of the department of history and geography of the college. One was titled "San-ts'ung i" ("On the Principle of Three Obediences [for Woman]"); the other, "Fu-shun shuo" ("On the Obedience of Woman"). His topic was the relation between the woman problem and mathematics. He referred to one of the thirteen Chinese classes which sets forth a "Principle of Three Obediences" for woman, namely, she should obey her father before her marriage, obey her husband after her marriage, and obey her son after her husband's death.[39] This he correlated with another classical work which presents a "magic square" as follows:

7
fire
2

5
8 wood 3 earth 4 metal 9
10

1
water
6

The iconoclastic fervor on the part of the young intellectuals may be made more clear if we list some of the conventions and superstitions pervading Chinese society which they opposed. They attacked the theories of rebirth and of the existence of ghosts, spiritualism,[41] as well as divination,[42] geomancy, fortunetelling, treating diseases by means of charms or incantations for controlling demons, magic pills for immortality, and Taoist breathing exercises.[43] They also criticized such traditionals as the queue for men, footbinding for women, the kowtow, the old calendar, and opium smoking.[44] The list is, of course, incomplete. And not all these ideas or customs were supported by every conservative. But many of them were upheld on traditional pretexts.

The problem of modernizing China's age-old ways was of such magnitude as to render petty the complaints about insubordination and instability of mind in the Chinese youth who tackled it during the May Fourth period. In the opinion of John Dewey, these manifestations were only phenomena of transition and evidence of an eager thirst for ideas. He says:

It [the instability of mind] is to be regretted. But it is genuine evidence of a general state of transition, with the hesitation, uncertainty and openness to novel stimuli that such periods are bound to exhibit. On the other hand, there is a maturity of interest far beyond that which marks American students of the same years. High school boys and girls listen soberly and intelligently to lectures on subjects that would create nothing but bored restlessness in an American school. There is an eager thirst for ideas — beyond anything existing, I am convinced, in the youth of any other country on earth. At present the zeal for ideas outruns persistence in getting knowledge with which to back up the ideas. But it supplies an extraordinary vitality to the growing desire for knowledge and scientific method. It means that knowledge is being acquired, not as a technical device nor as a conventional badge of culture, but for social application.[45]

The proliferation of publications and the fervor for criticism of tradition and for the introduction of new ideas did not exhaust all the activities of the new intellectuals after the May Fourth Incident. They also launched a campaign for social organization and social service.

The professor thought that the number "1" represented man and "2" woman. If there were no "1," there would be no "2"; consequently, if there were no man, there would be no woman. That was why woman should obey her father or husband. Furthermore, "1" plus "2" equaled marriage. Since it produced "3," an odd (yang, or male) number, instead of an even (yin, or female) number, woman should obey her son. Other explanations in the articles were even more illogical, in fact unintelligible. Anyway, the conclusion was drawn that it was a law of Heaven that woman should obey man. The author, absurd as he was, was retained as a professor and enjoyed a great reputation in the community as one of the leaders of the conservatives advocating the so-called "national quintessence." This caused a student to write a letter to the editor of New Youth protesting the articles in the Mathematics Magazine.[40]

New Intellectual, Social, and Political Organizations

Before the May Fourth Incident, there were in China few well-organized groups in the modern Western style existing among the merchants, workers, teachers, or even students.[46] In 1917 and 1918, with the launching of the new literature and new thought movements, students started to set up study organizations. But these were limited to a few active students; social organizations were not popular among the people. After the May Fourth Incident, an enthusiasm for organizations, similar to that for publications, spread throughout the cities of China. The intellectuals carried on the business of such organizations in a more or less democratic and open way which differed somewhat from previous Chinese practice.[47]

Some of the student organizations established during the period of demonstrations and strikes turned out to be temporary in nature and were dissolved within six to twelve months. But the student unions, which were established at individual schools or on a city-wide or province-wide basis, continued long afterwards as did many other coincident social organizations. The Student Union of the Republic of China with its headquarters in Shanghai became the most active and influential of these new organizations. Other important student organizations continuing after the incident were the World Chinese Students' Association, organized in 1905 and revived in 1919, the Japanese Returned Students' Union for National Salvation, and the Western Returned Students' Union reorganized and expanded from the American Returned Students' Union after the incident.

In addition to these bodies for self-government, students established with other intellectuals organizations for the purpose of study, discussion, popular education, social service, or other social, cultural, or political ends, such as the Society for the Discussion of Family Reconstruction, the Chinese Philosophical Society, the Society for Promoting the New Education, the Society for the Study of Socialism (*She-hui-chu-i yen-chiu-hui*), the Society for the Study of Russell (*Lo-su hsüeh-hui*), the Society for Lectures on the New Learning (or the Chinese Lecture Association, *Chiang-hsüeh she*), the Educational Survey Society, and the Popular Education Association. The Cooperative Study Society, which had been trying to induce a large number of students to study together, translated and published in the postincident period a number of realistic Western dramas and novels, especially those of France, Russia, and Germany, and later, communist literature. Older intellectuals joined the various campaigns with comparable enthusiasm. The Aspiration Society (*Shang-chih hsüeh-hui*), founded by ex-officials and writers such as Liang Ch'i-ch'ao, Fan Yüan-lien, Lin Ch'ang-min, and Chang Tung-sun, also made great efforts to introduce Western culture. Its leading members often supported, financially and otherwise, the visits of Western thinkers. It also published many Chinese translations of Western philosophic works.[48]

The new intellectuals also cooperated with other social groups. This was done mainly through the ambitiously entitled Federation of All Organizations of China which was established after the incident with headquarters in Shanghai. It was instituted to harmonize actions of various groups and secure internal and external support for their participation in national affairs.[49] The federation was composed of the Student Union of the Republic of China, the Society of Women Comrades for Patriotism, the Christian National Salvation Society, the National Chamber of Commerce, the All-China Journalists' Union, and representatives from the gentry, labor, and other social and religious groups.[50] A pattern of allied organizations such as this spread from Shanghai to most of the big cities, including Tientsin and Peking.[51]

The most active of these new organizations, aside from the student unions, were the many small societies established by young intellectuals within or outside of the schools. The Young China Association, for example, which had been initiated in 1918, did not become active until after the May Fourth Incident. Thanks to the stimulation of the incident, this association, after a year of preparation, was formally established in Peking on July 1, 1919. At the time it had seventy-four members, most of whom were students, educators, journalists, and writers in the major cities and abroad and who later became political, social, or educational leaders of modern China. At the inaugural meeting, the four aims of the association proposed in the early stage of initiation were changed, at the suggestion of Li Ta-chao and other members, to accord with the current intellectual tempo, and they stated: "Our association dedicates itself to social services under the guidance of the scientific spirit, in order to realize our ideal of creating a young China." Furthermore, four watchwords were adopted to guide the activities of all members, i.e., "strife, practicality, endurance, and thrift." Although the association was not strictly organized, its members maintained frequent correspondence with the headquarters and with each other expressing their various viewpoints on important social and cultural problems and reporting their impressions of the economic and social situations, at home or abroad. They also held a number of discussion meetings concerning various subjects. Besides its two organs, *Young China* and *Young World*, the association published small magazines in several cities and a number of pamphlets.[52]

Smaller societies similar to this, organized by students and youths, are too numerous to list. Actually, most of the hundreds of new periodicals were supported or established by one small society or another, such as the Dawn Society, the Common Study Society, the Association for Practical Promotion of Society, the Society for the Progress of Youth, and the Truth Society. These organizations varied in nature, being liberal, socialistic, or of other political tints, and in them many of the later Chinese political leaders, leftist or rightist, started their careers.

Organizations of an outright political character also attracted the youth. Some of the young men joined the Kuomintang, and others the numerous small political groups of the time. From the fall of 1919, many political or semi-political organizations were established or strengthened by students who later became leaders of the Chinese Communist Party though before 1920 they only leaned to idealistic socialism or liberalism instead of adopting communism as their creed. Mao Tse-tung became more active in the New People's Study Society after the incident. He was editor of the organ of the Student Union of Hunan Province, the *Hsiang River Review* (*Hsiang-chiang p'ing-lun*), a weekly founded on July 14, 1919. The magazine vehemently promoted the students' cause and criticized the government. Consequently the union and the weekly were suppressed by the Military Governor of Hunan, Chang Ching-yao, early in August. This intensified Mao's activities against the Governor and led to his revisit to Peking in February 1920 and his subsequent conversion to communism in the summer. In Wuchang in the fall of 1919, Yün Tai-ying established with Lin Piao and Chang Hao (alias of Lin Yü-nan, Lin Piao's elder cousin, who was later a communist labor leader) the Social Welfare Society (*She-hui fu-li hui*) and the Social Benefit Book Store (*Li ch'ün shu-she*); the latter had business relations with Mao's Culture Book Store (*Wen-hua shu-she*), which was established in Changsha in September 1920. The Awakening Society (*Chüeh-wu she*) was founded in Tientsin on September 16, 1919, by active boy students from the Student Union of Tientsin and girl students from the Tientsin Association of Women Patriotic Comrades. Most of the members were students at the Nankai School and the Chihli Industrial College; among the most active were Chou En-lai, Ma Chün, Teng Ying-ch'ao, Sun Hsiao-ch'ing (later secretary of the Canton committee of the Kuomintang), Kuo Lung-chen, and Kuan Hsi-pin. The society was founded with the assumption that social progress must be based on self-awakening of the individual and developed strong leanings toward guild socialism, anarchism, and humanitarianism. It started to publish its magazine, *Awakening,* on January 20, 1920, and received some advice from Li Ta-chao. In Peking there was another society with the same name as well as a like organization called the Resurgence Society (*Fu she*). Similar societies were established in Shanghai, Hangchow, and Hankow.[53]

There was also a tendency shortly after the May Fourth Incident for some of the different groups mentioned above to band together to further their common goals. For instance, a Reform Alliance (*Kai-tsao lien-ho-hui*) was formed by the Young China Association, the Humanity Society, the Dawn Society, the Peking Awakening Society, and the Youth Cooperative Corps (*Ch'ing-nien hu-ch'u t'uan*). The alliance published a manifesto and a charter, though it was only short-lived.

The idealism characterizing almost all of the new organizations may be illustrated by a few examples of movements started after the incident by new intellectuals. A Japanese utopian social movement called "atarashiki mura" (new village) developed by Mushakoji Saneatsu had caught the fancy of some Chinese professors and students. The theory and organization underlying the new village were set forth in 1919 in both *New Youth* and *New Tide* magazines by Chou Tso-jen, his elder brother Lu Hsün, and other writers.[g] The movement was based on the philosophy of mutual assistance and humanitarianism espoused by Kropotkin, Tolstoy, and certain idealistic socialists. Members of the village gave up all their private property. They aimed to carry out the ideal "from each according to his capacity, to each according to his needs." *New Youth* published a letter and poem written by Mushakoji to "Chinese friends unknown," along with the enthusiastic responses of the Chinese intellectual leaders, Ts'ai Yüan-p'ei, Ch'en Tu-hsiu, and the Chou brothers.[55] As presented in this and other Chinese periodicals, Mushakoji's idealistic socialism and humanitarianism produced a notable impression on the Chinese new intellectuals in the period after the May Fourth Incident.

The intellectuals' enthusiasm for a new society was also displayed in one of their attempts to create a new life for themselves. In the winter of 1919 some

---

[g] Chou visited the Japanese "new villages" in Tokyo, Hiuga, and Ueno in July 1919. Lu Hsün translated Mushakoji's drama, *A Youth's Dream*, first published in the *Kuo-min kung-pao* starting in Aug. 1919. After the daily was suppressed by the Peking government on Oct. 25, the play was reprinted and continued in *New Youth*, VII, 2 (Jan. 1, 1920), pp. 65–103, and the next three issues. The idea of the new village was opposed by Hu Shih who thought that it only promoted a kind of hermit's life.[54]

of the young intellectuals, including Wang Kuang-ch'i, Lo Chia-lun, and Hsü Yen-chih, with the support of Ts'ai Yüan-p'ei, Ch'en Tu-hsiu, Hu Shih, Li Ta-chao, and Chou Tso-jen, started — under the influence of the work-and-study scheme in France and of the new village — to organize the Work-and-Learning Mutual Assistance Corps (*Kung-tu hu-chu t'uan*) in Peking, Tientsin, Shanghai, and a few other big cities. Each member of the corps was expected not only to study, but in addition to work at least four hours a day. The income of every member belonged to the corps as a whole, and his living and other basic expenses such as tuition, medicines, room, clothes, books, and so forth were provided by the corps. The work included opening printing shops, restaurants, laundries, and engaging in handicraft and peddling.[56] Although the program was not carried out on a large scale and actually failed in the end, it put into practice at least temporarily the ideas of many of the new intellectuals and this practical experience influenced their later thinking about social problems. The supporters of the movement ranged widely in viewpoint,[h] and its failure provided a lesson to some of the new intellectuals, who subsequently realized that it was impossible for them to create a utopia in the established economy and society without the cooperation of either the urban workers or the capitalists, or both.[i]

Public Education Sponsored by the New Intellectuals

More successful and far-reaching were the programs of public education widely carried on throughout the country by these organizations. These included the following:

Academic and popular lectures

These became a vogue in China after 1919. Several prominent Western thinkers were invited to visit China for the purpose of lecturing and were

[h] At the beginning the corps had to depend on the financial support of its sympathizers. Among the contributors to the Peking branch of the corps were, for example, Ch'en Tu-hsiu (30 *yuan*), Hu Shih (20 *yuan*), Chang Lan (leader of the Democratic League after World War II) (30 *yuan*), Li Ta-chao (10 *yuan*), Lan Chih-hsien (Chinputang) (10 *yuan*), Chang Chi (10 *yuan*), Chiang Kai-shek (10 *yuan*), and Ch'en Po-sheng (145 *yuan*). Hu Shih compared the corps to the practice of American students working to support themselves; whereas some of the other sponsors viewed it as an experiment and the start of a new way of life and of a new society.

[i] Tai Chi-t'ao, Sun Yat-sen's follower and at the time one of the pioneer Chinese supporters of Marxism, suggested that it was better for the students in the program to enter the capitalists' factories, work together with the urban workers, and lead them.[57] Some of the worker-students of the corps later became famous, such as Shih Ts'un-t'ung (Shih Fu-liang), the economist, and the writer Chang T'ieh-min.

enthusiastically received. John Dewey was one of the first of these visitors. At the invitation of an educational association, he stayed in China for two years and two months, traveling to eleven provinces (Fengtien, Chihli, Shansi, Shantung, Kiangsu, Kiangsi, Hupei, Hunan, Chekiang, Fukien, Kwangtgung). He delivered numerous academic and public speeches, especially in Peking, Nanking, and in Shansi Province. His five major lectures given at Peking University and interpreted for the most part by Hu Shih were: (1) "Social Philosophy and Political Philosophy" (explored in the light of pragmatism for the first time); (2) "Philosophy of Education"; (3) "Ways of Thinking"; (4) "Three Philosophers of Our Times" (Bergson, Russell, James); and (5) "On Ethics." These lectures appeared in newspapers and periodicals, and later were published in a book which went through fourteen Chinese printings of 10,000 copies each in two years. His other lectures were also often attended not only by students and teachers but by other intellectuals and were reported fully and widely in the local and national newspapers. Indeed, it was the first time that a Western philosopher had made so many speeches in modern China. His books on philosophy, logic, and education were also translated and widely circulated.[58]

On September 5, 1920, the Society for Lectures on the New Learning, which had been established by Liang Ch'i-ch'ao to sponsor public lectures by distinguished Chinese and foreign scholars, proposed that the government should provide twenty thousand *yuan* each year to bring famous scholars to China to lecture. By that time, while Dewey was still in China, Liang and others invited Bertrand Russell to China following his visit to the Soviet Union. He arrived in China on October 12 and remained there for nearly a year delivering many public speeches as well as five academic lectures in Peking: (1) "Mathematical Logic"; (2) "The Analysis of Matter"; (3) "The Analysis of Mind"; (4) "The Problem of Philosophy"; and (5) "On the Structure of Society." Both before and after his stay in China, a number of Russell's works in social, political, and philosophical fields were translated into Chinese and became popular among Chinese reformers and progressives. As had been mentioned, a Society for the Study of Russell was soon organized and a *Russell Monthly* (*Lo-su yüeh-k'an*) was established in January 1921.[59] Russell's philosophy and personality impressed the Chinese intellectuals, especially active youths, in the latter stage of the May Fourth period more deeply than those of any other contemporary Western thinker.

Besides Dewey and Russell, the American educator Paul Monroe was invited to China on September 5, 1921. The German philosopher Hans Driesch came to China in 1922. And Rabindranath Tagore, the Indian philosopher-poet, was invited in 1923.[60] The Chinese new intellectuals also planned to invite Bergson and Eucken, but the plans did not materialize.

Meanwhile, Chinese students were carrying on a widespread popular speech campaign among the illiterate masses of the people. In these popular lectures they propagated scientific knowledge, patriotism, new ethics, and many new social and political ideas. One group presenting lectures was the Mass Education Speech Corps (*P'ing-min chiao-yü chiang-yen t'uan*) established on March 23, 1919, by students of Peking University, Liao Shu-ts'ang, Teng Chung-hsia, Lo Chia-lun, K'ang Pai-ch'ing, Yi K'e-ni, Chou Ping-lin, Hsü Te-heng, Chang Kuo-t'ao, Wang Kuang-ch'i, and others. The work of the corps was greatly intensified after the May Fourth Incident. Members made numerous lectures in cities and in the countryside, and distributed printed lectures and popular magazines to the people. The corps carried on its work, sometimes despite police intervention, until 1923. Similar organizations existed at the Peking Higher Normal College and other schools.[61]

Popular education and free schools

After the May Fourth Incident, many schools opened free night sessions for workers and the children of the poor. During the years of World War I, some Chinese schools and universities had instituted night schools for their janitors. Peking University started its Night Classes for Janitors (*Hsiao-yü yeh-pan*) in 1917.[62] On January 18, 1920, the student union of the university opened its Night School for the Plain People (*P'ing-min yeh-hsiao*). These steps were a break with the tradition of Chinese higher education which had prevented the common man from entering school, especially college. In older times, a sign was often put at the front door of schools reading, "The school is an important place; extraneous persons are excluded."[j] By the end of 1919 the night school established by the School of Science of Peking University had more than five hundred students of ages ranging from seven to thirty. Similar night classes were opened at other schools.[64] There were other free schools cosponsored by students and merchants with the latter's financial support. It is said that after the May Fourth Incident free popular schools established by student unions "spread all over the country."[65] An American correspondent reported from China in August 1919: "The students have organized on a per-

---

[j] Soldiers could, of course, not be refused entry. The warlords often invaded and closed schools and converted them into barracks as they liked.[63] This seemed true throughout the period from the establishment of the Republic to recent times.

manent basis to educate the masses and the poor children of the country. In Shanghai alone, sixteen free schools have been opened for children who cannot afford to pay for their education, and similar action has been taken in every city of the country. Students are going among the peasants in the villages, to carry on a campaign for national integrity."[66] In 1920, Y. C. James Yen, on the basis of his experience in teaching Chinese workers in France, started his famous "Mass Education Movement," and it enjoyed a great expansion in the ensuing decade because of the students' enthusiasm for popular education during this period.[67] The social services carried out by students and intellectuals also included wall newspapers, public libraries, and work for the improvement of public health.

Increasing Support for the New Culture Movement

As the events described above developed, their interrelation became clear. Their unity of purpose was recognized in the term "new culture movement" which gradually came into use to encompass all these developments. The idea of creating a new culture or civilization had developed only a few years earlier. Ch'en Tu-hsiu paid some attention to this concept after his founding of *New Youth* in 1915. In the first issues of the magazine he had written an article, "The French and Modern Civilization," and translated the third chapter of Charles Seignobos' *Histoire de la Civilisation Contemporaine.*[68] At the beginning of 1916, Ch'en wrote that the characteristic quality of human life was the creation of civilization, and that man of the twentieth century should create a civilization for the twentieth century instead of following that of the nineteenth century.[69] In the first issue of *New Tide* published in January 1919, the students also declared that the foremost duty of their magazine was to lead China to adjust itself to the civilization of the modern world.[70] These ambitious ideas and the related activities were not, however, systematically advocated by the new intellectuals as a new culture movement until after the incident.

The designation "new culture movement" gained currency in the half year following May 4, 1919. In December of that year, the editor of *New Tide*, in a reply to a reader, indicated that their movement was a "culture movement."[71] By the beginning of 1920 the movement had become very popular.[72] To be sure, from the spring of 1918 many newspapers of the Chinputang had begun to support the new thought movement. Members of the Kuomintang had also become enthusiastic supporters individually. But in January 1920, Sun Yat-sen gave his official approval. He summarized all these new tides as a new culture movement and asked all his followers to support it. He wrote to the overseas members of the Kuomintang:

After the May Fourth Movement was initiated by the students of the National University of Peking, all patriotic youths realized that intellectual reform is the preparation for reform activities in the future. By this means public opinion develops rapidly and publications become prosperous with public support. Numerous and varied new magazines and newspapers are established by enthusiastic youths, growing as fresh and beautiful flowers each at its best. Society thus has been considerably influenced by the movement. Even the extremely corrupt and reactionary puppet Peking government dares not run counter to it. This kind of new culture movement reflects indeed an unprecedented change among the intellectuals of China today. As for the origin of the movement, it started only by the advocacy of one or two enlightened publications at the beginning. As a result, public opinion has developed rapidly and gloriously; students' strikes erupt all over the country; and with awakened consciousness and determination to strive unto death, almost everybody joins in the patriotic activities. There is no doubt that the movement will produce great and everlasting effects if it continues to grow and expand. The success of the revolution which is carried on by our party must depend on a change of thought in China, just as the ancient *Book of Strategy* (*Ping-fa*) by Sun Tzu says that to attack the mind is more effective than to attack a city, and as the old saying has it that a renovation of the mind is prerequisite to a revolution. Therefore, the new culture movement is really a most valuable thing.[73]

By this letter, Sun acknowledged and pointed out to his followers the great influence of the May Fourth Movement upon Chinese society, the initiative of *New Youth, New Tide*, and some other magazines in the movement, and also the close connection existing between the student movement and the development of the new culture movement. Actually, from the time of the May Fourth Incident, many leaders of the Kuomintang and other progressive intellectuals had joined or positively supported the new culture movement.

The term "cultural movement" as used by most of the new intellectuals at this time was conceived in a broad sense, broader than was acknowledged in later years. In the spring of 1920 Ch'en Tu-hsiu, in a discussion of the new culture movement, restricted the meaning of "culture" to that which dealt with science, religion, morality, literature, music, the arts, and the like, and did not use it in its sociological connotation to include practical political, social, and economic actions. Early in 1921, he further asserted that the cultural and social movements were two different things; the former could not include the latter or vice versa. It is apparent that the activities of the new intellectuals after the May Fourth Incident actually exceeded the scope of a cultural movement in this narrower sense. But until a year after the incident, the intellectuals seemed to place more emphasis on activities in the more narrowly cultural sphere than on practical social or political action. Consequently, it was with this implication that the term "the new culture movement" gained wide acceptance among the Chinese at the time.

The far-reaching development of the new culture movement in the year following the incident gave China a new outlook and great hope. John Dewey, after a long analysis of the new culture movement, reached the conclusion:

> One may assert that, with all its crudities and vacillations, the new culture movement provides one of the firmest bases for hope for the future of China. It cannot take the place of better means of communication — railways and highways — without which the country will not be unified and hence will not be strong. But in China there is need, too, for a unified mind, and that is impossible without the new intellectual movement. It also makes a great deal of difference whether the mind when unified looks to the past or is in sympathy with modern thought in the rest of the world.[74]

As for the young Chinese intellectuals, they were even more optimistic. They looked to the new cultural reform activities as a ray of light in the darkness illuminating a hopeful way to save the country. It was so attractive to the young Chinese that many intelligent and ambitious students abroad decided to return to China to join the movement. Kuo Mo-jo, then still a student in Japan, and a fervent Goethian poet, inspired by the new tide in China, started to write a number of new poems in the vernacular in praise of the new era and the new China. He wrote that "China after the May Fourth Incident seemed in my mind a lively and lovely young girl with a progressive manner; she simply appeared to be my sweetheart."[75] Indeed, in the postincident period most of the dedicated Chinese youth were swept off their feet by love of their country.

CHAPTER VIII

FOREIGN ATTITUDES TOWARD THE MOVEMENT

Foreign influence upon the development of the May Fourth Movement was significant from the beginning, as was true of other major reform movements of modern China, which were usually touched off by contacts with foreign countries. In the case of the May Fourth Movement, foreign actions or reactions often interwove with its events and sometimes drew it in new directions. This was notable especially after the May Fourth Incident developed into a nation-wide uprising, and again when the new intellectuals started to split the movement. In order to facilitate the understanding of these developments and particularly the split which we will deal with in the following chapter, a short account of the differing and changing attitudes of foreign countries toward the movement and toward the Chinese situation of the period is provided in the following sections.

Among those foreign countries principally concerned with the movement, Japan was the one directly involved; Western countries such as the United States, Great Britain, and France exercised both positive and negative influences to some degree upon the new intellectuals in different periods; and the Soviet Union came to exert a stirring appeal for them after the movement had reached its acme.

The Japanese Reaction

It is understandable that the conservative Japanese government was from the beginning very much annoyed by the anti-Japanese sentiments of the Chinese consequent on the Twenty-one Demands. It periodically requested the Peking regime to take severe measures to suppress the student movement and the boycott against Japan. Moreover, right after the May Fourth Incident, the Japanese-owned and -controlled press in China started to allege that the student movement had been nurtured by the United States. On June 16, 1919, the Japanese Minister for Foreign Affairs bitterly complained of this to the American ambassador to Japan, Roland S. Morris. In the same talk, he also suggested that the movement would encourage the rapid development of "anti-foreign sentiment" in general.[1] Meanwhile, the Japanese press widely reported that British and American agents were inflaming the Chinese students against Japan, "taking advantage of the movement to extend their markets."[2] It also attributed the May Fourth Incident to the conflicting ambitions of Chinese politicians, to Bolshevik propaganda, and, according to Morris, to "everything except Japanese aggressiveness."[3] Conservative Japanese newspapers after the incident often referred to the Chinese students as "student bandits" (gakuhi).[a]

The rumor that the student movement was instigated and financed by the American Minister to China was spread in China in May, probably by pro-Japanese groups or the Japanese consular authorities in China. It was said that Reinsch had appropriated the proceeds of the United War Work campaign to finance the student movement.[b] This charge Reinsch denied flatly, as he later wrote in his memoirs:

No one could fail to sympathize with the aims and ideals of the Chinese students, who were striving for national freedom and regeneration. I, too, felt a strong sympathy, though I, of course, abstained from all direct contact with the movement, as it was a purely Chinese matter. Nevertheless, the Japanese papers reported quite in detail how I had organized the student movement, and how I had spent $2,000,000 in getting it under way. As everybody knew how spontaneous and irrepressible the movement of the students was, these items excited only amusement.[6]

The charge was also widely circulated in Japan by the conservative Japanese press, which made the additional accusation that the British and American residents and missionaries in China had assisted the student movement. Morris stated in Tokyo in June 1919: "The Kokumin in its issue of the 19th reports that the barracks of the American troops, as well as Red Cross and Y.M.C.A. rooms are being used as meeting places by Chinese and Americans engaged in anti-Japanese propaganda, and that the American Legation has distributed sums amounting to five million yen for financing such movements."[7]

The Japanese charge that Reinsch financed the student movement is, as has

[a] As a protest against this, Kuo Mo-jo, then a student studying medicine in Japan, wrote at the end of 1919 a poem titled "In Praise of Bandits" (Fei-t'u sung).[4]

[b] According to Reinsch's report, during May there was offered to the American Legation for purchase a photograph of the rough draft of a pamphlet of this charge against him. It was said that thousands of copies of this pamphlet had been distributed throughout China. It was thought that the draft was in the handwriting of Ts'ao Ju-lin or from the pen of some member of the New Communication Clique, to which Ts'ao belonged, but the authorship was not established by the photograph.[5]

been related before, not supported by evidence.[c] Since the movement embraced a great number of rather naive boys and girls who could not have kept a secret for long, such financial aid on his part would have been known almost immediately. It is also very apparent that such a vast movement could not, as John Dewey repeatedly stressed, have been instigated by a few foreign residents or diplomats.

As for the Japanese government's claim that the Chinese were developing general antiforeign sentiments, it was those conservative Japanese themselves who charged that the Americans and Britons, both foreigners to the Chinese, had instigated and supported the movement. According to the American and Chinese views of the time, in June, when the Chinese situation appeared grave, the Japanese government, facing a rice shortage and social unrest within Japan, adopted a policy which attempted to divert the anti-Japanese sentiments of the Chinese against all white foreigners. Reinsch and other American diplomats in China and Japan repeatedly reported this policy, warning that Japanese agents were "doing everything to direct the popular mind also against other foreigners particularly British and Americans," and "of Americans particularly American missionaries." [8]

It is true that after the Paris decision of the Shantung question, the Chinese intellectuals harbored deep resentments against the Great Powers. Nationalist feeling was rising among the general public. But the Chinese resentment of the time mainly concentrated on opposing international power politics instead of foreigners in general. So far as most of the new intellectual leaders were concerned, narrow nationalism did not develop during the period of the May Fourth Movement.[d] It was obvious that, although the movement bore a strong nationalist imprint, it was not essentially an antiforeign movement. From the onset of World War I through 1919 Americans and many other foreigners actually enjoyed their greatest popularity in China.[11] The fact that so many prominent Western intellectuals were welcomed to China to lecture during this period and a few years later was just one of the manifestations of that truth. Indeed, the May Fourth Movement was to a great degree a Westernization movement. Fundamentally, "antiforeignism" was the opposite of what the movement stood for.

---

[c] Above, Chap. V, pp. 121–122; Chap. VI, n.e.
[d] Ch'en Tu-hsiu even denounced "selfish nationalism and patriotism" which he thought were "inferior goods" imported from Japan which should be "boycotted by China." He suggested humanitarianism and the love of justice as substitutes for nationalism and patriotism.[9] Referring to the Japanese racial appeal, Ch'en went so far as to say that, if China had to be subdued, it seemed no better to be subdued by the yellow race than by the white.[10]

Furthermore, considering the fact that so many Chinese intellectuals were influenced by Japanese liberals and socialists,[e] one may assert that the anti-Japanese movement in China during the May Fourth period, so far as the leading Chinese intellectuals were concerned, was not aimed at Japanese or Japanese ideas in general, but rather at aggressive Japanese militarists. This is, of course, not a denial of the fact that a furious anti-Japanese sentiment had been developing among the general public and some hardships were suffered by Japanese individuals in China.

On the other side, Japanese liberals took a view of the matter different from the conservatives. Yoshino Sakuzō,[f] a famous liberal professor at Tokyo Imperial University, pointed out in an article published right after the May Fourth Incident that the Japanese press' report of foreign instigation of the movement was untrue, and that anti-Japanese sentiments in China were directed at Japanese bureaucracy and militarism and not at the Japanese people.[13] Besides several other articles with similar views he also wrote shortly after the incident a letter to a Chinese friend of his at Peking University, saying, "Aggressive Japan is not only opposed by the youths of your country, but also by us." [14]

Another Japanese writer, Fukuda Tokuzō,[g] an anti-communist socialist, professor at Keio University, declared that the Japanese foreign policy was actually directed by a "voracious capitalistic chauvinism," and the anti-Japanese movement in China was the "immediate result of such a policy." [15]

The famous *Central Review* (*Chūō kōron*) took a similar view, though it went farther, suggesting that the Japanese should "restrain the China policy of the bureaucrats and the capitalists" of Japan and stop aggravating "the dissatisfaction of the Chinese people by rendering assistance to Tsao, Chang, and other so-called pro-Japanese." It declared that "the object for which the Chinese students are struggling must be described as the same as our own

---

[e] Li Ta-chao's access to Marxism through Kawakami Hajime, and the popularity of the Japanese humanitarian new village movement among Chinese liberal and progressive intellectual leaders during the postincident period are but two examples.

[f] Yoshino Sakuzo (1877–1933), a leader of the Dawn Society (*Reimei-kai*), was in China in 1905 as Yüan Shih-k'ai's adviser and tutor of his son, as well as a teacher at Peiyang University in Tientsin. Later he studied in Great Britain, Germany, and the United States. After returning to Japan in 1913 he became a professor of political science at Tokyo Imperial University and contributed greatly to the democratic and progressive movement in Japan. He published more than thirty books on political history and theory. The Japanese Dawn Society was most sympathetic with the Chinese student movement. In June or July 1919, the Student Union of the Republic of China exchanged correspondences with it.[13]

[g] Fukuda Tokuzō (1874–1930) studied economics in Germany and was influenced by British economic thought and the historical school before he became interested in the social welfare aspects of economics. The Chinese Communists labeled him in 1958 a "capitalistic economist."

object," and their success would "emancipate Japan from the baneful influence of the bureaucrats and militarists." [16]

Two Contrasting Western Attitudes: Sympathy and Suspicion

Discounting the Japanese charges that the Chinese movement was instigated by the United States, one may still assert that most of the well-informed Westerners in China sympathized with the students and in many cases supported their cause as far as the Shantung question and the anti-Japanese movement were concerned. A number of reports and articles by American and British correspondents and writers in China at the time, ranging from Witter Bynner and George Sokolsky to John Dewey, and later Bertrand Russell, praised the Chinese intellectual movement as representing the hopeful and enlightened awakening of an old nation.[17] Almost all of the major Western diplomats in China were sympathetic, including Reinsch, the British Minister John Jordan, and the French Minister Boppe.

As a career diplomat and political scientist, Reinsch sympathized with the student movement of 1919 both in the light of the American conflict of interest with Japan in the Far East and in the light of his own conscience and political beliefs. He strongly objected to the Paris resolution concerning the Shantung question, because he thought that it was not only contrary to the interests of the United States and China, but also "a lamentable denial of every principle put forward during the war" by Wilson.[18] Meanwhile, as a former professor, Reinsch had kept a close relation with Chinese intellectuals and saw clearly that the aims and ideals of the youth of China found no support in the activities of Chinese bureaucrats and warlords. According to his observation, during the movement Western democracy was taking roots in the old country and an articulate public was being born. Among foreign diplomats in China he became one of the most earnest sympathizers with the Chinese youth, who were, as he believed, fighting for their national freedom and regeneration.

Reinsch's attitude toward the student movement, especially with regard to the Shantung question, was shared by a number of Westerners in China and was actually acknowledged for some time by the United States government. Late in May after the incident, many American and British organizations in China, including the American Chamber of Commerce of China, the American University Club of China, the Peking Missionary Association, and the Anglo-American Association of Peking, expressed their opposition to the Paris resolution and extended their sympathy to China.[19]

But the Westerners' sympathy with the movement was not uniform. While most of them supported the anti-Japanese sentiment, the intellectual agitation which interested Western writers, correspondents, and some missionaries roused the suspicions of Western merchants and other residents. The favorable attitude of the British and French authorities of the concessions in Shanghai and other cities toward the May Fourth Movement was affected and reversed by the Japanese government's propaganda and by an hysteria among some foreign businessmen in China concerning "radicalism" — Bolshevism was translated into Chinese as the "doctrine of workers and peasants" (*lao-nung-chu-i*), or, following the Japanese practice, as radicalism (*kuo-chi-chu-i*), at the time, while the term Bolsheviks was sometimes translated as *Kuang-i p'ai* — in the movement, after the merchants' and workers' strikes in June. Even before the May Fourth Incident, as Morris reported from Tokyo in March 1919, the Japanese press gave "currency to various distorted reports calculated to create alarm at America's sinister designs on Japan and the world." He quoted one of these reports which said "that America is aligning herself with Bolsheviks in order to throw the Far East into confusion and calls upon Japan to put a stop to these activities." [20]

The foreign concessions area in Shanghai, which consisted of the International Settlement and the French Concession, had been set up, like many in other Chinese cities, by treaties concluded after China's defeats in wars with the Great Powers in the last century and, under the protection of treaty privileges, had become a country within a country, with its own police force, troops, and post office, and many civil rights denied to the multitude of Chinese residents.[h] In 1919, the administration of the International Settlement

---

[h] The Shanghai International Settlement was governed, as were many other concessions in China, by a municipal council. Except in the British and Italian Concessions at Tientsin, Chinese residents were not eligible for election to the councils of any of the concessions. In the case of Shanghai, the Chinese residents in the International Settlement had no voice and representation in the municipal council, though they constituted over 97 per cent of the population of the area and contributed 80 per cent of the taxes of the municipality. The council was dominated by nine foreign members who actually represented the interest of a small number of businessmen, nationals of the Great Powers. It was governed in the traditional colonial manner which differed radically from the democratic systems of the mother countries. In 1915, the International Settlement of Shanghai had 18,519 foreign residents and 620,400 Chinese. In 1920, the numbers were 23,307 and 759,839 respectively. The settlement provided in the same year 211,400 taels for foreign pupils as educational funds, but only 87,500 taels for Chinese pupils. The French Concession was more undemocratic than the International Settlement. Its basic law had been granted by the French Emperor Napoleon III in 1868 and still remained in effect unchanged. There were cases of the police assaulting innocent people and damaging goods in shops. Once for a time, signs were posted in the parks by the authorities of the French Concession reading "Dogs and Chinese not allowed." Actually, according to the regulation of the parks founded in 1909, dogs accompanied by their owners were allowed, but not the Chinese. The regulation was reversed in 1928.[21]

showed great concern for the Chinese popular movement. Before the merchants' and workers' strikes of June, it often expressed its sympathy with the students and new intellectuals, though mass demonstrations of Chinese students were usually not approved in its area. All the news in its organ, *The North-China Herald*, before this date indicated that the student movements in Shanghai, Peking, and other cities were carried on in good order. Even on June 7, the magazine still acknowledged that "the students had in the meantime succeeded in gaining sympathy and promises of support from most of the merchants." It also reported that, at the large gathering of merchant representatives on June 5, in which students and the press also participated, the merchants' views in favor of supporting the merchants' strike were "unanimous." [22]

But on June 6, the day following the start of the merchants' and workers' strikes, the International Settlement showed it had begun to change its attitude toward the student movement by issuing a notification warning the public against the distribution in the settlement of handbills and prohibiting there the exhibition of flags bearing characters which would further excite the people. Warning was also given against the assembling of crowds in the streets. It was announced that offenses of these sorts would be punished. These warnings were not heeded by the Chinese students, merchants, and workers. In a meeting on Sunday night (June 8), the municipal council resolved to prohibit "unauthorized persons from appearing in the streets or in any public place in uniform or wearing any distinctive dress or badge or headgear signifying membership of any particular organization, association or body." [23] It also resolved to suppress all strikes, boycotts, street lectures, and other student activities, and to expel the Student Union of Shanghai from the settlement. It, at the same time, decided to carry out these resolutions by force starting on June 9 at 4 p.m.

The proposed action of suppression was supported by some of the foreign merchants and by the British, French, and Belgian Consuls in Shanghai, but — according to Reinsch — Thomas Sammons, the American Consul-General in Shanghai, as well as Reinsch and the British and French Ministers in China objected to it. Reinsch reported to the State Department on June 24: "When, on June 9, I received a telegram from the [American] Naval Intelligence Officer at Shanghai concerning the critical situation brought about by the proposed action of the Municipal Council to enforce rigid measures of repression, I was greatly concerned, fearing that this narrow-minded and short-sighted action would have the result of involving both the British and ourselves in the national Chinese movement." [24] He had then on June 9 immediately telegraphed to the American Consul-General in Shanghai asking him to "exert every possible effort to induce" his "colleagues and the Municipal Council to modify such action." [25] Reinsch later recalled this event in his memoirs, saying:

The Japanese, who were feeling the full force of the popular thrust, tried to brand it anti-foreign and to reawaken memories of the Boxer period. Some of the influential British in Shanghai, frightened by the successful efforts of the merchants and students among the industrial workers, began to call them anti-foreign, too. I was told that the Municipal Council in Shanghai might take very stringent action against the boycott and strike. The British minister had gone to the seashore, and I sent him word that the situation was serious.

It would have been the height of folly had either we or the British let ourselves be dragged into the disturbance, which was directed solely against the Japanese, and was fortunately not our concern, and in no sense anti-foreign. I sent specific instructions to the consulate-general at Shanghai advising the American community neither to encourage nor oppose this movement, which was the affair of the Chinese. The Americans saw the point clearly, and realized how undesirable it would be to entangle the Municipal Council in the business. I told the Consul-General that, illegal and overt acts excepted, the foreign authorities in China had nothing to do with the strike; being happily free of Chinese ill-will, we wished to remain free. In order to avoid all danger of more general trouble, Americans exerted considerable influence with the Chinese leaders to cause them to abstain from action that would tend to involve foreigners generally. They responded willingly.[26]

But the effort to induce modification of the proposed suppression failed. There were two Americans on the municipal council, but only one of them sided with Reinsch. The British and French Ministers had no power over the concession authorities. And the British Consul-General had to consider the interests of the British merchants, who were most powerful in the International Settlement. Therefore, the council mobilized all its forces to carry out the drastic resolutions. Distribution of handbills and displaying of Chinese flags were prohibited. Meetings, processions, and street demonstrations were forbidden. The Student Union of Shanghai was expelled from the settlement on June 9. (It then moved its office to the French Concession, and on June 11 was expelled again by the French police and consequently moved to the Chinese section.) All Chinese wearing boycott badges were forced to leave the area.

From June 9 on, *The North-China Herald* completely changed its tune, calling the student movement a "riot." Reversing its own previous encouraging opinions, it started to warn the students that their duty was to study. After explaining that it had previously always supported the student movement, its editorial of June 9 declared:

But just now, he [the Chinese student] is posing as a critic of things political. How dangerous that ground is he does not comprehend, and he will pardon our making a quotation from the speech of a most capable and wise American statesman: — "Democracies," this gentleman said, "have their dangers, and they have their dangers in foreign affairs, and these dangers arise from the fact that the great mass of the people haven't the time or the opportunity, or in most cases, the capacity, to study and understand the intricate and complicated relations which exist necessarily between nations." . . . The speaker whose opinion this is, was no less an authority than Mr. Elihu Root. The people of whom he spoke were the Americans, amongst the most enlightened people politically that the world knows. If he could speak so of such a people, what would he say of things in China today? Would he not recommend the student to stick to his books? *Ne sutor ultra crepidam.*[27]

The magazine now also contradicted its previous reports by accusing the students of "intimidating" and "blackmailing" the merchants to join the strike. "There can be no question," said the *Herald*, "that whatever their opinions, the Chinese students have no right to come into this International Settlement and impose a tyranny upon its inhabitants any more than have the blackmailers who from time to time attempt to extort money from ex-officials and others who find in this port an asylum from their political opponents."[28]

Later, on June 12, after the news of the dismissal of the three officials reached Shanghai, Chinese shopkeepers, students, and workers celebrated the event by holding meetings and processions in the Chinese quarter. When one of the processions, mainly merchants and workers with some students, entered the French Concession, it was attacked and broken up by French police. Another was prevented from entering the International Settlement. A number of Chinese workers and merchants were killed and wounded by the municipal police in street fighting.[29] Reinsch's report on the matter to the State Department on June 24 is worth quoting at length:

The British Minister . . . Sir John Jordan . . . substantially agreed with me, as had the French Minister from the start, concerning what should be our proper attitude. Unfortunately, the British Consul-General and the Municipal Council in Shanghai, notwithstanding the solitary opposition of Mr. Harold Dollar, a member of the Council (the other American member, Mr. Merriman, having been always closely allied with the British interest), had already taken action which, if the Chinese leaders had not been very cool-headed and well-advised, would have invited very serious trouble.

The American community, from the start, seems to have taken the view that the Chinese national movement was essentially sound and that it was not our affair to interfere with it. The [American] Consul-General used every proper effort to discourage and avoid action which would entangle us in unwise measures. As a result of the American attitude in Shanghai, I believe that not only was the traditional friendship between America and China strengthened but even the British were benefitted by being protected against the natural results of the short-sighted action of the Municipal Council.

Consul-General Sammons had reasonable ground to complain of the attitude of the British Consul-General. In his despatch No. 3256 of June 14th, Mr. Sammons reports that the British and Belgian Consuls had expressed the opinion that the students should not be allowed to return to their quarters in the International Settlement and that the American Consul-General had taken emphatic exception to this proposal. When a British gunboat had been placed alongside the Customs' jetty, Consul Sammons notified a senior Consul that such procedure is not legal and ought not to be considered a precedent since there was no previous Consular recognition. The British Consul-General stated that the movement of British Naval vessels is controlled entirely by the senior Naval Officer. The mooring at that point is considered as particularly likely to incite the Chinese population.

. . . When the acceptance of the resignations of these men [Ts'ao, Lu, and Chang] had been verified through telegrams from the British, French, and American Legations to their Consulates at Shanghai, the active movement there came to an end and the strike was called off both at Shanghai and elsewhere. The boycott of Japanese goods, however, continues. Unfortunately, the hot-headed action of a Municipal police official on June 10th [12th?] caused the deaths and wounding of a number of Chinese. The manner in which the national movement has thus far been conducted has commanded the respect of foreigners.[30]

The American Consul-General at Shanghai made a further report concerning "some very sinister incidental elements in the repressive policy of the Municipal Council," but this was not made public.[31]

The narrow policy of the British Consul-General in Shanghai and the municipal council vis-à-vis the student movement was bitterly resented by British and American residents in China. In its issue of June 21, the British *North China Daily News* published an editorial expressing appreciation of the place of the student movement in the future of China. The American newspaper in Shanghai, *The China Press*, in an editorial of the same date urged "the Consular Body to order a public investigation not only of the handling of the strike but of the whole machinery of defense of the International Settlement — its methods and its personnel." [32] Reinsch frankly pointed out that the municipal council was "representing narrow Shanghai commercialism." [33]

The French Concession in Shanghai adopted a similar repressive policy towards the student and new culture movements. On June 18, 1919, a week after the end of the strikes, August Wilden, the French Consul-General in Shanghai, informed the municipal council that the Chinese *Chiu-kuo jih-pao* (*Save-the-Nation Daily*), which was published in the French Concession, had been permanently closed, and that its editor had been sentenced to the maximum penalty provided by Chinese law on the charge that his paper had incited the

Chinese masses to join the boycott against Japanese goods. On June 26 the consul-general proclaimed an ordinance restricting all publications. It provided: "No printed matter, tract, magazine or newspaper, shall be put into circulation without the previous lodgment of a copy with the French police and the French Consul-General." [34] Offending publishing firms could be closed at any time by the police, and were subject to punishment.[35] The ordinance was immediately put into effect in the French Concession.

But when the French authorities attempted to secure the passage by the International Settlement of a restrictive amendment to a bylaw so that a parallel policy might be followed there, a very considerable opposition was immediately forthcoming both from the Chinese and the foreign residents. Scores of Chinese societies, including those representing the merchants, newspapermen, publishers, bankers, clerks, students, industrialists, workers, all joined in protest. At a joint meeting of the executive committees of the Ameriman Chamber of Commerce of China and the American Association of China a resolution was adopted opposing the proposed amendment "because it is against American principles and because it will not accomplish the object for which it is proposed." [36] It was also opposed by most of the consuls. As a result of this strong opposition, it was decided to submit the proposal to a meeting of the ratepayers. There it was defeated, for the ratepayers were completely indifferent. All of the meetings of the ratepayers called by the council in each year from 1919 to 1925 to consider the proposal were abortive because the ratepayers failed to attend the meetings and there was never a quorum. But, as a matter of fact, the repressive policy of the concession authorities was carried out on most occasions.

After the May Fourth Incident, however, the Chinese residents of Shanghai started to organize themselves more effectively into groups like the street unions, the Chinese Ratepayers' Association, and others. They continually protested that "the Chinese ratepayers had no voice at the Ratepayers' Meetings and were deprived of their civil rights." [37] The Chinese struggle for civil rights in the Shanghai concession area thus accelerated by the May Fourth Incident characterized the municipal history of that city in subsequent years, and extended to all other big cities wherever there were concessions.

This struggle for civil rights in the Shanghai concessions exerted great influence upon the mental attitude of the young Chinese intellectuals in the early twenties, because during this period a great number of important intellectual leaders, political workers, active and ambitious young men and women, and the energetic students of the new China tended to gravitate to that city. The Western administration of the concessions did not present a good showcase for Western democracy. In view of the miserable conditions endured there by factory workers and their experiences with Shanghai commercialism and the narrow-minded policies of the concession authorities, these intellectuals soon felt disappointed in the West.

One event which the concessions' authorities in Shanghai considered a menace and a justification for their repressive policies was the workers' strike and its potential consequences. Most of the factories in Shanghai were owned or controlled by foreigners. The exploitation of labor in China had long been flagrant. Women and children, as John Dewey and many other writers had reported, worked day and night for long hours — often twelve to thirteen and a half hours a day, seven days a week — for incredibly low pay, ranging from twenty cents Chinese money a day to no payment at all except board. Despite such conditions, most of the workers had not yet awakened to the possibilities of strikes. The factory owners were alarmed for they believed that the students went among the workers and explained to them ideas of freedom and democracy and the nature of Western labor movements, although the strike staged by the workers in Shanghai early in June was in support of the students, not a protest against management, and the students had actually advised the workers in Western-owned factories to avoid strikes in order to prevent international complications.[38]

The action of the concessions' authorities was also influenced by the atmosphere of a Red scare which existed in Eastern as well as Western countries in 1919.[i] While there was no genuinely influential communist group in China before 1920, an hysterical fear of Bolshevism permeated traditional Chinese society and Western residents in China. People with liberal leanings, or who advocated reforms, such as Hu Shih, were regarded as Bolsheviks.[40] The Chinese, like the Western public, often confused Bolshevists with anarchists and socialists[j] who actually differed from each other to a very great degree. It is quite safe to say that Bolshevik influence upon the May Fourth Movement in 1919 and before hardly equaled liberal and democratic influences.[k]

---

[i] A Chinese publisher of the time refused to publish a book on sociology (she-hui hsüeh), fearing that the government would ban it, because the word "sociology" in the title had the same root characters "socio" (she-hui) as "socialism" (she-hui chu-i).[39]

[j] For example, Kotenev stated that the Shanghai municipal police regarded "books and documents of pronounced socialist and anarchist tendencies" as "Bolshevist literature." Two book stores raided by the police at the time actually published most of the liberal publications. One of them, the Oriental Book Co. (Ya-tung t'u-shu-kuan) published New Youth and almost all of Hu Shih's works.[41]

[k] John Dewey, writing in the summer of 1921, asserted this point, basing his conclusion on

The Soviet Appeal

It was during this critical period, when the Chinese intellectuals, trying to imbibe the liberal and democratic tradition of Western thinkers, were encountering the stern realities of commercial and colonial practice in China, that the Soviet Union made its tempting appeal to them. China by the time of the May Fourth Movement was a country which permitted the exercise within her national boundaries of all kinds of extraterritorial rights and privileges. There existed within her territory "spheres of influence," "spheres of special interest," war zones, leased territories, treaty ports, concessions, settlements, and the Legation Quarter. The foreigners maintained their own law courts and post offices in China; even the Chinese who had law suits with foreign residents were subject to foreign courts. There were a great number of special privileges granted to the Great Powers in respect to commercial and industrial rights, railroads and mines, loans, and currency. Two of China's chief revenue sources, i.e., the maritime customs and the salt tax, and their administration, were completely under foreign control or direction. Their proceeds, as well as other revenues, were pledged to meet fixed charges on foreign loans — loans in most cases concluded publicly or secretly by warlords for the financing of the numerous civil wars that accompanied their personal struggle for power. The national tariff rates were fixed by the Great Powers. Firearms and narcotics were smuggled and dumped on the Chinese market by Chinese and foreign importers. In many strategic places within her borders, there were stationed considerable bodies of foreign troops and warships under foreign command. All these facts, and many others, had made China a geographic term instead of a sovereign state, a market instead of a nation.[43] In spite of the criticism of some far-sighted Westerners, the official policies of the Western Great Powers toward China still adhered to the traditional, colonial lines. Russia, on the other hand, in the period following the October Revolu-

---

personal observation. "A selection of writings," said he, "could be made which would show it [the May Fourth Movement] to be dangerous to society, to the peace of the world. Japanese writers who have paid attention to it have mostly held it up as a subversive radicalism and have attributed it to Bolshevist propaganda. But in the nine provinces I have visited, I have yet to find a single trace of direct Russian influence. Indirectly, the Russian upheaval has, of course, had a tremendous influence as a ferment, but far subordinate to that of the World War and even to President Wilson's ideas of democracy and self-determination. For the New Culture Movement, though it cares nothing for what is politely called a republic in present China, is enthusiastically stirred by democratic ideas." Dewey went further: "For Bolshevism in the technical sense there is no preparation and no aptitude in China. But it is conceivable that military misrule, oppression and corruption will, if they continue till they directly touch the peasants, produce a chaos of rebellion that adherents of the existing order will certainly label Bolshevism." [42]

tion, adopted a more or less idealistic policy toward China and the colonies of Asia. Several Tsarist secret treaties made with Japan concerning China had been made public and annulled by the Soviet government. On July 25, 1919, Leo P. Karakhan, acting for the People's Commissariat for Foreign Affairs of the Soviet Government of Workers and Peasants (*Narkomindel*) in Moscow, issued a declaration, addressed "to the Chinese people and to the governments of China, North and South," proposing the abrogation of all the secret treaties and other unequal treaties concluded by the Tsarist government with China and the relinquishment of all its privileges and interests without compensation.[44]

The telegram containing this declaration was delayed in transmission, strangely, for eight months, and reached Peking only in March 1920. The Peking government refused to negotiate and, in a message to all provincial governors in June, declared that it could not accept the proposal formally because the communication was probably a forgery. The Western press in China also stated that they did not vouch for the genuineness of the document and that they had found no corroboration, while some "internal evidence" on several points militated against its genuineness. This allegation of forgery was quite groundless.[1] But the Anfu Cabinet summarily ignored the offer. So did its

---

[1] The Karakhan declaration actually had been published, albeit with a one-month delay, in the Moscow official publications, *Izvestiia* and *Pravda*, on Aug. 26, 1919, in the course of a report on a meeting of Chinese workers in Moscow.[45] A similar offer to restore their concessions and rights to China had been made by the Soviet government in 1918 and at the time had been officially revealed by Moscow.[46] In the middle of April 1920, before the Peking government alleged the forgery of the declaration, Soviet representatives had already arrived in Peking to conduct negotiations on the proposal.[47] As for the "internal evidence" suggested by the Western press, it was to the effect that, since the declaration said, "The Soviet government renounces all the conquests made by the government of the Tsar depriving China of Manchuria, and other regions," that this was contrary to the fact that Russia had not legally deprived China of all Manchuria. In other words, the declaration was too generous.[48] Later on, it was discovered that in the English translation of the declaration published in China in June 1920 there was a paragraph concerning the return of the Chinese Eastern Railroad to China, which the text published in Moscow does not have. Some Soviet officials later charged that the paragraph was planted by the translator or someone else to confuse the matter, but Western writers asserted or implied that it was a mystery and that the genuine offer was not as generous as the text available in China indicated. Other interpretations attributed the omission to the Soviet change in diplomatic attitude.[49] At any rate, the episode seemed not to have made much sense to the Chinese of that time because both the texts published in China and Moscow contain the over-generous statement that the Soviet Union would return "all the conquests made by the government of the Tsar depriving China of Manchuria, and other regions," which might well be interpreted as including the Chinese Eastern Railroad which was in Manchuria. The declaration also asked for negotiation for "all other questions" between the two countries. The intention of the Great Powers to prevent China from negotiating with the Soviet Union is very apparent. The French and Japanese Ministers in China even formally issued a protest against China's allowing the Siberian trade delegation of the Soviet government to enter China.[50]

successor, Wu P'ei-fu's regime. The Soviet proposal was never entirely put into practice.[m] This was attributed by some to the Peking regime's reluctance to negotiate and by others to the shift in Soviet policy from a revolutionary diplomacy of self-denial to a traditional diplomacy of self-interest along with the retreat of Kolchak's counterrevolutionary forces from eastern Russia from August to October 1919.

The delay of the telegram to China might be attributed to Western and Chinese anti-Soviet efforts. Its delay proves that there were no organized or influential Bolsheviks in China at this time, or, at least if there were, that there was little contact between those in China and Russia. Otherwise, they would have spread the news much earlier, at the time when the Chinese student movement and strikes were at their height.[n] Moreover, the Karakhan declaration was made more than two months after the occurrence of the May Fourth Incident and one month after the Chinese refused to sign the German Peace Treaty, that is, after the settlement of the incident. If the Bolsheviks had played an important role in the student movement and strikes in this period, as the Tokyo, Peking, and concession authorities alleged and later the Chinese Communists asserted, the declaration should have been made earlier. Nevertheless, major Soviet reaction to the May Fourth Incident was expressed in *Izvestiia* in September 1919. The author, A. Voznesenskii, then chief of the eastern section of Narkomindel, held an optimistic view on the opportunity the incident provided for Bolshevism in China.[53]

This is not the place to judge the motives for the Soviet proposal and to predict whether it would have been carried out had the Peking government been willing to negotiate. What is important here is that after the Chinese intellectuals learned late in March 1920 of the existence of the declaration, the development of the May Fourth Movement was greatly influenced. They be-

---

[m] The Soviet Union sent troops into Outer Mongolia in 1921 to liquidate the remnants of the anti-Bolshevik troops fleeing from Siberia under Atman Semenoff. They stayed there and supported the establishment of the Mongolian People's Revolutionary Government. In 1922 a secret Soviet-Mongolian Agreement was signed. But on May 31, 1924, when the Sino-Russian Treaty and Agreements were signed, the following points were secured: (1) The Soviet Union renounced all previous treaties and agreements between China and Tsarist Russia, and all concessions Tsarist Russia had acquired in China before the Russian Revolution. (2) The Soviet Union recognized Outer Mongolia as an integral part of China, promising to respect China's sovereignty therein and to withdraw the Soviet troops from there. (3) The Soviet Union agreed to the joint Sino-Soviet management and redemption of the Chinese Eastern Railroad by China.

It is hard to evaluate the sincerity of the Karakhan declaration because of the complicated political changes in China in later years.[51]

[n] As for the Russian immigrants in China, the official figure for 1917 was 51,310 and it increased to about 200,000 in 1920 because of the October Revolution. Most of them were anti-Bolsheviks or former officials.[52]

lieved that under the circumstances, in contrast with the Japanese Twenty-one Demands and other pressures on China and the Western powers' insistence on privileges and discrimination in the country, there was no reason why the Chinese should not enthusiastically welcome the offer. The Peking government's policy toward Russia and its apathy toward the proposal were incomprehensible to the Chinese intellectuals.

Before the overthrow of the Tsarist government, China had tried to refuse to pay the Boxer indemnity to Russia, which amounted to about 120,000,000 haikwan taels. While all other powers agreed to forego the indemnity for a period of five years dating from China's entrance into the World War, the Tsarist government agreed to give up only about one fourth of its share. Actually the Chinese had failed to pay this for some time. Now the Tsarist government had been overthrown for more than three years. Tsarist Russia could no longer finance the maintenance of the large staff of its legation and consulates in China. But the Peking government was now paying the indemnity to the old Russian legation in Peking despite its earlier refusal to do so to the former Tsarist government. (After the February Revolution of 1917 the Chinese government seemed to have informally recognized Russia's provisional government. But the Russian legation in China retained its Tsarist staff and maintained more or less the traditional attitude toward China. Thus, it was often regarded by the Chinese as a Tsarist legation.) These payments were then sent to support Kolchak, Semenoff, and others who were attempting to overthrow the Soviet government. These Russian forces in Siberia had been playing the Japanese game and had shown no regard for China's interests. When the Peking government sent gunboats to the Amur to protect Chinese interests, the gunboats were fired on and held by the Russians as a result of Japanese persuasion.[54] The old Russian legation still insisted on the enforcement of all those treaties which had been secured by the Tsarist government from China by force.[55] It, of course, seemed absurd to the Chinese people that the Peking government still recognized this Russian legation, which had no government at all, and refused to negotiate with the Soviet government, which offered unconditionally to give up all Russia's concessions and privileges in China.

Consequently, upon learning of the Karakhan declaration, the Chinese press and various societies, including those of students, teachers, merchants, industrialists, workers, and women, responded with fervid demonstrations of gratitude. It was notable that the declaration made a deep impression not only on the new intellectuals, but also upon the industrialists and merchants, who under ordinary circumstances would not have been inspired by communist actions.

The whole body of parliamentary members, regardless of their political beliefs, also joined in the enthusiasm. By early April, more than thirty important organizations had communicated directly with the Soviet government on the matter. These included the All-China Journalists' Union, Student Union of China, Federation of Street Unions of Shanghai, Merchants' Save-China Association, Chinese Federation of Labor, Chinese Industrialists' Association, Women's Association, all members of Parliament, and other social and political organizations.[56]

In its reply to the Soviet government and people, dated April 11, 1920, the Student Union of the Republic of China declared:

> We really feel extremely grateful to you for your recent gracious proposal. We will do our best to advocate the formal restoration of diplomatic relations with your country, and hope with enthusiasm that, based on the justice of liberty, equality, and mutual assistance, the Chinese and Russian people will with profound friendship strive to wipe out international oppression and the discrimination of country, race, and class, in order to create new conditions for genuine equality, liberty, and fraternity.[57]

The other societies expressed similar hopes.

Meanwhile, most of the Chinese newspapers and periodicals, liberal or conservative, responded with similar enthusiasm, demanding the establishment of diplomatic relations with the Soviet government. The well-known Chinese paper, the *Social Welfare Daily*, which was owned by an American syndicate,[58] was one of the first papers to support this demand.[59] The Chinputang organ thought that the Karakhan declaration was based on those Wilsonian principles which Wilson himself had been unable to carry out.[60] The Kuomintang organ said:

> Since the May Fourth Incident, all the attention of the Chinese people has been focused on the problem of their relations with Japan. But this problem cannot be solved by merely dealing with the Japanese government. Henceforth, we ought to transfer our attention to the problem of our relations with Russia. This problem is not one of relations with one country but with the whole world. How to resolve the conflict between the capitalist class and the laboring class, between aggression and pacifism, and between nationalism and internationalism is related to each country's attitude toward Russia. We hope that all the press circles, student circles, industrial circles, and other citizens of China will awake, study, and face squarely this problem.[61]

During the latter phase of the May Fourth Movement after the spring of 1920, the Chinese intellectuals thus started to pay more attention to the Soviet

Union than ever before. Their attitudes towards it were divided. Although there were a number of groups which were still hostile to the Soviet Union, the pro-Soviet tide was rising.

Under heavy pressure from public opinion, the Peking government had to send a diplomatic delegation to Moscow and on September 20, 1920, it discontinued its recognition of the old Russian government.[62] On September 27, the Soviet government published a second proclamation signed by Karakhan containing proposals similar to the first one but with more reservations concerning the Chinese Eastern Railroad.[63] Some of the Chinese intellectuals arranged to keep in contact with Soviet representatives in China as early as 1920, four years before the Peking government's recognition of the Soviet government. In August 1922 when the Soviet envoy, Adolph A. Joffe, arrived at Peking, he was enthusiastically welcomed by Chinese students and social groups, though the Peking government treated him coolly. In a welcome meeting, fourteen important social and student organizations, including the New Tide Society, the Great Federation of Antireligionists, and the Society for the Study of Socialism, joined, as did educational leaders such as Ts'ai Yüan-p'ei. Thus, the selfish attitudes of the Western commercial interests in China and the appeal the Soviet Union had for the Chinese intellectuals profoundly influenced the trend of the May Fourth Movement.

The trend of Chinese intellectuals to the left in later years may be attributed in part to the lack of a tradition of individualism in China and to the impatience of the intellectuals with a prosaic and apparently everlasting program. The backwardness of China in terms of practical politics in contrast to a Western world with far more progressive ideas and practices made patience a difficult quality to maintain. But more important, Western democracy as practiced at home was distorted in China by the Western "self-interest and hidden groups," as John Dewey termed them.[64] The imperialist and colonial attitudes of the Western concessions in China towards the new intellectual movement and the foreign policies of the Great Powers towards China were too obviously contradictory to the ideas preached by the Western thinkers and statesmen, such as Dewey, Russell, and Wilson. The Soviet appeal to China was directed at the rising tide of nationalism and the independence movement in which China was attempting to shake off the political and economic control of the Great Powers. Under these circumstances, the suppression of the news of the Karakhan declaration in China and the Peking regime's refusal to negotiate made the Soviet appeal all the more dramatic and effective.

CHAPTER IX

THE IDEOLOGICAL AND POLITICAL SPLIT, 1919–1921

THE spirit of unity prevalent among the new intellectuals during the months immediately following the May Fourth Incident was only superficial, a temporary result of the fact that they all faced a common opposition. Beyond their shared intention to re-evaluate tradition and promote new learning, there was little evidence of a single mind among them. The Western ideas introduced into China had always been extremely diverse. When traditional Chinese thinking and institutions appeared shaken, Western ideas such as democracy, science, liberalism, pragmatism, humanitarianism, anarchism, socialism and so on all entered a free market for thought. Moreover, the contemporary problems of China were exceedingly complicated. To face them, the new reformers had to be concerned with practical politics and controversy. Turning from their common hostility to the traditional order to the task of finding positive solutions, they were confronted with a diversity of social philosophies and models. Therefore, after 1919, discord among the new intellectuals increased, first in ideas and then in actions, and the movement was split wide open in its later years.

Major Intellectual Groups Involved in the Split

The currents of Chinese thought in the period after the incident are too complicated to be easily classified. Because of the high rate of illiteracy, average people did not appreciate the contradictions among the various new ideas as clearly as the new intellectuals who became involved in the disputes. For convenience of discussion, we may ignore minor complications and classify the new intellectuals into four major groups: the liberals, the leftists, some members of the Kuomintang, and some of the Chinputang. The first two groups and some nationalistic elements of the latter two had actually taken the leadership of the May Fourth Movement both in ideology and action. Other individual members of the latter two parties had also extended considerable support to it, especially in the protest against the government's foreign and domestic policies.

The leftists at this time included various elements which were not actually referred to as "leftists" during the May Fourth period. Here we use the term to include all the radical factions who advocated extreme social, economic, and political changes, except the purely nationalistic revolutionaries. In the early years of the period, the leading leftists were idealistic and democratic socialists, anarchists, guild socialists, and syndicalists. Later on, there were various Marxists and communists. In 1919 and 1920 there was a tendency among the new intellectuals to promote some general socialist ideals without subtle ideological distinctions; but except for the fact that they all attacked private ownership of property, these groups differed greatly from each other. It also must be noted that many of the prominent leftist intellectuals such as Ch'en Tu-hsiu and Li Ta-chao did not swing strongly in this direction until after the middle of the May Fourth period.

On the other side, the liberals, as was natural, took less to organizational activities and in many cases were not to be easily identified as a group. When we ask what is the common ground of all those we call "liberals," we find that, in various degrees, they advocated freedom of thought and expression. While some of them might have been considered radical in aspects of their philosophy, in the sphere of action they tended to stress democratic procedures. Some intellectuals and writers who had been previously affected by British or French liberalism or constitutionalism, such as Chang Shih-chao, had refrained from participating in the new reform movement and often abandoned their early convictions. Other eminent intellectual leaders with liberal views like Ts'ai Yüan-p'ei and Wu Chih-hui were influenced by anarchist and nihilist ideas. They did not undertake any systematic exposition of liberalism. In the study of liberalism and Western democratic theories, there were only a handful of scholars who were well versed, such as Chang Wei-tz'u, Kao I-han and T'ao Meng-ho. Among these liberal writers the most articulate and widely read was Hu Shih. John Dewey's other disciples such as Chiang Monlin and T'ao Hsing-chih were also influential liberal educators and his works and lectures attracted the attention of most young intellectuals. In the post-incident period, the pragmatists actually took the lead in the liberal camp in China.

Besides these groups were the two major political parties, which embraced more complicated elements in their membership. A number of the intellectual leaders of the Chinputang associated with Liang Ch'i-ch'ao and under the influence of Bertrand Russell and Henri Bergson came close to guild socialism. Chang Tung-sun, Chiang Po-li, Carsun Chang, and Lan Kung-wu (Lan Chih-fei or Chih-hsien) were, besides Liang, the most prominent writers in this party. Some leaders were liberal gentry and Wilsonian idealists, such as Lin Ch'ang-min, a foremost and enthusiastic supporter of the student movement. As for the large part of the party's membership, i.e., bureaucrats and politicians, they made less contact with young intellectuals.

By the time of the May Fourth Incident, the Kuomintang had split into Southern revolutionary and Northern parliamentarian factions. Sun Yat-sen and his close followers had been in Canton and Shanghai in an effort to overthrow the Peking regime, joined by a few members of the Chinputang and Southern warlords and politicians. Other factions of the Kuomintang, such as the remnants of the Hua-hsing-hui originally led by Huang Hsing and Sung Chiao-jen and those of the Kuang-fu-hui originally led by Chang Ping-lin as well as some party members with anarchist background, remained in Peking. Among the leaders of the party who had great appeal to the new intellectuals and students were Sun Yat-sen, Ts'ai Yüan-p'ei, Wu Chih-hui, Hu Han-min, Tai Chi-t'ao, Yeh Ch'u-ts'ang, Shen Ting-i (Shen Hsüan-lu), Shao Li-tzu, Chu Chih-hsin, and Liao Chung-k'ai, most with socialist and nationalist tendencies by the time of the incident, though Ts'ai and Wu were actually loosely related to the party.

That the May Fourth reforms were tending in opposite directions became evident with the leftist wing's zeal for socialist studies and propaganda and the liberal wing's concern with the proper approach to practical problems. The split became overt in a debate between Hu Shih on the one side and the socialists and some Chinputang members on the other. Meanwhile, the liberals tended to avoid political entanglement and advocated that reform should be achieved by way of educational and cultural movements, whereas the socialists and the Kuomintang were more politically minded, with the Chinputang as a party falling in the center. Furthermore, the vital question of what kind of economic and political systems China should adopt came to the fore. And more immediately, what attitude should be taken toward the Peking regime? In all these questions, the leftist intellectuals found themselves closer to the Kuomintang in advocating a political revolution against the Peking government, while the Chinputang remained within the latter and the liberals gradually retreated to academic work after some criticism and ineffectual protest against the warlord regime.

"Problems and Isms"

The split of the new intellectual group actually began in the field of ideas and developed shortly after the incident. Chinese youths, almost overwhelmed with reform fervor, thought the problems of China might be solved in a total, overall fashion with some specific Western doctrine. This enthusiasm and naiveté were especially apparent among the various kinds of leftists. On the other side, the liberals felt that the solution could be achieved only piecemeal, and consequently shunned any suggestion of a "basic solution." Such a discrepancy in ideology gradually came to the surface when from July to September 1919 a furor was caused among the new intellectual leaders by Hu Shih's article, "More Study of Problems, Less Talk of 'Isms,'" published in *Weekly Critic* on July 20 of that year. This short-lived debate may be considered a signal for the start of the split.

Hu's argument was based on pragmatism. He declared in the article that no doctrine or "ism" was more than an instrument for the solution of this or that practical problem. The formulation of a doctrine, in Hu's opinion, should be based on and grow from the study of specific, practical problems. High-toned, all-embracing isms might be facilely advocated by anybody. Indeed, after the May Fourth Incident, even the leaders of the warlord Anfu Club talked of socialism or the "principle of the people's livelihood," interpreting it in their own light manner. Moreover, imported isms, as Hu pointed out, might not fit the practical needs of the time. Finally, abstract isms expressed only on paper could be utilized by politicians as vague slogans to serve their own ambitions instead of to solve problems. Hu thought the problems of China could not be solved altogether, but must be tackled individually. There was no single prescription which could cure every kind of disease.[1]

Hu's article provoked immediate opposition on the part of a journalist of the Chinputang, Lan Kung-wu, and Li Ta-chao, who was fervently studying Marxism. Lan pointed out that the problems were often interrelated and not simply isolated. Many problems could not be recognized as problems without "subjective reflection" or the help of certain theories; the Chinese had not considered despotism intolerable for several thousand years until the doctrine of Western democracy was introduced into China.[2] To both Lan and Li, all problems were linked together in all embracing structures, and all-embracing isms were groups of ideas with similar character. Isms were needed both as standards for the judgment of situations and problems, and as instruments for the solution of such linked problems. Li Ta-chao agreed with Hu Shih that practical problems should be studied closely, and that doctrines should not be talked about vaguely; but he did not think there was any contradiction between the study of problems and the talk of isms. The fact that isms were utilized by warlords and politicians as slogans for their own purposes did not prove that isms were themselves at fault, but, rather, emphasized the necessity for careful study and rigorous implementation of the various doctrines. Having by then accepted in part Marx's materialism and his theory of class struggle, Li argued further that, in an unorganized and stagnant country, problems could not be solved separately without a basic change in economic structure.[3]

Replying to these arguments, Hu insisted that isms might be studied and selectively adopted as instruments and hypotheses. They should not, however, be accepted as creeds or iron laws, but ought to be studied in the light of evolution and by a "genetic method."[4]

Later, on November 1, Hu wrote another article to summarize his view on the new thought tide and concluded thus:

> The spirit of the new thought tide is "a critical attitude."
> The methods of the new thought tide are the study of problems and the introduction of academic theories.
> The future tendency of the new thought, from my personal observation, should be to lay emphasis on the study of problems important to life and society, and to carry out the task of introducing academic theories through studies of these problems.
> The attitude of the new thought tide toward the old civilization is, on the negative side, to oppose blind obedience and to oppose compromise, and, on the positive side, to reorganize our national heritage with scientific method.
> What is the sole aim of the new thought tide? It is to re-create civilization.[5]

At the end of the article, Hu insisted that civilization was not created *in toto*, but by inches and by drops; that liberation or reform meant only the liberation or reform of this or that system, idea, or individual by inches and by drops; that the first step in the re-creation of civilization was the study of individual problems; and that the progress of the re-creation lay in the solution of such individual problems. It may be noted that the term "to reorganize the national heritage" suggested earlier by Chang Ping-lin and redefined here by Hu Shih was later used in a sense quite different from the early antitraditionalist new thought tide, a fact we will discuss in Chapter XIII.

The above interpretation of the new thought movement by Hu Shih was theoretically sustained but also qualified by John Dewey's lectures on "Social

Philosophy and Political Philosophy" at Peking University in the winter of 1919. In the sixteen lectures on this subject, Dewey, on the basis of his major principle that knowledge is a form of doing, criticized and rejected both extreme idealism and extreme materialism. He said that society has gradually evolved in the course of history and theories for the solution of problems originate in events. Consequently, social scientists should pay more attention to events and evidence, maintain an attitude of experimentation, and regard all principles as hypotheses. In other words, the new social and political philosophy emphasizes experimentation, the study of particular events, and the "continuous improvement" of society.[6]

The questions raised by Hu's article and Dewey's lectures concerned the problem of methodology in social science and proper attitudes towards theories and practical reforms. Their major point was the warning that problems could not be solved *in toto* with any all-embracing doctrine and isms should not be accepted as cure-alls but as hypotheses and instruments for solving specific problems at specific times. In view of the development of dogmatism among many Chinese intellectuals in thought and political action in later years, the warning was quite significant and far-sighted.

The danger, however, was not apparent to the leftists and most of the other new intellectuals in this early time. In fact, few eminent intellectuals close to socialism or other doctrines had then dogmatically accepted their isms as a whole. Li Ta-chao acknowledged in August 1919 that isms were but instruments for the solution of practical social problems.[7] Ch'en Tu-hsiu maintained even in September 1920: "It is better to promote the practical movement of education and emancipation of workers than vaguely to talk anarchism and socialism."[8] It was not until the end of the year that Ch'en declared that isms provided necessary guidance for social reforms just as a destination was necessary for a voyage. But he maintained at the same time that revolution or social reforms could not be achieved *in toto* in a short time but in continuous endeavors inch by inch.[9] In this aspect Ch'en was quite close to Hu Shih, and to his last days he maintained that he had never liked to talk vague isms. Even as late as the summer of 1921 a communist writing in the Chinese Communist organ declared: "All kinds of socialism are only temporarily true; they should never be regarded as permanent and absolute truth."[10]

With such views similar, at least superficially, to those of the liberals, these leftist leaders side-stepped the issue at this point. But the fact remained that a number of the youth during this period were really susceptible to the fashion of isms, and some of them had firmly if vaguely committed themselves to this or that specific doctrine. They enthusiastically talked of isms and ideals but had not carefully studied them. Their conceptions were in general shallow and confused. This defect was obvious not only among the anarchists, socialists, and Marxists, but also among the liberals and conservatives. It was important to warn all of them that practical problems must not give way to abstract theories and that isms and theories should be studied in detail rather than treated as slogans.

On the other hand, while the proposal for "more study of problems" was to the point and timely, the liberals did not seem to have done better in this respect than the zealots of other competing isms. It may be correct to say that, under the circumstances, economic and social problems were among the most crucial problems China had to face squarely. The liberals, however, failed at least as much as others to study these urgent problems and suggest any hypothetical or final solutions. In practice, it is difficult to perceive what were the really controversial issues on which they disagreed with the advocates of the other theories. The Deweyites, of course, had paid more attention to educational problems and suggested a solution of them; yet most of the youth of that time remained unconvinced that education alone could solve all economic, political, and social problems. It is also ironical that in 1920, just after their suggestion of "more study of problems," very few liberals joined the social survey or labor movements, whereas many of the socialists and their associates started to go among the workers and peasants to study their living conditions.[a] After 1922 quite a few liberals tended to specialize in esoteric academic work such as verifying ancient texts. It was not until several years later that some leading liberals tried to study urgent Chinese problems. They seem to have overlooked in these early years the fact that the potential contributions of pragmatism and liberalism were more than mere carping criticism.

Moreover, pragmatism and liberalism were, of course, themselves isms, and the introduction and competition of so many contradictory and vague isms in China at one time was a further problem. The pragmatists and liberals could not sway the Chinese intellectuals without involving themselves in an ideological contest in detail with the proponents of the other isms. Such a struggle was actually evaded by both sides. Few of them at the time made any thorough and critical study of each other's theories. Under such circumstances, the pragmatists occupied a rather disadvantageous position, since in effect they only told

---

[a] The May 1920 issue of *New Youth* was in some aspects a result of this trend. The magazine hereafter paid some attention to social and economic surveys and labor problems, while the liberals refrained from this. *Young China* and *Young World* showed attitudes similar to *New Youth*, early in the twenties.

the others: "You should give up all isms and accept our ism, because, according to our ism, no ism should be accepted as a creed." This argument was obviously too feeble to be advanced at the beginning of a vast intellectual movement when isms were accepted by many as slogans only. Indeed, it was a case of the dilemma produced by a "doctrine of no doctrine at all."[11]

Although the debate did not change the ideological trend of the time, it made a little clearer to the liberal-minded and even some radical intellectuals that they should refrain from sheer slogan shouting. The establishment of *Young World* with its emphasis on practical surveys might be a proof of this influence. In the fall of 1919 Mao Tse-tung and his friends also became aware of the issue and organized the Society for the Study of Problems (*Wen-t'i yen-chiu hui*) in Changsha. The society proposed to study more than 140 problems in the fields of politics, economics, sociology, education, labor, international affairs, and the like, such as how to unite the people, the feasibility of socialism, and the problem of Confucianism. Mao rather accepted the argument that the study of problems should be related to that of isms, but his proposal had never been fully carried out.[12] Meanwhile, the warning "less talk of isms" was, if not totally ineffective, inadequate to deal with the issues between the liberal and other ism zealots, especially with regard to various practical problems.

Sociopolitical Activism versus Cultural Activism

Another fundamental difference between the attitudes of the liberals and the leftists was reflected in their views on the relative priority of political action and cultural reform. The liberals in general veered away from politics and paid more attention to educational and cultural reforms, whereas the leftists (in cooperation with the nationalists) favored direct political action.

As mentioned before, from the beginning of the alliance of the new intellectual leaders in 1917, some of them were reluctant to become involved in political affairs or to talk politics. This was true even in the case of Ch'en Tu-hsiu, who was so much disappointed by warlordism and the old bureaucracy that he thought at this time the hope of saving China lay not in political action but in a cultural renovation of the entire nation. But after 1918, foreign and domestic policies of the Peking government drew his attention more and more to politics. In *New Youth* he and other writers like Li Ta-chao, Kao I-han, and Chang Wei-tz'u, of whom the last two were scholars in the field of political science, found it difficult to avoid touching upon political problems.

Disregarding the opposition of other members of the magazine, Ch'en insisted on writing about such subjects and often urged Kao and Chang to do so also.[13] Meanwhile, many youthful readers of the magazine and of similar publications thought that more political problems should be dealt with in positive fashion by those periodicals. In Ch'en's opinion, politics might be discussed, but what he meant by politics was much broader than conventional administrative trifles or the doings of politicians. He approached the problem in a new way, wanting to "build a social foundation for the new politics."[14] This attitude was shared by many of his associates. Consequently political problems in the broad sense were among the important subjects discussed by them.

On the other side, people who advocated keeping remote from the politics of the time were not few. According to Ch'en Tu-hsiu, they included at least three groups: certain scholars and intellectuals such as Hu Shih and Chang Tung-sun; merchant groups exemplified by the Chamber of Commerce and the newly-established Federation of Street Unions in Shanghai; and the anarchists. Ch'en thought that this last group positively and fundamentally rejected politics as a means to achieve their goals while the other two were merely negative and temporary escapists from the practical political situation.[15] This account of the three groups is not completely accurate, since neither the anarchists such as Wu Chih-hui, the guild socialists such as Chang Tung-sun, nor the merchant groups as a whole, as in the case of the street unions, completely shunned practical politics. Nevertheless, it is true that a number of people, including the liberal intellectuals, were reluctant to take political action. Even the scholars specializing in political science were inclined to avoid practical political entanglement.

The liberals' abhorrence of practical politics was based on the one hand upon their pessimistic views of the warlord and bureaucratic government, and on the other upon their assumption that political reform could be achieved only after a social and cultural transformation which must be promoted by way of education. As Hu Shih explained later, he himself, though originally interested in politics, decided to avoid involvement in it for twenty years only because, on his way back to China in the summer of 1917, he was discouraged by the news of Chang Hsün's restoration movement. He thought that the restoration movement was natural under the circumstances — that the circumstances themselves must be changed. So he set out to participate in the reforms of Chinese literature and Chinese thought in order to lay the foundations for political reform.[16] The same view was explained systematically by John Dewey. Since "democracy was a matter of beliefs, of outlook upon life, of habits of mind, and not merely a matter of forms of government," as he pointed out, it demanded "universal education," and the first step towards achieving universal education was to establish the spoken language as a written literary language.[17] Speaking of "the comparative failure of the Revolution" of 1911, Dewey asserted at the end of 1919 that it was "due to the fact that political change far outran intellectual and moral preparation; that political revolution was formal and external; that an intellectual revolution is required before the nominal governmental revolution can be cashed in." Accordingly, China should be built "by spreading a democratic education, raising the standard of living, improving industries and relieving poverty."[18] On another occasion, after an analysis of the history of Westernization movements in China, Dewey came to the same conclusion that "China could not be changed without a social transformation based upon a transformation of ideas. The political revolution was a failure, because it was external, formal, touching the mechanism of social action but not affecting conceptions of life, which really control society."[19] And another thing for the Chinese to do would be to learn scientific methods from the West.[20]

With these views in mind, the liberals went further and asserted that the student movement and the reform currents were not political movements. "When most political in its outward expression," said Dewey, the student revolt of May 4, 1919, "was not a political movement. It was the manifestation of a new consciousness, an intellectual awakening in the young men and young women who through their schooling had been aroused to the necessity of a new order of belief, a new method of thinking. The movement is secure no matter how much its outward forms may alter or crumble."[21] Since Dewey held that the new culture movement was "concretely and practically" "associated with the Student Revolt," his view on the student activities might be actually applicable to the May Fourth Movement in this aspect. Furthermore, he not only held that the movement was not a political one, but also asserted that "it was in its deeper aspect a protest against all politicians and against all further reliance upon politics as a direct means of social reform."[22] Acknowledging the political appearance of the student movement, he believed that its main emphasis was on matters outside the political sphere. He gave two reasons for this: first, China was traditionally "apathetic towards governmental questions. The Student Revolt marked a temporary exception only in appearance." Second, "the hopelessness of the political muddle, with corrupt officials and provincial military governors in real control is enough to turn the youth away from direct politics."[23]

While the liberals tried to emphasize the educational and cultural reforms of the movement, the leftists stressed and capitalized on its political nature. This attitude may be exemplified by Ch'en Tu-hsiu's argument in 1921. The students succeeded in the May Fourth Incident, as Ch'en saw it, mainly because they had taken well-organized action and awakened a mass movement which from the beginning had strong political significance.[24] As the warlord government appeared more unbearable to him than before, Ch'en thought the intellectuals should take a variety of actions to achieve their political goal. On the one hand, he held that the new culture movement should help this cause. Although he accepted the assumptions that military, political, and economic activities should be excluded from the field of culture, that the cultural movement ought to deal solely with science (social and natural), religion, morality, literature, music, and the arts, and that, as far as political affairs were concerned, the movement should merely concern itself with problems of political science, he insisted that it must be oriented in the following directions. First, it should emphasize organizational activities to build up the public spirit of the people. Second, it should emphasize a creative spirit to develop a new culture rather than merely to abandon the Eastern culture in favor of the Western. Third, it should influence all other movements, i.e., indirectly influence practical politics, military, and economic affairs, but not be infiltrated by them.[25]

On the other hand, Ch'en suggested that the new culture movement was not the sole activity in which the new intellectuals should participate. They might join in social movements which dealt with social problems, such as those relating to the position of women, the condition of labor, population questions, and the like. In Ch'en's opinion, those who worked for the cultural movement might or might not work at the same time for the social movement, and vice versa. He also held that a man of letters or a scientist might maintain his standing in the cultural movement even if he expressed somewhat conservative views on social questions. He objected to using the cultural movement as a direct instrument for political and social reforms. A cultural movement would influence political and social reforms in the long run. But it was a herculean task for a nation, demanding much time and continuous effort. It could not, and should not be expected to, achieve success in a short time.[26]

Ch'en's distinction between the cultural and social movements seems to reveal an intention on his part to explain the necessity of the latter for the solution of the pressing political and social problems of China. There is no doubt that he was from the beginning to the end an enthusiastic supporter and promoter of the new culture movement. But in later years, his activities seemed to center more around the social movement if we follow his definitions of the two types. His approach to the solution of Chinese social, political, and economic problems was by way of the social movement. This seemed consistent with his idea of building a new social foundation for the new politics, although it probably differed somewhat from his views expressed in 1915 when he started the *Youth Magazine*. The cultural movement in the narrow sense wou.d, of course, also help to build this foundation. Nevertheless, in his opinion, this was an indirect way of dealing with things. It did not rule out the necessity of social and political action for the solution of China's problems. On this point, therefore, his view differed in essence from that of the liberals.

Turning to the existing political parties, we find that both the Kuomintang and the Chinputang leaders recognized the political significance of the May Fourth Movement. As has been mentioned, Sun Yat-sen was one of those who first realized the political character of the student and new thought movements, and regarded them as the prerequisites of a political revolution. The Kuomintang leaders in the few years following the incident actually sensed the political implications and potentialities of the movement more than its cultural facets.

As for the Chinputang, a moderate attitude was expressed by one of its leaders, Liang Ch'i-ch'ao. Early in 1921, discussing the development of the May Fourth Movement during the year following the incident, he stated that, although it was beneficial to shift the bias of the movement in the direction of cultural activities, it was a mistake to neglect political matters. A veteran political reformer, he cited Chinese and Western histories to support his point that political progress was often achieved by continual "political movement." This he defined as "a means adopted by a group of citizens dissatisfied with a part or the whole of the body politic, to achieve the common purpose of political reform or political revolution with continual and united propaganda and activities joined by a mass of people in a public manner with the preservation and development of the state as their ideal." [27] He pointed out that it was "the most crucial problem" of the time for the Chinese people to decide whether political activities should be encouraged now or postponed indefinitely. On the other hand, he realized that to nurture a political movement in a country without freedom of speech and assembly and among a people largely illiterate would engender the following dangers: The movement might be manipulated by politicians and political parties for their own ends. The majority of the people would not be interested enough to join it. Or, if they did join it, it would be dominated by mob emotion and not by rational considerations. For these reasons, it seemed better to build first a foundation for future political reform by way of a cultural movement or of an economic and social reform movement. But, as he observed, a political movement had long been an urgent need in China, because: (1) With the unfavorable political circumstances, in which political freedom was denied to the people, no reform movement, not even a cultural movement, could be pushed forward. (2) The Chinese people were too passive and apathetic towards public affairs; without a political movement, the society could not be changed into a dynamic one and no social reform could be achieved. (3) It was true that a genuine political movement could not be started without the citizens having political knowledge and interest; but the reverse was also true, namely, citizens' political knowledge and interest would not increase if they were not brought into contact with political activity. (4) A political movement might improve the consciousness of unity and the capacity for self-government of the Chinese people.

Consequently, though he was not sure whether or not politics should be a major activity of the Chinese people of the time, he suggested that in the existing transitional period, political activities should be directed at eliminating obstructions hindering the cultural and social movements, and the political education of the people should be commenced in order to lay the foundations for effective political movements in the future.[28]

It seems clear that Liang's position was somewhere between that of Hu Shih and Ch'en Tu-hsiu, while the Kuomintang leaders' interest in the political potentialities of the new movement attracted some of the leftist intellectuals to that party.

It is true that the May Fourth Movement was in essence an intellectual revolution; but it was so only because of a rising political interest among the new intelligentsia. Almost invariably in Chinese history, every major student movement was a manifestation of a tendency away from the traditional apathy and towards political action. The May Fourth Incident apparently was part of a similar tendency not only among the new youth, but also among the masses of the people, at least city dwellers, who were awakened by the students' campaign. A Western observer, referring to the student movement of May 1919, reported the situation thus, "Literally millions of farmers, dealers, and artisans are talking for the first time of national and international affairs which it never entered their minds that they could express an opinion on, not even when stirred up by the recent revolutions. One can go to any food shop among any group of laborers on the job and hear it all about him. The signs in the tea shops: 'Don't talk politics' are out of date. It is a remarkable thing which these young crusaders [students] are doing — perhaps the real awakening of China at last." [29] It is true that the discouraging political circumstances were enough to turn the new youth away from aspiring to official careers in the existing government, but the very hopelessness of the political muddle was at the same time a factor which could (and did) drive them into direct politics in the sense of political revolution.

Democracy, Capitalism, Socialism, and Westernization

The foregoing sections have been concerned only with the attitudes and methods of the reformers. The more urgent and vital questions were still what kind of political and economic system and what kind of culture China should build up for herself. While some polemics on academic and philosophical problems are reserved for a later chapter on the ideological controversies which developed early in the twenties, we will present here those various responses to these vital questions which fundamentally influenced the split of the May Fourth Movement.

Democracy, one of the catchwords most often used by the new intellectuals during the May Fourth period, had never been sufficiently discussed and understood. Among those who first analyzed the subject in Western terms and published in the Chinese spoken language, Dewey deeply impressed the new Chinese intellectuals with his lectures on the problem. In a lecture delivered in the winter of 1919, Dewey divided democracy into four elements. These were (1) political democracy: principally constitutionalism and representation in legislation; (2) democracy in people's rights: such as freedom of speech, press, belief, residence, and the like; (3) social democracy: the abolition of social inequality; and (4) economic democracy: the equalization of the distribution of wealth.[30] These were what Dewey considered the essentials of modern democracy which should be upheld.

In discussing the application of democracy and individualism in China, Dewey suggested a gradual and progressive program which would modify the traditional individualistic ideals of the West. He traced the history of political individualism in the West in two stages. In the first stage people struggled for individual freedom against state or organization control. After this stage, inequality among individuals became a problem and the recent tendency of Western democracy had been to eliminate inequality by social legislation limiting individual freedom. Dewey then suggested that China should carry out the two stages in one step as follows: (1) Since China lacked a tradition of individualism, its traditional "principle of protection" (of the individual by social groups or the state) might be democratized. (2) China might achieve equality of opportunity for the people by means of popular education. (3) In order to solve its specific problems China might develop specialization of knowledge, which, as he said, Western democracy trusted too little.[31] These suggestions were attempts by Dewey to tailor his ideal to the Chinese reality. But despite Dewey there was always the danger that individual freedom and rights might be slighted by the Chinese since they had not sufficiently experienced the first stage, the struggle for individual freedom and rights, and state and government authority had until recently scarcely been seriously challenged in China. Nevertheless, his program appeared quite agreeable to the Chinese of the time.

Furthermore, in his analysis of existing economic theories and institutions Dewey adopted a kind of progressive or radical liberalism, rejecting the theories of both orthodox capitalism and Marxian socialism. He attacked the traditional theory of free contract on two counts. First, it failed to realize that free contracts could not be achieved without the existence of equal standing and capacity of the two parties concerned. A large supply of surplus labor would compel workers to accept a contract unfavorable to them. Second, the theory of free contract also erred in considering that contracts between employers and employees merely affected the interests of the parties concerned, whereas in fact they affected the interests of the whole society. On the other hand, Dewey thought that Marxian socialism was not acceptable because in an economy under the control of the state, individual initiative would be eliminated, as it had been under feudalism, and because a minority of the able and experienced elite would still be able to manipulate the state economic organization.[32]

Following this analysis, Dewey discussed guild socialism and syndicalism, elements of which he thought had been borrowed by the new Soviet constitution. He did not accept guild socialism as a creed, but seemed less critical of this kind of "industrial democracy," as he labeled it. Consequently, he made two concrete suggestions for the solution of Chinese economic problems: (1) the Chinese state should own important resources, such as roads, mines, forests, and waterways instead of leaving them to private ownership; (2) China should utilize and reform its old guild system as one of the elements with which to build a democracy, transforming the professional guilds into political organizations — a point which had been suggested by some Chinese writers such as Chang Tung-sun. In concluding his long lectures Dewey urged as the guiding principle for Chinese economic reconstruction that the major aim of all economic enterprise should be to further the interests of society rather than private profit. Thus he, though far from a socialist, cast doubt upon one of the major premises of traditional capitalism, i.e., that the private profit incentive will spontaneously promote the interests of society.[33]

Dewey's rejection of Marxism and traditional capitalism in theory was further reinforced by his observation of China's economic condition. In his judgment, labor problems and the uneven distribution of wealth had not yet become serious in China because of the underdevelopment of its industry. Hence, socialism and Marxism should have no roots in China.[34] He fully recognized, however, that China had been a "paradise" for exploiters due to the lack of labor laws.[35] He said, "China is after all in the early stage of the industrial revolution, and, if it is not to repeat the experience of the rest of the world, with all the evils and dangers of the welfare of capital and labor, with sweated industries, child and woman labor, oppression by capital and sabotage by the worker; if it is going to profit by the nineteenth-century experience of the rest of the world, it has to come to the problem prepared." [36] Therefore, like many Chinese intellectuals including Sun Yat-sen, Liang Ch'i-ch'ao, and Ch'en Tu-hsiu at this time, Dewey thought that economic measures to prevent a future social revolution should be adopted. Indeed, when he classified in his lectures all social problems into three categories — economic, political, and intellectual — Dewey pointed out that economic problems were the most important, because, as he said, "economic life is the foundation of all social life." [37]

But the significant economic problem discussed by Dewey did not attract enough attention from his Chinese students and friends and other Chinese liberals. Chinese liberals at this time were preoccupied with educational reform, academic research, and the re-evaluation of national classics. Few of them considered seriously the problem of the application of democracy in China in terms of economic organization and practice. This was undoubtedly one of the major causes of their waning influence on the public following their dramatic role in attacking the traditional ideology and institutions.

On the other hand, a number of Chinese intellectuals, even those already inclined to some form of socialism, were influenced for a time by Dewey's concept of democracy and especially his economic reforming ideas. In his article, "The Basis for the Realization of Democracy," published in the December 1919 issue of New Youth wherein the first installment of Dewey's lectures on social and political philosophy also appeared, Ch'en Tu-hsiu agreed in essence with Dewey's analysis of the four elements of democracy with only one addition. That is, he thought a system of representation and constitutionalism was not enough to protect political democracy; it was better for it to be supplemented with "direct legislation," a term which he did not define but by which he presumably meant initiative, referendum, and recall. Ch'en also noted that social and economic democracy were more important than the other elements, i.e., political democracy and democracy in people's rights.[38]

Ch'en was very optimistic about democracy in this broader sense being applied in China. He recognized that democracy in the sense of political and civil rights elements was more fully developed in Great Britain and the United States than in other countries, while social and economic democracy had still not been achieved by "any country." In asserting this, he did not make any exception of the Soviet Union. Further, basing himself on Dewey's analysis of the development of democracy in the United States, he recognized that American democracy had its grass roots in self-government in village, town, and county, rather than in the activities of the federal government.[39] Ch'en went on to suggest: "In implementing democracy, we must follow the British and American models, paying attention to social and economic aspects, and laying a strong foundation; that is, the foundation must consist of small units built by the people themselves."[40]

Starting from this principle, Ch'en proposed for the task of building democracy in China two concrete programs: local self-government and "professional unions." The idea of the former was largely based on Dewey's description of the growth of self-government in the villages and towns of the United States. The latter was actually an embodiment and expansion of Dewey's suggestion for the utilization of the traditional Chinese guild system. It is interesting to note that Ch'en also pointed out that the "professional union" which he proposed as one of the bases of social and economic democracy differed from the conventional commercial chamber or medieval guild which was organized only by the employers, and from the Western trade union which was joined only by the workers. The professional union proposed by him would be joined by both the employers and employees on a basis of equality. "In the industrial and commercial circles of China today," said Ch'en, "the status of most of the employers and employees in commerce and industry differs very little, except in a few big factories, railroads, and mines in Shanghai, Hankow, and Tientsin, where considerable unequal status exists. Before the existence of apparent conflict of interests between capital and labor all those who engage in the same profession, no matter whether they are owners or workers, may join the same unions."[41] Therefore, in his proposals for self-governing local units and professional unions, which very much resembled the street unions developed in Shanghai after the May Fourth Incident, Ch'en rejected at least for the time being the necessity of class struggle in China, and his conceptions showed strongly the influence of guild socialism.

Although even those who leaned to socialism had agreed with Dewey in certain aspects of his interpretation of democracy, their special emphasis on economic problems, neglect of democratic procedure, and oversimplification of the political situation were remarkable. A check of their writings in these years, including Li Ta-chao's, shows that they had little genuine understanding of Western political institutions. In this respect, Ch'en Tu-hsiu was probably better educated than his associates. But when he criticized constitutionalism and party politics in principle in June 1919, he stated his conclusion very simply: "What is politics after all? Everybody must eat — that is important."[42] The appalling economic situation of China and the postwar world not only led the leftists to distrust Western political institutions, but also induced some leading liberals such as T'ao Meng-ho to doubt that Western political institutions, especially representative government, were useful in general to cope with the existing political and economic problems both in China and in the West.[43] In addition, the corrupt Chinese political practice and the aggressive, colonial policies of the West towards China overshadowed any theoretical consideration of Western democratic political systems and legal devices. It was not until the last few years before his death in 1942 that Ch'en Tu-hsiu realized that even a socialist society should accept some Western democratic political devices and experience, such as parliamentary government, legal procedure in guarantee of civil rights, such as freedom of thought, speech, the press, and workers' right of strike, protection for the opposition parties, and free elections.[44]

In the trend to undervalue political achievements of the Western democracies, the Chinese intellectuals started to be preoccupied with the discussion of economic systems in terms of capitalism and socialism. This was accelerated in 1920 upon the arrival of Bertrand Russell, when guild socialism and syndicalism showed some increasing influence and capitalism became a serious subject for discussion.

Russell's visit in China from the fall of 1920 to that of 1921 was sponsored by Chinputang leaders such as Liang Ch'i-ch'ao. As has been mentioned, this party from the beginning had some relations with the Peking government and consisted of complex elements. While its bureaucratic and conservative members often had some sort of relations with the warlords, its intellectual leaders and newspapers sympathized from 1918 with the student movement and the new culture movement, a policy which intensified, and also was intensified by, its feud with the Anfu group. The party members' political views were various and included guild socialism, democratic socialism, capitalism, and republican or monarchical constitutionalism. To a certain degree, its leaders' sponsorship of Russell's lectures was conducted in the hope of strengthening their ideological position.

But because of his prosocialist views, particularly before his visit to the Soviet Union in May 1920 which preceded his China trip, Russell was also welcomed by the Chinese leftists and liberals. In fact, among the politically minded Chinese youths he was more widely read than Dewey. By 1920, quite a few of his works had been translated into Chinese. These included the *Principles of Social Reconstruction, Roads to Freedom: Socialism, Anarchism and Syndicalism, Political Ideals,* and *The Problems of Philosophy.* G. D. H. Cole's *Self-Government in Industry* and J. H. Harley's *Syndicalism* were also available in Chinese by the end of 1920. The ideals of local small-scale democracy and self-government in guilds were prevalent among some of the new intellectuals. In October and November of 1920 *New Youth* carried a number of articles by or on Russell. At that time, Russell had already published articles criticizing the Soviet Union on the basis of his recent visit,[45] while Ch'en Tu-hsiu had actually committed himself to communism; yet the attitude of Ch'en and other leftists toward Russell was not critical until his views were interpreted by some Chinese intellectuals and conservatives to their own advantage. This involved the questions stemming from his speeches of whether capitalism might be adopted in China and what China should learn from Western civilization.

Russell's first impression of China was her extreme poverty. He considered development of her industry and education was China's most crucial and urgent task. To accomplish this, Russell urged, much against his own philosophy of less government, that the first requisite was to establish an orderly and competent government. In this respect, he suggested that a parliamentary government with the support of the Chinese constitutionalists and of a patriotic and world-minded populace with public spirit and energy to stop military usurpation and foreign control should be encouraged. This view was later well summarized and explained by him at the end of his trip.[46] But it was not popularized and thoroughly discussed by the Chinese during Russell's stay in China.

As for the economic aspect, Russell advocated a system which, if not qualified somewhat, might have been rather difficult to differentiate from the Soviet economic system. He thought that in a country "economically but not culturally backward" such as China, given good government, "State Socialism, or rather what Lenin calls State Capitalism," would have many advantages.[47]

Like Dewey, Russell believed that whether to establish genuine socialism was not an urgent question in China at the time. Noncapitalistic economic systems, including those of communistic anarchism, syndicalism, and guild socialism, would not fit undeveloped countries. To develop industry, there were, as he said in an interview with a Chinese economist, three possible ways: under the control of capitalists, of the state, or of workers. Since the Chinese workers were not organized and educated enough to run the economy, and political democracy could not be achieved in China in the near future, Russell believed that, of the three ways, state control would be the best for China and native private capitalism the second best. "The worst thing for China," said he, "is to allow her economy to be controlled by foreign capitalists." [48] In the Chinese translations based on his oral speeches and also in his "farewell address in China," Russell said that the Russian type of communism could not prevail in Western Europe and was not an ideal system for world peace, but with important qualifications it might be applied in China in the present stage of her economic development since her urgent problem was to increase production with great speed.[b] Consequently, he advised China to try for the time being state socialism, i.e., state capitalism, with an orderly and competent government but to avoid excessive bureaucratic dictatorship and overemphasis of economic factors at the expense of ethics, which the communists failed to avoid, and look for further liberal and democratic development.[50]

Russell's suggestions for governmental and economic systems were qualified by his opinions concerning the problem of the spread of education in China. He believed that education should develop political consciousness among the people. Chinese education, like her industry, should be free from foreign control which had made the Chinese students slavish toward Western civilization, and she should not always depend upon her returned students who had the stamp of the country in which they had been educated. As for "the aim which Young China should set before itself," Russell proposed "the preservation of

[b] Russell even publicly and definitely upheld in his lectures in China some of the ideals of communism and acknowledged the achievements of Russian Bolshevik economic practice. In the conclusion of a lecture, after a great deal of praise of the success of communism in Russia, such as the realization of economic and social equality, Russell asked all countries to help her to continue, and said: "I hope, furthermore, that every civilized country in the world should experiment with this excellent new doctrine." [49] Russell's views presented in the Chinese translations based on his oral speeches sometimes do not seem to completely accord with those in his own English writings. (The same is true of Dewey to a lesser degree.) In some cases, the translations must be incorrect, with some qualifications in the original being possibly left out. Hence, while their essentials are true, the translations should not be taken too literally as representing Russell's own views. But here we would rather base our account on the Chinese translations because it was these which were widely read by the Chinese public of the time.

the urbanity and courtesy, the candour and the pacific temper, which are characteristic of the Chinese nation, together with a knowledge of Western science and an application of it to the practical problems of China." [51] Unless China preserved her own pacifist philosophy of life instead of learning the Western aggressive attitude toward things, her adoption of Western government and industrialization would, as Russell believed, not necessarily improve the chance of world peace.[52]

This opinion of Russell's in regard to the aim of education was based on his broad view of Eastern and Western civilizations. As a pacifist, Russell flatly disapproved of the Western militant and aggressive attitude. In China he found instead a tranquil, pacific, humane, and tolerant life among the average people, those in the countryside in particular. Moreover, most of Chinese ethics and political philosophy, as Russell saw them, preached an ideal life along these lines. He was especially impressed by the Taoist teachings of Lao-tzu and Chuang-tzu, whose conception, "production without possession, action without self-assertion, development without domination," bore great similarity to Russell's own ideas of promoting creative impulses and eliminating possessive ones. Referring to the Westerners, Russell said, "In so far as there is a difference of morals between us and the Chinese, we differ for the worse, because we are more energetic, and can therefore commit more crimes *per diem*." [53] Contrary to Dewey and most of the Chinese new intellectuals in the early stage of the May Fourth period who had been advocating Western ideology in general against Chinese traditional ethics and philosophy, Russell maintained that what the Westerners "have to teach the Chinese is not morals, or ethical maxims about government, but science and technical skill," or more exactly, scientific method. On the other hand, Westerners should learn from the Chinese "a just conception of the ends of life." [54]

It is interesting to note here that, when the Deweyites and, to a lesser degree, the Y.M.C.A., together with the Marxists and anarchists, were attacking Confucianism and the Chinese tradition, and the Marxists were starting to attack imperialism, Russell, disliking war and imperialism more than or as much as the others did, tried to demolish all those Western factions by citing the traditional Chinese philosophy of life, especially the Taoist principle, the love of nature. He said that "the real problem for the Chinese intellectuals is to acquire Western knowledge without acquiring the mechanistic outlook." [55] By "the mechanistic outlook," Russell meant "the habit of regarding mankind as raw material, to be moulded by our scientific manipulation into whatever form may happen to suit our fancy," a habit "which exists equally in Imperialism, Bol-

shevism and the Y.M.C.A., which distinguishes all these from the Chinese outlook, and which I, for my part, consider very evil." [56]

Russell realized that what he considered of merit in the Chinese character
and civilization would not help to achieve the effective government and economic system he proposed. He also understood that, compelled by the aggressive attitude of the West and Japan, China would also have to resort to militant
measures, to give up the traditional Confucian and Taoist passive agricultural
and family ethic and develop public spirit or patriotism or Western nationalism. Recalling his visit to China, Russell later said, "I loved the Chinese, but it
was obvious that the resistance to hostile militarisms must destroy much of
what was in their civilization. They seemed to have no alternative except to be
conquered or to adopt many of the vices of their enemies." [57]

Russell's views were expressed at a time when socialism had become a much-
discussed subject; they provoked several controversies because of both distortion and misinterpretation and of the temper of the Chinese new thought tide
during the period. In respect to political and economic problems, Russell's
rejection of the broad aspects of Russian communist practice drew some Chinese intellectuals back from their hope to adopt it *in toto*. His emphasis on the
necessity of increasing production, on the other hand, brought out the question
whether native private capitalism was necessary for China. The Chinputang
guild socialists as a whole had been skeptical of capitalism.[58] But now the problem of efficient production came to the fore, and the guild socialists realized
that Chinese factory workers were too few and too weak to take over political
and economic responsibilities. Some of them such as Chang Tung-sun even
found no genuine working class in China but only soldiers and bandits. In their
opinion, what people needed was employment and a livelihood more than
freedom or anything else; and capitalism was the most effective means to
achieve these, even if it was unjust to the workers. They, therefore, suggested
that local capitalism or cooperativism be tried in the present stage. When
capitalism was fully developed and the working class became strong, the former
should be abandoned for socialism. For the time being, it was more necessary
to resist international capitalist control than to overthrow the native capitalists.
These views, which were in some aspects quite similar to the arguments of the
Russian legal Marxists such as Peter Struve and Tugan-Baranowsky late in the
last decade of the nineteenth century, were expressed in various ways in a series
of articles published in the Chinputang organ *La Rekonstruo* (*Kai-tsao*) early
in 1921.[59]

This reorientation of the viewpoint of the guild socialists at once drew criticism from both the Marxists and the Kuomintang members in Shanghai and gave rise to a debate on socialism published mainly in *New Youth* and the Kuomintang organs.[60] The leftists maintained that the aggression from foreign capitalist countries could not be halted without the establishment in China of a strong government of the working class, which, though admittedly nascent, should be helped to grow. The Kuomintang leaders of course believed in the necessity of a powerful government in place of the Peking regime.

Although the *La Rekonstruo* group was criticized for its "antisocialist" and "procapitalist" tendencies by the leftists, the genuine issue was not so clear-cut. Most of the former group which consisted of writers with different shades of opinions had never defended capitalism as a goal, nor had they conceded that they denied the ideal of socialism, though they said they did not accept either Marxism or anarchism.[61] A few writers among them raised the points that government ownership of production means would not necessarily be more reasonable and better than private enterprise, that an unchecked government could be very dangerous, and that a socialist transformation would cause chaos in the society.[62] These doubts, however, did not receive much attention from the majority of the new intellectuals and were not taken as key points in the argument, though they were seized upon by conservative circles as support for their cause. There seems to have been some truth in the report that, when Dewey and Russell stayed in Shanghai, quite a few members of the Chinputang and some merchants, industrialists, and compradors joined the welcoming parties and tried to paint the two philosophers as their partners.[63] Consequently, the opinions of Russell and the guild socialists on many points were distorted and utilized as a basis for supporting the policy of cooperation with the Peking government, the interests of the merchants and industrialists, and the preservation of the "national quintessence."

This final point was reinforced by Russell's views on Eastern and Western civilizations. His advocacy of industrialization without losing the passive and pacific character of the Chinese and their ethics developed in an agricultural society raised the question whether it was a too difficult thing to realize if not impossible. Whether the Taoist doctrine to "reject knowledge" and "return to and follow nature" was compatible with the modern scientific attempt to seek knowledge endlessly and conquer nature was also an open question. Russell's idea actually bears some similarity to the theory of "Chinese study as fundamental structure and Western study for practical use" advocated by some Chinese literati at the end of the last century and rejected by most of the new intellectuals during the May Fourth period and also by Dewey. Dewey thought that "this idea of the materialistic, technological nature of Western civilization" had been applied in Japan and resulted in evils because of the preservation of the traditional Japanese militarism.[64] To this argument, Russell certainly might have replied that, if Japan could learn scientific technology and at the same time keep her own ideology, why could not China achieve the same and would not the preservation of her pacifist and tolerant ethics result in the opposite of the Japanese practice?

Nevertheless, Russell's opinion on civilization was applied by the Chinese conservatives and traditionalists in other directions. It was argued that even an eminent Western philosopher conceded the superiority of the Eastern civilization which was essentially spiritual, and that science was not as important as generally acknowledged, points reiterated in the polemics on science and metaphysics and on civilizations, which we will discuss in a later chapter. Aside from this distortion and utilization by the conservatives and traditionalists, some of Russell's views were obviously not harmonious with the frame of mind of China's new intellectuals of the time, especially the Marxists who were launching a severe attack on guild socialists and anarchists in 1920 and 1921.

In a letter to the present writer in 1954, Russell still insisted on his view of China expressed three decades earlier, but pointed out that the Chinese conservatives' utilization of his opinion as a theoretical justification for attempting to halt the contemporary influx of Western learning in science into China was far from his intention. He said in part:

I am interested in what you say about the way that my views were interpreted in China. I can see how they might be used by reactionaries, although this was far from my intention. I stated what I thought ought to be done in a farewell address which I gave in Peking and in my book on "The Problem of China." I realize that China had decided to industrialize as fast as possible. The same thing is being done in all the less industrialized parts of the world. Very soon there will be a vast surplus of industrial goods and a vast deficiency of food. Both these troubles will be cured by a great war in which industrial products are used to diminish the number of mouths that have to be fed. This did not seem to me thirty years ago, and does not seem to me now, a road to the millennium.[c]

[c] Bertrand Russell, letter to Chow Tse-tsung, Aug. 26, 1954. In the same letter, Russell explained that he could not remember Ch'en Tu-hsiu's letter to him asking the real meaning of his remarks on capitalism, and his reply at the end of 1920. For Ch'en's letter to Russell see *New Youth*, VIII, 4 (Dec. 1, 1920), p. 8; also VIII, 5 (Jan. 1, 1921), editor's note; Russell's reply was scheduled for No. 6. The "farewell address" referred to in the letter is titled "China's Road to Freedom" and appeared in *Che-hsüeh* (*Philosophia*), No. 3 (Sept. 1921), Appendix, pp. 1–14, with a Chinese translation by Fu T'ung, pp. 357–68. Some of Russell's opinions expressed in the address, such as the suggestion of state socialism, were opposed by such former supporters in the Chinputang as Chang Tung-sun but sympathized with by such others as Fu T'ung, editor of *Che-hsüeh*.

The conflict of views on political and economic systems and on civilization among the Chinese, which was greatly influenced by Dewey and Russell in the two years after the May Fourth Incident, at first produced a rather confusing situation with few groups completely agreeing with others. But gradually the dividing line between economic and political considerations dominated the split of the movement. This was accelerated by the impact of practical politics.

Participation in Politics

Along with the ideological conflict which gradually intensified from 1920 on, there was a corresponding split in action on the part of the intellectuals. It was based on differing attitudes toward the Peking government and differing aspirations for sociopolitical and cultural reforms or revolutions. Whereas the liberals and conservatives tried in vain to demand moderate reforms under the warlord rule, the leftists and nationalists accelerated their organizational activities under the rising influence of Soviet Russia.

In the years immediately following the May Fourth Incident, a series of unsuccessful attempts to bring about political reforms were made by the new intellectuals, especially the liberals and some members of the Chinputang, with the support of a few leftists. Under the rule of the warlord government, the liberals often found it difficult to maintain their aloofness toward politics. Early in September 1919, just after Hu Shih had argued the question of "problems and isms" with Li Ta-chao in *Weekly Critic*, the weekly was suppressed by the Peking government, and the two men had to carry on their debate in *The Pacific Ocean* monthly, a magazine established by students returned from Europe and America.[65] On August 1, 1920, the liberals Hu Shih, Chiang Monlin, T'ao Meng-ho, Kao I-han, Wang Cheng (secretary to the new American Consortium), and Chang Tsu-hsün (Chang Wei-tz'u) joined with the new Marxist convert Li Ta-chao to publish a "Manifesto of the Struggle for Freedom," which began:

Basically we are not men who talk about practical politics, but practical politics has always been our stumbling block. It has been nine years since the 1911 Revolution. Under the rule of the pseudo republicanism of the last nine years, we have experienced every kind of suffering known to those who are not free. These sufferings remain the same regardless of political changes or the substitution of one political party in power for another. When politics brings us to such a dead end, we have to arouse ourselves and realize that genuine republicanism can never be achieved until politics is initiated by the people. In order to get the people to initiate politics, we must have as a prerequisite an atmosphere wherein a genuine spirit of free thought and free criticism can be nurtured. As we believe, in the history of mankind, no freedom has ever been secured in any country without the sacrifice of the blood and sweat of the people. If there are no people who wish to fight for freedom, there will be no genuine realization of freedom. The fact that the warlords and political parties have dared to behave so tyrannously in the last few years is just a manifestation of the lack of that genuine spirit of free thought and free criticism on the part of the people.[66]

In their manifesto they asked for the abolition of police oppression, and of the laws and regulations governing press, publication, and emergencies enacted in 1912 and 1914.[d] On the positive side, they demanded, firstly, freedom of speech, publication, assembly and association, and secrecy of communications; secondly, writ of habeas corpus; and thirdly, supervision of elections by nonpartisan organizations.

It must be noted that in this manifesto, the liberals and their associates definitely stressed two facts: One was the existence of warlords in China and their tyrannical behavior. The other was that freedom could be secured only by the people's fighting for it. When the warlord government merely turned a deaf ear to their declaration, what they should and could do about this immediately became an important question. But there was no definite answer nor any further action on this question.

When the above manifesto was published, Tuan Ch'i-jui and his Anfu Clique had just been turned out of power in the Peking government. Replacing them were two other warlords, Ts'ao K'un and Wu P'ei-fu, who were favored by most of the British interests in China.[e] The Chinese political situation went from bad to worse. On May 13, 1922, the same men who had published the manifesto two years earlier joined with other famous intellectual leaders and made another declaration — "Our Political Proposals." It was initiated by Liang Sou-ming and Li Ta-chao, and drafted by Hu Shih.[f] Its theme of "good govern-

---

[d] The laws and regulations referred to in the manifesto are those mentioned above, Chapter III, plus the "Regulation Governing Printing Enterprises" which was enacted in 1919. The regulation was intended to deprive the people of freedom of written public expression.

[e] Tuan's troops were defeated by the allied forces of Chang Tso-lin of Manchuria and Ts'ao K'un of the Chihli group, in July 1920. The Anfu Club was suppressed on Aug. 5. Wu was the most powerful lieutenant of Ts'ao and in actual control of North China. It was reported that Soviet Russia also had for a time regarded Wu as a possible ally but dropped him later in favor of Sun Yat-sen.

[f] The proposal was signed by the following sixteen persons: Ts'ai Yüan-p'ei (chancellor of Peking University), Wang Ch'ung-hui, Lo Wen-kan, T'ang Erh-ho (former chancellor of the Peking Medical College), T'ao Chih-hsing (W. T. T'ao, later changed to T'ao Hsing-chih, chairman of the department of education, National Southeastern University, Nanking), Wang Po-ch'iu (chairman of the department of political science, law, and economics, Southeastern University), Liang Sou-ming, Li Ta-chao (chief librarian and professor of Peking University), T'ao Meng-ho (chairman of the department of philosophy, Peking University), Chu Ching-nung, Chang Wei-tz'u,

ment" was also suggested by Hu and was probably inspired by the ideas of the American Good Government Association. In the declaration they suggested their "goal of political reform":

> We believe that we must have a practical, clear-cut goal which is intelligible to everybody if we talk of politics. And we believe that the goal of "good government" should be the most modest requirement for the present political reform of China, a goal which is commonly recognized by all the Chinese elite, regardless of what their ideal political institutions are — democratic, guild socialist, or anarchist. We ought to fight united against the evil forces of China under this one banner.[67]

Then they defined the term "good government." On the negative side, there had to be proper organizations supervising the officials in the government; and on the positive side, the government had to endeavor to improve the welfare of the society as a whole, and at the same time to permit adequate individual freedom and protect the development of the individual personality. Accordingly, they demanded a constitutional government to carry out political programs publicly instead of in secret. Their first step toward achieving their goal was to arouse "good men" to organize a fighting public opinion. Additional reforms they advocated included these: (1) the conflict between the North and the South should be resolved at a new peace conference, (2) disarmament should be realized, (3) the number of government personnel should be reduced, and (4) the election system should be reformed.

The declaration proved fruitless. The Northern warlords were still dreaming of unifying China by armed force. In the following year Ts'ao K'un was made President of the Peking government, in an election which has been since regarded as the most notorious in Chinese history. Almost all the votes in the Peking Parliament were bought by Ts'ao, at about five thousand *yuan* apiece. Those five-hundred-odd parliamentarians were later known in China as the "swinish representatives" (*chu-tsai i-yüan*).[68]

These reform proposals of the intellectuals were destined to fail because they were backed neither by power nor by organization, and because most of the proponents were too reluctant to take practical political action against the warlords. Some of them joined the warlord government but were quickly ousted.[g]

Kao I-han, Hsü Pao-huang, Wang Cheng (secretary to the New American Consortium), Ting Wen-chiang (V. K. Ting, former director of the Bureau of Geological Survey), and Hu Shih. All were professors at Peking University except those otherwise noted.

[g] On Sept. 19, 1922, four months after the publication of the "good government" declaration, three of its signatories joined the Peking government with Wu P'ei-fu's support. Wang Ch'ung-hui was made Prime Minister, Lo Wen-kan (d. 1941) Minister of Finance, and T'ang Erh-ho, Minister of Education. It was somewhat ironically called "the good men Cabinet" because of their previous declaration. But the Cabinet was disliked by Ts'ao K'un and some other warlords. Lo

Indeed, many of them were remote from the masses of the people and even from the majority of the young, active intellectuals. Moreover, although on the surface the good government proposal was made in a spirit of liberalism, actually not all its signatories were liberals. Some of them were rather conservative, and too moderate to carry out even a peaceful political reform, while, at the other extreme, Li Ta-chao had already joined the Chinese Communist Party. Hu Shih was at this time one of the central figures of the movement but his position was not made clear. When a group of youths wrote him raising the question as to how good government could be achieved short of a revolution, since the warlord government would never listen to mere verbal persuasion, Hu answered ambiguously that they should take both revolution and reform as their means.[70] But in fact many of the intellectual leaders in the good government movement were tolerating the Peking government for practical purposes. Because of his sober attitude, Hu's previous conservative opponents in the arena of the literary revolution came out to congratulate him saying, "your opinion on politics, avoiding extremity and fantasy, will greatly benefit society and is a thousand times better than your discussions of the vernacular and pragmatism."[71] On the other side, Hu's friends in the literary camp regretted that he had given up his previous career in literary reform.[72] Hu explained that he had returned to politics because now that "the slaves of Confucius and Chu Hsi have decreased in number, the slaves of Marx and Kropotkin have appeared."[73] Hu's stand against both the anarchists and Marxists and against those who advocated the overthrow of the Peking government certainly alienated some leftist and nationalist support of the reform. After the spring of 1923 when the Peking government completely ignored the liberals' suggestions, and suppressed them, the latter had to give up their participation in practical politics. Liberalism gradually became less active after a magnificent spurt in the first stage of the May Fourth period.[h]

On the other hand, in 1920 the Soviet Russians made contact with the Chi-

---

was soon falsely accused and imprisoned. On Nov. 25, the Cabinet resigned in protest. The case of Lo aroused stormy strikes by the professors and students of Peking University led by Ts'ai Yüan-p'ei in support of Lo. The incident seemed to be an excellent example of the inadequacy of the theory of "good government" under the warlords' rule.[69]

[h] It would exceed the scope of this book to discuss the development of Chinese liberalism in later years. It may be still an open question whether it was liberalism in the modern Western sense. The Chinese liberals regenerated their activities in 1930–31 when they published an article "Which Road Do We Take?" At this time, Hu Shih reversed his previous stand to the extent of declaring that there had been no warlords in China, and drew criticism from Liang Sou-ming and the leftists. But in 1934–35 when a number of writers and military men propounded dictatorship and fascism for China, the liberals, including Hu Shih, were among the strong opponents of them.[74]

nese leftists, nationalists, and other new intellectual leaders who leaned to socialism. As said before, in the few months following the May Fourth Incident, socialism had attracted greater interest among the new intellectuals than before. Under the influence of the spirit of protest and rebellion prevailing then, a number of them organized to study it collectively. Organizations for the study of socialism had become so popular among intellectuals in the fall of 1919 that even members of the Anfu Club and other conservatives had set up a few of them. In December 1919 a Society for the Study of Socialism was founded at Peking University with a membership of over one hundred college students and professors of the university as well as other colleges. Similar study groups were established in many other big cities. These intellectuals were not all converted to socialism in the strict sense but were more fervent and active than the earlier socialists such as Chiang K'ang-hu's followers, most of whom were close to national or democratic socialism. There were of course many other socialists who joined neither these study societies nor Chiang's Socialist Party. By the end of 1919, various kinds of socialism were considered; members of the Society for the Study of Socialism split and established different organizations for the study of guild socialism, anarchism, and syndicalism.[i]

It was under such circumstances, early in 1920, that the Comintern, impressed by the May Fourth fermentation, sent from the Far Eastern Secretariat of its Executive Committee a Russian, Gregori Voitinsky (alias Wu T'ing-k'ang), together with a Russian secretary and his wife, and a Chinese interpreter, Yang Ming-chai, to China to promote communist activities among the new intellectuals.[j] The group arrived in Peking and at first found no way to

---

[i] According to Chang Hsi-man, the Society for the Study of Socialism was founded under Ts'ai Yüan-p'ei's protection at Peking University. Chang also stated that, as time went on, its active members included Ch'en Tu-hsiu, Li Ta-chao, Chang Hsi-man, Ch'en Ku-yüan, Chu Ch'ien-chih, Ch'ü Ch'iu-pai, Meng Shou-ch'un, Teng Chung-hsia, Chang Kuo-t'ao, Yi K'e-ni, Yi Chia-yüeh [Yi Chün-tso], Kuo Meng-liang, Hsü Liu-chi, Fan T'i-jen, Fei Chüeh-t'ien, Mao Tse-tung, and Chou En-lai. Later Kuo Meng-liang and Hsü Liu-chi with others established the Society for the Study of Guild Socialism (*Chi-erh-t'e she-hui-chu-i yen-chiu hui*), Ch'en Ku-yüan and others organized the Society for the Study of Syndicalist Socialism (*Kung-t'uan she-hui-chu-i yen-chiu hui*), and Chu Ch'ien-chih and others established the Society for the Study of Anarchism (*Wu-cheng-fu-chu-i yen-chiu hui*).[75] Chang Kuo-t'ao denied in 1958 in the manuscript of his English memoirs that he had joined any organization as the Society for the Study of Socialism and doubted even the existence of this society at such an early date. But we find sufficient evidence to support the statement that early in 1920 societies bearing this name already existed in several big Chinese cities.

[j] Yang Ming-chai was born in Shantung of a poor family. He went to Tsarist Russia through Manchuria and Siberia, studying and working there for more than ten years. After the October Revolution he joined the Russian Communist Party. In Sept. 1921, together with Ch'en Tu-hsiu and Ch'en's wife, Kao Chün-man, and a few other communist members, such as Li Ta, Chou Fo-hai, and Pao Hui-seng, he was arrested for two days by the French Concession police in Shanghai. After this he seems to have become less active in communist organization work. In the twen-

approach the Chinese. After a while, with the introduction of the Soviet representative M. I. Yurin who had been in Peking with A. K. Paikes to arrange for the negotiation of the Karakhan declaration, Voitinsky met a Russian professor of the Russian language at Peking University, Sergei A. Polevoy (*Pao-li-wei*), who was starting to sympathize with the Soviet government at the time, and through him Voitinsky came into touch with Li Ta-chao and some other intellectuals who had been active in the May Fourth Movement. Li subsequently sent him to Shanghai to see Ch'en Tu-hsiu, who had been there since the fall of 1919 following his release from a Peking prison and was carrying on in the French Concession the publication of *New Youth*.

Because of this influence from the international communists and the accelerated split within socialist groups among the youth, a faction of the Society for the Study of Socialism joined with other students from Peking University, under the inspiration of Li Ta-chao, to initiate in March 1920 a Society for the Study of Marxist Theory (*Ma-k'e-ssu hsüeh-shuo yen-chiu hui*).ᵏ A Society

---

ties he stayed for some time in Peking writing. He published a Chinese translation of Leo Tolstoy's *The Forged Coupon* (*Chia li-ch'üan*) in 1922 and a book *Comments on Three Chinese Views of Chinese and Western Civilizations* (*P'ing Chung Hsi wen-hua kuan*) in 1924. In the latter book he did not take a Marxist standpoint and criticized only mildly the views of Liang Sou-ming, Liang Ch'i-ch'ao, and Chang Shih-chao on the civilization problem.

ᵏ Many writers, following Hatano Ken'ichi, give the date of the establishment of the Society for the Study of Marxist Theory at Peking University as early as 1918. But no reliable sources available so far support this assertion in any detail. There might have been a Ma-k'e-shih chu-i yen-chiu hui proposed in Peking after Oct. 1918 by Li Ta-chao and a very few other intellectuals. Its existence and the time of its establishment are still in question. Individual study of Marxism' in China of course may be traced to an early date (see above, Chap. II, nn. 67 and 68). Li Ta-chao probably had read some Marxist literature in 1918 when he wrote "Victory of Bolshevism," but his more serious study of the doctrine apparently did not start until the spring of 1919 when the May issue of *New Youth* which he edited was dedicated to Marxism. Informal and secret group study in Shanghai and Peking by some Kuomintang leaders, anarchists, and students may have begun in this year. The Society for the Study of Marxist Theory, initiated in March 1920, was not formally established until Oct. 1921 (Chang Kuo-t'ao thinks it was in Sept. 1920), four months after the First Communist Congress. It had a membership of nineteen students from the university, including Kao Ch'ung-huan, Wang Yu-te, Teng Chung-hsia, Lo Chang-lung, Huang Shao-ku, Wang Fu-sheng, Huang Jih-k'uei, Liu Jen-ching, Fan Hung-chi, Li Chün, Ho Meng-hung, and Chu Wu-shan. Chang Kuo-t'ao, who had been one of the most active Marxist students at the university at the time, was notably absent from the rolls as far as the records show. Public invitation for membership started on Nov. 17, 1921, and the society held a formal inaugural meeting in December. Early in Feb. 1922 its membership increased to sixty-three. From then on discussion meetings were held more often, at least once every week. Li Ta-chao, Ku Meng-yü, a Kuomintang member and contributor to *New Youth*, Ch'en Ch'i-hsiu (Ch'en Pao-yin), pioneering translator of a part of *Das Kapital* and a famous economic writer, and Kao I-han delivered lectures sponsored by the society. It founded a small library with about 40 English and 20 Chinese books, one third of which were by Marx, Engels, and Lenin, as well as general periodicals and newspapers. It developed some relations with the miners' strikes in Tangshan and Peking in 1922.⁷⁶ The somewhat detached, academic approach of Marxism by the members of the society is indicated by their use of *hsüeh-shuo* (theory) rather than *chu-i* (ism) in the society's name. It must also be pointed out that the meaning

for the Study of Russia (*O-lo-ssu yen-chiu hui*) was organized about the same time.

It should be remembered that, from the summer of 1919 after the merchants' and workers' strikes and the suppression of the student movement in the concessions, nationalists in Shanghai had tended more to the left and socialists and anarchists in the city had become more active. Marxism was studied and in some aspects propagated there more fervently than in Peking and any other cities. When Ch'en Tu-hsiu arrived in the city, with his prestige heightened in Peking, he soon met many able and active intellectuals with such leanings.[78] Besides anarchists such as Yüan Chen-ying, Chin Chia-feng, and I-hen (possibly pen name of Lien-ken), there were the Chinputang guild socialist, Chang Tung-sun, who was editor of the party's organ *Shih-shih hsin pao* (*The China Times*), and many of Sun Yat-sen's followers.

As has been pointed out, at the turn of the last century Kuomintang leaders had started to propagate socialist ideas. Sun Yat-sen had made contact with European and possibly Russian socialist revolutionaries in London in 1896–1898 after his release from the Chinese Legation. In 1906, Sun identified one of his "Three Principles of the People" (*San min chu-i*), "Principle of the People's Livelihood," with socialism.[1] To a degree Lenin had welcomed China's 1911 Revolution led by Sun, and Sun's party was the first to spread the news of the Russian October Revolution in China a few days after it took place. Frustrated in his dealing with the Southern warlords and politicians, Sun left Canton after May 1918 and set up his headquarters in Shanghai, studying and writing his revolutionary philosophy and reconstruction programs for China, as well as planning to recapture Canton as a base for the revolution. In the same year he started to maintain contact with Lenin and the latter sent representatives to see him in Shanghai. Prior to the May Fourth Incident, or at least before 1918, Sun had not been enthusiastic about the new thought tide and especially the new literature movement. He appeared reluctant to accept the view that the

---

of Marxism or Marxist theory was much broader in these years than it became in communist dogma at a later date. As late as 1921 Chinese communist leaders still acknowledged that Marxist socialism should include orthodox Marxism (represented by Kautsky), revisionary Marxism (represented by Bernstein), syndicalism, guild socialism, and Bolshevism (the last represented by Lenin and Trotsky). Before 1921 there were Chinese writers who often considered Bolshevism a faction of anarchism instead of Marxism. Some Chinese socialist writers in 1919 and 1920 thought that socialism consisted of two branches: one was collectivism, i.e., Marxism, and the other, communism, i.e., the anarchism promoted by Kropotkin. The terms were very much confused during this period. The term *kung-ch'an-chu-i* (communism) was probably first established in Chinese about 1914 by the anarchist Liu Shih-fu.[77]

[1] Sun said that the term "Principle of the People's Livelihood" (*Min-sheng chu-i*) was actually a Chinese translation of "socialism." [79]

vernacular language should be substituted for the literary, believing that the latter was more refined.[m] But as soon as he received the news of the incident, he gave positive support to the student movement as a turning point of thought transformation, the achievement of which would, in his opinion, lay a foundation for the realization of the Chinese revolution and strengthen his hands in fighting against the Peking government.[n]

As one of the founders of the Republic and a leading political figure, Sun, in his support of the May Fourth student activities, exerted great influence upon the split of the intellectuals and drew the youths to the revolutionary camp. Impressed by Lenin's success in the October Revolution and disappointed by the Western countries' unresponsiveness to his invitation to support financially his reconstruction plan and by their continuous recognition of the Peking regime, he gradually leaned to the left. Previously, the Kuomintang newspaper *Min-kuo jih-pao* (*Republic Daily*) in Shanghai edited by Yeh Ch'u-ts'ang and Shao Li-tzu had become a champion of the new culture movement. Shao was assisted by Ch'en Wang-tao who had become, like Shao, a member of the Shanghai Society for the Study of Socialism and was translating for the first time the full text of the *Communist Manifesto* into Chinese which was later (April 1920) published by the society. In June 1919 the party established in Shanghai a *Weekly Review* (*Hsing-ch'i p'ing-lun*), which was edited by Shen Ting-i and Tai Chi-t'ao. In August Sun's group further established in the same city a monthly *The Construction* (*Chien-she*) with Tai as its editor and Chu Chih-hsin its manager. Tai invited Li Han-chün, a student returned

---

[m] All of Sun's works were written in the classical literary language prior to the incident. But after it, his speeches were almost all in the vernacular, and much of the literature of the Kuomintang in the early twenties followed this example. Sun's first speech written in the vernacular was probably his "Kai-tsao Chung-kuo chih ti-i-pu" ("The First Step to the Reform of China"), delivered at the Y.M.C.A. of Shanghai on Oct. 8, 1919.[80]

[n] Although Sun Yat-sen supported the May Fourth Movement, his ideas in some aspects differed from the new thought of the period. In spite of the fact that he drew his principles largely from Western sources, he had a tendency to exaggerate his inheritance from Chinese orthodox tradition, possibly for the sake of convincing some conservative and nationalist elements. It was well known that in Kweilin, Kwangsi Province, in the winter of 1921, when the international communist agent Maring (alias of H. J. F. M. Sneevliet) asked him what was the nucleus of his revolutionary thought, he proudly replied, "In Chinese history there was an 'orthodox tradition of Tao' (*tao t'ung*) which was passed from the Emperors Yao, Shun, Yü, T'ang, Wen, and Wu, to the Duke of Chou and then to Confucius. I just carry on this orthodox tradition of Tao." In his lectures on nationalism, he also glorified the traditional Chinese ethical principles, such as the "four cardinal bonds" (ritual, righteousness, integrity, and sense of shame) and the "eight morals" (loyalty, filial piety, benevolence, love, honesty, righteousness, peace, and equality). Sun meant to provide a modern interpretation of traditional ethics. However, in later years, this aspect of Sun's thought often supplied backing for the traditionalist wing of the Kuomintang in its campaign for Confucian worship and study of the classics. So far as such aspects are concerned, Sun's thought was opposed to the beliefs of the new thought segment of the May Fourth Movement.[81]

from Japan and a fervent Marxist, to help him. (In October, Sun reorganized and strengthened his party, adopting its present name.) In 1919 and 1920 the two magazines, besides introducing some Western democratic theories and institutions, published a number of articles on socialism, anarchism, and Marxism.

Despite the fact that Sun Yat-sen and most of his followers had never accepted Marxism as a whole, prominent party leaders such as Tai Chi-t'ao, Hu Han-min, Chu Chih-hsin, Shen Ting-i, and Liao Chung-k'ai did defend and propagate some of its ideas from a nationalist standpoint. They accepted its materialistic concept of history and the ideal of equal distribution of wealth and suggested that ancient Chinese philosophers had already developed similar ideas. But regarding the theory of class struggle, most of the Kuomintang writers advocated preventive measures instead of the Marxist program. On the whole, they had reached in theory the position of democratic socialists.[82] Their socialist reconstruction and interpretation of Chinese history at one point raised some mild criticism from the liberals and resulted in an academic controversy.[°]

Moreover, Sun's party at the time proposed an elitist theory of revolution among the intellectuals. In speeches delivered at the Y.M.C.A. and the Student Union of China in Shanghai in the fall of 1919, he rejected the idea that the first step for the solution of China's problems was to carry out educational reform, industrialization, or local self-government. In his opinion, the existing corrupt government would not permit the accomplishment of such aims. The first step to build a new China must be a political revolution wherein the old bureaucrats, militarists, and politicians would be wiped out. Reconstruction work might be achieved only after this destruction had been accomplished.[84] In addition, he believed that China could be saved only by a party of professional revolutionaries. As he said, a revolutionary partisan would devote himself exclusively to revolution. Some liberal students were skeptical of this ideal but it had great appeal to active youths.[85] Immediately following the May Fourth Incident, Sun wrote in reply to letters from the student unions of Shanghai and Tientsin, encouraging the students to start upon their revolutionary careers. "I enthusiastically hope," said he, "that you will rally all your comrades to join the struggle in order to achieve the final goal of destruction." [86] It was reported that many student representatives from other cities also had

° The controversy was whether the "well-field" system (ching-t'ien chih-tu) described in Mencius, i.e., a kind of common ownership of land, really existed in ancient China. The Kuomintang writers, Hu Han-min, Liao Chung-k'ai, and Chu Chih-hsin, were on the affirmative side and Hu Shih and others on the negative.[83]

kept close contact with him in Shanghai.[87] As a result, from the end of 1919 a great number of youths participating in the May Fourth Incident began to be recruited into the Kuomintang. As Lo Chia-lun recalled:

There was a very practical political influence which drew the youths and the men of middle age, who had been aroused by the tide of the May Fourth Movement, to participate in the National Revolution. Dr. Sun Yat-sen was the one who felt this tendency most acutely and seized the opportunity most quickly. With great attention and maximum enthusiasm, he recruited those youths who had taken part in the May Fourth Movement. Each time he was interviewed by the student representatives of Peking, he would talk with them for three or four hours with increasing energy and spirit. This is a fact that I saw and experienced in person. Subsequently, around the time before and after 1924, when the Kuomintang was reorganized, most of the new party workers were drawn from among the participants in the May Fourth Movement, and this resulted in a new outlook for the National Revolution.[88]

While the nationalists, socialists, and anarchists were all active among the youths, Ch'en Tu-hsiu was seeking to increase similarly his own political influence. Soon he and Li Ta-chao developed some relation with the Kuomintang leaders and began to publish their writings in *New Youth* and *Weekly Critic*. When Voitinsky arrived in Shanghai, Ch'en introduced him to such people as Tai Chi-t'ao, Li Han-chün, Shen Ting-i, Shao Li-tzu, and Chang Tung-sun. After conferring many times, often secretly at Tai's residence, they agreed to establish a new revolutionary coalition by combining the forces behind *New Youth*, *Weekly Review*, and *The China Times*, as well as other groups, in order to organize a Chinese Communist Party or a new Chinese Socialist Party. However, when the draft party constitution was brought out for discussion, its class conception was unacceptable to some of the participants. Chang Tung-sun felt obliged to withdraw from the organization. After some consideration, a Chinese Communist Party (*Chung-kuo kung-ch'an tang*) was at last created in secret in May 1920. This should be considered the true date of the founding of the Chinese Communist Party, albeit it later officially set the date as July 1921. Among the initiating members were Ch'en Tu-hsiu, Tai Chi-t'ao, Li Han-chün, Shen Ting-i, Shao Li-tzu, Ch'en Wang-t'ao, Li Ta, Shih Ts'un-t'ung, Yü Hsiu-sung, and Yüan Hsiao-hsien. They passed the draft party constitution and established a provisional central organization in Shanghai. Ch'en Tu-hsiu was elected its secretary. Although Tai Chi-t'ao and Shao Li-tzu soon left the party, it is clear that Ch'en Tu-hsiu, who had allied himself with many young Kuomintang, anarchist, and socialist leaders in his revolutionary career in 1920, from then on concentrated on his new political adventure. Immediately after May 1920 the party established in Shanghai the Sino-Russian News Agency under the directorship of Yang Ming-chai, and the Foreign Language School, and in August the Socialist Youth Corps. On August 15 the party began to publish a weekly, *Labor Circles* (*Lao-tung chieh*), and on November 7, the third anniversary of the Russian October Revolution, its organ *The Communist* (*Kung-ch'an-tang*) appeared. Before the Communist First Congress of July 1–5 (Chang Kuo-t'ao recalled that the meeting lasted to the ninth or tenth), 1921, with the assistance of the Voitinsky mission, six party branches had been established in Shanghai, Peking, Changsha, Wu-Han, Canton, and Tsinan. In France, early in 1921, a similar organization, the Young China Communist Party (*Shao-nien Chung-kuo kung-ch'an-tang*), was established by the Chinese worker-students after a number of arguments between the leftists and rightists.[p]

[p] After the establishment of the central organization in Shanghai, Voitinsky and his staff went separately to other big cities to promote the communist movement. Lacking interpreters, they often talked with young Chinese intellectuals by pointing to the words in English-Russian and Chinese-English dictionaries. The Peking branch of the party and of the Socialist Youth Corps was established by Li Ta-chao and his students, such as Teng Chung-hsia, in Sept. 1920. At the same time, Mao Tse-tung, who was now teaching at the elementary school of Hunan Province First Normal School, established the Culture Book Store and the Changsha Society for the Study of Marxism, apparently on receiving orders from Ch'en Tu-hsiu and Li Ta-chao. The several scores of members of the society were in the main recruited from the New People's Study Society and the Hunan Student Union, most of whom were teachers, alumni, and students at the First Normal School. The members included Ho Shu-heng, Ch'en Ch'ang, Hsia Hsi, Kuo Liang, and Hsiao Shu-fan. In October, Mao received letters and the charter of the Socialist Youth Corps from Peking. About the same time Bertrand Russell delivered a number of speeches in Changsha pointing out the cruelty of the Russian Communist dictatorship and the possibility of realizing socialism by peaceful means like education and economic reform. The speeches stirred up fervid argument among the Chinese intellectuals in the city, including members of the New People's Study Society. Mao rejected Russell's conception and thought that to seize political power by force was a necessity. Consequently he started to purge the anticommunist members from the society, and in early Jan. 1921 founded a branch of the corps in Changsha. About the same time a similar organization was established in Wu-Han by Tung Pi-wu and Ch'en T'an-ch'iu under the guidance and help of Voitinsky's secretary and Palevoy. In France many of the sixteen hundred Chinese work-and-study students had become politically conscious by 1920. They contrasted in their weekly *Study in Europe* (*Lü Ou*) their inferior financial situation with the better position of the Chinese students in the United States and predicted their own leadership of China in the future: "Please wait and see to whom our country will belong." A split similar to that in Changsha took place among the 14 members of the New People's Study Society in France early in July 1920. One of the founders of the Society, Hsiao Tzu-sheng, led the anarchist and anticommunist faction and later joined the Kuomintang. On the other side, Ts'ai Ho-sen led the radical wing to join with Chou En-lai, Wang Jo-fei, and Li Li-san to establish the Young China Communist Party and a Socialist Youth Corps in France in 1921. The corps was in fact converted from the Work-and-Study Cooperative Society (*Kung-hsüeh hu-chu she*), whose members also include Li Fu-ch'un, Li Wei-han, Ts'ai Ch'ang, Hsiang Ching-yü, Chang K'un-ti, and Lo Hsüeh-tsan. These communists then had a number of struggles with the nationalists and anarchists among the work-and-study students. Subsequently in the fall of 1921 Ts'ai Ho-sen, Chang K'un-ti, Lo Hsüeh-tsan, and others were expelled to China by the French government.

This new political development made any attempts at unification of the new intellectuals very difficult to continue. In 1920 and 1921 many of the politically conscious intellectuals started to take different political stands and consequently caused the split of the organizations in which they had worked together previously. First of all, the New Youth Society was affected. Though its monthly was not yet the organ of the new Communist Party, it was under its control. The May 1920 issue of the magazine was devoted to Labor Day. Articles by leftists increased and those by liberals appeared less frequently in the monthly. On September 1, Ch'en Tu-hsiu established a new New Youth Society in Shanghai in charge of editing and printing the magazine. In the winter, Sun Yat-sen was invited by the self-styled revolutionary warlord Ch'en Chiung-ming to assume political leadership in Kwangtung. On Sun's or his followers' recommendation, Ch'en Tu-hsiu was appointed chief of the education board in Canton. On December 16, he departed Shanghai for the South and left the editorship of the magazine to Ch'en Wang-tao.

By this time, the left wing of the New Youth group, especially Ch'en and his associates in Shanghai, complained that their liberal partners in the group such as Hu Shih and T'ao Meng-ho had become too conservative and too close to the Chinputang.[89] As Li Ta-chao put it: "Now we in the universities are like a maiden; all cliques of the Chinputang are trying to lure us; if they fail, they smear us. And the Kuomintang is also jealous of this. What a bore!"[90] But the liberals felt that the magazine had become too politically colored and that it "now has almost become a Chinese version of *Soviet Russia* [the New York communist weekly pictorial whose articles it often translated]."[91] So Hu Shih proposed that they should either establish a new magazine philosophical and literary in nature and leave *New Youth* as a political organ or reaffirm their determination to refrain from discussing politics and move the editors' office of the magazine to Peking.[92] Ch'en Tu-hsiu disagreed; but after some patient consultation with other members in Peking, Hu succeeded in obtaining the agreement of Lu Hsün, Chou Tso-jen, Ch'ien Hsüan-t'ung, T'ao Meng-ho, Kao I-han, Chang Wei-tz'u, and Wang Hsing-kung to move the editors' office to Peking and keep the original philosophical and literary character of the periodical. In order to prevent a split, Li Ta-chao accepted the proposal.[93] But just then, i.e., late in January 1921 the magazine was suppressed by the French Concession in Shanghai; subsequently Ch'en moved it to Canton and converted it into an organ of the Chinese Communist Party. A year later, on May 7, 1922, Hu Shih, Kao I-han, and T'ao Meng-ho founded their own weekly *Endeavor* (*Nu-li chou-pao*) in Peking. Thus ended the four-year alliance of those new intellectual leaders. In September of 1922 Ch'en finally established in Shanghai a purely political organ, *The Guide Weekly* (*Hsiang-tao chou-pao*).

Other intellectual groups split in a somewhat similar way at about the same period. The New Tide Society started to expand its activities in November 1919, and reorganized on August 15, 1920. A few months later the magazine ceased to appear, because most of its leaders had gone to the United States and Great Britain to study. Most of the fifty members remained liberal scholars, writers, or educators, and a few later joined the Kuomintang. The society gradually withered away late in 1920 and in 1921.[94] The New People's Society led by Mao Tse-tung also started at the beginning of 1920 to divide into right and left wings. Some of the right wing later joined the Kuomintang, such as Hsiao Tzu-sheng, who became a follower of Li Shih-tseng and Yi P'ei-chi and a high official in the National government. The left wing insisted, according to Mao, on "a programme of far-reaching social, economic, and political changes." [95]

A split also took place in one of the most prominent social organizations, the Young China Association. The membership of the association was drawn largely from returned students from Japan and France as well as from the ranks of students, writers, teachers, and journalists. Although the number of its members did not exceed 108, they included many able and active young Chinese.[96] In the early days the association had forbidden all members to participate in politics. But in the postincident circumstances this was obviously impracticable. From 1920 its members took active roles in various social, political, or cultural movements. As a consequence, serious problems arose among them, that is, whether the members of the association should join in political activities and what their attitudes should be toward political and religious affairs. The problems provoked fervent arguments among the members. In 1921 a conference of representatives was held to discuss these issues. The most vital question on the surface was, as they put it, "whether the association should adopt a doctrine," but in effect was whether they "should turn the association into a socialist organization." By the time, as we know, some of the members had already joined in secret the Chinese Communist Party. Others, however, were averse to any left trends. The conference ended without an acceptable resolution on the issue. In July 1922 in another conference the problems of the adoption of an ism and of political action stirred up further fruitless arguments. Consequently the *Young China* monthly published in September a special issue on the controversy. Again, on October 4, 1923, a conference was held in Soochow. Facing a national crisis arising from a notorious election in Peking, in which bribery was used, and international intervention in the civil war, the conference published a manifesto, declaring that the aim of the association was "to achieve the national independence of China by way of uniting the youth." A nine-point program was also adopted which included "opposition to international imperialism, especially British and American," "promotion of self-determination of citizens and antiwarlordism," "advocation of a nationalistic education and opposition of the establishment of schools by religious groups," "advancement of the concept that economic reconstruction is the important way to improve the national virtue." These points, a mixture of the heightened nationalism and the communist programs developed shortly after the May Fourth period, were a result of anxious argument, persuasion, and compromise among the badly split membership. But the compromise could not last very long. In a number of other informal discussion meetings in Shanghai, Nanking, and Paris no genuinely common course could be agreed upon. As a result, the association ceased to function and its members went their different ways. Members of the left wing, such as Li Ta-chao, Yün Tai-ying, Chou Fo-hai, Teng Chung-hsia, Mao Tse-tung, Liu Jen-ching, Chang Wen-t'ien, Shen Tse-min, Huang Jih-k'uei, Chao Shih-yen, Kao Shang-te (Kao Chün-yü), Hou Shao-ch'iu, and Yang Hsien-chiang devoted themselves to the Chinese Communist Party. Members of the right wing, such as Tseng Ch'i, Tso Shun-sheng, Li Huang, Chang Meng-chiu, Ho Lu-chih, Yü Chia-chü, Ch'en Ch'i-t'ien, Liu Ssu-ying (Liu Cheng-chiang), Wei Ssu-luan (killed by the communists on April 1, 1951*), Ch'ang Nai-te, Chao Tseng-ch'iu, and Ch'en Teng-ch'ioh set to work to organize the Young China Party, later called the Chinese Youth Party, advocating nationalism and democracy. There were also a few that joined the Kuomintang or Chinputang, or established minor political parties.q Tso Shun-sheng, once the

---

* I based this statement on a contemporary Chinese account, but it has since been brought to my attention that the source was erroneous.

q One of the members, the poet K'ang Pai-ch'ing, changed his name to K'ang Hung-chang (after Li Hung-chang's name); he later went to the United States and organized with another member of the Young China Association, Meng Shou-ch'un, and others the short-lived New China Party (Hsin-Chung-kuo-tang). Another member, Hsü Te-heng, later became, as we have mentioned, the leader of the Chiu-san hsüeh-she, now a minority party in Mao's regime. The headquarters of the Young China Association was at first set in Peking but moved to Nanking after the Soochow conference of Oct. 1923. Nanking (later Peking), Chengtu, and Paris had branch offices. Among the 74 inaugurating members 9 were in France, 7 in Japan, 4 in Germany, 1 each in Great Britain and the United States, all students; 15 in Peking, 12 in Nanking, 4 each in Shanghai and Chengtu, all students, educators, journalists, editors, or translators; 15 entrepreneurs

leader of the Chinese Youth Party, recalls that, when Teng Chung-hsia left his house in Shanghai after the last hot argument between the members, Teng shook hands with him with emotion, dramatically saying, "Well, Shun-sheng, we will see each other again on the battle field." [98] Indeed, this remark summarizes the ominous split of the May Fourth Movement which foreshadowed the tragic struggle between the two broad groups of the Chinese intellectuals in the following decades.

and journalists scattered in Wuchang, Changsha, Tientsin, Tsinan, Sian, Canton, Fukien, Chekiang, and Fengtien; and 1 educator and 1 journalist in Malaya. In the Jan. 1925 issue of the *Young China* monthly a list of 95 members was published, among which beside the names we have mentioned were such famous persons as Tsung Pai-hua, poet, Fang Tung-mei, philosopher, Cheng Po-ch'i, T'ien Han, Li Ch'u-li, Chu Tzu-ch'ing, all prominent writers, Chou Ping-lin, Yang Liang-kung, Wu Pao-feng, T'ai Shuang-ch'iu, Chang Chih, Shu Hsin-ch'eng, Mu Chi-po, Ts'ao Ch'u, Ni Wen-chou, Wu Chün-sheng, Li Ju-mien, Yang Hsiao-ch'un, all eminent educators, Yüan T'ung-li, a leading librarian, Su Chia-jung, Lu Tso-fu, industrialists, Yang Chung-chien, paleontologist, Shen I, mayor of Nanking under the Kuomintang government, as well as Hsü Yen-chih, Li Chi-jen, Ch'en Pao-o, Yün chen, Lei Kuo-neng, Chu Ching-chou, and Jui Hsüeh-tseng. The association selected members very carefully in accordance with its high standards, one of which was that members should have positive and aggressive attitudes towards their careers. From the beginning to the end, the majority of the members opposed "the Marxist national socialism adopted by Lenin," which they considered harmful to individual freedom, though many of them entertained certain ideals close to socialism. They also rejected the class struggle and the Russian October Revolution on the ground that they were too ruthless and inhuman. The association was supported by contributions from its members and refused financial aid from outside. The Soochow conference had resolved to establish a middle school but the plan was not realized. After 1924 the association became inactive because of the split in political opinions among the members. In the fall of 1925 a five-man reorganization committee attempted to revive the association. The effort failed and subsequently the association ceased to exist. [97]

CHAPTER X

SOCIOPOLITICAL CONSEQUENCES, 1920–1922

THE May Fourth Movement and its split had immediate consequences and far-reaching influences on China's political, social, and educational developments. The following sections will concentrate on the major immediate consequences in 1920–1922 and refer only briefly to later developments, generally up to 1924.

Reorientation of Political and Economic Organizations

The political protests of the student movement were taken up by the parties. Riding the rising tide of nationalism and socialism, the alliance of the Kuomintang and the Chinese Communist Party, supported by the Soviet Union, developed rapidly. The catchwords "throw out the traitors" and "struggle for sovereignty" or "resist the Great Powers" initiated by the students were soon seized on by the political parties and expanded into formal antiwarlordism and anti-imperialism. The former was expressed in the disarmament movement to cut down military expenditures North and South, supported by the Chinputang leaders and liberals early in the twenties, and in the revolutionaries' campaign against the Peking regime. The latter was promoted by the new alliance of the leftists and nationalists. When the Great League of Anti-Imperialism (*Fan-ti-kuo-chu-i ta t'ung-meng*) was created by the Student Union of China, the National Labor Union, the National Chamber of Commerce, and other organizations in Peking on July 13, 1923, it soon secured enthusiastic support from many social forces. Twenty-four branches were established by the league in all the major cities in the nation within a month. Its program was to abolish all concessions, the conventional tariff, and extraterritoriality, to expel all foreign troops, to annul the unequal treaties, and to restore the lost territories, by means of boycotts, strikes, and cooperation with other oppressed peoples.[1] In such a climate of public opinion, the Kuomintang reorganized to admit the communists into the party early in 1924 and paved the way for the Northern Expedition or National Revolution (the communists later called it the Great Revolution) of 1926–27 which overthrew the Peking government and brought Chiang Kai-shek to power.

Another consequence of the May Fourth Movement in its sociopolitical aspect was the development of organizations and activities of the merchants and urban workers. In a sense, the May Fourth Incident taught the Chinese people that "their strength lay in organization."[2]

Shortly after the incident, merchants in big cities started to organize themselves in various ways. In Shanghai, their organizations were set up as "street unions" (ma-lu lien-ho-hui). The proprietors and residents on each street formed a union no matter what kind of business they carried on. Thus, the fifty-two streets in Shanghai which were located in the business districts were organized into fifty-two street unions. To unite all these, a central organization was established known as the Federation of Street Unions of Shanghai. Each street union instituted its own commercial night school for clerks and apprentices; it also had its own organizations to take care of sanitation and the other social welfare problems of the street.[3] The federation became the most influential organization in Shanghai. In later years, it also led some of the movements of the Chinese residents in the city in demanding civil rights from the government and the foreign concessions.[a] Merchants in other cities in general followed the practice of Tientsin, where merchants incorporated themselves into trade unions (t'ung-yeh kung-hui) along professional lines. All these new commercial organizations differed from the old commercial guilds (shang-wu kung-hui), which were often manipulated by the government.

Moreover, modern labor unions also started to develop after the May Fourth Incident. The June fifth strike of workers had actually brought the Chinese labor movement into a new era. Before the May Fourth period, Chinese labor organizations were almost all of the traditional guild type and not well arranged. During 1917 and 1918, this kind of guild union had developed rapidly, partly because of encouragement by Sun Yat-sen and some anarchists and partly because of the influence of the labor movement in Hong Kong. It was reported at the time that there existed in Canton sixty-two unions organized on the pattern of guilds and British trade unions. In March 1918 a monthly bearing the name Labor (Lao-tung) was for the first time established in China by the

---

[a] For a short time in 1949 after they took over the mainland, the communists also set up street organizations in Shanghai. They seem to have followed in some aspects the pattern of the street unions created during the May Fourth period.[4]

anarchist Wu Chih-hui. Proudhon's theory of labor and the syndicalist concept of labor unions were propagated in the magazine. After the May Fourth Incident, due to the increased activities of students among the workers, there sprang up many new labor organizations. In Shanghai a few months after the incident, for example, there were the Industrial Association of China (*Chung-hua kung-yeh hsieh-hui*), the Federation of Chinese Labor Unions (*Chung-hua kung-hui tsung-hui*), the Alliance of Electrical Workers (*Tien-ch'i kung-chieh lien-ho-hui*), and others.[5] At the same time when many Chinese workers returned from France after the end of World War I with new ideas, experiences, and ambitions, they formed in Shanghai the Chinese Returned Laborers' Association which became a backbone of the new labor movement in that city. In Canton alone, twenty-six modern unions were organized by such returnees in 1919. These were considered the first Chinese labor unions in the modern Western sense. Unions of this kind in Canton increased to 130 in the following year.[6] Labor Day was first introduced into China by the *Labor* monthly in April 1918 and celebrated in Canton on May 1 of that year and in Shanghai in 1920. In January 1921 the provisional central organization of the Chinese Communist Party set up a Committee for the Labor Movement (*Chih-kung yün-tung wei-yüan-hui*), headed by Yu Hsiu-sung and Li Ch'i-han (Li Sen), to organize workers in printing, tobacco, and textile factories. At the same time, Chang Kuo-t'ao and Teng Chung-hsia started to organize a few thousand railroad workers in Ch'ang-hsin-tien on the Peking-Hankow Railroad. Other communist adherents and Kuomintang members also started to organize workers in Shanghai during the same period. After its First Congress in July, the Communist Party set up a Chinese Labor Union Secretariat (*Chung-kuo lao-tung tsu-ho shu-chi-pu*) led by Chang Kuo-t'ao (using here the alias, Chang T'e-li). The secretariat aimed at coordinating and uniting the scattered labor unions established after 1918 and directing their strikes.

However, in the period from 1919 to 1923, with the rapid increase of labor organizations, the opinions of their leaders were widely divided. A group of them believed that Chinese workers should engage in political action and strikes, but were too weak to have independent organizations and had to rely on political parties, the Kuomintang in particular. A second group also thought that workers should depend on political parties but in more direct and radical political action and strikes. This group tended to accept the leadership of the Communist Party. Still a third group of labor unionists attempted to promote a labor movement independent of politics. These divergent groups were not united until the spring of 1924.[7]

Workers' strikes also increased after the May Fourth Incident. In 1918 there were only 25 strikes in China. But in 1919 the number increased to 66. The years 1920 and 1921 had fewer strikes, 46 and 49 respectively, because the labor movement, declining temporarily like the student movement, was in a state of wavering and preparation. The number of strikes rose to 91 in 1922. The number of workers involved in the strikes also increased after 1919. The average number of workers involved per reported strike in 1918 was 538; but in 1919 it was 3,520; in 1921 it increased to 4,910; and in the following year 4,635. Among the causes of the strikes, patriotic and political motives played a part in the postincident period. The rising tide of strikes ebbed in 1923 and 1924, but increased thereafter.[8]

The Emancipation of Women

The emancipation of women from their traditional social bondage was another significant consequence of the May Fourth Movement. "The Chinese woman's achievement of a life of independent personality," says a writer on the history of Chinese women's life, "was actually initiated by *New Youth,* and the May Fourth Movement provided the key to the achievement."[9]

It seems true that in the preceding centuries, Chinese women had often been harshly treated. They were isolated from many social relations and activities. The law never regarded them as independent citizens. In fact, daughters enjoyed no inheritance of property. Within the family, women occupied an inferior, passive, and obedient position. The traditional ideal of a woman was a dependent being, i.e., "a helpful wife and wise mother" (*hsien-ch'i liang-mu*). Footbinding, which started at the latest in the first part of the tenth century, made women as weak and disabled as cripples. Although there were a number of women poets and painters in Chinese history, the traditional view of Chinese ethics was that "lack of learning is a credit to a woman's virtue" (*nü-tzu wu ts'ai pien shih te*). One-sided chastity was forced on women. Concubinage was permitted by law. Association with courtesans was in many cases regarded as proper to the intellectual life. There were often cases where parents drowned their baby girls, and because of family economic pressures, girls were looked down upon in the society. All in all, women were traditionally treated unequally.

At the turn of the last century, Yen Fu and other reformers had remarked that the old family system was not appropriate to modern times. Early in 1916 Ch'en Tu-hsiu suggested a new family system and the emancipation of women.[10] Later in their attack on Confucian ethics Ch'en and Wu Yü often made this point. In January 1918 *New Youth* published T'ao Meng-ho's article on the position of women, introducing Western views of the woman's movement.[11] Four months later, Chou Tso-jen published in the monthly his translation from the Japanese of an article by Yosano Akiko (1878–1942) on chastity, opposing one-sided chastity and rejecting the idea that chastity is morality.[12] This view was supported by Hu Shih, Lu Hsün, and many other writers.[13] Such articles constituted the ideological preparation for women's emancipation.

After the May Fourth Incident, girls started to join the student movement and its attendant social and political activities. Coeducation was established. Before the incident there had been very few girls' schools of higher learning. In 1922, however, twenty-eight universities and colleges had girl students.[14] They were taught to be independent citizens instead of dependent beings in the family. After the incident, women were allowed to teach in boys' schools.[15] Professional opportunities for women increased. Free marriage was practiced more often. Morality concerning the sexes started to change and the concept of birth control was introduced.[b]

Meanwhile, new ideals of family life and women's social position attracted the attention of most of the Chinese young intellectuals. Women were to be emancipated from the heavy burdens of housekeeping and child care by cooperative arrangements, public nurseries, and social security. Ideas for the reform of women's life suggested by Western writers were discussed in China.[17] Public sympathy with feminism increased. Girls struggling against family or marriage bondage or for an education often obtained public support.[18]

More important, like the boys, the Chinese girl students developed a great interest in political affairs during the latter stages of the May Fourth Movement. The women's suffrage movement made great advances.[c] In 1920 a number of women in Changsha joined the citizens' demonstration, asking for marriage freedom and personal freedom. In February of the following year the Women's

---

[b] In April 1922, after being refused permission to go ashore in Japan by the Japanese government, Mrs. Margaret Sanger visited China, and delivered a speech at Peking University on "The What and How of Birth Control," interpreted by Hu Shih. Mrs. Sanger's visit to China aroused for the first time popular interest in the subject of birth control. Several organizations were then established in Peking and Shanghai to promote it.[16]

[c] During the 1911 Revolution quite a few girls had joined the revolutionary army. But after the inauguration of the Republic, the girls' army was disbanded by the Provisional Government in Nanking. Some woman's suffrage organizations petitioned the Provisional Parliament in 1912 and asked that the Constitution grant equal rights for both sexes. They were ignored. On March 19, a number of young women stormed Parliament, broke its windows and hurt its guards. This was, of course, an unprecedented event in Chinese history. Yet the event involved only a small circle, and, after that incident, the woman's suffrage movement was almost suspended.[19]

Association of Hunan (*Hu-nan nü-chieh lien-ho-hui*) was established, and proposed the realization of five rights for women, i.e., equal right of property inheritance, right to vote and to be elected to office, equal rights of education, equal rights to work, and the right of self-determination in marriage. This was later known as the "five proposal movement" (*wu-chung yün-tung*). It succeeded in December 1921 in obtaining provision for suffrage and women's personal freedom in the Hunan provincial constitution, and in electing a woman to the provincial legislature. Similar movements took place in Chekiang and Kwantung Provinces.[20]

The woman's suffrage movement became active in the summer of 1922 after the defeat of the Anfu troops, but also split into moderate and revolutionary wings.[d] The Peking government promised some reforms in the following year, such as a program to prohibit licensed prostitution and a statute to restrict concubinage. But the demand for woman's suffrage and equal rights for men and women was not in fact met for a long time to come.

Reforms in Education

A number of educational reforms had been continually suggested by the National Alliance of Educational Associations (*Ch'üan-kuo chiao-yü-hui lien-ho-hui*) at its annual meetings from October 1918 on. Educational principles, institutions, curricula, student self-government, and popular education were all considered. The China Society for the Promotion of New Education (*Chung-hua hsin chiao-yü kung-chin-she*), which was established in January 1919, and consisted of many prominent educators such as Ts'ai Yüan-p'ei, Chiang Monlin, T'ao Chih-hsing, Huang Yen-p'ei, Kuo Ping-wen, Hu Shih, Ho Ping-sung, and T'ao Meng-ho, was one of the major professional organizations in education which contributed to the reforms.

Among the educational reforms of the May Fourth period, was the development of vocational education. It reflected, in a sense, an increasingly close relation between the new intelligentsia and some of the new industrialists developed since 1916.[e] This promotion of vocational education and relations be-

---

[d] The Woman's Suffrage Association (*Nü-tzu ts'an-cheng-hui*) established in Peking on July 25, 1922, by girl students asked for constitutional equality for women. The Woman's Rights League (*Nü-ch'üan yün-tung t'ung-meng-hui*) established in the same city on Aug. 23 by other girl students made similar demands but at the same time called on women to join the revolution to overthrow the "feudal warlords" and to realize democracy.[21]

[e] The development of relations was first manifested in a joint meeting in March 1916, attended by all the principals of the vocational and technical schools of Kiangsu Province and by many leading industrialists of Shanghai. The two groups discussed how they might assist one another. On

tween schools and industrialists was advanced by the arrival of Paul Monroe in China on September 5, 1921, at the invitation of the Chinese Society for the Survey of Practical Education (*Hsi-chih chiao-yü tiao-ch'a she*). Monroe and many of his Chinese friends attempted to reform Chinese education along American lines. They thought that education and private enterprise should rely on each other in their development.[23] Broad surveys and discussions of Chinese educational problems proceeded in the following years. On November 1, 1922, a new educational system, modeled on the American, which actually laid the foundations of Chinese educational institutions for later decades, was promulgated by the President of the Republic.[24]

The above educational reforms were mainly sponsored by liberals but supported by some nationalists and conservatives. Despite some achievements, they also encountered great obstacles. The nascent Chinese private enterprises were not strong and enthusiastic enough to provide adequate financial support for vocational schools, let alone other private schools. Chinese education had to rely upon governmental support. The primary interest of the warlords, who in fact controlled the revenues of the central and local governments, lay in military affairs and in the civil wars wherein they hoped to defeat their rivals and seize power. Eighty per cent of the entire revenue of the nation was devoted to military affairs, and the very small allotment for education was often illegally diverted by the warlords.[25] Schools were often closed and occupied by soldiers as barracks. Consequently, from the winter of 1919 on, the liberals and some conservatives, who believed that education might be the means of moral, social, and political reforms, had to involve themselves in an ineffective struggle for the maintenance of educational funds and for disarmament.

In its fifth annual meeting held in October 1919, the National Alliance of Educational Associations resolved to press the government on disarmament

---

May 6 of the next year, a Chinese Association for Vocational Education (*Chung-hua chih-yeh chiao-yü she*) was established in Shanghai by Huang Yen-p'ei, Wu T'ing-fang, Liang Ch'i-ch'ao, Chang Chien, Wang Cheng-t'ing, Ts'ai Yüan-p'ei, and Kuo Ping-wen. In 1918, vocational, commercial, and industrial schools were improved and developed. Their contact with urban enterprises also increased. Early in 1919, some Chinese firms started to donate money to schools and to establish scholarships for students. The Ministry of Education promulgated regulations encouraging such contributions. After the May Fourth Incident, the National Alliance of Educational Associations passed resolutions advocating that educational circles should unite with agricultural associations, labor unions, and chambers of commerce. In March 1920, a joint conference of commercial and educational circles in Hankow adopted a plan of cooperation for the promotion of popular education. A month later, the Peking government decided to dispatch educational inspectors to local schools in order to encourage cooperation between the schools and private business enterprises. The National Association of Vocational Schools (*Ch'üan-kuo chih-yeh hsüeh-hsiao lien-ho-hui*) was organized in Aug. 1922.[22]

and the increase of educational expenditures. The proposal was repeated at the next meeting a year later.[26] From 1921 to 1922 the disarmament movement made some progress. Mass meetings on this subject were held by citizens in the fall of 1922.[27] But the attempt to reduce the armed forces was bound to fail so long as warlords or "strong men" ruled the country.

The struggle for independence of educational finances characterized Chinese education in the latter stage of the May Fourth Movement. Teachers were always underpaid at the time. Seventy to eighty per cent of their salaries was paid in paper money, which often could not be redeemed and was then worth nothing.[28] On December 4, 1919, because of the refusal of the Central Bank and the Bank of Communications to redeem this money, teachers of elementary schools and institutions of higher learning in Peking, under the leadership of the teachers union, asked payment from the government but failed to obtain it. A strike by all teachers and professors of the city resulted from this incident, beginning on the same day and lasting for more than one month, ending on January 12, 1920. It caused the President of the Republic to decree government maintenance of educational finances as a gesture of reassurance.[29] On March 14, 1921, professors in all the government colleges and universities in Peking again started a strike because the government had not financed the schools for the past three and a half months. The monthly budget for the eight government colleges and universities in Peking actually amounted to only two hundred thousand *yuan*, yet the government refused to meet it.[30] The strike lasted for several months and developed into a "movement for the independence of educational funds [i.e., fixed and guaranteed appropriations in the governmental budget]." On June 3, the professors of the eight schools, accompanied by the acting Minister of Education and followed by thousands of students, marched to the office of President Hsü Shih-ch'ang, to present a petition. They were halted at the gate of the palace office and were badly beaten as well as shot at by the President's armed guards.[31] Many professors and students were severely wounded. The strike ended on July 28, after the mediation of some influential people and after the government had established a special educational fund of two million *yuan* credit deposited in a bank for the Peking government schools.[32] The incident was known as the June Third Movement for Study (*Liu-san tu-shu yün-tung*). Teachers' strikes and incidents similar to those in Peking were numerous in other cities after 1921.[33]

The degree of failure of these struggles proved to the leftists and nationalists that the program of the liberals to reform China through pure education was not practicable under the circumstances. As a result, the former two groups obtained more favorable opportunities to attract the intellectuals to their cause, that of overthrowing the Peking regime by force. Meanwhile, the student movement was strengthened, even though the liberal teachers remained reluctant to participate in it and continued their criticisms of its political nature.

Later Trends in the Student Movement

The Chinese student movement after 1919 was often entangled with Sino-Japanese relations. Some of the events resulted from the lasting anti-Japanese boycott; others involved the government's policy toward Japan, especially the unsolved Shantung question. In their protests against the government, the students were often supported by political groups.[f]

The support given by the progressives and leftists to the students' and teachers' strikes strengthened them and provided them with some political coloration. This probably had both good and evil influences on the development of educational and student movements. It must be pointed out, however, that, given the great ideological difference between the views of the new intellectuals and the conservative government officials, not to mention the warlords, these movements were not all due to political influences outside the schools and educational circles. Many teachers' and students' strikes in later years, known in China as "school storms" or "student storms" (*hsüeh-ch'ao*), reflected a spon-

---

[f] On Nov. 16, 1919, a number of Chinese students were wounded by Japanese residents and consulate guards in Foochow, because of the former's activities in boycotting Japanese goods. The incident provoked wearisome diplomatic negotiations lasting for a year. It was solved on Nov. 12, 1920, by both governments apologizing and the Japanese government paying twelve hundred yen to the wounded Chinese students. Another event involved the old Shantung question, which had remained unsolved after China refused to sign the peace treaty with Germany. On Jan. 24, 1920, Obata Torikichi, the Japanese Minister in Peking, asked for direct negotiations between Japan and China. The Anfu Clique planned to accept the proposal. Other political leaders, such as Sun Yat-sen, Liang Ch'i-ch'ao, and the former President Li Yüan-hung, all opposed it. Among the opposition, the student unions were most active and energetic. On Jan. 28, four days after the Japanese proposal was published, the Student Union of Peking presented a letter to the President of the Republic raising objections to the proposal for direct negotiation and explaining the reasons for these objections. The problem soon developed into a controversy. On Feb. 4, two thousand students met at the T'ien-an Gate, to protest against the government's attitude, where nine months before the May Fourth demonstration had started. Forty of them were arrested by police and troops on the spot and indicted by the government in a civil court. Some of them were then sentenced to prison for several months on charges of disorderly conduct. When on April 26 Obata reopened the question of direct negotiations, it again drew the protests of students. But a nation-wide student strike proclaimed by the Student Union of China did not materialize. Only a few schools carried out the resolution, which was opposed by the merchants and industrialists. However, it might be noted that Chinese workers in Shanghai did carry out a sympathy strike which ended on the following day.[84]

taneous protest against the control of education by corrupt and stagnant social and political forces.

School storms had become after the May Fourth Incident a great annoyance and a major political and social issue in China. They were too numerous and complicated to describe and evaluate here. A general survey of these strikes by the newspapers of Shanghai and Peking showed that in 1922 China had 125 notable educational disturbances, of which 101 were conducted by students or teachers in individual schools and 24 involved more than one school or professional educational society.[35]

While the years following the May Fourth Incident had witnessed many school troubles, the students also engaged in a number of constructive and encouraging activities. These may be classified under the term, "student self-government." It has been mentioned that students, after the incident, became more active in private organizations and social service during the expansion of the new culture movement. Actually, in the years after 1919, various student organizations in the schools, besides the student unions, also developed greatly. Their activities became more autonomous, more dynamic, and more expressive. Many of these student organizations and activities were created at this time. Taking the National University of Peking as an example, the following student organizations at the university were established in the few years after the incident: Esperanto Instituto (established in October 1919), Drama Society (1919), Society for the Study of Geography (1920), Society for the Study of Socialism (December 1919), Bertrand Russell Society (December 1920), Students' Y.M.C.A. (1920), English Speech Society (1920), Society for the Study of Marxist Theory (October 1921), Political Science Association (1921), Law Association (1921), Economics Association, Mathematics Association, Society for the Study of Methods of Learning, Society for Research in Popular Education, and many others.

An interesting contrast in character between the student organizations and activities before and after the May Fourth Incident could be seen in the example of Tsing Hua College in Peking, which was financially supported by the American Boxer indemnity. Prior to the incident, from the establishment of the Republic to 1918, students had founded organizations for religious affiliation, such as the Y.M.C.A. and the Buddhist Club, for boxing, science, Confucianism, and the like. In the postincident period these organizations still existed, but their activities were expanded and sometimes changed to include more social survey and social service work. In the years 1919–1922, the students created a night school and library for servants and janitors, societies for the study of agriculture, art, political science, economics, poetry, fiction, drama, and music, and organizations for the promotion of public speeches and debating, and of Esperanto. A student court similar to American student judicial organizations was also founded.[36] And, most important, the student union established in 1919 became the nucleus of all the student activities at the college in the following years. This contrast in character of student organizations and activities in the pre- and postincident periods was also true in other colleges and schools.

To summarize the development of the student movement from the May Fourth period to the middle of the twenties, we may assert that in terms of political significance it passed through three stages. From 1915 or 1917 to 1919, it was often a patriotic and intellectual movement with developing political interests and activities. The petition of May 1918 and the incident of a year later signified its active intervention in political affairs. But at that time there were few close relations between the students and the existing political parties. In 1919 political parties were still supporters of the student movement rather than its active partners. The student movement in this stage also enjoyed almost unanimous support from all the progressive intellectual, social, economic, and political leaders.

In the second stage, from 1920 to 1921, the students' interest in politics increased along with strengthening political influence from outside. They began to develop closer relations with political parties and some of them joined partisan activities. Political parties began to throw open the columns of their newspapers to student contributors. A number of student editors and reporters were employed by those papers. At the same time, most of the liberals, industrialists, and merchants gradually withdrew their support from the student movement. Liberals like Ts'ai Yüan-p'ei, Hu Shih, Chiang Monlin, and T'ao Meng-ho, together with the new industrialists, such as Mu Ou-ch'u, during May 1920, all expressed their opinion that student demonstrations and strikes should cease and that the duty of students was to study.[37] On the other hand, the leftists and nationalists became enthusiastic about the student movement. Because of these new complications, the student movement had gradually weakened in 1921 and the following year. The oppression of the government and conflicts between the right and left wings among the students themselves also contributed to this temporary decline of the student movement. The lack of a unified, strict student organization during this period was another cause.

The years 1922 to 1924 comprised the third stage. During this period students started to take part in the work of party organization. Nation-wide student movement revived in 1923 and the left wing of the students, especially in South

China, almost dominated the movement. The trend culminated in the adoption of the policy of enlisting students as members of the Kuomintang in 1924 with the support of that policy by the Communist Party, most of whose members also joined the Kuomintang at the time. Student unions were henceforth formally listed as political factions in proposed government activities.[38]

PART TWO

ANALYSIS OF MAIN INTELLECTUAL CURRENTS

CHAPTER XI

THE LITERARY REVOLUTION

Aᴍᴏɴɢ those developments associated with the May Fourth Movement which have exerted a far-reaching influence upon the intellectual trends of China in later decades, two are notable: one was the literary revolution, the other, the introduction of Western thought and the re-evaluation of the traditional civilization. This chapter will be devoted to presenting the background and accomplishments of the literary revolution and the means by which it was achieved. The introduction of Western thought and the re-evaluation of the traditional ethics will be taken up in the next two chapters.

The Old Literature

Literature was the major profession of the traditional Chinese intellectuals. This fact immediately explains why the literary revolution played so significant a role in the May Fourth Movement, which was led by the intelligentsia.

Generally speaking, Chinese literature in the nineteenth century was dominated by three literary schools. In nonfictional prose writing, most of the famous writers followed the style of the T'ung-ch'eng school.[a] The leaders of this school drew up a list of "rhetorical principles" (*i-fa*), which they claimed were based on the style of Confucius.[1] They included: (1) "Literature is meant to convey principles" (*wen i tsai tao*); when this was applied to an extreme in later years, it meant that writers should write to propagate the doctrines of the sages and moral principles. In a broad sense, it may be rendered as "literature for tao's sake," and somewhat resembles the Western conception that "all literature is propaganda," though they are not completely the same. Since tao was at the time regarded primarily as a moral and ethical principle, the theory was sometimes conceived as "literature for morality's sake." (2) Literary writing should have its "mood, rhythm, and color"; diction should be strictly selected; vulgar

[a] For both this and the *Wen-hsüan* school see above, Chap. III, n. 1.

language should <u>not be countenanced</u>.[2] Literary leaders at the beginning of the twentieth century, leaders such as Lin Shu and Yen Fu, were consciously or unconsciously influenced by such principles.

Another literary group that appeared later than the T'ung-ch'eng school was the <u>Wen-hsüan school</u>. The writers belonging to this group, such as Wang K'ai-yün (1832–1916), Liu Shih-p'ei, and Huang K'an, imitated the style of the writers living in the period between the third century b.c. and the fifth century a.d. Some of their writings were "<u>parallel prose</u>" (*p'ien wen*), overburdened with <u>stale rhetoric</u>.

In <u>poetry</u>, the style of the <u>Kiangsi school</u> of the Sung dynasty was most copied.[b] Poets of this school strove to use <u>archaic, obscure</u>, and <u>whimsical words</u> and, except for a few nationalist and revolutionary poets, most of their writings were on either <u>trifling</u> or <u>conventional subjects</u>.

The above three schools dominated Chinese literature in the nineteenth century, only poetry and nonfictional prose being considered serious literature. <u>Fiction</u> and the <u>drama</u> were generally <u>regarded with contempt</u>. Many of the excellent novels, short stories, and plays written in the vernacular in the previous few centuries failed to achieve recognition as orthodox literature. To be sure, there was a period in the late nineteenth century when both original fiction and translations of Western fiction were used as media for political criticism by many writers and received considerable serious attention. But most of the popular contemporary writers of fiction produced only inferior ghost, detective, or "boy-meets-girl" stories.[3] With very few exceptions, Chinese literature of all the types discussed had become <u>stereotyped</u> and <u>stagnant</u> during the late Ch'ing period.

At the turn of the nineteenth century, embryonic ideas for literary reform were developed: (1) A <u>new poetry</u> was <u>advocated after 1895</u> by a few young poets and political <u>reformers of the Hundred Days' Reform</u>. They tried to bring into poetic writing some <u>prose diction, new or Western terms, and common words found in folksongs</u>.[c] (2) The style of Chinese <u>prose was in some instances</u> adjusted to <u>utilitarian purposes</u>. Examples were the translations of Yen Fu and Lin Shu, the popular essays of Liang Ch'i-ch'ao, and the political

[b] This school of poetry followed the style of the poet Huang T'ing-chien (1045–1105) of the Sung dynasty. Huang, a contemporary of Su Tung-p'o (1036–1101), was born in Kiangsi Province. Many Chinese poets in this school during the first two decades of the twentieth century were members of the Southern Society (*Nan she*), an organization of poets which included quite a few of the 1911 revolutionaries as well as conservatives.

[c] The major poet in this poetic reform was Huang Tsun-hsien (1848–1905). Others were K'ang Yu-wei (1858–1927), Liang Ch'i-ch'ao (1873–1929), T'an Ssu-t'ung (1865–1898), and Hsia Tseng-yu (1865–1924).

essays of Chang Shih-chao.[4] The works of these authors were influenced to some degree by foreign languages. (3) The spoken language, *pai-hua*, which had been employed to write philosophical discourses in the Sung dynasty, some dramas and governmental documents in the Yüan dynasty, and novels and popular short stories since the Sung dynasty, began to be used by a few scholar-reformers and foreign missionaries in publishing periodicals, newspapers, and other writings. Ch'en Tu-hsiu and Hu Shih joined this movement during their youth, in 1904 and 1906.[d] In the last quarter of the nineteenth century a great number of novels in the vernacular tradition had been produced, though they were not recognized as literary works.[5] (4) In the field of literary theory, the concept that literature should be "for the description of life" and that each generation had its own literature was propounded by Wang Kuo-wei (1877–1927), under the influence of the philosophies of Nietzsche and Schopenhauer.[6] (5) A few systems for alphabetizing Chinese were developed by scholars.[7]

All these late Ch'ing reforms and developments in Chinese literature were the work of only a few scholars, and the reformers did not seriously threaten the traditional literature and language.

Advocacy of Realism and the Vernacular in Literary Writing

The new literature movement which started in 1916 was different, however. First, the new reformers declared aggressively that literary Chinese was a dead language "because it is no longer spoken by the people."[8] Next, they averred that the spoken language, being a living language, was the only fit medium for the creation of a living Chinese literature. Works in the vernacular would henceforth constitute the main body of Chinese literature.[9] In the third place, the new literary reformers attacked the heart of the traditional literary theory, the idea that "literature is meant to convey the tao," or "moral principles," as too restrictive. The old theory was at last replaced, or at least reinterpreted. Literature was now to be either for literature's sake or for the sake of conveying some new ideals. In the fourth place, the proposed new alphabets were not considered merely as tools for the teaching of Chinese characters, but as substitutes for the characters themselves. Because it revolutionized written

[d] By the end of the Ch'ing dynasty there had been a few periodicals in the vernacular. Lin Shu contributed to the *Hangchow Vernacular Magazine* (*Hang-chou pai-hua pao*) at the end of the nineteenth century. Ch'en Tu-hsiu also became associated in 1906 with the *Wusih Vernacular Magazine* (*Wu-hsi pai-hua pao*) which was established in 1898. Hu Shih's association was with the *Ching-yeh Ten-day Magazine* (*Ching-yeh hsün-pao*) which was established in 1906. There were during this period at least seven or eight magazines entitled "vernacular magazine."

communication, the literary revolution was a crucial part of the May Fourth reforms, and of great significance in changing the Chinese way of thinking.

New literature and new thought movements on the model of the European Renaissance was first proposed by Huang Yüan-yung, one of the leading journalists of the day. He first advocated this program before 1915, and at the same time criticized the principle that literature is meant to convey the tao.[10] In 1915 just before he left Shanghai for the United States, Huang wrote a letter to Chang Shih-chao, the editor of the *Tiger* monthly in Tokyo and Ch'en Tu-hsiu's senior associate on the magazine, saying:

> In my humble opinion, politics is in such confusion that I am at a loss to know what to talk about. Ideal schemes will have to be buried for future generations to unearth. . . . As to fundamental salvation, I believe its beginning must be sought in the promotion of a new literature. In short, we must endeavor to bring Chinese thought into direct contact with the contemporary thought of the world, thereby to accelerate its radical awakening. And we must see to it that the basic ideals of world thought must be related to the life of the average man. The method seems to consist in using simple [plain] and simplified language and literature for wide dissemination of ideas among the people. Have we not seen that historians regard the Renaissance as the foundation of the overthrow of medievalism in Europe?[11]

Upon receiving this letter, Chang replied discouragingly that "all social reforms must presuppose a certain level of political stability and orderliness, and the promotion of a new literature cannot be an exception."[12]

Unlike Chang, Ch'en Tu-hsiu devoted much attention to the introduction of modern Western literature to China when he founded *New Youth* in September 1915. The first issue began a serial translation of Ivan Turgenev's novel *Spring Floods*, and from the second issue on, Oscar Wilde's comedy *An Ideal Husband* was translated, both into the vernacular.[13] In November, Ch'en Tu-hsiu published his article "A Discussion of the History of Modern European Literature" in which he pointed out, with oversimplification, that, in the eighteenth and nineteenth centuries, literary thought in Europe changed from classicism to romanticism, then, after the end of the nineteenth century, to realism and finally, to naturalism.[14] "Due to the rise of science since the end of the nineteenth century," said he, "the real nature of the universe and human life was discovered. Europe was unveiled and entered a new enlightened era; the face of Nature was stripped of the mask which had concealed its mysteries. All the old moral principles, old thoughts, and old institutions handed down from antiquity were destroyed. Literature and the arts followed the current, and passed from romanticism to realism and further to naturalism."[15] Following this statement, Ch'en described the success and increasing ascendancy of naturalism in France and Europe, highly praising Emile Zola and his follow- ers and friends — the Goncourts, Flaubert, Daudet, Turgenev, and Maupassant. Ch'en held that all modern European writers, no matter to what schools they belonged, were influenced by naturalism. He accepted the opinion that Tolstoy, Zola, and Ibsen were the three greatest literary men of the world and the idea that Ibsen, Turgenev, Wilde, and Maeterlinck were the four writers most representative of the modern world. Late in December, in reply to a reader's questions as to the editor's opinion on Chinese literature and whether or not he would promote naturalism in China, Ch'en said, "Chinese literature still remains in the stage of classicism and romanticism. Hereafter it will tend to realism." [16] This assertion of the classicism and romanticism of Chinese litera- ture was stretching a point. Ch'en apparently used the term romanticism to mean idealism and the term classicism with solely a traditionalist connotation, somewhat different from the Western implications. But his intention was to show the coming of realism in China. He advocated realism in China instead of naturalism because he feared that the bold description of explicit, painful, and ugly details of society and life by the naturalistic writers might not be accepted by contemporary Orientals — a view supported by events in Japan.[17]

This short discussion of Western and Chinese literary tendencies was probably the first manifestation of the new intellectuals' intention to reform Chinese literature in accordance with Western theories and foreshadowed trends of Chinese literary thought in later years. It did not draw much attention from readers in China, but elicited a letter from a Chinese student in the United States, supporting Ch'en's opinion that Chinese literature should be realistic. The correspondent was Hu Shih, who had just contributed to the magazine a vernacular translation of a short story by a Russian author.[18] In his letter, Hu criticized the poetry of the contemporary Southern Society (*Nan she*) and, more important, for the first time publicly suggested what he later called "eight-don'ts-ism," referred to in Chapter II above, for a Chinese "literary revo- lution": [19]

On the whole, the reason for the decay of contemporary Chinese literature is the overemphasis on style at the expense of spirit and reality. This means that writings have form but no spirit. They imitate the ancient works and superficially resemble them, but in content, they are vague. To overcome this defect, we must pay more attention to the meaning and reality of what we write, the spirit which is contained in the body. Our ancients said, "writing without elegant literary style will not spread widely." To this I answer, "If the writing does not mean anything or does not reflect reality, what is the use of having a literary style?"

As a result of my study and consideration of the matter during this year, I have come to the conclusion that we must start with the following eight principles if we now want to achieve a literary revolution:

(1) Avoid the use of classical allusions;

(2) Discard stale, time-worn literary phrases;

(3) Discard the parallel construction of sentences;

(4) Do not avoid using vernacular words and speech;

(5) Follow literary grammar;

(The above are suggestions for a revolution in literary form or style.)

(6) Do not write that you are sick or sad when you do not feel sick or sad;

(7) Do not imitate the writings of the ancients; what you write should reflect your own personality;

(8) What you write should have meaning or real substance.

(The above are suggestions for a revolution in content.) [e]

Ch'en responded to the letter with extreme enthusiasm, supporting all the principles except the fifth and eighth items. The eighth principle, Ch'en thought, might be interpreted as supporting the traditional theory that literature is meant to convey principles. Ch'en then felt strongly that literature was not a means or a tool which existed only to further some aim. He objected to overlooking the independent value of literature and fine art. The naturalistic writer should describe society as it was without subjective interpretation; and this was, he believed, the fundamental difference between realism and romanticism.[f]

With Ch'en's encouragement, Hu wrote an article titled "Some Tentative Suggestions for the Reform of Chinese Literature," which appeared in both the January 1, 1917, issue of *New Youth* and the March issue of *The Chinese Students' Quarterly* (*Liu Mei hsüeh-sheng chi-pao*), a magazine in Chinese printed in Shanghai by the Chinese Students' Alliance in the United States and with Hu Shih as its editor-in-chief at the time. The article was a further

[e] Hu's suggestions show the influence of Wordsworth's "Preface" to the second edition of *Lyrical Ballads* and Coleridge's *Biographia Literaria*, in addition to the American imagists' principles (which were in turn influenced by Chinese and Japanese poetry) as mentioned in Chapter II. Chou Tso-jen thought Hu's opinion was essentially similar to that of the Chinese literary reformers of the Ming dynasty.[20]

[f] Ch'en's reply to Hu, in "Letters to the Editor," *New Youth*, II, 2 (Oct. 1, 1916), pp. 3–4. This point was later made more clear by Ch'en in a letter answering a reader (Tseng I) in "Letters to the Editor," Vol. III, No. 2 (April 1, 1917), pp. 10–11. Ch'en thought the term tao in the phrase *wen i tsai tao* (literature is meant to convey principles) had been narrowly interpreted by the old literary scholars as "Confucian principles." But even if it were broadly interpreted as "principles" or "theories," he would not advocate the idea of *wen i tsai tao* because fundamentally literature did not exist to promote ideals. However, under existing circumstances, idealistic literature might be tolerable in contemporary China for the time being. What he wanted to attack was only classicism and the narrow interpretation of the tao.

explanation of the eight principles suggested in his letter, and was regarded later as the first trumpet call of the literary revolution. The notable thing is that Hu, in his explanation of the principle "do not avoid using vernacular words and speech," declared that the existing Chinese literature in the vernacular was the "standard" literature of China, and that the vernacular, not the literary, Chinese would be the fit medium for the creation of a "living literature." [21]

Hu Shih, encountering strong opposition from his Chinese fellow students in the United States, avoided the use of the term "literary revolution," and called the proposed movement a "reform." Ch'en received the article most sympathetically. He added a note at the end of it, specifically pointing out that spoken Chinese should be used as the medium of standard Chinese literature, and that he "had had the same firm belief and warm hope" that it would be.[22] In the very next issue, published February 1, Ch'en himself opened fire. His leading article, which bore the bold title "On the Literary Revolution," stated in part:

> What is the foundation stone of contemporary Europe which lies so brilliantly before us? It is the gift of revolutions. The term revolution in Europe means a change from the old to the new, which differs absolutely from what we call the change of dynasties. Since the Renaissance in Europe, there have been revolutions in the fields of politics, religion, ethics, morality, literature, and the arts, and because of these revolutions there have been rejuvenation and progress. The history of modern Europe is a history of revolution. So we say that the brilliance of contemporary Europe is the gift of revolutions.
>
> . . . In China we have undertaken three revolutions [in 1911, 1913, and 1916?], and yet darkness has not disappeared from the scene. This is partly because these revolutions each had "the head of a tiger but the tail of a snake." They began well enough, but were never carried to their logical conclusion. The old dirt was not washed away by blood. But the major cause for the continued prevalence of darkness in China is that even that kind of revolution "with a tiger's head and a snake's tail" has not been carried out by us in the fields of ethics, morality, literature, and the fine arts, which, laden with a great deal of "debris" and covered with a thick, dark "smoke screen," are the sources of our spiritual life. That is why the purely political revolution is incapable of changing our society. The fundamental cause of all these failures lies in the fact that we are afraid of revolution and ignorant of its function in the improvement of civilization.
>
> Today, happily, the validity of Confucianism is being hotly debated. This is a signal for the beginning of an ethical or moral revolution. As for the literary revolution, it has mushroomed for a not inconsiderable length of time, and the foremost in the vanguard, who first raised the revolutionary banner, is my friend Hu Shih. I am willing to brave the enmity of all the pedantic scholars of the country,

and hoist the great banner of the "Army of the Literary Revolution" in support of my friend. On this banner shall be written in big, clear characters my three great principles of the Revolutionary Army:

(1) To overthrow the painted, powdered, and obsequious literature of the aristocratic few, and to create the plain, simple, and expressive literature of the people;

(2) To overthrow the stereotyped and over-ornamental literature of classicism, and to create the fresh and sincere literature of realism;

(3) To overthrow the pedantic, unintelligible, and obscurantist literature of the hermit and recluse, and to create the plain-speaking and popular literature of society in general.[23]

The article bravely attacked the existing three literary schools and concluded with the following vivid and stirring sentences: "Is there any ambitious man in Chinese literary circles who is willing to become a Chinese Hugo, Zola, Goethe, Hauptmann, Dickens, or Wilde? Is there anyone who wishes to disregard whether the pedantic scholars are praising or criticizing us and to challenge in public these 'demons'? If there is any such man, I would like to drag out my largest cannons to be his advance guard." [24]

These articles by Hu and Ch'en immediately attracted the attention of other new intellectual leaders. The first strong and effective support came from Ch'ien Hsüan-t'ung, formerly a student of Chang Ping-lin. Ch'ien was at the time a famous professor at Peking University specializing in Chinese phonetics, semantics, and etymology. His support at once strengthened the "Army of the Literary Revolution" and attracted the attention of literary circles. He wrote a series of letters to Ch'en attacking the leaders of the existing literary schools, calling them the "black sheep of the T'ung-ch'eng school" (*T'ung-ch'eng miaochung*) and "demons of the *Wen-hsüan* school" (*Hsüan-hsüeh yao-yeh*).[25] Liu Fu also came out publicly in support of the revolutionaries.[26] By late 1917, the literary reform ideas had won enthusiastic support from many students of Peking University, among them Fu Ssu-nien and Lo Chia-lun, and Fu's articles in 1918 and 1919 advanced the popularity of the literary reform among students.[27]

After the spring of 1917 the discussion continued by means of letters and essays such as Hu Shih's "On the Historico-evolutionary Concept of Literature." [28] In these discussions, Ch'en Tu-hsiu and Ch'ien Hsüan-t'ung were the most steadfast advocates of the literary revolution, while Hu Shih's essays appeared more convincing to the average intellectual. On April 9, 1917, Hu Shih wrote to Ch'en Tu-hsiu from New York:

The validity of these principles [Hu's eight points and Ch'en's three principles on the literary revolution] cannot be determined overnight. It also cannot be determined by one or two persons. I hope my fellow countrymen will join with composure in the study of this problem. The more the discussion, the clearer the matter. Although we cannot retreat now that we have raised the revolutionary banner, yet we dare not regard our advocacy as absolutely right and leave no room for correction.[29]

Ch'en replied:

The voice of literary reform has been raised in the nation. The number of advocates and opponents is about equal. In my opinion, it is indeed a principle of academic development to tolerate opposition and to have free discussions; but the idea that in the reform of Chinese literature the vernacular language should be the only or principal medium for literature is obviously right, and there is no room for discussion by opponents. We must uphold the creed that our belief is absolutely right and does not need their correction. Why? Because it is an unchangeable requirement to write in the vernacular if the written language is to identify itself with the spoken language in China. Those who oppose literature in the "national language" and uphold the classical are similar to the Chinese in the eighteenth century who opposed Western astronomy and the theory of the rotation of the earth around the sun. We really do not have the leisure to argue with them over such a meaningless question.[30]

After 1917, the literary revolution moved to the stage of "construction." The reformers began to experiment with writing in the vernacular. From January 1918 on *New Youth*, now edited by six professors at Peking University, was published completely in the vernacular, which was later to be called the "national language" (*kuo yü*), a term which had been used by returned students in 1906.[g] In his article "On a Constructive Revolution in Chinese Literature" Hu Shih proclaimed the death of classical literature, actually far from proven, and suggested the creation of a living literature in the vernacular:

My purpose in the "Constructive Revolution in Chinese Literature" is simply to suggest the creation of "a literature in the national language and a national language suitable for literature." Our aim in the literary revolution is merely to create in China a literature in the national language. A national language may be established only after we have produced a literature in the national language; and the national language may be considered a genuine national language only after we have established a national language suitable for literature. . . .

Chinese literature produced by the literary men during the last two thousand years is a dead literature, written in a dead language. A dead language cannot produce a living literature. . . .

In short, from the time of the *Book of Odes* to the present, any Chinese literary work which has had value and life has been written in the vernacular or in lan-

[g] For the change in editorship of *New Youth* see above, Chap. III, n. d.; for the reference to *kuo-yü* see Chap. II, p. 34.

guage close to the vernacular. The others are all lifeless antiques, items for museums! . . .

If China needs a living literature, we must write in the vernacular, in the national language, and we must try to produce literary works in the national language.

. . . If we need to establish a national language, we must first create the literature in the national language. . . .[31]

The year 1918 may be regarded as the natal year of the new Chinese literature. New poetry in the vernacular was widely experimented with by the new intellectuals and was the first fruit of the vernacular movement. Most of the poems in Hu's *A Book of Experiments*, which was published in March 1920, were composed in 1918. Leading reformers in Peking, men such as Liu Fu, Lu Hsün, Shen Yin-mo, Yü P'ing-po, Chou Tso-jen, Chu Tzu-ch'ing, K'ang Pai-ch'ing, Ch'en Tu-hsiu, Li Ta-chao, Liu Ta-pai, Fu Ssu-nien, and Lo Chia-lun, joined in writing vernacular poems. A second development was the introduction of modern European literature in a new translation technique. Works of Ibsen, Strindberg, Andersen (Northern Europe); of Dostoyevsky, Kuprin, Tolstoy (Eastern Europe), as well as the modern Greek Ephtaliotis and the Pole Sienkiewicz, were translated into a written Chinese influenced by the grammar and style of the original European languages.[32] A third innovation was a new essay form. The column, "Random Thoughts" (*Sui-kan lu*) — consisting of a number of acute satiric short essays by various contributors — was established in *New Youth* starting with the April 1918 issue and in *Weekly Critic* a little later. Pieces by Ch'en Tu-hsiu, Liu Fu, Ch'ien Hsüan-t'ung, and later Lu Hsün and Chou Tso-jen appeared in *New Youth*. It marked the beginning of a new kind of Chinese short essay which, usually with a sarcastic tone, became a devastating political weapon in later years. Fourthly, the modern Chinese short story was created in 1918. Lu Hsün, joining *New Youth* at Ch'ien Hsüan-t'ung's insistence, first published his short story, "The Diary of a Madman" (*K'uang-jen jih-chi*) in the May issue of the monthly.[33] His collected short stories, the first collection of this type in Chinese, *Cries* (*Na-han*, published in September 1923) were all composed in the period between 1918 and 1922. Fifthly, the new drama movement was started in 1918. *New Youth* published a special issue on Ibsen in June and a special issue on the reform of the traditional Chinese opera and drama in October. Early essays on the new drama showed the great current influence of Ibsen.

But the spread of the new literary movement to wider circles did not start until 1919. By the spring of that year the literary revolution was arousing both more support and more opposition. After the May Fourth Incident, the vernacular language was widely used in the majority of student publications. Almost all magazines, newspapers, and literary writings began to change to the new literary medium. Hu Shih described in 1922 the incident's influence upon the literary revolution as follows:

> The student movement of 1919 was of great significance for the new literary movement in popularizing the use of the vernacular in writing all over the country; though the student movement and the new literary movement were two different things. Moreover, after the May Fourth Incident, the enlightened Chinese, gradually awakening to the significance of the "intellectual reform," either took an attitude of welcome, or of study, or of toleration, toward this new tide. Their previous hostile attitude toward it gradually decreased. As a result, the literary revolution was able to develop freely. After 1919, vernacular literature spread as though it wore seven-league boots.[34]

In October of 1919, the National Alliance of Educational Associations resolved to ask the government to promote the vernacular officially.[35] On January 12, 1920, the Ministry of Education issued an ordinance providing for the substitution of the vernacular for the classical literary language, from the fall of that year, in the Chinese language instruction in the first and second grades of the primary schools.[36] In March, it ordered the abandonment of text books in the classical language in all grades of these schools.[37] This adoption of the vernacular quickly spread to the middle and higher schools. In 1920 and 1921, the vernacular was officially and popularly recognized as the "national language." Meanwhile, a Chinese "national phonetic alphabet" was established in the years 1918 and 1919.[h]

Opposition to the Literary Reform

The opposition to the literary revolution was from the beginning very weak. The earliest opposition was provided mainly by the traditional scholars, represented by Lin Shu and Ku Hung-ming, the former writing in Chinese, and the latter in English, both in 1919. The opposition of the professors of classics at Peking University, men such as Liu Shih-p'ei, Huang K'an, Lin Sun, and Ma Hsü-lun, was not as influential as that of Lin Shu, because they were

[h] A committee for the standardization of Chinese pronunciation was established by the Ministry of Education in 1912. It proposed a set of 39 "phonetic symbols" (*chu-yin fu-hao*) to note pronunciation. It was established in Nov. 1918 as a phonetic "alphabet" by the ministry. In April 1919 a new sequence of the symbols was proclaimed. In Sept. 1919, a *Dictionary of National Phonetic Symbols* was published. The phonetic symbols were promoted for a time, as a simpler phonetic substitute for the complex ideographs, in the May Fourth period, but in later years interest in this dwindled.[38]

not as widely read and because some of them did not object as seriously as Lin Shu to the new literature.

But Lin Shu's opposition to the literary revolution as has been mentioned in Chapter III was also relatively ineffective. Firstly, in his discussion of the old and the new literature, he made much of traditional ethics. But since his defence of them tended to take the form of short stories such as "Cheng-sheng the Giant" rather than logical analysis, his arguments could do little to assist the cause of the classical language. Secondly, his own experience modified his all-out opposition. At the turn of the nineteenth century Lin had actually been a literary reformer himself. He did recognize to a certain extent the literary value of the old novels in the vernacular. He could only object mildly in his letter to Ts'ai Yüan-p'ei that people would not be able to write very well in the vernacular if they did not read a great number of classical works.[1] He even went so far as to say: "the literature in the classical language is the foundation of that in the vernacular. Without the former, there will not be the latter." [39] This seemed to be neither a strong nor a valid objection to the vernacular as a medium for a new literature. Thirdly, Lin could not argue persuasively that the archaic classical language should not be abandoned for current literature. "If we recognize," said he, "that Latin could not be discarded, there must be some reason too for the preservation of the writings in the classical language by Ssu-ma Ch'ien, Pan Ku, Han Yü, and Liu Tsung-yüan. I know the reason but cannot explain it." [40] He also said lamely, "We are too old to point out and rectify their [the new-literature advocates'] errors. In the ages that lie ahead, there must come someone who will appreciate this. Await his arrival wide-eyed." [41] Had Lin's objection been directed against Hu Shih's later exaggeration that "Chinese literature produced by the literary men during the last two thousand years is a dead literature," he would have taken a safer position. There were in fact a great number of old literary works in classical Chinese which were valuable and lively literature. But this did not help the case that living Chinese authors should still use the classical language in contemporary writing.

As for the ardent traditionalist Ku Hung-ming, he thought that a dead language should be defined as "a clumsy, inert, lifeless language incapable of producing a living literature" and, having so defined it, pointed out that classical Chinese was not a dead language in that sense. Instead, like Shakespeare's English, it was a "noble language." It was more beautiful than spoken Chinese, just as the language of Shakespeare was more beautiful than modern spoken

[1] See above, Chap. III, p. 69.

English. He also maintained that classical Chinese literature was not a dead literature because it conveyed the tao which he rendered into English as "the Law of Life." But the reformers, he said, brought in "a literature which makes men become ethically dwarfed," and this he then categorized as a truly dead literature.[42]

The reformers retorted that a dead language was one which was no longer spoken by the people and was unintelligible to the ear. Even if classical Chinese had its beauty, it was not spoken nor auditorily understandable. The language of Shakespeare was noble and beautiful, but the English-speaking people now used modern English and not the English of Shakespeare. Furthermore, about 90 per cent of the Chinese people were illiterate partly because the classical language was too difficult to learn. To get the people educated, it was better to adopt the spoken language for writing purposes.[43]

To these arguments Ku Hung-ming answered:

> The language most popularly used was not necessarily a better one. More bread and jam were consumed than roast turkey throughout the world; yet could we say that the latter was less delicious and nutritious than the former only because it was rarer and that we should all eat "only" bread and jam?[44]

Ku seemed to be unaware of, or at least chose to ignore, the fact that Shakespeare's English was actually spoken and intelligible to the ear in his time; Shakespeare did not use Latin when writing his plays, nor did Ku himself use Middle English in everyday writing. As for the problem of illiteracy, Ku simply retorted that it was a public blessing that 90 per cent of the population of China was illiterate; otherwise, a fantastic sum of money would have been spent on telegrams to the Chinese delegates at the Paris Conference on the Shantung question, if every literate person had copied the example of the students and intellectuals.[j] In a wily paragraph calculated to appeal to the moralists and traditionalists Ku argued further that, by the Confucian definition of an educated man, that is, the moral man, the illiterate 90 per cent were in fact the only "educated" people in China. How could those "uneducated" intellectuals talk of educating them?

Another old writer, Yen Fu, who was sixty-five years old and very sick in 1919, did not find it necessary, as we have mentioned in Chapter III, to publicly argue the case against the new literary movement. In a letter to a student of his, however, he gave two reasons to oppose the vernacular movement. He thought that the reformers rested their case only on precedents in the Western

---

[j] See above, Chap. IV, pp. 91–92.

literary reforms. They were wrong, in Yen's ill-founded opinion, because in the Western literary reforms spoken languages were adapted to the written, whereas the Chinese reformers now tried the opposite, to bring a written language close to a spoken. In addition, Yen believed quite arbitrarily that literary Chinese was richer in figurative dictions than the vernacular.

The opposition of these old conservatives quickly faded away but further opposition came from a group of conservative Western-educated professors in Nanking in 1922. Most of the members of this group were influenced by Western classicism. One of them had raised his objection to the new literary movement in the spring of 1919.[45] In January 1922 the professors of the Nanking Higher Normal College established the *Critical Review* (*Hsüeh heng*) monthly. Those associated with the magazine such as Wu Mi, Mei Chin-chuang (Mei Kuang-ti), and Hu Hsien-su, all under the influence of Irving Babbitt's new humanism, opposed both the new literature and the new culture movements.[k] While their opinions were not identical, the following are the main objections they held in common: (1) The spoken language changed too often. If it was adopted for writing purposes, both the old and the new literary works would be incomprehensible to posterity.[47] (2) The evolution theory of literature was not valid, as had been demonstrated by the British critic, Hazlitt. It was not true that modern Western literature had developed from classicism to romanticism, from romanticism to realism, and from realism to symbolism, futurism, and neoromanticism.[48]

Since these professors all wrote in classical Chinese, they were not widely read. They were so ineffective that the reformers did not even bother to argue with them. Lu Hsün simply remarked that "what I respect in you gentlemen [the *Critical Review* group] is only that you still have the courage to publish such articles."[49] In March 1922, Hu Shih declared, "The voice of the *Critical Review* probably utters the epilogue of the opposition to the literary revolution. I dare say that the revolution has passed the stage of discussion, and the opposition party has collapsed. From now on, we live in the period of the creation of the new literature."[50]

It is true that by 1922 the literary revolution had triumphed. But further skirmishes occurred from time to time. In July 1925 Chang Shih-chao, then Minister of Education and Minister of Justice in Tuan Ch'i-jui's new govern-

---

[k] Mei Kuang-ti and Wu Mi had been students of Irving Babbitt at Harvard University. They were influenced by his literary theories. Babbitt wrote early in 1922 that he recognized that "China needs to escape from the rut of pseudoclassic formalism" but he urged the reformers of China "to retain the soul of truth that is contained in its great traditions" and warned them not to imitate the Occident and pour out the baby with the bath water in their eagerness to become progressive.[46]

ment, established in Peking *The Tiger Weekly* (*Chia-yin chou-k'an*), a successor of the earlier monthly which had been published in Tokyo, and in its pages wrote against the literary revolution. This time, because of Chang's position and influence, a great deal of alarm was stirred up among writers. In rejoinder, Hu Shih published an article "Old Chang Rebels Again" (*Lao Chang yü fan-pan liao*) and Wu Chih-hui wrote satirically of "The Death of a Friend" (*Yu sang*), mourning for the "death" of Chang and of the old literature.[1]

Humanitarianism, Naturalism, and Romanticism: The Society for Literary Studies and the Creation Society

After the success of the literary revolution through their joint efforts during 1919 and 1920, the new intellectual leaders began to separate into natural groupings according to their special interests. A number of early leaders of the literary revolution actually dropped out of the drive to develop a new literature. Ch'en Tu-hsiu interested himself in social and political movements; Hu Shih gradually turned his attention to the study of the Chinese classics and the old vernacular novels; Ch'ien Hsüan-t'ung and Liu Fu concentrated on the study of linguistics; Fu Ssu-nien and Lo Chia-lun went abroad to study history; Shen Yin-mo and some others turned again to write poems in the classical language. On the other hand, Chou Tso-jen and Lu Hsün and many other young writers began the task of introducing more Western literary theories and works, and of producing creative literature in the spoken language. In this development, the literary revolution, just like the cultural and political movements, branched out in different directions.

One of the early consequences of the new literary movement was the organization of the Society for Literary Studies (*Wen-hsüeh yen-chiu hui*) in Peking on January 4, 1921.[51] Most of the prominent men of letters of the time joined the society, with the reformed *Short Story Monthly* and newly-founded *Ten-day Literary Publication* (*Wen-hsüeh hsün-k'an*, later changed to *Literary Weekly*) as its major organs. It had a membership of 172 leading writers, established many local branch organizations, and published a number of local periodicals. Though loosely organized, it was the most influential literary group after the creation of the New Youth and New Tide societies.[52]

Under the influence of Chou Tso-jen and Mao Tun, the Society for Literary

---

[1] Actually the classical language was still advocated in many kinds of writing by the Kuomintang government in later years. In 1934 there came another reaction against the vernacular, but in vain.

Studies at the beginning advocated a "literature of humanity." The theory had first been developed by Chou in 1918 when he published his article "Literature of Humanity" in *New Youth*, by which he meant a literature based on individualistic humanitarianism; [53] in 1920 he stated that literature should be for mankind's sake instead of for "literature's sake." [54] Later when the Society for Literary Studies was established, Chou embodied the theory in its manifesto, which he drafted. The manifesto declared: "Literature is a form of labor, and a form of labor very significant for humanity." [55]

The idea "literature for humanity's sake" was never adequately explained. At the beginning it was supposed to oppose both the traditional, orthodox theory that "literature is meant to convey the tao" and the light attitude taken toward literature by the contemporary Saturday Group (*Li-pai-liu p'ai*).[m] The society rejected both the ideas that literature is merely a tool of morality and that it is independent of humanity, i.e., the concept "art for art's sake." But in further interpretations of the literature of humanity, the members of the society did not seem to take a uniform stand. Their views are vague and ambiguous. Chou Tso-jen simply identified the idea of humanity with idealism.[56] On the other hand, Mao Tun showed a tendency towards realism and naturalism. In his opinion, "genuine literature" should be the "literature of humanity." "Literature at present," he said, "has become a kind of science whose subject matter for study is humanity — contemporary humanity — and whose tools of study are poetry, drama, and fiction. With artistic skill, the writer's revelation of humanity must be the life of all mankind, without an iota of selfishness or the least particle of subjectivity. Of course, the people described in literary works will have thoughts and feelings, but these thoughts and feelings must surely be common to the masses, common to the whole of mankind, and not just to the writer himself." [57] Mao Tun emphasized the objectivity of literature, accepting the Western idea that "literature is the reflection of life," or the mirror of society, the nation, the circumstances, the times, and the writer's personality.[58] (Mao Tun, whose name was originally intended to mean in Chinese "contradiction," did not see a contradiction between the claim he made at times that literature is a "science" in which the subjective bias should be completely suppressed and the personal view play no part, and the claim at other times that the writer's personality must after all be reflected in literature.) He also rejected both the ideas that "literature is meant to convey the tao" and "literature is for literature's sake." [59]

---

[m] The popular organ of this group, *Saturday* (*Li-pai-liu*), published in Shanghai, contained light fiction and other prose of no literary value.

In its later period, the works produced by members of the society tended to emphasize realism and naturalism, though quite a few were of a romantic nature. The members were not inclined to prescribe solutions for the plight of humanity, but in laying bare the real situation of humanity they felt that they were sensitizing their readers to an appreciation of the plight of their fellow human beings and a sense of solidarity with them. To the extent that they believed literature must serve a purpose beyond itself — a nonliterary purpose — they themselves were in a sense indirectly committed to their own "tao." While many of the members of the society engaged in creative writing and the study of the traditional Chinese literature, their major achievement was considered to be the introduction of Western, and some other Oriental, literature, especially the literature of "oppressed peoples," such as those of eastern Europe. Works translated by its members represented more than twenty countries, including Japan, Germany, France, the United States, Great Britain, Spain, Sweden, Norway, Hungary, Russia, Austria, Poland, Belgium, India, Jewish Palestine, Ireland, Italy, Holland, and Bolivia.[60] Scandinavian writers such as Bjornson, Bojer, Ibsen, and Strindberg; French writers such as Barbusse, Baudelaire, Anatole France, Maupassant, and Zola; and India's Tagore were all translated. Translations of Russian works were the most numerous, but few Soviet Russian authors were included, probably because the Soviet Union had not been established very long. Those translated from Russian were Andreyev, Artzybashev, Dostoyevsky, Gogol, Tolstoy, Turgenev, and Gorky.[61]

One might say broadly that the society performed the function of introducing Western realistic and naturalistic literature and theories into China. It helped to reveal the realities of the Chinese social scene. This, of course, reflected the temper of the new intellectuals during the May Fourth period; they were deeply interested in the study and reform of society. Meanwhile, the society's efforts prompted the development of an indigenous "literature of blood and tears," which reflected the spirit of protest of the Chinese intelligentsia of the time.[62]

Late in the May Fourth period, romantic and pessimistic feelings prevailed among many of the young intellectuals. The old civilization was shaken; traditional ethical principles and ideas of life were of uncertain value to the youth who were driven by the oppression of the warlords and bureaucrats and of society itself to join in the protest movement. After the excitement of participation in social protest, they were caught by the dream of a new and brighter future. But the burden of tradition was still heavy. Society, the government, the schools, all were far from being ideal. New ideas were divergent and confusing. Where should they stand? Where should they go? What should they do?

It was a time full of frustration, distress, fantasy, and hesitation. These feelings of protest, hesitation, and pessimism are seen in the characters of Lu Hsün's short stories, in his *Cries* and *Hesitation* (*P'ang-huang*). Yeh Shao-chün's novel *Ni Huan-chih*, about a teacher in a primary school, describes the trials and struggle of a typical young intellectual in the period of the May Fourth Movement.

Unsatisfactory family life was another source of distress to the youth. They were awakening to the needs for greater freedom in relations between the sexes and life in general; consequently, they found the traditional arranged marriage a serious problem.[n] Since divorce was still a serious matter, the situation certainly had a great influence on the psychology of the young intellectuals. Suicide became a problem of the time.

It was not surprising under such circumstances that a new literary group devoted to expressing these various rebellions of youth sprang into being. In the summer of 1921 a group of nostalgic Chinese returned students from Japan — Kuo Mo-jo, Yü Ta-fu (1897–1945), Chang Tzu-p'ing, Ch'eng Fang-wu, T'ien Han, Cheng Po-ch'i, and later Wang Tu-ch'ing (1896–1940) from France — organized in Shanghai the Creation Society (*Ch'uang-tsao she*), a rival of the Society for Literary Studies.[64] The slogan of these young men was "creative writing." Their organs, the *Creation Quarterly* (*Ch'uang-tsao chi-k'an*, May 1922–January 1924) and *Creation Weekly* (*Ch'uang-tsao chou-pao*, May 1923–May 1924), were influenced to different degrees by Western romanticism and individualism. In many cases, these authors were affected by a kind of *fin de siècle* feeling. They advocated "art for art's sake"; the development of the self, unrestricted expression of emotion, and freedom of organization.[65] They considered themselves literary heretics, bearing no relation to the adherents of *New Youth*, which they thought had already performed its duty of attack upon the old literature in the first stage of the new literary movement. The second stage was a time for creation and construction. Their duty now was to create new works and to attack the "opportunists" in the new literary camps, i.e., to criticize their coarse writings and translations. Their hostile attitude toward all other groups made themselves a target for attack.[66]

---

[n] A survey of the marital circumstances of 631 male college and high school students early in 1921 showed that, among the 184 married, only 5 had chosen their wives for themselves. The marriages of the other 179 were decided by their parents. Most of them did not meet their spouses before they were married; about half of them were found to have marital troubles. Among the 181 engaged students only 6 had chosen their own fiancées, while 158 of the engagements were arranged by parents without the consent of their offspring.[63]

The works of the Creation Society soon acquired a wide public among young Chinese. Kuo's romantic poetry such as *The Goddesses* (*Nü-sheng*, 1921) and later his translation (1928) of Goethe's *Die Lieden des Jungen Werther*, Chang Tzu-p'ing's love stories, and Yü Ta-fu's pessimistic writings attracted many young readers. A member of the society once said: "After the May Fourth Incident, romanticism indeed appeared prevalent among all the youth of the country. *Sturm und Drang* almost became a popular catchword for the average young person. New-born literary organizations of the time all more or less shared this tendency. Among them, the one that most strongly bore this imprint was the Creation Society." [67] During the early period of the society's history, it did represent this spirit of the time.

From Literary Revolution to Revolutionary Literature

As a whole the new literary revolution, in the period of the May Fourth Movement, was a manifestation of the trend against the idea that "literature is meant to convey the tao," and of the trend to establish the vernacular as a national language. Whether art was held to be for humanity's sake or for art's sake, for the most part literature remained in practice independent of all aims beside human interests and revelations or self-expression. The Society for Literary Studies and the Creation Society represented the main currents of the new literature in this period. The former emphasized the revelation of human and social realities; the latter emphasized unrestricted expression of personal feelings. In their works few of these writers suggested concrete solutions for the problems of society and life. Their spirit was one of protest and self-consolation. [68]

In later years the two societies were deeply affected by changing circumstances. After the May Thirtieth Incident of 1925 in connection with the Shanghai anti-British and anti-Japanese strikes, the Creation Society, as a result of the worsened political situation, moved into its second period, giving up its individualism, pessimism, and the idea of "art for art's sake." It adopted "revolutionary literature" as its battle cry and fought against imperialism and warlordism. The same incident also caused the split and collapse of the Society for Literary Studies. Lu Hsün and Chou Tso-jen went on to establish a new literary group, the Thread-of-Talk Society (*Yü-ssu she*), insisting on realism and humanitarianism; while Hsü Chih-mo, Hu Shih, Wen I-to, and Liang Shih-ch'iu organized the Crescent Moon Society (*Hsin-yüeh she*), advocating symbolism. After 1928, the Creation Society entered a third period, propagating "proletarian literature." Then in 1930 the League of Leftist Writers (*Tso-i tso-chia lien-meng*) was organized under the leadership of Lu Hsün; against it stood a group advocating "nationalist literature" (*min-tsu-chu-i wen-hsüeh*) led by Huang Chen-hsia, Wang P'ing-ling, Shao Hsün-mei, and others. Later controversies in literary circles involved such problems as whether or not literature should be independent of politics and whether or not literature had a class character. From the thirties on, leftist writings dominated China's new literature.

The practical aspects of the new literature movement, developed from 1917, were successful; as a consequence the archaic literary language and the old stereotyped literature declined rapidly. The vernacular came to be widely employed in writing and teaching. As the written language tended to become one with the spoken, knowledge and education became more easily popularized. Moreover, poetry, essays, short stories, novels, and the drama all took new directions. Literary criticism and literary theory also made great advances. Literature was thus brought closer to the realities of life and society. It also came to enjoy a greater popularity. Trends of the new literature toward naturalism and socialism in later years exercised a considerable influence upon the intellectual and psychological development of Chinese youth. It is in such senses as these that the literary revolution should be recognized as having played a significant role in modern China's intellectual and sociopolitical transformation.

CHAPTER XII

THE NEW THOUGHT AND RE-EVALUATION
OF THE TRADITION

IT is no exaggeration to say that, of all the activities of the new intellectuals, the new thought tide was the most significant. The main aim of the reformers in the May Fourth Movement was the creation of a new China; one method was to be the substitution of new thought for the old and traditional. From the time *New Youth* was established, this had become the major idea of the new reform movement. In a sense, the May Fourth Incident was a result and manifestation of this idea.

Most of the leading new intellectuals during the early period adopted an uncompromising attitude on ideological reform. This attitude is well exemplified in Ch'en Tu-hsiu's and Hu Shih's joint answer to a reader of *New Youth* in 1918: "The old literature, old politics, and old ethics have always belonged to one family; we cannot abandon one and preserve the others. It is Oriental to compromise and only go half way when reforming, for fear of opposition. This was the most important factor behind the failures of reform movements during the last several decades." [1]

The Hard Core of the Old Thought

To understand what the new thought innovators were fighting, it is necessary to examine briefly the Chinese philosophical tradition in general, and in particular how Confucianism was manipulated by political authorities to their own advantage in recent centuries.

For many centuries, China had been dominated by four schools of thought: Confucianism, Legalism, Taoism, and Buddhism. In their popular forms, Confucianism had been for long mixed with Legalist ideas, and Taoism and Buddhism had been corrupted by all kinds of superstitions such as spiritualism and divination. These superstitious ideas were further popularized by traditional Chinese operas and stories. In the sphere of systematic philosophy and ethics, the Chinese mind in the last century was greatly influenced by Neo-Confucianism dating from the Sung dynasty and the Han learning developed early in the Ch'ing dynasty.[2]

Neo-Confucianism, which was influenced by Buddhism and Taoism, asserted that everything is governed by *li* (principles, or reason, somewhat similar to Plato's ideas or the Western higher law of nature), and the one great *li*, the Supreme Ultimate, which was sometimes identified with the tao, was regarded as absolute truth, eternal and forever unchanging. According to the orthodox interpretation of the theory, the ideal type of political conduct conformed to *li* or tao. The actual government, if it corresponded to this ideal government, would be considered absolutely good. To achieve this ideal, the ruler should obtain virtue by investigating things to extend his knowledge, making his thought sincere, rectifying his heart to cultivate his character, and regulating his family.[3] By doing this, the ruler might achieve the goal of becoming a sage-king of absolute virtue. In practice, Chinese emperors or usurpers, by claiming that they possessed the "mandate of heaven" and absolute virtue, in accordance with Confucian orthodoxy, easily found justification for their absolute rule, although the people also made appeal to *li* or *tao-li* as a higher law in their struggle against political authority. Early in the Ming dynasty, the Neo-Confucianist interpretation of the classics or Canons by Chu Hsi (1130–1200) was approved by the government as the official interpretation, and it was adopted in 1313 as the standard for the civil service examinations until 1905 when the examination system was abolished. With this orthodox theory and the rising Legalist influence upon practical government, a monarch's power was made absolute.

In the late Ming and early Ch'ing periods, Neo-Confucianism was opposed by a few enlightened thinkers such as Huang Tsung-hsi, Ku Yen-wu (1613–1682), Yen Yüan (1635–1704), and Li Kung (1659–1733).[4] The stand taken against Neo-Confucianism by these men was based on the argument that its interpretation of Confucianism was not based on Confucius' own teaching, and that the idea of *li* could not be found in the five classics, i.e., the *Book of Odes*, *Book of History*, *Book of Changes*, *Book of Rites*, and *Spring and Autumn Annals*, or any other records of Confucius and Mencius. Ku and Huang even advocated individual liberty and emphasized Mencius' idea that "in a state the people are of first importance, the shrines of the state gods are next, and the ruler is least important." But these thinkers did not develop their theories. Later on, a number of prominent Ch'ing scholars devoted themselves to a careful analysis of classical texts. They studied more or less objectively the earliest commentaries on the classics, commentaries made in the Han dynasty (206 B.C.–A.D. 221), and turned up material which discredited Neo-Confucianism.[5] They criticized the ancient texts, extracted new meanings, and exposed forgeries. This group of classicists was known as the school of "Han learning," while the Neo-Confucianists were called the school of "Sung learning."

The discoveries of the classicists of the Han learning exerted some influence upon the new intelligentsia of the May Fourth Movement when the latter attacked orthodox Neo-Confucianism. In their textual criticisms the earlier scholars had spotted many ancient Chinese philosophers who were not Confucians. The educational philosophy of Yen Yüan and Li Kung was even considered by Liang Ch'i-ch'ao to be similar to John Dewey's.[6] But the influence of the Ch'ing scholars of the Han learning on the criticism of Confucian orthodoxy was limited. Their studies were confined to rather specialized and esoteric subjects such as phonetics, etymology, and semantics. In philosophy, some of them tended in the later years of the Ch'ing to follow the line of the Sung learning. Those who criticized Neo-Confucianism did so on the basis of a literal acceptance of original Confucianism itself. Their intention had been not to question or revise but to restore true Confucianism as they saw it. Consequently, Confucianism continued to retain its stereotype and predominance in the nineteenth century. Indeed, the most powerful slogan for Tseng Kuo-fan's (1811–1872) suppression of the T'ai-p'ing Rebellion was the need to defend Confucianism, the Sage's teachings, and the traditional ethics. K'ang Yu-wei's reform movement of 1898 was also based on his interpretation of Confucianism, namely, that Confucius himself was a reformer. At the other extreme, the Ch'ing ultra-conservatives displayed great enthusiasm in offering sacrifices to Confucius. In December 1906, Tz'u-hsi, the Dowager Empress, decreed that Confucius should receive the highest sacrificial rites.[7]

In the Yüan Shih-k'ai period (1912–1916) of the Republic, the Confucian controversy became more and more intense. In 1912 a Confucian Society (K'ung-chiao hui) was established in Shanghai by K'ang Yu-wei's disciple Ch'en Huan-chang and a number of famous old literati such as Shen Tseng-chih, Chu Tsu-mou, Liang Ting-fen, and Yen Fu. In July 1913 when the Constitutional Commission of Parliament started to draw up a draft constitution for the Republic of China, known as the "Temple-of-Heaven Draft," an article providing for the establishment of Confucianism as a state religion was proposed by members of the Chinputang. It was opposed by the members of the Kuomintang and soon became a heated debating point throughout the country. After long, weary arguments, the issue was temporarily settled by a compromise. Article XIX read "Confucius' principles (*tao*) shall be the basis for the cultivation of character in national education." [8]

Yüan Shih-k'ai, in his monarchical move, leaned heavily on the prop of Confucian orthodoxy. In preparing for his "coronation," he was careful to sacrifice to Confucius.[9] On January 1, 1916, the first day of his monarchy, Yüan decreed that K'ung Ling-i, who claimed descent from Confucius, should be given the title "Holy Duke" (*Yen-sheng-kung*) which was first conferred upon the lineal descendant of Confucius in A.D. 1055 by an Emperor of the Sung dynasty. Yüan went even further, and gave him an additional title of Prince.[10] A few societies and periodicals specializing in Confucianism were also established to support the monarchical movement.[a]

The struggle over Confucianism did not die away with the collapse of Yüan's monarchical movement. In August 1916, while Parliament was in session in Peking, Article XIX of the Temple-of-Heaven Draft Constitution became a crucial issue. Some parliamentary members resumed their efforts to establish Confucianism as a state religion. K'ang Yu-wei, after the failure of Yüan's utilization of Confucianism, wrote a letter to President Li Yüan-hung and Premier Tuan Ch'i-jui with the same suggestion. He even produced his own draft constitution embodying the idea. He asserted that all peoples had religions except the barbarians; that Confucius had been the founder of a religion; that if the people did not read the Confucian classics, they would not know how to behave; that Confucius' *Annals* was actually a traditional Chinese constitution according to which many judicial and other important cases after

---

[a] The Confucian Society founded the monthly *Journal of the Confucian Society* (*K'ung-chiao hui tsa-chih*) in Peking in Feb. 1913, advocating the establishment of Confucianism as a state religion. The society was one of the most enthusiastic supporters of Yüan's monarchical movement. Paul S. Reinsch recorded: "'The whole Chinese people hold the doctrines of Confucius most sacred,' declared President Yüan Shih-kai in his decree of November 26, 1913, which reintroduced much of the old state religion. He stopped a little short of giving Confucianism the character of an established religion, but ordered that the sacrificial rites and the biennial commemoration exercises be restored. 'I am strongly convinced,' he said, 'of the importance of preserving the traditional beliefs of China.' In this he was upheld by the Confucian Society at Peking, in the organization of which an American [Columbia] University graduate, Dr. Chen Huan-chang, was a leading spirit. Mr. Chen's doctoral dissertation had dealt with the economic principles of Confucius and his school; upon his return to China, his aim had been to make Confucianism the state religion under the Republic." [11] In 1913–1915 similar societies for a Confucian religion and a monarchical movement existed in many provinces, such as the Confucian Association (*K'ung she*) of Chihli, and that of Honan. Others were called *K'ung-tao hui* or *K'ung-chiao kung-hui* as in Hunan, Shantung, and Hehlungchiang (Amur River) Provinces.

the Han dynasty had been decided; that the ancient Chinese had advocated the recitation of the *Book of Filial Piety* for the suppression of bandits, and the use of the *Great Learning* for the pacification of evil spirits, and had claimed that the use of even half of the *Analects of Confucius* could govern the whole country.[12] K'ang also argued that, since Confucianism had dominated China for two thousand years, on its abandonment, China would be divided and eliminated. Every country had to have a spiritual base; Confucian teaching was the Chinese one: "No Confucianism, no China." [13] Therefore, he suggested: (1) All officials, from the President down to the local magistrates should sacrifice to Confucius every month and on important occasions. They should kowtow to the icons of the Sage. (2) All students from the university level down to the elementary school ought to read the Confucian classics. The schools should offer degrees in such studies, and the state should subsidize them. (3) Confucian "churches" should be established and subsidized by the state.[14] The opinions of the other supporters of Confucianism varied in degree. But all of them argued that Confucianism was the best teaching China had had and should be accepted as a basic code for the nation.

These proposals obtained strong support from the conservatives, who thought only of tradition, but they were furiously opposed by the new reformers. Consequently, after hot debates both within and without Parliament, the article concerning Confucianism in the draft constitution was amended to read: "The people of the Republic of China have freedom to worship Confucius and freedom of religion which shall not be restricted except by law." [15] The situation was such that, on the eve of the May Fourth Movement and in its early years, especially in 1916 and 1917, although Yüan Shih-k'ai was already dead, Ts'ai Yüan-p'ei, Ch'en Tu-hsiu, and many other intellectuals felt that his spirit was still alive; "there were numerous Yüan Shih-k'ais, thinking, talking, and acting in China." [b]

New Thought: Realism, Utilitarianism, Liberalism, Individualism, Socialism, and Darwinism

While the older generation and the conservatives clung to traditional thought and ethics, the new intellectuals, influenced by Western ideas, were rallying to the support of "Mr. *Te*" (Democracy) and "Mr. *Sai*" (Science), as they conveniently dubbed the new currents. It was in the names of these two gentlemen

---

[b] There was a rumor spread by the Chinese and Western newspapers in Shanghai in the winter of 1916 that Yüan had not, in fact, died.[16]

that Confucianism and its followers were attacked. An examination of the ideas of the new intellectuals during the early period of the May Fourth Movement reveals that they were a mélange of postseventeenth-century Western ones; especially highly regarded were ideas stemming from the American and French Revolutions.

During the two decades before 1919, various Western philosophic ideas had been popularized in China. Utilitarianism, the theory of evolution, and empiricism were introduced by Yen Fu's translations. These included Thomas Huxley's *Evolution and Ethics* (translated in 1894–1895, published in 1895 and April 1898); Adam Smith's *The Wealth of Nations* (translated from late 1897 to the fall of 1900, published late in 1901); John Stuart Mill's *On Liberty* (translated in 1899, published in October 1903) and *System of Logic* (only first half, translated in 1900–1902, published in 1902); Herbert Spencer's *Study of Sociology* (translated in 1898–1902, published in May 1903); Edward Jenks' *A Short History of Politics* (translated in 1903, published in February 1904); Montesquieu's *L'Esprit des lois* (translated in 1900–1905, published in September 1904–1909); and William Stanley Jevons' *Primer of Logic* (translated in the fall of 1908, published in the same year). Those intellectual leaders who were middle-aged at the time of the May Fourth Movement had been influenced mainly by these works. French revolutionary ideas were first introduced by Liang Ch'i-ch'ao at the beginning of this century. Rousseau was popularized by Liang's lucid essays. After 1906, Lamarck's *Philosophie Zoologique*, Kropotkin's *Mutual Assistance*, and other French philosophic works were introduced by Wu Chih-hui, Li Shih-tseng, Ts'ai Yüan-p'ei, Chang Chi, and Wang Ching-wei. Schopenhauer, Nietzsche, and Kant were introduced by Wang Kuo-wei and others. Some of Bertrand Russell's works were translated into Chinese before the May Fourth Incident. They reinforced the influence of British empiricism introduced earlier. Russell's work, with John Dewey's introduction of the Cartesian method later, laid a foundation for the study of mathematical logic in China.

At the beginning of the May Fourth period, all these ideas affected in various degrees the critical thinking of the new Chinese intellectual leaders, but realism and utilitarianism were the most widely prevailing principles. In the opening article of the first issue of *New Youth*, Ch'en Tu-hsiu suggested a utilitarian and realistic approach to the problems of life. He expressed his admiration of John Mill and Comte.[17] In Ch'en's opinion, one of the fundamental differences between East and West was that the latter paid more attention to practical matters while the former paid more to ceremony.[18] Therefore, for the rejuvenation of the Chinese people, he advocated the adoption of realism as one of the principles of Chinese education.[19] Utilitarianism was propagated also by many other writers.[20] These ideas were later merged with pragmatism. After the May Fourth Incident, though the young were gripped by fantasy, they still based, or at least pretended to base, their activities on practicality.

Liberalism was a catchword among the intellectuals in those early years. Individual freedom had been propounded by Liang Ch'i-ch'ao and the Kuomintang leaders at the beginning of the twentieth century. In the first issue of *New Youth*, Ch'en Tu-hsiu emphasized individual freedom, and came out in opposition to any kind of slavery.[21] In the second issue, he published his Chinese translation of Samuel F. Smith's "America" (American national hymn).[22] Edmund Burke's speech in the House of Commons supporting the resistance of the American colonists was also translated and published in the monthly.[23] In the main, the concept of freedom current among these Chinese intellectuals was derived from Rousseau's theory of general will and from British utilitarianism.[24] They talked of freedom in terms of human rights, and freedom of speech and the press.[25]

At a time when most people had become aware of the need for national unity and the importance of statehood, some new intellectuals tended to emphasize individualism. They maintained that the defense of a sovereign and independent republic should not be at the expense of individual freedom.[26] Most of the new intellectual leaders rejected the idea that statehood and nationalism should be ultimate ideals. They conceded only that these were temporarily necessary for the betterment of the welfare of the individual.[27] Ch'en Tu-hsiu realized that the most significant difference between East and West was that Western civilization, be it British, American, French, or German, was based on a thoroughgoing individualism, whereas the Eastern variety was based on family or clan units. As he understood them, Western ethics, moral principles, political theories, and law all tended to advocate individual rights and welfare, freedom of thought and speech, as well as the development of individuality. Under the Eastern system, a man was a member of his family or clan, and not an independent individual. This system destroyed individual dignity and self-respect, choked free will and independent thought, deprived a person of equal rights under the law, and encouraged people to rely on others. Consequently, he suggested the substitution of individualism for the family system.[28] Hu Shih also stimulated the spread of individualism by introducing Ibsen to China. He explained Ibsen's opposition to the conformity imposed by law, religion, and moral principles. Ibsen asserted, so Hu said, that society "destroyed individuality by force and suppressed the spirit of individual freedom and independence."[29] Ibsen's ideal was a life in which an "individual might develop to the full his talent and individuality."[30] Hu, influenced by Ibsen's plays, such as *A Doll's House, An Enemy of the People,* and *Ghosts,* drew attention to the inferior status of women in Chinese society, and encouraged Chinese women to protest and secure emancipation, as well as exalted independent thinking.

Among the pre-1919 intellectuals there were some who toyed with ideas of socialism or anarchism on the ground that only thus could the freedom of the individual be balanced by the equality of others. These ideas were derived mainly from the early French socialists and anarchists, but also owed something to traditional Chinese ideas. However, most of the vanguard intellectuals were not completely committed to socialism, perhaps because they felt that the same liberal program which would achieve individual freedom would also achieve equality. Therefore, they preferred to advocate the equality of every individual's right, and to propound the ideas of universal love and mutual assistance.[31] In discussing the French contribution to modern civilization, Ch'en Tu-hsiu hailed the socialist idea of economic and social equality as the latest tendency of modern European culture. Private property could not be abandoned immediately; the rich and the poor would be leveled by social policies.[32] These ideas had been promoted previously by Sun Yat-sen and by many socialists and anarchists. After 1919, they had increasing appeal for the youth of China.

Turning to science, we find that most of the new intellectuals emphasized Darwin's theory of evolution. It was on the basis of this theory that they attacked religion and tradition. Some of them, for example Tai Chi-t'ao, while accepting this theory, advocated mutual assistance. They thought that whereas life was maintained by struggle, mutual assistance was the best way to advance humanity in this struggle. In any case, Darwinism was the first scientific theory to exert a strong influence upon Chinese social thought.

Technology and the control of nature were also recognized as significant aspects of the scientific civilization of the West. The new intellectual leaders discarded the old idea that the spiritual civilization of the East was superior to the materialistic civilization of the West. Wu Chih-hui in particular was the champion of the beneficence of a material welfare achieved by the control and improvement of tools, although he himself lived a very simple, stoical life.[33] Wu believed in the "omnipotence of science."[34]

New Methods: Pragmatic, Skeptical, and Agnostic Approaches
and the Beginning of Marxist Influence

The fact that the new intellectual leaders had a better training in logical thinking made their arguments against the old gentry more effective. This was true especially in the case of Hu Shih who gave more emphasis to methodology than did other writers. In the re-evaluation of the Chinese tradition, Hu insisted that all inferences must be based on evidence and anything without proof should be held doubtful. As a means of verification, historical evolution or, in Dewey's phrase, the "genetic method," i.e., concentrating attention on the origin and evolution of the subject, was emphasized. This method owed a debt to Huxley's agnosticism, but stemmed immediately from Dewey's pragmatism. As Hu himself said:

My thought is influenced mainly by two persons: one is Huxley and the other is Mr. Dewey. Huxley teaches me how to doubt and teaches me to believe in nothing without sufficient evidence. Mr. Dewey teaches me how to think and teaches me to consider the immediate problems in all cases, to regard all theories and ideals as hypotheses which are in need of verification, and to take into account the effect of thoughts. These two persons make me understand the character and function of scientific method.[35]

In the prevalent climate of agnosticism, an iconoclastic spirit arose among the new intelligentsia. Ch'en Tu-hsiu, Hu Shih, Wu Chih-hui, and Lu Hsün were "laughing lions" who "annihilated with laughter," as Nietzsche said of Voltaire in Europe, and with all their strength called for the destruction of idols.[36] Ch'en said: "Destroy! Destroy idols! Our beliefs must be based on reality and reasonableness. All the fantasies handed down from ancient times, religious, political, and ethical, and other false and unreasonable beliefs are idols which should be destroyed! If these false idols are not destroyed, universal truth cannot be restored to the profound beliefs in our minds." [37] This was the call of the time.

On the whole, it is fair to say that, in the early period of the May Fourth Movement, pragmatism, skepticism, and agnosticism were the principal critical approaches found in the reformers' attack on traditional ethics and ideas. There was no strong competition from either materialism or dialectical materialism until the middle of the twenties.

However, as early as 1915, Ch'en Tu-hsiu had developed some interest in the economic interpretation of history and society.[38] Materialism in a vague sense was also advocated to some extent by a few writers.[39] In 1916 and 1918,

Li Ta-chao's writings showed some embryonic traces of dialectics in opposition to the "genetic method." [40] But no genuine Marxist theories could be found in Li's writings in this early stage. Beside Chu Chih-hsin's translation of a part of *The Communist Manifesto* in 1906 as we have mentioned, the earliest Chinese translation of Marx's major work published within China was his *Wage, Labor, and Capital*, which appeared with the title "Labor and Capital" (*Lao-tung yü tzu-pen*) in the Chinputang newspaper, *The Morning Post*, from May 9 to June 1, 1919. In the summer of 1919, following the vogue of pragmatism, dialectical materialism came to the attention of the Chinese intellectual leaders, but they took a more or less critical and skeptical attitude toward it, and did not accept it as a whole. The Society for the Study of Socialism established in about December of 1919 was not dedicated primarily to Marxism, but in the main to guild socialism, syndicalism, and anarchism. Organized study of Marxism did not begin until the spring of 1920.[41]

A notable critical introduction to Marxism was published in May 1919 by Li Ta-chao, who was in fact basically sympathetic to it. He said: "Recently there has appeared in philosophy a neoidealism which may rectify Marx's materialism and remedy its defects." [42] Li actually took a revisionist view of Marx's historical materialism: (1) He followed Eugenio Rignano's criticism of Marx that historical materialism was contradictory to the theory of class struggle. He imagined Marx might have replied that class struggle would ultimately be part of the process of economic change; "but," Li remarked, "even though this reply would be true, it would be a forced interpretation, and somehow self-contradictory." [43] (2) To Li, historical materialism had the defect of determinism or fatalism; but this was offset by the rallying cry of *The Communist Manifesto* which called upon the working classes to unite and struggle.[44] (3) Marx overlooked the function of ethics and the humanitarian movement in the course of history. It was here that Li prescribed the remedy of neoidealism. (4) Li remarked: "Marx's theory was a product of his time; in his time it was indeed a great discovery. However, history should not be interpreted forever by this theory which was formulated at a specific time and under specific circumstances, nor should Marxist theory be accepted as a whole and applied uncritically to modern society. On the other hand, we should not disregard its historical value and specific findings." [45]

It is striking that Li's criticism of Marx's materialistic interpretation of history was rejected by one of the Kuomintang leaders, Hu Han-min. His long article "A Criticism of Criticism of Historical Materialism" was almost a direct rebuttal, point by point, of Li's article.[c] Hu Han-min also seems to have been the first to study Chinese history, philosophy, ethics, and institutions in the light of historical materialism. His "A Materialistic Study of the History of Chinese Philosophy" was published in October 1919. The Chinese translation of Karl Kautsky's *Karl Marx's ökonomische lehren* (1887) published in *Ch'en pao* from June 2 and that by Tai Chi-t'ao from November were the first major, systematic introduction of *Das Kapital* into China.[47] Following these, Li Ta-chao published his "Material Change and Ethical Change" in December 1919 and "An Economic Interpretation of the Cause of Changes in Modern Chinese Thought" in January 1920.[48] The latter was the first attempt to explain the new thought movement in terms of materialism. But it must be noted that Tai and Hu approached Marxism differently from Li. The two former emphasized the nationalist implications of the theory, while Li followed the line of class struggle. This factor led to their later split.[49]

Meanwhile, a Chinese translation of the first section of *The Communist Manifesto* was published in the students' monthly, *The Citizens*, on November 1, 1919 (Vol. II, No. 1), and that of Marx's preface to *Das Kapital* on October 1, 1920 in the same magazine (Vol. II, No. 3). The manifesto was translated in full into Chinese by Ch'en Wang-tao and published in April 1920. After these translations, Part III of Engels' *Anti-Dühring* (1877) was translated in *The Construction* in December 1920 (Vol. III, No. 1). Marx's preface to *The Critique of Political Economy* (1859) was translated in *The Eastern Miscellany* in January 1921 (Vol. XVIII, No. 1), and Engels' *Socialism: Utopian and Scientific* was first rendered into Chinese by Shih Jen-yung and published in the *New World* (*Hsin shih-chieh*) fortnightly after 1912. A translation of the latter by Cheng Tz'u-ch'uan was published in book form by the Shanghai Ch'ün-i shu-chü in 1921. The above includes the list of almost all major works of Marx and Engels which Chinese students of Marxism could read in their own language in the years before 1921. It is notable that most of the works were translated by those who were not finally converted into Marxism.[50]

After 1923 dialectical materialism began to be accepted by some Chinese writers and from the latter part of the twenties onwards it had increasing influence on Chinese thinking. However, to pursue it further here would be a diversion from our immediate concern with the May Fourth period.

[c] At this time, Li Ta-chao had quite close relations with the Kuomintang leaders in Shanghai. Li was one of the agents in Peking in charge of selling the Kuomintang organ, *The Construction*.[46]

"Down With Confucius and Sons"

Aided by Mr. *Te* and Mr. *Sai*, the new intellectual leaders set out to attack traditional ethics. They aimed first of all at dethroning what became known in Hu Shih's catch phrase as "Confucius and Sons" (*K'ung-chia-tien*) [d] from its undisputed sway over ethics and ideas in China which had lasted two thousand years.

There had not been very many people who declared themselves anti-Confucian during these two thousand years. But some thinkers like Wang Ch'ung (A.D. 27–97) and Li Chih (Li Tso-wu, A.D. 1527–1602) had dared to take exception for anti-Confucian opinions had generally been suppressed by government and society. At the turn of the nineteenth century a few writers had expressed opinions skeptical or critical of Confucianism. Yen Fu had for a time raised his doubt of the traditional Chinese thinking as a whole, and Chinese anarchists and socialists provided devastating criticism of the general existing orthodoxy. Liang Ch'i-ch'ao had said, "I love Confucius, but I love truth more." Wu Yü [e] had written a series of essays attacking Confucianism, but had been forbidden to publish them, both by the Ch'ing dynasty and the Republican government.[52] In 1915 several articles in *New Youth* attacked the whole framework of traditional ethics and institutions. Yet they did not specifically point to Confucius' teachings. It was not until the spring of 1916, when Yüan Shih-

---

[d] A term first used by Hu in his preface to Wu Yü's selected essays to refer to Confucianism and its followers. It became popular later in the anti-Confucian movement.[51] For a more systematic study of this, see the present author's "The Anti-Confucian Movement in the Early Republic of China" (a paper for the Fourth Conference on Chinese Thought, 1958, to be published in Arthur F. Wright, ed., *The Confucian Persuasion* by Stanford University Press in 1960).

[e] Wu Yü (*tzu*: Yu-ling, *hao*: Ai-chih-lu chu-jen, or the Master of the Hut of Love for Wisdom, 1871–1949) was born in Chengtu, Szechwan. He went to Japan for study in 1905 (some say in 1896) and was influenced there by Western liberal and democratic ideas. Because of its anti-Confucian characteristics, his book, *Discussions of the Intellectual Trends in the Sung and Yüan Dynasties* (*Sung Yüan hsüeh-an ts'ui-yü*), was banned from sale by the Ministry of Education under the Ch'ing government. He escaped to the countryside and avoided the arrest ordered by the government. In 1913 he edited the *Awaken-the-Masses Magazine* (*Hsing ch'ün pao*) in Chengtu. It was also suppressed by the government because of its unconventional opinions. His poems had been published by Ch'en Tu-hsiu in *The Tiger* magazine in July 1915 before his anti-Confucian articles appeared in *New Youth* in 1917. Late in 1916 Wu was impressed by the anti-Confucian stand of *New Youth* and wrote a letter to Ch'en Tu-hsiu. Consequently, a number of Wu's articles were published in the magazine from February 1917 on. In 1919 Wu was invited to teach at Peking University where he remained until his return to Chengtu in the mid-1920's. There he taught at Chengtu University from about 1926 and at the National Szechwan University from 1931. In his last years he retired to the vicinity of Chengtu. Among his published works are *Collected Essays of Wu Yü* (*Wu Yü wen-lu*), *Supplements* (*Wu Yü wen pieh-lu*, Chengtu, 1936; *Wu Yü wen hsü-lu*, Chengtu, 1937), and a collection of poems in the literary language, *The Autumn Water* (*Ch'iu-shui chi*, Chengtu, 1913). Many of his essays were written in the vernacular.

k'ai's monarchical movement was in the doldrums, that anti-Confucianism began to gain ground. 🗡

In the February 1916 issue of *New Youth*, there first appeared an article by Yi Pai-sha (1886–1921), Yi P'ei-chi's younger brother who was a teacher at the Hunan Province First Normal School in Changsha and the Nankai School in Tientsin between 1916 and 1919, and later, as a nationalist with anarchist ideas, committed suicide because of his pessimistic view of the Chinese political outlook. The article, "A Discussion of Confucius," was intended by the author to "expose the secret of Confucian worship" during the previous two thousand years. Yi's analysis went as follows: Confucianism was originally but one of the "nine schools" of thought. Confucius and his disciples upheld the authority of the emperor, but they often joined rebellions against the kings of states. After their suppression by Ch'in Shih-huang-ti (the first emperor of the Ch'in dynasty) Confucians joined the rebellion that overthrew the Ch'in dynasty in 206 B.C. Aware of the causes of the Ch'in failure, the subsequent Han emperors adopted a placatory policy toward the Confucians and set up Confucius as an idol to be worshiped. Consequently, Confucianism became the official dogma, a tool for the suppression of other schools and of freedom of thought. Yi went further and said that the fact that Confucianism could be and was used as a tool by the rulers was Confucius' own fault. First, Confucius advocated, as Yi probably overstated, unlimited authority for the monarch and government by man instead of by law. He identified the emperor with Heaven, a being to be checked by nothing save his own conscience. This would, of course, easily make a ruler an autocrat. Secondly, in his teaching, Confucius often discouraged his disciples from asking questions, thus helping to lay the foundations of ideological orthodoxy. Thirdly, Confucius' advocacy of the "golden mean" was merely a way of evading making decisions in regard to practical problems. His ambiguity invited distortion. Fourthly, Confucius was too enthusiastic an office seeker, and neglected to ensure himself means for an independent livelihood. He visited and entreated seventy-two kings, hoping in vain to obtain an official appointment. He said that he would be in great perturbation if he did not live under the rule of a king for three months. On the other hand, he looked down upon material welfare and the effort of making a living. Therefore, his followers had to depend upon the rulers' financial support, and were utilized as tools. Thus Confucianism itself became the tool of the reigning monarch.[53] In the second part of the article, Yi said that Confucianism had no right to claim a monopoly of Chinese thought, because the Chinese intellectual tradition was rich with the ideas of diverse schools. He felt, however, that Confucius and his disciples were in fact political revolutionaries. They themselves wanted to be kings and joined many rebellions.[54]

The author in the above article intended to expose only the reasons why Confucian worship was imposed by rulers. He did not make a concentrated attack on Confucianism as a philosophic or ethical system, or point out why it should not be accepted in modern times as, after the publication of this article, was done by Ch'en Tu-hsiu, Wu Yü, and, in a different way, Lu Hsün in their later powerful and influential attacks on Confucianism.

While he saw some value in Confucius' teachings, Ch'en Tu-hsiu opposed the undiscriminating acceptance of Confucianism mainly on the grounds that it was a product of feudal ages, and did not fit the needs of modern society. His arguments which are to be found in various articles may be summarized as follows: (1) The Confucians advocated superfluous ceremonies and preached the morality of meek compliance and a yielding nature, decrying struggle and competition. This made the Chinese people too weak and passive to survive in the modern world.[55] (2) Modern society was composed of individuals acting as independent units, and its laws and ethics tended to protect individual freedom and rights. Confucianism was based on a feudal society composed of family and clan units. The individual was regarded only as a member of the family, and not as an independent unit in the society and state. Confucian ethics imposed on the individual filial piety to the family and loyal duty to the ruler, without providing him with individual rights. All these ethical principles of the feudal ages were highly inappropriate to modern individualistic society.[f] (3) Confucianism upheld a caste system, and the inequality of status of individuals in the state. This could not be retained in a republic.[57] (4) The ethical concept of the independence of the individual personality was required to sanction the individual's financial independence. In accordance with Confucian theory grown-up children could not possess private property until their parents died, and women were deprived of all financial rights. This clashed directly with modern economic conceptions.[58] (5) In modern democracies, sons and wives might join political parties other than those of their parents and husbands. But according to Confucianism, sons should accept their parent's beliefs, at least until three years after the latter's death. Furthermore, since women had to obey their fathers, husbands, or sons, women's suffrage was impossible.[59] (6) Confucianism demanded a one-sided female

---

[f] According to the [Han period] Confucian theory of "Three Bonds [duties]," the emperor was the master of his subjects, the father the master of his sons, and the husband the master of his wife.[56]

chastity. Widows could not marry again. And many trifling taboos concerning sexual relations were now impractical for everyday life.[g] (7) To oppose K'ang Yu-wei's proposal for an officially established Confucian religion, Ch'en argued that Confucianism was not a religion at all because Confucius refused to discuss the soul or life after death, and did not advocate religious worship. Therefore, it would be ridiculous to make Confucianism a state religion under the constitution. Even if it were a religion, the adoption of a state religion would be contrary to the principle of freedom of religious belief which had been accepted in the draft constitution.[61] (8) To enforce Confucianism as an official principle of education militated against freedom of thought and teaching. Ch'en thought that no theory should be regarded as the sole truth, since that would hamper the free development of thought and civilization.[62] (9) Confucius' apologists argued that Confucius' theories had been distorted and utilized for their own purposes by the scholars of the Han and Sung dynasties and that consequently he himself was not responsible for later interpretations. To this Ch'en retorted: why did those scholars not distort and utilize theories other than those of Confucius? Ch'en went further to assert that the Han and Sung scholars did in fact closely follow Confucius' teachings. In the main they only systematized his theories and did not change them in essence. The Neo-Confucianists should not be blamed any more than Confucius himself. Since Confucius' teachings were products of feudalism, their feudal characteristics were inevitable. The question was: after more than two thousand years, how could a feudalistic doctrine still be used for worship and applied to a modern republic?[63]

Ch'en's criticism of Confucianism was very straightforward. But the real champion of the anti-Confucianists was Wu Yü, a scholar who had studied law and political science in Tokyo. Wu criticized Confucianism not only as an abstract philosophic and ethical system, but also in its application to "the teachings of proprieties" (li-chiao), the law, institutions, customs, and the evaluation of historical events. For ten years he studied the traditional arguments and briefs in the judicial and ritual cases cited in Chinese historical rec-

[g] According to the *Book of Rites* (*Li chi*), which was attributed to Confucius' disciples and edited by a Han Confucian scholar, Tai Sheng, in order to avoid suspicion, widows had to refrain from weeping mournfully at night; and men had to refrain from befriending a widow's sons. In addition, according to the Confucian classics, women should not sit together. Women should not talk with their brothers-in-law; married women should not sit at the same table with their brothers when the former visited their parents' home; things should not be passed directly by hand between men and women; boys and girls of seven years of age or above should not sit at the same table to eat. Ch'en argued that all these teachings were respected by the traditional Confucianists, but could hardly be lived up to in the twentieth century.[60] We must point out here, however, that these teachings had never been carried out completely in Chinese history.

ords — arguments and briefs based on the allegedly Confucian classics or on traditional laws embodying them. He compared these cases and arguments with the theories of the two Taoist philosophers, Lao-tzu and Chuang-tzu, and with those of Montesquieu, Jenks, John Mill, Herbert Spencer, Endō Ryūkichi, and Kubo Tenzui (1875–1934) as well as with the principles of the constitutional, civil, and criminal laws of European countries and the United States.[64] In other words, in his attack on Confucianism Wu concentrated his attention on institutions, customs, and the philosophy of law.

Wu's major arguments against Confucianism were that it upheld the traditional family system; that its advocacy of paternalism had become the basis of despotism; and that its fundamental ethical principle, filial piety (hsiao), became the basis of the principle of unquestioning loyalty (chung) to the sovereign. Wu traced the development of the idea of filial piety and its relation to the idea of loyalty and to propriety.[h] In Wu's view, which cannot be completely justified so far as Confucius' own words are concerned, the Confucian idea was to eliminate any desire to protest or rebel on the part of the people. "Because filial piety and fraternal duty are virtues of obedience," a Neo-Confucianist of the Sung dynasty held, "those who possess these virtues will not offend their superiors, and there will be of course no rebellion." [66] In this matter Wu Yü remarked: "The effect of the idea of filial piety has been to turn China into a big factory for the manufacturing of obedient subjects." [67]

This combination or mixture of the idea of filial piety with the idea of loyalty, family with state, was certainly welcomed by all rulers, especially autocrats. Hence the rulers embodied the theory in institutions, laws, and customs. One of the principles of the philosophy of law set by the *Book of Filial Piety* said, "In the application of the three thousand categories of the five classes of punishment, the most severe crime is the committing of an unfilial act. Those who offend the sovereign are disloyal, those who reject the sages are lawbreakers, and those who commit an unfilial act are rejecting their parents: these

[h] According to the classics, the editorship or authorship of which was at the time attributed to Confucius or his disciples, filial piety was considered the very root of morality, the basis of proper behavior, and the source of education. Filial piety was defined in the classics as a duty "beginning with serving one's parents, developing in serving the emperor, and ending with benefitting one's self." The *Book of Filial Piety*, which has traditionally but erroneously been attributed to Confucius or his disciples, held that "to serve the emperor with filial piety means loyalty," and that "a gentleman who serves his parents with filial piety may transfer it to his loyalty to the emperor; who serves his elder brother with fraternal obedience may transfer it to his obedience to his superiors; since he manages his family well, he will govern well as an official." In this connotation, state was similar to family and emperor to father. The meaning of filial piety expanded in the *Book of Rites*: "One is not filial if one does not respect one's superiors in office." [65]

ways lead to turmoil." [68] In the teachings of propriety, there were numerous trifling regulations for the performance of acts of filial piety.

In the traditional laws of the Manchu dynasty and earlier periods an unfilial act was regarded as one of the "ten vices." And custom encouraged the performance of acts of filial piety to an extreme degree. There were legends of people who buried their infant sons alive in order to save money to feed their parents, and they were honored in history as "filial sons." [69] But, one who had no son was considered, as Mencius said, the most unfilial. As a result, concubinage prevailed, women were despised, and birth control was impossible. Confucius also taught that one should not travel afar when his parents were living; thus the spirit of adventure was discouraged. [70]

After exposing all the defects of the Confucian ethic, Wu Yü said that its principles had been opposed by many ancient Chinese philosophers. Han Fei (?–233 B.C.), one of the leaders of the Legalist School, pointed out the possible contradiction between filial piety and loyalty to the sovereign. He gave as an example a man whose father stole another's sheep. The son tipped off the government. By his act, which was disapproved by Confucius, he was loyal to the sovereign but not to his father.[i] In another case given by Han Fei there was a soldier who always retreated from battle when fighting in defense of his sovereign, not risking his life because he loved his old father. He was of course very filial, but was he loyal to his sovereign or state? [73]

The fierce attack on filial piety by Wu Yü and Ch'en Tu-hsiu was a great shock to the conservatives. They then accused Ch'en of changing the old proverb, "Adultery is the first of all sins, and filial piety, the first of all virtues" (*Wan o yin wei shou, po shan hsiao wei hsien*), into a new dictum, "Filial piety is the first of all sins, and adultery, the first of all virtues" (*Wan o hsiao wei shou, po shan yin wei hsien*). While the charge is unfounded, it well indicates the temper both of the attack on and the defense of the old ethical principles.

[i] Herbert Allen Giles translates the story as follows: "One of the feudal princes was boasting to Confucius of the high level of morality which prevailed in his own State. 'Among us here,' he said, 'you will find upright men. If a father has stolen a sheep, his son will give evidence against him.' 'In my part of the country,' replied Confucius, 'there is a different standard from this. A father will shield his son, a son will shield his father. It is thus that uprightness will be found.' " [71] Bertrand Russell, in contrasting the Confucian filial piety to the growth of public spirit in the West commented: "It is interesting to contrast this story with that of the elder Brutus and his son, upon which we in the West were all brought up." [72] Russell here referred to the legend of Junius Brutus who condemned to death his two sons for joining a conspiracy to restore to the throne a banished Roman king. It may be also interesting to compare these with Euthyphro's prosecution of his father for homicide in *The Dialogues of Plato*.

This attack on the traditional family ethics was carried forward enthusiastically by young students and created a furious reaction in the society. For instance, on November 8, 1919, Shih Ts'un-t'ung, a student of the Chekiang Province First Normal School in Hangchow (a school very similar in nature to its Changsha counterpart) with strong anarchist leanings who, though he was later one of the founders of the Chinese Communist Party, soon withdrew from the party and became an economic writer, published in a student magazine an article titled "Oppose Filial Piety." The author, as he conceded later, attempted to arouse a great controversy by severe criticism of filial piety in order to overthrow the traditional family system to prepare the way for the construction of a new society. The article achieved the purpose of creating a controversy. It was soon praised by supporters, including the Kuomintang newspaper, Min-kuo jih-pao, as a thunderstorm which would clear the air, but denounced by opponents, led by the Governor and legislature, as heresy and treason. It is interesting to note that in this issue Ch'en Tu-hsiu, Shen Ting-i, and Shen Chung-chiu, an anarchist and former teacher at the school, wrote letters to the students to support Shih, whereas Tai Chi-t'ao wrote one to support those students who opposed Shih. Because of the article, the magazine was immediately suppressed by the Peking government. Shih Ts'un-t'ung and his three schoolmates, Yü Hsiu-sung, Chou Po-ti, Yü T'an-fen, withdrew from the school and went to Peking to join the Work-and-Learning Mutual Assistance Corps. Shih was later helped by Ch'en Tu-hsiu to go to Japan. Under the influence of Ōsugi Sakae there, he was converted to anarchism. This episode and other disputes concerning the vernacular literature and classic studies led to a furious struggle between the provincial government and the students and teachers of the school. As a result, the head of the school, Ching Heng-i, was dismissed and the school forcibly closed by the government in the spring of 1920. But subsequently the students won a right to choose their new principal and teachers. On the government's side, the director of the education bureau of the province at that time was Hsia Ching-kuan, a famous poet of the Kiangsi school of the old style. On the other side, leading teachers at the school supporting the new thought included Liu Ta-pai, a distinguished poet of both the vernacular and literary languages, Hsia Mien-tsun, later a writer and translator, very influential among middle school students, and Ch'en Wang-tao. Among the students were Feng Hsüeh-feng, Wang Ching-chih, P'an Mo-hua, lyric poets, and Ts'ao Chü-jen, later a famous leftist writer and journalist. Shortly after this, Chiang Ch'i succeeded Ching as the principal and Chu Tzu-ch'ing and Yü P'ing-po joined the faculty, all recommended by

Chiang Monlin. Thus the school became a center of the new culture and new literature movements in Chekiang.[74]

In addition to the criticism of Confucian filial ethics, Wu Yü attacked Confucius' advocacy of the caste system and social inequality. According to Wu's interpretation, Confucius actually upheld the distinction between the superior and the inferior and it was by analogy with the basic concept of a superior Heaven and an inferior earth that Confucius regarded the sovereign, fathers, husbands, and officials as superior, and the ministers, sons, wives, and people as inferior.[75] Confucius said that such a relation between monarch and subjects could not be abandoned. While Mencius had the idea that in the state people are of most importance and monarch the least, he said, when he criticized Yang Chu (fourth century B.C.) and Mo Ti (fifth century B.C.), that those who rejected their parents and monarch were beasts.[76] The idea of universal harmony, or one world (ta-t'ung) in which there would be equality for all had long been attributed to Confucius. But Wu argued that since the Sung dynasty the Neo-Confucianists had suspected that Confucius was not the author of the paragraph containing this idea. It was, he said, actually borrowed from Lao-tzu. On this question, Ch'en Tu-hsiu held a very definite view. Even if the idea was really held by Confucius, it only meant that in this ideal world the sovereigns might freely choose able men as their successors in substitution for hereditary succession. The sovereign power was still transmitted from ruler to ruler instead of through popular elections. Therefore, such a world should not be accepted by a modern democracy as ideal.[77]

Since Wu's criticism of Confucianism was aimed not only at Confucius' own teachings or the original Confucian doctrine, but also at the application of the theory to Chinese institutions, laws, and customs and their practical effects on Chinese life and society, Hu Shih praised him for his unconscious application of the pragmatic method and for his correct criticism of Confucianism. In a preface to Wu Yü's works Hu called Wu "the old hero from Szechwan Province who beat 'Confucius and Sons single-handed.'"[j] Chiefly owing to Wu's efforts, "overthrow Confucius and Sons" (ta-tao K'ung-chia-tien) became a popular slogan among the Chinese intellectuals during the May Fourth period.

Wu's critical attitude toward Confucianism probably met the needs of the time. The real issue was not merely to re-examine Confucius' own teachings but to expose the falsity and cruelty of all the ethical principles and institutions

[j] Hu's remarks on Wu Yü was an allusion to a fight episode in the Chinese novel *All Men Are Brothers*, which, according to Wu, Hu was studying when he wrote his preface.[78]

imposed on the people by rulers and officials down the centuries, i.e., the inequitable principles and institutions which either were based on Confucius' original theories or pretended to adopt them. The vital battle was the fight against a stagnant tradition, of which Confucianism was the core.

Shortly after Wu's criticism there came the fiercer and more effective fighter, Lu Hsün. His attack on Confucian ethics extended to the whole of traditional society and life, and to the Chinese character. His approach was not via theoretical discussion, but by satiric, pungent, and humorous exposure. His excellent style and wit, and occasional flashes of irony, won a great number of readers.

Persuaded by Ch'ien Hsüan-t'ung, Lu Hsün joined the circle of *New Youth* in the summer of 1917. His first short story, "The Diary of a Madman," written in April 1918, and published in the May issue of the monthly, showed the influence of Gogol and Andreyev. It was a furious attack upon the old Chinese civilization and tradition. In the story he said through the madman: "I take a look at history; it is not a record of time but on each page are confusedly written the characters 'benevolence, righteousness, and morals.'" "Desperately unsleeping, I carefully look it over again and again for half the night, and at last find between the lines that it is full of the same word 'cannibalism!'" "Having unconsciously practiced cannibalism for four thousand years, I am awakening now and feel ashamed to face a genuine human being!" The madman's conclusion was: "There may be some children who haven't yet become cannibals? Save the children. . . ."[79]

In a later issue the story was interpreted by Wu Yü. He explained: the people who talk etiquette, morality, or ethics most enthusiastically, are literally the most brutal cannibals. Wu supported this proposition with a number of cases recorded in Chinese history and the classics.[k] He then jumped to the conclusion that, in extreme cases, cannibalism was the only means by which the Confucian ethics could be completely observed.

[k] For example, in the Chou dynasty, Duke Huan of Ch'i (*Ch'i Huan-kung*) was regarded as loyal and filial. When the Emperor exempted him from the kowtow on account of his old age, he insisted on performing it in order to affirm his loyalty and ethical principles. But once he told his obsequious courtier Yi Ya that he (the Duke) had enjoyed all the food Yi cooked for him but that he had unfortunately never eaten an infant's head. On learning this, Yi cooked his own son alive for the Duke. So the loyal and filial Duke was actually a cannibal.[80] Another example was: The first Emperor of the Han dynasty, Liu Pang (247–195 B.C.), who was also the first in Chinese history to worship Confucius, cooked the flesh of one of his rebel generals and gave it as a reward to his ministers to eat.[81] Chang Hsün (A.D. 709–757), the famous general of the T'ang dynasty, cooked his concubine to feed his soldiers while defending a besieged city for the Emperor. When the soldiers wept and dared not eat, he forced them to. Later, about twenty to thirty thousand women and children in the city were eaten. Subsequently, the general was praised as one of the most loyal and righteous in Chinese history.[82] The story about Yi Ya is actually a fable.

Lu Hsün's short essays and stories were directed not so much against ethics as against customs in general. His criticism of these was made largely from a realistic and humanitarian point of view though delivered with a satiric sting. In his re-evaluation of the Chinese tradition, what concerned him most was the well-being of the average Chinese. "What most people fear is that the *term* 'the Chinese race' will disappear, while what I fear is that the *Chinese* will be extinguished from among the 'world races.' "[83] The ultraconservative traditionalists often talked of the preservation of the "national quintessence"; Lu Hsün commented that what they wanted to preserve was not national quintessence but "national refuse." Against such people, Lu Hsün argued, "A friend of mine has said, 'the question is not whether we can preserve our national quintessence, but whether the national quintessence can preserve us.' To preserve ourselves is the first thing. We ask only whether it has or has not the power to preserve us, regardless of whether it is our national quintessence or not."[84] Lu Hsün declared that the Chinese should live for themselves instead of for their ancestors. To learn modern science and Western knowledge was more important than to recite the Confucian classics. "Even a cow cannot serve both as a sacrificial animal and as a draught animal, both for beef and for milking; how can a human being survive both for his ancestors and for himself?"[85] Hence Lu Hsün advocated creation instead of preservation. If one could not create, one should at least find something better — even a new idol, if it was better than the older one: "Rather than worship Confucius and Kuan Kung [A.D. 160?–219] one should worship Darwin and Ibsen. Rather than sacrifice to the God of Pestilence and the Five Classes of Spirits, one should worship Apollo."[86] Of this argument Lin Yutang, once a colleague and friend of Lu Hsün, remarked two decades later, "This has justified the witticism that the American bug is better than the Chinese bug and the American moon is better than the Chinese moon."[87] Lu Hsün was sincere from his realistic and utilitarian point of view; if the new was more useful than the old, he asked, in effect, why should one bother whether it was Chinese or foreign? In fact, in the same article criticized by Lin Yutang, Lu Hsün had advocated Western iconoclasm against idolatry, but it was ignored by Lin. Nevertheless there is evil inherent in any idol worship, no matter whether the idol is old or new, Eastern or Western — a proposition which proved tragically true in the case of many Chinese extreme leftist and rightist intellectuals in later decades.[1]

---

[1] Lu Hsün himself had never been an idol worshiper. He expressed himself strongly against any excessive praise of authority, either conservative or revolutionary, by men of letters when he came to oppose the "revolutionary literature" proposed by Kuo Mo-jo and other members of the

Lu Hsün was a wholehearted supporter of the new learning, ridiculing backward conservatives, both Chinese and foreign, in China. There were many concession authorities and foreign businessmen in China who insisted on the treaty privileges on the ground that traditional Chinese laws and customs were archaic; but at the same time they supported the backward Chinese conservatives who advocated the preservation of the traditional laws, institutions, customs, and ethics. These foreign interests joined in praising the Chinese national heritage and opposing the progressives in order that their own privileges in China might be preserved. In Lu Hsün's opinion, what these people wanted was to subdue China with an invisible knife. "Almost all of those who praise the old Chinese culture," he declared, "are the rich who are residing in the concessions or other safe places. They praise it because they have money and do not suffer from the civil wars." [90] He even pushed his point to an extreme: "Chinese culture is a culture of serving one's masters who are triumphant at the cost of the misery of the multitude. Those who praise Chinese culture, whether they be Chinese or foreigners, conceive of themselves as belonging to the ruling class." At the same time he exposed the falsity of the traditionalists by saying, "There is a favorite technique of those who know the old literature. When a new idea is introduced, they call it 'heresy' and bend all their efforts to destroy it. If that new idea, by its struggle against their efforts, wins a place for itself, they then discover that 'it's the same thing as was taught by Confucius.' They object to all imported things, saying that these are 'to

---

Creation Society in the middle of the twenties. Not a few of the Chinese new intellectuals who joined in the iconoclastic tide in the May Fourth period later became idol worshipers. The unconditional support and praise of Chiang Kai-shek by Wu Chih-hui and Tai Chi-t'ao, exemplify those who abandoned their early ideals and surrendered to nationalist authority. On the other hand, the Marxist poet and historian Kuo Mo-jo provides an example of those who submitted to leftist authority. Kuo wrote a paradoxical poem between May and June 1920 titled "I Am an Idol Worshiper":

> O I am an idol worshiper!
> I worship the sun, mountains, and oceans;
> I worship the water, the fire, volcanoes, and great rivers;
> I worship life, death, light, and night;
> I worship Suez, Panama, the Great Wall of China, and the Pyramids;
> I worship the spirit of creation, force, blood, and heart;
> I worship bombs, sadness, and destruction;
> I worship iconoclasts and myself!
> O I am also an iconoclast! [88]

These lines reveal the romantic pantheism which characterizes Kuo's poetry, as well as his self-contradiction which illuminates for us his later actions. In recent years his idolatry has predominated over his iconoclasm. Now president of the Chinese Academy of Sciences in Peking, he has published a collection of 21 short poems in which Stalin's and Mao Tse-tung's names are praised 55 times and the slogan "long live . . ." occurs 27 times (twice in Russian); 20 times this slogan refers to the two leaders and never to the people. [89]

convert Chinese into barbarians,' but when the barbarians become rulers of China, they discover these 'barbarians' are also descendants of the Yellow Emperor (*Huang-ti*)." [91]

Between 1918 and 1925, Lu Hsün wrote twenty-six short stories and many short commentaries.[92] The characters in the stories were almost all grotesque, caricatured to represent the shortcomings in character of the Chinese people under the influence of traditional ethics and institutions. "The True Story of Ah Q" (*Ah Q cheng chuan*), a brilliant satire which was published in December 1921 and has since been translated into thirteen different languages, was typical. The weaknesses of the Chinese exposed by Lu Hsün in his writings included intolerance, inertia, hypocrisy, servility toward a superior and arrogance toward a subordinate, opportunism, and hesitation. In his short commentaries, he fiercely attacked conservatism, superstition, and the old ethics. Lu Hsün always described the dark side of life and society. As a writer he was primarily a fighter. His pen was like a rapier. With one sudden stroke it would fatally pierce the very heart of its objective. Heinrich Heine asked in his own epitaph that a sword instead of a pen be laid beside his bier. Lu Hsün might have done the same.

Lu Hsün was undoubtedly one of the most influential and effective attackers of Chinese tradition. A Chinese writer who had been at one time critical of Lu Hsün concluded later that "Lu Hsün's place in the May Fourth Movement of China was like Voltaire's in the Enlightenment of France." [93] Lu Hsün's "The True Story of Ah Q" was compared also by a Western writer with Voltaire's *Candide*.[94]

It should be pointed out that the greater part of the "Confucianism" attacked by the new intellectuals in the early period of the May Fourth Movement was the currently orthodox interpretation of Confucianism. This interpretation and the attacks upon it, although neither was entirely groundless, did not necessarily take into account Confucius' whole theory or spirit. Whether the spirit of Confucius himself is precisely the same as the spirit of the later Confucianism attacked by the intellectuals still remains debatable. Confucius' doctrines are not free from ambiguities and limitations. Varying emphases or distortions will certainly paint a different Confucius. Indeed, he has been arbitrarily painted as a leading revolutionary since the May Fourth period by some Chinese writers such as Kuo Mo-jo. There are other interpreters including some Western writers, who go so far as to consider him a genuine democrat and maintain that his theories have influenced the Western Enlightenment and French and American democratic ideas.[95]

Very few effective defenses of Confucianism were offered in this early period. It was only after 1920 that some theoretical opposition to the attack was raised. Besides Liang Sou-ming, whose defense of Confucianism and Eastern civilization will be discussed in the next chapter, Bertrand Russell gave a short, rather sympathetic reappraisal of some Confucian principles. After a discussion of the shortcomings of the theory of filial piety, such as its militating against public spirit, Russell said that "it is certainly less harmful than its Western counterpart, patriotism," which, he thought, "leads much more easily to imperialism and militarism." [96]

Whatever the merits of Russell's argument, it could hardly appeal to the young Chinese intelligentsia during and after the May Fourth period, when a loosely organized China was facing an aggressive modern world dominated by nation-states. That patriotism, nationalism, and anti-imperialism developed in China was mainly due to a reaction against this situation. To many Chinese reformers, the traditional Chinese passive ethics would be ineffective in this struggle for the independence of China, unless the Great Powers and other nations also gave up the idea of the sovereign state and its aggressive policies.

Russell himself pointed out why so many foreign conservatives in China joined their Chinese counterparts in defending the Confucian tradition. He said: "In the present day, when China is confronted with problems requiring a radically new outlook, these features of the Confucian system have made it a barrier to necessary reconstruction, and accordingly we find all those foreigners who wish to exploit China praising the old tradition and deriding the efforts of Young China to construct something more suited to modern needs." [97] To question the motive of all the promoters of Confucianism in China in this way may have been unfair to honest Confucianists, but the "foreign exploiters," as Russell termed them, should themselves have heeded Confucius' teachings of self-restraint, moderation, and altruism. This was probably Russell's original intention when he acknowledged on the one hand that some of the Chinese tradition "has had to be swept away to meet modern needs," on the other hand, that he hoped something of value in the traditional Chinese ethics and institutions would not "have to perish in the struggle to repel the foreign exploiters and the fierce and cruel system which they miscall [Western] civilization." [98] In view of Russell's prestige, it was not strange that his praise of certain aspects of Confucianism and Chinese tradition should have intensified the debate between the reformers and their opponents.[m]

In the task of "overthrowing Confucius and Sons," there were, apart from

[m] See above, Chap. IX, pp. 234–238.

Ch'en Tu-hsiu, Wu Yü, and Lu Hsün, many other intellectuals who took important roles, men such as Ku Chieh-kang, Ch'ien Hsüan-t'ung, and Hu Shih. Their sober approach was more academic and fairer to the ancient philosophers but no less effective than that of the former writers.

CHAPTER XIII

THE NEW THOUGHT AND LATER
CONTROVERSIES

In the early period of the new thought movement the reformers encountered, as far as ideological conflict was concerned, only minor opposition to their attack on Confucianism and the traditional ethics because of the decline in status and lack of critical thinking of the old gentry. Meanwhile, the new intelligentsia who were introducing Western ideas had themselves failed to make a penetrating analysis of these ideas. This situation helped to keep their own front in harmony.

But as time went on, the ideological issues were examined in more detail. Those who were trained in modern thought found the problems of the intellectual tradition and transplantation of Western ideas more complicated than at first imagined, and in many cases they were driven to take divergent and controversial stands. In theoretical debate, opposition to the new thought grew stronger in the latter period. The main currents of iconoclasm and the critical spirit still prevailed among most of the new intellectuals but their minds were occupied by more controversial issues than those conceived previously. These included the study of antiquity, the re-evaluation and reorganization of the national heritage, the antireligious movements, as well as the controversies over Eastern and Western civilizations, and over science and one's view of life.

Doubts on Antiquity

After 1919 the study of the Chinese classics and history was characterized by a skeptical approach. Both the authenticity and the authorship of the classics were widely questioned. After these efforts, concepts of Chinese antiquity were considerably modified.

It is notable that the skeptical spirit of the time had various sources. One of these was the Modern Text School (*Chin-wen chia*) of the Han learning established during the Ch'ing dynasty. As has been pointed out, K'ang Yu-wei, one of the last leading scholars of this school and a leader of the Hundred Days' Reform, claimed that Confucius had actually been a reformer in antiquarian guise. Confucius wrote and revised, K'ang maintained, the six classics to support his own conception of reform. To bolster his political movement, K'ang also wrote several books to prove that many of the traditional Confucian classics were forgeries and that others, which suited his reform campaign, were genuine.[1] At the turn of the century he was regarded by the conservatives as a dangerous radical. But his skepticism in classical studies was merely a political tactic. Later, in the second decade of this century, his earlier views of Confucius damaged his own political career. Since he had supported the attempted monarchical restoration and Confucian worship, he was regarded by the younger generation as a leading conservative. Nevertheless, his work on forgeries in the classics exerted a great influence upon the new skepticism. It led the young Chinese scholars to speculate about Chinese antiquity.[2] K'ang's disciple Liang Ch'i-ch'ao carried still farther the skeptical spirit and approach in the field of Chinese historiography and influenced many young historians.[3]

On the other hand, Hu Shih's study of ancient Chinese philosophy based on agnosticism and the genetic method introduced a new technique for the study of the Chinese classics. Already in 1919, in discussing the new thought, Hu emphasized the need for a reappraisal of the national heritage. After 1920, he concentrated his own efforts on the verification of the authorship and evolution of the stories of some old Chinese vernacular novels such as *All Men Are Brothers* and *Dream of the Red Chamber*. His studies provided young Chinese scholars with material for the application of a scientific method and attitude in textual criticism and study.

Furthermore, the iconoclastic atmosphere in China after 1917 itself encouraged young Chinese students to study critically antiquity and the classics, and accelerated the popularization of skeptical writings on social problems in general. In the decade after the May Fourth Incident, works critical of tradition and authority became fashionable among the new intellectuals. The spirit of the time revolved about the re-evaluation of all tradition.

In this environment, skepticism and higher criticism in the study of ancient Chinese history and the classics achieved much. The leaders of this trend were Ku Chieh-kang and Ch'ien Hsüan-t'ung, both of whom had been students of Ts'ui Shih, a professor at Peking University and K'ang Yu-wei's follower in classical studies. Ku, a graduate of the university and one of the founders of *New Tide* magazine, began in late 1920 his critical study of ancient Chinese history under the influence of Hu Shih, concentrating on the discovery of false authorship and forgeries. In 1922, in a study of ancient Chinese legends, especially the legend of Yü, Ku developed a hypothesis that many records of ancient Chinese history were legends that had grown up over the centuries. The later the legends were added, the more deliberate and complete the fabrication and the earlier the period to which they were attributed.[4] According to his findings, Emperor Yü, who had been glorified by Confucius and his followers as one of the ideal sage-kings, was but a legendary and symbolic figure. And this theory was also applied to other ancient figures, such as the Yellow Emperor, Yao, and Shun. If this revolutionary assumption were true, recorded authentic Chinese history would be shortened from five thousand years to about three thousand years.[5]

Ku's study of ancient history was based on agnostic and genetic methods. He traced the evolution of legends in different times, comparing the ideas with current folklore and folksongs. He also used these methods to study the biographies of many historical figures. In this way he pointed out how Chinese views on Confucius changed from time to time and traced the development of the myths surrounding him. "Confucius was regarded," said Ku, "in the *Ch'un-ch'iu* period (722–481 B.C.) as a gentleman, in the time of the Warring States (403–221 B.C.) as a sage, in the Western Han (202 B.C.–A.D. 9) as a saviour, after the Eastern Han (A.D. 25–220) again a sage, and now is about to be regarded once more as a gentleman."[6]

Meanwhile, in order to ascertain the authenticity of the ancient historical records, Ch'ien Hsüan-t'ung and Ku Chieh-kang tackled the problem of authorship of the six classics. They rejected completely the conclusion reached by the Modern Text School that the six classics were written or revised by Confucius. The alleged lost *Book of Music*, as these young scholars maintained, did not exist at all. As for the other five classics, *Book of Odes*, *Book of History*, *Book of Rites*, *Book of Changes*, and *Spring and Autumn Annals*, they were but five unrelated works used by Confucius as text books in teaching. Eventually, these scholars deprived Confucius of the authorship and editorship of the classics and tore the accepted version of ancient Chinese history to pieces.

In the latter years of the May Fourth period, a group of "antiquity doubters" (*i-ku p'ai*) came into existence in Chinese historiography and classical studies, led by Ku, Ch'ien, Hu Shih, and Liang Ch'i-ch'ao.[a] Their methodology and

---

[a] Ch'ien Hsüan-t'ung was so fervent in suspecting the authenticity of the Chinese classics that in Aug. 1925 he changed his family name Ch'ien into "I-ku" (Doubting Antiquity, "Yiku" preferred) and from that time on always signed his name "Yiku Hsüan-t'ung."

conclusions were criticized by historians later and a "battle of the books" ensued which lasted from 1923 to the forties.[b]

The skeptics achieved the destruction of an unrealistic picture of antiquity. Once Confucius' authorship or editorship of the six classics in whole or part was denied and the denial was, in many cases, accepted by most historians, his true position in Chinese philosophy became clearer than ever before. The early attack on Confucianism was directed at Confucianism in the conventional sense. After the authenticity, authorship, and editorship of the classics had been subjected to critical review, the criteria for evaluating the classics and Confucius had, of course, to be changed.

Though the skeptics had helped to destroy an imaginary view of antiquity or at least to cast doubts on it, they were very cautious about building a new one. They thought that a broken ancient vase could not be restored to the original shape without examining the fragments carefully piece by piece; but China as a nation immediately needed a new vase. Later the question became involved with politics, like the new literary movement itself.[c]

Re-evaluation and Reorganization of the National Heritage

The re-evaluation of tradition according to the new thought was not limited to the attack on Confucianism, nor was skepticism confined to the classics and antiquity. Through the efforts of Hu Shih, Liang Ch'i-ch'ao, and other scholars came the "reorganization of the heritage" (cheng-li kuo-ku), a term redefined by Hu Shih in 1919, but often used later to denote developments in the field of

[b] As soon as Ku and Ch'ien published their opinions on ancient history and the classics, strong dissent was expressed by historians such as Liu T'an-li and Hu Chin-jen, Hu Shih's distant uncle and childhood companion. The letters and essays written on the controversy were collected in *A Symposium on Ancient Chinese History*, in seven volumes. The early opponents of Ku and Ch'ien defended the authenticity of the classics and legends with reasoning which was not too sound. It was not until later years that more reasonable objections were raised against the methods employed by the skeptical school. Some charged that Ku's conclusion was based on an "argument from silence," as described and rejected by Langbos and Seignobos in their *Introduction to the Study of History* (pp. 254–56), i.e., to disprove the occurrence of historical events by pointing out that there is no reliable record of them existing.[7] Others thought that the genetic method and a study of history based on comparisons with folklore and folksongs were unsound.[8] But all these objections still did not restore the traditional picture of antiquity. In any event, the antiquity doubters did not suggest that their opinions were conclusive. Their spirit of agnosticism actually prevailed in academic circles throughout the years following the May Fourth period.

[c] The Marxist historians, led by Kuo Mo-jo's *Chung-kuo ku-tai she-hui yen-chiu* (A Study of Ancient Chinese Society) published in 1930, intended to reconstruct Chinese antiquity and history on the basis of the concepts of historical and dialectical materialism. They were later embroiled in a complicated controversy within their own camp over the interpretation of the history of Chinese society.[9] On the other side, the nationalist conservative historians merely restored the original imaginary picture of the vase, as if the skeptics had never existed.[10]

classical studies more recent than the early "re-evaluation tide." Hu's contributions in this field, starting with his *Outline of the History of Chinese Philosophy*, may be summarized thus: (1) he was the first one to study with Western method the logic of ancient Chinese philosophers; (2) he paid more attention than the traditional scholars to the dates of the ancient philosophers and the authenticity of their works; (3) his excellent study on Mohism, and its logic in particular, was unique in Chinese scholarship; (4) his verification of the authorship, editions, and evolution of the stories of the old Chinese novels in the vernacular heightened public interest in popular literature and set an example for the application of scientific method to the study of the literary tradition.[11] Hu's work in these fields was severely criticized later by Marxists such as Li Chi and Yeh Ch'ing; but lacking classical training, they seemed not able conclusively to dispute Hu's work on the classics. Nor could they deny his contributions in these fields. Nevertheless, some of his conclusions were seriously challenged by scholars like the Marxist historian Kuo Mo-jo and the neorealist Fung Yu-lan.[12]

Under the influence of the new thought, Liang Ch'i-ch'ao began in 1919 his work on the reorganization of the heritage. His contribution was made in the study of Chinese historiography, Mohism, and the history of the political thought of ancient China; and his summarized descriptions of the development of Chinese scholarship in the previous three centuries were influential in the study of the subject. Liang, Hu, T'ang Yung-t'ung, and Liang Sou-ming reviewed critically the history of Buddhism in China. Fung Yu-lan's works on Taoism and the history of Chinese philosophy were also outstanding achievements and part of the same general tide of the reorganization of the traditional culture. By and large, the leading scholars in the heritage reorganization produced more constructive and possibly more judicious work on the Chinese tradition than the earlier writers attacking it.

On the other hand, the reorganization currents to a certain extent adversely affected the new thought movement. In the first place, the reorganization of the heritage by concentrating attention, insufficiently critical on the part of average writers, on the classics provided a pretext for the ultraconservatives to promote blind worship of the tradition. The scholars, in their study of the Chinese heritage, had to systematize the old theories and give them new interpretations in the light of Western thought. This gave the conservatives an opportunity to declare that many modern Western theories had been known in ancient China, and that the Chinese had no need to learn from the West. Using this pretext, the warlords and bureaucrats made every effort to discourage the study of Western culture, and required the Chinese people to read again the classics and to worship Confucius.[13]

In the second place, there were of course many valuable elements in the old Chinese civilization, but they were mixed with a great many backward and timeworn ideas which would hinder China from getting in step with the modern world, if they were allowed to retain their sway over the Chinese mind. Too few Chinese had been armed with training in logical thinking that could enable them to judge the heritage with a reasonable, critical attitude. Wu Chih-hui criticized the reorganization movement vigorously from this point of view. "What is the so-called 'national heritage?'" he asked. "What is its relation to our modern world? It is only a kind of antique, which should be preserved. That is all. . . . It may be continually studied by several highly specialized archaeologists. Why should it be used to educate the average child and to exhaust his energy?"[14] From the practical viewpoint, Wu declared:

This notorious "national heritage" was originally always associated with concubinage and opium-smoking; and concubinage and opium-smoking were always associated with the notion of seeking promotion in office and getting rich. In Chinese history any government under which the national learning flourished was corrupt. This is because Confucius, Mencius, Lao-tzu, and Mo-tzu were all the products of a country in turmoil during the periods of the Annals and the Warring States. Their books should be deposited in the privy for thirty years. For the present, let us encourage a dry and dull material civilization. When others shoot us with machine guns, we will shoot back at them. It will not be too late to reorganize the national heritage after China has ensured her survival.[15]

In the third place, although Wu Chih-hui and many other opponents of the reorganization movement did not fail to recognize the value of the old civilization, the trouble was that it could and did distract the attention of young Chinese from the study of modern science which was urgently needed in China. Because of their training in the classics and their personal interests, it was justifiable for Hu Shih and Liang Ch'i-ch'ao and other scholars to study old books. What alarmed the opponents was that, consciously or unconsciously, these scholars encouraged many young intellectuals to emulate their efforts. In 1919, Hu Shih in his article "The Significance of the New Thought" suggested that one of the important tasks of the new thought tide was the reorganization of the national heritage. In February 1921, he established the *Reading Magazine*, which encouraged youth to study old books.[16] Two years later he and Liang outlined for young students broad programs for the study of the national heritage. They asked average high school students, no matter what their fields, to read hundreds of volumes of Chinese classics which even etymologists and other specialists could not completely understand.

These advices to young students produced opposition from many other writers. Wu Chih-hui, normally an admirer of Hu Shih, hastened to warn the young Chinese student not to follow this line, otherwise he might become a Hu Shih, a creator of a "foreign eight-legged doctrine," [17] i.e., foreign formalism.[d] Later Hu Shih himself also became aware of the dangers endemic in the national heritage crusade.[e] When the "reading classics" and "worship of Confucius" measures were revived by the conservative officials, he put himself on record as opposing them, but in vain.

The Antireligious Movement

On the whole, organized religion has not been as strong in China as in the West, though some Westerners held that ancestor-worship was "the essential religion of China." [20] In the opinion of many, Confucianism and Taoism originally were not religions at all. Buddhism, though it has existed for centuries in China, has not for the most part been taken as seriously as the religions in the West and India. The Chinese literati have emphasized its philosophic implications for the present life no less than its view of the afterlife.

Under such circumstances, the reformers did not concentrate an attack on religion when they launched their iconoclastic campaign during and after 1916. But, in their opposition to the attempt to promote Confucianism as a state religion, they did show their distaste for religions in general. Their major argument, nevertheless, was still "religious freedom" rather than the abolition of all religions. This was manifested both in Ts'ai Yüan-p'ei's speech at the Society for Religious Freedom, which was published in *New Youth* at the end of 1916, and in many of Ch'en Tu-hsiu's articles published in 1916 and 1917. Meanwhile, in their attack on superstitions, the reformers rejected the ideas of the existence of ghosts or spirits and the immortality of soul. The

[d] In the traditional civil service examinations, "eight-legged" (*pa-ku*) essays were set as the official style (i.e., an essay must be composed in eight parts) and the form had become stale. Subsequently, the term "eight-legged" bore the connotation "stale and formalistic" in Chinese usage.

[e] In 1927, Hu Shih cautiously stated that his aim in reorganizing the national heritage was to exorcise the "evil spirits" in it rather than to worship it. "I am completely convinced," said he, "that in the 'worn-out paper stacks' there are numerous old evil spirits, more poisonous than the germs discovered by Pasteur, which will eat and possess human beings. I study it, because I have the self-confidence that, though I am not able to destroy the germs, I am quite able to 'exorcise evil spirits' and 'beat ghosts.' " [18] In the next year, Hu further warned the young that achievements of methodology were limited by the character of the material used. He asserted "the study of the old books is a dead end," and advised the young people to "change their tack and study instead the natural sciences." [19]

argument in an essay titled "On the Mortality of the Spirit" (*Shen mien lun*) by Fan Chen, a philosopher of the fifth century, was revived. Fan contended: "The body is the material basis of the spirit, and the spirit is only the functioning of the body. . . . The spirit is to the body what sharpness is to a sharp knife. . . . There will be no sharp knife without sharpness; and there will be no sharpness without the sharp knife. We have never known the existence of sharpness after the destruction of the knife. How can we admit the survival of the spirit when the body is gone?" [21] To accept this theory, of course, leads logically to the rejection of most conventional religions.

For the time being, the intellectuals judged religions in terms of their utility. Ch'en Tu-hsiu thought in 1917 that "the value of a religion is in direct proportion to the extent of its benefit to the society." [22] In reply to the planted letter under the false name "Wang Ching-hsüan" written by Ch'ien Hsüan-t'ung, which asked why *New Youth* had concentrated its attack on Confucianism and left out Western religions, Liu Fu, one of the editors, replied, "The editors of this magazine are not followers of any Western religion. The reason we have not attacked Western religions is because the poison spread in China by Western religions has not been as great as that spread by Confucianism, and so, comparatively speaking, we can postpone that discussion." [23] Actually, from the standpoint of humanitarianism and realism, many of the leading new intellectuals acknowledged some merits of the founders of the great religions. Ch'en Tu-hsiu, for instance, was an admirer of the personality of Jesus. He said in an article translated into English and published in the missionary organ, *The Chinese Recorder*, "We should try to cultivate the lofty and majestic character of Jesus and imbue our very blood with his warm and rich passion in order to save us from the pit of chilly indifference, darkness, and filth into which we have fallen." [24] But it is obvious that Ch'en accepted Jesus only as a human being, a humanitarian, or a social reformer rather than the Son of God. He believed that the doctrines of Creation and the Trinity were mere superstitions in the light of modern science and history. So he declared: "Aside from the character and passion of Jesus, we know no other Christian doctrines." [25] In general, Ch'en was antireligious; as he said, "All religions are useless as instruments of government and education. They are to be classed with the other discarded idols of a past age." [26]

After 1920, with the development of the agnostic, rational, and iconoclastic tide, the antireligious movement gathered force in China. In February 1920, Ch'en Tu-hsiu's partially sympathetic view of Christianity was criticized by Shen Ting-i, who declared that "in the life of our future society, we are going to reject all religions." [27] Another writer of the time, Chu Chih-hsin, held that Jesus was only an illegitimate child and that his character was not at all superior. Chu questioned the authenticity of the Bible, and claimed that the Cross was developed out of primitive phallic worship.[28]

The first powerful, organized antireligious movement was launched by the Young China Association in September 1920. Its executive committee in Peking passed at that time a resolution, introduced by its members who were studying in Paris, to the effect that persons with religious beliefs should not be accepted as members and that old members with such faith should voluntarily withdraw their membership. One may speculate that the passing of such a resolution at this time was not merely a result of intellectual consideration, given the circumstances of a rising tide of nationalist, socialist, and anti-imperialist emotions. The decision caused a controversy among its members, a number of them protesting against the resolution. T'ien Han, then a member studying in Japan and later a famous dramatist, wrote a letter to Paris contending that freedom of religious belief is provided in the Chinese Constitution, that a life of religious belief and a life of material and intellectual activities are not incompatible, and that the teachings of Jesus and the literary materials in the Bible should not be ignored, though T'ien did not believe in Jesus as the Son of God. T'ien said that he was trying to express in a most realistic way the spirit of religion, and suggested that the matter be reconsidered. The association at a conference in Nanking in July 1921 then canceled the resolution and adopted a policy of investigation and research on the religious question.[29] "We regard religion," its organ *Young China* monthly declared, "entirely as a problem to be studied. We do not wish to oppose or advocate religion without study, nor do we wish to show any partiality to the two opposite opinions." [30]

Consequently, a number of public lectures on the problem were sponsored by the association in Peking and Nanking. Among the lecturers, Bertrand Russell furnished additional reasons for the Chinese antireligious movement. All the lectures were later published in *Young China* which had three special issues on the "problems of religions" in 1921.[31] Meanwhile, its members in Paris, led by Li Huang, later a founder of the Young China Party, sent a circular letter, dated February 25, 1921, to some French professors at the University of Paris, asking the following questions: (1) Is man a religious animal? (2) Have the old and new religions any chance of survival in modern life? (3) Will new China need a religion? They received replies from three prominent professors, Marcel Granet (1884–1940), professor of Chinese history at the Sorbonne, Henri Barbusse (1873–1935), the famous novelist, and Célestin

Bouglé (1870–1940), professor of social philosophy and sociology at the Sorbonne. All of them answered in the negative. Barbusse stated that European religion was not a worthy agent for the spreading of new Western thought or morals, and that it was unfortunate that Christianity has been introduced into China as a means of extending economic and political power.[32]

Besides the Young China Association and its organ, there were a number of organizations and magazines in China which discussed the religious problem in 1920 and 1921, among them were the magazines *Wissen und Wissenschaft*, *Science*, *Philosophia*, and *The Critical Review*. Most of them took a skeptical view of religion.

It should be noted that the student movement, after 1919, exerted great influence on the controversy over religious problems. During the developments following the May Fourth Incident, most of the Chinese students in missionary schools joined or sympathized with the student patriotic movement. The Young Men's Christian Association had in fact supported the student movement against Japan and consequently was accused by the Japanese government of instigating the student disturbance. Some of the liberal missionaries tried to understand the new youth, but the conservative missionaries were shocked by the nature of the student movement. During the student strikes a number of incidents resulted from the prohibition of students' activities by missionary school administrators.[f] This action of the missionary educators drew protests both from the students of missionary schools and from those of nonmissionary government and private schools.

Aware of the antireligious tide, some international Christian organizations decided to hold a conference of the World's Student Christian Federation at Tsing Hua College in Peking in April 1922. The event provoked immediately

---

[f] The Deweys reported from Shanghai on May 13, 1919: "The story at St. John's here is very interesting. It is the Episcopalian mission school, and one of the best. Students walked to Shanghai, ten miles, on the hottest day to parade, then ten miles back. Some of them fell by the way with sunstroke. On their return in the evening they found some of the younger students going in to a concert. The day was a holiday, called the Day of Humiliation. It is the anniversary of the date of the twenty-one demands of Japan, and is observed by all the schools. It is a day of general meetings and speech-making for China. These students stood outside of the door where the concert was to be held and their principal came out and told them they must go to the concert. They replied that they were praying there, as it was not a time for celebrating by a concert on the Day of Humiliation. Then they were ordered to go in first by this principal and afterwards by the President of the whole college. Considerable excitement was the result. Students said they were watching there for the sake of China as the apostles prayed at the death of Christ and this anniversary was like the anniversary of the death of Christ. The President told them if they did not go in then he would shut them out of the college. This he did. They stood there till morning and then one of them who lived nearby took them into his house. Therefore St. John's College is closed and the President has not given in."[33] Later disputes developed between the students and the college authorities over the student strikes.

anti-Christian agitations and subsequently a general antireligious movement. A Great Federation of Antireligionists (*Fei-tsung-chiao ta-i'ung-meng*) was organized in Peking in March under the leadership of the veteran anarchist, Li Shih-tseng, and supported by communists and left Kuomintang leaders such as Ts'ai Yüan-p'ei, Chu Chih-hsin, Wu Chih-hui, Wang Ching-wei, Tai Chi-t'ao, and Ch'en Tu-hsiu. A few professors like Chou Tso-jen and Ch'ien Hsüan-t'ung dissented, and some Christians came out to defend their faith. The issue was centered on freedom of religion and educational independence of religious interference.[34]

In their antireligious movement, the Chinese widely cited Western thinkers such as Bacon, Descartes, Voltaire, Diderot, Holbach, Helvetius, Bentham, La Place, Lamarck, Comte, Hugo, Darwin, Cavour, Bernard, Bakunin, Marx, Boyer, Reclus, Napuet, and Kropotkin, principally French, English, and Russian writers. On the other side, the religionists used the theories of William James, Tolstoy, and Bergson to defend their cause. The issues and arguments were almost a repetition of those going on in the West in the last three or four centuries.

One of the popular arguments against religion at the time was based on the new confidence in science, knowledge, clear thinking, and agnosticism. It ran as follows: Religious faith does not come from logical thinking. The question whether or not there exists a superhuman power is beyond the knowledge of human beings. To worship something unknown only leads to blind faith and superstition. The subject matter of religious myths is only something which is still unknown for the time being. Its scope will be narrowed when the knowledge of human beings is broadened. Even if knowledge cannot solve everything, it is better to leave things unknown as unknown, rather than to believe in them blindly. All religious faith is dogmatic and hence unscientific, emotional instead of rationalistic. Science has become the major weapon against religion, since religion is in conflict with modern science. Bertrand Russell and many Chinese writers of the time expressed this opinion. In his attack on religion, Russell, interestingly enough, included Marxism as a kind of religion in addition to Christianity, Buddhism, and Islam. In October 1918 even Li Ta-chao agreed that Bolshevism was a mass movement similar to a religion.[35]

Another argument against religion was based on its origin and development. The antireligionists held that religion originated from the ignorance and fear of primitive peoples. It took advantage of the weaknesses of human beings and was based on superstition. As human knowledge develops, the role of religion decreases. History proved that, since the progress of science in the nineteenth century, religion has lost much of its vitality. The new astronomy rules out any possible existence of Heaven and Hell. Darwin's theory of evolution and later biological findings have overthrown the Biblical idea of Creation. "The religious view of the universe," said T'u Hsiao-shih, T'u Ching-shan's son and later a philosopher, "is teleological, whereas the scientific view of the universe is mechanical. This is the most important point at which the two are diametrically opposed to each other."[36] From an historical point of view, the role of religion in human society will be constantly diminished.

Furthermore, the antireligionists argued that religions are partisan and aligned against each other. Honest believers in any organized religion must insist upon its essential teachings as absolute and final truth. They are necessarily in conflict with followers of other religions. This dogmatic attitude will thwart the development of individuality and social advancement.[37]

Another reason for the rejection of religion is that there is no rational ground to believe that the soul or spirit may exist independent of the body or material. The theory of immortality of the soul is but a superstition. Moreover, religion has no connection whatsoever with morality. Morality based on religion is passive, unnatural, looking for reward, and hypocritical.[38]

The antireligionists also attacked specifically the Christian teachings. They pointed out that the legends in the Old Testament, Genesis, the accounts of the birth, miracles, and resurrection of Jesus, and Revelation are all unscientific and superstitious. The argument from the theme of Voltaire's *Candide* was reaffirmed — that is, the goodness and all-powerfulness of God is incompatible with the evils of the present world. They also charged that Christian teaching relies too much on superhuman power and underestimates the possibility of social reformation. In short, it trusts God and ignores man.[39] Other attacks were directed at the Christian churches. They accused them of suppression of free thinking and democratic ideas in Europe, and of support of colonialist and imperialist aggression in China.

In their criticisms of religion, some of the new intellectual leaders tried to propose substitutes. Ts'ai Yüan-p'ei suggested aesthetic cultivation in place of religion. Religion, his argument ran, is, for the most part, based on human "feeling"; the present religions are exclusive and consequently hurt the feelings; it is better to cultivate the aesthetic sense to overcome man's tensions since beauty possesses the quality of universality and transcends human distinctions. It may develop a sense of disinterestedness and help its adherents to understand the world of reality.[40] Ch'en Tu-hsiu, on the other hand, believed that science would replace religion. In his opinion, there are two kinds of laws. Natural laws are universal, permanent, and unchangeable. They belong to the realm of science. Man-made laws are partial, temporary, and changeable. They belong to the realm of religion, morality, and the like. Ch'en went so far as to declare that in the future course of human progress science will help to make man-made laws as valid as natural laws, and explain all the secrets of life and the universe. As he insisted this would be only a matter of time and man should not remain subject to the false concepts of religion.[41] Hu Shih suggested another theory. Since he did not believe in the immortality of the soul, he proposed the conception of "social immortality." Influenced by Leibniz's *Monadology*, Hu suggested that each individual self is connected with all others and with the whole of society and the universe of the past, present, and future. The individual self is the product of the accumulated effect of the social self or larger self which may be termed Society, or Humanity, or the Great Being. "The individual may die, but he lives on in this Great Self which is immortal." All his action, thought, and speech, significant or trivial, right or wrong, for good or for evil, live in the effect they produce on the Great Self. Through the immortality of this Great Self, each individual, no matter whether a hero or a vagabond, a genius or a fool, is immortal. Because of this fact, the individual self should be aware of his duty to the Great Self or Society or Humanity. Hu propounded this as his religion which had rid itself of the traditional religious myth.[42]

Countering these views, some Christian students argued that religion is both inevitable and useful. It gives human comfort to the distressed. Religion and science are not conflicting factors in modern society, and science cannot be the only solution of human problems. In defense of Christianity, they advanced a progressive plea. They said that those elements of the Christian religion which seem to be antagonistic to science are simply out-of-date doctrines, that the essence of Christianity is the supreme personality of Jesus, that the fact that the Church has committed sins in the past cannot be used as grounds for rejecting Christian teachings, and that socialism is an actual practice of the Christian principle which upholds that labor is sacred, slavery should be abolished, and cooperation should be promoted. They insisted that Christianity is the "gospel of the poor." [43]

The antireligious movement in this period exercised a considerable influence in promoting religious reforms in China. The Buddhist reform movement, led by the abbot T'ai Hsü, at the time began to pay more attention to sutra studies than to formal ceremonies.[44] A "church revolution" was re-

orted to have started at this time in various Christian churches in China, and
1ese churches made a point of affirming that they had no relations with im-
erialism and capitalism in response to the leftist charge that they were the
1strument of these institutions. Meanwhile, while the young intellectuals grew
1ore atheistic, this controversy aroused others, previously apathetic, to become
1ore concerned with religious problems.

The Controversy over Eastern and Western Civilizations

In the early attack on Confucianism and traditional Chinese civilization,
1e reformers did not seem to have encountered really strong opposition in
rgument. Most of their opponents were backward elements, old gentry, bu-
eaucrats, or warlords, few of whom possessed modern knowledge. Their voices
vere scarcely attractive to the young and to many thinking men. The contro-
ersies did not, however, end here. They developed into a chain of polemics
n the major problem of Eastern versus Western civilization, a problem which
rose in the process of acquiring Western learning and re-evaluating Chinese
adition.

As has been mentioned in the introduction, China's response to the West
vent through three stages. At first, Chinese leaders concluded that what China
eeded to learn from the West was only its material civilization, but soon it
ecame evident that changes in her institutions and laws were also necessary.
3y the time of the May Fourth period, it was clear that the ideas and prin-
iples underlying Western technology and institutions such as philosophy,
thics, science, literature, and the arts, had all to be studied. It was on the basis
f this realization that the new intellectuals savagely attacked Confucianism
nd the traditional civilization. Early opposition to this trend was feeble, be-
ause the old conservatives neither understood sufficiently what Confucianism
nd the tradition were, nor could they criticize Western civilization with under-
tanding. But toward the end of, and in the years following, the May Fourth
eriod, especially after 1921, a real opposition was formed by some scholars
vho based their work on a study of Eastern and Western civilizations, and
n some Western philosophic theories.

Shortly after World War I, a pessimism seized most of the intellectuals of
Europe that had been ravaged by war. They thought that the folly of de-
truction resulted from a material, scientific civilization. A number of Western
hilosophers such as Bergson, Eucken, and Russell looked to the presumed
acifism of Eastern civilization for salvation, especially to that of China and

India. At the end of 1918, Liang Ch'i-ch'ao led a semiofficial group of observers of the Paris Peace Conference, including Chiang Po-li, Carsun Chang, and Ting Wen-chiang (V. K. Ting), on a trip to Europe. Liang visited Eucken, Bergson, and Bergson's teacher, Boutroux, and many other philosophers as well as politicians, party leaders, and men of letters. The visit of Liang and his group to these philosophers and intellectuals was, according to Carsun Chang, motivated by their shock at the influx of new thought into China. They hoped to get advice from these European intellectuals.[45] The Europeans responded that the war was a manifestation of the bankruptcy of Western civilization, and that they hoped to learn from the Chinese heritage a wisdom to correct their own errors. Liang reported these views in China in March 1919 through a series of articles in his lucid, emotionally appealing style. He pointed out that because of the rapid development of science, the Western view of life was completely subject to mechanical principles and physical lust. Moral authority was overthrown. Struggle and war had become inevitable. Thus the whole of Europe was in despair. All in all, "the dream of the omnipotence of science" had been shattered. As Liang said:

> Those who praised the omnipotence of science had hoped previously that, as soon as science succeeded, the golden age would appear forthwith. Now science is successful indeed; material progress in the West in the last one hundred years has greatly surpassed the achievements of the three thousand years prior to this period. Yet we human beings have not secured happiness; on the contrary, science gives us catastrophes. We are like travelers losing their way in a desert. They see a big black shadow ahead, and desperately run to it, thinking that it may lead them somewhere. But after running a long way, they no longer see the shadow and fall into the slough of despond. What is that shadow? It is this "Mr. Science." The Europeans have dreamed a vast dream of the omnipotence of science; now they decry its bankruptcy. This is a major turning-point in current world thought.[46]

Further, Liang said that in the reconstruction of world civilization the Chinese would assume great responsibilities. The youth of China should love and respect their own civilization and contribute to that reconstruction. "O, our lovable youths!" said Liang, "Attention! March on! Millions of people on the other shore of the ocean are worrying about the bankruptcy of material civilization, sorrowfully and desperately crying for help, waiting for your aid. Our ancestors in Heaven, the sages, and the older generation are all earnestly hoping you will carry out their task. Their spirit is helping you!"[47]

These provocative articles by Liang were very influential in China. He made two main points. On the one hand, although he did say that he only criticized the "dream of the omnipotence of science," many of his readers ob tained the impression that he believed in the bankruptcy of science. On the other hand, he asserted the failure of Western civilization, which he thought was basically materialistic.

These were certainly serious challenges to the new thought movement. If Liang's assumptions were true, the learning from the West, the "Mr. Science" and "Mr. Democracy" advocated by the new thought, would be undermined.

On the second point, Liang Ch'i-ch'ao was reinforced by Liang Sou-ming, who delivered a number of lectures at Peking University and elsewhere in 1920 and 1921 on the subject "Eastern and Western Civilizations and Their Philosophies." These were published in 1921 in book form. They constituted the first systematized and strong defense of Confucianism and Eastern civilization since the challenge by the new intellectuals.

As a student of Indian philosophy and Neo-Confucianism who was also possessed of some Western learning, Liang Sou-ming argued that a civilization was only a "way of life," and life was the manifestation of infinite "will," using that term in a manner similar to Schopenhauer.[48] On the basis of this assumption, Liang classified world civilizations into three categories: (1) Western civilization since the Renaissance was based on the will going forward to seek satisfaction. It emphasized reason, rationalism, knowledge and the conquest of nature, and a life of struggle. This he called the first way of life. Liang recognized its splendid achievements — science and democracy — but pointed out its weakness in metaphysics or view of life. (2) Chinese civilization was based on the will's self-adjustment, self-sufficiency, and the golden mean. It looked neither forwards nor backwards, but sideways. The traditional way of the Chinese, which Liang called the second way of life, was not to change circumstances but to adjust to them. They found happiness in self-contentedness and in taking things for granted. The Chinese achieved great happiness in life, but suffered in material welfare by not following the Western way. (3) Indian civilization was based on the atrophy of the will. Encountering difficult problems, an Indian often tried to banish them from his mind instead of solving them either by satisfying the will or adjusting himself to circumstances. He was a good ascetic, capable of self-denial and austerity. This was the third way, by which spiritual life and religion were fully developed. But this attitude toward life contributed to the Indian's poor material conditions which were worse than those of the Chinese.[49]

According to Liang Sou-ming, the first way of life was now a dead end for Westerners. In capitalistic economic organization, man had become a slave of the machines instead of vice versa. The Western economic structure had to be

changed, and Western civilization would change too. Furthermore, after th
material welfare of man was adequately attended to, the concept of the stru
gle for existence would no longer be needed and problems of metaphysics an
of the interrelations of human beings would become more important. Conse
quently, the West was about to adopt the second way of life, that of Chin
Liang found signs of this change in the rise of anti-intellectualism, of ps
chology, and of the theories of Bergson, Eucken, Russell, Kropotkin, Tagor
James, Dewey, and Einstein, which, as he thought, all looked to the East.

As for China, Liang said that she should: (1) flatly reject the Indian wa
and (2) accept the Western way, but change the Western attitude toward lif
He also suggested that (3) the traditional Chinese attitude toward life shoul
be preserved after re-examination.[51] His major reason was: world civilizatio
must evolve according to the following sequences, the Western way to th
Chinese way, and finally to the Indian way. But China and India had skippe
the first way, so they should go back through it, though he believed the India
way was the final destination of world civilization.[52]

Liang went further and defended Chinese metaphysics and Confucianis
by pointing out that Chinese philosophy had from the start taken a way com
pletely different from those of the West and India. The core of Chinese philo
ophy was a theory of "change," which avoided the controversy over ontolog
Its method was intuition, and its characteristics were to advocate relativism an
the nonverbalization of many basic ideas. Starting from this point, Confuci
established the fundamental principles of his philosophy of life as: (1) prai
of life; (2) pliancy and moderation; (3) intuition; (4) benevolent love, whic
was conscientiousness secured by intuition; (5) actions without consideratio
of interest but justice; and (6) happiness in self-contentedness.[53] This interpr
tation of Confucius' doctrines in terms of intuition, indetermination, and nor
utilitarianism was to a certain degree influenced by Wang Yang-ming's an
other Neo-Confucianists' views and by Indian philosophy.

Liang Sou-ming's theory was essentially a reaction to the new thought
the May Fourth period. In spite of advocating the acceptance of certain a
pects of Western civilization in these lectures, he later rejected other Wester
ideas, including both democracy and socialism.[54] In his defense of Confucia
ism and traditional Chinese civilization, he actually deprecated Western learn
ing, and advocated in effect a sort of "Eastward Ho!"[55]

Since Liang was the first to defend Confucianism and the Chinese traditio
theoretically and systematically, he encountered both praise and criticism from
the intellectuals. His merit lay in the fact that his theory and his systematize

classification of world civilizations were based to some extent on original thought and analysis. Not only was he a renowned philosopher loyal to his own principles, but he also made determined efforts to popularize his opinions. Consequently, his views on the civilization problem exerted great influence upon the Chinese mind, in particular strengthening the conservative position.[g]

An examination of Liang's argument reveals firstly, albeit accompanied with insight, an oversimplification in the analysis of the three ways of life and civilization. He seemed to fail to realize the complex contents of a civilization but looked on it as an integrated whole; as a result, to him a civilization would either prevail in the world or disappear as a whole[56] — a proposition which had in fact plagued many of the reformers during the May Fourth period as well. Secondly, his assumption of the sequence of transition of the three civilizations in such a regular order, though based on laborious analysis, was actually fantastic and incredible. Thirdly, Liang's interpretation of Confucius' theory in terms of intuition, indetermination, and a nonutilitarianism might be correct, but to the reformers it could not be accepted as beneficial in a society which badly needed the development of science and clear logical thinking. Fourthly, since the physical desire of a human being knows no limit, the self-contented attitude toward life, though admirable, seemed impossible to obtain in modern times. Fifthly, in a world where the sphere of scientific knowledge was expanding more and more, one may doubt how the Indian religious way of life would be the final goal of world civilization.

On the whole, Liang contributed most by analyzing sympathetically certain characteristics of the three civilizations and by systematically criticizing previous views on the problem of Eastern and Western civilizations. In the latter case, he pointed out the inadequacy of the vague views on the problem held by Li Ta-chao, Hu Shih, and others. He also rejected, at least verbally, the old view that Western civilization was material and Eastern spiritual,[57] though many of his critics asserted that he eventually maintained this traditional position.[58] His view that the three civilizations originated fundamentally from the three different directions of development of human will toward the solution of problems, oversimplified in some aspects as it was, had its own merits. Hu Shih criticized this point by mentioning a few exceptions in order to discredit

---

[g] Liang's thought was naturally affected by his personal background and scholarly training. Faced with the rising tide of the new thought, his father, a famous former-official in the Ch'ing dynasty, committed suicide in 1918, declaring that he died for the failing old civilization. The young Liang was of course influenced by this tragedy. He had been teaching Indian philosophy at Peking University in 1917 when Ts'ai Yüan-p'ei began to lead the institution, and kept a friendly relation with the new thought leaders such as Ch'en Tu-hsiu and Li Ta-chao, but remained silent on the new intellectual reforms and quite disapproved of the student movement.

the theory. In his opinion, Indian ascetics who burnt their own fingers possessed a spirit of forward struggle similar to that of Westerners.[59] This of course missed the point that Liang made, namely that the Indian intended to control his will and banish his desire, whereas the Westerner wanted to satisfy them both. Though both possessed the spirit of struggle, their motives, approaches, or, as Liang put it, directions were different. Hu further suggested that the Chinese attitude of self-adjustment, self-contentedness, and the Confucian advocacy of moderation and the golden mean were to be found also in all other civilizations.[60] To this point, Liang might have replied, the question of degree made a great deal of difference. Whereas in his severe criticism of Liang, Hu Shih insisted that every civilization possessed the attitude of self-contentedness (*chih-tsu*) and rejected that it was a characteristic of only one civilization,[61] he sharply contradicted himself three years later by stating in another article: "The most significant characteristic of Eastern civilization is its self-contentedness (*chih-tsu*), and that of Western its nonself-contentedness (*pu-chih-tsu*)." [62]

Liang's argument intensified and complicated the controversy over the problem of Eastern and Western civilizations. The controversy was carried on in later decades in terms of such slogans as "wholesale Westernization" (*ch'üan-p'an Hsi-hua*), the "reconstruction of civilization on a Chinese base" (*Chung-kuo pen-wei wen-hua*), and the "national form" (*min-tsu hsing-shih*).[h]

[h] In 1929 and 1934, the slogan "wholesale Westernization" was adopted by Ch'en Hsü-ching and Hu Shih. It was misleading partly because to accept any foreign civilization as a whole was impossible and partly because Western civilization, or any civilization, consists of varied and contradictory elements. Hu Shih later suggested to substitute for it the term "wholehearted modernization." Shortly after this, on January 10, 1935, a manifesto, "Reconstruction of Civilization on a Chinese Base," was issued by ten famous professors, including Sa Meng-wu, T'ao Hsi-sheng, and Ho Ping-sung, most of them Kuomintang supporters. It gained a wide public and provoked hot discussions. In it the professors declared that they objected both to conservatism and to blind imitation and advocated preservation of the tradition with the addition of Western learning according to the immediate needs of China. The phrase "on a Chinese base" closely resembled the old idea of "Chinese studies as the fundamental structure, Western studies for practical use," suggested by Chang Chih-tung and other gentry late in the Ch'ing period. What the ten professors worried about most seemed to be the submersion of China in world civilization. They failed to see that China's greatest need was the rapid acquisition of Western learning and industrial techniques. China would not be lost. To concentrate on preservation of the Chinese base only resulted in the slowing down of the modernization of China. It provided, as Liang Ch'i-ch'ao and Liang Sou-ming had done, a pretext for the diehards to halt the modernization movement. During World War II, the Chinese communists suggested another formula: to adapt Western civilization to the Chinese form, that is, to apply Marxism and introduce socialist civilization to China in a "national form," adapting them to a Chinese pattern but preserving their essentials. From the middle of the nineteenth century through the May Fourth Movement and down to later years, Chinese were seeking a suitable standard for the re-evaluation of the heritage and the new learning. The school of wholesale Westernization did not suggest such a standard, while the ten professors suggested a nationalistic one. The communists were mainly concerned with the application of their doctrine,

The Polemic on Science and Metaphysics

Liang Ch'i-ch'ao's articles in 1919 not only raised the problem of civilization, but also questioned "the dream of the omnipotence of science." This was the first attack on "Mr. Science," who early in the May Fourth period had established a great reputation in the movement against Chinese tradition and "Confucius and Sons." Liang's message did not immediately provoke an argument since at the time the new intellectuals were fully occupied with the Shantung question and the May Fourth Incident. The controversy was deepened, however, by a speech titled "View of Life" delivered by Carsun Chang at Tsing Hua University in Peking on February 14, 1923. Chang thought that the problem of the re-evaluation and reconstruction of Chinese civilization would be "determined" by a "view of life" (*Lebensanschauung*), a term taken from the title of a book of Rudolf Eucken. What the Chinese should learn from the West ought to be decided, in Chang's opinion, by this viewpoint.[64] He felt that, after the May Fourth Incident, too many Chinese had obtained the impression that science was able to solve all problems.[i] In his opinion, science (the scientific attitude) differed in many ways from a view of life, which was a person's attitude toward his relation with the outside world;[j] the characteristics of the former were objective, logical, analytical, causative, and uniform, whereas the latter were subjective, intuitive, synthetic, undetermined, and unique. Discussing intuitiveness, he asserted that a view of life was not governed by logical principles, nor was it upheld by any definition

---

which they had unquestioningly accepted as a criterion. The present author believes that, in learning and choosing better elements from other civilizations, the lack of a yardstick results in confusion, and a nationalistic or dogmatic standard only produces intellectual inertia. Rational and realistic judgment is required as a guide in this problem.[63]

[i] In a discussion of the problem with the present author in Washington, D.C., in Jan. 1954, Chang emphasized that his speech of the time was in the main a reaction to this phenomenon. Chang was a student of Bergson and Eucken, and coauthor with the latter of *Das Lebensproblem in China und in Europa* (Leipzig, 1922). He founded in 1934 the Chinese National Socialist Party which was amalgamated later in 1946 with the Democratic Constitutionalist Party to form the Chinese Democratic Socialist Party with Chang as its leader. Important members of these parties had often previously associated with Liang Ch'i-ch'ao and the Chinputang.[65]

[j] In the speech Chang classified the different views of life into the following nine groups: (1) relation to the family: big family system or small family system; (2) relation to the opposite sex: man superior to woman or equality between the sexes, free marriage or marriage decided by others; (3) relation to property: private property system or common ownership; (4) attitude toward social institutions: conservative or reformist; (5) relation of mind to external matter: material civilization or spiritual civilization; (6) relation to the human race: individualism or socialism (or the doctrine of mutual assistance); (7) relation to other persons: egoism or altruism; (8) hopes concerning the world: pessimism or optimism; and (9) belief in whether or not a creator or creators exist: theism or atheism; monotheism, polytheism or pantheism (pp. 2–4).

or method, but by the command of one's own conscience. Purely psychological phenomena, he maintained, are not governed by laws of causality.[66] Consequently he reasoned, "No matter how far science develops, it is not able to solve the problem of a view of life." [67] This led to his conclusion that as Western civilization of the last few centuries, which he considered a material civilization achieved by science, had been doubted and "detested" by Europeans since World War I, China should value her own spiritual civilization.[68] In effect, Chang told the Chinese that the new thought reformers' advocacy of science could scarcely solve the problems of China, because, on the one hand, science had nothing to do with a view of life which, by his definition, included most of the social sciences and all of ethics, religion, and metaphysics — actually philosophy as a whole — and on the other, because Western civilization was not as satisfactory as Eastern, which the reformers were fiercely attacking.

Two months after Chang's speech, the supporters of the new thought poured forth a series of criticisms of it, led by an article titled "Metaphysics and Science" by Ting Wen-chiang (1887–1936), a leading geologist and a friend of Chang. Chang had been "possessed," said Ting, by "Ghost Metaphysics (*Hsüan-hsüeh kuei*)" which had "loitered in Europe for more than two thousand years and now becomes unemployed and dramatically marches on into China with newly forged signs and advertisements for deceit." [69] In the same article Ting made the following points: (1) A view of life is governed by scientific methods and, although it is not unified at the present, it will be in the future (pp. 3–6). (2) Both knowledge and psychology are the subject matter of science. "No knowledge can be recognized as knowledge, if it is not critically and logically studied" (pp. 7–14). Therefore, "science is omnipotent in the field of knowledge" (p. 16). (3) Metaphysics, politics, and education, not science, should be held responsible for the war (pp. 22–26). (4) Eastern and Western civilizations could not be distinguished as spiritual and material (pp. 27–28). In conclusion, what China needed was still "God Science (*K'o-hsüeh shen*)."

Ting's criticism was answered by Chang in a long article. The polemic was joined by a number of writers. Chang was supported by Chang Tung-sun, Lin Tsai-p'ing, Fan Shou-k'ang, Ch'ü Chü-nung, and eventually by Liang Ch'i-ch'ao, men usually associated with the Chinputang. Their articles appeared in its newspapers, *Shih-shih hsin-pao* in Shanghai and *Ch'en pao* in Peking. On the other side, writers Hu Shih, Wang Hsing-kung, Jen Shu-yung, Chu Ching-nung, T'ang Yüeh, Lu Chih-wei, and Wu Chih-hui hastened to help Ting in his defense of science. Their articles were published mainly in the

Endeavor Weekly, edited by Hu Shih in Peking; a few appeared in the *Pacific Ocean Monthly* of Shanghai. The debate lasted about a year and when the major articles in the polemic were collected by the end of 1923 they ran to more than 260,000 words.

In the course of these arguments many problems were raised. To name a few: (1) the definitions of science, metaphysics, and a view of life; (2) the relation of science to metaphysics and to a view of life, as well as the relation between the latter two; (3) the relation between science and scientific method or logic; (4) the difference and relation between metaphysics and philosophy; (5) the problem of epistemology and related controversies; (6) the validity of causality in the study of purely psychological phenomena; (7) the relation of emotion to a view of life; (8) the problem of mind and matter; (9) the scope of science and philosophy; (10) the right of some social sciences to be called sciences; and (11) the relation between science and religion.[70] All these problems were so big, so complex, and so confusing that the debate was bound to be inconclusive.

As a matter of fact, few of the debaters had grasped the central problem of the controversy, i.e., that of epistemology. The polemic started with the question of how far science could be applied in a view of life. It was an obscure problem since the latter term was very uncertain in meaning and in the debate nobody gave it a clear or lasting definition. After the debate started, it veered into a controversy over the relation between science and metaphysics and gradually shifted to other related issues. As epistemology was insufficiently discussed, other arguments were inevitably superficial.

After examining the controversial literature, one realizes that the arguments of Carsun Chang and his companions were based largely on the theories of Eucken, Bergson, Driesch, and Urwick, and those propagated by V. K. Ting, Hu Shih, and their partners were for the most part obtained from Dewey, James, Huxley, and Karl Pearson. The real controversy was therefore a controversy between activistic idealism and intellectualistic pragmatism or naturalism; and the epistemological problem might be reduced to an issue with intuitionism and personalism on the one hand and pragmatic empiricism on the other. The dispute between these philosophical schools might also have been understood, in the final analysis, as an issue between the argument for free will and determinism, an issue which could hardly have been settled in this kind of polemic.

The defenders of science were no doubt motivated by a desire ultimately to abandon metaphysics, almost an impossible task. As skeptical idealists, Ting and many other writers had to recognize that there are things in life and the universe not yet understood. Their intended exclusion of metaphysical speculation could not therefore be justified until they were able to prove that science would answer all the unsolved questions or to demonstrate that a new metaphysics based on science could be created. Since the question argued was whether a view of life might be governed by science, it would have been more effective for the defenders of science to produce a view of life, or even a new ontology and cosmology, which could be claimed to have been based on it.

On this point only the veteran anarchist, Wu Chih-hui (1864–1953), ventured to serve as such a "scientific" metaphysical ghost. In an essay of 70,000 words titled "A New Conception of the Universe and of Life, Based upon a New Belief," Wu built up his critically naturalistic and mechanistic theory of life and the universe — a universe that was "a dark and chaotic whole" and "a life that was bare desire." He simply "expelled the term 'God' and banished the soul or the spirit." [71] His universe originated from a chaotic oneness which was infinite in time and space, but also included nontime and nonspace, the logical and illogical, and being and not-being, and was a living universe (pp. 7, 12). Consequently, both being and not-being were living (p. 23). By "living" he meant "possessing matter and energy" (pp. 16, 22). Energy was only the manifestation of the function of matter, and energy and matter could not be separated (pp. 16, 22). Sense, emotion, rationality, mind, will, and soul were all reflections of energy and matter. Their difference was a difference of degree not one of kind (pp. 22–23).

In respect to a view of life, Wu defined man as the animal with two hands and a big brain which enabled him to make tools and create civilizations to satisfy his desires and better his living. This was achieved by science and its application. To Wu the morals of man had been bettered more by the advancement of science than by religions or vague moral philosophies; the improvement of man's morality would be obtained through material progress. [72] Subsequently he presented his view of life as threefold: (1) eating (to make everyone who works have a better living); (2) bearing children (to recognize as a fact that love and marriage are all based on sexual desire); and (3) greeting friends (to achieve universal love and morality by way of developing reason). [73] From this analysis of life, love, and morality in the light of physical desire and his materialistic view of the universe, Wu inferred that the whole universe and life could be explained by science, and that literature, the arts, religion, metaphysics, and philosophy all belonged to the field of science (p. 137). By saying this, Wu seemed to have asserted that logic could explain the illogical, as the latter was included in his universe.

Wu's view of the universe and life was later accepted by Hu Shih. With a few revisions and additions, Hu summarized it as follows: "This new credo is a hypothesis founded on the generally accepted scientific knowledge of the last two or three hundred years. To avoid unnecessary controversy, I propose to call it, not 'a scientific credo,' but merely the 'Naturalistic Conception of Life and the Universe.' " [74]

Although the polemic was inconclusive, it greatly influenced Chinese thought in the years following. In many respects the arguments on both sides appeared superficial and confusing. They were less academic discussions than popular debates. The event seemed to manifest both the poverty of philosophy and of science and the new enthusiasm over them in China at this time. This did not, nevertheless, diminish the significance of the event. On the contrary, because of the popular and humorous literature produced in the course of the controversy, public interest in the new thought and philosophy and in science was greatly stimulated. The statements on a naturalistic and skeptical view of life and the universe enjoyed greater publicity than did their rebuttal, partly owing to the lucid, pungent, and humorous style of their proponents and to the quantity of their writings.

In this dispute between the intuitionists and naturalists, the dialectical materialists remained aloof. Immediately after the debate, however, when Ch'en Tu-hsiu and Hu Shih came to review it at the end of 1923, they started a new controversy. Ch'en, a Marxian materialist at the time, began to challenge Hu and the other liberal writers as dualistic idealists.[75] The controversy extended to the thirties.

In sum, in the new thought movement of the May Fourth period, we see first the traditional orthodox Confucianism and ethics attacked by an alliance of Western utilitarianism, agnosticism, and pragmatism and by the Chinese criticism of the Han Learning. Later on, the Neo-Confucianism of the Sung Learning was reinforced by European intuitionism and activism. This led to controversies which resulted in the popularization of critical naturalism. In this main current, Chinese history, classics, religion, and civilization were all critically re-evaluated according to various schemes, and many complications later arose in the endless controversies.

CHAPTER XIV

CONCLUSION: VARIOUS INTERPRETATIONS AND EVALUATIONS

THE May Fourth Movement has been shown to have had repercussions in many fields. These have complicated, in later years, the problem of interpreting and evaluating the movement per se. The new intellectuals divided after 1919 in terms of ideology, professional interests, attitudes toward political theory and reality, and practical relations with politics. The nature and achievements of the movement and the identity of its true leadership rapidly became points of dispute. Of the various and confusing interpretations, the major ones are those of the liberals and other independents, the minor parties, the Kuomintang, and the Communist Party authorities.

A Renaissance, Reformation, or Enlightenment — The Liberals' Views

The earliest liberal or independent view of the movement, or, at least, of its cultural aspects, held that it was a "Chinese Renaissance." The term was first put forward by the journalist Huang Yüan-yung in 1915 before the movement actually started. From then to 1918, a number of authors had described the significance of the European Renaissance in transforming modern Western civilization. Their views may be found in *New Youth*, especially in the writings of Ch'en Tu-hsiu and Hu Shih. When in the winter of 1918 the student magazine *New Tide* was being prepared, the English subtitle selected was "The Renaissance" — a recognition of similarity between the current Chinese movement and the Renaissance in Europe. In June 1919, right after the May Fourth Incident, Chiang Monlin wrote of the European Renaissance as an "emancipating movement," and said "the recent May Fourth Movement is a first step toward this kind of emancipation. We are going to change our attitude toward life and bring about a Chinese Renaissance, emancipating emotions, emancipating thought, and demanding human rights." Chinese Christians in 1920 held similar views and called for a "Christian Renaissance" in China.[1]

After the twenties, many liberal authors took this view when writing about the movement. To support this claim, they emphasized that the movement had promoted "a new literature in the living language of the people to take the place of the old literature in the classical language"; that it was "a movement of reason versus tradition, freedom versus authority, and glorification of life and human values versus their suppression"; and that it was a humanist movement "led by men who knew their cultural heritage and tried to study it with the new methodology of modern historical criticism and research." [2] Other writers, with Marxist and liberal leanings, viewed the European Renaissance as a movement demanded by a nascent capitalistic society struggling in the bonds of the medieval order. Features of Greek and Roman civilizations met the needs of modern capitalism and subsequently were revived in Europe. In the May Fourth period the Chinese economy also evolved from a medieval condition toward a capitalist condition and made similar cultural demands. But, because modern European culture was more progressive than ancient Chinese culture, it was better to transplant the former into China rather than to revive the latter. Nevertheless, in their opinion, the basic nature of the May Fourth Movement was that of the Renaissance.[3]

It seems true that among the characteristics of the May Fourth Movement several may be found which resemble those of the European Renaissance. Semi-medieval economic and social conditions, the vernacular problem, and the need to emancipate the individual from the bondage of traditional ideas, institutions, and customs may be regarded, in some degree, as common settings of the two movements. Their differences, however, were numerous, and these differences force us to place them in two distinct categories. First of all, Europe in the late Middle Ages was the scene of a commercial revolution attended by a strong demand for the expansion of markets, and eventually for colonies abroad; while China, after World War I, was in transition from an agrarian to an infant industrial economy, and faced a fully industrialized capitalistic West and, to a lesser degree, Japan. As a consequence the Chinese economy had become semicolonial rather than expansive. This difference actually put the May Fourth Movement in an economic setting quite unlike that of the European Renaissance.

Moreover, the Chinese of the May Fourth period, although they demanded individual freedom and the emancipation of the individual from the bondage of tradition, mixed with these demands others that the medieval Europeans had not pressed for. Because of the economic and political situation of China and its experience of Western laissez-faire capitalism in the nineteenth century, the demand for the economic independence of China as a nation and for individual economic equality was strongly supported by the Chinese intelligentsia after the May Fourth Movement. Hence the attraction for them of nationalism and shortly afterwards a conflict of socialism with liberalism.

The Renaissance in Europe was in a sense the rebirth of interest in an ancient civilization, a seeking to substitute Greek and Roman ideas for those of medievalism. The study of these ancient civilizations was an aspect of the revolutionary side of the Renaissance as a whole. But the May Fourth Movement was far from being a restoration movement. On the contrary, it aimed at the transplantation of a modern civilization into an old nation, accompanied by bitter criticism of the old civilization.[4] A recognition of this point contradicts the conclusion that the May Fourth Movement was a Renaissance; and the assumption that the study of China's cultural heritage by modern methods resembled a feature of the European Renaissance is not even half true. The early critical study of Chinese antiquity and the classics was really an attack upon them aimed at replacing the old by new findings. "Down with Confucius and Sons" was the spirit of the time. The main current in the May Fourth Movement was never the restoration of the ancient spirit. If there was any restoration, it was a rediscovery of the real nature of antiquity as a result of the new learning from the West. The new learning of the modern world constituted a driving force of the movement, while the study of the heritage was only one of the fruits of this new learning. As for the "reorganization of the national heritage" it may be considered as being a later development of the May Fourth Movement; it was used to some extent by the ultraconservatives as a pretext to halt Western studies. Chinese antiquity and classics differed in essence from those of ancient Greece. Science and democracy were not features of ancient China. It would be a mistake to imply that the May Fourth Movement meant a rebirth of the ancient Chinese civilization.

The most eloquent argument for the interpretation of the May Fourth Movement as a Chinese Renaissance similar to the European may lie in the adoption of the vernacular as a national language and the establishment of the new literature. Yet even in this sense the similarity is very limited. In the European Renaissance, most of the great literary works in the vernacular languages were written during and after the movement, whereas in China a number of excellent novels in the vernacular had existed several hundred years before the May Fourth period. The movement created a new literature chiefly in the sense that the vernacular was thereafter recognized as a major medium for all literature and as a national language, and that the subject matter of literature changed. It seems that only in the former sense did the May Fourth Movement bear some similarity to the Renaissance in Europe. As to the latter sense, the new Chinese literature went through a short stage of humanitarian enthusiasm but swiftly developed into a mixture of realism, naturalism, and romanticism, and later became in the main a "revolutionary literature" used as a political instrument. In its spirit the literature of the May Fourth period resembles very little that of the European Renaissance.

Finally, the term Western Renaissance is itself an obscure and disputable one, but in Chinese writers' usage it became even more loose. In their broader interpretation, Renaissance applied not only to the May Fourth Movement, but also to four previous Chinese literary and intellectual reforms. This loose use of the term confuses rather than clarifies the meaning of the May Fourth Movement and the other reforms.[5]   Hu Shih

A similar comparison of the European Renaissance with Chinese events but with a different period in mind had been adopted earlier by Liang Ch'i-ch'ao and his friends. In 1902 Liang pointed out that the intellectual trends in the Ch'ing dynasty were similar to the European Renaissance, especially in the aspect of restoration of classical studies. This viewpoint was further strengthened by the visit of Liang and his associates, Chiang Po-li and others, in Europe early in 1919, where they studied enthusiastically the history of the European Renaissance. Chiang's book on the subject, published in 1920, elaborated the idea and interpreted in this light the radical changes in thought then taking place in China. With this preoccupation in mind, Chiang and Liang maintained that in the decade after the Ch'ing period the Chinese situation also fitted the European pattern of the post-Renaissance, that is, the coming of a "Reformation." What they meant was that there would be, besides a new literature and fine arts, a possible rise of a "Neo-Buddhism" in China.[6] This implied that the May Fourth period was a "Chinese Reformation." The implication reveals in effect the intention of Liang and his followers to promote a "spiritual civilization of the East" based on Chinese and Indian cultures as the height of civilization. In view of the increasing strength of antireligious movements and naturalism and materialism in China in the twenties, this analogy of the May Fourth period with a Reformation on the European pattern is far from convincing.

Besides the above interpretations, there were a few authors who suggested that the movement was an *Aufklärung* or a Chinese version of the French Enlightenment of the eighteenth century.[7] The reason for these suggestions was apparently the fact that rationalism and naturalism were the prevalent thought of the movement. The new intellectuals were almost as skeptical as Descartes and as iconoclastic as Voltaire. They advocated clear thinking and utilitarian criteria for the evaluation of everything. Their spirit was a spirit of criticism and destruction. They appealed to reason not custom, to nature not man-made law, and to humanitarianism and aesthetics not ethical rules and religion. They doubted everything which appeared to them not proved. Their role in history was to loosen old habits and conventions, to reform thought and feeling, to destroy tradition, and to open the mind to change. In short, they prepared the way for a great revolution. Indeed, in all these aspects the May Fourth Movement is closer to the Enlightenment than to the Renaissance. But there are also some basic differences between the May Fourth Movement and the European Enlightenment. For instance, in the latter, a feudal aristocracy was dethroned by a rising middle class; while in China the middle class did not play such a role independently, but rather there was a coalition of various rising social forces against a withering alliance of older groups.

Any interpretations in terms of Western history cannot avoid missing certain critical points and causing misunderstanding. The major mistake of these writers in their interpretations seems to be that they overlooked the significance of the new intellectuals' assuming the leadership of new political and social forces, and of the rising nationalistic and socialistic tides. However, their interpretations still had some merit in making clear certain features of the May Fourth Movement, especially during its early period.

On the other hand, the liberals' interpretations of the movement seem to have been in many cases the least dogmatic. To a certain degree liberals had given the new thought and new literature movements proper consideration and appreciated their achievements, especially in Chinese intellectual and academic life and in some social and ethical fields.[8] They had grasped one of the essential parts of the movement in its early stage, the emancipation of the individual.[9] Their neglect of the political nature of the movement in later interpretations of it was quite understandable in view of the early liberals' concentration on educational reforms and academic improvements during the movement.

A Catastrophe to China — Criticisms by the Conservative Nationalists and Traditionalists

The nationalist and traditionalist views of the movement were represented by the leaders and writers of the Kuomintang and the Chinese Youth Party. As has been mentioned, before his death, Sun Yat-sen had supported the student and new culture movements on political grounds, but had never completely agreed with the new literature and new thought on nationalistic grounds. This ambivalent attitude of Sun's toward the movement often led in later years to controversial and confusing situations within his party. The progressive and liberal wing, and some members who had previously had roles in the movement, took a view more or less approximating some of the liberals' views described above. This faction, however, generally had no power in the party. The conservative wing, and especially its more nationalistic and traditionalist elements, either derided the movement as a whole or criticized its iconoclastic attitude toward the national heritage.

To understand the official attitude of the Kuomintang toward the movement, it will be best to review briefly Chiang Kai-shek's opinions on the matter. In ideology, Chiang's training was far from the new thought tide, but the movement certainly impressed him.[a] There is no question that before 1927 Chiang adopted Sun Yat-sen's policy of supporting the May Fourth Movement. Chiang's success in the Northern Expedition was helped by this policy. As for the meaning of the May Fourth Movement, Chiang seems to have emphasized the significance of the national sentiments against warlordism and particularly against the aggression of the Great Powers. After mentioning the Chinese resentment against the Twenty-one Demands and other Sino-Japanese secret treaties, Chiang said in 1943, "These national humiliations were in direct conflict with the aspirations of the Chinese people and constituted an insulting

---

[a] After receiving his military education at the Tokyo Military Officers' Academy in Japan, Chiang lived in retirement from 1917 to 1923, which covers the whole May Fourth period. In 1917 and 1918 he lived in Shanghai. From the fall of 1918 to the summer of 1919 Chiang spent most of his time in mountainous Fukien Province as a regimental commander in the Canton Army under Ch'en Chiung-ming. By 1918 Chiang was already a believer in the Neo-Confucianism of the Sung and Ming dynasties, especially in Wang Yang-ming's intuitionism and activism. (In later years he became one of the most fervent admirers of that Confucianist and loyal minister of the Manchu dynasty, Tseng Kuo-fan.) The intellectual trend of the May Fourth period seems to have had some influence on him. At the end of July 1919 he intended to go to Europe and America to study. In addition to a number of orthodox texts on Chinese philosophy and history, and Neo-Confucian works, he started to read modern social science and literature, e.g., Marshall's *Principles of Economics*, a history of the Russian Revolution, books about the Japanese new village movement, a biography of Ibsen, as well as *New Youth* and *New Tide*. He also busied himself studying the English and Russian languages. In October he visited Japan and published a few articles on foreign relations, advocating the reconsideration of policies toward the Russian government. From then on he became optimistic about his own future and the Chinese situation and interested in Soviet party organization and the methods of the Red Army. Consequently, he was sent by Sun Yat-sen in Aug. 1923 to Russia with Wang Teng-yün, a Kuomintang member, Chang T'ai-lei, a communist, and Shen Ting-i, who was a member of both parties, and remained there for more than three months. Returning to China on Dec. 15, Chiang became anti-imperialistic and suspicious of the Russian communists' intention towards China.[10]

challenge to their self-confidence. Thereupon a strong demand for revolution was aroused which found an unmistakable expression in the May 4th Student Movement. In the face of the people's strong demand for revolution the political system of the militarists and bureaucrats was doomed." [11] Following this, Chiang described the later National Revolution as a revolution to "struggle for the uprooting of warlordism and the abolition of unequal treaties." [12]

Thus Chiang's approval of the May Fourth Movement, in the main, was a result of its patriotic or nationalist aspects, for he severely criticized its new thought and student movement aspects. He attacked both liberals and communists on the grounds that they did not give due respect to the traditional Chinese civilization; that this caused the Chinese people to lose their national self-confidence; that both the liberals and communists blindly worshiped foreign ideas which were incompatible with the psychology and temperament of the Chinese nation; and that both groups only imitated the superficial aspects of Western theories without paying proper attention to the needs of China. [13]

As for intellectual and student life, Chiang accused the intellectual reformers of corrupting the youth by teaching them to act contrary to moral principles, law, and government orders. [14] Indeed, Chiang not only severely criticized the reformers for their iconoclastic teachings, but also rejected the whole idea of the new culture movement, in spite of the fact that Sun Yat-sen had so highly praised its achievements and asked his followers to support it. Chiang said:

> Let us see what the so-called new culture movement of that time [the May Fourth period] means. In view of the practical situation of the time, we really do not see that it has concrete content. Does the new culture movement mean the advocacy of the vernacular literature? Does the new culture movement mean the piecemeal introduction of Western literature? Does the new culture movement mean the overthrow of the old ethics and the rejection of national history? Does the new culture movement mean the demand for individual emancipation and an ignorance of nation and society? Does the new culture movement mean the destruction of all discipline and the expansion of individual freedom? Or, does the new culture movement mean the blind worship of foreign countries and indiscriminate introduction and acceptance of foreign civilization? If it does, the new culture we seek is too simple, too cheap and too dangerous! [15]

In Chiang's opinion, the remedy for this decline of intellectual and cultural life was the carrying out of "faithful action" on the part of the intellectuals and the coordination of civil and military matters. As for science and democracy, Chiang disagreed with the intellectual reformers on the question of their meaning. In 1951 he interpreted "the spirit of democracy" as "discipline," and "the meaning of science" as "organization." He said that as a complement to science and democracy, nationalism or ethics should be promoted as the third slogan.[16] With his orthodox and activist Neo-Confucian background, Chiang was probably quite sincere in objecting to the attitude of the new intellectuals in their re-evaluation of the tradition. From the thirties to the present, the conservative wing under Chiang continually promoted a generally traditionalist policy. They were cold toward the new literature and the vernacular and tended to glorify the national heritage, especially traditional ethics such as the principles of loyalty and filial piety. They also required the average person to read the classics and to pay homage to Confucius.[b] Most of the new Chinese intellectuals, and the youth in particular, who had been so thoroughly influenced by the iconoclastic tide of the May Fourth Movement sternly opposed this official policy. This conflict was one of the factors that drove students and young intellectuals into opposition to the Nationalist government.

It is apparent that the Kuomintang conservatives consciously or unconsciously emphasized the nationalist sentiments of the May Fourth Movement while rejecting its antitraditionalism. Nationalist feeling was, of course, strong among the Chinese people during the May Fourth period; few people would have denied that an independent and free China must be based on the building of a strong nation. However, most of the intellectual reformers questioned the capacity of the traditional heritage in general, and the old ethics in particular, to aid national salvation. The history of the latter part of the nineteenth century had proved that tradition can not make China strong and independent. It is in this sense that, to the reformers, traditionalism is less useful for the

[b] In 1952, three years after the Kuomintang government was driven off the mainland, Chiang Kai-shek repeated his advocacy of "reading classics" and his criticism of the May Fourth Movement. He said: "The classics are the quintessence of our excellent national culture and a powerful weapon in the fight against the communists. There is no reason why they should be abandoned. I have heard that most of the members of our party at Peking University in the early years of the Republic opposed the study of the classics. They thought that there could be no revolution or reform without such a policy. This is really a misunderstanding of the meaning of revolution and reform. I have said that, through a failure to consider the fundamental problem of national salvation, the May Fourth Movement had many defects and troubles in spite of its advocacy of science and democracy. Peking University was the birthplace of the May Fourth Movement and it was also this institution that proposed those two principles [i.e., science and democracy]. But after more than thirty years we have seen that these two principles cannot save our country." He went on to propose that the classics should be reorganized and studied by all students of literature, law, history, geography, and philosophy. This article strengthened once more the hands of the traditionalists. High ranking officials on Formosa suggested again that the classics should be a subject in all civil service examinations and taught in all schools. Some liberals resumed their moderate objections and the old issue was debated anew. In the debate the conservatives accused the May Fourth Movement of bearing full responsibility for the defeat of the Kuomintang and the rise of the Communist Party on the mainland; whereas their opponents retorted that the conservative view was but a repetition of the absurd old idea that one could ward off bandits by reciting the *Book of Filial Piety.*[17]

purposes of nationalism than is iconoclasm. And the materialists' and progressives' idea of returning machine gun shots for machine gun shots proved more attractive to the average person with strong nationalist sentiments.

Moreover, there is no doubt that traditional Confucianism, ethics, and institutions, whatever their merits, embodied many archaic elements contrary to the principles and spirit of modern democracy and science. It is very clear that in requiring the people to worship Confucius and tradition, all previous governmental authorities, from the emperors of the Han to the Empress Dowager and Yüan Shih-k'ai, emphasized the antidemocratic elements in Confucianism in order to stabilize a despotic rule on a basis of orthodoxy and the institutions of an agricultural society. The Kuomintang government seemed to have not been aware of this tendency when it promoted "the worship of Confucius and the reading of classics" while its official interpretation of democracy was "discipline" and of science, "organization."

Chiang's condemnation of the intellectual reformers' blind worship of the West might be justifiable so far as the "wholesale Westernization" proposal was concerned. But this proposal was initiated by some liberals only after the May Fourth period and was soon amended. When one compares Chiang's charge of blind worship of foreign countries with the view of the Japanese government and of the authorities of the foreign concessions, as well as some other Westerners, that the movement was "antiforeign" in character, one cannot fail to be amused at such a conflict of opinion.

Except for some ultraconservatives, few Kuomintang authorities publicly attacked the May Fourth Movement *in toto*. But because of their dislike of the iconoclastic trends of the new thought, they have since 1927 become, in general, opponents of the movement. The few liberal members in the party, such as Wu Chih-hui and Lo Chia-lun, who still defended in later years some of the causes of the movement, did not remain in power; and they finally became even a little cool to the principles which they advocated during the May Fourth period. In the thirties the National government so abhorred the May Fourth Movement that anyone who even mentioned it in public became unpopular with the government.[18] Its fight against the student movement in the thirties and forties, using the police and armed forces, proved that it had been driven to occupy the position of the old Peking government.

However, some of the objections of the Nationalists may warrant further consideration. The attempt on the part of some extremists and iconoclasts to reject the Chinese past *in toto* was, from a nationalistic point of view, detrimental to national self-confidence. There can be no objection to an undogmatic re-evaluation of the Chinese past, to a willingness to find some positive values in Chinese civilization. All this should be done in a realistic manner however and not in the spirit of a bigoted, traditionalist nationalism.

Similar to the views of the Kuomintang were those of the leaders of the conservative and nationalist Chinese Youth Party. Though they did not criticize the unconventional side of the movement as much as did the Kuomintang leaders, they regarded it as a nationalistic student and popular movement which had exalted statism under the anti-traitors and anti-Great Powers slogans. They praised highly its patriotic and anti-Japanese sentiments, but disapproved of the new literature and new thought tides. Like the liberals, but for a different reason, they concluded that the alliance of the Kuomintang and the communists at the end of the movement was a disaster to the nation, and that the communists who came into existence during the movement had betrayed patriotism in a treacherous surrender to Soviet Russia.[19]

An Anti-Imperialist and Antifeudal Movement Called Forth by Lenin — The Communist Interpretation

The Chinese Communist Party has tried since the thirties to make the movement a dividing line in its periodization of modern Chinese history and a starting point of the record of its political career. It has been mainly concerned with the two questions: what was the nature of the movement and who led it?

To these questions early communist leaders did not provide unified answers. Those early leaders such as Ch'en Tu-hsiu and Li Ta-chao who had played important roles in the May Fourth Movement had realized its political significance and considered that to some extent they were carrying on some of its spirit in their party activities. They, however, never claimed that the movement was inspired by the Russian October Revolution or led by communists. Writing on October 12, 1919, in *The Citizens* monthly Li Ta-chao regarded the May Fourth Movement as a movement "against the Pan-Asianism and aggression, but not for hating the Japanese." He also said that it was not merely a patriotic movement but, rather vaguely, "a part of human liberation." Ch'en Tu-hsiu, writing in 1938 an article, "Is the May Fourth Period a Thing of the Past?" a criticism of the "agricultural Soviet" and "mountain Marxism" of the Mao Tse-tung faction of the Chinese Communist Party, insisted that the May Fourth Movement was a "democratic revolution." In his opinion, the movement should be regarded as one of the related events of the "whole era of democratic revolution," which had begun with the 1911 Revolution and was still going on. The popular demands of the May Fourth period, as he understood them, were for democracy and national independence and might be listed as follows:

To oppose the aggression of the Japanese imperialists and the traitors.

To oppose the bondage of the old ethics and promote the emancipation of thought and women in order to wipe out the remnants of feudalism.

To promote science, the destruction of superstition, and the construction of industry.

To oppose the classical literature and promote the vernacular as a means of educational and cultural popularization.

To promote the people's rights and oppose bureaucracy.[20]

According to Ch'en, all these demands were basically the same at present. What was needed now was to achieve them. Ch'en acknowledged that the May Fourth Movement had had the defect of being mainly carried on by young intellectuals and not by the working masses, but strongly repudiated the prevailing communist idea that the May Fourth period had passed away.

This view of the movement was not accepted by the Chinese Communist Party which had been dominated by Mao Tse-tung's generalized interpretation on the subject. Mao was in fact awakened by the movement and started his political career with it. From the beginning he grasped the opportunity of the student and new culture movements in their impact on the political and economic aspects of society.[c] The formation of his major theory, the so-called

---

[c] Mao was a student at the Hunan Province First Normal School in Changsha from the spring of 1913 to the summer of 1918. In the early years of this period, Mao read, besides the orthodox Chinese histories, some Western works translated by Yen Fu and others, such as Adam Smith's *Wealth of Nations*, Darwin's *Origin of Species*, John Mill's *Logic*, Spencer's *Sociology*, Montesquieu's *The Spirit of the Laws*, Rousseau's works, and Greek and Roman literature. But he was soon attracted by *New Youth* and discarded his earlier ideals. As we have mentioned, during his first stay in Peking from Sept. 1918 to early 1919, he was deeply influenced by anarchism and liberalism in Peking University. Mao returned to Changsha from Shanghai in March 1919. He joined the students of that city in supporting the May Fourth student movement of Peking, as soon as he learned the news of the incident. There is no doubt that the incident provided Mao with a great opportunity. His support of, and activities in, the student movement snatched him, a high school graduate, from an obscure position and placed him in the national limelight. The short-lived student magazine edited by Mao, *Hsiang River Review*, was at once recognized by Fu Ssu-nien, editor of *New Tide*, as one of the five or six best magazines of the nation, ranking with *New Youth, The Construction, Emancipation and Reconstruction, Young China*, and *Weekly Critic*. And Mao's article, "The Great Alliance of the People," published in *Hsiang River Review* (July 21–Aug. 4, 1919) in support of the May Fourth Incident was immediately recommended by another student leader, Lo Chia-lun, as an accurate interpretation of the student movement.[21] Mao pointed out in his article that the movement was an awakening to the need for unification by the students, merchants, and workers in their struggle for civil rights and social organization. Early in August of 1919 Mao's magazine was suppressed by the provincial government, and subsequently

"new democracy," [d] may have been influenced by his experience in and interpretation of the movement.

Early in May 1939 Mao wrote a short article titled "The May Fourth Movement," for the newspapers in Yenan in commemoration of the twentieth anniversary of the movement. In the beginning of the article, Mao said:

> The May Fourth Movement of twenty years ago laid bare the fact that the anti-imperialist and antifeudal bourgeois-democratic revolution of China had developed into a new stage. The initiation of the May Fourth Movement as a cultural reform movement was but a form of expression of China's anti-imperialist and antifeudal bourgeois-democratic revolution. Because of the growth and expansion of the new social forces of that time a strong front came into existence in this revolution, that is, the united front composed of the Chinese worker class, students, and the newly rising national bourgeoisie [bourgeoisie who were, according to Mao's usage, neither bureaucratic capitalists nor capitalists affiliating with foreign imperialists]. And, in the May Fourth period, appeared the several hundred thousand students bravely standing at the head of the movement. This means that the May Fourth Movement advanced one step further than the 1911 Revolution.[23]

His brief explanation of the May Fourth Movement contained the essence of Mao's thought that developed in the six months following the publication of the article. It made clear three points: (1) The May Fourth Movement was the jumping-off point of the "anti-imperialist and antifeudal bourgeois-democratic revolution" leading to a new period. (2) The national bourgeoisie might and did join the revolution in a united front together with the proletariat and the intelligentsia. (3) The intelligentsia provided the leadership of this united front in the revolution. Mao also emphasized in the same article: (1) The

---

he went again to Peking and Shanghai to seek support for the Hunanese student movement against warlordism. In the fall of 1920 Yi P'ei-chi, a famous scholar and revolutionary, became principal of the normal school. A number of new teachers with liberal and anarchist leanings came to serve on the faculty. They included K'uang Hu-sheng, the anarchist who had played a hand in the May Fourth Incident, Shen Chung-chiu and Hsia Mien-tsun, former teachers at the Chekiang First Normal, Yü Chia-chü, Ch'en Ch'i-t'ien, and Yün Tai-ying, graduates from Chung-hua University in Wuchang, Hsiung Jen-an, Kuang's schoolmate and comrade in the May Fourth Incident, Shu Hsin-ch'eng and Sun Lang-kung, famous writers. Mao at the time, from the fall of 1920 to the winter of 1922, was head of the elementary school in Changsha, which belonged to the Hunan First Normal.

[d] It may be pertinent to point out that the term "new democracy" is not entirely Mao's creation. It had been introduced into China by Lo Chia-lun early in 1919 when he cited Walter Edward Weyl's book, *The New Democracy*, in *New Tide*. On Jan. 28, 1922, Chiang K'ang-hu had used "new socialism and new democracy" (*hsin she-hui-chu-i hsin min-chu-chu-i*) for the doctrine of his Socialist Party, which two years later he changed into the New Socialist Democratic Party of China (*Chung-kuo hsin she-hui min-chu tang*). The term the new people (*hsin-min*) had been used by Liang Ch'i-ch'ao earlier and might be traced to the ancient Confucian classics such as the *Great Learning* and *Book of History*. This term has different meanings from Mao's. Mao also drew from many other writers in his interpretation of the May Fouth Movement.[22]

Chinese revolution in the past hundred years since the Opium War was bourgeois-democratic in nature. Its aim was to establish a democratic society from the ruins of a semicolonial and semifeudal society which had replaced the traditional feudal society since the middle of the previous century. The communists should join this struggle to establish the bourgeois-democratic society first and then transform it into a socialist society. This was considered an "inevitable path of history." (2) The achievement of the Chinese revolution depends on a united front of certain social forces, that is, workers, peasants, intelligentsia, and progressive bourgeoisie. (3) "In the Chinese democratic revolution, the intelligentsia are the first awakened element. The 1911 Revolution and the May Fourth Movement both clearly manifested this point. And the intelligentsia in the May Fourth Movement became more awakened and larger in number than those of the 1911 Revolution. But the intelligentsia will achieve nothing if they do not unite with workers and peasants. The only dividing line between revolutionary and nonrevolutionary or counterrevolutionary intellectual elements lies in whether or not they are willing to and do unite with workers and peasants." [24]

A few days after he wrote the above article, Mao delivered a speech at a mass meeting of youth in Yenan held on May 4, 1939, also for the twentieth anniversary of the movement. In this speech he elaborated and developed the views expressed in the previous article, and stressed the points that the May Fourth Movement was an anti-imperialist and antifeudal revolutionary movement, and that in the task of arousing the masses of the people, Chinese students and youths had started to perform "a vanguard function" since the May Fourth Movement. But the movement failed because in the later years a section of the intellectuals did not join the task of arousing and organizing the workers and peasants.[25]

The above speech has been officially regarded by the Chinese Communist Party as the first expression of the ideas which were later expanded into the theory of "new democracy."[e] Later, on January 15, 1940, Mao published his "On New Democracy," in which he systematically set forth the main features of the above article and speech.

In the essay "On New Democracy," Mao pointed out that the May Fourth Movement had marked the dividing line between "old democracy" and "new democracy" in China. Old democracy was the characteristic of the first eighty

---

[e] This is noted by the editors of the Communist Party in Mao's *Selected Works*: "Comrade Mao Tse-tung developed in this speech [at the May Fourth Movement memorial meeting] his thoughts about the problem of Chinese revolution." [26]

years before the movement, while new democracy was that of the twenty years after the movement.[27] The reason for this demarcation was, as Mao asserted, that, before the May Fourth Movement, "the political guiding force of the Chinese bourgeois-democratic revolution was the Chinese petty bourgeois and bourgeois classes (the intelligentsia of both)," while after the movement, "the political guidance of the bourgeois-democratic revolution in the main no longer rested solely upon the bourgeois class, but upon the proletariat."[28] That is to say, after the movement, the Chinese proletariat became a conscious, independent political force. But because of the colonial or semicolonial circumstances of contemporary China, the Chinese bourgeois class, suffering from imperialist oppression, still possessed an instinctive aversion to foreign imperialism and internal bureaucratic government and consequently might cooperate with the proletarian class in the present revolution. This was the difference, as Mao said, between the Chinese bourgeoisie and that of Tsarist Russia, which did not have a comparable revolutionary character.[29]

Mao asserted further in his "On New Democracy" that in the field of culture the May Fourth Movement marked also the dividing line between the two historical periods. "Before the May Fourth Movement, the struggle in the field of Chinese culture was the struggle between the new culture of the bourgeois class and the old culture of the feudal class."[30] The new, Western knowledge in China before the May Fourth Movement was for the most part derived from the natural and social sciences useful to the bourgeois class. The new culture movement and cultural revolution of that time were also led by that class and was part of the world-wide capitalist cultural revolution. "But the situation after the May Fourth Movement was quite different. From this time on, an entirely new cultural force was born in China, the cultural thought of communism under the leadership of the Chinese Communist Party, i.e., the communist world view and its theory of social revolution."[31]

Although Mao fully realized the political significance of the May Fourth Movement he seemed to consider it more especially a cultural revolution. The Chinese cultural revolution in the years from 1919 to 1940 was as Mao said based on a united front similar to that in the political sphere. It had undergone four stages: (1) the two years between the May Fourth Incident of 1919 and the establishment of the Chinese Communist Party in 1921; (2) the six years from 1921 to the end of the Northern Expedition in 1927; (3) the nine years from 1927 to 1936, a period of civil war between the Kuomintang and the Chinese Communist Party; (4) the three years from the beginning of the Sino-Japanese War in 1937 to 1940. Mao thought that the May Fourth Movement with its twofold program of attack against the old ethics and against the old literature was the main feature of the first stage of this Chinese cultural revolution. It "was so great and so thorough a cultural revolution that it was unprecedented in Chinese history." [32]

Coincidentally with this assertion that the May Fourth Movement was a dividing line between the old and new democracies, Mao declared in the same essay: "It was at the summons of this world revolutionary upheaval, of the Russian Revolution and at the call of Lenin, that the 'May 4th' movement actually took place. The 'May 4th' movement formed a part of the then world revolution of the proletarian class." [33]

This view of Mao's on the nature of the May Fourth Movement has since been accepted by the Chinese Communist Party as the official interpretation of the movement. A great number of communist writers have written on the subject and almost all of them follow this line. Unorthodox views have drawn severe rebuke from dogmatic partisan historians, who often produce mere mouthings of interpretation rather than factual accounts.[f]

Judging Mao's interpretation of the movement involves one in the general ideological controversy in China concerning the term "feudalism" or "semifeudalism" — a controversy, the solution to which cannot be attempted in this book. Mao's view on this problem is based on his, and the official Chinese Communist Party's, interpretation of modern Chinese society in terms of class division and as "semicolonial and semifeudal." One who does not accept this in-

---

[f] For example, in June 1940, Kuo Mo-jo made a comparison of the May Fourth Movement with the literary development reflected in the works of the patriotic poet Ch'ü Yüan (339?–272? B.C.). Kuo said that Ch'ü's poetry was written in a kind of vernacular, a substitute for the classical literary language. This and the May Fourth Movement, asserted Kuo, were the two greatest "literary revolutions" in Chinese history. As a Marxist, Kuo attributed the basic causes of these two literary revolutions to economic changes: "All changes in ideological forms must follow changes in economic systems. In the transition from slavery to feudalism, and from feudalism to capitalism, there had to be new languages arising." According to Kuo, in the period of the *Annals* and the Warring States, when Ch'ü Yüan was living, Chinese society had started to change from slavery to feudalism. This caused the literary revolution manifested in Ch'ü's poetry. And in recent decades, because Chinese society was further transformed from feudalism into capitalism and democracy, there came the May Fourth Movement. "We also had," said Kuo, "a May Fourth Movement two thousand years ago. And Ch'ü Yüan was the vigorous leader of this ancient 'May Fourth Movement.'" This unorthodox view of the May Fourth Movement was critized by a communist historian of the movement, Hua Kang. He pointed out three mistakes in Kuo's interpretation: (1) The social change in the May Fourth period was from a "semifeudal and a semicolonial society" to a new democratic society, rather than from feudalism to capitalism. (2) The May Fourth Movement should not be regarded as a purely literary revolution. To regard the May Fourth Movement in this way, as Hu Shih and others did, reflects an intention to diminish deliberately the significance of its anti-imperialist and antifeudal nature. (3) The May Fourth Movement is an unprecedented event in Chinese history, which should not be misunderstood as a "reprinting" of a literary reform of two thousand years before.[34]

terpretation of Chinese society and the class idea will naturally reject their view of the movement. On the other hand, among the left wing of the Chinese intelligentsia, which gradually grew in numbers in later years, this interpretation of Chinese society is accepted as a matter of course.

But actually, even without defining the nature of contemporary Chinese society, we can examine whether the May Fourth Movement was carried on as an anti-imperialist and antifeudal, class-conscious movement. A ghost-exorcising campaign may be carried on, even if the question of whether ghosts exist remains debatable. Under these circumstances one can best determine whether the movement was regarded by its participants as anti-imperialist and antifeudal by judging the events of the movement itself. In evaluating Mao's interpretation of the movement from this point of view, it will be found that he has confused and exaggerated some points while recognizing some of its significant features.

Mao thought that the May Fourth Movement was "a form of expression" of the "bourgeois-democratic revolution." He also acknowledged that the main ideas in the movement were those of the "urban petty bourgeois and bourgeois intelligentsia," and that the methods they employed were still the methods of the capitalist class. In the same breath, he said that "the May Fourth Movement formed a part of the then world revolution of the proletarian class" and that he considered the movement the "dividing line" between the old and the new democracies in China. These self-contradictory remarks confuse the issue. They arose from the fact that the movement was actually a transitional phase which covered several years rather than a single event, and that the thought and activities of participants in the movement underwent great changes and developments during this period. It can only be said that at the very end of the period, communist influence started to manifest itself. Taking the period as a whole into consideration, it cannot be said that the movement "formed a part of the then world revolution of the proletarian class." After 1919, to be sure, numerous Chinese student leaders were impressed by the October Revolution as reflected in *New Tide*. But it must be remembered that the new thought and the new literature movements had started to take form in 1916 and to gather force after the summer of 1917, all these before the October Revolution. Mao did not deny the fact that the intelligentsia in the May Fourth Movement only "possessed some elementary knowledge of communism" and lacked "the Marxist spirit of criticism." He also acknowledged that he himself was only a subscriber to anarchism in 1919 and still one of the admirers of Hu Shih, Ch'en Tu-hsiu, and Li Ta-chao.

Ch'en did not commit himself to Marxism until 1920, and Li still did not accept it as a whole before the end of 1919. Mao also said that, at the end of 1919, he himself was "a strong supporter of America's Monroe Doctrine and the Open Door." [35] All this, of course, does not so much deny the great influence of the world revolutionary situation following World War I upon the later development of the movement, as contradict the assumption that the movement took place "at the summons" of the October Revolution and "at the call of Lenin."

Furthermore, the anti-imperialist and antifeudal ideas seem to have been in the main developed after 1920. At least, most of the participants in the movement were not conscious of these ideas before that time. Their intentions were to fight against an aggressive Japan and the pro-Japanese officials. This fact has been acknowledged by another communist leader and one of the participants in the movement, Teng Ying-ch'ao, Chou En-lai's wife, when she said:

The May Fourth patriotic movement and the new culture movement themselves were anti-imperialist and antifeudal in nature. But at that time, this was not clearly conceived in our minds. It was not until 1921, when the Chinese Communist Party was established and it pointed out that the Chinese revolution was an anti-imperialist and antifeudal revolution, that this aspect of the movement gradually became clear to us. In the May Fourth period, we also did not know that the intelligentsia should unite with the workers and the peasants. We only knew that Lenin was the leader of the Soviet Revolution, who merely intended to seek emancipation for the oppressed workers and peasants. But we indeed at the time had also a kind of spontaneous and intuitive realization that to save our country we must carry our activities beyond student circles. We students alone could not save our country. We should "awaken our fellow citizens." Consequently we paid much attention to propaganda and organized a number of speech corps. [36]

Teng then belonged to the radical wing of the students. As for the others, who constituted the majority of the student body, it is interesting to note that they seldom used the words "imperialist" or "feudal," and, while anti-imperialism and antitraditionalism were at the heart of the movement, the specific Leninist interpretations of "imperialism" and "feudalism" were not evident in their statements, although the term "imperialism" (ti-kuo chu-i) in a non-Leninist sense had been introduced into China through Japanese as early as 1895.[g]

[g] Ukita Kazuomi's (1858–1945) *Imperialism* (*Teikoku-shugi*) was translated into Chinese by the Ch'ü-yang hsüeh-sheng pien-chi-so in 1895, and Kōtoku Denjirō's (1871–1911) *Imperialism, the Spectre of the Twentieth Century* (*Niju seiki no kaibutsu teikoku-shugi*) (1901) was translated by Chao Pi-chen in 1902. Ukita was a progressive liberal and Kōtoku a social democrat when they wrote these books. Li Ta-chao mentioned in the Feb. 10, 1919, issue of *The Citizens*

The antifeudal idea was probably voiced earlier than the anti-imperialist conception by some intellectual leaders in the new thought movement, even before the May Fourth Incident. One of the major accusations raised against Confucianism by Ch'en Tu-hsiu, Ts'ai Yüan-p'ei, and others was that it was produced by a feudal society and remained, in many aspects, feudal in nature. Their strong objection to preserving a feudal doctrine in a modern and different society implies that they did not consider contemporary Chinese society to be feudal in nature. Moreover, "feudalism," like "imperialism," was never used during this period in the Marxist sense.

Who Led the Movement?

Another problem specifically concerned with the communist interpretation of the May Fourth Movement arises from the questions whether the movement took place on the basis of class divisions and who led it. Although Mao Tse-tung analyzed the movement in terms of class in his later writings, he was seemingly conscious that this was inexact, since he said in his first interpretation of it in 1939 that the movement was actually a united front of different "social forces" instead of classes. With regard to the composition of this united front Mao enumerated "the Chinese workers, students, and the newly rising national bourgeoisie." Later, in 1940, in "On New Democracy," he added more class character by saying:

Though there was no Communist Party in China at the time of the Movement, there were a great many among the intelligentsia, who welcomed the Russian revolution and possessed some elementary knowledge of Communism. The 'May 4th' Movement from its very inception was a revolutionary movement of the united front consisting of the Communist intelligentsia, the revolutionary petty-bourgeois intelligentsia, and the bourgeois intelligentsia (the last-mentioned forming the right wing of the united front). The weakness of this stage of the Movement was that it

magazine that: "The Pan-Asianism promoted by the Japanese is not a doctrine of national self-determination but an imperialism that will subdue small and weak nations." Even this concept of imperialism from a purely nationalist viewpoint was not very often mentioned during the May Fourth period. Lenin wrote his *Imperialism, the Highest Stage of Capitalism* in 1916, based somewhat upon J. A. Hobson's *Imperialism* which was published in 1902. Lenin thought the term "imperialism" had been "more and more adopted" by Western social reformers and pacifists after 1898. Modern imperialism in the economic sense had been criticized earlier by the physiocrats of France and even by Adam Smith. Lenin's work was not translated into Chinese and published in China until Sept. 1, 1919, when his "Rejections and Demands of the Bolsheviks" appeared in the first issue of the *Emancipation and Reconstruction* fortnightly. Then on Nov. 1, 1920, a part of his "Report on the Party Program at the Eighth Congress of the Russian Communist Party" appeared with the Chinese title, "National Self-determination" (*Min-tsu tzu-chüeh*), in *New Youth*, VIII, 3, pp. 6–10. After this, there were about ten articles of his translated into Chinese in 1920 and 1921.[37]

lacked the participation of the workers and peasants. In contrast, later on when it developed to the June 3rd Movement not only the intelligentsia but also the vast masses of the proletariat, the petty bourgeoisie and the bourgeoisie were drawn in. Consequently, it became a revolutionary movement on a nation-wide scale.[38]

In this analysis, although he exaggerated the role of the "communist intelligentsia," which in fact hardly came into existence until after 1920, Mao still did not state which wing of the intelligentsia had played the leading role in this united front. However, in later years, Chinese communist writers often carried Mao's idea further, and asserted that in the coalition of the May Fourth Movement, the communist intelligentsia played the leading role. One of these writers, for example, interpreted the three kinds of intelligentsia mentioned by Mao in the following terms: "Representative figures of the communist intelligentsia were Li Ta-chao and Mao Tse-tung, representative figures of the revolutionary petty-bourgeois intelligentsia were Lu Hsün and Ch'en Tu-hsiu, and a representative figure of the bourgeois intelligentsia was Hu Shih. In this revolutionary movement of a united front, the communist intelligentsia were the major leading force." [39] The reason for this inference, according to this communist historian, is that, "the proletarian thought of the communist intelligentsia in this movement was less in quantity, yet higher in quality, and more effective in mobilizing the vast masses of the revolutionary people [than the thought of other groups]." [40] If one could not prove, by reference to evidence, that the May Fourth Movement had been led by communists and influenced by the proletarian idea, especially in its early period, how could effectiveness of mobilization justify this argument?

As a matter of fact the question as to who had led the May Fourth Movement has, from the time of the movement to the present, been a controversial and perplexing one. Shortly after the May Fourth Incident, the Japanese and Peking governments accused the Bolsheviks of inciting the movement. This was denied by the intellectual leaders and by many foreign observers and diplomats. After the June fifth strikes, however, the Western concession authorities started to follow the line of the Japanese government, though some of them conceded that they did not find any evidence for this charge. In the decades following the May Fourth period, when the reputation of the movement rose high among the Chinese public, various groups often claimed leading roles in it. Chinese liberals and Western missionaries and writers often overemphasized the liberal leadership, especially Hu Shih's role in the literary movement. The Kuomintang leaders, even though they were at the same time critical of the aims of the movement, sometimes declared, or implied, that members of their party, such as Ts'ai Yüan-p'ei, Wu Chih-hui, Lo Chia-lun, and Tuan Hsi-p'eng, actually had led or influenced the movement.[41] The ultraconservatives took a different viewpoint. They, still clinging to the assertion of the Japanese government, simply attributed the leadership of the movement to the communists, because they regarded it as an open riot. On the other hand, the Chinese communists enthusiastically claimed for themselves the leading role and stressed the influence of the October Revolution as mentioned above, while belittling the influence of the liberals and Nationalists. Since 1949, Hu Shih has been denounced by the communists as a "traitor" in the movement, and Dewey and Russell have been called "spies" sent into China by imperialists to damage the movement. A communist biographer of Mao Tse-tung even said, ignoring all historical facts, that Russell was always "an imperialist warmonger." Ch'en Tu-hsiu's claim to a leading role in the movement was eliminated from communist literature after 1927, because he had become a Trotskyite and "betrayed the Communist Party." Even Ch'en's "flag of the Literary Revolution Army" was, according to Ch'ü Ch'iu-pai, the renowned communist leader who succeeded Ch'en Tu-hsiu in 1927, "not a Red Flag of the Red 'Bandits' but the Blue and White Flag of the Kuomintang." Subsequently, Li Ta-chao, Lu Hsün, Mao Tse-tung, and Ch'ü Ch'iu-pai were described by communist writers as leading figures in the movement, more important than Ch'en Tu-hsiu and Hu Shih. Noncommunist historians in China are even restrained from obtaining reprints of *New Youth* and of the early communist organ, *The Guide Weekly*.[42] The problem of who actually led the movement is thus confused by partisan considerations on the part of the various interested political and social groups.

The same question was raised by Ch'en Tu-hsiu at the end of 1923. Ch'en, trying to interpret the new literature movement in terms of historical materialism, remarked: "People often asserted that the adoption of the vernacular in literary writing was brought about by Hu Shih, Ch'en Tu-hsiu, and their company. This is, in fact, an accomplishment attributed to us which we never deserved. Vernacular literature was created and established in order to meet the needs of the recent industrial development and population concentration of China. If Hu and others had promoted vernacular literature three decades ago, their plan would have been utterly wiped out by a single article by Chang Shih-chao; but now who will listen to Chang's lofty and vehement arguments against it?"[43] Hu Shih rejected this attribution to economic "first causes." In 1935 he answered this claim by elaborating many other causes such as the historical, social, political, and international factors, adding that "if there had not

been 'Hu Shih, Ch'en Tu-hsiu, and their company,' the adoption of the ver
nacular in literary writing would have been delayed for at least two or three
decades." [44] In 1940, on the occasion of Ts'ai Yüan-p'ei's death, Ch'en Tu-hsiu
said again, "The May Fourth Movement was a necessary result of the develop
ment of modern Chinese society. Regardless of its merits or demerits, it should
not be viewed as having been originated by any few individuals. But Mr. Ts'ai,
Mr. Hu Shih, and I were the persons mainly responsible for the ideology and
public opinion of that time." [45] These statements on the causes of the literary
revolution by Ch'en and Hu shed some light on their views of the leadership
of the literary revolution and the movement. While Ch'en sometimes under
estimated the importance of individual leadership, Hu minimized the eco
nomic element and the demand of society for a plain written language. Their
views indicated other angles from which the question of who led the May
Fourth Movement might be posed.

Mao Tse-tung seems to have grasped some of the sociopolitical significance
of the movement and to have paid due attention to the coalition of the variou
social forces particularly with regard to the participation of merchants, in
dustrialists, and workers in a movement against foreign aggression and domes
tic warlordism — the coalition which was first manifested in the June fifth
strikes. This realization helped in the formation of his theories of "new
democracy" in 1940 and of "coalition government" in 1945. This seems, in turn
to have been of some help in the Communist Party's mobilization of the dif
ferent forces of society to support its causes during and after World War II
Moreover, Mao, in his experience with the May Fourth Movement, fully real
ized the importance of the intellectuals' leadership of the workers and peasants
and was aware that students and teachers were in this sense the great resource
of the Chinese revolution. He understood that the crucial question was to rally
the new intelligentsia to go among the peasants and workers in order to lead
and utilize them, presumably to fight for their interests. This had been real
ized by Sun Yat-sen earlier but ignored by the Kuomintang leaders in later
years. In spite of these realizations, Mao's interpretation of the movement is,
as we have shown, sometimes characterized by dogmatism, distortion, and self-
contradictions.

The Real Nature of the Movement — A Suggested Interpretation

The May Fourth Movement was actually a combined intellectual and
sociopolitical movement to achieve national independence, the emancipation

of the individual, and a just society by the modernization of China. Essentially, it was an intellectual revolution in the broad sense, intellectual because it was based on the assumption that intellectual changes were a prerequisite for such a task of modernization, because it precipitated a mainly intellectual awakening and transformation, and because it was led by intellectuals. This also accelerated numerous social and political and cultural changes. The most important purpose of the movement was to maintain the existence and independence of the nation, a goal which had actually generated all of the major reforms and revolutions in China since the latter half of the nineteenth century.

In order to do this, the intellectual reformers, unlike the previous generations, advocated the modernization or Westernization of China in all important aspects of her culture, from literature, philosophy, and ethics to social, political, and economic institutions and customs. They started by attacking tradition and by re-evaluating attitudes and practices in the light of modern Western civilization, the essence of which they thought to be science and democracy. The basic spirit of the movement, therefore, was to jettison tradition and create a new, modern civilization to "save China."

The emancipation of the individual was one of the dominant conceptions especially in the first stage of the May Fourth period. After 1915, most of the young energetic intellectual reformers started to conceive that, to rejuvenate the nation, the individual should be freed from the bondage of the traditional stagnant ethics and institutions. To have all individuals liberated from the old passive thinking and from the self-sufficing and paternalistic family and clan system based on an agricultural society would strengthen the nation. Hence destruction of tradition and convention by iconoclasm and criticism became the most colorful phenomenon of the movement. Its attack on the conventional Confucianism, assault on the classical language and literature, exposure of the defects of the national character and customs, ridicule of the "spiritual" culture of the Orient, demolition of the legends of antiquity, as well as revolt of youth against the old marriage arrangements and family life — all manifested this spirit of iconoclasm, criticism, and furious destruction. Though the construction of a modern civilization was the proclaimed goal of the leading reformers, their efforts in this respect were overshadowed by their destructive activities. As a result, conservatism and traditionalism lost their appeal for the young Chinese literati.

In the early process of this critical re-evaluation, idealism, liberalism, pragmatism, rationalism, utilitarianism, realism, and agnosticism infused the minds of the young intellectuals. In general, the reformers believed ideological and institutional changes must precede a material and sociopolitical transformation. They preferred individual freedom to conformity as far as the traditional restraints were concerned. Moreover, in spite of their emotionalism and patriotism, they attacked their problems with rationalism and logic or at least proclaimed their intention to do so. This phenomenon, though nascent, was remarkable in view of the way of thinking which had characterized, with a few exceptions, their forebears in the Chinese gentry since the late Ch'ing period. Their ideal in intellectual activities was clear thinking. They challenged authorities, cast doubts on the existing social order and moral principles, and re-evaluated all these in a utilitarian manner. "Prove all things" and "give us the evidence" were their catchwords, though not always carried out in action.[46] They left unchallenged virtually no tradition that appeared to them doubtful.

The trend toward the emancipation of the individual, however, did not mean the same as the exaltation of individualism as in the West, nor was liberalism promoted exactly in the Western sense. To many young Chinese reformers, emancipation of the individual was as much for the sake of saving the nation as upholding individual rights. The value of individual and independent judgment was indeed appreciated more in the May Fourth period than ever before, yet the individual's duty to society and the nation was also emphasized. This situation differed from the rise of individualism in the modern West, since a nation-state was still to be born in China as she faced aggressive imperialist powers. Consequently the Chinese emancipation of the individual from tradition, especially from the big family system, was soon balanced by the demand for a well organized society and state and therefore a strong government. Moreover, liberalism was exalted in a broad sense in the period by groups with divergent ideological commitments. Besides the liberals influenced by the French and British trends of the eighteenth and nineteenth centuries and the pragmatists there were anarchists, nihilists, and various kinds of socialists, all of whom at the time regarded themselves as champions of freedom and provided vigorous stimuli for the break with tradition and convention.

The divergencies of these groups and the emphasis on the primacy of the nation, in addition to the influence of foreign and domestic political interference, facilitated the rise of nationalist and socialist forces after the May Fourth Incident which overwhelmed the individualistic trend. Modern Western patriotism and nationalism and the conception of an independent, socialist-inclined nation-state developed rapidly in China. The intelligentsia soon became aware that they must awaken the masses of the people to the national crisis and to the people's own interests and then organize and lead them if the nation were to be saved and strengthened. Mass movement, propaganda, organization, and revolutionary discipline were consequently regarded by the young intellectuals as significant and justifiable techniques for their struggle against world power politics and warlordism. The socialist and Marxist-Leninist preaching of liberation of the impoverished classes and colonies and of internationalism and brotherhood in the future provided more moral justification for these conceptions and practices. As a result, trends that were antiliberal and anti-individualistic from the Western point of view were developing by the end of the May Fourth period, and this development may have prepared the way for the later nationalist paternalism and communist totalitarianism. But to most of the Chinese intellectuals, under the circumstances in the few years following the May Fourth Incident, direct, organized activities and mass demonstrations appeared to be the best possible way to promote genuine democracy in China. Their aim was to bring social pressure on the government by way of popular action.[47] Organized activities of this type seemed a particularly desirable form of protest against a government oppressive to its own people but weak to foreign aggression, since the sole alternative, given the existing conditions, was probably a bloody revolution, which was not the aim of most participants in the movement.

On the whole, the basic aspect of the movement was its transitional nature. Examining China before and after the movement, one cannot fail to appreciate that she had undergone a fundamental and thorough intellectual and sociopolitical change. This was carried through amid vigorous altercations, and organized struggles swiftly developed after the attack on tradition. In the process ancient Cathay suffered the birth pangs of producing a new nation-state and society. Different features stood out in the successive stages of the reform activities. In a sense the movement appears to have been a microcosmic repetition, with some varying emphases and sequences, of the intellectual evolution of the West over the last three or four centuries. From a long range point of view, it undoubtedly constitutes a dividing line in the intellectual, cultural, and sociopolitical history of modern China and marks the initiation of a new era, just as definitely as the 1911 Revolution marked the abolition of an established political institution.

Achievements and Shortcomings Reappraised

The movement has often been judged as to whether it was a success or a failure as a whole. This has led to oversimplifying an unplanned and complicated event which cannot be analyzed in these terms. It has also been evaluated

from partisan viewpoints. Mao Tse-tung suggested that the movement ha
made great achievements in establishing a strong anti-imperialist united fron
in provoking in its antifeudal aspect the revolt against the old ethics and th
old literature, in preparing the ground for the formation of the Communis
Party and later revolutionary actions, and in starting to produce a gloriou
new culture of the new democracy forming a part of the world socialis
cultural revolution and led by the proletarian class.[48] As for the defects of th
movement, Mao said that "the cultural movement of the time was not broa
enough to reach down to the masses of workers and peasants"; [49] that bour
geois thought, which had previously performed a revolutionary function i
fighting against feudal ideology, was soon defeated by the right wing forme
by the bourgeois intelligentsia and other bourgeoisie, a group which bega
toward the end of the movement to take the "reactionary position" of "the er
slaving thought of foreign imperialism and the back-to-antiquity thought c
Chinese feudalism"; [50] and that "many leading figures of the time still did no
possess the Marxist spirit of criticism." Mao continued, "The method they em
ployed was, in general, still the method of the capitalist classes; in other word
it was a formalistic method. It was quite correct for them to oppose the ol
formalism and the old dogmas, and to promote science and democracy; bu
they did not apply the critical spirit of dialectical materialism and historica
materialism to the contemporary situation, history, or things foreign." [51] Nor
Marxist critics using the same evidence might well reverse this evaluation. Fc
instance, the absence of Marxist method among many leading figures migh
be regarded as a credit to, instead of a liability of, the movement. Meanwhil
the defects Mao mentioned, if they were true, cast some doubts on his ow
assertion that the movement had become a part of the then world proletaria
revolution.

From our viewpoint, the most important achievement of the movement wa
the ideological and, to a lesser degree, practical transformation in social equi
librium which took place during the period. With the accelerating collapse c
the old political structure and the agricultural economy and with the rise c
new native industry and commerce, the traditional alliance of the gentry, lanc
lords, and the bureaucracy in support of their mutual interests started to brea
down and to be succeeded by the formation of a new alignment. The new in
telligentsia launched a revolt against the ruling powers. The young intellectual
most of whom still came from landlord and bureaucratic families — with som
from the new merchant and industrialist class — rebelled against tradition
ideas, institutions, and customs and the interests of the warlords and bureaucrat

Significantly, they were supported in their anti-imperialist activities by workers, merchants, and industrialists. In such changes of the social order, it is often the intellectuals who start the ideological revolt against the status quo — a phenomenon which was called by some historians of revolution the "transfer of the allegiance of the intellectuals" and by others "the desertion of the intellectuals." [52] The May Fourth Movement provides a good example of this kind of transformation.

In this process of social transformation fundamental ideological changes among the people and among young intellectuals in particular were most striking. Traditional ethical principles and dogmas were effectively shattered. Idols and authorities trembled before the movement. The prestige of tradition has not since been restored, despite the efforts of later traditionalists and conservatives. The worship of the old was replaced by enthusiasm for the new. Eagerness for new learning among the youth of this period has never been surpassed. New standards began to take form. Among the literati, views of life and the world were broadened and changed.

These ideological changes were accompanied and helped by the adoption of the vernacular as a medium for writing, by the creation of a new literature variously based on humanitarianism, romanticism, realism, and naturalism, and by the rapid development of the press and of popular education. The vernacular became the popular form of writing, even though conservative authorities later tried to encourage the preservation of the classical literary language. This new literature has since dominated Chinese literary circles. New poetry, new short essays and stories, and new drama all came into existence during the movement, and new novels appeared immediately afterwards. As "revolutionary literature," these new forms were later supported and effectively used by the leftists and progressives in their ideological struggle against the conservatives and Nationalists, who produced almost no popular or distinguished works in the literary field. Other fine arts such as painting, sculpture, and music were also greatly influenced by the cultural upheaval.

The Chinese press and public opinion made great progress after the May Fourth Incident. If one compares newspapers and periodicals published before the movement with those published after, the latter show great improvement in both technique and contents. The speedy increase in the number of such publications was unprecedented in Chinese history. They also enjoyed a much bigger audience, and were regarded as considerably more important by both the government and the public than ever before.

Meanwhile, popular education spread, other educational reforms took hold, and general intellectual life and scholarship were greatly improved. Modern knowledge was increasingly taught in the schools as a result of the movement. Industrial training started to develop closer connection with the new national industry. Teachers and students established more and stronger organizations, and their social and academic activities considerably increased. Western philosophy and logic were introduced. Social science and a new historiography soon spread. Modern economics, political science, and sociology began to take roots in China. Natural science achieved a remarkable degree of progress in a short space of time during and after the period. Most of the prominent Chinese associations for the study of natural science were created during the decade following 1915. Notable advances were made in the fields of biology, geology, paleontology, meteorology, physics, physiology, and biochemistry.[53] Most important of all, scientific methods and attitudes were introduced and used far more than in earlier times.

Along with these ideological changes and intellectual developments there occurred social transformations. After the movement the traditional family system gradually declined. Marriage based on love was more frequently demanded. Against the old family and clan systems, Chinese youth strove to assert their personalities and rights in society. A tendency toward a larger social cohesion as a substitute for the family and clan bonds made itself felt during and after the period. The social status of women began to rise. Coeducation was established. Women began to be emancipated from traditional ethical, social, and political shackles. The movement nurtured a more active woman's suffrage movement and brought women into political and social activities. Truly, the movement started and propelled a "revolution of the family."

China's economic structure also underwent notable changes during the period. These were accompanied by the progressive decline of the landlords' position, unrest among the peasantry, an increase of political activities on the part of urban dwellers, and the increasing significance of the labor problem. The May Fourth Movement was in a sense a consequence of such economic developments, but it in turn focussed attention on these phenomena. After the split of the movement, the conflict of interests between urban workers and capital became more obvious, and, under the influence of the young intellectuals, the labor movement started to gain in strength and organization and to take on a political coloration. Though labor did not become a major force in Chinese politics, it became, through cooperation with the movement, one of the forces in the general political and social struggle, and provided much stimulus for the new intelligentsia.

Accompanying all this was the movement's effect on political processes in China. It facilitated the adoption of new principles and methods of party organization and activity. Political parties since then have developed closer relations with the masses of the people and especially with the young intellectuals. At the same time they laid more emphasis on social problems in their platforms and policies. The consciousness of China as a nation-state was strengthened. Socialism, democracy, and the ideas of national freedom and independence gained repute among the intelligentsia, while warlordism, imperialism, and colonial policy became political targets and met more effective resistance by the public.

By and large, the tendencies of the May Fourth Movement almost determined China's intellectual, social, and political development in the following decades. The deep social and national consciousness, which had started to take shape in this intellectual fermentation, persisted. After the May Fourth period, the demands of the new intellectuals for a modern "scientific culture" and for an effective government to guarantee the independence and equality of the nation in the family of nation-states were continued and intensified. History proved that political leaders and groups who acted against these trends, such as the traditionalists and conservatives, brought their own downfall, whereas those "boys who played and rode with the tide," even with distortion and manipulation, gained advantages. The lasting effect of the drive to emancipate the individual and the propaganda for democracy and independent thinking, albeit countered by the later emphasis on subordination to organizational activities, should not be underestimated. The seeds of iconoclasm sown in the minds of the Chinese intelligentsia during the May Fourth period could not be easily removed. The prestige of democracy had been exalted so much that thereafter even those who most strongly opposed it had to do so by devious means. A faithful account of the movement would be a menace to any authoritarianism.

If these are the major achievements of the reforms during the May Fourth period, a few general shortcomings may also be pointed out. In criticizing the Chinese tradition, few of the reformers gave it fair or sympathetic consideration. They felt that several thousand years of social stagnation had left a great many obstacles in the way of progress and reform. In order to sweep these away, excessive attacks on the whole tradition and an underestimation of its merits could hardly be avoided. Consequently, many excellent features of Confucianism and the national legacy were overlooked or left unmentioned. From a long range view, the criticism by the reformers seems in some respects shallow, indiscriminate, and oversimplified. It, nevertheless, may have been necessary under circumstances of such national inertia.

On the other hand, the new intellectuals were too credulous of the new ideas introduced into China during the period. Critical study was professed but inadequately practiced. Vague "isms" were fervently discussed without careful, detailed examination of their contents. As a result, they were often advocated or rejected *in toto* and with much ambiguity and confusion, in spite of some warnings against unclear thinking. This is probably a natural phenomenon in any early period of massive intellectual transition.

Another defect of the Chinese reformers of the period may have been overconfidence that what they thought was correct and good might be achieved in China in a short space of time. A lack of patience and persistence characterized their dealings with a number of difficult and complex problems. So vast a cultural and social transition, involving so many aspects of the national situation, needed long and patient constructive work. To expect to achieve in China in a matter of a few years what had taken the West centuries of effort and had still not been completely accomplished was, of course, quite illusory. Nevertheless, few of the young Chinese during the May Fourth period were sufficiently aware of this. Such impatience, however, was no monopoly of the reformers in the movement, but characterized also their critics and opponents in later years. Many of the latter, in criticizing the failure of the movement to achieve its goals, did not realize the factor of time.[h]

Some Further Considerations

Still further questions and controversies arise from this reappraisal of the movement. As mentioned above, a major assumption of the new thought movement was that ethical and ideological change was fundamental to building a new Chinese civilization. This idea was a reaction against the earlier conception that military technology and political institutions were the most significant things to be learned from the West. The new intellectuals, unlike earlier reformers, paid more attention to ethics, ideas, and principles than to techniques of industrialization or material construction. Later critics, such as

[h] At the end of the May Fourth period, John Dewey ventured to predict that China might achieve in "a century or so the intellectual, scientific, industrial, political, and religious progress for which the rest of the world has taken several centuries. It cannot, like the United States, make the change with plenty of elbowroom, but must accomplish it in a civilization crowded with traditions and superstitions as well as with people."[54] In her autobiography, Pearl S. Buck also gave an account and criticism of the Chinese intellectual trends during and following the May Fourth period based on her personal observations in China.[55]

Fung Yu-lan, felt that the movement as a whole had overlooked the urgency of industrialization. They believed that "after a certain material civilization was achieved, a corresponding spiritual civilization would spontaneously follow," although they also acknowledged the fact that industrialization depends on both spiritual and material factors.[56] However, this criticism does not counter the reasoning of the new intellectuals that ideological backwardness constituted one of the strongest obstacles preventing the industrialization of China. Moreover, it may be pointed out that mere material construction will not necessarily or spontaneously carry with it desirable ideological or institutional achievements. The example of Japan after the Meiji Restoration should not be ignored. In fact, the May Fourth Movement was a preparatory work for the industrialization of China. Industrialization is a further step, not a rejection, of the major theme of the movement.

The conservatives' charge that the movement was responsible for the rise of socialism and communism in China provides another interesting question. There is no doubt that Chinese communism sprouted from the movement. In this sense, the charge has some truth in it. But actually, the charge seems to imply that the whole movement was wrong from the beginning and that liberals and nationalists should neither have started nor joined it. If this is the meaning of the charge, certain questions may be raised: was the movement a product of historical circumstances and could it have been avoided; or, more important, is it correct to say the subsequent rise of socialist currents was due to the participation of liberals and nationalists in the movement, or rather to their subsequent rejection of, and withdrawal from, its political aspects?

Several points may be made in answering the above questions. The movement started shortly after the end of World War I when the fortunes of capitalism, nationalism, and liberalism were or appeared to be rising. The people's desire for national independence from external aggression and intervention, and the new intelligentsia's demand for freedom and the sharing of political power had become stronger and stronger during the war period. In the early stage of the movement, the enthusiasm of the liberals, nationalists, and to a lesser degree capitalists for the struggle against Japan's position in China and against Chinese tradition was natural and understandable. The turning point for the decisive rise of socialism and communism did not arrive until the postincident stage. During this stage there also arose the question of the attitude of Westerners toward the movement. On the one hand prominent Western intellectuals in China, such as John Dewey, Bertrand Russell, and Paul S. Reinsch, supported the modernization movement which, if carried out, would have resulted in an independent and stronger China. On the other hand, most representatives of Western economic interests in China clung to the policy of preserving their special privileges. They supported the corrupt ruling forces in China which guaranteed them the most privileges in making profit, no matter to what extent these forces ran counter to the will of the majority of the Chinese people and no matter how illiberal or antidemocratic their conduct was. When the Western policies toward China were finally decided in favor of these interests, the young Chinese felt bitterly disappointed. Then came the Soviet declarations giving up all concessions in China which, under the circumstances, made a profound impression. This certainly contributed to driving the progressive and left wings of the movement, as well as the nationalists, to reorient their thinking and their activities. A consideration of this juxtaposition of events seems important in any attempt to understand later Chinese attitudes toward communism and the Soviet Union. The Chinese liberals turned conservative or inactive and provided no significant political counterweight. Their ignoring of pressing economic problems, their reluctance to become involved in politics, their failure to realize the intelligentsia's leading role among other social forces, the nature of warlordism in China, and the Chinese people's abhorrence of imperialism and colonialism, and finally, their retreat to academic work all caused them to lose contact with the majority of the youth and the masses of the people. At last, after the unification of the country by an ill-fated coalition with the communists, the Kuomintang leaders adopted a traditionalist and conservative attitude toward reforms promoted in the movement.

Considering the above situation, one may conclude that, besides the communist intrusion in the political scene, the change in attitude and policy of the Kuomintang and the Western Great Powers toward the movement and the weakness of the Chinese liberals are two of the most significant phenomena in and after the latter stage of the movement. This change and weakness were crucial factors in the later political and social development of China.

Forty years have passed since the beginning of the May Fourth Movement. China has undergone more fundamental change in these years than in any previous period of its history. The currents set in motion at that time continue to dominate the scene; the profound problems raised then remain to be reconsidered and solved.

A CHRONOLOGY OF RELEVANT EVENTS
1914–1923

APPENDIXES

NOTES

A CHRONOLOGY OF RELEVANT EVENTS
1914–1923

1914

January 4: President Yüan Shih-k'ai dissolved the first Parliament of the Republic and annulled the Constitution of 1912.

February 8: Yüan Shih-k'ai ordered the whole country, from officials to families, to worship Heaven and Confucius formally.

March 2–December 4: A series of press laws proclaimed to restrict publication.

Program of work-and-study in France expanded by Li Shih-tseng, Wu Chih-hui, and Tsai Yüan-p'ei.

September 2: Japanese troops sent to China.

November 7: Japanese troops occupied Tsingtao, Shantung.

1915

January 18: Japan served on China the Twenty-one Demands.

Huang Yüan-yung proposed a new literature using the vernacular language as in the European Renaissance.

March–December: Boycott against Japanese goods protesting the Twenty-one Demands.

May 7: Japan presented China with ultimatum demanding acceptance of the Twenty-one Demands.

May 9: Chinese government accepted Japan's terms set in the ultimatum.

May 25: Sino-Japanese Treaty based on the Twenty-one Demands concluded.

Chinese students in Japan returned to China as a body in protest against the Twenty-one Demands.

August 23: The Society to Plan for Stability, which was initiated on August 14, founded in Peking.

September 15: *Youth Magazine* (later *New Youth*) established in Shanghai by Ch'en Tu-hsiu.

November 15: Ch'en Tu-hsiu proposed in *New Youth* a new Chinese literature based on realism and naturalism.

December 12 (to March 22, 1916): Yüan Shih-k'ai abolished the Republic and declared himself Emperor.

1916

January 1: Yüan Shih-k'ai bestowed on Confucius' descendant the title of Prince.

February 15: Intensified attack on Confucianism began in *New Youth*.

Spring (to spring 1919): 200,000 Chinese laborers recruited to France for war work in aid to Allied governments.

Summer: Hu Shih discussed the vernacular problem with friends in New York.

June 6: Yüan Shih-k'ai died. Succeeded by Li Yüan-hung as President. Tuan Ch'i-jui appointed Premier.

August: Peking Parliament discussed the issue of providing for Confucianism as a state religion in the Draft Constitution.

October 1: Hu Shih's letter suggesting a Chinese literary revolution published in *New Youth*.

December 26: Ts'ai Yüan-p'ei appointed chancellor of Peking University.

1917

January 1: Hu Shih's article "Some Tentative Suggestions for the Reform of Chinese Literature" appeared in *New Youth*.

January 20 (to September 28, 1918): Tuan Ch'i-jui secured the Nishihara loans from Japan.

February 1: Ch'en Tu-hsiu's article "On the Literary Revolution" appeared in *New Youth*.

February: Japan concluded secret agreements with Britain, Russia, France, and Italy, securing their approval of her claims in China.

Spring: Ch'en Tu-hsiu appointed dean of the School of Letters, Peking University.

March 4: Tuan Ch'i-jui proposed to cease diplomatic relations with Germany.

March 16: Tsarist government overthrown by the February Revolution in Russia.

May 23: President Li Yüan-hung dismissed Tuan Ch'i-jui as Premier.

From summer: Chou Tso-jen, Hu Shih, and Liu Fu joined the faculty of Peking University.

June 13: Li dissolved Parliament.

July 1–13: Chang Hsün restored the Manchu boy Emperor to the throne. Chang was defeated by Tuan Ch'i-jui.

July 14: Li Yüan-hung resigned as President. Tuan Ch'i-jui resumed premiership.

July 17: Sun Yat-sen left Shanghai for Canton advocating to restore the Constitution of 1912.

August 1: Feng Kuo-chang became acting President.

August 14: China declared war on Germany and Austria.

September 1: Sun Yat-sen established the Military Government in Canton.

October 6: Civil war between North and South began.

November 2: The United States recognized Japan's "special interests" in China by signing the Lansing-Ishii Agreement.

November 7: October Revolution in Russia.

November 22: Tuan Ch'i-jui resigned as Premier.

1918

January 8: Wilson's Fourteen Points proclaimed.

January 15: *New Youth* started to publish all articles in the vernacular.

February: Li Ta-chao appointed chief librarian at Peking University.

March 7: Anfu Club established by Tuan Ch'i-jui, Hsü Shu-cheng, Ts'ao Ju-lin, etc. (possibly initiated in August 1917).

March 23: Tuan Ch'i-jui resumed premiership.

March 25: Sino-Japanese Military Mutual Assistance Convention concluded. Tuan Ch'i-jui gave Japan the right to send troops to North Manchuria and Outer Mongolia.

April 18: The New People's-Study Society founded by Mao Tse-tung in Changsha.

May 4: Sun Yat-sen resigned as the head of the Canton Military Government.

May 5: The Corps of Chinese Students in Japan for National Salvation established in Tokyo.

May 6: Forty-six Chinese students arrested by Japanese police in Tokyo.

May 12: Chinese students in Japan returned to China as a body in protest against the Sino-Japanese Military Mutual Assistance Convention.

May 15: Lu Hsün's short story "The Diary of a Madman" published in *New Youth*.

May 20: Sun Yat-sen left Canton and established headquarters in Shanghai.

May 21: Over 2,000 college students petitioned President Feng's office in Peking protesting the Sino-Japanese Military Mutual Assistance Convention.

Summer: The Students' Society for National Salvation founded in Shanghai.

June 30: The Young China Association initiated in Peking by Tseng Ch'i, Wang Kuang-ch'i, Li Huang, Li Ta-chao, etc.

August 1: The Soviet Russian foreign minister Chicherin wrote to Sun Yat-sen proposing alliance.

August: Rice riots in Japan.

Fall: Mao Tse-tung appointed assistant librarian at Peking University.

September 4: Hsü Shih-ch'ang elected President of the Republic by the new Parliament in Peking.

September 24: Sino-Japanese exchange of notes on the Tsi-Shun and Kao-Hsü Railroads made in secret.

October 10: Hsü Shih-ch'ang assumed office as President. Tuan Ch'i-jui resigned premiership. Ch'ien Neng-hsün appointed acting Premier.

October 13: The New Tide Society established at Peking University by students.

November 11: World War I armistice signed.

November 16: Truce between North and South ordered.

December 22: *Weekly Critic* established in Peking by Ch'en Tu-hsiu.

Imports of Japanese goods into China doubled over previous year, because of the lack in Western competition.

1919

January 1: First issue of *New Tide* and of *The Citizens Magazine* appeared.

January 18: Paris Peace Conference opened.

January: The China Society for the Promotion of New Education established by Ts'ai Yüan-p'ei, Chiang Monlin, T'ao Hsing-chih, etc.

New Education, a monthly, established in Shanghai.

January 27: Japan made public in Paris her secret agreements with Britain, France, and Italy on China secured in February 1917.

February 20: Peace conference between Peking and Canton held in Shanghai.

February–April: A number of telegrams from Chinese students, merchants, etc., protesting Japan's claim on Shantung sent to Paris Peace Conference.

February: Hu Shih's *Outline of the History of Chinese Philosophy* published.

March 1: March First Movement took place in Korea.

March 2–6: Communist (Third) International organized and its First World Congress held in Moscow.

March 18: Lin Shu's letter to Ts'ai Yüan-p'ei criticizing Peking University published. Ts'ai's reply written.

March: Ch'en Tu-hsiu compelled to resign as dean of the School of Letters of Peking University.

Liang Ch'i-ch'ao's article doubting the omnipotence of science and the value of Western civilization published.

April 30: Japan's claim for Shantung agreed to in secret by Wilson, Lloyd George, and Clemenceau at Paris Peace Conference.

April 30: Peking student groups resolved to demonstrate on May 7 in protest of the Paris decision.

May 1 (to July 11, 1921): John Dewey and wife visited China.

May 4: Over 3,000 college students demonstrated in Peking against Paris decision on the Shantung problem and the government's foreign policy. Ts'ao Ju-lin's house burned. Chang Tsung-hsiang beaten, and 32 students arrested in the May Fourth Incident.

May 5: The Student Union of the Middle Schools and Institutions of Higher Learning in Peking established.

May 6, 8: Hsü Shih-ch'ang, President of China, issued two orders to discipline the students.

May 9: Ts'ai Yüan-p'ei left Peking in secret and submitted resignation of the chancellorship.

May 12: Fu Tseng-hsiang, Minister of Education, left office.

May 14: Government ordered suppression of student activities by military force.

May 14–18: Student unions established in major cities. Widespread demonstrations in support of Peking students.

May 15: Fu Tseng-hsiang permitted to resign; Vice Minister Yüan Hsi-t'ao promoted to acting Minister of Education.

Peace conference in Shanghai broken off.

Mid-May: The Alliance of Teachers' Unions of the Middle Schools and Institutions of Higher Learning in Peking established.

May 18: Emergency meeting of student union in Peking; resolved to call general strike.

May 19: Students' general strike in Peking. The boycott intensified. Six demands by students presented to the President.

May 20–June 10: Student strikes or unrest spread to more than 200 cities.

May 21: Japan served protest on Chinese government demanding suppression of students' anti-Japanese activities.

May 21: Premier Ch'ien Neng-hsün answered the students' demands but not to the latter's satisfaction.

May 23: Peking government suppressed student press and activities.

May 25: Ministry of Education ordered all students to return to classes within three days. Students refused to comply.

June 1: President Hsü issued orders to close student unions. Martial law proclaimed in Peking.

June 2, 3, 4: Mass arrests of 1,150 students in Peking. Student street speeches intensified.

June 4: Minister of Education Yüan Hsi-t'ao resigned, succeeded by Fu Yo-fen.

June 5: Strikes of merchants and workers in support of students started in Shanghai.

June 6: Merchants' and workers' strikes spread to other cities.

June 8: *Weekly Review* established in Shanghai by the Kuomintang (then still named Chung-hua ke-ming-tang).

Foreign concessions in Shanghai started to suppress student activities.

June 10: Ts'ao Ju-lin, Chang Tsung-hsiang, and Lu Tsung-yü permitted to resign.

June 11: Ch'en Tu-hsiu arrested by Peking Government because of his support of the student movement.

June 12: All merchants' and workers' strikes ended.

June 13: Premier Ch'ien Neng-hsün resigned. Finance Minister Kung Hsin-chan succeeded as acting Premier.

June 16: The Student Union of the Republic of China established in Shanghai.

June 28: Chinese delegation to the Paris Peace Conference refused to sign the Peace Treaty with Germany. Immediate goals of the May Fourth demonstration achieved.

July 1: The Young China Association formally established in Peking.

July 14: *Hsiang River Review*, a weekly, established by student union in Changsha, edited by Mao Tse-tung.

July 15: *Young China*, a monthly, established in Shanghai by the Young China Association.

July 20–November: Polemics on "problems and isms" carried on between Hu Shih, Lan Kung-wu, and Li Ta-chao.

July 22: Students' strikes ended.

July 25: Soviet Union made the Karakhan declaration promising to give up all Russian concessions in China.

August 1: *The Construction*, a monthly, established in Shanghai by the Kuomintang.

August 31: *Weekly Critic* suppressed by the Peking government.

September 1: *Emancipation and Reconstruction*, a semimonthly, established in Shanghai by the Chinputang.

September 20: Ts'ai Yüan-p'ei returned to Peking University as chancellor.

September: The New Youth Society organized by Ch'en Tu-hsiu, Hu Shih, Chou Tso-jen, Li Ta-chao, Lu Hsün, etc.

October 10: Sun Yat-sen reorganized his party under the name Chung-kuo Kuomintang.

November 19: Expansion of the New Tide Society's membership and activities.

December 1: "Manifesto of *New Youth*" published.

December: The Society for the Study of Socialism established in Peking. Similar groups set up in Shanghai, Canton, Hong Kong, etc.

December 4 (to January 12, 1920): Teachers' strike in Peking demanding payment of salaries.

By the end of the year: Co-education established at Peking University.

1920

January 1: *Young World*, a monthly, established in Shanghai.

January: Voitinsky arrived in China, meeting Li Ta-chao in Peking and, later, Ch'en Tu-hsiu in Shanghai.

January 12: Peking government ordered the vernacular to be taught in primary schools, and later (March) in all grade schools.

January 29: Sun Yat-sen telegraphed his followers to support the student and new culture movements.

March: Hu Shih's new poems, *A Book of Experiments*, published.

First steps to initiate the Society for the Study of Marxist Theory taken at Peking University.

March 21: The Karakhan declaration made public in China.

April: Chinese social and political organizations enthusiastically welcomed the Soviet declaration.

May: Chinese Communist Party organized in Shanghai by Ch'en Tu-hsiu, Tai Chi-t'ao, Shen Ting-i, Li Ta, etc.

June 1: *New Tide* suspended for 16 months.

June 6: Last issue of *Weekly Review* appeared.

July 14–18: Tuan Ch'i-jui's troops defeated by the allied force of Chang Tso-lin and Ts'ao K'un. North China under control of Wu P'ei-fu.

July 19–August 7: Second World Congress of the Comintern held in Moscow and Petrograd.

August 5: Anfu Club suppressed by the new Peking government.

August: "Manifesto of the Struggle for Freedom" published in Peking by Hu Shih, Chiang Monlin, T'ao Meng-ho, Kao I-han, Li Ta-chao, etc.

Socialist Youth Corps (S.Y.) established by the Chinese Communist Party in Shanghai (after July 1921 called Communist Youth Corps, or C.Y.).

Fall (to end of 1921): Polemics on capitalism and socialism between *La Rekonstruo, New Youth*, etc.

Fall: Antireligious movement gathered force under the influence of the Young China Association.

August: Last issue of *The Construction* appeared.

September 20: Peking discontinued recognition of the old Russian government.

September 27: Second Karakhan declaration to China made by Soviet Union.

October 12 (to October 1921): Bertrand Russell and Dora Black visited China.

October 29: Ch'en Chiung-ming (joined by Chiang Kai-shek) recaptured Canton.

November 7: *The Communist*, a monthly, established in Shanghai by the Chinese Communist Party.

November 29: Sun Yat-sen returned to Canton resuming political leadership.

December 16: Ch'en Tu-hsiu left Shanghai for Canton, appointed director of education board there.

This year woman suffrage movement became active in several provinces.

1921

Liang Sou-ming's *Eastern and Western Civilizations and Their Philosophies* published.

January 4: The Society for Literary Studies organized in Peking by Chou Tso-jen, Mao Tun, Lu Hsün, Cheng Chen-to, etc.

January: *Critical Review*, a monthly, established in Nanking by Wu Mi, Hu Hsien-su, and Mei Kuang-ti; critical of the new culture and new literature movements.

Labor Movement Committee established in Shanghai by the Chinese Communist Party.

Late in January: *New Youth* suppressed by the French Concession in Shanghai.

February: *New Youth* moved to Canton, liberals withdrawing from the magazine.

Reading Magazine, advocating the "reorganization of the national heritage," established in Peking by Hu Shih, Ku Chieh-kang, etc.

March 14–July 28: Teachers' strike in Peking demanding the independence of educational funds; became known as June Third Movement for Study.

May: Last issue of *The Citizens* appeared.

Summer: The Creation Society organized in Shanghai by Kuo Mo-jo, Yü Ta-fu, Chang Tzu-p'ing, Ch'eng Fang-wu, T'ien Han, etc.

June 22–July 12: Third Congress of the Comintern held in Moscow.

July 1–5: First National Congress of the Chinese Communist Party held in Shanghai and Chiahsing.

August: Chinese Labor Union Secretariat established in Shanghai by the Chinese Communist Party.

Kuo Mo-jo's new poems *The Goddesses* published.

Early in September: Ch'en Tu-hsiu arrested by the French Concession police in Shanghai.
September 5: Paul Monroe arrived in China.
December: Lu Hsün's short story "The True Story of Ah Q" published.
December 23: Comintern sent Maring to Kwangsi to see Sun Yat-sen.
During the year: The Young China Association started to split.

1922

"Doubting antiquity" studies published by Ku Chieh-kang and Ch'ien Hsüan-t'ung.
January 12–March 5: Hong Kong seamen's strike (directed by the Chinese Communist Party).
February 4–6: Washington Conference. Nine-Power Treaty to restrain Japan's activities in China and keep China's door open.
March: Great Federation of Antireligionists established in Peking.
March: Last issue of *New Tide* appeared.
April 4–9: The World's Student Christian Federation held its conference in Peking.
May 1–6: First Congress of the All-China Labor Federation held in Canton, attended by delegates from more than 100 labor unions.
May 5: Socialist Youth Corps held its first conference in Canton.
May 7: *Endeavor Weekly* established in Peking by Hu Shih, Kao I-han, V. K. Ting, etc.
May 13: "Our Political Proposals," published by Ts'ai Yüan-p'ei, Wang Ch'ung-hui, Liang Sou-ming, Hu Shih, Li Ta-chao, etc., demanding "good government."
June 2: President Hsü Shih-ch'ang resigned. Succeeded by Li Yüan-hung on June 11.
June 16: Ch'en Chiung-ming rebelled against Sun Yat-sen.
July 1: Last issue of the *New Youth* monthly appeared in Canton.
July: Chinese Communist Party held its second congress in Hangchow; resolved to ally with the Kuomintang.
August: Li Ta-chao saw Sun Yat-sen in Shanghai and announced his intention to join the Kuomintang as a communist member.
September: The Kuomintang resolved to permit Chinese communists to join the party. *The Guide Weekly* founded in Shanghai by Ch'en Tu-hsiu.
September 15: Last issue of *La Rekonstruo* appeared.
September 19: "Good men cabinet" formed in Peking by Wang Ch'ung-hui and other members of the "good government" group.
November 5–December 5: Ch'en Tu-hsiu attended in Moscow the Fourth World Congress of the Comintern which called for a Kuomintang-Communist alliance.
November 25: The "good men cabinet" fell because of lack of support from Ts'ao K'un and other military men.
Winter: Citizens' disarmament meetings to reduce Chinese armed forces of North and South held in Peking.

1923

January 16: Kuomintang troops recaptured Canton from Ch'en Chiung-ming.
January 26: Joint manifesto by Sun Yat-sen and A. Joffe issued in Shanghai.
February–December: Polemics on science and metaphysics carried on by Carsun Chang, V. K. Ting, Liang Ch'i-ch'ao, Hu Shih, Wu Chih-hui, etc.
June 15: *New Youth* quarterly published by the Chinese Communist Party in Canton.
July 13: The Great Alliance for Anti-Imperialism established in Peking by student, labor, and educational groups.

APPENDIX A

A BRIEF ANALYSIS OF THE SOCIAL FORCES IN THE MAY FOURTH PERIOD *

As the old social order disintegrated, four new social forces, which exerted great influence on the May Fourth Movement, came to the fore. They were the new intelligentsia, the new commercial and industrial groups, the urban workers, and, finally, the poor and landless peasants and the unemployed.

The new intelligentsia, the most important element in the May Fourth Movement, grew out of the impact of Western civilization on China in the latter half of the nineteenth century. Although the first new-style school was established in China in 1862, a Western-style educational system did not actually begin functioning on a large scale until 1907, about ten years before the beginning of the new literature revolution. In those ten years a group of intellectuals with a certain degree of Western learning emerged in China.

According to Table 1, there were about 5,500,000 people in school or graduated in the

TABLE 1. STATISTICS OF NEW-STYLE SCHOOLS IN CHINA, 1905–1923
(Including all elementary, middle schools, and higher educational institutions)

Year	Number of schools	Number of students	Number of graduates	Number of teachers	Number of administrators
1905 [a]	4,222	102,767	. . . . . .	. . . . . .	. . . . . .
1906 [b]	. . . . . .	468,220	. . . . . .	. . . . . .	. . . . . .
1907 [c]	37,888	1,024,988	. . . . . .	. . . . . .	. . . . . .
1908 [c]	47,995	1,300,739	. . . . . .	. . . . . .	. . . . . .
1909 [c]	. . . . . .	1,626,720	. . . . . .	. . . . . .	. . . . . .
1910	. . . . . .	. . . . . .	. . . . . .	. . . . . .	. . . . . .
1911 [a]	52,650	1,625,534	. . . . . .	. . . . . .	. . . . . .
Aug. 1912– July 1913 [d]	87,272	2,933,387	173,207	129,297	98,929
1913–1914 [d]	108,448	3,643,206	232,221	164,607	122,174
1914–1915 [d]	122,289	4,075,338	257,889	189,853	122,116
1915–1916 [d]	129,739	4,294,251	235,372	198,976	130,799
1916–1917 [d e]	121,119	3,974,454	334,519	182,583	129,221
1917–1918	. . . . . .	. . . . . .	. . . . . .	. . . . . .	. . . . . .
1918–1919 [f]	. . . . . .	4,500,000	. . . . . .	. . . . . .	. . . . . .
1919–1920	. . . . . .	. . . . . .	. . . . . .	. . . . . .	. . . . . .
1920–1921	. . . . . .	. . . . . .	. . . . . .	. . . . . .	. . . . . .
1921–1922 [b]	. . . . . .	4,987,647	. . . . . .	. . . . . .	. . . . . .
1922–1923 [b]	. . . . . .	6,615,772	. . . . . .	. . . . . .	. . . . . .

[a] Cited in Ernest R. Hughes 657, *Invasion of China by the Western World* (London, 1937), Chap. IV, p. 168.
[b] From Chu Ching-nung and others, comps., *Chiao-yü ta tz'u-shu* (The Encyclopedia of Education) (Shanghai, 1930), p. 1052.
[c] From the Ministry of Education, Ch'ing government, Statistical Tables and Charts of the First Survey of Education (1910), of the Second Survey (1910), of the Third Survey (1911), also in Ting Chih-p'ing 444, ed., Chronological Records of Chinese Education in the Last Seventy Years (Shanghai, 1935), pp. 29, 31–32, 34.
[d] From the Ministry of Education, Peking government, Statistical Tables and Charts of the Fifth Survey of Education, also in Yüan Hsiang and others, comps., *Chung-kuo nien-chien* (China Year Book), No. I (Shanghai, 1924), pp. 1863–64, 1906–10.
[e] Figures exclude Szechwan, Kwangsi, and Kweichow Provinces.
[f] The figure represents enrollment in government schools. There were 500,000 students in mission schools in 1919. See Paul Hutchinson 660, *China's Real Revolution* (New York, 1924), Chap. II, p. 36.

* This survey does not attempt to be comprehensive. Statistics in China early in this century were often scanty and far from reliable. The numbers given in the following tables are not exceptions, but they provide a general picture of the situation.

five academic years from 1912 to 1917, inclusive. Roughly speaking, at the beginning of the May Fourth Movement there might have been 10,000,000 persons who had received some form of the new education. In proportion to the whole population this new intelligentsia was very small, perhaps 3 per cent; but its great significance to Chinese society has been set forth in the text.

The new merchants, many of whom supported the May Fourth Movement, had, because of the collapse of the rural economy, veered from their traditional ties with the landlords and bureaucrats and joined forces with the new industrialists. To get an estimate of the size and growth rate of this new group in the decade before the May Fourth Movement is difficult. But the figures on Chinese chambers of commerce, shown in Table 2, provide some indication since these organizations were a modern innovation aimed specifically at developing mutual cooperation by members of this new group. The growth of the merchant class in some hinterland provinces was even more remarkable. For example, in Shansi the numbers of chambers of commerce and their membership in 1912 were respectively 28 and 4,220, but in 1918 they were 104 and 7,878; in Anhwei the numbers in 1912 were 17 and 2,943, but in 1918 they were 65 and 13,684; and in Shantung the numbers in 1912 were 47 and 6,043, but in 1918 they were 101 and 14,160. [See Yüan Hsiang and others, comps., China Year Book, No. I, pp. 1539–71; Chou Ku-ch'eng, *Chung-kuo she-hui chih pien-hua* (Changes in Chinese Society) (Shanghai, 1931), Chap. III, pp. 227–53; Yen Chung-p'ing, *Chung-kuo mien-yeh chih fa-chien* (The Development of China's Cotton Enterprise) (Chungking, 1943), V, pp. 121–23, Chap. VI, pp. 157–59.]

TABLE 2. NUMBER OF CHINESE CHAMBERS OF COMMERCE
AND THEIR MEMBERSHIP, 1912–1918

Year	Number of chambers of commerce	Number of members
1912	794	196,636
1913	745	192,589
1914	1,050	203,020
1915	1,242	245,728
1916 [a]	1,158	193,314
1917 [a]	1,148	206,290
1918 [a]	1,103	162,490

[a] Numbers in these years are incomplete.
· Sources: The Ministry of Agriculture and Commerce, *The Seventh Statistics of Agriculture and Commerce of China* (Peking, 1922), also in Yüan Hsiang and others, comps., China Year Book, No. I, pp. 1539–43.

The term "new industrialists and merchants" refers to those groups which manufactured (or imported) and distributed modern machine products and which were consequently tied to foreign financial interests. As contrasted with their predecessors they were more concerned with developing nation-wide than local markets. They were also more articulate and influential in national politics. In the early twenties, for example, there was even a group of important people advocating a "government by merchants," instead of by the warlords and bureaucrats. [See *Chung-kuo kuo-min-tang ti-i-tz'u ch'üan-kuo tai-piao ta-hui hsüan-yen* (The Manifesto of the First Congress of the Kuomintang) (Canton, 1924), Appendix 2 of Li Chien-nung 289, Political History of China in the Last Thirty Years (Shanghai, 1930), Chap. XI, pp. 559–60.]

The new urban labor emerged in China when members of the rural population were drawn into the modern industrial centers. In an estimate of 1915, the total number of Chinese workers was given as 10,759,971, which equaled that of the United States in the same year. (Yüan Hsiang and others, comps., China Year Book, No. I, p. 1421.) But this number of Chinese workers must have included the manual workers and artisans of the old workshops. The number of Chinese factory workers before World War I was very small. It remained about 650,000 throughout the period from 1912 to 1915 inclusive (*ibid.*, p. 1430). According to the official statistics (Table 3), it rose in 1918 to 1,749,339.

TABLE 3. NUMBER OF CHINESE INDUSTRIAL WORKERS, 1918

Manufacture	638,641
Transportation	221,811
Mines	530,885
Municipal utilities	12,000
Agricultural factories	......
Government employed	21,640
Foreign factories employed	324,362
Total	1,749,339

Sources: Statistics by the Ministry of Agriculture and Commerce in 1918, cited in Hu Hua and others, eds., *Chung-kuo hsin min-chu-chu-i ke-ming ts'an-kao tzu-liao* (Source Materials of the New Democratic Revolution of China) (Shanghai, 1951), pp. 59–61.

Another estimate gave the number of Chinese workers in urban factories, mines, and railroads (excluding mariners and rickshaw pullers) as 2,000,000, and the family handicraft workers also as 2,000,000 during the period 1920–1927. [See Ch'en Ta *43*, The Labor Problem in China (Shanghai, 1929), pp. 7–21.] A communist writer estimated the total number of Chinese workers of 1919 as 3,000,000, including 1,100,000 factory workers, 850,000 miners, 400,000 workers in factories owned by foreigners, 300,000 longshoremen, 200,000 workers in railroads and communications, and 150,000 seamen. [See Hung Huanch'un *235*, The Chinese Revolutionary Movement During the May Fourth Period (Peking, 1956), Chap. I, pp. 14–17.]

The landless peasantry was greatly increased in this period by the collapse of the rural economy and of the self-sufficient family and village systems. The percentage of tenant peasants to the total number of peasants during the years 1917–1924 is shown by two surveys, official and private, in Table 4, which are somewhat contradictory.

TABLE 4. PERCENTAGE OF LAND TENANCY IN CHINA, 1917–1924

	1917	1918	1919	1920	1921	1921–1924
Survey A [a]	49.7%	46.7%	41.4%	40.0%	46.3%	...
Survey B [b]	36.0%	...	...	...	...	60.0%

[a] The figures are from a survey of the whole country by the Ministry of Agriculture and Commerce, Peking government.

[b] The figure of 1917 is from a survey of seventeen important areas and that of 1921–1924 is from a survey of thirty-seven areas, all by private statistical agencies.

Sources: Liu Ta-chün, *Wo-kuo tien-nung ching-chi chuang-k'uang* (Economic Conditions of Chinese Tenant Peasants) (Shanghai, 1929), pp. 2–8; also Chou Ku-ch'eng, Changes in Chinese Society, Chap. III, pp. 195–199.

Another set of official figures on tenant and landowning farmers, shown in Table 5, was issued by the Nationalist government after its break with the Communists had changed its political orientation. Before that, the National government in Hankow had announced in 1926 that 45 per cent of the peasants were landowners and 55 per cent of them did not own any land.

TABLE 5. PERCENTAGE OF TENANT FARMERS AND FARMERS
OWNING LAND IN CHINA

	1912	1931	1932	1933
Tenant farmers	28%	31%	31%	32%
Farmers owning land	49%	46%	46%	45%

Sources: Chung-kuo yin-hang, *Chung-hang yüeh-k'an* (The Bank of China Monthly) (Shanghai, Aug. 1933).

In respect to this matter of land ownership in China, different statistics were used by the rightists and leftists to support their variant views and political needs. Some more scientific surveys in later years show that concentration of land ownership in China varied greatly in different areas. Generally speaking, the problem was more severe in fertile areas, such as southern and central China. [See Wang Hsiao-wen and Ch'en Ch'uan-kang, *Chung-kuo t'u-ti wen-t'i* (The Land Problem of China), in *Wan-yu-wen-k'u*, Collection II, No. 700 (Shanghai, 1936), Vol. II, Chap. IV, pp. 106–28. In his *Land and Labor in China* (New York, 1932), R. H. Tawney adopted the figures from Chang Hsin-i's survey published in his article, "A Statistical Study of Farm Tenancy in China," *China Weekly Review*, III, 39 (Shanghai, Sept. 25, 1930). Also see Wu Ching-ch'ao, "Ts'ung tien-hu tao tzu-ken-nung" ("From Tenant to Peasant Owning Land"), *The Tsing Hua Journal*, IX, 4 (Peiping, October 1934), pp. 973–92. Cf. J. L. Buck, *Land Utilization in China* (Chicago, 1937).]

It is hardly an exaggeration, however, to say that in the second and third decades of the twentieth century, half of the Chinese peasants were landless, and that among those who owned land, half of them were poor and middle peasants, holding from one to thirty Chinese acres. (A Chinese acre, *mou*, is regarded at Shanghai by custom as equivalent to one sixth of an English acre [7,260 sq. ft.], but it varies throughout China from 3,840 sq. ft. to 9,964 sq. ft. A standard of 18,148 sq. ft. has even been cited.) Under such straitened circumstances many poor peasants left their villages. In various districts these were estimated to include 8–20 per cent of the population. Furthermore, a huge proportion of the population was displaced because of famines and civil wars. A survey of the calamity-stricken people in half the provinces of China in the twenties gave their number as 56,559,000. Some of these poor peasants and displaced people may have gone to cities and factories; but, as the capacity of the infant Chinese industry was limited, most of them had to try to find some other source of income or starve. A great number probably became professional soldiers, others bandits or roamers. This roaming population was of great significance to modern China since it nourished warlordism, particularly during the years just prior to the May Fourth Movement. This disruption of the peasantry also contributed to the collapse of social morality and to the increase of social instability.

From the above analysis, we see that, during the May Fourth period, Chinese society was undergoing a great transition. The old social equilibrium had been thrown off balance. The landlords and the old gentry were declining; the new intelligentsia, and, in various degrees, the new industrialists, the merchants, the financiers, and the urban workers, were gradually coming to the fore. The peasants were to a large extent impoverished, uprooted, and restless, while the warlords took advantage of the total situation to seize power. [See

Nagano Akira, *Shina no shakai soshiki* (The Social Organization of China) (Tokyo, 1926), Bk. II, Chap. IV, pp. 262–86. Or see the Chinese translation by Chu Chia-ch'ing, *Chung-kuo she-hui tsu-chih* (Shanghai, 1930), pp. 368–402. The chapter deals with "The Roaming Class" of China. See also Nagano Akira, *Shina-hei, dohi, koso-kai* (Chinese Soldiers, Bandits, and the Red Spear Society) (Tokyo, 1938); Chiang Fang-chen, "Tsui-chin wu-shih-nien-lai Chung-kuo chün-shih pien-ch'ien shih" ("History of Military Changes of China in the Last Fifty Years") in Shun Pao *414*, The Past Fifty Years (Shanghai, 1923); Yada Tadao, *Chūgoku nomin mondai to nomin undo* (The Peasant Problem and Peasant Movement of China), p. 184. For information about the calamity situation see *Chung-kuo chien-she* (Construction of China), I, 1 (Nanking, Jan. 1930), p. 79; the fourteen provinces surveyed are Kiangsu, Chekiang, Kwangtung, Kiangsi, Hunan, Hupei, Shantung, Shansi, Honan, Hopei, Shensi, Kansu, Suiyuan, and Chahar. Chou Ku-ch'eng estimated the total number of calamity-stricken people of China at 100,000,000, which may be an overestimate.]

APPENDIX B

THE NUMBER OF SCHOOLS AND STUDENTS INVOLVED IN THE MAY FOURTH INCIDENT

The question of the numbers of students and schools involved in the meeting and the demonstration of May 4, 1919, has been a matter of some confusion. There are at least two categories of accounts giving different figures:

(A) Some reports state that the number of students attending the meeting and joining the general demonstration was markedly greater than that of the students parading to the Legation Quarter and attacking Ts'ao's house: (1) "About thirty schools were present with more than 10,000 students" in the meeting and demonstration, but "three thousand of us paraded to the Legation Quarter," says a student of the National University of Peking, quoted in Tsi C. Wang, *The Youth Movement in China* (New York, 1928), Chap. X, pp. 165, 166. (2) "In the morning students from thirty-three schools and colleges in Peking, fifteen thousand strong, paraded the streets as a demonstration against the Shantung decision. Three thousand of them went to the Legation Quarter to ask the Allied ministers to use their good offices to secure justice for China." See Chiang Monlin, "The Student Movement," in E. C. Lobenstine and A. L. Warnshuis, eds., *The China Mission Year Book, 1919* (1920), p. 46. But later, in 1947, Chiang gave the number of students as 3,000 without mentioning the difference between the numbers participating in the meeting, the parade, or the visit to the Legation Quarter. See his *Tides from the West* (New Haven, 1947), Chap. XV, p. 120. (3) An early source says that 3,000 students gathered at the front of T'ien-an-men, and later at the Legation Quarter a great number of citizens joined the throng. See Ts'ai Hsiao-chou and Yang Ching-kung, *Wu-ssu* (May Fourth), p. 50. (4) Ts'ao Ju-lin reported in his letter of resignation that he saw "over one thousand" students approaching his home. C. F. Remer asserts that the demonstrators were dispersed at the Legation Quarter and gathered again to march to Ts'ao's house, where students "about a thousand strong arrived and demanded entrance." See "The Revolt of the Chinese Students," *Asia* (Sept. 1919), p. 932. These figures are an underestimate, and the demonstrators were not dispersed at the Legation Quarter.

(B) Other accounts concerning the Incident give no difference in number between the students taking part in the meeting and general demonstration and those going to the Legation Quarter and attacking the residence of Ts'ao. Most of them agree that thirteen colleges and universities were represented (Kung Chen-huang reported that there were fourteen schools since he counted the North China Union College separately; see his *Ch'ing-tao ch'ao* [The Storm of Tsingtao], published in Shanghai on Aug. 10, 1919), but they give different numbers for the students involved in the affair: (1) *Over 5,000.* Reported in "Special Record," *Chung-hua chiao-yü chieh* (Chinese Educational Circles), VIII, 2 (Aug. 1919), p. 1. Also accepted by Ch'en Shou-sun, ed., *She-hui wen-t'i tz'u-tien* (Encyclopedia of Social Problems) (Shanghai, 1929), p. 117; Ting Chih-p'ing 444, ed., Chronological Records of Chinese Education in the Last Seventy Years (Shanghai, 1935); Ch'en Tuan-chih 73, An Historical Evaluation of the May Fourth Movement (Shanghai, 1936), p. 232. Hsü Te-heng gives this figure too. (2) *5,000.* This figure was reported in the statement issued to the Paris Peace Conference by the Chinese delegation. See *The New York Times*, May 10, 1919, p. 3, a dispatch of the Associated Press from Paris dated May 9. The same figure was also given in a report dated May 9 in *The North-China Herald* (Shanghai, May 10, 1919), p. 347; and Ch'a-kung 6, "A Record of the Student Strikes," Chinese Educational Circles, III, 1 (July 1919), p. 121. (3) *Over 3,000* students of thirteen schools was the official report given by the Peking police department cited in the President's mandate of May 8, 1919. The *Ta-kung-pao* (Tientsin) gave the same number in its report dated May 5, 1919. This is accepted by many writers such as Ta Chung-hua Kuo-min [pen name], ed., *Mai-kuo-tse chih-i, Chang Tsung-hsiang* (Chang Tsung-hsiang the Traitor, No. I), published in Shanghai by the end of May 1919; Chia I-chün, Short History of the May Fourth Movement (Peking, 1953), p. 15. (4) *3,000.* Rodney Gilbert reported on May 4, 1919: "Three thousand young men (representing nearly every school in and about Peking, and ranging in age from 13 to 25)" joined the demonstration. See *The North-China Herald*, May 10, 1919, p. 348. Wu Chung-pi uses the same figure, in *Shang-hai pa-shih chiu-wang shih* (A History of the Shanghai Strike and National Salvation Movement), published in Shanghai in July 1919. (5) *About 2,000 or 3,000.* Reported in Kung Cheng-huang, ed., The Storm of Tsingtao. (6) *Over 1,000.* A report by a gendarme officer on May 5, 1919, gives this figure. See Hua-chung Kung-hsüeh-yüan 228, ed., Collected Articles on the May Fourth Movement (Wu-Han, 1957), p. 173.

·While the exact number of the students involved cannot be secured now, the figure of over 3,000 participating in the meeting and demonstration seems to be the most reliable. The number of students who subsequently paraded through the streets to Ts'ao's house was apparently smaller, but their ranks were swelled to some extent by the general public.

APPENDIX C

UNIVERSITIES AND COLLEGES INVOLVED IN THE MAY FOURTH INCIDENT

The matter of what schools were involved in the incident has been confused by various reports. Writers often make wrong identification of the thirteen schools joining the demonstration. For example, the report by the gendarme officer on May 5, 1919, indicates that students from the Shantung Middle School were present; others did not note this. Ch'en Tuan-chih does not give the list of the schools but indicates that the Preparatory School for Study in France (*Liu Fa yü-pei hsüeh-hsiao*) was one of the thirteen involved. (See his 73, An Historical Evaluation of the May Fourth Movement [Shanghai, 1936], Chap. XIII, p. 236.) Others list the National Institute of French Language (*Kuo-li Fa-wen chuan-hsiu-kuan*) and the National Institute of Russian Language (*Kuo-li O-wen chuan-hsiu-kuan*). The identical accounts in the *Wu-ssu* (May Fourth) by Ts'ai Hsiao-chou and Yang Ching-kung, in *Mai-kuo tse chih-i Chang Tsung-hsiang* (Chang Tsung-hsiang the Traitor, No. I) by Ta Chung-hua Kuo-min, and in the *Wu-ssu li-shih yen-i* (Chap. IX, p. 127) by Ch'iang-wei-yüan-chu are more correct.

An article entitled "Pei-ching chuan-men i-shang hsüeh-hsiao hsin tiao-ch'a" (A New Survey of the Institutions of Higher Learning in Peking) by Ching-kuan (published in *Shen Pao* [Shanghai, June or early July 1919], and reprinted in *The Eastern Miscellany* [Shanghai, September 15, 1919], pp. 186–88) listed twenty-five such institutions in Peking at that time. The Institute of French Language, which had been left out, should be added to the list and makes the total 26. Among these, several did not join the demonstration on May 4 but became involved later. These were the National Girls' Higher Normal College of Peking, the Institute of French Language, the Institute of Russian Language, Tsing Hua School, and one of the five military schools. (It was probably the Army Cadets Academy, but early reports called it *Lu-chün hsüeh-hsiao* (Army School). Of the latter schools, the Army Cadets Academy (*Lu-chün ta-hsüeh*) had over 500 cadets; the Army Survey School (*Lu-chün ts'e-liang hsüeh-hsiao*), about 80; the Military Medical School (*Chün-i hsüeh-hsiao*), about 300; the number of students in the School of Logistics (*Chün-hsü hsüeh-hsiao*) was unknown; and the Academy of Aviation (*Hang-k'ung hsüeh-hsiao*), which had about 120 cadets, was out of the immediate vicinity. All were under the chiefs of staff or the Army Department.

All figures are based on Ching-kuan's article cited above unless otherwise noted. For Hui-wen University the figure is furnished by its successor, Yenching University. The total number of students enrolled in the ten schools involved insofar as the figures are known is 6,111. That of the three uncounted schools is estimated not to have exceeded 400.

THE INSTITUTIONS AND NUMBER OF STUDENTS

1. National University of Peking (*Kuo-li Pei-ching ta-hsüeh*): 2,411 *

2. National Higher Normal College of Peking (*Kuo-li Pei-ching kao-teng shih-fan hsüeh-hsiao*): 925

3. National College of Law and Political Science of Peking (*Kuo-li Pei-ching fa cheng chuan-men hsüeh-hsiao*)

4. National Industrial College of Peking (*Kuo-li Pei-ching kung-yeh chuan-men hsüeh-hsiao*): over 200

---

* The figure in Ching-kuan's article is 3,000. Tsi C. Wang gave 2,228 for 1919. The number of 2,411 was reported about February 1919 by *Shen Pao*.

5. National Agricultural College of Peking (*Kuo-li Pei-ching nung-yeh chuan-men hsüeh-hsiao*): over 200

6. National Medical College of Peking (*Kuo-li Pei-ching yi-hsüeh chuan-men hsüeh-hsiao*): over 200

7. Academy of Police Officers, Ministry of the Interior (*Nei-wu-pu ching-kuan hsüeh-hsiao*): one class only; no figs. given

8. Institute of Railroad Administration, Ministry of Communications (*Chiao-t'ung-pu t'ieh-lu kuan-li hsüeh-hsiao*) [b]: 200

9. Peking Institute of Tax Administration, Bureau of Tax Administration (*Shui-wu-ch'u Pei-ching shui-wu hsüeh-hsiao*)

10. China University (private) (*Ssu-li Chung-kuo ta-hsüeh*) [c]: 1,400

11. Hui-wen University (private) (American missionary) (*Ssu-li hui-wen ta-hsüeh*) [d]: 75

12. University of the Republic (private) (*Ssu-li min-kuo ta-hsüeh*) [e]: 300

13. Ch'ao-yang University (private) (*Ssu-li ch'ao-yang ta-hsüeh*): over 200

[b] It may be noted that the Institute of Railroad Administration belonged to the Ministry of Communications, the head of which was Ts'ao Ju-lin himself. The participation of the Police Academy was probably due to the attitude of the constabulary chief, Wu Ping-hsiang. Chap. IV, n. c', p. 111.

[c] The founders of the China University had some relations with the Kuomintang. The chancellor of the university then was Yao Han.

[d] Hui-wen University, known as "Peking University" during 1902–1918, was a Methodist college for men. By the time of the incident it was in the process of being merged with the North China Union College (*Hsieh-ho ta-hsüeh*), a Congregational college for men in T'ungchou, and the North China Union Women's College in Peking to form Yenching University. In the summer of 1919, Leighton Stuart succeeded Liu Hai-lan, who had been the head of Hui-wen, as the chancellor of Yenching. The Hui-wen University, and later Yenching, was under the control of a trustee board in the United States and was registered in New York State until 1926, when it was required to register with the Chinese Ministry of Education.

[e] The University of the Republic had been established in February 1917 by some parliamentary members, and after 1918 had some relations with Feng Kuo-chang and other military leaders and with overseas Chinese in Southeast Asia.

APPENDIX D

DATA ON WORKERS' STRIKES IN CHINA 1918–1926

TABLE 1. NUMBER OF WORKERS INVOLVED IN STRIKES

Year	Actual number of strikes	Number of formally reported strikes	Total number of workers in reported strikes	Average number of workers involved per reported strike
1918	25	12	6,455	538
1919	66	26	91,520	3,520
1920	46	19	46,140	2,428
1921	49	22	108,025	4,910
1922	91	30	139,050	4,635
1923	47	17	35,835	2,108
1924	56	18	61,860	3,437
1925 [a]	318	198	784,821	3,964
1926 [b]	535	313	539,585	1,723.91
Total	1,233	655	1,813,291	2,768.38

[a] Of the strikes in 1925, 135 were provoked by the May Thirtieth Incident of that year; 95 of these were formally reported with 381,487 workers involved.
[b] The Hong Kong-Canton Strike covered the period 1925–1926. It is counted as a unit in both years.
Sources: Adjusted from Ch'en Ta *42*, "An Analysis of Strikes in China in the Last Eight Years," *The Tsing Hua Journal*, III, 1 (Peking, June 1926), p. 810; also Ch'en Ta *44*, "An Analysis of the Strike Situation in China from 1918 to 1926," *The Economic Fortnightly*, II, 4 and 5, condensed in Wang Ch'ing-pin, Fan Hung, and others *479*, comps., Chinese Labor Yearbook, No. I (Peiping, 1928), Part II, Chap. 2, p. 139.

TABLE 2. DURATION OF STRIKES

Year	Actual number of strikes	Number of formally reported strikes	Total number of days reported strikes lasted	Average number of days per reported strike
1918	25	15	124	8.27
1919	66	52	294	5.65
1920	46	22	157	7.14
1921	49	21	155	7.38
1922	91	54	452	8.37
1923	47	21	134	6.38
1924	56	26	241	9.27
1925 [a]	318	120	2,266	18.88
1926	535	340	2,335	6.87
Total	1,233	671	6,158	9.18

[a] Of the 120 reported strikes, 25 were provoked by the May Thirtieth Incident of 1925. These 25 strikes lasted 1,761 days in all.
Sources and other notes same as Table 1.

TABLE 3. CAUSES OF STRIKES

Number of strikes caused by:	Year									Total
	1918	1919	1920	1921	1922	1923	1924	1925	1926	
1. Demands for Wage Raises	15	23	32	33	61	28	34	105	250	581
2. Opposing Overwork and Ill-Treatment	7	7	11	9	12	4	9	52	172	283
3. Patriotic Movements	..	35	..	..	1	1	1	141	19	198
4. Organization of Labor Unions	..	..	..	..	4	2	..	4	11	21
5. Conflict with Other Groups	..	..	..	3	3	3	2	4	15	30
6. Sympathy Strikes	..	..	..	1	2	2	1	..	16	22
7. Miscellaneous	3	1	2	3	3	4	7	11	23	57
8. Causes Unknown	..	..	1	..	5	3	2	1	29	41
Totals	25	66	46	49	91	47	56	318	535	1,233

Sources: Same as Table 1.

NOTES

The Arabic numerals in italic type immediately following an author's or editor's name or, when the author or editor is not mentioned, immediately preceding a source refer to the source number as listed in the Bibliography in *Research Guide to "The May Fourth Movement,"* the separately published volume of additional reference matter. Those titles of books or other bound volumes not in italics indicate sources in the Chinese or Japanese language. For original Chinese and Japanese titles of works not in the Bibliography, see the Glossary in the same separately published volume.

CHAPTER I

INTRODUCTION

1. The term was first used by the Student Union of Peking on May 18, 1919, in a telegram to other social organizations transmitting its "Manifesto for a General Strike"; see Chap. V, below. Hu Shih thought that the term appeared for the first time in the May 26, 1919, issue (No. 23) of *Mei-chou p'ing-lun* (Weekly Critic) in *236*, "The Spirit of the May Fourth Movement," by an author pen-named "I"; see Hu Shih *199*, "In Memory of May Fourth," Independent Critic, No. 149 (Peking, May 5, 1935), p. 4.

2. Chou Yü-t'ung *124*, "The Departed May Fourth," The Middle School Students (Shanghai, May 4, 1930).

3. See Ts'ai Shang-ssu *447*, Biography of Ts'ai Yüan-p'ei, with Emphasis on His Scholarship and Thought (Shanghai, 1950), Chap. I, pp. 18–19.

4. Hu Shih *226*, "Twenty-eighth Anniversary of 'May Fourth,'" L'Impartial (Shanghai, May 4, 1947), p. 1.

5. See Kiang Wen-han *666*, *The Chinese Student Movement* (New York, 1948), Chap. I, pp. 35–40; p. 147, n. 1.

6. Fung [Feng] Yu-lan *153*, "The Main Tendency of the National Movement of Modern China," The Sociological World, No. 9 (Peiping, 1936), p. 264.

7. Li Ch'ang-chih *286*, Welcome to the Chinese Renaissance (Chungking, 1944), Chap. II, p. 12.

8. The definition of the May Fourth Movement has not been sufficiently discussed by any author. As far as the question of whether there were certain main currents in the movement, see Fu Ssu-nien *162*, "The Twenty-fifth Anniversary of 'May Fourth,'" L'Impartial (Chungking, May 4, 1944), p. 1.

9. See Chang Hsi-jo *15*, "Cultivation of the People's Personality," and Hu Shih *210*, "Individual Freedom and Social Progress — A Further Discussion of the May Fourth Movement," both in Independent Critic, No. 150 (May 15, 1935), pp. 2, 15. See also Ho Kan-chih *170*, History of the Chinese Enlightenment (Shanghai, 1947), Chap. V, p. 151.

10. Chinese materials on the subject are massive. For a short account of the event in English see William Ayers *568*, "Shanghai Labor and the May 30th Movement," *Harvard Papers on China* (Cambridge, Mass., April 1950), mimeographed, Vol. 5, pp. 1–38; also Dorothy Borg, *American Policy and the Chinese Revolution, 1925–1928* (New York, 1947).

11. Ch'en Tu-hsiu 69, "Is the May Fourth Period a Thing of the Past?" Political Review, I, 11 (Chungking, May 15, 1938), pp. 8–9.

12. In the *Ta Ch'ing lu li* (Laws and Cases of the Ch'ing Dynasty) it provided that "the family property, except for those with official noble rank, whose eldest sons have priority of inheritance of property, shall be equally divided among the sons, no matter whether they were born to wives or concubines. The illegitimate son shall have half as much as a legitimate son." Since noble rank under the Empire in most cases was in each succeeding generation lowered by one grade or inherited only in a limited number of generations, even the property of the noble could not accumulate for long.

13. See Weng Wen-hao, "Chin wu-shih nien lai ti Chung-kuo ching-chi chien-she" ("Economic Reconstruction of China in the Last Fifty Years"), in P'an Kung-chan, ed., *Wu-shih nien lai ti Chung-kuo* (China in the Last Fifty Years) (Chungking, 1945), p. 9. See also Kung Chün, *Chung-kuo hsin kung-yeh fa-chan shih ta-kang* (An Outline of the Development of China's New Industry) (Shanghai, 1933), Chaps. VII, VIII, pp. 92–262.

14. This panic of China's native industry shortly after the end of World War I shows its imprint in the statistics concerning many major industries. For a long analysis of this problem see Tse-tsung Chow 599, *The May Fourth Movement and Its Influence upon China's Socio-political Development* (Ann Arbor: University of Michigan Microfilms, 1955; publication No. 12,553; Library of Congress card number: MICA 55–2195), Chap. II, "Economic, Social, and Political Background." Statistics may be found in Ch'en Ming-hsün, *Ching-chi kai-tsao chung chih Chung-kuo kung-yeh wen-t'i* (Chinese Industrial Problems in the Process of Economic Reconstruction) (Shanghai, 1928), II, 48–51; *Hua shang sha-ch'ang lien-ho hui chi-k'an* (The Quarterly of the Association of Cotton Mills Owned by Chinese), III, 4 (Shanghai, Winter 1921), p. 63; Yen Chung-p'ing, *Chung-kuo mien-yeh chih fa-chan* (The Development of China's Cotton Enterprise) (Chungking, 1943; rev. ed. with title *Chung-kuo mien-fang-chih-yeh shih kao* or *A Draft History of China's Cotton Textile Enterprise* [Peking, 1955], VI, 163–205); and Hamada Minetarō, *Shina ni okeru bōseki-gyō* (The Textile Industry in China) (Shanghai, 1923), p. 21. For Chinese Communist works concerning the problem see Hu Hua *193*, ed., Source Materials for the History of the New Democratic Revolution in China (Shanghai, 1951), p. 57; Hung Huan-ch'un *235*, The Chinese Revolutionary Movement during the May Fourth Period (Peking, 1956), Chap. I, pp. 4–20; and Chou Hsiu-luan, *Ti-i-tz'u shih-chieh ta chan shih-ch'i Chung-kuo min-tsu kung-yeh ti fa-chan* (The Expansion of China's National Industry during World War I) (Shanghai, 1958).

15. Yüan Hsiang and others, comps., *Chung-kuo nien-chien* (China Year Book), No. I (Shanghai, 1924), pp. 54–55; Kung Chün, *Chung-kuo tu-shih kung-yeh-hua ch'eng-tu chih t'ung-chi fen-hsi* (A Statistical Analysis of the Industrialization of Chinese Cities) (Shanghai, 1933), pp. 15–28; also Julean Arnold, *Commercial Handbook of China* (Washington, D.C., 1919), p. 321.

16. For a short survey of major wars in China during these years see Chow Tse-tsung *125*, "Chinese Political Trends in the Last One Hundred Years," New Understanding, VI, 3–4 (Chungking, Dec. 15, 1942), pp. 15–17.

17. *Tso Chuan*, Bk. IX, Year XXXI of Duke Seang [Hsiang] (542 B.C.), James Legge's translation *Chinese Classics*, Vol. V, Part II.

18. Fan Yeh, *Hou-Han shu* (History of the Later Han Dynasty), Vols. 97, 109; cf. Kiang Wen-han 666, *The Chinese Student Movement*, p. 8; also Liu I-cheng 326, "Student Storms in Chinese History," The Critical Review, No. 42 (Nanking, June 1925), pp. 1–14.

19. *Sung shih* (History of the Sung Dynasty), in the series of *Nien-ssu shih* (The Twenty-four Histories), edition of the fourth year of Ch'ien-nung era (1739 A.D.), Vol.

346, p. 1a; Vol. 23, p. 2a; Vol. 455, p. 1a–b; Vol. 23, pp. 4a–5a; Vol. 352, p. 4b; Vol. 362, p. 10a; Vol. 399, p. 8; Vol. 455, pp. 1b–3a; Vol. 58, p. 5a; see also Vol. 377, pp. 17b–18b; Vol. 392, p. 9; Vol. 455, pp. 14b–15a; and Vol. 418, p. 7a–b; Ch'en Tung, *Sung t'ai-hsüeh-sheng Ch'en Tung chin-chung lu* (Documents and Memoirs of the Sung Student Ch'en Tung) (1878, transcript), 8 *chüan*, 6 *ts'e*. Also Yeh Shao-weng, *Ssu-ch'ao wen-chien lu* (Memoirs), series of the *Chih-pu-tsu-chai ts'ung-shu*, Bk. I, pp. 42b–43b; Wu Ch'i-ch'ang *507*, "A Study of the Student Movements Which Interfered in Politics in the Sung Dynasty," The Tsing Hua Journal, III, 2 (Peking, Dec. 1926), pp. 999–1046.

20. *Ming shih* (History of the Ming Dynasty), Vol. 231.

21. Huang Tsung-hsi, "Hsüeh-hsiao p'ien" ("On Schools"), in *Ming-yi tai-fang lu* (English translation by W. T. De Bary titled *A Plan for the Prince* [New York, 1957]). See also Hu Shih, "Huang Li-chou's Discussion on Student Movements," written on May 2, 1921, reprinted in Hu Shih *207*, Collected Essays of Hu Shih, Collection II (Shanghai, 1924), III, 11–15. For a criticism of Huang's theory see Chang Ping-lin *23*, Collected Essays of Chang Ping-lin, Chap. I.

22. Lo Chia-lun *342*, "A Retrospect of the Past [May Fourth Movement] in the Light of Current Affairs," in Lo Chia-lun *339*, From Dark Clouds, to Cloudbursts, to Bright Sunset (Chungking, 1943), p. 71.

23. Chow Tse-tsung *126*, "On the Significance and Characteristics of the May Fourth Movement," L'Impartial (Shanghai, May 4, 1947), p. 2, written for the anniversary of the May Fourth Movement.

24. For this problem see *Hsin Jen-shih* (New Understanding), VI, 3 and 4 (Chungking, Dec. 15, 1942), articles by Chow Tse-tsung, Li Ch'ang-chih, and Tsou Yün-t'ing on Chinese political and cultural movements of the last one hundred years; also Chow Tse-tsung and Feng Ta-lin *127*, "On the Great Changes of China in the Last Hundred Years," The Three People's Principles Fortnightly (Chungking, 1945).

25. Bertrand Russell *729*, *The Problem of China* (London, 1922), Chap. I, p. 1.

26. Wang Yün-sheng *499*, "The May Fourth; It Makes Me Feel Uneasy Again," L'Impartial (Shanghai, May 4, 1947), p. 1.

27. *Ibid.*

CHAPTER II

FORCES THAT PRECIPITATED THE MOVEMENT, 1915–1918

1. Paul S. Reinsch *707*, *An American Diplomat in China*, Chap. XII, pp. 129–31; and Wang Yün-sheng *498*, Sixty Years' Relation between China and Japan (Tientsin, 1934), Vol. VI.

2. For the full texts of the Twenty-one Demands and the consequent Sino-Japanese Treaty and other relevant documents see John V. A. MacMurray *688*, ed., *Treaties and Agreements with and concerning China, 1894–1919* (New York, 1921), Vol. II, No. 1915/8, pp. 1216–37; U.S. Department of State, *Papers Relating to the Foreign Relations of the United States, 1915* (Washington, D.C., 1924), pp. 79–206. For the Chinese texts see Wang Yün-sheng *498*, Sixty Years' Relation, VI, 80–400.

3. MacMurray *688*, Treaties and Agreements, II, 1235; the English version is from the official Japanese statement.

4. Wang Yün-sheng *498*, Sixty Years' Relation, VI, 398.

5. Telegram of Lu Tsung-yü, Chinese Minister to Japan, to Chinese Ministry of Foreign Affairs, Feb. 3, 1915, in Wang Yün-sheng *498*, Sixty Years' Relation, VI, 121; another telegram, Feb. 16, 1915, *ibid.*, pp. 142–43.

6. "Minutes of Sino-Japanese Negotiations, Feb. 22, 1915," *ibid.*, pp. 145–56.

7. *Ibid.*, p. 216.

8. Reinsch *707*, *American Diplomat*, Chap. XII, p. 141.

9. See Yüan's handwritten marginal comments in red ink on the Chinese text of Japan's demands, in Chinese Government Files; see also "Minutes of Second Negotiative Meeting of Feb. 5, 1915," Files of the Ministry of Foreign Affairs; and China's first revised terms presented to Japan on Feb. 9, 1915, Files of the Chinese Legation in Tokyo. Cited in Wang Yün-sheng *498*, Sixty Years' Relation, VI, 94, 131, 139.

10. "Home News" (Hu Shih, ed.), in *The Chinese Students' Monthly*, X, 7 (Ithaca, N.Y., April 1915), pp. 451–52.

11. Min-ch'ien T. Z. Tyau *762*, *China Awakened* (New York, 1922), Chap. IX, p. 141; Chap. VII, p. 119.

12. Chu Kung-ching, ed., *Pen-kuo chi-nien-jih shih* (A History of the Chinese Commemoration Dates) (4th ed.; Shanghai, 1929, 1932), XIV, 92–120; P'ing Lin, ed., *Chi-nien-jih shih-liao* (Source Materials for the Commemoration Dates) (Darien, 1948), pp. 79–83.

13. Lu Tsung-yü's Telegram to the Chinese Foreign Ministry, June 10, 1915, Files of Chinese Legation in Japan.

14. "Foreign and Domestic Current Affairs," *Tung-fang tsa-chih* (The Eastern Miscellany), XII, 6 (June 15, 1915), pp. 34–36.

15. "Main Chinese Current Affairs," *ibid.*, 7 (July 15, 1915), pp. 1–2.

16. Scott Nearing *697*, *Whither China? An Economic Interpretation of Recent Events in the Far East* (New York, 1927), Chap. II, p. 48.

17. Cited by W. K. Chung, "Korea or Belgium?" *The Chinese Students' Monthly*, X, 6 (March, 1915), p. 334; see also pp. 330–31, 335, 342–44.

18. Frederick Moor, "Telegram to the Associated Press," Feb. 11, 1915, *Papers Relating to Foreign Relations, 1915*, p. 92; *The Chinese Students' Monthly*, X, 6, p. 380. For the Kuomintang leaders' attitudes toward Japan and Yüan Shih-k'ai during this period see Marius B. Jansen, *The Japanese and Sun Yat-sen* (Cambridge, Mass., 1954), Chap. VIII, pp. 175–201, and Chap. IX, pp. 202–12.

19. Li Chien-nung *289*, Political History of China in the Last One Hundred Years, Vol. II, Chap. XI, pp. 419–20. English translation by Ssu-yü Teng and Jeremy Ingalls titled *The Political History of China, 1840–1928* (Princeton, N.J., 1956), pp. 310–12.

20. Meng Shih-chieh, *Chung-kuo tsui-chin-shih shih* (History of China in Most Recent Times) (Peiping, 1921), Vol. III, Chap. VI, p. 169; Pan-su [pseudonym of Li Chien-nung], *Chung-shan ch'u-shih hou Chung-kuo liu-shih nien ta-shih chi* (Chronological Records of the Important Events of China in the Sixty Years after Sun Yat-sen's Birth (enlarged ed.; Shanghai, 1929), p. 156. Cf. Charles F. Remer *708*, *A Study of Chinese Boycotts* (Baltimore, 1933), Chap. VI, pp. 46–54.

21. Dispatch from Hankow, May 14, 1915, *The New York Times* (May 16, 1915), Sec. II, p. 5.

22. Wen-yü [Chiang Wen-yü] *98*, "A Short Account of the Boycotts against Japanese Goods in the Last Twenty-five Years," Culture Monthly, III, 8 (Shanghai, 1932), p. 4.

23. Dispatch from Tokyo, June 16, 1915, *The New York Times* (June 17, 1915), p. 3; also *The Chinese Students' Monthly*, X, 8 (May 1915), p. 512.

24. Pan-su, Chronological Records of Important Events of China, pp. 157–58.

25. Lu Tsung-yü's Telegram to the Chinese Foreign Ministry from Tokyo, June 10, 1915, Files of the Chinese Legation in Tokyo; Meng Shih-chieh, History of China in Most Recent Times; also *The New York Times* (June 20, 1915), Sec. III, p. 5; Willard Price, "China's Fighting Blood Up," *World's Work*, XXX (Oct. 1915), p. 725; Remer *708*, *A Study of Chinese Boycotts*, p. 48.

26. Chinese Maritime Customs, *Returns of Trade* (Shanghai, 1915), p. 1.

27. Special Correspondence from Peking, May 15, 1915, *The New York Times* (June 20, 1915), Sec. III, p. 5. See also Huang Yüan-yung, "Hsin-wen jih-chi" (A Daily Account of Current Affairs) (April 1, 9, 1915) in *Huang Yüan-sheng i-chu* (Collected Works of Huang Yüan-yung) (Shanghai, 1920), Vol. IV.

28. Ch'en Tu-hsiu, "Ti-k'ang li" ("The Force of Resistance"), New Youth, I, 3 (Shanghai, Nov. 15, 1915), pp. 2–3.

29. Liang Ch'i-ch'ao *306*, An Introduction to the Scholarship of the Ch'ing Period, 1644–1911 (Shanghai, 1927), Sect. 29, p. 163; translation ours. Cf. the English translation by Immanuel C. Y. Hsü titled *Intellectual Trends in the Ch'ing Period* (Cambridge, Mass., 1959), p. 114.

30. Ch'ang Tao-chih, "Liu Mei hsüeh-sheng chuang-k'uang yü chin-hou chih liu-hsüeh cheng-ts'e" ("Situation of the Chinese Students in the United States and Future Policy for Our Sending Students Abroad"), *Chung-hua chiao-yü chieh* (Chinese Educational Circles), XV, 9.

31. See *The Chinese Students' Monthly*, X, 7 (April 1915), pp. 410–11.

32. Dean W. K. Chung, "Korea or Belgium?" *ibid.*, 6 (March 1915), pp. 333–34; Hsu-kun Kwong [Kuang Hsü-k'un], "China Shall Not Be Japanned," *ibid.*, pp. 335–41; "Our Duty" (editorial), *ibid.*, p. 331.

33. "Military Training Camps for Chinese Students" (editorial), *ibid.*, p. 413.

34. For his early life, see Hu's *220*, My Autobiography Written at Forty (Shanghai, 1933; enlarged ed., Taipei, 1954), and *205*, Hu Shih's Diary While Studying in the U.S.A. (2nd ed.; Shanghai, 1947, 1948).

35. Hu Shih *647*, "A Plea for Patriotic Sanity, an Open Letter to All Chinese Students," *The Chinese Students' Monthly*, X, 6 (March 1915), pp. 425–26. Capitalization and italics are in the original. The letter also appears in Hu Shih *205*, Diary, IX, 591–96.

36. *Living Philosophies* (New York, 1931), pp. 253–54.

37. H. K. [Hsu-kun] Kwong *672*, "What Is Patriotic Sanity? A Reply to Suh Hu," *The Chinese Students' Monthly*, X, 7 (April 1915), p. 429.

38. T. S. Yeh, "Is Our Duty to Study Only?" (A Letter to the Editor), *ibid.*, 8 (May 1915), pp. 515–16.

39. Hu Shih *205*, Diary, IX, 566; see also XI, 784.

40. "Letter to Professor H. S. Williams," Jan. 31, 1916, *ibid.*, XII, 843.

41. *Ibid.*, XI, 784.

42. *Ibid.*, p. 790.

43. *Ibid.*, XIII, July 5, 1916, p. 938; Sept. 6, 1916, pp. 939–45. Also Hu Shih *652*, *The Chinese Renaissance*, Chap. III, p. 50.

44. Yüan R. Chao, *588*, "The Problem of the Chinese Language," *The Chinese Students' Monthly*, XI, 6 (April 1916), pp. 437–43; 7 (May 1916), pp. 500–09; Suh Hu and Yüan R. Chao *588*, *ibid.*, 8 (June 1916), pp. 567–93.

45. Ch'en Tzu-chan *76*, The Evolution of Modern Chinese Literature (Shanghai, 1929), Chap. II, pp. 6–29.

46. Hu Shih *196*, "The Author's Preface to *A Book of Experiments*," written on Aug. 1, 1919, reprinted in Hu Shih *207*, Selected Essays of Hu Shih (Shanghai, 1930), pp. 217–

41; also Hu Shih *216*, "Compelled to rebel — The Beginning of the Literary Revolution," in Chao Chia-pi *33*, ed., A Corpus of China's New Literature (Shanghai, 1935), I, 3–27.

47. Louis Untermeyer, Preface, *Modern American Poetry* (New York, 1950), pp. 12–13.

48. Henry Steele Commager, "He Sings of America's Plain People," in Francis Brown, ed., *Highlights of Modern Literature* (New York, 1949), pp. 176–77.

49. Horace Gregory and Marya Zaturenska, *A History of American Poetry, 1900–1940* (New York, 1946), p. 141.

50. Commager, "He Sings of America's Plain People," p. 176.

51. A sketch of his ideas in the May Fourth period may be found in Albert Borowitz *573*, "Chiang Monlin: Theory and Practice of Chinese Education 1917–1930," *Harvard Papers on China* (Cambridge, Mass., 1954), VIII, 107–35.

52. Hu Shih *205*, Diary, XIV, 979.

53. "Mei Chin-chuang's letter to Hu Shih," July 24, 1916, *ibid.*, p. 981.

54. Hu's reply, July 30, 1916, *ibid.*, pp. 982–83.

55. Ezra Pound, "A Few Don'ts," *Poetry, A Magazine of Verse*, I, 6 (Chicago, March 1913). See also Henri Van Boven, *766*, *Histoire de la Littérature Chinoise Moderne*, Ser. 1 (Peiping, 1946), pp. 21ff.

56. Hu Shih *205*, Diary, XV, 1070–73.

57. See Chap. VII below, p. 192. See also Dewey's letter to Hu Shih and Hu's to Ts'ai Yüan-p'ei concerning Dewey's visit to China, published in *Pei-ching ta-shüeh jih-k'an* (The Peking University Daily), March 28, 1919, and May 18, 1919.

58. Shu Hsin-ch'eng *412*, A History of Chinese Students Studying Abroad in the Modern Period (3rd ed.; Shanghai, 1927, 1933), IV, 21–27; VI, 46–71; Sanetō Keishu *397*, Draft History of Chinese Students in Japan (Tokyo, 1939); Chinese translation of first two chapters by Chang Ming-san, *Chung-kuo liu Jih t'ung-hsüeh hui chi-k'an* (Quarterly of the Association of Chinese Returned Students from Japan) (Peking, Sept. 1942; Jan. 1943).

59. Shu Hsin-ch'eng *412*, History of Chinese Students Studying Abroad, Chap. XV, pp. 224–31, esp. pp. 230–31; also Chap. XI, pp. 147–48.

60. *Ibid.*, Chap. VI, pp. 56–64.

61. *Ibid.*, Chap. XV, pp. 212.

62. See text of oaths required of cadets entering Shimbu Military School, a preparatory institute for Tokyo Military Officers' Academy, in the *Shimbu Gakkō ichiran* (A Guide to the Shimbu Military School) (April 1908); also Shu Hsin-ch'eng *412*, History of Chinese Students Studying Abroad, VI, 63–64.

63. Sanetō Keishū, *Jih-pen wen-hua chih Chung-kuo ti ying-hsiang* (Influences of Japanese Civilization upon China), Chinese trans. Chang Ming-san (Shanghai, 1944), pp. 4–37.

64. Kuo Mo-jo, "Cho-tzu ti t'iao-wu ("The Dance of the Table") *Ch'uang-tsao yüeh-k'an* (Creation Monthly) (Jan. 1928).

65. See Nakamura Tadayuki, "Chūgoku bungei ni oyoboser Nippon bungei no eikyō" ("The Influence Exerted by Japanese on Chinese Literature"), *Taidai bungaku* (Taiwan University Literature), VII, 4 (Dec. 1942), pp. 214–43; VII, 6 (April 1943), pp. 362–84; VIII, 2 (Aug. 1943), pp. 86–152; VIII, 4 (June 1944), pp. 27–85; VIII, 5 (Nov. 1944), pp. 42–111; also his other articles listed in John K. Fairbank and Masataka Banno, *Japanese Studies of Modern China* (Tokyo, 1955), pp. 161–62.

66. Ts'ai Yüan-p'ei, *"She-hui-chu-i shih* hsü" ("Preface to the Chinese Translation of *A History of Socialism*"), New Youth, VIII, 1 (Shanghai, June 1, 1920); the *History* was by Thomas Kirkup (5th ed.; London, 1892, 1913), Chinese trans. Li Mou-yu.

67. See *Hsin min ts'ung-pao*, No. 18 (Yokohama, 1902), p. 22; see also combined issue of Nos. 42 and 43 (1903), Liang Ch'i-ch'ao's articles; *Min pao*, No. 2 (Tokyo, Jan. 22, 1906; 2nd printing, April 10, 1906), and No. 4 (April 28, 1906), Chu Chih-hsin's (under pseudonyms Chih-shen and Hsien-chieh) articles, and Sun Yat-sen's speech in No. 10 (Dec. 20, 1906). See also Robert A. Scalapino and Harold Schiffrin, "Early Socialist Currents in the Chinese Revolutionary Movement," *The Journal of Asian Studies*, XVIII, 3 (Ann Arbor, Mich., May 1959), pp. 321–42.

68. Fukui Junzō, *Chin-shih she-hui chu-i* (Modern Socialism) (Shanghai, 1903). For manifesto see "Short Biographies of German Social Revolutionaries," *Min pao*, No. 2. For Chinese publications of nationalism, socialism, anarchism, and other revolutionary ideas by the end of Ch'ing dynasty see Chang Yü-ying, "Hsin-hai ke-ming shu-cheng" ("An Annotated Bibliography of Publications Concerning the 1911 Revolution"), *Hsüeh-lin* (Scholars' Circles), No. VI (Shanghai, April 1941), reprinted in Chang Ching-lu 9, comp. and noted, Source Material for the History of Publication in Modern China, Part I (Shanghai, 1953), pp. 140–83; also Chang Yü-ying, "Hsin-hai ke-ming tsa-chih lu" ("An Annotated Bibliography of Periodicals Concerning the 1911 Revolution"), *Hsüeh-lin*, No. VI, reprinted in Chang Ching-lu 9, Source Material for Publication History, pp. 97–103; the list of Chinese publications abroad and at home before 1911 in Feng Tzu-yu's *Ke-ming i-shih* (An Informal History of the 1911 Revolution), III, reprinted in Chang Ching-lu *10*, Source Material for Publication History, Part II (Shanghai, 1954), pp. 276–96.

69. Ching Mei-chiu, *Tsui-an* (The "Criminal" Case), pp. 72–76.

70. Chiang [Kiang] K'ang-hu, *Chin-shih san ta chu-i yü Chung-kuo* (The Three Grand Isms of the Modern Times and China) (Peking, 1924), pp. 37–38; also *Ming-ho chi* (Chiang K'ang-hu's Will) (Peking, 1927), p. 21.

71. Sanetō, Influences of Japanese Civilization upon China, pp. 105–06.

72. Shu Hsin-ch'eng *412*, History of Chinese Students Studying Abroad, pp. 278–79; Sanetō, Influences of Japanese Civilization upon China, pp. 65–84, 106–61; Pan-su, Chronological Records of Important Events of China, p. 188; *Chiao-yü tsa-chih* (The Chinese Educational Review), X, 6 (May 1918), p. 45; and Li Chien-nung *289*, Political History of China, Vol. II, Chap. XII, p. 517.

73. Yü Chia-chü and others, ed., *Chung-kuo chiao-yü tz'u-tien* (Encyclopaedia of Chinese Education) (3rd ed.; Shanghai, 1928, 1930), p. 46; Shu Hsin-ch'eng *412*, History of Chinese Students Studying Abroad, p. 279; The Chinese Educational Review, X, 6, p. 45.

74. "Ko-sheng liu-Hu hsüeh-sheng tsung-hui ti-i-tz'u chien-chang" ("The Draft Program of the Alliance of Students in Shanghai from All Provinces"), in *Chiang-ning hsüeh-wu* (Educational Affairs of Chiang-ning-fu) (Nanking, 1906), reprinted in Shu Hsin-ch'eng *410*, comp., Source Material for an Educational History of Modern China (Shanghai, 1928), IV, 169.

75. *Ibid.*, pp. 168–70.

76. See Chu Ching-nung and others, comps., *Chiao-yü ta tz'u-shu* (Encyclopaedia of Education) (Shanghai, 1930), pp. 1549–50.

77. Hu Shih *205*, Diary, Vol. IV, No. 42, "A View of Japanese Civilization Expressed by A Chinese Student in Japan," May 2, 1915, pp. 621–22; Sanetō, Influences of Japanese Civilization Upon China, pp. 85–105. Although not very good fiction, the novel by [P'ing-chiang-] Pu-hsiao-sheng [pseudonym of Hsiang K'ai-jan], *Liu-tung wai-shih* (Romances of Chinese Students in Japan) (2nd printing; Shanghai, 1925), described some of the real situations of Chinese students in Japan. Ch'en Tu-hsiu thought that many Chinese students in Japan might be classified in two categories: they learned from Japan either patriotism

or the doctrine of treason (New Youth, VII, 2 [Jan. 1, 1920], pp. 155–56). This is of course an oversimplification.

78. See John Dewey *620*, "New Culture in China," *Asia*, XXI, 7 (New York, July 1921), p. 583.

79. Hu Shih *198*, "Ch'en Tu-hsiu and the Literary Revolution," in Ch'en Tung-hsiao *74*, ed., Discussions on Ch'en Tu-hsiu (Peiping, 1933), pp. 53–54. Hu said, "He [Ch'en] was greatly influenced by French civilization; he could read both English and French."

80. New Youth, I, 1 (Shanghai, Sept. 15, 1915), pp. 7–10.

81. The weekly was suspended in the summer of 1910. The articles published in it were later collected and reprinted as *Hsin shih-chi ts'ung-shu* (The New Century Series) and *Wu cheng-fu chu-i ts'ui-yen* (The Quintessence of Anarchism). See Wen-ting, "The Biography of Liu Shih-fu," in T'ieh-hsin, ed., *Shih-fu wen ts'un* (Collected Essays of [Liu] Shih-fu (2nd printing; Canton, 1927–1928), pp. 3–4; Jung Meng-yüan, "Hsin-hai ke-ming ch'ien Chung-kuo shu-k'an shang tui Ma-k'e-ssu chu-i ti chieh-shao" ("Introduction of Marxism in Chinese Publications before the 1911 Revolution"), *Hsin chien-she* (New Construction), No. 54 (Peking, March 1953), p. 7; also see John Dewey, "New Culture in China," p. 585.

82. Liu Fa chien-hsüeh-hui *387*, "Pei-ching liu Fa chien-hsüeh-hui chien-chang" ("Regulations of the Society for Frugal Study in France of Peking"), New Youth, III, 2 (April 1, 1917). Also see Shu Hsin-ch'eng *412*, History of Chinese Students Studying Abroad, Chap. VIII, pp. 86–88.

83. *Ibid.*, pp. 88–91; "Liu Fa ch'in-kung chien-hsüeh ti li-shih" ("A History of Frugal Study by Means of Labor"), *Kung-hsüeh* (Work-and-Study), No. 2 (Peking 1921) mimeographed.

84. Anonymous *148*, "Fa-kuo chao chih Hua kung" ("The French Recruitment of Chinese Workers"), The Eastern Miscellany, XIV, 2 (Feb. 15, 1917); Ch'en Ta *590*, *Chinese Migrations, with Special Reference to Labor Conditions*, Bulletin of the U.S. Bureau of Labor Statistics, Department of Labor, No. 340 (Washington, D.C., 1923), Chap. IX, p. 143.

85. *Ibid.*, pp. 143–46.

86. W. Reginald Wheeler, *China and the World War* (New York, 1919), Chap. VIII, pp. 150–51. Ts'ai Yüan-p'ei said that at the end of the war there were about 150,000 Chinese workers working for the Allies in France, in his *456*, "The Divinity of Labor," New Youth, V, 5 (Nov. 15, 1918), 438.

87. See "Council of Ten, Jan. 15, 1919, 10:30 a.m.," in U.S. Department of State, *The Paris Peace Conference* (Washington, D.C., 1919), III, 567. Ts'ui Shu-ch'in gave the same number in "The Influence of the Canton-Moscow Entente upon Sun Yat-sen's Political Philosophy," *Chinese Social and Political Science Review* (Peiping, April–Oct. 1934). H. F. MacNair gives 50,000 Chinese with the French and 150,000 with the British in *The Chinese Abroad* (Shanghai, 1924), p. 235. For various estimates of the number, see also Min-ch'ien T. Z. Tyau *762*, *China Awakened*, Chap. XIII, p. 239; and "China at the Peace Conference," in The Diplomatic Association, *Far Eastern Political Science Review* (in English), special number (Canton, Aug. 1919), p. 113; Judith Blick *572*, "The Chinese Labor Corps in World War I," *Harvard Papers on China* (Cambridge, Mass., 1955), Vol. 9, pp. 111–45.

88. Anonymous *148*, "The French Recruitment of Chinese Workers," The Eastern Miscellany, XIV, 2; Ch'en Ta *590*, *Chinese Migrations*, pp. 142–43.

89. Yü Chia-chü and others, Encyclopaedia of Chinese Education, pp. 353–54.

90. Ch'en Ta *590*, *Chinese Migrations*, pp. 147–48.

91. "Hui Min Contract for Common Laborers" (Articles 13, 17), *ibid.*, pp. 207–10.

92. See Ch'en Ch'un-sui [Ch'en Teng-ch'ioh], Romances of the Chinese Students in the West (2nd ed.; Shanghai, 1927, 1928), a novel imitating Pu-hsiao-sheng's Romances of Chinese Students in Japan.

93. Ch'en Ta *590, Chinese Migrations,* pp. 152–54. Also Min-ch'ien T. Z. Tyau *762, China Awakened,* p. 239; Y.M.C.A., National War Work Council, *Summary of World War Work of the American Y.M.C.A.* (New York, 1920), p. 239; and Y.M.C.A., *Service With Fighting Men,* 2:365–6 (New York, 1922).

94. "Records of Current Affairs," The Chinese Educational Review, XIX, 9 (Sept. 1927), p. 2; Pearl S. Buck, *Tell the People — Mass Education in China* (New York, 1945), p. 8–9.

95. Kuo-wu-yüan ch'iao-kung-shih-wu-chü (The Bureau of Labor Emigration, State Council), ed., *Tiao-ch'a tsai Fa Hua kung ch'ing-hsing shu* (Report on Conditions of Chinese Laborers in France), No. 3 (Peking, Dec. 1918), pp. 29–31; No. 5 (April 1919), p. 23–25; No. 7 (Sept. 1919), pp. 27–28; also Ch'en Ta *590, Chinese Migration,* pp. 150–1.

96. *Ibid.,* p. 157; Yü Chia-chü and others, Encyclopaedia of Chinese Education; Shu Hsin-ch'eng *412,* History of Chinese Students Studying Abroad, pp. 90–99. Some sources give the year as 1919; it seems to be 1920. See also *Ch'in-kung chien-shüeh hsüeh-sheng ü chiao-yü-hui sheng ssu kuan-t'ou* (The Life and Death Struggle between the Work-and-Study Students and the Societé Franco-Chinoise d'Education), mimeographed pamphlet signed by 74 students in France on May 8, 1920.

97. Min-ch'ien T. Z. Tyau *762, China Awakened,* pp. 238–41; see also Harold R. Isaacs *661, The Tragedy of the Chinese Revolution* (rev. ed.; Stanford, 1951), Chap. IV, p. 55.

98. See Wu Yü-chang *532,* "In Memory of Ts'ai Yüan-p'ei," Chinese Culture, No. 2 (Yenan, April 1940); see also Chou-mo-pao she (The Week-End News), ed., *Hsin Chung-kuo jen-wu chih* (Who's Who of New China) (Hong Kong, 1950), pp. 30ff; and Edgar Snow *739, Red Star over China* (New York, 1938, 1944), Part IV, Chap. IV, pp. 157–58.

CHAPTER III

THE INITIAL PHASE OF THE MOVEMENT:
EARLY LITERARY AND INTELLECTUAL ACTIVITIES, 1917–1919

1. See Ch'en Tung-hsiao *74,* ed., Discussions on Ch'en Tu-hsiu (Peiping, 1933), pp. 176–79, 203, 247; Ch'en Tu-hsiu, "Shih-an tzu-chuan" ("Autobiography"), in Yü-chou-feng she *562,* ed., A Chapter from Autobiographies (Kweilin, Kuangsi, 1938), pp. 14–33; Ho Chih-yü *169,* ed., galley proof of Complete Works of Ch'en Tu-hsiu (Shanghai, 1948), Vol. ; Wang Sen-jan *488,* Critical Biographies of Twenty Modern Chinese (Peiping, 1934), pp. 249–76; Benjamin Schwartz *734,* "Ch'en Tu-hsiu and the Acceptance of the Modern West," *Journal of the History of Ideas,* XII, 1 (Jan. 1951), pp. 61–62. Hu Shih did not believe, as he told the author, that Ch'en had been in France. But we find such record in 1919.

2. The Provisional Constitution of the Republic of China, Chap. II, Art. VI, Sec. 4.

3. *Ibid.,* Art. XV.

4. The law was promulgated in Dec. 1912. For a partial text of it see [Li] Chien-nung 288, "The Right of Freedom of Speech and Publication in the Chinese Constitution," The Pacific Ocean, II, 1 (2nd printing; May 5, 1920), p. 3.

5. See Kao I-han 256, "Comments on the Security and Police Regulations," New Youth, VII, 2 (Jan. 1, 1920), pp. 15–23. The regulation was first proclaimed on March 2, 1914, by Yüan as Ordinance No. 28 and later approved by his controlled State Council.

6. The regulation was promulgated on March 3, 1914. See Hu Shih, Chiang Monlin, etc. 227, "Manifesto of Struggle for Freedom," reprinted in The Eastern Miscellany, XVII 6 (Aug. 25, 1920), p. 134. Also see Kao I-han, "Pao-lü ssu-i" ("An Individual Discussion of the Press Law"), Chia-yin jih-k'an (The Tiger Daily) (1918).

7. The Press Regulation was promulgated on April 2, 1914. See Hu Shih, Chiang Mon lin, etc. 227, "Manifesto of Struggle for Freedom," p. 134. For the text of Chinese press laws of the period 1901–15, see Ko Kung-chen 260, History of Chinese Journalism (2nd ed.; Shanghai, 1927, 1928), Chap. VI, Sec. 17, pp. 332–71, reprinted in Chang Ching-lu 9 and 10, comp., Source Material of the Publication History of Modern China, Part I (Shanghai, 1953), pp. 311–13; Part II (Shanghai, 1954), pp. 397–418.

8. The law was promulgated on Dec. 4, 1914. See [Li] Chien-nung 288, "The Right of Freedom of Speech and Publication," pp. 3–5.

9. Ko Kung-Chen 260, History of Chinese Journalism, Chap. V, pp. 181–84.

10. Wang Sen-jan 488, Critical Biographies, pp. 250–51.

11. See Yang Chih-hua 535, ed., Historical Materials on Chinese Literary Circles (Shanghai, 1944), pp. 361–62; "Editor's Note," New Youth, IX, 1; also article by Fu Ssu-nien on Ch'en Tu-hsiu, in Ch'en Tung-hsaio 74, Discussions on Ch'en Tu-hsiu. For the latest Communist interpretation of New Youth see Chung-kung chung-yang 556, ed., An Introduction to the Periodicals in the May Fourth Period (Peking, 1958), I, 1–40.

12. See Ko Kung-chen 260, History of Chinese Journalism, Chap. III, pp. 67–70.

13. Ch'en Tu-hsiu 49, "Call to Youth," New Youth, I, 1 (Sept. 15, 1915), pp. 1–2; a complete English translation may be found in Ssu-yü Teng and John K. Fairbank 745, China's Response to the West, a Documentary Survey, 1839–1923 (Cambridge, Mass. 1954). Chap. VII, Doc. 59, pp. 240–41. The necessity of awakening the intellectuals was also emphasized in Ch'en's article 67, "Our Final Awakening," New Youth, I, 6 (Feb. 15, 1916), pp. 1–4. See Kiang Wen-han 666, The Chinese Student Movement (New York, 1948), Chap. I, p. 23.

14. Ch'en Tu-hsiu 49, "Call to Youth," p. 2.

15. Ch'en's answer to Ch'ang Nai-te, "Letters to the Editor," New Youth, III, 1 (March 1, 1917), pp. 15–16.

16. See Ts'ai Yüan-p'ei 462, "My Experiences in Educational Circles," in Yü-chou-feng she 562, ed., Chapter from Autobiographies, pp. 1–13; Ch'eng Chün-ying, Chung-kuo ta chiao-yü-chia (Great Educators of China) (Shanghai, 1948), Chap. XVI, pp. 89–91; Chia I-chün, ed., Chung-hua-min-kuo ming-jen chuan (Biographies of Famous People of the Republic of China) (Peiping, 1932), Vol. II, Chap. I, pp. 21–47; Ts'ai Shang-ssu 447, Biography of Ts'ai Yüan-p'ei, with Emphasis on His Scholarship and Thought (Shanghai, 1950); Robert K. Sakai 732, "Ts'ai Yüan-p'ei as a Synthesizer of Western and Chinese Thought," Harvard Papers on China (Cambridge, Mass., May 1949), Vol. 3, 170–92.

17. "Records of Current Affairs," The Chinese Educational Review, IX, 1 (Jan. 1917), p. 5.

18. Kung-shih [pen name] 270, "The Establishment and Development of Peking University," The Eastern Miscellany, XVI, 3 (March 15, 1919), pp. 161–63; Lo Tun-yung, "Ching-shih ta-hsüeh-t'ang ch'eng-li chi" ("A Record of the Establishment of the Im-

perial University"), in Shu Hsin-ch'eng *410*, ed., Source Materials for a History of Modern Chinese Education (Shanghai, 1923), Vol. I, Chap. I, pp. 157–61; *Kuo-li Pei-ching ta-hsueh i-lan* (A General View of the National University of Peking) (Peking, 1935), pp. 1–2; W. A. P. Martin, *The Awakening of China* (New York, 1907), p. 120; and Renville Clifton Lund *685*, "The Imperial University of Peking," doctoral dissertation for the University of Washington, 1956.

19. Ching-kuan [pen name] *112*, "Present Situation of the National University of Peking," The Eastern Miscellany, XVI, 3 (March 15, 1919), p. 164; and Paul Monroe *691*, "A Report on Education in China (for American Educational Authorities)," *Bulletin* of the Institute of International Education, Ser. III, No. 4 (Oct. 20, 1922), p. 34. Also anonymous *386*, "An Account of the Peking Government-Schools' Movement for the Independence of Educational Finance," Educational Magazine, II, 2, 3, 4 (Peking, 1921), also in Shu Hsin-ch'eng *410*, ed., Source Materials for a History of Modern Chinese Education, III, Chap. 20, p. 152.

20. The figures for both tables are from Kung-shih *270*, "Establishment of Peking University," p. 162; See also Ching-kuan *112*, "Present Situation of Peking University," p. 164 and Tsi C. Wang *771*, *Youth Movement in China*, Chap. VII, p. 109.

21. The number in parentheses is based on the account of Ching-kuan *112*, "Present Situation of Peking University," p. 165, with a minor revision. This version has perhaps included some auditing or special students.

22. Ts'ai Yüan-p'ei *462*, "My Experience in Educational Circles," in Yü-chou-feng she *562*, ed., Chapter from Autobiographies, pp. 1–13 and Ts'ai's *463*, "My Experiences at Peking University," The Eastern Miscellany (Jan. 1934), pp. 5–7; and Lo Tun-wei *346*, Reminiscences of the Last Fifty Years (Taipei, Taiwan, 1952), Chap. IV, p. 18; also Ts'ai Yüan-p'ei *457*, "The Aims of the Society for the Promotion of Virtue of Peking University," in his *461*, Life and Works of Ts'ai Yüan-p'ei (Peking, 1920), II, 310–11.

23. Ts'ai Yüan-p'ei *450*, "The Inaugural Address on Taking the Chancellorship of Peking University," *ibid.*, pp. 292–96.

24. Ts'ai Yüan-p'ei *458*, "Preface," National University of Peking Monthly, No. 1 (Peking, Nov. 1918), reprinted in his *461*, Life and Works of Tsai, I, 226–30; also see Kiang Wen-han *666*, *Chinese Student Movement*, Chap. I, p. 26; and Ts'ai's letter to Lin Shu, below, pp. 71–72.

25. See "Record of Current Affairs," The Chinese Educational Review, IX, 3 (Sept. 1917), p. 18. For the text of the order see Kuo-wu-yüan (State Council), *Fa-ling-chi-lan hsü-pien* (Collection of Laws and Orders, Supplement) (Peking, 1920), Vol. III, Part 12, Chap. I, pp. 3–4; also Yüan Hsiang and others, comps., *Chung-kuo nien-chien* (China Year Book), No. 1 (Shanghai, 1924), p. 2001.

26. See Ts'ai Yüan-p'ei *461*, Life and Works, I, 276–80.

27. Ts'ai Yüan-p'ei *457*, "The Aims of the Society for the Promotion of Virtue of Peking University," in *ibid.*, II, 303–10; also Ts'ai *462*, "My Experience in Educational Circles," pp. 91–101; Tsi C. Wang *771*, *Youth Movement in China*, Chap. VII, p. 109. For the origin of the Society see *Min-li pao* (Feb. 27, 1912).

28. See T'ieh-hsin, ed., "Editor's Introduction," *Shih-fu wen-ts'un* (Collected Essays of [Liu] Shih-fu) (2nd ed.; Canton, 1927, 1928), p. 1, and Wen-ting, "The Biography of [Liu] Shih-fu," *ibid.*, p. 4.

29. Ts'ai Yüan-p'ei, "Tui-yü chiao-yü fang-chen chih i-chien" ("Views on the Aims of Education") in Ts'ai *461*, Life and Works, pp. 189–203, esp. pp. 197–98. Complete English translation of text in Ssu-yü Teng and John K. Fairbank *745*, *China's Response to the West*, Chap. XXIV, pp. 235–38.

30. T'ang Leang-li *743*, *The New Social Order in China* (Shanghai, 1936), Chap. IX, p. 143.

31. See Ts'ai Yüan-p'ei, "Tu-hsiu wen-ts'un hsü ("Preface to the *Collected Essays of Ch'en Tu-hsiu*"), in Ch'en Tu-hsiu *62*, Collected Essays (12th ed.; Shanghai, 1922, 1939), pp. i–iii; New Youth, II, 5 (Jan. 1, 1917); Ts'ai Yüan-p'ei *463*, "My Experience at Peking University," pp. 5–8; also Kuo Chan-po *271*, An Intellectual History of China in the Last Fifty Years (2nd ed.; Peiping, 1935, 1936), pp. 100–01.

32. Books and articles in Chinese on Lu Hsün's life and works have been voluminous. The most recent and comprehensive biographies are Ts'ao Chü-jen *468*, A Critical Biography of Lu Hsün (Hong Kong, 1956), and his *467*, "A Chronological Biography of Lu Hsün," The Literary Century, No. 1 (Hong Kong, June 1957), pp. 26–27, and the following issues. See also Wang Shih-ching *491*, Biography of Lu Hsün (Shanghai and Hong Kong, 1948), and the English thesis by Huang Sung-k'ang *656*, *Lu Hsün and the New Culture Movement of Modern China* (Amsterdam, 1957). All the above are more or less from leftist viewpoints. See also Oda Takeo *379*, Biography of Lu Hsün (Chinese translation, Shanghai, 1946). For an unfavorable biography by a Trotskyist see Cheng Hsüeh-chia *82*, The True Story of Lu Hsün (Chungking, 1942).

33. See Lao Yung, "Wu-ssu yün-tung ti ling-tao-che Li Ta-chao" ("Leader of the May Fourth Movement, Li Ta-chao") in Wu-ssu sa chou-nien chi-nien chuan-chi pien-wei-hui *524*, ed., A Symposium for the Thirtieth Anniversary of "May Fourth" (Shanghai, 1949), pp. 139–49; Chin Yü-fu *111*, "Li Ta-chao and the May Fourth Movement," Observer, VI, 13 (Shanghai, May 1, 1950), pp. 12–14; and Li Lung-mu, "Li Ta-chao t'ung-chih ho Wu-ssu shih-ch'i Ma-k'e-ssu chu-i ssu-hsiang ti hsüan-ch'uan" ("Comrade Li Ta-chao and the Spread of Marxist Thought in China during the May Fourth Period"), *Li-shih yen-chiu* (Historical Studies), V (Peking, May 1957), pp. 1–18. For Li's works see his *301*, Collected Essays of Li Ta-chao (Shanghai, 1933, 1949, 1950).

34. See Fu Ssu-nien *157*, "Retrospect and Outlook of the *New Tide*," New Tide, II, 1 (Oct. 1919), pp. 119–205; Hsü Yen-chih *183*, "A Record of the New Tide Society," *ibid.*, II, 2 (Dec. 1919), pp. 398–402; Meng Shou-ch'un *372*, "A record of the Society," *ibid.*, II, 5 (Sept. 1920), pp. 1073–76.

35. Hu Shih *198*, "Ch'en Tu-hsiu and the Literary Revolution," a speech delivered at Peking University on Oct. 30, 1932, when Ch'en was imprisoned and tried in Nanking by the National Government, in Ch'en Tung-hsiao *74*, ed., Discussions on Ch'en Tu-hsiu, p. 51.

36. Ch'en Tu-hsiu, letter to Ch'eng Yen-sheng, "Letters to the Editor," New Youth, II, 6 (Feb. 1, 1917).

37. Ch'en Tu-hsiu *56*, "Our Answer to the Charges against the Magazine," *ibid.*, VI, 1 (Jan. 15, 1919), pp. 10–11.

38. [Fu Ssu-nien] *158*, "Aims of the Establishment of New Tide," New Tide (Peking, Jan. 1, 1919), pp. 1–3. English translation in Tsi C. Wang *771*, *Youth Movement in China*, Chap. VII, pp. 111–12, here revised by us.

39. Lo Chia-lun *336*, "The New Tide of the World of Today," New Tide, I, 1 (Jan. 1919), p. 19.

40. *Ibid.*, p. 20.

41. Fu Ssu-nien *159*, "Social Revolution — the Russian Type of Revolution," *ibid.*, pp. 128–29.

42. Lo Chia-lun *336*, "New Tide of the World Today," pp. 20–21.

43. *Ibid.*, p. 22.

44. Ching-kuan *112*, "Present Situation of Peking University," p. 165.

45. See *Kung-yen pao* (Public Opinion Daily) (Peking, March 18, 1919). The daily was owned by the warlords. See also Li Ho-lin *292*, On the Thought Tide of Chinese Literature in the Last Twenty Years (3rd ed.; Shanghai and Hong Kong, 1939, 1948), Chap. I, p. 10.

46. Tsi C. Wang *771*, *Youth Movement in China*, Chap. IX, p. 144.

47. See Yen Fu *552*, "Selected and Abridged Letters to Hsiung Shun-ju," The Critical Review, No. 20 (Aug. 1924), pp. 1–5; the letters were not dated, but apparently written between 1914 and 1920. Also in Chang Jo-ying *20*, ed., Source Materials for China's New Literature Movement (Shanghai, 1934), Chap. III, p. 110. See also Chou Chen-fu, *Yen Fu ssu-hsiang shu-p'ing* (An Account and Evaluation of Yen Fu's Thought) (Shanghai, 1940), Part III, pp. 251–310, especially pp. 301–10; Wang Chü-ch'ang, *Yen Chi-tao nien-p'u* (A Chronological Biography of Yen Fu) (Shanghai, 1936).

48. See Han-kuang *165*, Biography of Lin Shu (Shanghai, 1935), Chap. IV, pp. 65–135; Yang Yin-shen, *Chung-kuo wen-hsüeh chia lieh chuan* (Biographies of Chinese Men of Letters) (Shanghai, [1936?]), pp. 485–86. Also Chow Tse-tsung, "Lin Shu nien-p'u" ("A Chronological Biography of Lin Shü") (in manuscript).

49. Ch'ien Hsüan-t'ung *107*, "Letter to the Editor," New Youth, III, 1 (March 1, 1917), pp. 6–7.

50. Cited in Hu Shih, "Letter to the Editor," *ibid.*, III, 3 (May 1, 1917), pp. 4–5.

51. Cheng Chen-to *80*, "Introduction to the *Anthology of Essays concerning the Literary Controversy*," in Chao Chia-pi *33*, ed., A Corpus of China's New Literature (Shanghai, 1935), II, 5–6; "Wang Ching-hsüan" *108*, "Reaction to the Literary Revolution," New Youth, IV, 3 (March 15, 1918), pp. 265–68; and the editor's answer by Liu Fu, *ibid.*, pp. 268–85.

52. Lin Shu *315*, "Ching-sheng the Giant," reprinted in Chao chia-pi *33*, ed., A Corpus of China's New Literature, I, 174–75.

53. Lin Shu *319*, "The Nightmare," reprinted in *ibid.*, II, 431–33.

54. See Liu Fu, "*Ch'u-ch'i pai-hua shih kao pien-che hsü*" ("Editor's Preface to Manuscripts of Poems in the Vernacular in the Early Period") (Peiping, 1933), pp. 3–4.

55. Lin Shu *312*, "Letter to Ts'ai Yüan-p'ei," Public Opinion Daily (Peking, March 18, 1919).

56. Ts'ai Yüan-p'ei *444*, "Letter to the *Public Opinion Daily* and Answer to Lin Shu," reprinted in *461*, Life and Works, II, 314–35. The last part of the letter has been translated in Teng and Fairbank *745*, *China's Response to the West*, Chap. XXIV, pp. 238–39.

57. "K'ung Jung chuan" ("Biography of K'ung Jung"), *Hou-Han shu* (History of the Later Han), Chap. 100.

58. Pei-ching-jen pi-pao-she *382*, "A Short Account of the May Fourth Movement," The World Daily (Peiping, May 4, 1947), p. 4.

59. Cheng Chen-to *80*, "Introduction to *Literary Controversy*," p. 7; Li Ho-lin *292*, Thought Tide of Chinese Literature, Chap I, p. 10.

60. "Shen-mo hua" ("What Nonsense"), New Youth, VI, 4 (April 15, 1919), p. 446. For rumors of government intervention and public opinion backing of Peking University see Ch'en Tu-hsiu's article of March 16, 1, 19, "Kuan-yü Pei-ching ta-hsüeh ti yao-yen" ("Rumors concerning Peking University"), in Ch'en Tu-hsiu *62*, Collected Essays, I, 601–05.

61. Tsi C. Wang *771*, *Youth Movement in China*, Chap. VI, p. 100.

62. Chang Ching-lu *10*, comp., Source Material for the History of Publication in Modern China, Part II, pp. 315–16.

63. Pi Yün-ch'eng, "Letter to the Editor," New Youth, II, 1 (Sept. 1, 1916), p. 6.

64. See Edgar Snow 739, *Red Star over China* (New York, 1944), pp. 144–45; Hsiao San *178*, The Youth of Comrade Mao Tse-tung (3rd ed.; Shanghai, 1949, 1950), pp. 61–62, 81–82; Lo Tun-wei *346*, Reminiscences of the Last Fifty Years, Chap. IV, p. 18.

65. Edgar Snow 739, *Red Star over China*, pp. 146–47; Hsiao San *178*, The Youth of Mao, pp. 82–84.

66. See Shen I-chia, "An-hui liu-Fa ch'in-kung chien-hsüeh-sheng ti-i-tz'u pao-kao shu" ("Report on the Anhwei Work-and-Study Students in France, No. I"), *An-hui chiao-yü yüeh-k'an* (Anhwei Education Monthly), Nos. 24, 25; Hsiao San *178*, The Youth of Mao, pp. 89–90, 95; Snow 739, *Red Star over China*, pp. 149, 151–52.

67. *Ibid.*, pp. 146–48.

68. Materials for the history of the Kuomintang abound. The standard one is still Tsou Lu's *Chung-kuo kuo-min-tang shih-kao* (Draft History of the Kuomintang), 4 Vols. (Shanghai, 1929; rev. ed., Chungking, 1944).

69. See Yang Yu-chiung 547, A History of Chinese Political Parties (2nd ed.; Shanghai, 1936, 1937), Chap. VI, p. 109; Hsieh Pin, *Min-kuo cheng-tang shih* (History of Political Parties in the Republic of China) (rev. 4th ed.; Shanghai, 1926), Chaps. VII–IX, pp. 53–87; T'ao Chü-yin, *Chiang Po-li hsien-sheng chuan* (Biography of Chiang Po-li) (Shanghai, 1948), Chap. IX, p. 77; New Youth, VI, 4 (April 15, 1919), pp. 398–426.

70. See "Letter to the Editor," *ibid.*, VI, 3 (March 15, 1919), pp. 337–38.

71. Gotō Shimpei, "Jih-Chih ch'ung-t'u chih chen-hsiang" ("Real Situation of the Conflict between Japan and China"), cited in Wang Yün-sheng *498*, Sixty Years' Relation between China and Japan, Vol. VII, Chap. LXIII, pp. 58–71.

72. See Wang Yün-sheng *498*, Sixty Years' Relation (Tientsin, 1934), Vol. VII, Chap. LXVIII, pp. 128–31; Shōda Kazue, narrator, *Kiku no newake, Nisshi keizaijō no shisetsu ni tsuite* (The Separation of the Chrysanthemums' Roots, on the Institution of a Sino-Japanese Economy) (printed for private distribution by the Jijokai, 1918; 2nd printing, 1933).

73. See Hayashi's article cited in Wang Yün-sheng *498*, Sixty Years' Relation, Vol. VII, Chap. LXVIII, pp. 131–34.

74. See U.S. State Department *764*, *Papers Relating to the Foreign Relations of the United States, 1919* (Washington, D.C., 1934), I, 361–62; Yang Yu-chiung *547*, History of Chinese Political Parties, Chap. VI, pp. 107–10; Fei Ching-chung, *Tuan Ch'i-jui* (in Chinese) (Shanghai, 1921); Chia I-chün, *Chung-hua min-kuo shih* (History of the Republic of China) (Peiping, 1930), Chap. VI, pp. 52–54; and T'ao Chü-yin, *Pei-yang chün-fa t'ung-chih shih-ch'i shih-hua* (An Informal History of the Period Under the Rule of the Northern Chinese Warlords) (Peking, 1957), Vol. IV.

75. For text of some of the four secret agreements see Wang Yün-sheng *498*, Sixty Years' Relation, Vol. VII, Chap. LXII, pp. 42–44.

76. See Wang Yün-sheng *498*, *ibid.*, Chap. LXIX, pp. 212–37; William C. Dennis (legal adviser to the Peking government) *608*, "Notes on Secret Diplomacy," *The Chinese Social and Political Science Review*, V, 2 (Peking, June 1919), p. 104.

77. See Chia I-chün, ed., Biographies of the Famous People of the Republic of China, I, 31–32; also *Who's Who in China, 1926* (Shanghai, 1927). In the fall of 1917 the paper reported that Tuan Ch'i-jui was able to retain premiership because of Japanese interference. This drew the protest from the Japanese minister in Peking on Nov. 20. The paper was consequently suppressed. The two events might be related. See *Wai-chiao pu chiao-she chieh-yao* (Abridged Records of the Negotiations of the Foreign Ministry) (Peking, Nov. 1917), pp. 2a–3b.

78. See Kuo Mo-jo *273*, Autobiography of a Revolutionary (Shanghai, 1947, 1951), pp. 35–37, 60–61.

79. For the organization of the Corps of Chinese Students in Japan for National Salvation see "Records of Current Affairs," The Chinese Educational Review, X, 6 (Shanghai, June 20, 1918), pp. 45–46. For the Chinese students' episode with the Japanese police on the eve of May 7, 1918, see Wang Kung-pi, *Tung-yu hui-han lu* (Memoir on Study in Japan Written in Sweat) (Shanghai, 1919), Chapter "Ch'i-nien wu-ch'i chih ch'ien-hsi" ("The Eve of May 7, 1918"), reprinted in Chung-kuo k'o-hsüeh-yüan, li-shih yen-chiu-so ti-san-so, ed., *Chin-tai shih tzu-liao* (Source Material of Modern Chinese History), No. 5 (Peking, April 1955), pp. 108–18.

80. For the full text of the order see "Current Affairs," The Chinese Educational Review, X, 6 (June 20, 1918), pp. 37–38.

81. See *Chui-tao Tseng Ch'i hsien-sheng chi-nien k'an* (A Memorial Pamphlet in Mourning for Tseng Ch'i) (Washington, D.C., 1951), pp. 1–2.

82. Tso Shun-sheng *472*, Recollections of the Last Thirty Years (Kowloon, 1952), Chap. II, pp. 3–4.

83. Chang Pao-en *24*, "Concerning the Young China Association," Freedom Front Weekly, XV, 1 (Kowloon, Dec. 3, 1949), pp. 18–19.

84. Tso Shun-sheng *472*, Recollections of the Last Thirty Years, pp. 4–5. Article VIII of the Organizational Regulation of the Association.

85. Ch'en Tu-hsiu published in the *Shao-chung hui-wu pao-kao* (Official Report of the Young China Association) his article "Wo-men ying-kai tsen-yang" ("What Should We Do?"), which was reprinted in New Youth, VI, 4 (April 15, 1919), pp. 447–49.

86. Hua Kang *230*, History of the May Fourth Movement (Shanghai, 1951, 1952), Chap. VI, p. 111.

87. See "Current Affairs," Chinese Educational Review, X, 6 (June 20, 1918), pp. 44–45.

88. "Records of Chinese Affairs," The Eastern Miscellany, XV, 7 (Shanghai, July 15, 1918), p. 195.

89. Kua Kang *230*, History of the May Fourth Movement, Chap. VI, p. 111.

90. Ts'ai Yüan-p'ei *454*, "Opening Article for the *Citizens Magazine*," written in Jan. 1919, reprinted in Ts'ai's *461*, Life and Works, II, 417–20. See also Chang Kuo-t'ao's English memoir (in manuscript).

91. See Li Tien-yi *681*, *Woodrow Wilson's China Policy, 1913–1917* (New York, 1952), Chap. V, "Wilson's Support of Yuan Shih-k'ai," pp. 139ff; Wang Yün-sheng *490*, Sixty Years' Relation, Vol. VII, Chap. LXI, pp. 1–6, 8–14, 23–24; Paul S. Reinsch *707*, *An American Diplomat in China* (Garden City and Toronto, 1922), Chap. XV, pp. 175–76, 178–80, 187, 191.

92. *Ibid.*, Chap. XXIII, p. 275.

93. For the demands see *The North-China Herald*, CXXXI, 2700 (Shanghai, May 10, 1919), p. 388. The *Herald* translated the name as the Commercial Federation of Shanghai.

CHAPTER IV

THE MAY FOURTH INCIDENT

1. "Japanese Ultimatum to Germany," in John V. A. MacMurray *688*, ed., *Treaties and Agreements with and concerning China* (New York, 1921) II, 1167; see also Kung Chen-huang, ed., *Ch'ing-tao ch'ao* (The Storm of Tsingtao) (Shanghai, 1919), Chap. I,

reprinted in 523, Source Materials for the May Fourth Patriotic Movement (Peking, 1959), pp. 9–11, and *Ch'ing-chi wai-chiao shih-liao* (Diplomatic Documents in the Late Ch'ing Period), Vol. 130.

2. "The Kiao Chou [Kiaochow] Question" (editorial), *The Chinese Students' Monthly*, X, I (Ithaca, N.Y., Oct. 1914), p. 15; Suh Hu [Hu Shih], "Japan and Kiao-Chou," *ibid.*, p. 27.

3. "Special correspondence of the *New York Times*" from Peking, May 15, 1915, *New York Times*, June 20, 1915, Sec. III, p. 5.

4. See T. Z. Tyau 762, *China Awakened* (New York, 1922), Chap. XVIII, pp. 313–15.

5. Ch'en Tu-hsiu, "K'e-lin-te pei" ("The Von Ketteler Monument"), New Youth, V, 5 (Nov. 15, 1918), p. 449. The monument was known to the people in Peking as the "stony monument."

6. Ts'ai Yüan-p'ei 456, "Lao-kung shen-sheng" ("Divinity of the Laborer"), New Youth, V, 5 (Shanghai, Nov. 15, 1918), pp. 438–39; Li Ta-chao, "Shu-min ti sheng-li" ("Victory of the Plain People"), *ibid.*, pp. 436–38.

7. T'ao Li-kung [T'ao Meng-ho], "Ou-chan i-hou ti cheng-chih" ("Politics after the First World War"), *ibid.*, pp. 439–41; Hu Shih, "Wu-li chieh-chüeh yü chieh-chüeh wu-li," ("Solution by Armed Force or Solution of Armed Force"), *ibid.*, V, 6 (Dec. 15, 1918), p. 571–74. The four articles by Ts'ai, Li, T'ao, and Hu cited above were originally speeches on the occasion of celebration of the Allied victory in World War I.

8. See Russell H. Fifield 636, *Woodrow Wilson and the Far East* (New York, 1952), Chap. IV, p. 194.

9. *Ibid.*, Chap. III, pp. 144–45; Wang Yün-sheng 498, Sixty Years' Relation Between China and Japan (Tientsin, 1934), VII, 380–81; T. Z. Tyau 762, *China Awakened*, p. 316; also "China at the Peace Conference" (in English), in The Diplomatic Association, ed., *Far Eastern Political Science Review*, special number (Canton, Aug. 1919), pp. 106–7.

10. For an interesting account of this matter see Fifield 636, *Wilson and the Far East*, Chap. IV, pp. 182–87, 189; Tyau 762, *China Awakened*, pp. 315, 316.

11. See *The North-China Herald* (The weekly edition of the *North-China Daily News*), CXXXI, 2700 (May 10, 1919), p. 346.

12. See Wang Yün-sheng 498, Sixty Years' Relation, Vol. VII, Chap. 65, pp. 84–88, and Chap. 70, pp. 239–40. For the secret treaties see John V. A. MacMurray 688, ed., *Treaties and Agreements with and concerning China*, II, 1167–89; Chang Chung-fu, *Chung-hua min-kuo wai-chiao shih* (Diplomatic History of the Republic of China) (Chungking, 1943), Chap. VII, pp. 285–327, Chap. VIII, p. 329; Ch'en Po-wen, *Chung-Wo wai-chiao shih* (History of Diplomacy Between China and Russia) (Shanghai, 1928), Chap. IV, pp. 93, 100. For both English texts and the history of the secret understandings between Japan and the four powers see "The Correspondence of the *New York Times* from Paris," April 21, 1919, cited in The Diplomatic Association, ed., *Far Eastern Political Science Review* (Aug. 1919), pp. 25–31.

13. Wang Yün-sheng 498, Sixty Years' Relation, VII, 184–87; Tyau 762, *China Awakened*, pp. 422–25.

14. MacMurray 688, *Treaties and Agreements with and concerning China*, II, 1445–46; Chinest text of the notes in Wang Yün-sheng 498, Sixty Years' Relation, VII, 184–87; different English versions of the notes in T. Z. Tyau 762, *China Awakened*, pp. 425–26; see also the memorandum of an interview on Feb. 2, 1919, between Reinsch and Ch'en Lu about representations made by Obata earlier on Feb. 2, 1919, March 20, 1919, Paris Peace Conference 185.1158/51, cited in Fifield 636, *Wilson and the Far East*, Chap. III, pp. 145–47.

15. The Diplomatic Association, *Far Eastern Political Science Review*, p. 132.

16. See Fifield *636*, *Wilson and the Far East*, Chap. IV, p. 187.

17. See *ibid.*, Chap. III, pp. 144, 145; also Chap. IV, p. 187.

18. Lu Cheng-hsiang, "Confidential Telegram to the Chinese Ministry of Foreign Affairs" (in Chinese), Jan. 27, 1919, cited in Wang Yün-sheng *498*, Sixty Years' Relation, VII, 239–40.

19. See "Reinsch to Lansing," Feb. 15, 1919, Department of State 793.94/759.

20. See William C. Dennis *608*, "Notes on Secret Diplomacy," *The Chinese Social and Political Science Review*, V, 2 (Peking, June 1919), p. 104.

21. "The Claim of China for Direct Restitution to Herself of the Leased Territory of Kiaochow, the Tsingtao-Tsinan Railway and Other German Rights in Respect of Shantung Province," Feb. 15, 1919, cited in Tyau *762*, *China Awakened*, p. 397; Kung Chen-huang, ed., The Storm of Tsingtao, Chap. I, reprinted in *523*, Source Materials for the May Fourth Patriotic Movement, pp. 12–27.

22. Japanese Delegation to the Conference, Paris Peace Conference, "Quelques Observations sur le memorandum chinois demandant la restitution directe du territoire cédé à Bail de Kiaochéou," 1919.

23. For text of the treaty see MacMurray *688*, *Treaties and Agreements with and concerning China*, II, 1488; see also Kung Chen-huang, ed., the Storm of Tsingtao, Chap. I, reprinted in *523*, Source Materials for the May Fourth Patriotic Movement, pp. 32–39.

24. For text of the two memoranda submitted in April see Paris Peace Conference, 185.1158/75 and 185.1158/57. "The Questions for Readjustment submitted by China to the Peace Conference at Paris, April 1919" is also in Tyau *762*, *China Awakened*, pp. 430–59. For the Chinese texts see Wang Yün-sheng *498*, Sixty Years' Relation, VII, 311. An analysis of all the Chinese claims at the conference may be found in Fifield *636*, *Wilson and the Far East*, Chap. IV, pp. 197ff.

25. Ch'ien I-shih, *Chung-kuo wai-chiao shih* (History of Diplomacy of China), Chap. V, p. 156.

26. Stephen Bonsal, *Suitors and Suppliants* (New York, 1946), pp. 235, 238; also Fifield *636*, *Wilson and the Far East*, Chap. IV, pp. 194–95.

27. Ch'a-kung *6*, "A Record of the Student Strikes," Chinese Educational Circles, VIII, I (July 1919), reprinted in Shu Hsin-ch'eng *410*, ed., Source Materials for a History of Modern Chinese Education (Shanghai, 1928), Vol. III, Chap. 20, pp. 119–46; the article was also printed in book form under the name, Ch'a-an, ed., *Hsüeh-chieh feng-ch'ao chi* (A Record of the Student Strike) (Shanghai, Sept. 1919), and reprinted in *523*, Source Materials for the May Fourth Patriotic Movement, pp. 239–315; and The Diplomatic Association, *Far Eastern Political Science Review*, p. 125.

28. Pan-su, *Chung-shan ch'u-shih hou Chung-kuo liu-shih nien ta-shih chi* (Chronological Records of the Important Events of China in the Sixty Years after Sun Yat-sen's Birth) (enlarged ed.; Shanghai, 1929), p. 195.

29. Fifield *636*, *Wilson and the Far East*, Chap. IV, p. 188, 197; Wang Yün-sheng *498*, Sixty Years' Relation, VII, 241–44.

30. See *Telegrams Received by the Chinese Delegation in Support of Their Stand on the Shantung Question* (in English) (Paris, 1919). Most of the telegrams concerned the Shantung question.

31. *Ibid.*, p. 4.

32. *Ibid.*, p. 20.

33. Ku Hung-ming *670*, "Returned Student and Literary Revolution — Literacy and Education," *Millard's Review of the Far East*, IX, 11 (Shanghai, Aug. 16, 1919), p. 433.

34. Lu Cheng-hsiang, "Confidential Telegram to the Chinese Foreign Ministry" (in Chinese), April 22, 1919, cited in Wang Yün-sheng *498*, Sixty Years' Relation, VII, 314.

35. Quoted in Ch'ien I-shih, History of Diplomacy of China, Chap. VI, p. 161.

36. The Shanghai Students' Union, *The Students' Strike — An Explanation*, a leaflet published in English in 1919. It is preserved in the Missions Library of Union Theological Seminary, New York, and cited in Kiang Wen-han *666*, *The Chinese Student Movement* (New York: New Republic, Inc., 1948), Chap. I, p. 36.

37. An interview with an alumnus of the National University of Peking recalling his student days, as quoted in Tsi C. Wang *771*, *The Youth Movement in China* (New York, 1927), Chap. X, pp. 161–62.

38. *Ibid.*, p. 162.

39. Paul S. Reinsch *707*, *An American Diplomat in China* (Garden City: Doubleday, Page & Co., 1922), Chap. XXXI, pp. 361–62.

40. Bertrand Russell, *The Conquest of Happiness* (New York, 1930, reprinted as a Signet Book, 1951), Part II, Chap. 10, p. 88.

41. Pei-ching fu-wen she *384*, comp., Who's Who of Contemporary Officials and Eminent Gentry of China (Peking, 1919).

42. Cf. Chou Yü-t'ung *124*, "The Departed May Fourth," The Middle School Students Monthly (Shanghai, May 4, 1930), reprinted in Ts'ao Chü-jen, ed., *San-wen chia hsüan* (Selected Prose, No. I) (Shanghai, 1931), pp. 56–57.

43. See *ibid.*, p. 37; Ch'en Tuan-chih *73*, An Historical Evaluation of the May Fourth Movement (2nd ed.; Shanghai, 1935, 1936), Chap. XIII, p. 226; also Teng Chung-hsia *439*, A Short History of the Chinese Labor Movement (2nd ed.; [Yenan ?], 1930, 1949), Chap. I, pp. 5–6; also T'ieh-hsin, ed., *Shih-fu wen-ts'un* (Collected Essays of [Liu] Shih-fu) (2nd ed.; Canton, 1927, 1928), pp. 1–8, 53–56.

44. See Liang Ch'i-ch'ao *306*, An Introduction to the Scholarship of the Ch'ing Period, 1644–1911 (Shanghai, 1927), Chap. XXIV, pp. 132–37; Chap. XXVII, pp. 150–57; Takashi Oka, "The Philosophy of T'an Ssu-t'ung," *Harvard Papers on China* (Cambridge, Mass., Aug. 1955), Vol. 9, pp. 1–47; and T'an Ssu-t'ung ch'üan-chi (Complete Works of T'an Ssu-t'ung) (Peking, 1954), pp. 3–90, 515–16.

45. Chou Yü-t'ung *124*, "The Departed May Fourth," p. 37; Ch'en Tuan-chih *73*, Historical Evaluation of the May Fourth Movement (2nd ed.; Shanghai, 1933, 1936), p. 229.

46. Reinsch *707*, *An American Diplomat in China*, Chap. XXXI, p. 359.

47. Ch'a-kung *6*, "A Record of the Student Strikes," p. 121.

48. Ch'en Tu-hsiu, "Sui-kan-lu" ("Random Thoughts"), Weekly Critic (April 27, 1919), reprinted in *62*, Collected Essays of Ch'en Tu-hsiu, II, 32.

49. Ch'a-kung *6*, "A Record of the Student Strikes," p. 121; Wu Chung-pi, *Shang-hai pa-shih chiu-wang shih* (A History of the Shanghai Strike and National Salvation Movement) (Shanghai, 1919), reprinted in *523*, Source Materials for the May Fourth Patriotic Movement, p. 550.

50. *The North-China Herald*, CXXXI, 2700 (Shanghai, May 10, 1919), p. 347.

51. Ch'en Tuan-chih *73*, Historical Evaluation of the May Fourth Movement, Chap. XIII, p. 231.

52. A description by C. C. Su, trans. Tsi C. Wang *771*, *Youth Movement in China*, p. 163.

53. "Translated from a Chinese Document Written by a Student of the National University of Peking," trans. Tsi C. Wang, *ibid.*, pp. 163–64. See also Ts'ai Hsiao-chou and Yang Ching-kung *446*, eds., May Fourth (Peking, 1919), reprinted in part in Chung-kuo k'o-hsüeh-yüan, Li-shih yen-chiu-so (Department of Historical Studies, Academy of Sci-

ences), ed., *Chin-tai shih tzu-liao* (Source Materials for Modern Chinese History), No. 5 (Peking, April 1955), pp. 47–48; and Weekly Critic, No. 21 (May 11, 1919).

54. Hsü Te-heng *181*, "In Remembrance of May Fourth," *Wen-hui pao* (Shanghai, May 4, 1950).

55. See "Translated from a Chinese Document Written by a Student of the National University of Peking," trans. Tsi C. Wang *771*, *Youth Movement in China*, p. 163.

56. John and Alice Chipman Dewey *631*, *Letters from China and Japan*, ed. Evelyn Dewey (New York: E. P. Dutton & Co., 1920), pp. 246–47.

57. Ch'en Tuan-chih *73*, Historical Evaluation of the May Fourth Movement, p. 163.

58. For Ts'ao's brief in this case, see Chin-hsia-ko chu (Master of the Pavilion Cloaked in Rosy Clouds) 109, ed., Choice Examples of the Knife and Stylus [i.e., Judicial Decisions], (14th, rev. ed.; Shanghai, 1924, 1930).

59. *The North-China Herald*, CXXXI, 2701 (May 17, 1919), p. 417; see also Yüeh-tung hsien-ho [pen name], ed., *Mai-kuo-tse chih-erh, Ts'ao Ju-lin* (Ts'ao Ju-lin the traitor, No. 2) (Shanghai, 1919), reprinted in *523*, Source Materials for the May Fourth Patriotic Movement, pp. 652–53.

60. Ch'en Tuan-chih *73*, Historical Evaluation of the May Fourth Movement, p. 233. But according to C. F. Remer, "The students say this attack [on Ts'ao's house] was no part of the pre-arranged plan"; see his *771*, "The Revolt of the Chinese Students," *Asia*, Vol. XIX, No. 9 (New York, 1919), p. 932.

61. See Chou Yü-t'ung *124*, "The Departed May Fourth," p. 58.

62. Pao Tsun-p'eng *382*, History of the Youth Movement of Modern China (Taipei, 1953), Chap. II, p. 26.

63. Some reports say the meeting was held at T'ang-tzu hu-t'ung. For details see [Chu] Wen-shu *506*, "History of the May Fourth Movement," The Students' Magazine, X, 5 (Shanghai: May 5, 1923), p. 4; Weekly Critic, No. 21 (May 11, 1919); and Peking University: Pei-ching-jen pi-pao-she (Pekinese Wall-newspaper Society) *385*, ed., "A Short Account of the May Fourth Movement," in The World Daily (Peking, May 4, 1947), p. 4.

64. *Ibid.*; also Wen-shu *506*, "History of the May Fourth Movement," p. 4. According to the recollection of a student at the National University of Peking, "representatives of about eighteen leading schools in Peking" attended this meeting; Tsi C. Wang *771*, *Youth Movement in China*, p. 164.

65. "Translated from a Chinese Document Written by a Student of the National University of Peking," *ibid.*, p. 165.

66. Lo Chia-lun, "Wu-ssu yün-tung hsüan-yen" (The Manifesto of the May Fourth Movement), in his *339*, From Dark Clouds, to Cloudbursts, to Bright Sunset (Chungking, 1943), p. 1. About the meeting and the demonstration see Kung Chen-huang, ed., The Storm of Tsingtao, Chap. VI, reprinted in *523*, Source Materials for the May Fourth Patriotic Movement, pp. 39–42; and the novel by Ch'iang-wei-yüan-chu (Master of the Red Rose Garden) *100*, The Story of May Fourth (Shanghai, 1937), Chap. IX, pp. 127ff. The novel was in some respects based on facts, despite many fictitious but relevant names adopted.

67. "Pei-ching hsüeh-chieh T'ien-an-men ta-hui hsüan-yen" ("The Declaration of Students of Peking for the Meeting at the T'ien-an Gate"), Kung Chen-huang, ed., The Storm of Tsingtao, Appendix I, reprinted in *523*, Source Materials for the May Fourth Patriotic Movement, p. 181; also in Hsin-hsing shu-chü, ed., Min-kuo t'ung-su yen-i (A Popular Story of the Republic of China) (Taipei, 1956), Chap. 105, p. 657; and in Chia I-chün *89*, A Short History of the May Fourth Movement, pp. 37–38.

68. See *ibid.*, p. 15; Weekly Critic (May 11, 1919); Ts'ai Hsiao-chou and Yang Ching-kung *446*, May Fourth, pp. 48–49; Tsi C. Wang *771*, *Youth Movement in China*, pp. 164–65; Chiang Monlin *594*, *Tides from the West*, p. 120; Ch'en Tuan-chih *73*, Historical Evaluation of the May Fourth Movement, p. 121; Wen-shu *506*, "History of the May Fourth Movement," p. 4; Rodney Gilbert *641*, "Downfall of Ts'ao the Mighty," *The North-China Herald* (May 10, 1919), p. 348.

69. Wen-shu *506*, "History of the May Fourth Movement," p. 5; Tsi C. Wang *771*, *Youth Movement in China*, p. 166.

70. Bertrand Russell, *The Problem of China*, Chap. III, p. 54.

71. Tsi C. Wang *771*, *Youth Movement in China*, p. 166.

72. Reprinted in *475*, Collected Essays in Commemoration of May Fourth (Mukden, 1950), pp. 173–74.

73. Wen-shu *506*, "History of the May Fourth Movement," p. 5.

74. See Weekly Critic, No. 21 (May 11, 1919).

75. Hua Kang *230*, History of the May Fourth Movement (Shanghai, 1951, 1952), Chap. VI, pp. 113, 114.

76. See Rodney Gilbert *641*, "Downfall of Ts'ao the Mighty," *The North-China Herald*, CXXXI, 2700 (May 10, 1919), p. 348.

77. Reinsch *707*, *An American Diplomat in China*, Chap. XXXI, p. 358.

78. Ch'en Tuan-chih *73*, Historical Evaluation of the May Fourth Movement, p. 233; Ch'iang-wei-yüan-chu *100*, The Story of May Fourth; Chia I-chun *89*, A Short History of the May Fourth Movement, p. 16.

79. *The North-China Herald* (May 10, 1919), p. 347.

80. Chou Yü-t'ung *124*, "The Departed May Fourth," p. 59.

81. Gilbert *641*, "Downfall of Ts'ao," p. 348.

82. See Ts'ai Hsiao-chou and Yang Ching-kung *446*, May Fourth, pp. 50, 51; Weekly Critic, No. 21 (May 11, 1919).

83. Chiang Monlin *593*, "The Student Movement," in *The China Mission Year Book*, *1919*, p. 46.

84. See Pei-ching-jen pi-pao-she *385*, "A Short Account of the May Fourth Movement," p. 4.

85. See *525*, "Special Column for the Panel on May Fourth," *Chieh-fang jih-pao* (Liberation Daily) (Shanghai, May 3, 1950); Yi Chün-tso, "Wu-ssu jen-wu cha-i" ("Miscellaneous Reminiscences of My Friends in the May Fourth Movement"), *Tsu-kuo chou-k'an* (China Weekly), XVIII, 6 (Kowloon, May 13, 1957), pp. 8–10.

86. Pei-ching-jen pi-pao-she *385*, "A Short Account of the May Fourth Movement," p. 4. Some writers report that it was the back door which was opened first. See Ch'en Tuan-chih *73*, Historical Evaluation of the May Fourth Movement, p. 234.

87. See *ibid.*, p. 234; Wen-shu *506*, "History of the May Fourth Movement," p. 5; also Chang I-p'ing, *Ch'uang-hsia sui-pi* (Sketches by the Window) (Shanghai, 1932), p. 86.

88. See C. F. Remer *711*, "The Revolt of the Chinese Students," *Asia*, XIX, 9 (New York, Sept. 1919), p. 932; Kung Chen-huang, ed., The Storm of Tsingtao, Chap. VI, reprinted in *523*, Source Materials for the May Fourth Patriotic Movement, p. 40; and Pei-ching-jen pi-pao-she *385*, "A Short Account of the May Fourth Movement," p. 4.

89. See The Eastern Miscellany, XVI, 6 (June 15, 1919), p. 223; Ch'a-kung *6*, "A Record of the Student Strikes," pp. 121–22.

90. See *The North-China Herald* (May 10, 1919), p. 347; also Wu Chung-pi, ed., A History of the Shanghai Strike and National Salvation Movement, reprinted in *523*, Source Materials for the May Fourth Patriotic Movement, p. 552.

91. See Ts'ai Hsiao-chou and Yang Ching-kung *446*, May Fourth, p. 52; Ta-Chung-hua-kuo-min [pen name] *356*, ed., Chang Tsung-hsiang the Traitor, No. 1 (Shanghai, 1919), reprinted in *523*, Source Materials for the May Fourth Patriotic Movement, p. 638.

92. Tsi C. Wang *771*, *Youth Movement in China*, p. 167.

93. See Ch'en Tuan-chih *73*, Historical Evaluation of the May Fourth Movement, p. 234.

94. See Chia I-chün *89*, A Short History of the May Fourth Movement, pp. 15, 16; Hua Kang *230*, History of the May Fourth Movement, pp. 113–14.

95. For his life in Peking and his last years there, see Itō Takeo's article in *Chūgoku kenkyū* (Chinese Studies), No. 12 (April 1950), pp. 60–71. See also John K. Fairbank and Masataka Banno, *Japanese Studies of Modern China* (Cambridge, Mass., 1955).

96. Wang Yün-sheng *498*, Sixty Years' Relation, VII, 335–36; Chia I-chün *89*, A Short History of the May Fourth Movement, p. 32; Ch'en Tuan-chih *73*, Historical Evaluation of the May Fourth Movement, pp. 234–35.

97. See Ts'ai Hsiao-chou and Yang Ching-kung *446*, May Fourth, p. 51.

98. A Tientsin telegram dated May 6, 6 p.m., in *The North-China Herald* (May 10, 1919), p. 347; also Ch'a-kung *6*, "A Record of the Student Strikes," p. 122.

99. See Pei-ching-jen pi-pao-she *385*, "A Short Account of the May Fourth Movement," p. 4; and Ts'ao's communication to the President cited below.

100. See Chia I-chün *89*, A Short History of the May Fourth Movement, p. 33.

101. See *The North-China Herald*, CXXXI, 2700 (Shanghai, May 10, 1919), p. 345.

102. Tsi C. Wang *771*, *Youth Movement in China*, pp. 166–67.

103. See Chiang Monlin *594*, *Tides from the West*, p. 120; also his article *593*, "The Student Movement" in *China Mission Year Book, 1919*, pp. 46–47.

104. For the full text of Ts'ao's letter to the President see Ch'a-an, A Record of the Student Strike, Appendix IV, reprinted in *523*, Source Materials for the May Fourth Patriotic Movement, pp. 300–301. For Paul Reinsch's description of the scene see his *707*, *An American Diplomat in China*, Chap. XXX, pp. 358–59.

105. Telegram of the Associated Press from Peking, May 5, *New York Times* (May 9, 1919), p. 2.

106. Kung Chen-huang, ed., The Storm of Tsingtao, Chap. VI, reprinted in *523*, Source Materials for the May Fourth Patriotic Movement, pp. 58–60; Wen-shu *506*, "History of the May Fourth Movement," p. 5.

107. See Meng Shih-chieh, *Chung-kuo tsui-chin-shih shih* (History of China in Most Recent Times), III, 269–70; and Wang Yün-sheng *498*, Sixty Years' Relation, VII, 336.

108. Wen-shu *506*, "History of the May Fourth Movement," p. 5; Pei-ching-jen pi-pao-she *385*, "A Short Account of the May Fourth Movement"; Chia I-chün *89*, A Short History of the May Fourth Movement, p. 16; Ma Hsü-lun *353*, My Life before I Was Sixty Years of Age (Shanghai, 1947), p. 65. Since the number of students arrested was not officially published at first and the arrests were not all made at one time, the number has been in doubt: (1) The earlier reports were uncertain of the exact number. Rodney Gilbert reported on May 4, 1919, that 10 students were arrested and none were the leaders or organizers. The report by a gendarme officer on May 5 gave the figure as "over twenty" (see Hua-chung kung-hsüeh-yüan *228*, ed., Collected Articles on the May Fourth Movement [Wu-Han, 1957], p. 173). The telegram of the Associated Press dated May 5 reported "several arrests," *New York Times* (May 9, 1919), p. 2. A dispatch of May 7 in *The North-China Herald* (May 10, 1919), p. 347 said: "There were over 30 arrests made," although the same issue recorded an earlier telegram from Peking dated May 5 implying the number was ten. The President stated in his mandate of May 8 that the police reported

to the Premier that "many" students were arrested on the spot (see The Eastern Miscellany, XVI, 6 [June 15, 1919], p. 224). The same issue of the magazine gave the number as "several dozen." So did Ts'ai Yüan-p'ei in his "My Experience at the Peking University." Ch'a-kung recorded in June 1919, "There is still no accurate estimate of the number of students arrested, some say over 30, some say 22" (see his 6, "A Record of the Student Strikes," p. 122). (2) The number was later fixed at 32. Wu Chung-pi, A History of the Shanghai Strike and National Salvation Movement (written and published in July 1919) and Kung Chen-huang, The Storm of Tsingtao (written in June and published on Aug. 10, 1919), Chap. XIV, give more detailed reports on this matter, both reprinted in 523, Source Materials for the May Fourth Patriotic Movement, pp. 161, 165. Chiang Monlin also gives this figure in his article published in 1919 (see 593, "The Student Movement," China Mission Year Book, 1919, p. 47). But later in 1947 he said, "Meanwhile, the armed police and gendarmery had thrown a cordon around the house [of Ts'ao Ju-lin]. They arrested some sixty students and sent them to headquarters. The rest — about a thousand strong — followed after, each claiming individually to have been responsible for the outbreak and asking to be arrested. Finally all were put under heavy military guard in the compounds of the Law College of the university" (Chiang's 594, Tides from the West, pp. 120–21). The latter account is obviously mistaken, confusing the arrests of May 4 with those of June 2, 3, and 4. (3) Ch'en Kung-lu recorded the number as 7 in his History of Modern China, p. 763. Meng Shih-chieh gave 7 too in History of China in Most Recent Times, p. 270. Chung-hua chiao-yü chieh (Chinese Educational Circles) VIII, 1 (cited by Ting Chih-p'ing 444, ed., A Chronological Record of Chinese Education) asserted, "more than a thousand students were arrested." This is also confused with those arrested on June 2, 3, and 4 (see Ts'ai Shang-ssu 447, Biography of Ts'ai Yüan-p'ei, pp. 420–21). (4) Wang Yün-sheng gave the number 36, in his 498, Sixty Years' Relation, VII, 336. The number 32 is accurate. Rodney Gilbert reported that the arrests were made "half a mile from the scene of action and an hour after the event by a corpulent officer who arrived very late upon the scene with 20 soldiers" (The North-China Herald [May 10, 1919], p. 349; see also Hsü Te-heng 181, "In Remembrance of May Fourth," Bulletin of the Chiu-san Society, No. 3 [May 1951]).

109. Ts'ai and Yang 446, May Fourth, p. 52.

110. See Wen-shu 506, "History of the May Fourth Movement," p. 5; also Ch'en Tuan-chih 73, Historical Evaluation of the May Fourth Movement, p. 236; Ts'ai Shang-ssu 447, Biography of Ts'ai Yüan-p'ei, p. 421.

111. Tsi C. Wang 771, Youth Movement in China, p. 167, trans. by Wang and slightly revised by us; Kung Chen-huang, ed., The Storm of Tsingtao, Chap. XIV, reprinted in 523, Source Materials for the May Fourth Patriotic Movement, p. 165; see also Pei-ching-jen pi-pao-she 385, "A Short Account of the May Fourth Movement," p. 4.

112. The North-China Herald (May 10, 1919), p. 347. Another report said that martial law was proclaimed in the Legation Quarter.

113. Rodney Gilbert 641, "Downfall of Ts'ao," The North-China Herald (May 10, 1919), p. 349.

CHAPTER V

DEVELOPMENTS FOLLOWING THE INCIDENT:
STUDENT DEMONSTRATIONS AND STRIKES

1. Wen-shu 506, "History of the May Fourth Movement," Student Magazine, X, 5 (Shanghai, May 5, 1923), p. 7.

2. Chia I-chün 89, A Short History of the May Fourth Movement (Peking, 1951), p. 32, n. 8; a dispatch of May 5 reports that Ts'ao had gone with Chang Tsung-hsiang to Tientsin at 5 on that morning. Another report of May 6 says that he did not go to Tientsin but was taking shelter in the house of a prominent member of Tuan Ch'i-jui's party (*The North-China Herald* [May 10, 1919], p. 346). Some reports state that his resignation was submitted on May 6 instead of May 5. See Wen-shu 506, "History of the May Fourth Movement," p. 7.

3. *Ibid.*, For the text of Lu's letter see Yang Ch'en-yin, *Min-ch'ao ch'i-jih chi* (A Record of the Seven Days' Storm of the People) (Shanghai, 1919) and Ch'a-an, *Hsüeh-chieh feng-ch'ao chi* (A Record of the Student Strikes) (Shanghai, 1919), Appendix IV, both reprinted in 523, Source Materials for the May Fourth Patriotic Movement (Peking, 1959), pp. 554–55, 229–300.

4. *The North-China Herald* (May 10, 1919), p. 347.

5. *Shen pao* (Romanized *Shun Pao*, Shanghai daily) (May 8, 1919); Wen-shu 506, "History of the May Fourth Movement," p. 7; Ch'a-kung 6, "A Record of the Student Strikes," Chinese Educational Circles, VIII, 1 (July 1919), p. 123.

6. *Ibid.*

7. Ts'ai Yüan-p'ei 463, "My Experiences at Peking University," The Eastern Miscellany (Jan. 1934), p. 11.

8. Ch'a-kung 6, "A Record of the Student Strikes," p. 123.

9. See Kung Chen-huang, ed., *Ch'ing-tao ch'ao* (The Storm of Tsingtao) (Shanghai, 1919), Chap. VI, reprinted in 523, Source Materials for the May Fourth Patriotic Movement, p. 41; Wen-shu 506, "History of the May Fourth Movement," p. 7; and telegram dated May 7, *The North-China Herald* (May 10, 1919), pp. 345, 347.

10. Lin Shu, "Ti-chih Jih huo chih kung-tu" (A Public Letter Concerning the Boycott against Japanese Goods), in Chin-hsia-ko chu (Master of the Pavilion Cloaked in Rosy Clouds) 109, ed., Choice Examples of the Knife and Stylus [i.e., Judicial Decisions], Supplement (Rev. ed.; Shanghai, 1924, 1930), IV, 13–15.

11. Ch'en Tuan-chih 73, An Historical Evaluation of the May Fourth Movement (Shanghai, 1935, 1936), Chap. XIII, p. 236.

12. Tsi C. Wang 771, *The Youth Movement in China* (New York, 1928), Chap. X, p. 169.

13. Ch'en Tuan-chih 73, An Historical Evaluation of the May Fourth Movement, Chap. VIII, p. 236.

14. *Ibid.*, pp. 236–37. Also Ts'ai Hsiao-chou and Yang Ching-kung 446, May Fourth (Peking, 1919), p. 53.

15. Wen-shu 506, "History of the May Fourth Movement," p. 4; Ts'ai Hsiao-chou and Yang Ching-kung 446, May Fourth, pp. 53–54; and Kung Chen-huang, ed., The Storm of Tsingtao, Chap. VI, reprinted in 523, Source Materials for the May Fourth Patriotic Movement, p. 49.

16. Reinsch 707, *An American Diplomat in China* (Garden City, 1922), Chap. XXXIII, p. 376; U.S. State Department 764, *Papers Relating to the Foreign Relations of the United States, 1919* (Washington, D.C., 1934), p. 370.

17. Ch'en Tuan-chih 73, An Historical Evaluation of the May Fourth Movement, p. 237.

18. Pei-ching-jen pi-pao-she 385, "A Short Account of the May Fourth Movement" (May 4, 1947), p. 4; Kung Chen-huang, ed., The Storm of Tsingtao, Chap. VI, reprinted in 523, Source Materials for the May Fourth Patriotic Movement, p. 50.

19. *Ibid.*, pp. 49–50; Ch'en Tuan-chih 73, An Historical Evaluation of the May Fourth Movement, pp. 237–38.

20. See Chou yü-tung *124*, "The Departed May Fourth," The Middle School Students (Shanghai, 1930); Ts'ai Hsiao-chou and Yang Ching-kung *446*, May Fourth, pp. 62–63.

21. See Hsü Yen-chih, "Pei-ching ta-hsüeh nan-nü-kung-hsiao chi" (An Account of the Start of Coeducation at Peking University), *Shao-nien shih-chieh* (Young World), I, 7 (July 1, 1920), pp. 36–47; Chou Yü-t'ung *124*, "The Departed May Fourth"; also Chinese Educational Review, XII, 3 (March 1920); Ts'ai Yüan-p'ei *463*, "My Experiences at Peking University," The Eastern Miscellany, XXX, 1 (Jan. 1, 1934), p. 12; and Ts'ai Shangssu *447*, Biography of Ts'ai Yüan-p'ei, pp. 422–23.

22. Wen-shu *506*, "History of the May Fourth Movement," p. 5; some reports say that there were 14 chancellors (see Ts'ai Hsiao-chou and Yang Ching-kung *446*, May Fourth, p. 55; Ch'a-kung *6*, "A Record of the Student Strikes," p. 122).

23. *Ibid.*

24. Wen-shu *506*, "History of the May Fourth Movement"; Ts'ai Hsiao-chou and Yang Ching-kung *446*, May Fourth.

25. Chiang Monlin *594*, *Tides from the West* (New Haven, 1947), Chap. XV, p. 121.

26. *Ibid.;* Pei-ching-jen pi-pao-she *385*, "A Short Account of the May Fourth Movement," p. 4.

27. Tsi C. Wang *771*, *The Youth Movement in China*, pp. 170–71.

28. Wen-shu *506*, "History of the May Fourth Movement," p. 7.

29. *The North-China Herald*, CXXXI, 2700 (May 10, 1919), p. 345; see also Wu Chung-pi, *Shang-hai pa-shih chiu-wang shih* (A History of the Shanghai Strike and National Salvation Movement) (Shanghai, 1919), reprinted in *523*, Source Materials for the May Fourth Patriotic Movement, pp. 556–57.

30. *The North-China Herald*, CXXXI, 2700 (May 10, 1919), p. 345. For the Chinese text of T'ang's and Chu's telegrams to the Peking government see Hsin-hsing shu-chu, ed., *Min-kuo t'ung-su yen-i* (A Popular Story of the Republic of China) (Taipei, 1956), Chap. 106, pp. 666–67, and Ta-chung-hua-kuo-min [pen name], ed., *Mai-kuo-tse chih-i, Chang Tsung-hsiang* (Chang Tsung-hsiang the Traitor, No. I) (Shanghai, 1919), pp. 639–40. For their joint telegram see Kung Chen-huang, ed., The Storm of Tsingtao, Chap. XIII, reprinted in *523*, Source Materials for the May Fourth Patriotic Movement, p. 155.

31. See Lo Chia-lun *342*, "A Retrospect of the Past Year [May Fourth Incident] in the Light of Current Affairs," p. 70; see also Kung Chen-huang, ed., The Storm of Tsingtao, Chap. XIII, reprinted in *523*, Source Materials for the May Fourth Patriotic Movement, pp. 147–48.

32. Lo Chia-lun *342*, "A Retrospect of the Past Year," pp. 70–71.

33. Li Chien-nung *289*, Chinese Political History of the Last Thirty Years (Shanghai, 1936), pp. 439–50; Russell H. Fifield *636*, *Woodrow Wilson and the Far East* (New York, 1952), Chap. VI, p. 303.

34. K'ang's telegram addressed to the public in Kung Chen-huang, ed., The Storm of Tsingtao, Appendix III, reprinted in *523*, Source Materials for the May Fourth Patriotic Movement, 218–220; also cited in Chia I-chün *89*, A Short History of the May Fourth Movement, p. 33, n. 9.

35. Wu's telegram, *ibid.* For the telegrams by Chang, Ch'en, and others see Ch'a-an, A Record of the Student Strikes, Appendix II, and Kung Chen-huang, ed., The Storm of Tsingtao, Appendix III, both reprinted in *523*, Source Materials for the May Fourth Patriotic Movement, pp. 275–78, 220–22.

36. Pao Tsun-p'eng *382*, History of the Youth Movement of Modern China (Taipei, 1953), p. 32.

37. Ch'a-kung *6*, "A Record of the Student Strikes," p. 122.

38. *Ibid.; The North-China Herald* (May 10, 1919), pp. 343, 346; Ts'ai Hsiao-chou and Yang Ching-kung *446*, May Fourth, pp. 55–57.

39. Tsi C. Wang *771*, *The Youth Movement in China*, p. 172.

40. The following account of the student activities in various cities is based mainly upon Wen-shu's record *506*, "History of the May Fourth Movement," pp. 5–7, and Kung Chen-huang, ed., The Storm of Tsingtao, Chap. VII, reprinted in *523*, Source Materials for the May Fourth Patriotic Movement, pp. 60–97.

41. Teng Ying-ch'ao *440*, "A Memoir on the May Fourth Movement," in Wu-ssu sa-chou-nien chi-nien chuan-chi pien-wei-hui (Committee of Editors for the Symposium for the Thirtieth Anniversary of the May Fourth Movement), A Symposium for the Thirtieth Anniversary of the May Fourth Movement (Shanghai, 1949), pp. 162–65; also Ma Hui-ch'ing, "Wu-ssu yün-tung tsai T'ien-chin" ("The May Fourth Movement in Tientsin"), in Chung-kuo k'o-hsüeh-yüan, ed., *Chin-tai shih tzu-liao* (Source Materials for Modern Chinese History), No. 19 (Peking, April 1958), pp. 79–129.

42. Chiang Monlin *594*, *Tides from the West*, p. 121.

43. Hsin-hsing shu-chü, ed., A Popular Story of the Republic of China, Chap. 106, pp. 665–68; Pao Tsun-p'eng *382*, History of the Youth Movement of Modern China, p. 28.

44. *Ibid.*

45. Wang Kung-pi, "Pa-nien 'wu-ch'i' chih hsiang-chan" ("Street Fighting [between the Chinese students and the Japanese police in Tokyo] on May 7, 1919"), *Tung-yu hui-han lu* (Memoir on Study in Japan Written in Sweat) (Shanghai, 1919), reprinted in Chung-kuo k'o-hsüeh-yüan, ed., Source Materials for Modern Chinese History, No. 5 (Peking, April 1955), pp. 118–21; see also Tsi C. Wang *771*, *The Youth Movement in China*, p. 173.

46. *Ibid.;* Wen-shu *506*, "History of the May Fourth Movement," p. 6; Ch'a-kung *6*, "A Record of the Student Strikes," p. 126; Wang Kung-pi "Street Fighting on May 7," pp. 121–23.

47. *Ibid.*

48. *Ibid.*, p. 127; Wen-shu *506*, "History of the May Fourth Movement," pp. 6–7; also Wang Kung-pi, "Street Fighting on May 7."

49. *Ibid.*, p. 7.

50. *The North-China Herald*, CXXI, 2700 (Shanghai, May 10, 1919), p. 347. Chinese text in The Eastern Miscellany, XVI, 6 (June 15, 1919), pp. 223–24.

51. Wen-shu *506*, "History of the May Fourth Movement," p. 7; Kung Chen-huang, ed., The Storm of Tsingtao, Chap. XII, and Wu Chung-pi, ed., A History of the Shanghai Strike and National Salvation Movement, both reprinted in *523*, Source Materials for the May Fourth, pp. 137–38, 557.

52. *The North-China Herald*, CXXXI, 2701 (May 17, 1919), p. 411. Chinese text in The Eastern Miscellany, XVI, 6 (June 15, 1919), pp. 223–24.

53. Wen-shu *506*, "History of the May Fourth Movement," pp. 6–7.

54. John Dewey *628*, "The Student Revolt in China," *The New Republic*, XX, 248 (Aug. 6, 1919), p. 16; also Ts'ai Hsiao-chou and Yang Ching-kung *446*, May Fourth, pp. 57–58; Tsi C. Wang *771*, *The Youth Movement in China*, p. 174.

55. See Chiang Monlin *594*, *Tides from the West*, Chap. XV, pp. 122–23.

56. Ts'ai Yüan-p'ei *463*, "My Experiences at Peking University," The Eastern Miscellany, XXXI, 1 (Jan. 1, 1934), p. 11; *The North-China Herald*, CXXXI, 270 (May 17, 1919), p. 412.

57. See "Pa-nien wu-yüeh chiu-jih tz'u-chih ch'u-ching ch'i-shih" ("Notice of Resignation and Leaving Peking on May 9, 1919") and Professor Ch'eng Yen-sheng's letter to his

student Ch'ang Hui, May 10, 1919, in Hsin ch'ao she *461*, ed., The Life and Works of Ts'ai Yüan-p'ei (Peking, 1920), II, 335–37.

58. See Ts'ai Shang-ssu *447*, Biography of Ts'ai Yüan-p'ei (Shanghai, 1950), Chap. I, pp. 1–44.

59. Wen-shu *506*, "History of the May Fourth Movement," p. 7; Ts'ai Hsiao-chou and Yang Ching-kung *446*, May Fourth, p. 61.

60. Kung Chen-huang, ed., The Storm of Tsingtao, Chap. XIV, reprinted in *523*, Source Materials for the May Fourth Patriotic Movement, pp. 169–70; and Pei-ching-jen pi-pao-she *385*, "A Short Account of the May Fourth Movement," p. 4.

61. From a student's diary, cited in Tsi C. Wang *771*, *The Youth Movement in China*, p. 175.

62. Ch'a-kung *6*, "A Record of the Student Strikes," p. 124.

63. The Eastern Miscellany, XVI, 6 (June 15, 1919), p. 226.

64. For the text of the mandates see Kung Chen-huang, ed., The Storm of Tsingtao, Chap. XIV, reprinted in *523*, Source Materials for the May Fourth Patriotic Movement, pp. 166–67; see also Tsi C. Wang *771*, *The Youth Movement in China*, p. 175, n. 13; see also the students' manifesto for the general strike published on May 18, English translation of which appears in this chapter.

65. See M. T. Z. Tyau *762*, *China Awakened* (New York, 1922), p. 126; see also Kung Chen-huang, ed., The Storm of Tsingtao, Chap. VI, reprinted in *523*, Source Materials for the May Fourth Patriotic Movement, pp. 58–60.

66. Ch'a-kung *6*, "A Record of the Student Strikes," pp. 123–24.

67. See Ma Hsü-lun *353*, My Life before I was Sixty Years of Age (Shanghai, 1947), pp. 20, 67, 80–85, 90.

68. See Chuang Yü *136*, "Tsu-chih ch'üan-kuo chiao-yüan lien-ho-hui" ("Organize the Teachers' Union of All China"), The Chinese Educational Review, XI, 7 (July 20, 1919), pp. 1–4.

69. Ch'a-kung *6*, "A Record of the Student Strikes," pp. 124–25. Wen-shu gives the date as May 17.

70. Ts'ai Hsiao-chou and Yang Ching-kung *446*, May Fourth, pp. 63–64; see also Kung Chen-huang, ed., The Storm of Tsingtao, Chap. VI, reprinted in *523*, Source Materials for the May Fourth Patriotic Movement, pp. 52–55.

71. *Ibid.*, p. 52; Tsi C. Wang *771*, *The Youth Movement in China*, pp. 175–76; Ts'ai Hsiao-chou and Yang Ching-kung *446*, May Fourth, pp. 64–65.

72. See Paul Jones *663*, "The Students' Revolt in China," *The Independent*, Vol. 99, No. 3693 (New York, Sept. 20, 1919), p. 399. A Chinese translation of the article may be found in Chang I-chih *19*, ed., Collected Publications on the Shantung Question (Shanghai, 1921), II, 288–91.

73. See *The North-China Herald*, CXXXI, 270 (Shanghai, May 17, 1919), pp. 415–16.

74. See "A Brief History of the Chinese Communist Party" in *416*, Collection of Documentary Evidence of the Soviet Russian Conspiracy, ed. and trans. from the Russian by Peking Metropolitan Police Headquarters (Peking, 1928), p. 10; English version in C. Martin Wilbur and Julie Lien-ying How, eds., *Documents on Communism, Nationalism, and Soviet Advisers in China, 1918–1927* (New York, 1956), p. 47.

75. C. F. Remer *708*, "The Revolt of the Chinese Students," *Asia*, XIX, 9 (New York, Sept. 1919) p. 933. Wen-shu said that it was May 23.

76. Ts'ai Yüan-p'ei also sent his younger brother, Ts'ai Ku-ch'ing, to mediate; see Ch'a-kung *6*, "A Record of the Student Strikes," p. 125. On the strike and demonstration see Ts'ai Hsiao-chou and Yang Ching-kung *446*, May Fourth, pp. 78–79. For the text of the

students' manifesto for the strike see Hsin-hsing shu-chü, ed., A Popular Story of the Republic of China, Chap. 106, pp. 678–79, also Kung Chen-huang, ed., The Storm of Tsingtao, Appendex I, reprinted in *523*, Source Materials for the May Fourth Patriotic Movement, pp. 183–84.

77. Ch'a-kung *6*, "A Record of the Student Strikes," p. 126; Wen-shu *506*, "History of the May Fourth Movement," p. 8.

78. See Ch'a-kung *6*, "A Record of the Student Strikes," p. 135.

79. *Ibid.*, p. 136.

80. Tsi C. Wang *771*, *The Youth Movement in China*, p. 176; Wen-shu *506*, "History of the May Fourth Movement," p. 8; Paul Jones *663*, "The Students' Revolt in China," p. 399; Chung-kuo k'o-hsüeh yüan *523*, ed., Source Materials for the May Fourth Patriotic Movement, pp. 789–863. There are a few variations in the dates when the strikes started; uncertain dates have been omitted.

CHAPTER VI

FURTHER DEVELOPMENTS: SUPPORT FROM MERCHANTS, INDUSTRIALISTS, AND WORKERS

1. Wen-shu *506*, "History of the May Fourth Movement," Students' Magazine, X, 5 (May 1923), p. 8.

2. *Ibid.;* Ch'a-kung *6*, "A Record of the Student Strikes," Chinese Educational Circles, VIII, 6 (July 1919), p. 129.

3. *Ibid.* Wang was appointed on July 31; see The Eastern Miscellany, X, 9 (Sept. 15, 1919), p. 228.

4. See Hsiung Shao-hao, "Wu-shih nien lai pei-fang pao-chih chih shih-lüeh" ("A Short Sketch of Events Concerning the Press of North China in the Last Fifty Years"), in *Shun [Shen] Pao* (newspaper) *414*, ed., The Past Fifty Years, in Commemoration of the *Shun Pao's* Golden Jubilee (Shanghai, 1923), Part III, p. 25; Weekly Critic, No. 24 (June 1, 1919).

5. Ch'a-kung *6*, "A Record of the Student Strikes," p. 129; Kung Chen-huang, ed., *Ch'ing-tao ch'ao* (The Storm of Tsingtao) (Shanghai, 1919), Chap. VI, reprinted in *523*, Source Materials for the May Fourth Patriotic Movement (Peking, 1959), pp. 55–57.

6. Some say that the date is June 2, see *ibid.* and C. F. Remer *711*, "The Revolt of the Chinese Students," *Asia*, XIX, 9 (New York, Sept. 1919) and Stanley High *642*, *China's Place in the Sun* (New York, 1922), Chap. VII, p. 130. Wen-shu gives the date as June 1. For the text of the mandates see Hsin-hsing shu-chü, ed., *Min-kuo t'ung-su yen-i* (A Popular Story of the Republic of China) (Taipei, 1955), Chap. 108, pp. 675–78; and Kung Chen-huang, ed., The Storm of Tsingtao, Chap. XIV, reprinted in *523*, Source Materials for the May Fourth Patriotic Movement, pp. 167–69.

7. Reinsch *707*, *An American Diplomat in China* (Garden City, 1922), Chap. XXXII, p. 370. Tseng Ch'i *471*, "The May Fourth Movement and Statism," a speech delivered on May 4, 1926, reprinted in *471*, Collected Works of Tseng Ch'i (Taipei, 1954), Part II, p. 139.

8. Cited in Ch'a-kung *6*, "A Record of the Student Strikes," p. 129.

9. See *Shun-t'ien shih-pao*, a conservative daily close to the government (Peking, June 7, 1919).

10. Cited in Ch'a-kung *6*, "A Record of the Student Strikes," p. 130.

11. *Ibid.*, pp. 129–30; see also Wu Chung-pi, *Shang-hai pa-shih chiu-wang shih* (A

History of the Shanghai Strike and National Salvation Movement) (Shanghai, 1919), and Yüeh-tung hsien-ho, *Mai-kuo-tse chih-erh*, *Ts'ao Ju-lin* (Ts'ao Ju-lin the Traitor, No. 2) (Shanghai, 1919), both reprinted in *523*, Source Materials for the May Fourth Patriotic Movement, pp. 583–84, 665–75.

12. John and Alice Dewey *631*, *Letters from China and Japan* (New York, 1920), pp. 209–11. The letter was mistakenly dated June 1.

13. C. F. Remer gave the number 1,200. See Remer *711*, "The Revolt of the Chinese Students." A Chinese reporter of *The North-China Herald* reported on June 7, 1919, that 1,150 students were arrested by the Peking government on June 3 and 4; see the *Herald*, CXXXI, 2704 (Shanghai, June 7, 1919), p. 650. Reinsch says: "Nearly a thousand students were under forcible detention in Peking," in his *707*, *An American Diplomat in China*, p. 370. According to Ts'ai Hsiao-chou and Yang Ching-kung, about 800 were arrested on June 3, making the total about 1,000; see Ts'ai and Yang *446*, May Fourth (Peking, 1919), p. 68. Both Ch'a-kung and Wen-shu give the number as "more than one thousand"; see Ch'a-kung *6*, "A Record of the Student Strikes," p. 132; Wen-shu *506*, "History of the May Fourth Movement," p. 9. A reporter of the *Ch'en pao* visited two school-prisons and interviewed some representatives of the student prisoners there on the afternoon of June 6 from 4 to 6 o'clock. He reported that at the School of Science were imprisoned 139 students from Peking University, the French Institute, Tsing Hua School, the Fourth Middle School (*Ti-ssu chung-hsüeh-hsiao*), and the Shantung Middle School (*Shan-tung chung-hsüeh-hsiao*), and at the School of Law, 827 students from the following 20 schools: Peking University, the College of Law and Political Science, the Russian Institute, the Higher Normal College, the University of the Republic, Tsing Hua School, Hui-wen University, Peking Teachers' College (*Pei-ching shih-fan hsüeh-hsiao*), the Agricultural College, the Financial and Commercial College (*Ts'ai-cheng shang-yeh hsüeh-hsiao*), the Industrial College, and several middle schools. This makes the total number of prisoners in the two buildings 966. There were probably some in other places; see *Ch'en pao* (June 7, 1919). But the telegram of the Student Union of Peking to the associations of education, chambers of commerce, associations of agriculture, labor unions, schools, and newspapers of all provinces, dated June 6, says, "In the two days of June 3 and 4, there were over 700 student lecturers arrested by the government. More than 5,000 students went out to deliver speeches on June 5. The government made no more arrests but dispersed them with armed forces and police"; cited in Ch'a-kung *6*, "A Record of the Student Strikes," p. 133. There were some students who volunteered to go to prison.

14. See M. T. Z. Tyau *762*, *China Awakened* (New York, 1922), Chap. IX, p. 144.

15. *Ibid.*

16. Reinsch *707*, *An American Diplomat in China*, p. 370; *Ch'en pao* (Peking, June 4, 1919).

17. See Tsi C. Wang *771*, *The Youth Movement in China*, p. 179; *Ch'en pao* (June 7, 1919).

18. Wu Chung-pi, A History of the Shanghai Strike and National Salvation Movement, and Yüeh-tung hsien-ho, Ts'ao Ju-lin the Traitor, No. 2, both reprinted in *523*, Source Materials for the May Fourth Patriotic Movement, pp. 585, 671–72. Reinsch said that 700 petitioned, see his *707*, *An American Diplomat in China*, p. 370; some estimated 600; see Ts'ai Hsiao-chou and Yang Ching-kung *446*, May Fourth, p. 69. Other reports give the number 1,000; see Weekly Critic, No. 25 (June 8, 1919); see also John and Alice Dewey *631*, *Letters from China and Japan*, pp. 209–12.

19. Ma Hsü-lun *353*, My Life Before I was Sixty Years of Age (Shanghai, 1947), p. 68; Ch'a-kung *6*, "A Record of the Student Strikes," pp. 130–31.

20. *Ibid.*, p. 131. For the situation of the students in the prisons, see also the Deweys' letter of June 5 in John and Alice Dewey *631, Letters from China and Japan*, pp. 219–20; this letter was apparently written by Alice Dewey.

21. Ts'ai Hsiao-chou and Yang Ching-kung *446*, May Fourth, pp. 68–69.

22. See Ch'en Tuan-chih *73*, An Historical Evaluation of the May Fourth Movement (Shanghai, 1935, 1936), Chap. XIV, pp. 253–54; pp. 260–61, n. 4.

23. See Ch'a-kung *6*, "A Record of the Student Strikes," p. 137.

24. Hai-shang-hsien-jen (A loafer in Shanghai — pen name) *164*, ed., A Factual Account of the Shanghai Merchants' and Workers' Strikes [of June 1919] (Shanghai, 1919), I, 1–6.

25. *Ibid.*, p. 6.

26. Ch'en Tuan-chih *73*, An Historical Evaluation of the May Fourth Movement, Chap. XIV, p. 255; Ch'a-kung *6*, "A Record of the Student Strikes," p. 139; *The North-China Herald*, CXXXI, 2704 (Shanghai, June 7, 1919), pp. 650–51; and the statement made on June 3, 1919 by the police department of the International Settlement of Shanghai, in *523*, Source Materials for the May Fourth Patriotic Movement, pp. 717–18.

27. Ch'a-kung *6*, "A Record of the Student Strikes," pp. 139–40; Wen-shu *506*, "History of the May Fourth Movement," p. 9.

28. See G. H. W. Woodhead *784*, ed., *The China Year Book, 1921–22* (Peking & Tientsin, 1922), p. 21.

29. Hai-shang-hsien-jen *164*, ed., A Factual Account of the Shanghai Strikes, pp. 129ff.

30. *Ibid.;* Wen-shu *506*, "History of the May Fourth Movement," p. 10.

31. *The North-China Herald*, CXXXI, 2704 (June 7, 1919), p. 650. For details regarding the federation see Chap. VII below.

32. Chia I-chün *89*, A Short History of the May Fourth Movement (Peking, 1951), pp. 19–20.

33. John Dewey *628*, "The Student Revolt in China," *The New Republic*, XX, 248 (Aug. 6, 1919), p. 17.

34. For this problem see Chap. VIII below.

35. Yang Ch'en-yin, *Min-ch'ao ch'i-jih chi* (The Seven-Days' Storm of the People) (Shanghai, 1919) and Wu Chung-pi, A History of the Shanghai Strike and National Salvation Movement, both in *523*, Source Materials for the May Fourth Patriotic Movement, pp. 528–29, 562–97. Ch'en Tu-hsiu, "Shan-tung wen-t'i yü Shang-hai shang-hui" (The Shantung Question and the Chamber of Commerce of Shanghai), editorial of Weekly Critic, reprinted in *62*, Collected Essays of Ch'en Tu-hsiu (Shanghai, 1922, 1939), I, 635–42.

36. Lo Chia-lun *340*, "The Success and Failure of our Student Movement During the Past Year and the Future Path to be Taken," New Education, II, 5 (May 1920), p. 603; also in New Tide, II, 4 (May 1920).

37. See Ch'a-kung *6*, "A Record of the Student Strikes," p. 129.

38. Ch'en Ta *42*, "An Analysis of Strikes in China in the Last Eight Years," The Tsing Hua Journal, III, 1 (Peking, June 1926), pp. 810ff. Teng Chung-hsia says that the workers' strike was started by the copper and iron machinery workers; see his *439*, A Short History of the Labor Movement in China (2nd ed.; Hsin-Hua shu-tien, 1930, 1949), I, 8. Ch'a-kung's report is similar to Teng's; see Ch'a-kung *6*, "A Record of the Student Strikes," p. 140. Neither Teng nor Ch'a-kung gives the dates of the individual strikes, while Ch'en Ta does.

39. Hai-shang-hsien-jen *164*, ed., A Factual Account of the Shanghai Strikes.

40. Ch'en Ta *42*, "An Analysis of Strikes in China," Teng Chung-hsia *439*, A Short History of the Labor Movement of China, pp. 8–9; Wen-shu *506*, "History of the May

Fourth Movement," p. 10; and Shang-hai-shih she-hui-chü (Bureau of Social Affairs, the City Government of Greater Shanghai) *401*, ed. (in Chinese and English), Strikes and Lockouts in Shanghai since 1918 (Shanghai, 1933), Appendix I, pp. 3–6.

41. *Ibid.*

42. Hua Kang *230*, History of the May Fourth Movement (3rd ed.; Shanghai, 1951, 1952, 1954), p. 124.

43. *Shun Pao*, cited in Chia I-chün *89*, A Short History of the May Fourth Movement, pp. 20–21.

44. Hai-shang-hsien-jen *164*, ed., A Factual Account of the Shanghai Strikes; also George E. Sokolsky *740* (manager, Chinese Bureau of Public Information in Shanghai [an American agency]), "China's Defiance of Japan," The *Independent*, Vol. 99, No. 3693 (New York, Sept. 20, 1919), p. 388.

45. John and Alice Dewey *631*, *Letters from China and Japan*, p. 309; see also "Laws and Orders," The Eastern Miscellany, XIV, 7 (July 15, 1919), p. 223.

46. See *Pei-ching ta-hsüeh i-lan* (A General View of Peking University) (Peking, 1935), pp. 1–4.

47. See John and Alice Dewey *631*, *Letters from China and Japan*, p. 232.

48. Ch'a-kung *6*, "A Record of the Student Strikes," p. 132.

49. See the letter of June 5 in John and Alice Dewey *631*, *Letters from China and Japan*, p. 221; this letter was apparently written by Alice Dewey.

50. See Ch'a-kung *6*, "A Record of the Student Strikes," pp. 132–33.

51. *Ibid.*, p. 133.

52. Tsi C. Wang *771*, *The Youth Movement in China*, pp. 180–81.

53. John and Alice Dewey *631*, *Letters from China and Japan*, p. 231.

54. *Ibid.*, pp. 229–30.

55. Wen-shu *506*, "History of the May Fourth Movement," p. 10; Ts'ai Hsiao-chou and Yang Ching-kung *446*, May Fourth, pp. 85–86.

56. *Ibid.*, p. 82; and Wen-shu *506*, "History of the May Fourth Movement," p. 10.

57. *Ibid.*

58. *Ibid.*

59. *Ibid.*, pp. 10–11; Ch'a-kung *6*, "A Record of the Student Strikes," p. 140; Ts'ai Hsiao-chou and Yang Cheng-kung *446*, May Fourth, pp. 81–90; Ch'en Tuan-chih *73*, An Historical Evaluation of the May Fourth Movement, pp. 255–56; Hai-shang hsien-jen *164*, ed., A Factual Account of the Shanghai Strikes, pp. 10, 113.

60. Teng Chung-hsia *439*, A Short History of the Labor Movement of China, p. 9.

61. Wen-shu *506*, "History of the May Fourth Movement," p. 11; also Ma Hui-ch'ing *335*, "The May Fourth Movement in Tientsin," in Source Materials for Modern Chinese History, No. 19 (Peking, April 1958), pp. 84–90.

62. John Dewey *628*, "The Student Revolt in China," p. 17; see also John and Alice Dewey *631*, *Letters from China and Japan*, p. 236; Ch'en Tuan-chih *73*, An Historical Evaluation of the May Fourth Movement, p. 257.

63. "Laws and Orders," The Eastern Miscellany, XVI, 7 (July 15, 1919), p. 233; Wen-shu *506*, "History of the May Fourth Movement," p. 11; Ch'en Tuan-chih mistakenly gives the date of the publication of the orders as June 9; see Ch'en *73*, An Historical Evaluation of the May Fourth Movement, p. 257; see also *Ch'en Pao* (Peking, June 12, 1919).

64. Hsü Chih-yen, ed., *Min-kuo shih-chou chi-shih pen-mo* (A Record of Facts of the Republic of China, 1912–1921) (Shanghai, 1922), Chap. VIII, p. 24.

65. See Hai-shang-hsien-jen *164*, ed., A Factual Account of the Shanghai Strikes, II, 14, 137–39.

66. "Laws and Orders," The Eastern Miscellany, XVI, 7 (July 15, 1919), p. 223.

67. John and Alice Dewey *631*, *Letters from China and Japan*, p. 269.

68. Ch'a-kung *6*, "A Record of the Student Strikes," pp. 136–37.

69. Li Chien-nung *289*, Political History of China in the Last One Hundred Years (Shanghai, 1947), Chap. XIV, pp. 606–7; translation ours. Cf. the English translation of this book by Ssu-yü Teng and Jeremy Ingalls, *The Political History of China, 1840–1928* (Princeton, 1956), Chap. XIV, pp. 438–39.

70. See the Cabinet's telegram to the provinces, The Eastern Miscellany, XVI, 6 (June 15, 1919), pp. 225–26.

71. Chang Chung-fu, *Chung-hua-min-kuo wai-chiao-shih* (Diplomatic History of the Republic of China) (Chungking, 1943), Vol. I, Chap. VI, pp. 277–78.

72. Wang Yün-sheng *498*, Sixty Years' Relation Between China and Japan (Tientsin, 1932–34), VII, 359–61, 365; *The North-China Herald*, CXXXI (June 21, 1919), pp. 760–61; (June 28, 1919), pp. 832–33. For text of the telegram of June 24 see Ch'a-an, A Record of the Student Strikes, Appendix II, reprinted in *523*, Source Materials for the May Fourth Patriotic Movement, pp. 273–74.

73. Ch'en Tuan-chih *73*, An Historical Evaluation of the May Fourth Movement, Chap. XIV, pp. 257–58.

74. See "Reinsch to Polk," July 3, 1919, Paris Peace Conference 185.1158/169; Stanley K. Hornbeck, "Shantung at the Peace Conference," in H. W. V. Temperley, ed., *A History of the Peace Conference of Paris* (London, 1924), VI, 388; and Russell Fifield *636*, *Woodrow Wilson and the Far East* (New York, 1952), Chap. VI, p. 332.

75. The Diplomatic Association, ed., *Far Eastern Political Science Review*, II, 2 (Canton, Feb. 1920), pp. 84–85.

76. *Ibid.*

77. Lou Tseng-tsiang [Dom Pierre-célestin, Lu Cheng-hsiang], *Ways of Confucius and of Christ*, trans. Michael Derrich (London, 1948), p. 42. See also Lo Kuang, *Lu Cheng-hsiang chuan* (Biography of Lu Cheng-hsiang) (Hong Kong, 1949).

78. The Eastern Miscellany, XVI, 6 (June 15, 1919), pp. 223–25; also the English daily *North China Star*.

79. See Fifield *636*, *Woodrow Wilson and the Far East*, p. 164.

80. Wang Yün-sheng *498*, Sixty Years' Relation, VII, 361–63.

81. The Diplomatic Association, ed., *Far Eastern Political Science Review*, II, 2 (Feb. 1920), p. 84.

82. Wang Yün-sheng *498*, Sixty Years' Relation, VII, 366–68.

83. "Laws and Orders," The Eastern Miscellany, X, 9 (Sept. 15, 1919), p. 228. Before his return, Ts'ai sent Chiang Monlin, one of his former students, to the university to take charge for him. Chiang went to Peking in July with one of the student delegates and urged the students to return to serious study; see Chiang *594*, *Tides from the West* (New Haven, 1947), Chap. XV, p. 123; also A General View of Peking University, pp. 1–4. According to Ma Hsü-lun, Chiang's entering Peking University caused some suspicion among the faculty; see Ma *353*, My Life before I was Sixty, pp. 70–71.

84. John Dewey *626*, "The New Leaven in Chinese Politics," *Asia* (April 1920), reprinted in his *611*, *Characters and Events* (London, 1929), I, 245, with the new title "Justice and Law in China."

85. *Ibid.*, pp. 245–46.

86. John and Alice Dewey *631*, *Letters from China and Japan*, pp. 296–98.

87. For the brief written by Liu Ch'ung-yu and the case, see Chin-hsia-ko-chu *199*, ed., Choice Examples of the Knife and Stylus [i.e., Judicial Decisions], Supplement, VII, 19a–25a; Hsü Chih-yen ed., A Record of Facts of the Republic of China, Chap. VIII, p. 8.

88. John Dewey *626*, "Justice and Law in China," in his *611, Characters and Events*, I, 246.

89. *Ibid.*, p. 251.

90. Ch'en Tu-hsiu, "Tuan-p'ai, Ts'ao, Lu, An-fu chü-lo-pu" ("Tuan Clique, Ts'ao, Lu, Anfu Club"), New Youth, VII, 1 (Dec. 1, 1919), pp. 119–20; reprinted in Ch'en's *62*, Collected Essays, II, 73–76.

CHAPTER VII

EXPANSION OF THE NEW CULTURE MOVEMENT, 1919–1920

1. Chiang Monlin and Hu Shih *97*, "Our Hopes for the Student," New Education, II, 5 (May 1920), p. 592.

2. *Shen pao* reported in Shanghai on June 15, 1919, that Ch'en was arrested on June 11 at 2:00 p.m. at the Hsin shih-chien market. According to Liu Pan-nung's [Liu Fu] poems, which were written on Sept. 15, 1919, to celebrate Ch'en's release from the prison, he had "not seen you for over eighty days"; another says, "They [the police] got in trouble for three months"; see New Youth, VI, 6 (Nov. 1919), pp. 585–87, 588; also see Hu Shih *198*, "Ch'en Tu-hsiu and the Literary Revolution," in Ch'en Tung-hsiao *74*, ed., Discussions on Ch'en Tu-hsiu, pp. 51–52; and *Chung-kuo ming-jen chuan* (Who's Who in China) (5th ed.; Shanghai, 1936). For text of the "Peking Citizens' Manifesto" see *523*, Source Materials for the May Fourth Patriotic Movement (Peking, 1959), p. 848, also p. 782.

3. Hu Shih, "Wei-ch'üan" ("Authority"), New Youth, VI, 6 (Nov. 1, 1919), p. 588.

4. Liu Pan-nung, "D—!" *ibid.*, pp. 585–87. "D" stands for the initial of Ch'en's first name "Tu" (pronounced *du*).

5. See Ch'en Tu-hsiu *62*, Collected Essays, II, 50.

6. See Lo Chia-lun, "Chin-tai Hsi-yang ssu-hsiang tzu-yu ti chin-hua" ("Evolution of Freedom of Thought in the Modern West"), New Tide, I, 2 (Dec. 1919), p. 239.

7. Li Ta-chao, "Huan-ying Tu-hsiu ch'u yü" ("Welcoming Tu-hsiu on His Release from Prison"), New Youth, VI, 6 (Nov. 1, 1919), pp. 588–89; this is the third and last stanza of the poem.

8. Ch'en Tu-hsiu, "Ta Pan-nung ti D— shih" ("An Answer to Pan-nung's Poem 'D—,'" New Youth, VII 2 (Jan. 1, 1920), pp. 55–57.

9. See Hu Shih *204*, "The Significance of the New Thought Tide," New Youth, VII, 1 (Dec. 1, 1919), p. 6.

10. Ts'ai Yüan-p'ei *452*, "Floods and Beasts," New Youth, VII, 5 (April 1, 1920), pp. 1–2.

11. [Ch'en Tu-hsiu] *52*, "The Manifesto of *New Youth* Magazine," *ibid.*, 1 (Dec. 1, 1919), pp. 1–4. It was drafted by Ch'en Tu-hsiu and approved by other editors; translated here by us in full except for the omission of a few unimportant introductory sentences.

12. The French original was published in the newspaper *Humanité* (Paris, June 29, 1919); English translations were published in the *Cambridge Magazine* weekly (July 19, 1919), the *World Tomorrow* (Sept. 1919), and *The Nation* weekly (London, Oct. 11, 1919).

13. Chang Sung-nien [Chang Shen-fu] *27*, trans., "Déclaration d'indépendance de l'esprit," New Youth, VII, 1 (Dec. 1, 1919), pp. 30–48; also New Tide, II, 2 (Dec. 1919), pp. 374–94.

14. Hsü yen-chih, "Hsin-ch'ao she chi-shih" ("Records of the New Tide Society"), *ibid.*, pp. 398–402; and *ibid.*, 5 (Sept. 1920), pp. 1073–76.

15. Lo Chia-lun, "Chin-jih Chung-kuo chih tsa-chih chieh" ("China's Magazines Today"), New Tide, I, 4 (April 1, 1919), pp. 625–34.

16. Hu Shih *211*, "Miscellaneous Feelings on My Returning to China," New Youth, IV, 1 (Jan. 15, 1918), pp. 20–27; also see Chih-hsi [Lo Chia-lun] *337*, "China's Press Today," written on Nov. 5, 1918, New Tide, I, 1 (Jan. 1, 1919), pp. 117–23.

17. Hu Shih *211*, "Miscellaneous Feelings on My Returning to China," pp. 23, 26.

18. See Lo Chia-lun *340*, "The Success and Failure of Our Student Movement During the Past Year and the Future Path to Be Taken," New Tide, II, 4 (May 1, 1920), p. 848. For the other estimates see Chiang Monlin *593*, "The Student Movement," in E. C. Lobenstine and A. L. Warnshuis, eds., *The China Mission Year Book, 1919* (Shanghai, 1920); p. 51; John Dewey *627*, "The Sequel of the Student Revolt," *The New Republic*, XIX, 273 (New York, March 3, 1920), p. 381; Tsi C. Wang *771*, *The Youth Movement in China* (New York, 1928), Chap. IX, p. 154; Hu Shih *225*, "Chinese Literature of the Last Fifty Years," in Hu's *207*, Collected Essays, Collection II, II, 206; and Ching [sic], "1919–1927 nien chüan-kuo tsa-chih chien-mu" ("A Short List of Periodicals Published in China, 1919–1927"), in Chang Ching-lu *11*, comp., Source Material for the Publication History of Contemporary China, Part I (Shanghai, 1954), pp. 86–106.

19. See John Dewey *620*, "New Culture in China," *Asia*, XXI, 7 (New York, July 1921), p. 585; Tsi C. Wang *771*, *The Youth Movement in China*, pp. 154–55; Ko Kungchen *260*, History of the Chinese Journalism (Shanghai, 1927), Chap. V, pp. 188–95; Ah-ying 2, comp., Source Material: Indices for the New Literature, Vol. X of Chao Chia-pi *33*, ed., A Corpus of China's New Literature (Shanghai, 1935); also Wang Che-fu *478*, History of the Chinese New Literature Movement (Peiping, 1933), Appendix; and Ching [sic], "A Short List of Periodicals Published in China, 1919–1927," pp. 86–106. For the reprinted manifestos and tables of contents of about a hundred periodicals of the May Fourth period see Chung-kung chung-yang *556*, ed., An Introduction to the Periodicals Published during the May Fourth Period, 3 vols. (Peking, 1958–59).

20. John Dewey *620*, "New Culture in China," p. 585; also a list of periodicals in the separately published volume, *Research Guide to "The May Fourth Movement."*

21. "Pen-she hsin ting t'ou-kao chien-chang" ("New Regulations of this Magazine on the Contribution of Articles"), The Eastern Miscellany, XVI, 6 (June 15, 1919), front page.

22. Ching-ts'ang, "Chung-kuo tsa-chih-chieh ying-yu-chih piao-chun" ("The Necessary Standard of Chinese Magazines"), *ibid.*, XVI, 7 (July 15, 1919), pp. 1–7.

23. Sun Yat-sen *425*, "A Letter to the Overseas Comrades of the Kuomintang," Jan. 29, 1920, in Hu Han-min *424*, ed., Complete Works of Dr. Sun Yat-sen (Shanghai, 1930), III, 348.

24. Chang Ching-lu, *Chung-kuo ti hsin-wen-chi-che yü hsin-wen-chih* (Newspapers and Newspapermen of China) (Shanghai, 1932), Part II, Chap. III, pp. 33–34.

25. Li Tse-chang, "San-shih-wu nien lai Chung-kuo chih ch'u-pan yeh" ("The Publication Enterprise of China in the Last Thirty-five Years"), in Chuang Yü, etc., eds., *Tsuichin san-shih-wu nien chih Chung-kuo chiao-yü* (The Education of China in the Last Thirty-five Years) (Shanghai, 1931), pp. 266–67. Slightly different statistics are in Ho Sheng-nai's article on the development of printing technology in China, *ibid.*

26. *Ibid.*, pp. 273–74.

27. *Ibid.*, pp. 269–70; also Ko Kung-chen *260*, History of the Chinese Journalism, Chap. VI, pp. 254–56.

28. John Dewey *627*, "The Sequel of the Student Revolt," pp. 381–82.

29. Dewey *620*, "New Culture in China," p. 584.

30. Dewey, "Public Opinion in Japan," *The New Republic*, XXVIII, Sup. to 363 (Nov. 16, 1921), pp. 15–18, reprinted in his *611*, *Characters and Events* (London, 1929), I, 178, with the title, "Japan Revisited: Two Years Later."

31. Timothy Tingfang Lew [Liu T'ing-fang], an address in Tientsin in May 1921, published in *The Chinese Recorder* (Journal of the Christian Movement in China), in English (Shanghai, May 1921); cited in both Tsi C. Wang *771*, *The Youth Movement in China*, Chap. I, pp. 1–2, and Stanley High *642*, *China's Place in the Sun* (New York, 1922), Chap. VIII, p. 149.

32. John Dewey *620*, "New Culture in China" (The Asia Publishing Co.), p. 585.

33. *Ibid.*

34. Chang I-p'ing, *Chen-shang sui-pi* (Sketches Written in Bed) (5th ed.; Shanghai, 1929, 1932), pp. 66–72. Chang was a humorous prose writer, once Hu Shih's assistant, T'ieh-min was Chang T'ieh-min, also a writer, who had joined the Work-and-Study Mutual Assistance Corps in 1919; see Chap. VII, n. i.

35. Hu Shih *197*, "The Problem of Chastity," New Youth, V, 1 (July 15, 1918), pp. 5–8. About this problem see a series of articles by Hu Shih, Lan Chih-hsien, and Chou Tso-jen, *ibid.*, VI, 4 (April 15, 1919), pp. 398–426.

36. See Chüeh-an, "I-ko chen-lieh-ti nü-hai-tzu" ("A Rigorously Chaste Girl"), New Youth, VII, 2 (Jan. 1, 1920), pp. 121–23. Although this is a short story about how parents starve their daughters to death in order to get a reward from the county magistrate, it seems to reflect a custom and a social problem in China of the time. Similar stories and news items could be found elsewhere. See also T'ang-ssu (another pseudonym of Lu Hsün) *351*, "My View on Rigid Chastity," New Youth, V, 2 (Aug. 15, 1918), pp. 92–101.

37. Wu Yü *528*, "The Old Family and Clan System Is the Basis of Despotism," New Youth, II, 6 (Feb. 1, 1917); Meng-chen [Fu Ssu-nien] *160*, "The Source of All Evils," New Tide, I, 1 (Jan. 1, 1919), pp. 124–28. Though Fu confined his argument to the "corrupt Chinese family system," the anarchist magazine *Shih-she tzu-yu lu ti-er chi* (Record of Freedom, No. II) even went so far as to say without reservation that a family system *in toto* is the origin of all evil.

38. See the order given by the governor of Kiangsu Province forbidding students to buy and read the new periodicals which criticized the traditional literature and ethics, April 9, 1919, reprinted in New Youth, VI, 4 (April 15, 1919), p. 446, with a headline "Shen-mo hua" ("What Nonsense") added by the editor of the monthly.

39. See *I Li* (The Book of Ritual), "Sang-fu" ("Costume for Mourning"), Sec. 3.

40. See "Ching k'an Yao Ming-hui ti San-ts'ung i ho Fu-shun shuo" ("Please look at Professor Yao Ming-hui's 'On the Principle of the Three Obediences' and 'On the Obedience of Woman'"), letter to the editor, New Youth, VI, 6 (Nov. 1, 1919), pp. 654–57. (The two articles were reprinted in New Youth.) See also Kao Kua, "Lo-shu shih shen-mo" ("What is that Magic Square Out of the Lo River?"), *ibid.*, VII, 3 (Feb. 1, 1920), pp. 37–46.

41. See Ch'en Tu-hsiu *70*, "My Doubts on the Theory of the Existence of Ghosts," New Youth, IV, 5 (May 15, 1918), pp. 408–09; Yi Pai-sha, "Chu-tzu wu-kuei-lun" ("Theories of the Nonexistence of Ghosts by Ancient Chinese Philosophers"), *ibid.*, V, 1 (July 15, 1918), pp. 15–26; Yi Yi-hsüan, "Ta Ch'en Tu-hsiu Yu-kuei-lun chih-i" ("An Answer to Ch'en Tu-hsiu's Doubts on the Theory of the Existence of Ghosts"), *ibid.*, 2 (Aug. 15,

1918), pp. 131–36; Liu Shu-ya, "Nan Yi Yi-hsüan chün" ("To Contend with Yi Yi-hsüan"), *ibid.*, pp. 137–42; Mo Teng, "Kuei-hsiang chih yen-chiu" ("A Study of Photographs of Ghosts"), letter to the editor, and answers by Wang Hsing-kung, Ch'en Ta-ch'i, and Ch'en Tu-hsiu, *ibid.*, 6 (Dec. 15, 1918), pp. 616–24; Hu Shih *217*, "Pu-hsiu" ("On Immortality"), *ibid.*, VI, 2 (Feb. 15, 1919), pp. 96–106; Liu Shu-ya, introduction to his translation of Haeckel's *Die Lebenswunder*, *ibid.*, pp. 107–8.

42. See Ch'en Ta-ch'i, "P'i ling-hsüeh" ("Expose the Fallacies of the Theory of Divination"), *ibid.*, IV, 5 (May 15, 1918), pp. 370–85; Ch'ien Hsüan-t'ung and Liu Pan-nung, "Sui-kan lu" ("Random Thoughts"), *ibid.*, pp. 456–68.

43. See Ch'en Tu-hsiu in "Sui-kan lu" ("Random Thoughts"), *ibid.,* V, 1 (July 15, 1918), pp. 76–77; Ssu [Lu Hsün], in "Random Thoughts," *ibid.*, 4 (Oct. 15, 1918), pp. 405–09; *ibid.*, 5 (Nov. 15, 1918), pp. 514–15.

44. Ch'ien Hsüan-t'ung, in "Random Thoughts," *ibid.*, 3 (Sept. 15, 1918), pp. 295–96.

45. John Dewey *620*, "New Culture in China," p. 586.

46. Lo Chia-lun *340*, "The Success and Failure of Our Student Movement During the Past Year and the Future Path to Be Taken," New Education, II, 5 (May 1920), p. 603.

47. Timothy Tingfang Lew *680*, "China's Renaissance," in *China Today through Chinese Eyes* (London, 1922), p. 31.

48. *Ibid.*, pp. 32–33; H. C. Hu *645*, "The New Thought Movement," *The Chinese Recorder*, LIV, 8 (Aug. 1923), p. 451. For discussion of the Society for Study of Socialism and other similar organizations see below, Chap. IX, pp. 243ff.

49. Tsi C. Wang *771*, *The Youth Movement in China*, Chap. X, p. 184.

50. *Ibid.*, pp. 184–85.

51. *Ibid.*, pp. 184.

52. Tso Shun-sheng *472*, Recollections of the Last Thirty Years (Kowloon, 1952), Chap. II, p. 5.

53. See Edgar Snow *739*, *Red Star over China*, pp. 146–48. Hsiao San gives the name of Yün's organization as Li-ch'ün hsüeh-she (The Study Society for the Welfare of the Masses); see Hsiao San, "Wei-ta-ti wu-shih nien ti i chang" ("A Chapter from 'The Great Five-Decades'"), in Hsiao San and others *179*, Selected Biographic Sketches Concerning Mao Tse-tung (Kalgan, 1945), pp. 30–31.

54. See Hu Shih *203*, "Fei ko-jen-chu-i ti hsin sheng-huo" ("A New Life of Non-individualism") written on Jan. 22, 1920, Hu's *207*, Collected Essays, Collection I, IV, 173–89; also Chou Tso-jen *120*, "The Atarashiki Mura of Japan," New Youth, IV, 3 (March 15, 1919), pp. 266–77; Kuo Shao-yü *279*, "A Study of the Atarashiki Mura," New Tide, II, 1 (Oct. 1919), pp. 59–67; Chou Tso-jen *116*, "A Visit to the Atarashiki Mura in Japan," *ibid.*, pp. 69–80; and Chou Tso-jen *117*, "The Spirit of Atarashiki Mura," an address to the Society for Academic Lectures in Tientsin, Nov. 8, 1919, New Youth, VII, 2 (Jan. 1, 1920), pp. 129–34.

55. Mushakoji Saneatsu's "Yü Chih-na wei-chih-ti yu-jen" ("A Letter to My Chinese Friends Unknown"), his poem "Chih i-ko Chih-na-ti hsiung-ti" ("To a Chinese Brother"), and the answers of Ts'ai, Ch'en, and Chou were all printed in New Youth, VII, 3 (Feb. 1, 1920), pp. 47–52.

56. For the regulations of the corps, its budget, and information on its Peking branches, see New Tide, II, 2 (Dec. 1919), pp. 395–98; New Youth, VII, 2 (Jan. 1, 1920), pp. 183–86; *ibid.*, 3 (Feb. 1, 1920), pp. 151–53.

57. See the series of articles reviewing problems of the corps by Hu Shih, Tai Chi-t'ao, Li Ta-chao, Wang Kuang-ch'i, and Ch'en Tu-hsiu, in New Youth, VII, 5 (April 1, 1920), pp. 1–17.

58. See Hu Shih, "Tu-wei hsien-sheng yü Chung-kuo" ("Mr. Dewey and China"), in *Hu Shih wen hsüan* (Hu Shih's Selected Essays) (Shanghai, 1930), p. 13; Ts'ai Yüan-p'ei *465*, "Chinese Philosophy of the Last Fifty Years," in Shun [Shen] Pao *414*, ed., The Past Fifty Years, in Commemoration of the *Shun Pao's* Golden Jubilee (Shanghai, 1923); Jane M. Dewey, ed., "Biography of John Dewey" in Paul Arthur Schilpp, ed., *The Philosophy of John Dewey* (2nd ed.; New York, 1951), pp. 40–42. The Deweys' day-to-day impressions of the May Fourth Movement were for the most part preserved in their *631, Letters from China and Japan*, ed. Evelyn Dewey (London, 1920). Several scores of articles on the Chinese problem of this period by Dewey can be found in the *New Republic* and *Asia*. Many of them have been reprinted in his *614, China, Japan and the U.S.A.* (New York, 1921); *617, Impressions of Soviet Russia and the Revolutionary World, Mexico-China-Turkey* (New York, 1929); and *611, Characters and Events, Popular Essays in Social and Political Philosophy*, ed. Joseph Ratner (New York, 1929); but quite a few, especially those on the Chinese students' revolt, were left out. His numerous speeches as translated into Chinese are scattered in Chinese newspapers and magazines. They do not seem to have been collected yet, except for the three pamphlets *146*, Five Major Lectures of Dewey (Peking, 1920); *145*, Dewey's Speeches in Fukien (Fukien, 1920); and Chang Ching-lu *12*, ed., Collected Speeches of John Dewey and Bertrand Russell (Shanghai, 1923); all published in Chinese. For Dewey's influence on Chinese philosophy and his works translated into Chinese see O. Brière, S.J. *576, Fifty Years of Chinese Philosophy, 1898–1950*, trans. Laurence G. Thompson (London, 1956), pp. 24–26, 120; also H. C. Hu *545*, "The New Thought Movement," pp. 453–54.

59. Ts'ai Yüan-p'ei *465*, "Chinese Philosophy of the Last Fifty Years"; Timothy Ting-fang Lew *680*, "China's Renaissance," pp. 33–34; Yang Tuan-liu *543*, "Some Thoughts on Bertrand Russell's Leaving China," The Eastern Miscellany, XVIII, 13 (July 10, 1921); Bertrand Russell and Dora Black *394*, Collected Speeches of Russell and Black (Peking, 1921); also *Lo-su wu ta chiang-yen* (Five Major Lectures of Russell); all in Chinese. See also Bertrand Russell *723*, "My Mental Development," in Paul Arthur Schilpp, ed., The Philosophy of Bertrand Russell (New York, 1951), pp. 17–18. Russell's articles on China of the period appeared in the *Nation* (London), the *Atlantic Monthly*, *The New Republic*, *Dial*, and *Century*. Most of them were reprinted in *The Problem of China* (London and New York, 1922). For Russell's influence on Chinese thought and his works translated into Chinese see O. Brière, S.J. *576, Fifty Years of Chinese Philosophy*, pp. 26, 121. For a short and interesting description of his trip in China see Alan Wood, *Bertrand Russell: The Passionate Skeptic* (New York, 1958), Chap. XIV, pp. 134–40. See also Russell's letter to the present author, below, Chap. IX, p. 238.

60. See "Meng-lu chuan-hao" ("Monroe Issue"), *Hsin chiao-yü* (New Education), IV, 4 (Shanghai, April 1, 1922). For Tagore's visit in China in 1924 see Stephen N. Hay, "India's Prophet in East Asia: Tagore's Message of Pan-Asian Spiritual Revival and Its Reception in Japan and China, 1916–1929" (Ph.D. thesis, Harvard University, 1957).

61. See *Pei-ching ta-hsüeh jih-k'an* (Peking University Daily), March 7, 1919–Jan. 15, 1923. For a description of popular lectures in Tientsin in the summer of 1920, see Tsung-yin, "T'ien-chin ti she-hui chiao-yü chuang-k'uang" ("The Situation of Social Education in Tientsin"), The Chinese Educational Review, XII, 7 (July 20, 1920), p. 5.

62. See Ts'ai Yüan-p'ei, "Pei-ching-ta-hsüeh hsiao-yü yeh-pan k'ai-hsüeh-shih yen-shuo" ("An Address at the Opening Ceremony of the Night Classes for Janitors at Peking University"), in Hsin-ch'ao she *461*, ed., The Life and Works of Ts'ai Yüan-p'ei, I, 278–80.

63. See Ts'ai Yüan-p'ei, "Tsai P'ing-min-yeh-hsiao k'ai-hsüeh-jih ti yen-shuo" ("An

Address at the Opening Ceremony of the Night School for the Plain People"), *ibid.*, pp. 280–84.

64. Chiang Monlin *96*, "The Education of Social Movement," New Education, II, 4 (Dec. 1919), pp. 400–01.

65. Kao Chien-ssu, "San-shih-wu-nien lai Chung-kuo chih min-chung chiao-yü" ("Popular Education in China in the Last Thirty-five Years"), in Chuang Yü, etc., eds., The Education of China in the Last Thirty-five Years, p. 167.

66. George E. Sokolsky *740*, "China's Defiance of Japan," *The Independent*, Vol. 99, No. 3693 (New York, Sept. 20, 1919), p. 390.

67. Chuang Yü, etc., eds., The Education of China in the Last Thirty-five Years, pp. 167–69.

68. New Youth, I, 1 (Sept. 15, 1915), pp. 7, 1–14; I, 2 (Oct. 1, 1915), pp. 9, 1–14.

69. Ch'en Tu-hsiu *54*, "The Year 1916," *ibid.*, 5 (Jan. 1916), p. 1.

70. [Fu Ssu-nien] *158*, "A Declaration of the Aims of the Publication of *New Tide*," New Tide, I, 1 (Jan. 1, 1919), pp. 1–2.

71. *Ibid.*, II, 2 (Dec. 1, 1919), p. 370.

72. T'ien-min *442*, "The Cultural Movement and Self-education," The Chinese Educational Review, XII, 1 (Jan. 20, 1920), pp. 2–4.

73. Sun Yat-sen *425*, "A Letter to the Overseas Comrades of the Kuomintang," Jan. 29, 1920, in Hu Han-min *424*, ed., Complete Works of Dr. Sun Yat-sen, III, 347–48.

74. John Dewey *620*, "New Culture in China," p. 586.

75. Kuo Mo-jo *275*, Ten Years with the Creation Society (Shanghai, 1932), Chap. IV, p. 88. For latest communist study and interpretation of the new culture movement see Ting Shou-ho and Yin Hsü-i, "Wu-ssu hsin wen-hua yün-tung" ("The May Fourth New Culture Movement"), *Li-shih yen-chiu* (Historical Studies), No. 4 (Peking, April 1959), pp. 1–35. Generally following Mao Tse-tung's line, the authors tried to show how the new culture movement developed from antifeudal activities into antiwarlord activities and was linked with the anti-imperialist trend; and how it changed from an intellectual movement into a revolutionary mass movement.

CHAPTER VIII

FOREIGN ATTITUDES TOWARD THE MOVEMENT

1. U.S. State Department *763*, *Papers Relating to the Foreign Relations of the United States, 1919* (Washington, D.C., 1934), I, 702.

2. The Japanese newspaper *Asahi's* view cited in Morris' report to the U.S. Acting Secretary of State, Tokyo, June 20, 1919, *ibid.*, p. 706; see also an article written on behalf of the Japanese Army General Staff (*Sambō hombu*) by the famous Inaba Kunzan [Iwakichi] "Shina no gairyoku riyō" ("China's Utilization of Foreign Force"), *The Taiyō* (The Sun), XXV, 5 (Tokyo, April 27, 1919), pp. 163–71. For a moderate view see the famous educator, Sawayanagi Masatarō *400*, "On Sino-Japanese Coexistence," *ibid.*, 13 (Oct. 27, 1919), pp. 108–16; and 14 (Nov. 27, 1919), pp. 63–70.

3. U.S. State Department *763*, *Papers Relating to Foreign Relations, 1919*, I, 707. For editorials of some Japanese newspapers on the Shantung problem see Kung Chen-huang, ed., *Ch'ing-tao ch'ao* (The Storm of Tsingtao) (Shanghai, 1919), Chap. XV, reprinted in *523*, Source Materials for the May Fourth Patriotic Movement (Peking, 1959), pp. 173–80.

4. See Kuo Mo-jo *275*, Ten Years of the Creation Society (Shanghai, 1932), IV, 88; for the poem see his *Nü-shen* (The Goddesses) (Shanghai, 1921), II, 131–35.

5. See Paul S. Reinsch, "Report on Political and Economic Conditions for the Quarter Ending June 30, 1919," to U.S. Secretary of State, Peking, Sept. 10, 1919, in U.S. State Department 763, *Papers Relating to Foreign Relations, 1919*, p. 370.

6. Reinsch 707, *An American Diplomat in China*, Chap. XXXIII, p. 376.

7. Morris' report in U.S. State Department 763, *Papers Relating to Foreign Relations, 1919*, pp. 705–06. For further opinions of the Japanese press on the Chinese student movement and on the American role in it, see *Asian Review* [a Japanese magazine in English], Vol. I (1920), pp. 244–388, especially p. 378.

8. U.S. State Department 763, *Papers Relating to Foreign Relations, 1919*, pp. 386, 696, 700, and 705.

9. See Ch'en's "Hsüeh-sheng-chieh ying-kai p'ai-ch'ih ti Jih huo" ("The Japanese 'Goods' that Chinese Student Circles Should Boycott"), New Youth, VII, 2 (Jan. 1, 1920), pp. 155–56.

10. See "Kung-t'ung kuan-li" ("International Control"), in Ch'en's 62, Collected Essays, II, 38–39; also "Wang kuo yü mai kuo" ("To Have the Country Subdued and to Sell It Out"), *ibid.*, pp. 16–17.

11. The friendly feelings of the Chinese towards Americans were fully appreciated by Reinsch, even at the most critical times; see Reinsch 707, *An American Diplomat in China*, Chap. XXXI, pp. 361–62.

12. See Shinouchi Yasaburo, comp., *Shinsen daijinmei jiten* (The New Encyclopedia of Famous Persons of Japan) (Tokyo, 1939), VI, 483. For text of the letter of the Student Union of China to the society see Ch'a-an, *Hsüeh-chieh feng-ch'ao chi* (A Record of the Student Strikes) (Shanghai, 1919), Appendix III.

13. Yoshino Sakuzo 561, "My View on the Recent Student Strikes in China"; the original was published in the *Shinjin* (New Man) magazine, June 1919, translated into Chinese in *Chung-hua hsin pao*, reprinted in The Eastern Miscellany, XVI, 7 (July 15, 1919), pp. 191–94.

14. *Ibid.*, p. 191. See also Yoshino 559, "The Rise of the New Thought Tide in Peking University," *Chūō kōron* (The Central Review), No. 370 (June 1, 1919), pp. 94–96; and his 560, "The Anti-Japanese Incident in China," *ibid.*, No. 371 (July 1, 1919), pp. 84–86.

15. Fukuda Tokuzo 640, "Japan's Shortsighted Diplomacy," *The New Era* (July 1919), reprinted under a subtitle "Liberal Japanese View of Far Eastern Problems" in *The Far Eastern Fortnightly* (the Bulletin of the Far Eastern Bureau), VI, 19 (New York, Sept. 1, 1919), p. 6.

16. Cited in Morris' report to the acting Secretary of State, June 20, 1919, U.S. State Department 763, *Papers Relating to Foreign Relations, 1919*, pp. 707–08. See "Pekin gakusei-dan no kōdō o mamba suru nakare" ("Do Not Scold at the Activities of the Peking Students") (editorial), The Central Review, No. 370 (June 1, 1919), p. 1; "Kyoran seru Shina yōchō-ron" ("The Foolish and Confusing Opinion for Punishing China") (editorial), *ibid.*, No. 371 (July 1, 1919), p. 1.

17. See Witter Bynner's poem, "Shantung" in *The Nation* (May 1919) and George E. Sokolsky 740, "China's Defiance of Japan," *The Independent*, Vol. 99, No. 3693 (New York, Sept. 20, 1919), pp. 388, 390. Sokolsky reported on p. 390: "China is awake. Her people have become democratically articulate." Sokolsky, a Russian Jew, had been editor of the *Russian Daily News* in Petrograd in 1917. He became assistant editor of the *North China Star* in Tientsin in 1918. In the summer of 1919 he was in Shanghai as a newspaperman having close relations with the student unions, and was suspected by the police of the International Settlement of being a Bolshevist.

18. Reinsch 707, *An American Diplomat in China*, Chap. XXXII, p. 373.

19. *Ibid.*, pp. 373–74; U.S. State Department 763, *Papers Relating to Foreign Relations, 1919,* pp. 694; 698–99; 701–14; for the cautious support by Western missionaries in China of the Chinese student movement right after the May Fourth Incident see a series of editorials of the American mission monthly, *The Chinese Recorder,* L, 7 (Shanghai, July 1919), pp. 434–37. For Chinese translation of the editorials of Western newspapers in China sympathetic with the student strike see Kung Chen-huang, ed., The Storm of Tsingtao (Shanghai, 1919), Appendix IV, reprinted in 523, Source Materials for the May Fourth Patriotic Movement (Peking, 1959), pp. 227–36.

20. Morris' telegram to the U.S. acting Secretary of State, Tokyo, March 23, 1919, in U.S. State Department 763, *Papers Relating to Foreign Relations, 1919,* p. 689.

21. See Shang-hai t'ung-hsin she, comp., *Shang-hai yen-chiu tzu-liao* (Source Material for the Study of Shanghai) (Shanghai, 1936), pp. 127–53, 483; Chang Chün-mai [Carsun Chang], "Shang-hai Kung-kung tsu-chieh Fa tsu-chieh chih tzu-chih tsu-chih chi Shang-hai shih-min tui-yü tzu-chih chih tse-jen" ("The Organization of Self-government of the International Settlement and French Concession of Shanghai and the Responsibility of Shanghai Citizens Toward Self-government"), The Eastern Miscellany, XIX, 7 (April 10, 1922), pp. 119–24; H. G. W. Woodhead 784, ed., *The China Year Book, 1921–22* (London, 1922), pp. 731–34; E. C. Pearce, "How Shanghai is Governed," *Millard's Review,* XIV, 9 (Oct. 30, 1920), pp. 444–46.

22. [Editor] 690, "Merchants' Strike in Shanghai," *The North-China Herald,* CXXXI, 2704 (Shanghai, June 7, 1919), p. 650.

23. *The North-China Herald,* CXXXI, 2705 (June 14, 1919), p. 685.

24. Reinsch to the acting Secretary of State, Peking, June 24, 1919, U.S. State Department 763, *Papers Relating to Foreign Relations, 1919,* p. 708.

25. *Ibid.*

26. Reinsch 707, *An American Diplomat in China,* Chap. XXXII, p. 371.

27. [Editor] 746, "The Chinese Student," *The North-China Herald,* CXXXI, 2705 (June 14, 1919), p. 684; written and first published in the daily on June 9.

28. "Lawlessness in Shanghai" (editorial), *The North-China Herald,* CXXXI, 2705, p. 684, first published on June 10.

29. For this incident and other measures taken by the International Settlement in dealing with the students, merchants, and workers see "Shang-hai kung-kung tsu-chieh kung-pu-chü ching-wu-ch'u tang-an" ("Files from the Police Department of the Municipal Council of the Shanghai International Settlement") trans. from English into Chinese by the police department of Shanghai and printed in 523, Source Materials for the May Fourth Patriotic Movement, pp. 711–86; Hai-shang-hsien-jen 164, ed., A Factual Account of the Shanghai Strikes, Vol. II; see also Anatol M. Kotenev 667, *Shanghai: Its Municipality and the Chinese, Being the History of the Shanghai Municipal Council and Its Relations with the Chinese, etc.* (Shanghai, 1927). Kotenev wrongly gave the date of the incident as June 11.

30. Reinsch to the acting Secretary of State, June 24, 1919, U.S. State Department 763, *Papers Relating to Foreign Relations, 1919,* pp. 709–10.

31. The report is titled "Shanghai Despatch No. 3297," June 21, 1919; see *ibid.*, p. 711.

32. *Ibid.*, pp. 711–12. For public opinion of the Western newspapers in Shanghai see Hai-shang-hsien-jen 164, ed., A Factual Account of the Shanghai Merchants' and Workers' Strikes (Shanghai, 1919), Vol. I.

33. Reinsch's telegram to the acting Secretary of State, Peking, June 11, 1919, U.S. State Department 763, *Papers Relating to Foreign Relations, 1919,* p. 700.

34. French Consular Ordinance N5, Article 3, translated in Kotenev 667, *Shanghai: Its Municipality and the Chinese*, Chap. VII, pp. 83–89; see also Article 1.

35. *Ibid.*, Articles 4, 5, 6, and 7.

36. J. B. Powell, secretary of the American Chamber of Commerce of China, to E. C. Pearce, chairman of the municipal council of the International Settlement, July 8, 1919, in Kotenev 667, *Shanghai: Its Municipality and the Chinese*, pp. 83–89.

37. See a joint protest signed by 26 different Chinese organizations which represented practically the entire Chinese mercantile and professional communities of Shanghai, April 12, 1924, *ibid.*

38. See the letter of the Shanghai Student Union to E. C. Pearce, chairman of the Shanghai municipal council, June 5, 1919, in *The North-China Herald*, CXXXI, 2704 (Shanghai, June 7, 1919), p. 650; also Reinsch 707, *An American Diplomat in China*, Chap. XXXII, p. 373.

39. See [Li] Chien-nung 288, "The Right of Freedom of Speech and Publication in the Chinese Constitution," The Pacific Ocean, II, 1 (2nd printing; May 5, 1920), p. 6; see also Hollington K. Tong, "Is China Drifting Toward Bolshevism?" *Millard's Review*, X, 8 (Oct. 25, 1919), pp. 309–14. The same hysteria prevailed in the United States at the time; see "Editorially Speaking," *The Independent* (June 5, 1919), p. 17.

40. See Hu Shih 222, "More Study of Problems, Less Talk of 'Isms,' " Weekly Critic, XXXI (July 20, 1919); and Li Ta-chao 302, "One More Discussion of Problems and Isms," Weekly Critic, XXXV (Aug. 17, 1919).

41. See Kotenev 667, *Shanghai: Its Municipality and the Chinese*, pp. 83–89.

42. Dewey 620, "New Culture in China," *Asia* (July 1921), p. 584.

43. See Westel Woodbury Willoughby 782, *Foreign Rights and Interests in China* (Baltimore, 1927), Vol. I, Introduction; W. W. Langer, *The Diplomacy of Imperialism* (New York and London, 1935); also John K. Fairbank 635, *The United States and China* (Cambridge, Mass., 1948), Chap. VII, pp. 135ff (1958 ed., pp. 120–23).

44. For the Russian text of the declaration see Vladimir Vilenskii [Sibiriakov], *Kitai i Sovetskaia Rossiia* (China and Soviet Russia) (Moscow, 1919), pp. 14–16; English translation based on French, cited in Hollington K. Tong 750, "Russian Soviet Would Befriend China," *Millard's Review*, VIII, 1 (June 5, 1920), pp. 25–26; reprinted in *The Far Eastern Fortnightly*, VII, 25 (Dec. 6, 1920), pp. 4–5; another English translation in Jane Degras, ed., *Soviet Documents on Foreign Policy*, Vol. I, 1917–1924 (London, 1951), pp. 158–61; and with omission supplied in Allen S. Whiting 777, *Soviet Policies in China, 1917–1924* (New York, 1954), Chap. I, pp. 16–21. For the Chinese text see New Youth, VII, 6 (May 1, 1920), Appendix, pp. 1–3. For a revised Chinese translation in the literary language by the Kuomintang see Lo Chia-lun, ed., *Ke-ming wen-hsien* (Documents of the Chinese Revolution) (Taipei, 1955), IX, 1–17.

45. See *Izvestiia*, No. 163 (715) (Aug. 26, 1919), p. 1, and *Pravda*, No. 188 (Aug. 26, 1919), p. 1.

46. See 595, Chicherin's report to the Fifth Congress of Soviets on July 4, 1918, in *Izvestiia*, No. 138 (402) (July 5, 1918), p. 7; and Allen S. Whiting 777, *Soviet Policies in China*, Chap. II, pp. 28–29.

47. See *Millard's Review*, 13 (June 5, 1920), p. 26; and Hollington K. Tong 750, "Russian Soviet Would Befriend China," pp. 25–26.

48. *Ibid.*; *The Far Eastern Fortnightly*, VII, 25 (Dec. 6, 1920), p. 4.

49. See Allen S. Whiting 777, *Soviet Policies in China*, Chap. II, pp. 29–38; also Whiting 778, "The Soviet Offer to China of 1919," *The Far Eastern Quarterly*, X, 4 (Aug. 1951), pp. 355–64.

50. See John Dewey *615*, "China's Nightmare," *Millard's Review*, XIII, 12 (Aug. 21, 1920), p. 630; also in *New Republic*, XXIII (June 30, 1920), pp. 145–57; Hollington K. Tong *751*, "Soviet Delegation to Arrange Commercial Relations with China," *Millard's Review*, XIV, 1 (Sept. 4, 1920), pp. 4–6, also in *The Far Eastern Fortnightly*, VII, 25 (Dec. 6, 1920), p. 4.

51. See Leo Pasvolsky *700*, *Russia in the Far East* (New York, 1922), Appendix II; *Izvestiia* (Nov. 6, 1921); and Weigh Ken-shen *775*, *Russo-Chinese Diplomacy* (Shanghai, 1928), Appendix C, pp. 349–63.

52. "China and Russians in China" (editorial), *Millard's Review*, XIV, 5 (Oct. 2, 1920), p. 213.

53. A. Vozenesenskii *769*, "Revoliutsionnyi pozhar na Vostoke" ("Revolutionary Conflagration in the East"), *Izvestiia*, No. 204 (765) (Sept. 14, 1919), p. 2.

54. "Russian Interests in China and the Chinese," *Millard's Review*, reprinted in *The Far Eastern Fortnightly*, VII, 25 (Dec. 6, 1920), pp. 3–4.

55. "Protests of Prince Koudatcheff, Russian Minister at Peking, over Chinese Government's Action in Withdrawing Recognition [on Sept. 23, 1920]," Sept. 24, 1920; reprinted *ibid.*, pp. 6–7.

56. See "Tui-yü O-lo-ssu Lao-nung cheng-fu t'ung-kao ti yü-lun" ("Public Opinion on the Proclamation of the Russian Government of Workers and Peasants"), New Youth, VII, 6 (May 1, 1920), Appendix, pp. 3–10.

57. *Ibid.*, p. 5.

58. Reinsch, "Report on Political and Economic Conditions for the Quarter Ending June 30, 1919," Peking, Sept. 10, 1919, in U.S. State Department *764*, *Papers Relating to the Foreign Relations of the U.S., 1919*, p. 389.

59. "Public Opinion on the Proclamation of the Russian Government of Workers and Peasants," New Youth, VII, 6 (May 1, 1920), pp. 10–11.

60. *Shih shih hsin pao* (Shanghai) (editorial), reprinted in *ibid.*, p. 11.

61. *Hsing-ch'i p'ing-lun* (Weekly Review) (Shanghai) (editorial), reprinted in *ibid.*, p. 22.

62. Text of the Chinese presidential mandate *596*, "China's Declaration of Policy Toward Russia," dated Sept. 23, 1920, reprinted in *The Far Eastern Fortnightly* (Dec. 6, 1920), pp. 5–6. See also Hollington K. Tong *754*, "The New Development of Sino-Russian Relations," *Millard's Review*, XIV, 6 (Oct. 9, 1920), pp. 281–84; and Hu Sheng, *Imperialism and Chinese Politics* (Peking, 1949), Chap. VI, p. 284.

63. Chinese text of the second Karakhan proclamation in Hu Hua *193*, ed., Source Materials for the History of the New Democratic Revolution in China (Shanghai, 1951), Part I, pp. 35–38. For the English translation see Allen S. Whiting *777*, *Soviet Policies in China*, Appendix C, pp. 272–75.

64. John Dewey *618*, "Is China a Nation or a Market?" *New Republic*, XLIV (Nov. 11, 1925), 298–99; reprinted in Dewey *611*, *Characters and Events*, I, 318.

CHAPTER IX

THE IDEOLOGICAL AND POLITICAL SPLIT, 1919–1921

1. Hu Shih *222*, "More Study of Problems, Less Talk of 'Isms,'" Weekly Critic, No. 31 (July 20, 1919).

2. [Lan] Chih-fei *283*, "Problems and Isms," *Kuo-min kung-pao* (Citizens' Gazette), reprinted in The Pacific Ocean, II, 1 (2nd printing; May 5, 1920), pp. 4–10.

3. Li Ta-chao *302*, "One More Discussion of Problems and Isms," Weekly Critic, No. 35 (Aug. 17, 1919).

4. Hu Shih *218*, "The Third Discussion of Problems and Isms" and "The Fourth Discussion of Problems and Isms," The Pacific Ocean, II, 1 (2nd printing; May 5, 1920), pp. 15–25.

5. Hu Shih *204*, "The Significance of the New Thought Tide," New Youth, VII, 1 (Dec. 1, 1919), p. 11. An abridged English translation of the article may be found in Ssu-yü Teng and John K. Fairbank *745*, *China's Response to the West, a Documentary Survey 1839–1923* (Cambridge, Mass., 1954), Chap. XXVI, pp. 252–55.

6. John Dewey *144*, "Social Philosophy and Political Philosophy," New Youth, VII, 1 (Dec. 1, 1919), pp. 121–34; VII, 2 (Jan. 1, 1920), pp. 163–82.

7. See Li Ta-chao *302*, "One More Discussion of Problems and 'Isms.' "

8. Ch'en Tu-hsiu, "Pi-chiao-shang ken shih-chi ti hsiao-kuo" ("Comparatively More Practical Effects"), in "Random Thoughts," New Youth, VIII, 1 (Sept. 1, 1920), p. 2.

9. Ch'en Tu-hsiu *50*, "Chu-i yü nu-li" ("Isms and Endeavor"), in "Random Thoughts," New Youth, VIII, 4 (Dec. 1, 1920), pp. 2–3.

10. C. T. [Shih Ts'un-t'ung], "Wo-men yao tsen-mo-yang kan she-hui-ke-ming" ("How Should We Carry on Social Revolution"), *Kung-ch'an-tang* (The Communist), No. 5 (Shanghai, June 7, 1921), p. 10.

11. For a discussion of this dilemma of John Dewey's theory in the field of education in the United States, see Robert M. Hutchins, *Freedom, Education, and the Fund, Essays and Addresses, 1946–1956* (New York, 1956), Part II, Chap. 3, pp. 126–37.

12. The society's program for the study of the problems was sent by Mao to Teng Chung-hsia in Peking. Teng distributed it among his friends and reprinted it in the *Pei-ching ta-hsüeh jih-k'an* (Peking University Daily), No. 467 (Oct. 23, 1919).

13. Ch'en Tu-hsiu *60*, "Discussion on Politics," New Youth, VIII, 1 (Sept. 1, 1920), pp. 1–2.

14. *Ibid.*

15. *Ibid.*

16. Hu Shih's letter in answer to Sun Fu-lu and Ch'ang Nai-te, June 16, 1922, in Hu Shih *207*, Collected Essays, Collection II, p. 101.

17. John Dewey *620*, "New Culture in China," *Asia* (July 1921), p. 581.

18. John Dewey *627*, "The Sequel of the Student Revolt," *The New Republic*, XXI, 273 (March 3, 1920), pp. 380–81.

19. John Dewey *620*, "New Culture in China," p. 581.

20. *Ibid.*

21. John Dewey *627*, "The Sequel of the Student Revolt," pp. 380–81.

22. John Dewey *620*, "New Culture in China," pp. 581–82.

23. John Dewey *627*, "The Sequel of the Student Revolt," p. 380.

24. Ch'en Tu-hsiu, "T'ao-lun wu-cheng-fu chu-i ti hsin" ("Letters in Discussion of Anarchism, No. 2, to Ch'ü Sheng-pai"), in Hsin-ch'ing-nien-she pien-chi-pu *180*, ed., Collected Essays in Discussion of Socialism (Canton, 1922), pp. 105–06.

25. Ch'en Tu-hsiu *53*, "What Is the New Culture Movement?" New Youth, VII, 5 (April 1, 1920), pp. 1–6.

26. Ch'en Tu-hsiu *66*, "Cultural Movement and Social Movement," in Ch'en *62*, Collected Essays of Ch'en Tu-hsiu, II, 114–17.

27. Liang Ch'i-ch'ao *307*, "The Significance and Value of Political Movements," in Liang *310*, Collected Works of Liang Ch'i-ch'ao (Shanghai, 1936), Essays, Vol. XIII, Sec. 36, pp. 12–13.

28. *Ibid.*, pp. 18–19.

IDEOLOGICAL AND POLITICAL SPLIT · 433

29. Upton Close, article in *Weekly Review of the Far East* (Aug. 2, 1919), cited in Stanley High *642*, *China's Place in the Sun* (New York, 1922), VII, 133–34; see also T'ao Meng-ho's article *438*, "Our Political Life," New Youth, V, 6 (Dec. 15, 1918).

30. John Dewey, "Mei-kuo chih min-chih ti fa-chan" ("The Development of Democracy in the United States"), *Mei-chou p'ing-lun* (Weekly Critic), No. 26 (Peking, June 15, 1919), also in *Ch'en Pao*, "Supplementary" (Peking, June 17–20, 1919), and cited in Ch'en Tu-hsiu *59*, "The Basis for the Realization of Democracy," New Youth, VII, 1 (Dec. 1, 1919), p. 16.

31. John Dewey *144*, "Social Philosophy and Political Philosophy," New Youth, VII, 1 (Dec. 1, 1919), pp. 1–6.

32. *Ibid.*, 3 (Feb. 1, 1920), pp. 125–27, 129–30.

33. *Ibid.*, pp. 130–32.

34. John Dewey *627*, "The Sequel of the Student Revolt," *The New Republic*, XXI, 273 (Feb. 25, 1920), p. 381.

35. John and Alice Dewey *631*, *Letters from China and Japan* (New York, 1920), pp. 150, 170.

36. John Dewey *620*, "New Culture in China," p. 642.

37. Dewey *144*, "Social Philosophy and Political Philosophy," New Youth, VII, 3 (Feb. 1, 1920), p. 118.

38. Ch'en Tu-hsiu *59*, "The Basis for the Realization of Democracy," pp. 13–14; also Benjamin Schwartz *735*, *Chinese Communism and the Rise of Mao*, Chap. 1, pp. 19–20.

39. This was based on Dewey's lecture, "The Development of Democracy in the United States," Weekly Critic, No. 26 (June 15, 1919), cited in Ch'en Tu-hsiu *59*, "The Basis for the Realization of Democracy," p. 16.

40. *Ibid.*, pp. 16–17.

41. *Ibid.*, pp. 17–18.

42. Ch'en Tu-hsiu, "Li-hsien-cheng-chih yü cheng-tang" ("Constitutionalism and Political Parties"), in *Ch'en 62*, Collected Essays, II, 47; also "Ch'ih-fan wen-t'i" ("A Problem of Eating"), *ibid.*, p. 8. Both written between June 1–8, 1919.

43. T'ao Li-kung [T'ao Meng-ho], "Yu Ou chih kan-hsiang" ("Some Thoughts during my European Trip"), New Youth, VII, 1 (Dec. 1, 1919), pp. 49–55.

44. Ch'en Tu-hsiu *47*, Ch'en Tu-hsiu's Final Views (Hong Kong, 1950; 3rd ed., Taipei, 1959), Ch'en's letter to Lien-ken, July 31, 1940, pp. 15–16; Letter to Hsi-liu, Sept. 1940, pp. 19–24; and Ch'en's article, "Wo-ti ken-pen i-chien" ("My Basic Views"), Nov. 28, 1940, pp. 25–29; see also Hu Shih's preface, pp. 1–11.

45. Parts of Russell's articles on his impression of Russia, later reprinted in *Bolshevism: Theory and Practice* (New York, 1920), were translated into Chinese and published in The Eastern Miscellany; and some of the Russian's answers to his criticism were translated and published in New Youth, VIII, 3 (Nov. 1, 1920) and the following issues.

46. Bertrand Russell *729*, *The Problem of China* (London, 1922), Chap. XV, pp. 242–45.

47. *Ibid.*, p. 246; see also Russell *720*, "Industry in Undeveloped Countries," a speech delivered at the Chinese Social and Political Science Association in Peking on Dec. 10, 1920, *The Chinese Social and Political Science Review* V (a), 4 (Dec. 1920), pp. 239–54; a Chinese translation of the article, by Yang Tuan-liu, appeared in Chang Ching-lu *12*, ed., Collected Speeches of Dewey and Russell, pp. 24–51.

48. Yang Tuan-liu *554*, "A Talk with Russell," in Ch'en Tu-hsiu and others *71*, "Discussions of Socialism," New Youth, VIII, 4 (Dec. 1, 1920), pp. 15–16 (later enlarged as a book edited by the New Youth Society in Canton under the title *180*, Collected Essays in Discussion of Socialism, cited in n. 24); also Yang Tuan-liu *542*, "Talks with Mr. Ber-

trand Russell," 3 speeches delivered in Changsha by Yang, The Eastern Miscellany, XVII, 22 (Nov. 25, 1920), pp. 9–17.

49. See Russell's lecture *393*, "Bolshevik Thought," *Lo-su yüeh-k'an* (Russell Monthly), No. 1 (Shanghai, Jan. 1921), Appendix II, p. 11.

50. Bertrand Russell, "Chung-kuo-jen tao tzu-yu chih lu" ("China's Road to Freedom"), in *Che hsüeh* (Philosophia), No. 3 (Sept. 1921), pp. 357–68, also Chang Ching-lu *12*, ed., Collected Speeches of Dewey and Russell, pp. 15–23.

51. Bertrand Russell *729*, *The Problem of China*, Chap. XV, p. 250; see also pp. 248–51.

52. *Ibid.*, p. 251.

53. *Ibid.*, Chap. IV, p. 81.

54. *Ibid.*, Chap. XI, p. 185.

55. *Ibid.;* also Chap. XI, pp. 185–98; Chap. XII, pp. 199–213.

56. *Ibid.*, Chap. IV, pp. 81–82.

57. Bertrand Russell *723*, "My Mental Development," in Schilpp, ed., *The Philosophy of Bertrand Russell* (3rd ed.; New York, 1944, 1951), p. 17.

58. See [Chang] Tung-sun, "P'ing tzu-pen-chu-i ti pan-shih fang-fa" ("A Comment on Capitalist Method in Management"), *Chieh-fang yü kai-tsao* (Emancipation and Reconstruction), II, 3 (Feb. 1, 1920), pp. 1–3.

59. The discussion was brought about by Chang Tung-sun's short article "Hsien-tsai yü chiang-lai" ("The Present and the Future"), *Kai-tsao* (La Rekonstruo, or Reconstruction), III, 4 (Dec. 15, 1920). See also a series of articles by Liang Ch'i-ch'ao, Lan Kung-wu, Chiang Po-li, Chang Tung-sun, et al., "A Study of Socialism," *ibid.*, 6 (Feb. 15, 1921), pp. 17–58. For the Russian legal Marxists see Bertram D. Wolfe, *Three Who Made A Revolution* (Boston, 1948), Chap. VII, pp. 118–26.

60. See Ch'en Tu-hsiu and others *71*, "Discussions of Socialism," New Youth, VIII, 4 (Dec. 1, 1920).

61. See Liang Ch'i-ch'ao's conclusion and Chiang Po-li's opinion in La Rekonstruo, III, 6 (Feb. 15, 1921), pp. 25–26, 36.

62. Lan Kung-yen, "She-hui-chu-i yü tzu-pen-chih-tu" ("Socialism and Capitalist System"), *ibid.*, pp. 51–54.

63. Ch'en Tu-hsiu, "San lun Shang-hai she-hui" ("Third Discussion of the Shanghai Community"), New Youth, VIII, 3 (Nov. 1, 1920), p. 2.

64. John Dewey *620*, "New Culture in China," p. 583.

65. See Hu Shih's foreword *218*, for the discussions in The Pacific Ocean, II, 1 (2nd printing [1st printing, Jan. 5?]; May 5, 1920), p. 1.

66. Hu Shih and others *227*, "Manifesto of Struggle for Freedom," reprinted in The Eastern Miscellany, XVII, 16 (Aug. 25, 1920), pp. 133–34.

67. See Ts'ai Yüan-p'ei and others *466*, "Our Political Proposals," reprinted in The Eastern Miscellany, XIX, 8 (April 25, 1922), pp. 138–40.

68. Yang Yu-chiung *547*, A History of Chinese Political Parties (Shanghai, 1936), VII, 120–40; Li Chien-nung *289*, Political History of China in the Last One Hundred Years (Shanghai, 1947), Vol. II, Chap. XIII, pp. 596–601.

69. See *ibid.*, pp. 592–93; Chia I-chün, *Chung-hua-min-kuo shih* (The History of the Republic of China) (Peiping, 1930), Chap. IX, pp. 94–96; Ts'ai Yüan-p'ei *463*, "My Experiences at Peking University," The Eastern Miscellany, XXX, 1 (Jan. 1, 1934), pp. 5–13.

70. See Hu Shih, "Kuan-yü 'Wo-men ti cheng-chih chu-chang' ti t'ao-lun" ("Discussions of 'Our Political Proposals'"), appendix in Hu Shih *207*, Collected Essays, Collection II (Shanghai, 1924), II, 35–40.

71. Mei Kuang-ti [Mei Chin-chuang], letter to Hu Shih, May 13, 1922, in Hu's "Wo-ti ch'i-lu" ("My Cross Roads"), *ibid.*, p. 91.

72. Letters by Sun Fu-lu and Ch'ang Nai-te to Hu Shih, June 8 and June 2, 1922, respectively, *ibid.*, pp. 91–94.

73. Hu's answer to the above letters, June 16, 1922, *ibid.*, p. 101.

74. See Hu Shih, "Wo-men tsou na-t'iao lu" ("Which Road Do We Take?"), and Liang Sou-ming, "Chin i ch'ing-chiao Hu Shih-chih hsien-sheng" ("Some Humble Questions to Hu Shih"), together with Hu's answer, in 206, Recent Academic Writings of Hu Shih (Shanghai, 1935), pp. 439–67; Hu Shih and others, *Chung-kuo wen-t'i* (China Problems) (Shanghai, 1932). See also articles in the weekly edited by Hu Shih, *Tu-li p'ing-lun* (Independent Critic), in 1934–35.

75. See *Pei-ching ta-hsüeh jih-k'an* (Peking University Daily) (Nov. 17, 1921–Jan. 15, 1922); and Chang Hsi-man *18*, My Memory of Modern Historical Episodes (Shanghai, 1949), Chap. 38, pp. 136–48. For a short account of the development of socialism in China before 1920, see Feng Tzu-yu *152*, Socialism and China (Hong Kong, 1920).

76. See Peking University Daily, Nov. 17, 1921, to Nov. 20, 1922.

77. See Li Ta, "Ma-k'e-ssu-p'ai she-hui-chu-i" ("Marxist Socialism"), written on June 2, 1921, in *180*, Collected Essays in Discussion of Socialism, pp. 171–91; see also Feng Tzu-yu *152*, Socialism and China, pp. 18–19.

78. Fang-lu, "Ch'ing-suan Ch'en Tu-hsiu" ("Liquidating Ch'en Tu-hsiu"), in Ch'en Tung-hsiao *74*, ed., Discussions on Ch'en Tu-hsiu, p. 66; Benjamin Schwartz *735*, *Chinese Communism and the Rise of Mao*, Chap. II, p. 31.

79. See Sun's speech of 1906, "San min chu-i yü Chung-kuo chih ch'ien-t'u" ("The Three Principles of the People and the Future of China"), in Hu Han-min *424*, ed., Complete Works of Dr. Sun Yat-sen, II, 74–78; also "T'i-ch'ang kuo-chia she-hui chu-i" ("To Promote State Socialism"), *ibid.*, pp. 98–100; "She-hui chu-i chih p'ai-p'ieh yü fang-fa" ("The Kinds and Methods of Socialism"), *ibid.*, pp. 100–22; "Min-sheng chu-i yü she-hui ke-ming" ("The Principle of the People's Livelihood and Social Revolution"), *ibid.*, pp. 122–28; and "San min chu-i," written in 1919, in *Tsung-li ch'üan shu* (Dr. Sun Yat-sen's Complete Works) (Taipei, 1954), V, 399.

80. See Hu Han-min *421*, ed., Complete Works of Sun, II, 177–80; also see Hu Shih, "Kuo-yü ti chin-hua" ("The Progress of the National Language [Vernacular]"), New Youth (Feb. 1, 1920), pp. 2–3.

81. See Chiang Kai-shek *91*, "Cheng-li wen-hua i-ch'an yü kai-chin min-tsu hsi-hsing" ("Reorganization of the Cultural Heritage and Improvement of the National Character"), in Central Reform Committee of the Kuomintang, ed., *Tsung-ts'ai yen-lun hsüan-chi* (Selected Works of the Director General of the Kuomintang) (Taipei, Taiwan, 1952), p. 230.

82. See Hu Han-min, "Meng-tzu yü she-hui-chu-i" ("Mencius and Socialism"), *Chien-she* (The Construction), I, 1 (Aug. 1, 1919), pp. 157–68; also Hu Han-min *187*, "A Materialistic Study of the History of Chinese Philosophy," *ibid.*, 3 (Oct. 1, 1919), pp. 513–43; 4 (Nov. 1, 1919), pp. 36–69; and other articles by Tai Chi-t'ao and Lin Yün-kai.

83. See their letters under the title "Ching-t'ien chih-tu yu wu chih yen-chiu" ("A Study of the Problem Whether the Well-Field System Existed"), *ibid.*, II, 1 (Feb. 1, 1920), pp. 149–76; 2 (March 1, 1920), pp. 241–50; 5 (June 1, 1920), pp. 877–914; and 6 (Aug. 1, 1920), pp. 1245–60.

84. Sun Yat-sen *423*, "The First Step to the Reform of China," in Hu Han-min *424*, ed., Complete Works, II, 178–80; and *421*, "Chiu-kuo chih chi wu" ("The Urgent Task of Saving the Nation"), delivered at the Shanghai World Alliance of Chinese Students which was possibly also at the time the headquarters of the Student Union of China, on Oct. 18, 1919, *ibid.*, pp. 180–85.

85. K'ang Pai-ch'ing mentioned Sun's opinion and expressed his own doubt in a letter

to Tai Chi-t'ao; see Tai, "Ke-ming! ho-ku? wei-ho?" ("Revolution! Why? For What?"), The Construction, I, 3 (Oct. 1, 1919), pp. 567–97. For Sun's elitist theory and its similarity with Lenin's, see Benjamin Schwartz 735, *Chinese Communism and the Rise of Mao*, Chap. I, pp. 15, 22, n. 33 on p. 213, and Chap. II, p. 32; see also Ts'ui Shu-ch'in 474, Sun Yat-sen and Communism (Hong Kong, 1954).

86. Sun Yat-sen's letter to Ch'en I-hsün, a student of Peiyang University and representative of the Student Union of Tientsin. The manuscript of the letter was shown in the "Exhibit of the Party's Historical Materials in Commemoration of the Golden Jubilee of the Kuomintang."

87. According to Ch'eng T'ien-fang, during the period of strikes in 1919 many students went to see Sun in his Shanghai residence; see Ch'eng 84, "Wo ts'u-tz'u yeh-chien Tsung-li" ("My First Interview with Dr. Sun Yat-sen"), Sao-tang pao (Chungking, May 5, 1945).

88. Lo Chia-lun 342, "A Retrospect of the Past Year [1919] in the Light of Current Affairs," in Lo 339, From Dark Clouds, to Cloudbursts, to Bright Sunset (Chungking, 1943), p. 69. An interesting description of the students' interview of Sun Yat-sen in 1919 may be found in Chang Kuo-t'ao's English memoirs, in manuscript.

89. Ch'en Tu-hsiu's letter to Hu Shih and Kao I-han, Shanghai, Dec. 16, 1920, manuscript in Peking University; see Chang Ching-lu 11, ed., Source Material for the Publication History of Contemporary China, Part I (Shanghai, 1954), p. 7.

90. Li Ta-chao's letter to Hu Shih, no date, written in Peking about Jan. 1921, manuscript in Peking University, *ibid.*, p. 12.

91. Hu Shih's letter to Li Ta-chao, Lu Hsün, Ch'ien Hsüan-t'ung, T'ao Meng-ho, Chang Wei-tz'u Chou Tso-jen, Wang Hsing-kung, and Kao I-han, Peking, Jan. 22, 1921, *ibid.*, pp. 9–10.

92. Hu Shih's letter to Ch'en Tu-hsiu, no date, written in Peking about early Jan. 1921, *ibid.*, p. 8.

93. See Hu's letter to Li, Lu Hsün, Ch'ien, T'ao, etc., and the recipients' comments, the last of which is dated Peking, Jan. 26, 1921, *ibid.*, pp. 9–11; and Ch'en Tu-hsiu's letter to Hu Shih, Canton, Feb. 15, 1921, *ibid.*, p. 13.

94. Meng Shou-ch'un 372, "A Record of the New Tide Society," New Tide, II, 5 (Sept. 1920), pp. 1073–76.

95. Edgar Snow 739, *Red Star over China* (New York, 1938, 1944), p. 153.

96. Tso Shun-sheng 472, Recollections of the Last Thirty Years (Kowloon, 1952), Chap. II, p. 5.

97. See *ibid.*, pp. 9–10; Edgar Snow 739, *Red Star over China*, p. 150; and Shu Hsin-ch'eng 413, Education and I (Shanghai, 1945).

98. Tso Shun-sheng 472, Recollections of the Last Thirty Years, p. 9.

CHAPTER X

SOCIOPOLITICAL CONSEQUENCES, 1920–1922

1. Kao Hsi-sheng and others, comps., *She-hui k'o-hsüeh ta tz'u-tien* (Encyclopedia of Social Science) (Shanghai, 1929), pp. 116–17.

2. Chiang Monlin 593, "The Student Movement," in China Mission Year Book, *1919*, p. 50.

3. *Ibid.;* Lo Chia-lun *340*, "The Success and Failure of the Student Movement," New Tide, II, 4 (May 1920), p. 603.

4. See Anatol M. Kotenev *667, Shanghai: Its Municipality and the Chinese* (Shanghai, 1927), Chap. I, pp. 1–8, Chap. VII, pp. 83–89.

5. Teng Chung-hsia *439*, A Short History of the Chinese Labor Movement (2nd ed.; no publication place, 1930, 1949), Chap. I, pp. 11–12; Lo Chia-lun *340*, "The Success and Failure of the Student Movement," pp. 603–04.

6. Percy Finch, *Shanghai and Beyond* (New York, 1953), Chap. VII, p. 106; Wang Ch'ing-pin, Fan Hung, and others *479*, comps., China Labor Yearbook, No. 1 (Peiping, 1928), Part II, Chap. I, pp. 5–6.

7. Li P'ing-heng, "Chung-kuo kung-hui yün-tung chih kuo-ch'ü chi hsien-tsai" ("The Past and Present of China's Labor Union Movement"), *Lao-kung yüeh-k'an* (Labor Monthly), I, 2 (Nanking, May 15, 1932), pp. 9–11.

8. See Appendix D.

9. Ch'en Tung-yüan *75*, History of the Life of the Chinese Woman (Shanghai, 1928), Chap. X, p. 365. See also Lin Yutang *684, My Country and My People* (New York, 1935), Chap. V, p. 169.

10. Ch'en Tu-hsiu *54*, "The Year 1916," New Youth, I, 5 (Jan. 1916), pp. 1ff.

11. T'ao Meng-ho *437*, "The Woman Problem," *ibid.*, IV, 1 (Jan. 1918).

12. Yosano Akkiko *559*, translated by Chou Tso-jen, "On Chastity," *ibid.*, 5 (May 15, 1918).

13. Hu Shih *197*, "The Problem of Chastity," *ibid.*, V, 1 (July 15, 1918); T'ang Ssu [Lu Hsün] *351*, "My View on Rigid Chastity," *ibid.*, 2 (Aug. 15, 1918); Liu Pan-nung, "Nan kuei tsa-kan" ("Miscellaneous Thoughts on Returning Home in the South"), *ibid.;* Hu Shih *214*, "The American Woman," *ibid.*, 3 (Sept. 15, 1918); also Hu's short play "Chung-shen ta-shih" ("The Significant Event of Life" [marriage]), *ibid.*, VI, 3 (March 15, 1919).

14. Ch'en Tung-yüan *75*, History of the Life of the Chinese Woman, pp. 387–96.

15. *Ibid.*, p. 396.

16. *Ibid.*, pp. 410–16; also Lin Yutang *684, My Country and My People*, Chap. V, p. 170.

17. Ch'en Tung-yüan *75*, History of the Life of the Chinese Woman, pp. 423–29.

18. For some cases see Hu Shih, "Li Ch'ao chuan" ("Biography of Li Ch'ao"), in Hu Shih *207*, Collected Essays, and Ts'ai Yüan-p'ei, "Tsai Li Ch'ao nü-shih chui-tao-hui ti yen-shuo" ("A Speech at the Funeral Service for Miss Li Ch'ao"), in Ts'ai Yüan-p'ei *461*, Life and Works, II, 465–68.

19. See Ch'en Tung-yüan *75*, History of the Life of the Chinese Woman, Chap. IX, pp. 351–61; also Kao Hsi-sheng and others, comps., Encyclopedia of Social Science, pp. 69–70, 71.

20. *Ibid.*, pp. 127–29.

21. Paul Hutchinson *660, China's Real Revolution* (New York, 1924), Chap. V, pp. 101–02; Ch'en Tung-yüan *75*, History of the Life of the Chinese Woman, Chap. X, pp. 417–19; and Kao Hsi-sheng and others, eds., Encyclopedia of Social Science, pp. 70–72.

22. "Records of Current Affairs," *Chiao-yü tsa-chih* (The Chinese Educational Review), VIII, 5 (Shanghai, May 1916), p. 35; and *ibid.*, IX, 4 (April 1918), p. 33; X, 3 (March 1918), p. 15; X, 6 (June 1919), p. 44; X, 11 (Nov. 1918), p. 23. "Educational Documents," *Chiao-yü pu kung-pao* (Bulletin of the Ministry of Education), 5th year, No. 4 (1918), pp. 3, 9; "Special Materials," *ibid.*, No. 5, p. 7; "Educational Documents," *ibid.*, No. 5, p. 12. See also "Records of Current Affairs," The Chinese Educational Review, XI, 4 (April 1919), p. 32; "Records of Current Affairs," XII, 4 (April 1920), p. 6; XII, 5 (May 1920),

p. 1; and Chu Ching-nung and others, comps., *Chiao yü ta tz'u-shu* (Encyclopedia of Education) (Shanghai, 1930), p. 356.

23. See Monroe's speech at the welcoming meeting in Shanghai on Sept. 8, 1921, "Chiao-yü yü shih-yeh chih kuan-hsi" ("Relation between Education and Enterprise"), New Education, IV, 4, "Monroe Issue" (April 1922), pp. 585–88.

24. "Decrees," in *Chiao-yü pu kung-pao* (Bulletin of the Ministry of Education), 9th year, No. 19 (1922), p. 2; "Laws and Statutes," in *ibid.*, p. 1; also Yüan Hsiang and others, comps., *Chung-kuo nien-chien* (China Yearbook), No. I (Shanghai, 1924), p. 1831.

25. The North-China Herald CXXXI, 2700 (May 10, 1919), p. 388; John and Alice Dewey *631*, *Letters from China and Japan* (New York, 1920), p. 204; see also Lin Yutang *684*, *My Country and My People*, Chap. VI, p. 174.

26. "Records of Current Affairs," *Chiao-yü tsa-chih* (The Chinese Educational Review), XI, 11 (Nov. 20, 1919), p. 108; XII, 11 (Nov. 1920), p. 7.

27. See Liang Ch'i-ch'ao, "Tui-yü Pei-ching kuo-min ts'ai-ping yün-tung ta-hui ti kan-hsiang" ("Some Thoughts on the Peking Citizens' Meeting for a Disarmament Movement"), a speech delivered in the Y.M.C.A., Tientsin, Oct. 10, 1922, reprinted in *310*, Collected Works of Liang, Essays, XII, 20–24, and XIV, 35–39 (duplicated).

28. Ching-kuan *112*, "Present Situation of the National University of Peking," The Eastern Miscellany, XVI, 3 (March 15, 1919), p. 164.

29. "Records of Current Affairs," *Chiao-yü tsa-chih* (The Chinese Educational Review), XIII, 1 (Jan. 1920), p. 1; XII, 2 (Feb. 1920), pp. 3, 1; also see Ma Hsü-lun *353*, My Life Before I Was Sixty Years of Age (Shanghai, 1947), p. 72.

30. "Records of Current Affairs," *Chiao-yü tsa-chih* (The Chinese Educational Review), XIII, 4 (April 20, 1921), pp. 2–6.

31. *Ibid.*, 7 (July 20, 1921), p. 3; also Ma Hsü-lun *353*, My Life Before Sixty, pp. 72–75. Ma was at the time chairman of the teachers' union of the 8 colleges and among those wounded.

32. "Records of Current Affairs," *Chiao-yü tsa-chih* (The Chinese Educational Review), XIII, 8 (Aug. 20, 1921), p. 3.

33. *Ibid.*, XIII, 6 (June 20, 1921), p. 4; "Kuo-nei hsüeh-ch'ao hui-chih" ("A Survey of Educational Strikes in China, the Second Half of 1921"), *ibid.*, XIV, 1 (Jan. 20, 1922); "Educational Finance," *I nien lai chih An-hui chiao-yü* (The Education of Anhwei Province in the Past Year) (Feb. 1930), p. 1; "Educational News," *Chiao-yü tsa-chih* (The Chinese Educational Review), XIV, 3 (March 20, 1922), p. 4.

34. Yih T. Chang [Chang I-chih] *9*, ed., Collected Publications on the Shantung Question, II, 233–39; for the text of the letter see *ibid.*, pp. 230–33; for text of the lawyer Liu Ch'ung-yu's brief in defense of the students, May 12, 1920, see Chin-hsia-kuo chu *109*, ed., Choice Examples of the Knife and Stylus [i.e., Judicial Decisions], Supplement, VII, 25a–29b; for text of the court's sentence see *ibid.*, VI, 5b–7a; see also Lo Chia-lun *340*, "The Success and Failure of Our Student Movement in the Last Year and the Future Path to be Taken," New Education, II, 5 (May 1920), pp. 604–05.

35. Yang Chung-ming *537*, "School Storms in 1922," New Education, VI, 2 (Feb. 15, 1923), pp. 295–312; another survey showed that in 1922 there were 106 school strikes in 100 schools reported by the Peking *Ch'en pao* (Morning Post), and by the *Shun Pao*, the *Times*, the *China Times*, and the *Republic Daily* in Shanghai. See T. D. Shan *32*, "Investigation of the [School] Strikes in 1922," The Chinese Educational Review, XV, 4 (April 1923); also statistics in XV, 1 (Jan. 1923); see also Huang Ti *232*, "Chinese Student Storms Since May Fourth," The Sociological World, VI (Peiping, June 1932), pp. 287–303; see also New Education, V, 5 (Dec. 1922), pp. 1061–62; cited in Tsi C. Wang *771*,

The Youth Movement in China, XII, 223–25. For a partial survey of the student strikes in 1921 see The Chinese Educational Review, XIV, 1 (Jan. 1922).

36. Tsi C. Wang *771*, *The Youth Movement in China*, XII, 229–33.

37. See Ts'ai Yüan-p'ei *453*, "The Retrospect and Outlook of the Student Strikes in the Last Year — Since May Fourth of Last Year," New Education, II, 5 (May 1920), pp. 589–90; Chiang Monlin and Hu Shih *97*, "Our Hopes for the Students," *ibid.*, pp. 597–600; Mu Ou-ch'u *377*, "The Opinions of Business Circles on the Students," *ibid.*, pp. 617–19.

38. Hu Shih *650*, "Renaissance in China," in the Royal Institute of International Affairs, *Journal*, V (London, Nov. 1926), pp. 265–83; reprinted in Julia E. Johnsen *664*, ed., *Selected Articles on China, Yesterday and Today* (New York, 1926), p. 144.

CHAPTER XI

THE LITERARY REVOLUTION

1. The term derived from the historian Ssu-ma Ch'ien's description of Confucius' alleged writing in the *Annals;* see his introduction to "Shih-erh chu-hou nien-piao" ("The Chronological Tables of Twelve Princes"), *Shih chi* (Historical Record), Bk. XIV.

2. Fang Pao, "Ta Ch'eng K'uei-chou shu" (Letter to Ch'eng K'uei-chou), in *Fang Wang-ch'i hsien-sheng ch'üan-chi* (Complete Works of Fang Pao) (Ssu-pu ts'ung-k'an, ed.), *chuan* VI, pp. 30b–31a; Yao Nai, "P'ing Shen Chiao-yüan wen" (A Comment on Shen Chiao-yüan's writings), and *"Ku-wen-tz'u lei-tsuan hsü-mu"* (Preface to the *Anthology of the Old Literature*). See also Chiang Shu-ko, T'ung-ch'eng wen-p'ai p'ing-shu (An Introduction to the T'ung-ch'eng Literary School) (Shanghai, 1930); Liang K'un, T'ung-ch'eng wen-p'ai lun (On the T'ung-ch'eng Literary School) (Shanghai, 1940); and Wang Feng-yüan *480*, A Critical Account of the New Literature Movement in China (Peiping, 1935), Chap. II, p. 45.

3. See Ah-ying, "Wan-Ch'ing hsiao-shuo ti fan-jung" (The Prosperity of Fiction in the Late Ch'ing Period) (revised from Chapters I and XIV of the author's book *Wan-Ch'ing hsiao-shuo shih* [History of Fiction in the Late Ch'ing Period]), in Chang Ching-lu *9*, comp. and annotator, Source Materials for the History of Publication in Modern China, Part I (Shanghai, 1953), pp. 184–203, esp. 191–202; and Ah-ying, "Ch'ing-mo hsiao-shuo tsa-chih liao" (A Brief Survey of Fiction Periodicals at the End of the Ch'ing Dynasty), in *Hsiao-shuo hsien-t'an* (Speaking of Fiction) (Shanghai, 1936), reprinted in Chang Ching-lu *9*, Source Materials for the History of Publication in Modern China, Part I (Shanghai, 1953), pp. 103–10.

4. Hu Shih *225*, "Chinese Literature of the Last Fifty Years," in Shun [Shen] Pao *414*, ed., The Past Fifty Years [1872–1922] (Shanghai, 1923), Part II, reprinted in Hu *207*, Collected Essays, Collection II, Vol. II, pp. 92–94.

5. *Ibid.*, pp. 166–88; T'ang Pi-an, *Wan-Ch'ing ti pai-hua-wen yün-tung* (The Vernacular Movement in the Late Ch'ing Period) (Wu-Han, 1956).

6. See Wang Kuo-wei, *Wen-hsüeh hsiao-yen* (On Literature); and *"Sung Yüan hsi-ch'ü k'ao* tzu-hsü (Author's Preface to *A Study of the Drama and Opera in the Sung and Yüan Dynasties*), in *Hai-ning Wang Ching-an hsien-sheng i-shu* (Collected Works of Wang Kuo-wei) (Hai-ning, 1936), Vol. 43.

7. Hu Shih *652*, *The Chinese Renaissance* (Chicago, 1934), Chap. III, pp. 48–49; also Hu Shih, *"Chien-she li-lün chi* tao-yen" ("Introduction to the *Anthology of Essays Con-

cerning the Literary Construction"), in Chao Chia-pi *33*, ed., A Corpus of China's New Literature (Shanghai, 1935), I, 6–13.

8. Hu Shih, "The Problem of the Chinese Language," *The Chinese Students' Monthly*, XI, 8 (June 1916), p. 567.

9. *Ibid.*, pp. 567–68.

10. Huang Yüan-yung *234*, "Preface to [Liang Sou-ming's] *Selected Essays of Late-Chou, Han, and Wei Periods*," in *Yüan-sheng i-chu* (Collected Works of Huang Yüan-yung) (Shanghai, 1920), IV, 184–87.

11. Huang Yüan-yung, "Letter to Chang Shih-chao," *Chia-yin* (The Tiger), Vol. I, No. 10 (Tokyo, Feb. 1915), English translation by Hu Shih in his *653*, "The Literary Renaissance," in Sophia H. Chen Zen, ed., *Symposium on Chinese Culture* (Shanghai, 1931), VII, 129.

12. *Ibid.* Also see Chang Shih-chao *25*, Writings Collected from the *Tiger* Monthly (Shanghai, 1922), II, 94–98.

13. See Ch'en Ku's translation of the *Spring Floods* (*Ch'un-ch'ao*) in New Youth, I, 1 (Sept. 15, 1915) and the following three issues. Miss Hsüeh Ch'i-ying's translation of the drama by Wilde "An Ideal Husband" (*I-chung-jen*) was the first item in the vernacular to appear in the magazine, in I, 2 (Oct. 15, 1915) and the following issues.

14. Ch'en Tu-hsiu, "Hsien-tai Ou-chou wen-i shih t'an," New Youth, I, 3 (Nov. 15, 1915); I, 4 (Dec. 15, 1915). Ch'en's article seems to have been influenced greatly by Georges Pellissier (1852–1918), *Le mouvement littéraire contemporain* (Paris, 1901), although he was aware of Pellissier's opposition to naturalism.

15. Ch'en Tu-hsiu, "A Discussion of the History of Modern European Literature," New Youth, I, 3 (Nov. 15, 1915), p. 1.

16. "Letters to the Editor," New Youth, I, 4 (Dec. 15, 1915), p. 2.

17. "Letters to the Editor," *ibid.*, 6 (Feb. 15, 1916), pp. 1–2.

18. Hu's translation of Nikolai Dmitrievitch Teleshov's "The Duel" (*Chüeh-tou*) appeared in New Youth, II, 1 (Sept. 1, 1916). It was the first time Hu came into contact with Ch'en and his first appearance in the magazine.

19. Hu Shih *223*, Letter to Ch'en Tu-hsiu, "Letters to the Editor," *ibid.*, 2 (Oct. 1, 1916), pp. 1–3; see Tsi C. Wang *771*, *The Youth Movement in China* (New York, 1928), Chap. VIII, pp. 125–27; also see Henri Van Boven *766*, *Histoire de la Littérature Chinoise Moderne* (Peiping, 1946), Chap. V, pp. 25–28.

20. See Chou Tso-jen *115*, Sources and Currents of China's New Literature (Peiping, 1932), Lecture II, pp. 42–52; Lecture V, pp. 102–12.

21. Hu Shih *224*, "Some Tentative Suggestions for the Reform of Chinese Literature," New Youth, II, 5 (Jan. 1, 1917); also published in *Liu Mei hsüeh-sheng chi-pao* (The Chinese Students' Quarterly), IV, 1 (Shanghai, March 1917), pp. 1–14.

22. New Youth, II, 5 (Jan. 1, 1917), p. 11.

23. Ch'en Tu-hsiu *65*, "On the Literary Revolution," *ibid.*, 6 (Feb. 1, 1917), p. 1. Cf. the English translations in Carsun Chang [Chang Chün-mai], *The Third Force in China* (New York, 1952), Chap. I, pp. 48–49, in Hu Shih *652*, *The Chinese Renaissance* (Chicago, 1934), Chap. III, p. 54, and in Tsi C. Wang *771*, *The Youth Movement in China* (New York, 1928), Chap. IX, pp. 131–32.

24. Ch'en Tu-hsiu *65*, "On the Literary Revolution," p. 2.

25. New Youth, II, 6 (Feb. 1, 1917); also III, 1 (March 1, 1917) both in "Letters to the Editor."

26. Liu Pan-nung *324*, "My View on the Literary Reform," *ibid.*, 3 (May 1, 1917).

27. For Fu's articles on the literary reform published in New Youth and New Tide in 1918 and 1919 see his *156*, Complete Works of Fu Ssu-nien (Taipei, 1952), Vol. 1.

28. Hu Shih *212*, "On the Historico-evolutionary Concept of Literature," New Youth, III, 3 (May 1, 1917).

29. "Letters to the Editor," *ibid.*, p. 4.

30. *Ibid.*, p. 6.

31. Hu Shih *201*, "On Constructive Revolution in Chinese Literature, *ibid.*, IV, 4 (April 15, 1918), pp. 289–306.

32. Hu Shih *225*, "The Chinese Literature of the Last Fifty Years," p. 200.

33. See Lu Hsün *349*, Complete Works of Lu Hsün (Shanghai, 1938), I, 277–91. Lu Hsün also recalled that Ch'en Tu-hsiu was most enthusiastic in encouraging him to write stories. See his "Wo tsen-mo tso-ch'i hsiao-shuo lai" ("How Did I Start to Write Stories?"), written on March 5, 1933, in *Nan-ch'iang pei-tiao chi* (Collected Gibberish) (Shanghai, 1934), in *349*, Complete Works, V, 107.

34. Hu Shih *225*, "The Chinese Literature of the Last Fifty Years," p. 207.

35. "Records of Current Affairs," The Chinese Educational Review, XI, 2 (Nov. 20, 1919), p. 108.

36. For text of the ordinance see "Records of Current Affairs," *ibid.*, XII, 2 (Feb. 20, 1920), p. 1.

37. For text of the ordinance see "Record of Current Affairs," *ibid.*, 4 (April 20, 1920), pp. 5–6.

38. See John de Francis *607*, *Nationalism and Language Reform in China* (Princeton, 1950), pp. 69, 129, 220, 237, 245–46.

39. Lin Shu *317*, "On the Rise and Fall of the Classical Language and the Vernacular," reprinted in Chao Chia-pi *33*, ed., A Corpus of China's New Literature, Vol. II; see also Wang Yao *496*, Draft History of China's New Literature (Peking, 1951), Vol. I, Chap. 1, p. 34.

40. Lin Shu *316*, "Chinese Literature in the Classical Language Should not Be Discarded," *Min-kuo jih-pao* (Republic Daily) (Shanghai, Feb. 8, 1917), cited in Hu Shih *223*, "Letter to Ch'en Tu-hsiu," New Youth, III, 3 (May 1, 1917), p. 4; see also *205*, Hu Shih's Diary While Studying in the United States (Shanghai, 1947, 1948; new ed., Taipei, 1959), April 7, 1917, IV, 1116–17.

41. Lin Shu *317*, "On the Rise and Fall of the Classical Language and the Vernacular."

42. Ku Hung-ming *669*, "Against the Chinese Literary Revolution," *Millard's Review*, IX, 6 (Shanghai, July 12, 1919), pp. 221–23.

43. S. K. Hu, "China's Literature 'Too Literary' for 90 Per Cent of the Population," *ibid.*, 7 (July 19, 1919), p. 282.

44. Ku Hung-ming *670*, "Returned Students and Literary Revolution — Literacy and Education," *ibid.*, 11 (Aug. 16, 1919), pp. 432–38.

45. See Hu Hsien-su *189*, "On the Chinese Literary Reform," *Nan-ching kao-teng shih-fan yüeh-k'an* (Monthly of the Nanking Higher Normal College); Lo Chia-lun *341*, "Criticism of Hu Hsien-su's 'On the Chinese Literary Reform,'" New Tide, I, 5 (May, 1919).

46. Cited in H. C. Meng *689*, "The New Literary Movement in China," *The Weekly Review of the Far East* XX, 7 (Shanghai, April 15, 1922), p. 250; see also Wu Mi *786*, "Old and New in China," *The Chinese Students' Monthly*, XVI, 3 (Boston, Oct. 1920), pp. 198–209. Following the argument in *Old and New: Sundry Papers* (1920) by Professor C. H. Grandgent of Harvard University, Wu attacked various phases of the new movement, from the new literature to coeducation.

47. Hu Hsien-su *189*, "On the China Literary Reform."

48. Mei Kuang-ti, "P'ing t'i-ch'ang hsin wen-hua che" (Criticism of Those who Promote the New Culture), *Hsüeh heng* (The Critical Review), No. I (Jan. 1921).

49. Lu Hsün *347*, "An Evaluation of *The Critical Review*," written in Feb. 1922, reprinted in *Je feng* (Hot Wind) (Peking, 1925), in Lu Hsün *349*, Complete Works, II, 101.

50. Hu Shih *225*, "The Chinese Literature of the Last Fifty Years," p. 207.

51. For a short English survey of the society see William Ayers *568*, "The Society for Literary Studies, 1921–1930" (mimeographed), in *Harvard Papers on China*, No. 7 (Cambridge, Mass., 1953), pp. 34–79. See also Henri Van Boven *766*, *Histoire de la Littérature Chinoise Moderne*, Chap. VI, pp. 39–60.

52. Chao Ching-shen, *Wen-t'an i-chiu* (Reminiscence of the Literary Circles) (Shanghai, 1941); Yang Chih-hua *529*, Historical Materials on Chinese Literary Circles (Shanghai, 1944), pp. 367–68.

53. Chou Tso-jen *119*, "Literature of Humanity," New Youth, V, 6 (Dec. 1918); see also his *122*, "Intellectual Revolution," Weekly Critic, No. 11 (Peking, Feb. 2, 1919); and his *121*, "Plain People's Literature," reprinted in Hu Shih, ed., *Chien-she li-lün chi* (Anthology of Essays on Constructive Theories of the New Literature) (Shanghai, 1935), pp. 210–13.

54. Chou Tso-jen *118*, "Requisites for the New Literature," a speech delivered at the Young China Association in Peking, Jan. 6, 1920, in Cheng Chen-to, ed., *Wen-hsüeh lun-cheng chi* (Anthology of Essays Concerning the Literary Controversy) (Shanghai, 1935), pp. 141–44.

55. [The Society for Literary Studies] *501*, "Wen-hsüeh yen-chiu hui hsüan-yen" (The Manifesto of the Society for Literary Studies), The Short Story Monthly, XII, 1 (Shanghai, Jan. 10, 1921), Appendix, p. 1.

56. Chou Tso-jen *118*, "Requisites for the New Literature," p. 144.

57. Shen Yen-ping [Mao Tun] *364*, "The Relations of Literature to Man and Ancient China's Mistaken Ideas on the Position of Men of Letters," The Short Story Monthly, XII, 1 (Jan. 10, 1921), p. 10. Cf. Ayer's English translation *568*, "The Society for Literary Studies," p. 51.

58. Shen Yen-ping [Mao Tun] *362*, "The Responsibility and Efforts of the Researchers of the New Literature," reprinted in Cheng Chen-to, ed., Anthology of Essays Concerning the Literary Controversy, pp. 145–49; also Mao Tun *365*, "Literature and Life," *ibid.*, pp. 149–53.

59. Shen Yen-ping [Mao Tun] *363*, "What is Literature?," *ibid.*, pp. 153–59.

60. Yang Chih-hua *535*, Historical Materials on Chinese Literary Circles, pp. 367–68.

61. See Ayers *568*, "The Society for Literary Studies," p. 62; also Cheng Chen-to *80*, "Wen-hsüeh lun-cheng chi tao-yen" ("Introduction to the *Anthology of Essays Concerning the Literary Controversies*"), p. 9. For a list of Chinese translations of literary works of Western and Eastern countries published from the end of the 19th century to March 1929, see P'u-shao [pen name of Hsü T'iao-fu], ed., "Han-i Tung Hsi yang wen-hsüeh tso-p'in pien-mu" (Bibliography of Chinese Translations of Western and Eastern Literature) (Shanghai, 1929), revised and reprinted in Chang Ching-lu *11*, ed., Source Materials for the Publication History of Contemporary China, Part I (Shanghai, 1954), pp. 271–323.

62. *Ibid.*

63. See Ch'en Ho-ch'in *40*, "A Study of the Marriage Problems of the Student," The Eastern Miscellany, XVIII, 4 (Feb. 25, 1921), pp. 101–12; 5 (March 10, 1921), pp. 97–108; and 6 (March 25, 1921), pp. 109–22.

64. For a short survey in English of the society see Clarence Moy *695*, "Kuo Mo-jo and the Creation Society" (mimeographed), in *Harvard Papers on China*, No. 4 (Cambridge, Mass., April 1950), pp. 131–59; also Henri Van Boven *766*, *Histoire de la Littérature Chinoise Moderne*, Chap. VII, pp. 61–83.

65. Ku Feng-ch'eng *265*, "The Creation Society and the Cultural Movement in China," in Huang Jen-ying [Ku's pen name], ed., Discussions on the Creation Society (Shanghai, 1932), Chap. XI, pp. 104–13; Li Ho-lin *292*, On the Thought Tide of Chinese Literature in the Last Twenty Years (Shanghai, 1948), Part II; Wang Feng-yüan *480*, A Critical Account of the New Literature in China (Peiping, 1935), Chap. V, pp. 162–66.

66. Kuo Mo-jo *274*, "Ch'uang-tsao she ti tzu-wo p'i-p'an" (Self-criticism of the Creation Society), cited in Wang Feng-yüan *480*, A Critical Account of the New Literature in China, Chap. V, pp. 120–121; see also Kuo Mo-jo *276*, "Wen-hsüeh ke-ming chih hui-ku" (In Retrospect of the Literary Revolution, 1918–1928), in Wen-i chiang-tso (Forum of Literature), Vol. I (Shanghai: Shen-chou kuo-kuang she, 1930).

67. Cheng Po-ch'i, "Hsin wen-hsüeh ta-hsi hsiao-shuo tao-yen" (Introduction to the Anthology of Short Stories), in Chao Chia-pi *33*, A Corpus of China's New Literature, Vol. 3.

68. For a list of titles of Chinese new literature published in 1919–1923 see P'u-shao, "Ch'u-ch'i hsin wen-i ch'u-pan-wu pien-mu" (A Bibliography of Publications of the New Literature, 1919–1923), in Chang Ching-lu *9*, comp. and annotator, Source Materials for the Publication History of Contemporary China, Part I, pp. 107–121.

CHAPTER XII

THE NEW THOUGHT AND RE-EVALUATION OF THE TRADITION

1. Hu Shih and Ch'en Tu-hsiu, "Lun *Hsin ch'ing-nien* chih chu-chang" ("A Discussion on the Advocacies of *New Youth*"), letter in reply to Yi Chung-k'uei, New Youth, V, 4 (Oct. 15, 1918), p. 433.

2. For a summary of the development of Neo-Confucianism and later reaction to it see H. C. Creel *602*, *Chinese Thought: From Confucius to Mao Tse-tung* (Chicago, 1953), pp. 204ff; and W. Theodore de Bary, "A Reappraisal of Neo-Confucianism," in Arthur F. Wright *785*, ed., *Studies in Chinese Thought*, Vol. 55, No. 5, Part 2 of *The American Anthropologist* (Chicago, Dec. 1953), pp. 81–111.

3. James Legge, trans., *The Great Learning*, pp. 357–58. Also Chu Hsi's commentary.

4. See Arthur W. Hummel, ed., *Eminent Chinese of the Ch'ing Period (1644–1912)* (Washington, D.C., 1943–44). 5. See *ibid.*

6. Liang Ch'i-ch'ao, "Yen Li hsüeh-p'ai yü hsien-tai chiao-yü ssu-ch'ao" ("The School of Yen Yüan and Li Kung and Modern Educational Thought"), in *310*, Collected Works of Liang Ch'i-ch'ao, Essays (Shanghai, 1936, 1941), Vol. XIV, Part 41, pp. 3–27.

7. Pan-su [Li Chien-nung], *Chung-shan ch'u-shih hou Chung-kuo liu-shih nien ta-shih chi* (Chronological Records of the Important Events of China in the Sixty Years after Sun Yat-sen's Birth) (enlarged ed.; Shanghai, 1929), p. 86.

8. For this issue see Wu Tsung-tz'u, *Chung-hua min-kuo hsien-fa shih* (A Constitutional History of the Republic of China) (Peking, 1924), Vol. I, Chap. 3, p. 38; Kuo-hsien ch'i-ts'ao wei-yüan-hui (Committee for the Drafting of the National Constitution) *272*, ed., *Ts'ao-hsien pien-lan* (A Guide to Constitutional Drafting) (Peking, 1925), Part 3, pp. 2–4; Part 4, p. 28; Wu Ching-hsiung [John C. H. Wu] and Huang Kung-chüeh, *Chung-kuo chih-hsien shih* (A History of Constitution-making in China) (Shanghai, 1937), Sec. 3, p. 53; Ch'en Ju-hsüan, *Chung-kuo hsien-fa shih* (A History of the Chinese Constitution) (Shanghai, 1933), Chap. V, p. 51.

9. For an interesting description of the ceremony, see Paul S. Reinsch *707*, *An American Diplomat in China* (Garden City, 1922), Chap. III, pp. 26–27. See also Pai Chiao, *Yüan Shih-k'ai yü Chung-hua min-kuo* (Yüan Shih-k'ai and the Republic of China) (Shanghai, 1936), p. 162.

10. Pan-su, Chronological Records of the Important Events of China, p. 162.

11. Reinsch *707*, *An American Diplomat in China*, Chap. III, p. 23.

12. K'ang Yu-wei *249*, A Proposed Draft Constitution for the Republic of China (2nd

printing; Shanghai, 1916), pp. 1–5, 134–40; originally published in *Pu-jen* (Compassion), No. 3 (Shanghai, April 1913), pp. 1–54, written in 1898–99. Most of K'ang's writings on Confucian problem may be found in this monthly. Ch'en Tu-hsiu *57*, "Refutation of K'ang Yu-wei's Letter to the President [Li Yüan-hung] and the Premier [Tuan Ch'i-jui]," New Youth, II, 2 (Oct. 1, 1916).

13. K'ang Yu-wei *249*, A Proposed Draft Constitution, pp. 135–36.

14. *Ibid.*, p. 140.

15. Wu Ching-hsiung and Huang Kung-chüeh, A History of Constitution-making in China, Part I, Chap. II, p. 64.

16. See Ch'en Tu-hsiu, "Yüan Shih-k'ai fu-huo" ("The Resurrection of Yüan Shih-k'ai"), New Youth, II, 4 (Dec. 1, 1916).

17. Ch'en Tu-hsiu *49*, "Call to Youth," New Youth, I, 1 (Sept. 15, 1915), p. 5.

18. Ch'en-Tu-hsiu *63*, "Differences of Basic Thought between the Eastern and Western Peoples," *ibid.*, 4 (Dec. 15, 1915), pp. 2–4.

19. Ch'en Tu-hsiu *48*, "The Principles of Education of Today," *ibid.*, 2 (Oct. 15, 1915), pp. 3–4.

20. See Li I-min, "Jen-sheng wei-i chih mu-ti" ("The Sole Aim of Life"), *ibid.;* and Kao I-han *225*, "Utilitarianism and Life," *ibid.*, II, 1 (Sept. 1, 1916).

21. Chen Tu-hsiu *49*, "Call to Youth," p. 2.

22. Chen Tu-hsiu, trans., "Ya-mei-li-chia (Mei-kuo kuo-ko)" ("America — the American National Hymn"), *ibid.*, I, 2 (Oct. 15, 1915).

23. Liu Shu-ya, trans., "Mei-kuo-jen chih tzu-yu ching-shen" ("The Spirit of Liberty in the American Colonies") (from Burke's speech "Conciliation with America"), *ibid.*, 6 (Feb. 15, 1916).

24. See Kao I-han *253*, "The Republic and the Self-awakening of Youth," *ibid.*, 1 (Sept. 15, 1915); and his *257*, "Self-government and Freedom," *ibid.*, 5 (Jan. 15, 1916).

25. Ch'en Tu-hsiu, "Fa-lan-hsi-jen yü chin-tai wen-ming" ("The French and Modern Civilization"), *ibid.*, I, 1 (Sept. 15, 1915); Kao I-han, trans., "Tai-hsüeh Yin-kuo yen-lun tzu-yu chih ch'üan-li lun" ("A. V. Dicey's Discussion on the Right of Freedom of Speech in Great Britain") [from Chap. VI of his *The Law of the Constitution*], *ibid.*, 6 (Feb. 15, 1916).

26. Kao I-han *253*, "The Republic and the Self-awakening of Youth," p. 7.

27. Kao I-han *254*, "State Is Not the Final Goal of Life," New Youth, I, 4 (Dec. 15, 1915); also Ch'en Tu-hsiu *48*, "The Principles of Education Today," *ibid.*, I, 2 (Oct. 15, 1915), pp. 4–5; and his *54*, "The Year 1916," *ibid.*, I, 5 (Jan. 1916), p. 3.

28. Ch'en Tu-hsiu *63*, "Differences of Basic Thought between Eastern and Western Peoples," pp. 1–2.

29. Hu Shih *209*, "Ibsenism," New Youth, IV, 6 (June 15, 1918), p. 497. Hu conceded that Ibsen's individualism was one of the most fundamental principles of his (Hu's) view of life and his religion. See his *200*, "An Introduction to My Own Thought," preface (written on Nov. 27, 1930) to Selected Essays of Hu Shih, pp. 8–10.

30. *Ibid.*, p. 502.

31. See Wang Shu-ch'ien *494*, "The Problem of the New and the Old," New Youth, I, 1 (Sept. 1, 1915), p. 3; I Pai-sha, "Shu Mo" ("A Study of Motzu"), *ibid.*, 2 (Oct. 15, 1915) and 5 (Jan. 15, 1916).

32. Ch'en Tu-hsiu, "The French and Modern Civilization," pp. 2–3.

33. Wu Chih-hui, "Ch'ing-nien yü kung-chü" ("Youth and Tools"), New Youth, II, 2 (Oct. 1, 1916); "Tsai lun kung-chü" ("Second Essay on Tools"), *ibid.*, 3 (Nov. 1, 1916).

34. Wu Chih-hui *510*, "A New Conception of the Universe and of Life, Based Upon a

New Belief," in Wu Chih-hui's Academic Works and Other Essays (Shanghai, 1925, 1926), p. 118.

35. Hu Shih 200, "An Introduction to My Own Thought," p. 3.

36. Georg Brandes, *Main Currents in Nineteenth Century Literature* (New York, 1905), III, 57.

37. Ch'en Tu-hsiu 58, "On Iconoclasm," New Youth, V, 2 (Aug. 15, 1918), p. 91; see also [Chu] Chih-hsin 128, "Inviolable Sacredness and Iconoclasm," *Chien-she* (The Construction), I, 1 (Shanghai, Aug. 1, 1919), pp. 169–72.

38. Ch'en Tu-hsiu 48, "The Principles of Education Today," p. 5.

39. Li I-min, "The Sole Aim of Life," pp. 2–3.

40. Li Ta-chao 298, "Youth," New Youth, II, 1 (Sept. 1, 1916); "Chin" ("The Present"), *ibid.*, IV, 4 (April 15, 1918), pp. 307–10.

41. Hu Shih's article 219, "Experimentalism [or Pragmatism]," New Youth, VI, 4 (April 1, 1919); the next issue (May 1) was the special one on Marxism; see also above, Chap. IX.

42. Li Ta-chao 303, "My View on Marxism," New Youth, VI, 5 (May 1919), p. 536.

43. *Ibid.*, p. 533.

44. *Ibid.*, p. 534.

45. *Ibid.*, p. 537.

46. Hu Han-min 188, "A Criticism of Criticism of Historical Materialism," The Construction, I, 5 (Dec. 1919), reprinted in Hu Han-min, A Study of the Historical Conception of Materialism and Ethics, ed. Huang Ch'ang-ku (Shanghai, 1927), pp. 1–61.

47. Hu Han-min 187, "A Materialistic Study of the History of Chinese Philosophy," The Construction, I, 3 (Oct. 1919) and the following issues; also in Hu Han-min 188, A Study of the Historical Conception of Materialism and Ethics, pp. 63–153. Tai Chi-t'ao's retranslation from Japanese of most of Kautsky's book, which was given the Chinese title "Ma-k'e-ssu Tzu-pen-lun chieh-shao" ("Introduction to Marx's *Capital*") appeared in The Construction, I, 4 (Nov. 1, 1919), pp. 811–21, and the following issues. The translation was later completed by Hu Han-min and published in book form in Shanghai in 1927. (Kautsky's book was written before his split with the orthodox Communists).

48. Li Ta-chao 304, "Material Change and Ethical Change," New Tide, II, 2 (Dec. 1919), pp. 207–24; and his 305, "An Economic Interpretation of the Cause of Changes in Modern Chinese Thought," New Youth, VII, 2 (Jan. 1, 1920), pp. 47–53. See also Benjamin Schwartz 735, *Chinese Communism and the Rise of Mao* (Cambridge, Mass., 1951), Chap. I, pp. 17, 23–24. Ho Kan-chih considered Li Ta-chao's latter article as the first by a Chinese to survey intellectual history in the light of Materialism. He did not mention Hu Han-min. See Ho's 170, History of the Chinese Enlightenment (Shanghai, 1947), Chap. IV, p. 117.

49. Benjamin Schwartz 735, *Chinese Communism and the Rise of Mao*, Chap. II, pp. 32–33.

50. See above, Chap. IX, n. k.

51. See below, Chap. XII, n. j.

52. Wu Yü, "Letter to Ch'en Tu-hsiu," New Youth, II, 5 (Jan. 1, 1917), pp. 3–4.

53. Yi Pai-sha 554, "A Discussion of Confucius," Part I, New Youth, I, 6 (Feb. 15, 1916).

54. Part II, *ibid.*, II, 1 (Sept. 1, 1916).

55. Ch'en Tu-hsiu, "Ti-k'ang li" ("The Force of Resistance"), *ibid.*, I, 3 (Nov. 15, 1915), p. 4; also 63, "Differences of Basic Thought between Eastern and Western Peoples," *ibid.*, 4 (Dec. 15, 1915), p. 1.

56. *Ibid.*, pp. 1–2. Also Ch'en Tu-hsiu *55*, "Confucius' Principles and Modern Life," *ibid.*, II, 4 (Dec. 1, 1916), p. 3; and his *54*, "The Year 1916," p. 3.

57. Ch'en Tu-hsiu *67*, "Our Final Awakening," New Youth, I, 6 (Feb. 15, 1916), p. 4.

58. Ch'en Tu-hsiu *55*, "Confucius' Principles and Modern Life," New Youth, II, 4 (Dec. 1, 1916), pp. 3–4.

59. *Ibid.*, p. 4.

60. Ch'en Tu-hsiu *55*, "Confucius' Principles and Modern Life," pp. 3–4.

61. Ch'en Tu-hsiu *57*, "Refutation of K'ang Yu-wei's Letter to the President [Li Yüan-hung] and Premier [Tuan ch'i-jui]," p. 2; also Ch'en *61*, "One More Discussion of the Problem of Confucianism," New Youth, II, 5 (Jan. 1, 1917), pp. 1–2.

62. Ch'en Tu-hsiu, "Letter in Reply to Wu Yü," *ibid.*, p. 4.

63. Ch'en Tu-hsiu, "Letter in Reply to Ch'ang Nai-te," *ibid.*, 4 (Dec. 1, 1916), pp. 5–6; *ibid.*, 6 (Feb. 1, 1917), p. 10. According to Ch'en a contemporary writer, Ku Shih, was one of the apologists for Confucius at the expense of the Neo-Confucianists of the Sung dynasty. See also Ch'en *51*, "The Constitution and Confucianism," *ibid.*, 3 (Nov. 1, 1916), pp. 3–5.

64. Wu Yü, "Letter to Ch'en Tu-hsiu," *ibid.*, 5 (Jan. 1, 1917), p. 3. For a preliminary study of the early Confucian ethical principle, *li*, see Chow Tse-tsung, "Hsün-tzu li yüeh lun fa-wei" (An Introduction to Hsün-tzu's Theory of *Li* and *Yüeh*), *Hsüeh-shu shih-chieh* (Academic World), II, 3 (Shanghai, Jan. 1937), pp. 69–71; 4 (April 1937), pp. 61–66.

65. See Wu Yü *528*, "The Old Family and Clan System is the Basis of Despotism," New Youth, II, 6 (Feb. 1, 1917), pp. 1–2. For a bibliography concerning the problem of authorship and time of the *Book of Filial Piety* see n. 4 of William Hung, "A Bibliographical Controversy at the T'ang Court, A.D. 719," in *Harvard Journal of Asiatic Studies*, XX, 1–2 (June 1957), p. 99.

66. Ch'eng Hao's comment on "Tseng-tzu ta hsiao p'ien" (Tseng-tzu's Inquiry of Filial Piety") of the *Ta-tai chi*, or *Ta-tai li*, a work attributed to the Han dynasty Confucian scholar, Tai Te; see also Wu Yü, "Shuo hsiao" ("On Filial Piety"), in *531*, Collected Essays of Wu Yü (6th printing; Shanghai, 1921, 1929), pp. 15–16.

67. *Ibid.*, pp. 1–2.

68. *Ibid.*, p. 17.

69. *Ibid.*, pp. 19–20.

70. Ibid., pp. 19–23.

71. See Herbert Allen Giles, *Confucianism and Its Rivals* (London, 1915), p. 86. Confucius' remark on the story is in *Analects*, Bk. XIII, Chap. XVIII. See also the translations by James Legge and Arthur Waley.

72. See Bertrand Russell *729*, *The Problem of China* (London, 1922), Chap. II, p. 40.

73. Wu Yü, "Tao-chia Fa-chia chün fan-tui chiu tao-te shuo" ("An Explanation of the Fact That the Taoists and Legalists Were All Opposed to the Old Ethics"), in Wu *531*, Collected Essays, pp. 4–41.

74. See Shih Ts'un-t'ung, "Fei hsiao" ("Oppose Filial Piety"), *Che-chiang hsin-ch'ao* (The Chekiang New Tide), No. 2 (Hangchow, Nov. 8, 1919); also "Pei-t'ing ch'a-chin *Che-chiang hsin-ch'ao* tien" ("The Peking Government's Telegram to Suppress the *Chekiang New Tide*"), *Min-kuo jih-pao* (Republic Daily) (Shanghai, Dec. 15, 1919); and [Shih] Ts'un-t'ung, "Hui-t'ou k'an erh-shih-erh nien lai ti o" ("A Retrospect of My Past Twenty-two Years"), *ibid.* (Sept. 23, 1920), in its supplementary magazine, *Chüeh-wu* (Awakening), pp. 20–24. See also Ts'ao Chü-jen *469*, Three Recollections of the Literary Circles (Hong Kong, 1954), pp. 9–57.

75. Wu Yü *530*, "Disadvantages of Confucianists' Advocacy of the Caste System," New Youth, III, 4 (June 1, 1917), p. 1.

76. Wu Yü, "Hsiao-chi ke-ming chih Lao Chuang" ("The Passive Revolutionists Lao-tzu and Chuang-tzu"), *ibid.*, 2 (April 1, 1917), p. 1.

77. Wu Yü, "Ju-chia ta-t'ung chih i pen-yü Lao-tzu shuo" ("The Confucian Conception of One World Originated in Lao-tzu"), *ibid.*, 5 (July 1, 1917), pp. 1–3; Wu Yü, "Letter to Ch'en Tu-hsiu" and Ch'en's reply, *ibid.*, pp. 4–5.

78. Hu Shih, *"Wu Yü wen-lu* hsü" ("Preface to the *Collected Essays of Wu Yü"*), written on June 16, 1921, in *531,* The Collected Essays of Wu Yü, pp. 5–7.

79. Lu Hsün *348,* "The Diary of a Madman," New Youth, IV, 5 (May 15, 1918), pp. 414–24, reprinted in *Na-han* (Cries) (Shanghai, 1923), pp. 13–22.

80. From *Tso Chuan,* "Hsi-kung chiu nien" [651 B.C.]; and *Han Fei Tzu,* Vol. II, Chap. VII, "Erh-ping"; Vol. III, Chap. X, "Shih ko"; and Vol. XV, Chap. XXXVI, "Nan-i"; cited in Wu Yü *529,* "Cannibalism and [the Traditional Chinese] Ethics," New Youth, VI, 6 (Nov. 1, 1919), p. 578.

81. From "Biography of Ching Pu," in Ssu-ma Ch'ien's *Shih-chi* (Historical Records), cited in Wu Yü *529,* "Cannibalism and Ethics," New Youth VI, 6, p. 579.

82. "Biographies of the Loyal and Righteous," in Ou-yang Hsiu and others, comps., *Hsin T'ang-shu* (The New History of the T'ang Dynasty), cited in Wu Yü *529,* "Cannibalism and Ethics," New Youth, VI, 6, p. 580.

83. [T'ang] Ssu (another of Lu Hsün's pen names), "Sui-kan lu" ("Random Thoughts"), No. 36, *ibid.,* V, 5 (Nov. 15, 1918), p. 514.

84. T'ang Ssu, "Random Thoughts," No. 35, *ibid.,* pp. 513–14. Cf. Lin Yutang's English translation in *The Wisdom of China and India* (New York, 1942), p. 1089.

85. T'ang Ssu, "Random Thoughts," No. 46, New Youth, VI, 2 (Feb. 15, 1919), p. 212.

86. *Ibid.,* p. 213, trans. Lin Yutang, *The Wisdom of China and India,* p. 1090.

87. *Ibid.*

88. In *Nü-shen* (The Goddesses), his collected poems, first published in Shanghai, Aug. 1921; reprinted in Peking, 1953.

89. See Kuo Mo-jo, *Hsin-Hua sung* (In Praise of New China [collected poems]) (Peking, 1953).

90. Lu Hsün, "Lao tiao-tzu i-ching ch'ang wan" ("The Old Tune Has Been Sung Enough"), a speech delivered in Hong Kong on Feb. 19, 1927, in *349, Lu Hsün hsüan-chi* (Selected Works of Lu Hsün) (Peking, 1952), p. 666; see also Ho Kan-chih *171,* A Study of Lu Hsün's Thought (rev. ed.; Peking, 1940, 1950), I, 23–24.

91. "The Old Tune Has Been Sung Enough"; cf. the translation by Lin Yutang, *The Wisdom of China and India,* p. 1089.

92. The stories were collected by him into 2 volumes, titled *Na-han* (Cries) (Peking, 1923) and *P'ang-huang* (Hesitation) (Peking, 1926). Most of his short commentaries concerning the period of the May Fourth Movement were reprinted in *Je feng* (Hot Wind) (Peking, 1925) and *Fen* (The Grave) (Peking 1927).

93. Hsü Mou-yung, "Lu Hsün hsien-sheng yu i pi" ("Another Comparison with Lu Hsün"), cited in Wang Shih-ching *491,* Biography of Lu Hsün (Shanghai, 1949), Chap. X, p. 504.

94. Edgar Snow, "The Chinese Voltaire," cited *ibid.,* pp. 504–05.

95. Confucius was hailed by Kuo Mo-jo as a revolutionary in his *Shih p'i-p'an shu* (Ten Critiques of Ancient Chinese Thoughts) (Chungking, 1945). We may also note Yi Pai-sha's article in New Youth, cited above. H. C. Creel tried to prove that Confucian theory has influenced Western democratic thinkers such as Voltaire, Leibniz, Quesnay,

Franklin, and Jefferson; see his *603, Confucius, the Man and the Myth* (New York, 1949), Chap. XV, pp. 254–78.

96. Bertrand Russell *729, The Problem of China*, Chap. II, pp. 38–44, esp. p. 41.

97. *Ibid.*, p. 40.

98. *Ibid.*, p. 47.

CHAPTER XIII

THE NEW THOUGHT AND LATER CONTROVERSIES

1. See K'ang Yu-wei, *Hsin-hsüeh wei-ching k'ao* (A Study of the Classics Forged in the Hsin Period [A.D. 8–22]) (Canton, 1891); *K'ung-tzu kai chih k'ao* (A Study of Confucius' Institutional Reforms) (Canton, 1897; reprinted Peking, 1922); see also Liang Ch'i-ch'ao *306*, An Introduction to the Scholarship of the Ch'ing Period (Shanghai, 1923); Ch'ien Mu, *Chung-kuo chin san-po-nien hsüeh-shu shih* (History of Chinese Scholarship in the Last Three Hundred Years) (Chungking, 1945), Chap. XIV, pp. 498–514; Ku Chieh-kang *263*, Contemporary Chinese Historiography (Nanking, 1947); Chou Yü-t'ung, "Wu-shih nien-lai Chung-kuo chih hsin shih-hsüeh" ("The New Chinese Historiography in the Last Fifty Years"), *Hsüeh lin* (Scholars' Circles), No. 4 (Feb. 1941), pp. 1–36; S. Y. Teng, "Chinese Historiography in the Last Fifty Years," *The Far Eastern Quarterly*, VIII, 2 (Feb. 1949), p. 134.

2. Ku Chieh-kang *264, "Ku-shih pien* ti-i ts'e tzu-hsü" ("Preface to Volume One of the *Symposium on Ancient Chinese History*"), Vol. I (Peking, 1926), p. 78; Arthur W. Hummel's English translation of this preface titled *The Autobiography of a Chinese Historian* (Leyden, 1921); Ch'ien Hsüan-t'ung's letter to Ku Chieh-kang *264*, ed., A Symposium on Ancient Chinese History, Vol. I (Peking, 1926), p. 30.

3. See Liang Ch'i-ch'ao, *Chung-kuo li-shih yen-chiu fa* (Methodology in the Study of Chinese History) (Shanghai, 1922), and *Chung-kuo li-shih yen-chiu fa pu-pien* (Supplement to Methodology in the Study of Chinese History) (Shanghai, 1933).

4. Ku Chieh-kang, *The Autobiography of a Chinese Historian*, trans. Arthur W. Hummel.

5. Ku Chieh-kang *264*, ed., A Symposium on Ancient Chinese History, I, 59–66.

6. Ku Chieh-kang *262*, "The Confucius of the Ch'un Ch'iu Period and the Confucius of the Han Dynasty," in Ku Chieh-kang *264*, ed., A Symposium on Ancient Chinese History, Vol. II (Peiping, 1930), pp. 130–39; and other related articles in the volume. See also Fung Yu-lan, "K'ung-tzu tsai Chung-kuo li-shih chung ti ti-wei" ("Confucius' Place in Chinese History"), *Yen-ching hsüeh-pao* (Yenching Journal of Chinese Studies), No. 2 (Dec. 1927), pp. 233–47.

7. See Chang Yin-lin, "P'ing chin-jen tui-yü Chung-kuo ku-shih chih t'ao-lun" ("Comments on the Contemporary Discussions of Ancient Chinese History"), *Hsüeh heng* (The Critical Review), No. 40 (Nanking, April 1925), pp. 1–18.

8. See Liang Yüan-tung, "*Ku-shih pien* ti shih-hsüeh fang-fa shang-ch'üeh" ("A Discussion of the Method Employed in the *Symposium on Ancient Chinese History*"), The Eastern Miscellany, XXVII, 22 (Shanghai, Nov. 25, 1920), pp. 65–73, and 24 (Dec. 25, 1930), pp. 77–90. Also see Ku Chieh-kang *264*, ed., A Symposium on Ancient Chinese History, Vol. II, Part III, pp. 271ff.

9. For this controversy see Benjamin Schwartz, "A Marxist Controversy on China,"

The Far Eastern Quarterly, XIII, 2 (Feb. 1954), pp. 143–53. Materials on the subject in Chinese are massive.

10. S. Y. Teng, "Chinese Historiography in the Last Fifty Years," pp. 138–39.

11. See Ts'ai Yüan-p'ei, *"Chung-kuo che-hsüeh shih ta-kang* hsü" ("Preface to Hu's *Outline of the History of Chinese Philosophy"*); also Kuo Chan-po *271,* An Intellectual History of China in the Last Fifty Years (2nd ed.; Peiping, 1935, 1936), Part VI, Chap. V, pp. 296–98.

12. See Yeh Ch'ing *550,* Critique of Hu Shih, 2 vols. (Shanghai, 1933); also Li Chi, *Hu Shih Chung-kuo che-hsüeh shih ta-kang p'i-p'an* (Criticism on Hu Shih's *Outline of the History of Chinese Philosophy*) (Shanghai, 1931). Since 1954, Hu Shih's (and John Dewey's) thought and his role in the May Fourth Movement have been severely criticized by the Chinese communists. More than three million words have been produced in this campaign. The articles are collected in 8 volumes under the title *Hu Shih ssu-hsiang p'i-p'an* (Criticism of Hu Shih's Thought) (Peking, 1955–56). See also Li Ta, *Hu Shih fan-tung ssu-hsiang p'i-p'an* (A Critique of Hu Shih's Reactionary Thought) (Hankow, 1955); and Sun Ting-kuo, *Hu Shih che-hsüeh ssu-hsiang fan-tung shih-chih ti p'i-p'an* (Criticism of the Reactionary Nature of Hu Shih's Philosophy) (Peking, 1955). For a short answer see Hu Shih's paper, "John Dewey in China," delivered at the 1959 summer conference at the University of Hawaii. A Chinese translation of it, "Tu-wei tsai Chung-kuo," appears in *Tzu-yu Chung-kuo* (Free China Fortnightly), XXI, 4 (Taipei, Aug. 16, 1959), pp. 104–7.

13. See Wu Chih-hui *509,* "A Warning to Foreign-formalized [foreign eight-legged] 'Neo-confucianism,' " in Ya-tung t'u-shu-kuan *533,* ed., Science and View of Life (Shanghai, 1923), II, 7–8.

14. *Ibid.,* p. 9.

15. *Ibid.,* p. 8–9.

16. See Hu Shih, "Fa-ch'i *Tu-shu tsa-chih* ti yüan-ch'i" ("The Origin of the Establishment of the *Reading Magazine"*), written on Feb. 22, 1921, reprinted in *207,* Collected Essays, Collection II (Shanghai, 1924), I, 29.

17. Wu Chih-hui *509,* "A Warning to Foreign-formalized 'Neo-Confucianism,' " p. 10.

18. See Hu Shih, "Cheng-li kuo-ku yü 'ta kuei' " ("Reorganizing the National Heritage and 'Exorcising Evil Spirits' "), letter to Hao-hsü, Feb. 7, 1927, reprinted in *207,* Collected Essays, Collection III (Shanghai, 1930), II, 211.

19. See Hu Shih *202,* "Methods and Materials of Study," written in Sept. 1928, reprinted in *ibid.,* p. 205.

20. W. E. Soothill, *The Three Religions of China* (Oxford, 1913), p. 213.

21. See above, Chap. VII, n. 41; also Hu Shih *655,* "What I Believe," *Forum* (Jan. and Feb. 1931); Kiang Wen-han *666, The Chinese Student Movement* (New York, 1948), Chap. II, p. 59.

22. Ch'en Tu-hsiu, reply to Liu Ching-fu, New Youth, III, 3 (May 1, 1917).

23. Liu Fu [Pan-nung], reply to "Wang Ching-hsüan," *ibid.,* IV, 3 (March 15, 1918). See above, Chap. III, p. 66.

24. Ch'en Tu-hsiu, "Chi-tu-chiao yü Chung-kuo-jen" ("Christianity and the Chinese"), New Youth, VII, 3 (Feb. 1, 1920); trans. Kiang Wen-han *666, The Chinese Student Movement,* p. 61; also trans. Y. Y. Tsu in *The Chinese Recorder,* LI, 7 (Shanghai, July 1920), pp. 453–58.

25. Ch'en Tu-hsiu, "Christianity and the Chinese"; and Kiang Wen-han *666, The Chinese Student Movement,* p. 61.

26. Cited in Hu Shih *652, The Chinese Renaissance* (Chicago, 1934), Chap. V, p. 90;

see also Ch'en Tu-hsiu, "Chi-tu-chiao yü Chi-tu-chiao-hui" ("Christianity and the Christian Church"), in Neander C. S. Chang [Chang Ch'in-shih] 8, The Tide of Religious Thought in China During the Last Decade (Peking, 1927), pp. 190–93.

27. Shen Hsüan-lu [Shen Ting-i], "Tui-yü 'Chi-tu-chiao yü Chung-kuo-jen' ti huai-i" ("My Doubt on 'Christianity and the Chinese'"), Hsing-ch'i p'ing-lun (Weekly Review) No. 36 (Shanghai, Feb. 8, 1920).

28. Chu Chih-hsin, "What is Jesus?" reprinted in Neander C. S. Chang 8, The Tide of Religious Thought in China, pp. 23–37; see also Kiang Wen-han 666, The Chinese Student Movement, p. 61.

29. Shao-nien Chung-kuo (Young China), II, 8 (Peking, Feb. 1921) and 11 (May 1921) and III, 1 (Aug. 1921). See Tsi C. Wang 771, The Youth Movement in China (New York, 1928), Chap. XI, pp. 194–95; Kiang Wen-han 666, The Chinese Student Movement, p. 54.

30. Ibid.

31. Young China, II, 8 and 11, and III, 1.

32. Ibid.; Neander C. S. Chang 8, The Tide of Religious Thought in China, p. 147; Tsi C. Wang 771, The Youth Movement in China, pp. 197–98; Kiang Wen-han 666, The Chinese Student Movement, pp. 55–56.

33. John and Alice Dewey 631, Letters from China and Japan (New York, 1920), pp. 174–75.

34. For the religious controversy during the following years see Neander C. S. Chang 586, "The Antireligious Movement," The Chinese Recorder, LV, 8 (Shanghai, Aug. 1923), p. 459; and his 8, The Tide of Religious Thought in China, pp. 189–90; also Tatsuro and Sumiko Yamamoto, "Religion and Modernization in the Far East: II, The Anti-Christian Movement in China, 1922–1927," The Far Eastern Quarterly, XII, 2 (Ann Arbor, Mich., Feb. 1953), pp. 133–47, and Harold D. Lasswell's "Commentary," ibid., pp. 163–72.

35. Yün Tai-ying, "Lun hsin-yang" ("On Faith"), New Youth, III, 5 (July 1, 1917); Wang Hsing-kung's lecture on religion in Young China, II, 8 (Feb. 1921), reprinted in Neander C. S. Chang 8, The Tide of Religious Thought in China, pp. 59–72; Bertrand Russell, ibid., p. 73, also in Chang Ching-lu 12, ed., Collected Lectures of Dewey and Russell, Part 2, pp. 1–14; Liu Po-ming 331, "A Critical Discussion of the Antireligious Movement," Hsüeh heng (The Critical Review), No. 6 (June 1922). For Li Ta-chao's view on the similarity of Bolshevism and religion, see his 297, "The Victory of Bolshevism," New Youth, V, 5 (Oct. 15, 1918).

36. Neander C. S. Chang 8, The Tide of Religious Thought in China, p. 89; Kiang Wen-han 666, The Chinese Student Movement, p. 57.

37. Neander C. S. Chang 586, "The Antireligious Movement," pp. 463–64.

38. Ibid.; also Russell's lecture, in Young China, II, 8 (Feb. 1921), reprinted in Neander C. S. Chang 8, The Tide of Religious Thought in China, p. 73.

39. Neander C. S. Chang 586, "The Antireligious Movement," pp. 463–64.

40. Ts'ai Yüan-p'ei, "I mei-yü tai tsung-chiao" ("Substitute the Culture of Beauty for Religion"), in 461, The Life and Works of Ts'ai Yüan-p'ei (Peking, 1920); also in Neander C. S. Chang 8, The Tide of Religious Thought in China, p. 2.

41. Ch'en Tu-hsiu 61, "One More Discussion of the Problem of Confucianism," New Youth, II, 5 (Jan. 1, 1917).

42. Hu Shih 217, "Immortality," New Youth, VI, 2 (Feb. 15, 1919); the idea was further embodied in an article in English published in Feb. 1920; see his 655, "What I Believe," Forum (Jan. and Feb. 1931), and Hu 207, Collected Essays, Collection I, Vol. IV, pp. 105–18.

43. See Tsi C. Wang *771*, *The Youth Movement in China*, pp. 209–12.

44. *Ibid.*, p. 215; T'ai Hsü, "Wo-ti Fo-chiao ke-ming shih-pai shih" ("The History of Failure of My Buddhist Revolution"), Yü-chou-feng she *562*, ed., A Chapter from Biographies (Kweilin, 1938), p. 33.

45. Chang Chün-mai, "Tsai lun jen-sheng-kuan yü k'o-hsüeh ping ta Ting Tsai-chün" ("Further Discussion of View of Life and Science as an Answer to Ting Wen-chiang"), in Ya-tung t'u-shu-kuan *533*, ed., Science and View of Life, I, 96. See also Ting Wen-chiang, ed., *Liang Jen-kung hsien-sheng nien-p'u ch'ang-pien ch'u-kao* (Draft Chronological Biography of Liang Ch'i-ch'ao (Taipei, 1958), III, 551–74.

46. Liang Ch'i-ch'ao *309*, "Impression of a European Journey," *Shih shih hsin pao* (The China Times) (Shanghai, March 1919), collected in *Liang Jen-kung chin chu* (Recent Writings of Liang Ch'i-ch'ao), p. 23.

47. *Ibid.*

48. Liang Sou-ming *313*, Eastern and Western Civilizations and Their Philosophies (8th ed.; Shanghai, 1921, 1930), Chap. II, p. 24.

49. *Ibid.*, Chap. III, pp. 53–55.

50. *Ibid.*, Chap. V, pp. 161–91.

51. *Ibid.*, p. 202.

52. *Ibid.*, p. 202–09.

53. *Ibid.*, Chap. IV, pp. 114–38.

54. See Liang Sou-ming *311*, The Final Awakening of the Chinese National Self-salvation Movement (Shanghai, 1933), pp. 97–108.

55. *Ibid.*, p. 22.

56. Liang Sou-ming *313*, Eastern and Western Civilizations and Their Philosophies, p. 9. For criticisms of this point of Liang's see Hu Shih, "Tu Liang Sou-ming hsien-sheng ti *Tung Hsi wen-hua chi ch'i che-hsüeh*" ("After Reading Liang Sou-ming's *Eastern and Western Civilizations and Their Philosophies*"), written on March 28, 1923, reprinted in Hu Shih *207*, Collected Essays, Collection II, II, 57–89; and Wu Chih-hui *510*, "A New Conception of the Universe and of Life, Based upon a New Belief," in Ya-tung t'u-shu-kuan *533*, ed., Science and View of Life, II, 123–29.

57. Liang Sou-ming *313*, Eastern and Western Civilizations and Their Philosophies, Chap. I, pp. 10–11.

58. Such as Kuo Chan-po in his *271*, An Intellectual History of China in the Last Fifty Years (2nd ed.; Peiping, 1935–36), Part 3, Chap. VI, p. 177; Part 7, Chap. II, p. 317; and Ch'en Hsü-ching *36*, Outlet of Chinese Civilization (Shanghai, 1934), Chap. IV, p. 80.

59. Hu Shih, "After Reading Liang Sou-ming's *Eastern and Western Civilizations*," p. 79.

60. *Ibid.*, pp. 71–73. At this point Ho Lin made a strong defense of Liang Sou-ming in his *173*, Contemporary Chinese Philosophy (Nanking, 1947), Chap. I, pp. 9–13.

61. Hu Shih "After Reading Liang Sou-ming's *Eastern and Western Civilizations*," p. 71.

62. Hu Shih, "Wo-men tui-yü Hsi-yang chin-tai wen-ming ti t'ai-tu" ("Our Attitude toward Modern Western Civilization"), written on June 6, 1926, reprinted in *207*, Collected Essays, Collection III, I, 13.

63. See Ch'en Hsü-ching *36*, Outlet of Chinese Civilization, Chap. IV, p. 80; Hu Shih, "Ch'ung-fen shih-chieh-hua yü ch'üan-p'an hsi-hua" ("Wholehearted Modernization and Wholesale Westernization"), Hu's *206*, Recent Academic Writings of Hu Shih (Shanghai, 1935), pp. 558–61; and his article in the *Christian Year-book, 1929*; see also *Wen-hua chien-she* (Cultural Reconstruction) (monthly), I, 4 (Jan. 10, 1935).

64. Chang Chün-mai *13*, "View of Life," in *Tsing Hua chou-k'an* (Tsing Hua Weekly), No. 272, reprinted in Ya-tung tu-shu-kuan *533*, ed., Science and View of Life, I, 12; also in Kuo Meng-Liang, ed., *Jen-sheng-kuan chih lun-chan* (The Polemic on View of Life) (3rd ed.; Shanghai, 1923, 1928).

65. See Ch'ien Tuan-sheng, *The Government and Politics of China* (Cambridge, Mass., 1950), Chap. XXIII, pp. 354–55, 426.

66. Chang Chün-mai *13*, "View of Life," p. 8.

67. *Ibid.*, pp. 4–9.

68. *Ibid.*, pp. 9–11.

69. Ting Wen-chiang *445*, "Metaphysics and Science — A Criticism of Carsun Chang's 'View of Life,'" written on April 12, 1923, in *Nu-li chou-pao* (Endeavor Weekly), Nos. 48, 49; reprinted in Ya-tung tu-shu-kuan *533*, ed., Science and View of Life, I, 1–30.

70. Cf. T'ang Yüeh, "'Hsüan-hsüeh yü k'o-hsüeh' lun-cheng ti so-kei-ti an-shih" ("Some Revelations Coming Out of the Controversy on 'Metaphysics and Science'"), in Ya-tung tu-shu-kuan *533*, ed., Science and View of Life, II, 4–6.

71. Wu Chih-hui *510*, "A New Conception of the Universe and Life, Based upon a New Belief," *ibid.*, pp. 12–29.

72. *Ibid.*, pp. 38–40, 47–49; see also Hu Shih *652*, *The Chinese Renaissance*, Chap. V, pp. 91–93.

73. Wu Chih-hui *510*, "A New Conception of the Universe and Life, Based upon a New Belief," pp. 89–112, 151, 165.

74. Hu Shih *655*, "What I Believe," *Forum* (Jan. and Feb. 1931), reprinted in *Living Philosophies* (New York, 1931), pp. 260–63; see also Hu Shih, *"K'o-hsüeh yü jen-sheng-kuan hsü"* ("Preface"), Ya-tung tu-shu-kuan, *533*, ed., Science and View of Life, I, 25–29.

75. See both Ch'en Tu-hsiu's and Hu Shih's prefaces to *533*, Science and View of Life, I, 2, 11, 29–42. For Carsun Chang's criticism of the naturalists' views see his preface to Kuo Meng-liang, ed., The Polemic on View of Life; also Chang *14*, "A Retrospect of the Polemic on View of Life," The Eastern Miscellany, XXXI, 13 (July 1, 1934), pp. 5–13. For Hu Shih's latest review of the polemic see his *221*, Biography of Ting Wen-chiang (Taipei, 1956), Chap. XII, pp. 41–59.

CHAPTER XIV

CONCLUSION

1. Chiang Monlin *94*, "Change Our Attitude toward Life," New Education, No. 5 (Shanghai, June 1919), reprinted in his *95*, Thought and Education in the Transitional Period (Shanghai, 1933), p. 27. Also Hsü Pao-ch'ien, "The Christian Renaissance," a paper read at the meeting of International Christian Fellowship, Peking, Dec. 5, 1920, in *The Chinese Recorder*, LI, I (Jan. 1920), pp. 459–67; and "Christian Renaissance in China — Statement of Aims of the Peking Apologetic Group," trans. T. C. Chao, *ibid.*, 9 (Sept. 1920), pp. 636–39.

2. Hu Shih *652*, *The Chinese Renaissance* (Chicago, 1934), Chap. III, p. 44.

3. Yeh Ch'ing *551*, "Discussion of the May Fourth Cultural Movement," Cultural Reconstruction, I, 8 (Shanghai, May 10, 1935), pp. 22–23.

4. See Nathaniel Peffer *703*, *China: The Collapse of a Civilization* (New York, 1930), Chap. VIII, pp. 144–48.

5. Hu Shih *652*, *The Chinese Renaissance*, Chap. III, p. 45. For the problem of the interpretation of the movement see Chow Tse-tsung *126*, "On the Significance and Characteristics of the May Fourth Movement," L'Impartial (Shanghai, May 4, 1947).

6. See Chang Chün-mai, "Further Discussion of View of Life and Science as an Answer to Ting Wen-chiang," Ya-tung t'u-shu kuan *533*, ed., Science and View of Life (Shanghai, 1923), I, 96; also T'ao Chü-yin, *Chiang Po-li hsien-sheng chuan* (Biography of Chiang Po-li) (Shanghai, 1948), Chap. IX, p. 74. The result of the study were Chiang Po-li's *Ou-chou wen-i-fu-hsing shih* (History of the European Renaissance) and Liang Ch'i-ch'ao's famous introduction (written in Sept.–Oct. 1920) which was longer than the book itself. Liang's introduction was later reprinted in book form with the title *306*, An Introduction to the Scholarship of the Ch'ing Period (7th ed.; Shanghai, 1921, 1927).

7. See Li Ch'ang-chih *286*, Welcome to the Chinese Renaissance (Chungking, 1944), Chap. III, pp. 15–19; Ho Kan-chih *170*, History of the Chinese Enlightenment (Shanghai, 1947), Chap. I, p. 10; Chap. V, p. 151.

8. See Hu Shih *652*, *The Chinese Renaissance*, Chap. III, p. 45; and Fu Ssu-nien *162*, "The Twenty-fifth Anniversary of 'May Fourth,'" L'Impartial (Chungking, May 4, 1944), p. 1.

9. Chang Hsi-jo *15*, "Cultivation of the People's Personality," L'Impartial (May 5, 1935), written for the anniversary of the May Fourth Movement, reprinted in Independent Critic, No. 150 (May 12, 1935), pp. 14–17; Hu Shih *210*, "Individual Freedom and Social Progress — Further Discussion of the May Fourth Movement," *ibid.*, pp. 2–5.

10. Mao Ssu-ch'eng, etc., eds., *Min-kuo shih-wu nien i-ch'ien chih Chiang Chieh-shih hsien-sheng* (Biography of Chiang Kai-shek before 1926) (Nanking, 1937), Vol. II, Bk. VI, pp. 65–66, 72, 75, 89–90; also Chiang Kai-shek, *Su-O tsai Chung-kuo* (Taipei, Taiwan, 1956), Chap. II, pp. 19–26; English version of the book titled *Soviet Russia in China* (New York, 1957).

11. Chiang Kai-shek *592*, *China's Destiny*, authorized trans. Wang Ch'ung-hui (New York, 1947), Chap. II, Sec. 3, p. 51. In the Chinese original, the text reads "the May 4 Movement" instead of "the May 4 Student Movement."

12. Chiang Kai-shek *592*, *China's Destiny*, trans. Wang Ch'ung-hui, Chap. II, Sec. 3, p. 52.

13. *Ibid.*, Chap. III, Sec. 5, pp. 81–82.

14. *Ibid.*, Chap. VI, Sec. 2, pp. 199–200.

15. Chiang Kai-shek, "Che-hsüeh yü chiao-yü tui-yü ch'ing-nien ti kuan-hsi" ("The Relation of Philosophy and Education to Youth"), a speech delivered in July 1941, *Tsung-ts'ai yen-lun hsüan-chi* (Selected Speeches) (Taipei, 1953), III, 245.

16. Chiang Kai-shek *92*, "The Relation of Education to Revolution and National Reconstruction," in Youth and Education (Taipei, 1952), pp. 12–13.

17. See Chiang Kai-shek *91*, "Reorganization of the Cultural Heritage and Improvement of the National Character," China Weekly, No. 112 (Taipei, June 16, 1952), reprinted in Selected Works of the Director-General of the Kuomintang (Taipei, 1952), p. 231. For the controversy see also Huang Li-sheng, ed., *Tu ching wen-t'i* (The Problem of Reading the Classics) (Taipei, 1953).

18. Hu Shih *210*, "Individual Freedom and Social Progress," p. 2.

19. Tseng Ch'i *471*, "The May Fourth Movement and Statism," in Collected Works of Tseng Ch'i (Taipei, 1954), Part II, pp. 136–40; also "Chih Lo Chia-lun shu" ("Letter to Lo Chia-lun"), dated 1934, *ibid.*, Part III, pp. 191–92.

20. Ch'en Tu-hsiu *69*, "Is the May Fourth Period a Thing of the Past?" Political Review, I, 11 (Chungking, May 15, 1938), pp. 8–9.

21. See Fu Ssu-nien *157*, "Retrospect and Outlook of *New Tide*," New Tide, II, 1 (Oct. 21, 1919), p. 204; Fu's article was written on Sept. 5, 1919. See also Lo Chia-lun *340*, "The Success and Failure of Our Student Movement in the Last Year and Its Future Path," New Education, II, 5 (May 1920), p. 604; also in New Tide, II, 4 (May 1, 1920), p. 849.

22. See Chiang K'ang-hu, *Ming-ho chi* (Chiang K'ang-hu's Will) (Peking, 1927), p. 21; and Chiang's *Chung-kuo hsin she-hui min-chu tang* (The New Socialist Democratic Party of China, Its Manifesto, Advocacy, Attitude, Temporary Political Program, and Outline of Organization) [Nanking, 1926?]. It was reported that Chiang died later in a Chinese communist prison. For Mao's new democracy see also comments in Brandt, Schwartz, and Fairbank *575*, *A Documentary History of Chinese Communism* (Cambridge, Mass., 1952), pp. 260–63.

23. Mao Tse-tung *361*, "The May Fourth Movement," in Selected Works of Mao Tse-tung (Peking, 1952), II, 545; cf. the English trans. in Mao Tse-tung *687*, *Selected Works* (New York, 1955), III, 9.

24. Mao Tse-tung *361*, "The May Fourth Movement," p. 546.

25. Mao Tse-tung *357*, "The Direction of the Youth Movement in China," in Selected Works, pp. 549–57; English version of the article in Mao *687*, *Selected Works*, III, 12–21.

26. Mao Tse-tung *357*, "The Direction of the Youth Movement in China," Selected Works (in Chinese), Vol. II, footnote on p. 550.

27. Mao Tse-tung *359*, "On New Democracy," *ibid.*, p. 689.

28. *Ibid.*, pp. 665–66.

29. *Ibid.*, p. 666.

30. *Ibid.*, p. 689.

31. *Ibid.*, p. 690; trans. Brandt, Schwartz, and Fairbank *575*, *A Documentary History of Chinese Communism*, p. 271.

32. Mao Tse-tung *359*, "On New Democracy," pp. 692–93; trans. by Sharaf Ather Ali (Bombay, n.d.), reprinted in U.S. Congress, House of Representatives, Committee on Foreign Affairs, *Communism in China*, Appendix B, "Mao Tse-tung, *China's New Democracy*," pp. 86–87. For a discussion of the problem of English translations of the article see Lin Yutang, "Mao Tse-tung's 'Democracy,'" *The China Magazine*, XVII, 4 (New York, April 1947), pp. 14–24; 5 (May 1947), pp. 15–26.

33. Mao Tse-tung *359*, "On New Democracy," pp. 692–93.

34. See Kuo Mo-jo, "Ke-ming shih-jen Ch'ü Yüan ("Ch'ü Yüan the Revolutionary Poet"), in *Ch'ü Yüan — Wu mu shih-chü chi ch'i-t'a* (Ch'ü Yüan — A Five-act Historical Play and Others) (Chang-chia-k'ou or Kalgan, 1946), pp. 131–32; Kuo Mo-jo, "Ch'ü Yüan ti i-ju yü ssu-hsiang" ("Ch'ü Yüan's Craftsmanship and Thought"), in *ibid.*, pp. 155–56; also Hua Kang *230*, History of the May Fourth Movement (2nd rev. ed.; Shanghai, 1951, 1952), Chap. IX, pp. 196–98.

35. Edgar Snow *739*, *Red Star over China*, Part IV, Chap. III, p. 154.

36. Teng Ying-ch'ao *440*, "A Memoir on the May Fourth Movement," in A Symposium for the Thirtieth Anniversary of the May Fourth Movement, pp. 163–64. This point is also upheld by other participants in the movement. See Kuo Shao-yü *280*, "An Examination of Myself on the Anniversary of May Fourth"; and Chao Ching-shen *34*, "The Change of My View of May Fourth," both in Liberation Daily (Shanghai, May 3, 1950), p. 6.

37. For the last reference see Liu Li-k'ai, "Tsai Shih-yüeh ke-ming ying-hsiang hsia Ma-k'e-ssu Lieh-ning chu-i tsai Chung-kuo ti ch'u-ch'i ch'uan-po" ("The Spread of

Marxism-Leninism in China in the Early Stage under the Influence of the October Revolution), *Hsüeh-hsi* (Learning), No. 123 (No. 21) (Peking, Nov. 3, 1957), pp. 23–25.

38. Mao Tse-tung *359*, "On New Democracy," trans. by Sharaf Ather Ali, p. 87; cf. English version in Mao *687*, *Selected Works*, III, 146.

39. Hua Kang *230*, History of the May Fourth Movement, Chap. VIII, p. 160.

40. *Ibid.*, p. 173.

41. See Chiang Kai-shek *92*, "The Relation of Education to Revolution and National Reconstruction," pp. 10–11; also Pao Tsun-p'eng *382*, History of Youth Movement of Modern China, Part II, Chaps. II, III.

42. Ch'ü Ch'iu-pai, *Luan t'an chi ch'i-t'a* (Scattered Shots and Others — Selected Essays of Ch'ü Ch'iu-pai) (Shanghai, 1938), p. 122. For the remark on Russell see Li Jui, *Mao Tse-tung t'ung-chih ti ch'u-ch'i ke-ming huo-tung* (Comrade Mao Tse-tung's Early Revolutionary Activities) (Peking, 1957), p. 135, n. 3. For the communist restriction of sale of the early magazines to a few party leaders see *Kuang-ming jih-pao* (Peking, June 20, 1957), p. 3, and (Oct. 10, 1957), p. 3. The communists justified this action by saying that party leaders were more important in the revolution than other people. For a remark on the communists' interpretation of the movement see Wolfgang Franke *639*, *Chinas Kulturelle Revolution — Die Bewegung vom 4. Mai 1919* (München, 1957).

43. Ch'en Tu-hsiu, "Ta Shih-chih" ("An Answer to Hu Shih"), preface, written Dec. 9, 1923, in Ya-tung t'u-shu-kuan *533*, ed., Science and View of Life, I, 40.

44. Hu Shih, "Tao-yen" ("Introduction") to his An Anthology of Essays on Constructive Theories of the New Literature in Chao Chia-pi *33*, ed., A Corpus of China's New Literature (Shanghai, 1935), I, 15–17.

45. Ch'en Tu-hsiu, "Ts'ai Chieh-min hsien-sheng shih-shih hou kan-yen" ("Some Thoughts after the Death of Ts'ai Yüan-p'ei"), *Chung-yang jih-pao* (The Central Daily News) (Chungking, March 24, 1940).

46. See Ch'ien Chih-hsiu, "Kung-li-chu-i yü hsüeh-shu" ("Utilitarianism and Scholarship"), The Eastern Miscellany, XV, 6 (June 1918); Hu Shih *204*, "The Significance of the New Thought Tide," New Youth, VII, 1 (Dec. 1, 1919).

47. Chung-chiu [Shen Chung-chiu] *403*, "A Review of the May Fourth Movement," The Construction, I, 3 (Oct. 1, 1919), pp. 599–612.

48. Mao Tse-tung, "Fan-tui tang-pa-ku" ("Oppose Party Formalism"), speech delivered Feb. 8, 1942, in *Cheng-feng wen-hsien* (Documents on the Correction of Unorthodox Tendencies) (rev. ed.; Chieh-fang she, 1946, 1949), p. 21; English translation in Brandt, Schwartz, and Fairbank *575*, *A Documentary History of Chinese Communism*, p. 393; also Mao's *359*, "On New Democracy," p. 693; and *ibid.*, pp. 690–91, trans. by Sharaf Athar Ali (later Chinese version has some textual changes in this paragraph).

49. *Ibid.*, p. 693.

50. *Ibid.*, p. 690.

51. Mao Tse-tung, "Oppose Party Formalism," pp. 21–22; English translation in Brandt, Schwartz, and Fairbank *575*, *A Documentary History of Chinese Communism*, p. 394.

52. For the former term see Lyford P. Edwards, *The Natural History of Revolution* (Chicago, 1927), Chap. IV, pp. 38–66, and for the latter see Crane Brinton, *The Anatomy of Revolution* (rev. ed.; New York, 1938, 1958), Chap. II, pp. 41–52.

53. See Fu Ssu-nien *162*, "Twenty-fifth Anniversary of the 'May Fourth,'" L'Impartial (Chungking, May 4, 1944); Li Ch'ang-chih *286*, Welcome to the Chinese Renaissance, Chap. III, pp. 20–21; also Hu Shih *652*, *The Chinese Renaissance*, Chap. IV, pp. 73–74.

54. John Dewey *620*, "New Culture in China," *Asia*, XXI, 7 (New York, July 1921), p. 642.

55. Pearl S. Buck *579*, *My Several Worlds, a Personal Record* (New York, 1954), especially Parts II, III, and IV.

56. Fung Yu-lan *153*, "The Main Tendency of the National Movement of Modern China," The Sociological World, IX (Peiping, 1936), pp. 264–65.

INDEX

cott, 128–129; influence upon teachers, 138–139; "Manifesto for a General Strike," 139–140; six demands, 140–141; publication suppressed, 146; mass arrests, 148b, 149–150; financial situation, 151, 198–199; founding of Student Union of China, 163, 164t; and Peace Treaty, 165; and Sino-Japanese negotiation, 262f
Student Union of Peking University: financial situation, 121–122; organized, 121c; and student union of Peking city, 122; news of Ts'ao Ju-lin's resignation, 162
Student Union of The Republic of China (Student Union of China): office, 35g; established, 123, 163–164; influence, 164, 187; in Federation of All Organizations, 188; and Japanese Dawn Society, 200f; and Groups of Ten, 141; terminated strikes, 167; and Karakhan declaration, 213; and Sun Yat-sen, 247; in anti-imperialist campaign, 254; proclaimed strike (1920), 262f
Student Union of Shanghai: office, 35g; established, 130; activities among merchants and workers, 143, 153; letter to foreign consulates, 153–154h; meeting of social groups, 154; expelled from International Settlement, 203–204
Student Union of Tientsin, 129, 130, 142, 163, 189
Student Union of Wu-Han, 144
Students' Magazine, 181
Students' Society for National Salvation, 82
"Study and the Prison, The," 173b
Study Clique (Constitutional Study Society), 76, 90, 169. See also Chinputang
Study in Europe, 249p
Study of Ancient Chinese Society, A, 317c
"Study of Athletics, A," 74x
Study of Sociology, 294, 348c
"Study of the Development of Logical Method in Ancient China, A," 30
Su Man-ju, 42a
Sugawara Michizane, 13d
"Sui-kan-lu" (Random Thoughts), 278
Sun Chia-nai, 48
Sun Fu-yüan, 56, 112e'
Sun Hsiao-ch'ing, 189
Sun Lang-kung, 349c
Sun Yat-sen: view of movement, 3, 343, 344; established Military Government, 10; after Twenty-one Demands, 23; reorganized party, 35, 247; relation with Ts'ai Yüan-p'ei, 47f, 51; and Liu Shih-fu, 97m; supported May 4 demonstration, 125–126, j; and Federation

of All Organizations, 155; and new culture movement, 194–195; among intellectuals, 217; and student movement, 226, 247–248, 358; economic view, 230; accepted socialism, 244, 296; on the vernacular, 245–246; and Lenin, 245–246, 343a; orthodox tradition, 246n; recommended Ch'en Tu-hsiu, 250; organized labor unions, 255; opposed to Sino-Japanese negotiation, 262f; mentioned, 42a, 191i. See also Kuomintang, Nationalism, Socialism
Sung Chiao-jen, 217
Sung dynasty: student movements in, 11, 127; prose style, 271; Confucian worship, 292. See also Neo-Confucianism
Sung learning, 291, 337
Symposium on Ancient Chinese History, A, 317b
Syndicalism: Dewey's view, 229–230; introduced, 233, 256; and Russell, 234; Society for the Study of, 243i
Sze, Sao-ke Alfred (Shih Chao-chi), 86c

Ta-tao K'ung-chia-tien (overthrow Confucius and Sons), 307. See also Anti-Confucianism
Ta-t'ung (universal harmony, or one world), 307
Ta-t'ung shu (The One World Philosophy of K'ang Yu-wei), 98
Tagore, Rabindranath, 193, 285, 330
Tai Chi-t'ao (Tai ch'uan-hsien): view of work-and-learning, 191i; among intellectuals, 217; edited Weekly Review and Construction, 246; Marxism, 247, 299; founded Chinese Communist Party, 248; Darwinian ideas, 296; opposed to anti-Confucian movement, 306, antireligion, 324; mentioned, 310l
Tai Sheng, 303g
T'ai Hsü, 326
T'ai Shuang-ch'iu, 252
T'an P'ing-shan, 75
T'an Ssu-t'ung, 98, n, 270c
T'an-yen t'uan (the Brothel Brigade), 49
T'ang dynasty, 12
T'ang Erh-ho: relation with government, 124g; recommended Ch'en Tu-hsiu, 52k, 138–139v; "Our Political Proposal," 240f; in "good men Cabinet," 241g
T'ang Hua-lung, 54n.o
T'ang Ping-yüan, 164t
T'ang Shao-i, 125, 127
T'ang Yung-t'ung, 318
T'ang Yüeh, 334
Tangshan Station, 161